TRAFFIC ENGINEERING
for ISDN Design and Planning

NORTH-HOLLAND
STUDIES IN TELECOMMUNICATION
VOLUME 9

International Teletraffic Congress
International Advisory Council
The Development and Application of Teletraffic Theory

The first International Teletraffic Congress, entitled 'On the Application of the Theory of Probability in Telephone Engineering and Administration', took place in 1955 in Copenhagen. Every 3 years since then, specialists from tele-administrations, industry, and universities have gathered to present new methodologies and applications of the theory of teletraffic and teleplanning. Their audience is composed of experts and users, and the main focus is on issues of telecommunication traffic, as they affect customer service, and efficient telecommunication equipment loading, with special emphasis on probabilistic and other mathematical handling of traffic problems.

The International Advisory Council – with representatives from each past Congress country and the two future Congress countries – is responsible for the Congresses. Up till now, the following have served on the Council:

Denmark: Arne Jensen (Chairman, since 1955).
The Netherlands: L. Kosten (Hon.), J.W. Cohen.
France: R. Fortet (Hon.), P. Le Gall.
United Kingdom: E.P.G. Wright (Hon.), J. Povey (Hon.), A.C. Cole.
United States: R. Wilkinson (Hon.), Walt Hayward (Hon.), S. Katz.
Germany: Konrad Rohde (Hon.), P. Kühn (Vice-Chairman since 1985).
Sweden: Chr. Jacobäus (Hon.), Bengt Wallström.
Australia: Clem Pratt.
Spain: Eduardo Villar.
Canada: J. J. O'Shaughnessy.
USSR: V. Neiman.
Japan: H. Inose (Hon.), M. Akiyama.
Italy: P. de Ferra.

CCITT: E.P.G. Wright (U.K.); Clem Pratt (Australia); Ingvar Tånge (Sweden);
   G. Gosztony (Hungary); A. Lewis (Canada).

NORTH-HOLLAND – AMSTERDAM • NEW YORK • OXFORD • TOKYO

TRAFFIC ENGINEERING

for ISDN Design and Planning

Proceedings of the Fifth ITC Seminar held at Lake Como, Italy, May 4–8, 1987

Edited by

Mario BONATTI

ITALTEL
Central Research Laboratories
Milano, Italy

and

Maurizio DECINA

Politecnico of Milano
Milano, Italy

1988

NORTH-HOLLAND – AMSTERDAM ● NEW YORK ● OXFORD ● TOKYO

ISBN: 0 444 70405 1

Published by:
ELSEVIER SCIENCE PUBLISHERS B.V.
P.O. Box 1991
1000 BZ Amsterdam
The Netherlands

Sole distributors for the U.S.A. and Canada:
ELSEVIER SCIENCE PUBLISHING COMPANY, INC.
52 Vanderbilt Avenue
New York, N.Y. 10017
U.S.A.

Legal Notice:
All opinions expressed in these proceedings are those of the authors and are not binding on the International Advisory Council of the International Teletraffic Congress.

FOREWORD

The Lake Como Seminar on May 4-8, 1987 is the second ITC Seminar dedicated to the ISDN issue. The first one, which took place in Brussels during the first week of May 1986, concentrated on the micro-problems of ISDN. It resulted in an extensive exchange of ideas and experiences.

The Lake Como Seminar concentrated its efforts on the macro-problems. This required new approaches to, and more involvement in, systems engineering and design activities.

The organizers were very successful in building-up a stimulating program reflecting the dynamic development created by the rapidly changing new technological possibilities.

The program covered system engineering views on teletraffic issues, teletraffic contributions to system engineering problems and specific teletraffic studies. The result was a well-balanced program of ISDN theory and applications.

In Como, we were presented with both concrete results and new challenges for future ISDN work. This will assist us in solving the problems of the complex communication system created by the new revolutionary technological possibilities.

We are very grateful to P. de Ferra, M. Decina, M. Bonatti and to Italtel, the host organization. Their enthusiasm and devotion made this seminar possible just-in-time.

Arne Jensen
Chairman of the International Advisory Council
of the International Teletraffic Congresses

Copenhagen, October 1987

ISDN DESIGN AND PLANNING: A CHALLENGE TO TRAFFIC ENGINEERING

(Preface of the Chairman of the Program Committee)

M. Bonatti
ITALTEL, Italy

The V ITC Seminar on Traffic Engineering for ISDN Design and Planning has been promoted by the International Advisory Council (IAC) of the International Teletraffic Congress (ITC), since the beginning of the year 1984.

The IAC recognized that the progress of Traffic Engineering Community in confronting the problems posed by the emerging ISDN would be accelerated if a group of experts could have the opportunity to discuss together in a working environment.

The V ITC seminar has been, therefore, programmed after the ITC11 in Kyoto (September 1985) and the 4th ITC Seminar on ISDN traffic issues in Brussels (May 1986) and before the ITC12 in Torino (June 1988), with three main objectives:

- to learn from ISDN experts (mainly from CCITT SG XVIII experts);
- to understand what kind of Traffic Engineering work ISDN needs;
- to understand how must and could the Traffic Engineering work change to respond to these needs.

In the mean time, the traffic people have cooperated, within various administrations and manufacturing companies, with system engineers and designers to the first ISDN implementations and experiments.

Furthermore, four ad hoc meetings of the CCITT SG II Group of Experts for ISDN Traffic Engineering took place in '85 and in '86 (Paris, Rome, Budapest, Milan) and more liaison was undertaken with SG XI and SG XVIII.

These events matured the state of the art in a significant way, offering to the seminar quite advanced premises.

Some of the problems traffic engineering people are confronted with may be highlighted by a provocative view on traffic engineering history: from the rationalization of existing networks and systems to the performance design of communication based applications.

The first phase (at the top during the fifties) was characterized by a continuous progress in traffic knowledge based on the network management experience and practice and by significant contributions to the improvement of the networks performances in terms of grade of service, resources utilization and economy of scale. The actions have been mostly corrective; the logical attitude mostly deductive.

In the second phase, the traffic people have been confronted with problems originated by the introduction of SPC systems and of new routing disciplines: overloads, repeated call attempts, faults, all resulted in critical behaviours for systems and networks designed with a naive extrapolation of the current experience. Some preventive actions were required and developed, a lot of work was made in order to correct "badly performing" designs after the field experience. The logical attitude continued to be mostly deductive.

ISDN closes this second phase.

Some concepts have demonstrated their usefulness in the transition between the first and the second phase. In particular:
- a call flow diagram showing the possible sequences of events from the Call Demand to the Call Release;
- models for the offered traffic;
- performance models of basic systems, serving as reference for modeling more complex ones.

The various ITC, until ITC11 in Kyoto, testify the progress of the state of the art in dealing with POTS problems. Practically all problems have been solved, with the following exceptions:
- models allowing an integrated performance analysis of systems and networks taking into account overloads and faults (overload & fault tolerant design);
- complete and coherent process for the definition of GOS and End–to–End performance parameters, their targets and for their allocation to the Network Segments, to the links and to the nodes.

These problems will be, by now, confronted within ISDN.

Other problems, successfully solved for POTS, have been reopened because of the new ISDN context. They include:
- the definition of the various users in terms of Protocol Reference Model;
- the assessment of an ISDN call flow diagram;
- new models for the offered traffic and new procedures to forecast and measure it;
- performance models for the basic systems required by the Architecture Reference Model;
- strategic planning methods taking into account the multiplicity of utilization contexts and, therefore, of optimization criteria.

Furthermore, a deep, fundamental investigation on the nature of the communication seems required in cooperating to the realization of a new global communication environment.

The following format has been chosen for the Seminar:
a) an opening session to introduce the main general topics and their connections under three main points of view: technological and architectural evolution, standardization and traffic modeling;
b) three working days dealing respectively with services, networks and systems;
c) a panel, as closing session, to summarize the results of the seminar connecting the various topics already discussed.

Each working day consisted of two sessions: in the morning session a tutorial and two invited papers were given to introduce the main topics; in the afternoon session, five normal papers were presented and some written contributions were taken into account during the discussion (only two exceptions were decided in order to accommodate in the better place a tutorial on networks and a tutorial on systems).

The full program is reproduced in the table of content.

The solution of some of the problems mentioned (in particular those referring to fundamental investigation on the nature of the communication) could take profit of the knowledge of the state of the art of similar problems in other disciplines.

In the moment we are passing, a careful resort to an encyclopedic attitude could be useful (Encyclopedia, agkukliospaidea: learn to articulate the different points of view of the knowledge in active cycles and configurations around specific problems).

"The exploration of connections between domains traditionally held to be separated could help in removing outdated views, coming from the specialistic work, and obstructing the route toward needed new concepts and formulations".[1]

"Following a concept "outside" of the specific domain in which we have dealt with it, could be both pertinent and effective. The danger of rigid analogies that efface important differences, must be avoided, but "imported metaphors" moving across artificial and encrusted boundaries have at time been, and could in the future be, at the heart of fertile and rigorous innovations within particular contexts."[1]

The program of the seminar includes, in the form of Tutorials, presentations of some knowledge and methods in disciplines other than teletraffic that could be useful in the above mentioned spirit. The seminar was asked to evaluate possible crossfertilizations.

The Tutorials were chosen from the following fields:

Information Theory	Cybernetics
Linguistics	Catastrophe Theory
Irreversible Thermodynamics	Taxonomy
Morphological Analysis	Multivariate Statistical Analysis
Econometric Forecasting	Technological Forecasting
Industrial Dynamics	Game Theory
Ecology	Computer Science
Fault–Tolerance	Neurophisiology.

The Proceedings include introductions and conclusions of the Session Chairmen as well as the record of the discussions held after the presentation of the papers. Only the questions, the answers and the comments received in written form after the seminar have been taken into account. Tutorials have been invited by the program chairman on the basis of suggestions received by the program committee.

Submitted papers have been selected by a conventional refereeing process: each paper has been evaluated by all the members of the Paper Committee: 6 papers were selected as invited, 15 as normal and 6 as written contributions. The opening session includes papers directly invited by the Paper Committee. The following persons have served as referees in the selection process of submitted papers:

M.	Decina	J.	Labetoulle
I.P.	Dartois	P.	Le Gall
G.	Gosztony	K.	Nivert
D.	Grillo	P.	Pandya
S.	Katz	M.	Reiser
K.	Kawashima	D.	Songhurst
P.	Kuehn	R.	Van Der Ven
K.	Kummerle		

---

[1] from P. Livingston Ed. **Disorder and Order,** Proceedings of the Stanford International Symposium, september 1981, Amna Libri 1984

Thanks are due to all person above, for their generous and competent contributions. Particular gratitude goes to all the members of the International Program Committee for the support of their experience. The contribution of M. Decina and the support by A. Jensen, P. Kuehn and P. de Ferra have been of key importance for the success of the seminar.

The author of the Tutorials, of the Invited and the normal papers, of the contributions and all the participants contributed with their faith in the event to its realization and its success. But our gratitude also goes to authors we were unable to invite or to accept, mainly because of the choice of the program. We hope to have them with us in Turin, ITC12 and in further meetings on ISDN. Finally thanks are due to The Italian Ministry of Post and Telecommunication for its auspices; to Italtel as organizer; to Stet, Cselt, Fub and SIP for technical cooperation.

We hope that all these efforts have further contributed to the progress of the state of the art and of the Teletraffic Engineering profession, and we look forward to ITC12 in Turin with renewed enthusiasm.

Mario Bonatti
Milano, November 1987

TABLE OF CONTENTS

*Invited Papers.
**Tutorial Lectures.

ORGANIZATION

General Chairman: M. Decina, Italtel, Italy

Program Committee

Chairman: M. Bonatti, Italtel, Italy
National Technical Committee of ITC 12, Italy

Paper Committee

J.P. Dartois, Itt, France
G. Gosztony, Bhg Telecom, Hungary
D. Grillo, Fondazione Bordoni, Italy
S.S. Katz, AT&T Bell Laboratories, U.S.A.
K. Kawashima, Ntt, Japan
P. Kuehn, Itc, University of Stuttgart, F.R.G.
K. Kuemmerle, IBM, Switzerland
J. Labetoulle, Cnet, France
P. Le Gall, Cnet, France
K. Nivert, Televerket, Sweden
R. Pandya, Bnr, Canada
D. Songhurst, British Telecom, U.K.
P. Van Der Ven, Ptt-Caff, The Netherlands

International Members

M. Akiyama, University of Tokyo, Japan
M. Bicknell, British Telecom International, U.K.
G. Bocq, Regie des Telegraphes et des Telephones, Belgium
K. Boe, Norwegian Telecommunication Administration, Norway
V.A. Bolotin, IEEE Consoc/Bell Communications Research, U.S.A.
J. De Boer, AT&T Philips Telecommunications, The Netherlands
J.R. De Los Mozos, Itt, Spain
M. Gerla, University of California, U.S.A.
H. Hofstetter, Siemens AG, F.R.G.
A. Lewis, Teleglobe, Canada
J. Lubacz, University of Warsaw, Poland
M. Mori, Kdd, Japan
R.M. Potter, Bell Communications Research, U.S.A.
G. Pujolle, Inria, University of Paris IV, France
J. Roberts, Cnet, France
G. Robin, Itt, Belgium

Under the Auspices of

The Italian Ministry for Post and Telecommunication

Organized by

Italtel

In Cooperation with

Stet, Societa' Finanziaria Telefonica
Cselt, Centro Studi e Laboratori Telecommunicazioni
Fub, Fondazione Ugo Bordoni
Sip, Societa' Italiana per l'Esercizio delle Telecommunicazioni

TRAFFIC ENGINEERING for ISDN Design and Planning
M. Bonatti and M. Decina (Editors)
Elsevier Science Publishers B.V. (North-Holland)
© IAC, 1988

DRIVING FORCES IN ISDN EVOLUTION AND TRAFFIC ENGINEERING CONTRIBUTION

(Co-Chairman Introduction to the Opening Session)

Mario Bonatti

ITALTEL, Italy

The evolution of the ISDN will follow from the combined effect of

- Successfull services deployment strategies,

- Convenient network(s) deployment strategies,

- Adequate standardization support,

- Progress in the relevant technologies, and

- Progress in System Engineering.

The Opening Session has been organized in order to introduce the Seminar on these main aspects.

M. Decina was asked to introduce the impact of the progress in technology and in system engineering on the network and system evolution and to highlight the main driving forces and the main obstacles.

G. Gosztony, as chairman of SG II, was asked to present the state of the standardization work within CCITT and to indicate the future work needed.

Finally, P. Kuehn was asked to introduce the specific scope of the seminar in the context of the previous considerations with particular reference to Traffic Theory and Traffic Engineering contributions to ISDN design and planning.

The session was introduced by the chairman P. de Ferra, in his quality of Italian representative of IAC of ITC; he introduced all the previous mentioned topics with a very concrete reference to the present situation and to the development guidelines of Italian Telecommunications.

L. Gimpelson in his liaison statement with the previous ITC Seminar on ISDN (Bruxelles, May 1986), introduced the provocative question about the large scale take-off of ISDN and the "egg-chicken" situation that seems keep it late.

TRAFFIC ENGINEERING for ISDN Design and Planning
M. Bonatti and M. Decina (Editors)
Elsevier Science Publishers B.V. (North-Holland)
© IAC, 1988

ISDN IN ITALY AND TELETRAFFIC

Prof. Paolo de Ferra - STET - Italy

Summary: In this introductory contribution to the Lake Como Seminar, the present situation and the evolutionary guidelines of the Italian telecommunications are firstly described. Data on existing TLC terminals (mainly for telephony and data communication) are given, as well as development forecasts drawn from the present National Plan 1985 - 1994. The penetration of digital techniques in the network is then considered, with particular reference to the switching exchanges. Information on R&D activities and on the development trends in the subject of future switching is given, and the evolutionary steps of ISDN are defined. The plans for the introduction of ISDN in Italy and in other European countries are considered. On the basis of previous experiences, a policy for the introduction of future ISDNs is outlined, in the form of a sequence of specialized and general purpose networks. The relevant problems are evidenced, mainly concerning network architecture and technology, CCITT recommendations for interfaces and protocols, cost-efficient design and planning. Finally, the importance of a close participation of teletraffic specialists for the solution of all these problems is stressed.

1. ITALIAN TELECOMS

A suitable introduction to this Seminar, which is the first Teletraffic Seminar held in Italy, may be to start by briefly describing the present situation and development guidelines of Italian telecommunications. Probably, the fundamental bases of Italian telecoms are already well known; in substance, they can be summarized as follows:

- clear orientation towards digital techniques;
- clear orientation towards techniques and services integration;
- in particular, orientation towards research of solutions, being on one hand economically valid and, on the other, not preclusive for the integration of any service;
- in this framework, orientation towards the adoption of multi-services signalling systems, interfaces and protocols, coming from international standardization.

Concerning the size of Italy, Fig. 1 shows the relationship between the surface of Italy and that of the United States. The ratio is 1:30 or even less. But it should be noted that, to represent the relationship between the numbers of telephone subscribers, Italy should have an area 4 or 5 times larger.

The number of telephone subscribers was 18.2 millions at the end of 1986. Considering the relationship between number of subscribers, population and national wealth, Fig. 2 shows the GNP in abscisses and the telephone density in ordinates. The area of each circle expresses the quantity of subscribers in a single country. The position of Italy can be seen, in comparison with other European countries at the end of '85. This position fully respects all previous national plans for telecommunications. The present plan ranges from 1985 to 1994. Following this plan it is expected to reach, in '94, a density of more than 43 subscribers per 100 inhabitants and 94 home-subscribers per 100 families.

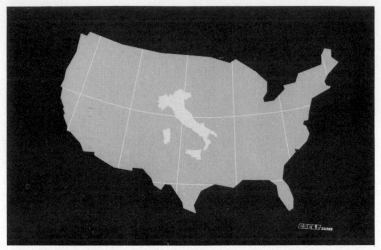

FIGURE 1: GEOGRAPHICAL SIZE OF ITALY

At the same time, considerable increases, far larger than for telephony, are expected for other services such as teletex, facsimile, information handling and message transfer. For data communication, more than 220 thousand terminal installations are in operation, but most of them are connected via leased circuits. By the year 1994 it is foreseen that this number will more than double, that new networks for specific users will enter into service, but also that terminal installations on leased lines will fall below 50%.

Increases by an order of magnitude are foreseen for mobile radio and radio paging services.

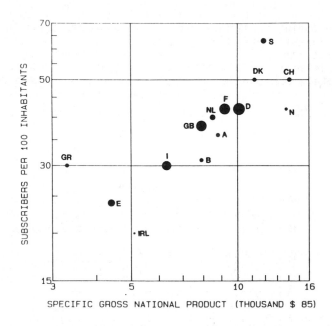

FIGURE 2: TELEPHONE SUBSCRIBERS AND NATIONAL PRODUCT

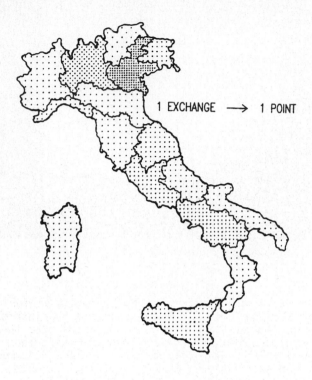

FIGURE 3: ELECTRONIC EXCHANGES IN SERVICE

Concerning the evolution of the transmission network, there has been a considerable digitalization effort for several years, with optical fibers playing
by now, a first rank role. In parallel, for the switching systems that are
essential for integration, all the supply of transit switching equipment is by
now fully digital. Its penetration into the network will reach 70% in '94.

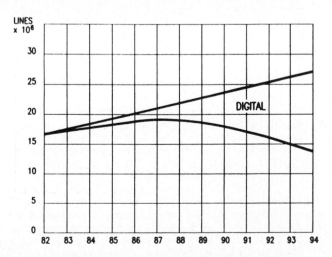

FIGURE 4: TOTAL SWITCHING DEPLOYMENT

FIGURE 5: AN EXCHANGE OF THE "LINEA UT" SYSTEM

With regard to local switching, Fig. 3 shows the amount of fully electronic exchanges already in operation at the end of last year: each point corresponds to one exchange. The penetration level was already 8.5%. Fig. 4 shows the plan for the future. By next year it is foreseen to conclude the conversion of production plants to digital, and to reach by '94 a penetration in the network of 45%.

A large part of the exchanges involved has been fully developed in Italy. Primary reference has to be made to the development of the national system "Linea UT". A large part of the local exchanges already in service are made up by UT modules interconnected with a fully meshed structure. Fig. 5 gives a picture of an exchange of this system. The peripheral module contains 2000 ports, thus permitting a final capacity of 20000 subscribers for these exchanges.

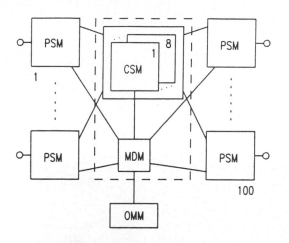

PSM: Periph. & Switching Module

CSM: Circuit Switching Module

MDM: Message Distribution Module

OMM: Oper.n & Maintenance Module

FIGURE 6: UT STRUCTURE (MAXIMUM CAPACITY)

FIGURE 7: UT SWITCHING MATRICES (2 x 512 x 512)

2. R&D ACTIVITIES

At present, the development activity mainly concerns the inter-module circuit and message switching networks represented in the middle of Fig. 6, allowing for a capacity beyond 100000 subscribers per exchange. The fundamental brick of the circuit switching network is the card with two 512 by 512 channels switching matrices, represented in Fig. 7.

FIGURE 8: A CONCENTRATOR-MULTIPLEXER MC 240

Several other developments are carried out at the same time, for example on common channel signalling or on user line concentrators and multiplexers of the type represented in Fig. 8. Further developments in switching concern other systems, for example the switching part of the ITALSAT satellite system.

Moreover, a quantity of R&D activities are dedicated to future switching techniques and architecture. At this moment the Italian industry is not planning a new switching system in the near future. It is considered more convenient to enhance present switching systems through the development of new modules (in particular for fast packet switching) and through the common use of already existing resources where possible. This is mainly for timing reasons, for savings in development resources, for the convenience of gradually developing and evolving the most suited modules, and to testing their markets. Therefore, it is expected that these R&D activities will not generate a revolution, but very important and further evolutions, after the progress by now generated in all telecom fields from the penetration of digital technologies.

An important consideration at the basis of the evolution is that the diffusion of digital transmission media and digital exchanges with common channel signalling is becoming wide enough to allow for a wide-coverage introduction of ISDN services starting immediately. Moreover, the most recent R&D results (particularly in the field of asynchronous time division techniques) clearly show that the trend towards services integration will become increasingly easy in the future than in the past, and extendable to a wide range of services.

3.   ISDN

The previous considerations open the way for the primary subject of this Seminar: ISDN. In particular, they open the way for considering ISDN as an evolutionary subject, to be approached by means of evolutionary strategies.

Reference can be made to the following five steps, marking the first evolution of the ISDN concept. These have been already presented in 1985 at the International Teletraffic Congress in Kyoto (ref. 7):

- Transparent digital connectivity at 64 kbit/s,
- ISDN including packet communications, with various multiservice customer interfaces;
- "Bearer ISDN (OSI), convergence point for existing networks by means of gateways;
- ISDN with high-level OSI functions for communication-oriented application services (e.g. MHS);
- "Intelligent" ISDN with high-level functions for for application services in general (VAS).

Considering the effects of the present diffusion of digital telephone exchanges with common channel signalling, the conclusion is that with few complementary adaptations it becomes possible to put ISDN into service now, with both digital connectivity at 64 kbit/s and with the capacity of also handling packet communications. So, it is possible to put into service an ISDN corresponding at least to the second evolutionary step mentioned above. In effect, this is what is presently in progress in Italy. Fig. 9 shows the network made up by standard exchanges, with the provision for a pilot ISDN service in Italy beginning next year, 1988. Starting in 1990, the same services integration features will be inserted in all the digital exchanges operating throughout the country.

Of course, all the advanced countries are introducing the ISDN approximately at the same time. At the International Switching Symposium held in Phoenix (Arizona) in March of this year, the word ISDN recurred 54 times in the titles of the 171 papers presented. All the six key speakers, from USA, Germany F.R., Japan, France, Canada and Italy, specifically stressed the introduction of ISDN in their respective countries (ref. from 1 to 6). This means that, when in 1990 an extended ISDN will commence functioning in Italy, the same network will be interconnected with all the other ISDNs emerging in other European countries.

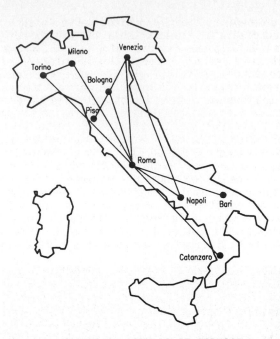

FIGURE 9: ISDN PILOT SERVICE

4. INTRODUCTION POLICIES

In the above said framework, considering now the process of introduction of ISDN in the previously mentioned sense of addition of specific equipment to the 64 kbit/s telephone exchanges already equipped with common channel signalling, it is reasonable to foresee that there will be no heavy problems of a technical nature to be solved (in particular, teletraffic problems).

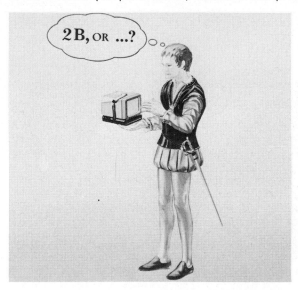

FIGURE 10: THE PRESENT HAMLET'S DILEMMA

May be, marketing or organizational problems (and delays) will emerge. For example, it seems reasonable to forecast that the success of ISDN will be measured mainly by its capacity to attract large users in the "business" area. Consequently, except in cases of large diffusion of Centrex, the success of ISDN should correspond to a wide use of the primary access (in Europe at 2 Mbit/s). Where Centrex has little diffusion or doesn't exist, the provision of the ISDN access 2B only would generate a Hamlet dilemma on the ISDN success, as shown in Fig. 10.

In effect, sooner or later ISDN will certainly be successful. However, in the meantime, circuit and packet switched specialized networks have been developed, both for public use and for exclusive use of specific customers. Enhancement and growth of these networks are expected, and particular mention should be given to the public specialized networks. For example, in Italy, the so-called speech and data network presently in operation and equipped with Nr. 7 CCITT common channel signalling makes it already possible to offer services such as digital connectivity, virtual network service (SDN/PVN-like) and an 800-like access from the telephone network. Moreover, regarding compatibility,

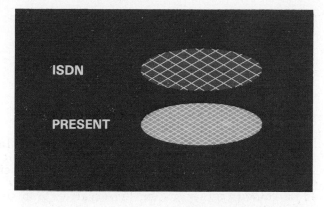

FIGURE 11: OVERLAY ISDN

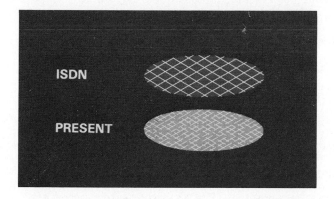

FIGURE 12: ABSORPTION OF THE PRESENT NETWORK

it can be foreseen that the specialized networks will not generate problems
for the introduction of ISDN, because in general they use the same standards,
that have been developed for ISDN (standard transmission interfaces, standard
common channel signalling, and so on).

All these considerations appear to be valid not only for the present situation, but also for the future in general. In effect, it seems reasonable to
foresee that, on one hand ISDN will develop further and further through subsequent evolutionary steps and that, on the other hand, at least the most important of these steps will be preceded by specialized networks anticipating this
or that feature.

In order to represent this concept in a graphical way, Fig. 11 shows how ISDN
has been seen from the beginning as a network layered over the previous analogue one. At birth, the upper network is quite thin and less equipped than the
lower one. Fig. 12 shows how, after a certain time, through the equipment replacement process, the lower network begins to crumble and to be absorbed into
the new one.

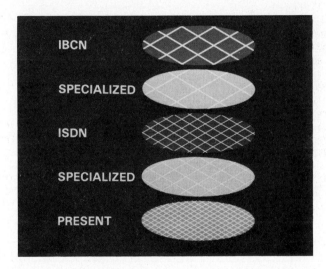

FIGURE 13: SPECIALIZED AND GENERAL PURPOSE NETWORKS

All this is evident, but it also takes time. It takes time before, in the expectation of the birth of the overlayed network, but also later in the expectation of introduction of evolutionary steps into the already existing ISDN.
In the meantime, the users (with particular reference to business users) cannot wait for the new ISDN. So, new specialized networks may emerge.

To give an idea of the entire process, Fig. 13 shows, in the lowest layer, the
previous analogue network. First generation ISDN is represented in the middle
layer while, between them, there is the class of specialized networks presently in operation. The uppermost layer represents second-generation ISDN. It may
represent for example an integrated broadband asynchronous time-division network of the future. The class of intermediate specialized networks that will
precede this second-generation ISDN is represented immediately below. This is
in some way a dynamic picture, with sequences of specialized and general purpose networks, repeated in various evolutionary stages.

5. PROBLEMS TO BE SOLVED

In this dynamic picture, compatibility between a specialized network and the subsequent ISDN will become essential. Certainly, the second generation ISDN will pose many problems in this sense. Once more, the importance of international standards will emerge. Standards shall come in time, have few options, and be the development requirements for all resources, either related to specialized networks or to ISDN.

But the application of standards implies the solution of alternatives for the definition of future switching systems, and these alternatives are numerous. The variability applies to several parameters ranging from the choice of efficient time-sharing utilization of the total band to the choice of a way for sharing the total band among signals having diverse bandwidths, to the choice of a method for rendering the delay compatible with different service needs, and so on. In order to reach cost-effective solutions, all these fields shall be rationalized.

6. TELETRAFFIC ASPECTS

In conclusion, mention has been made here to the three most important aspects to be considered with reference to ISDN, and in particular to a second-generation broad-band asynchronous time-division ISDN. They are:

- aspects concerning the evolution of the network architecture and technology for the ISDN;
- aspects concerning new standards for transmission, switching, signalling, in general new CCITT recommendations for future interfaces and protocols;
- aspects concerning the rationalization of all parameters involved in a cost-efficient ISDN design and planning.

These are the subjects dealt with successively in the next presentations, given by the three outstanding speakers that have accepted to give their contributions to the Opening Session of this Seminar dedicated to Teletraffic and ISDN.

In effect, it is a largely shared conviction that, for an efficient and practical solution to all the problems concerning the three aspects above, the support and close participation of teletraffic specialists are needed. This concept has already been clearly expressed at the International Teletraffic Congress held in Kyoto in 1985. Moreover, several problems related to Teletraffic and ISDN have already been underlined at the Teletraffic Seminar held in Bruxelles in 1986.

Following the lines above, the Lake Como Seminar is essentially a workshop dedicated to ISDN, in preparation for the International Teletraffic Congress to be held in Torino next year with the theme· "Teletraffic Science for new cost-effective Systems, Networks and Services". On this occasion the teletraffic science will demonstrate its practical validity and dynamic vitality, giving considerable contribution to the solution of important cost-effectiveness problems.

7. REFERENCES

1.- B.R. DeMaeyer: "Forces of Change in the United States Telecommunications Industry" - ISS'87.
2.- H. Schoen: "Introduction and Development of the ISDN in the Federal Republic of Germany" - ISS'87.

3.- J. Dondoux: "Telecommunications in France: Building a Nationwide ISDN" - ISS'87.
4.- M. Shiromizu: "Telecommunications Networks and Switching Systems in Japan" - ISS'87.
5.- W.B. Hewat: "Canada - In the Forefront of Telecommunications" - ISS'87.
6.- P. de Ferra: "Italian Telecoms in View of ISDN" - ISS'87.
7.- P. de Ferra: "Teletraffic and Management" - Proceedings of ITC 11 (North-Holland, Amsterdam, 1986).

TRAFFIC ENGINEERING for ISDN Design and Planning
M. Bonatti and M. Decina (Editors)
Elsevier Science Publishers B.V. (North-Holland)
© IAC, 1988

PROGRESS IN TRAFFIC ENGINEERING FOR ISDN: FROM KYOTO (1985) TO TORINO (1988)

Lester Gimpelson

ALCATEL, Belgium

This meeting in Como is a natural extension of the Kyoto and Brussels meetings and a preparation for the Torino ITC. In Kyoto initial investigations of ISDN were largely theoretical, as there were no major installations by that time, and indeed still much design work and standards setting ahead. Trials could be reported in Brussels, together with much more definite information on standards and the beginnings of traffic estimates. Now in Como we see from the strength and diversity of papers that progress is being made in ISDN and it is being supported actively and enthusiastically by the teletraffic community.

On the other hand, in my remarks at the last ITC in Kyoto, I asked this question: is the level of teletraffic work and the "inventiveness" of this work sufficient to prevent "unforeseen" problems as voice and data mix contentiously on national networks, or is there the potential for a major surprise (as we had twenty years ago with congestion of common controlled networks?). While I'm impressed by the scope and quality of the work being presented at this Como meeting, I'm still not completely sure that that two-year-old question has been answered.

This worry aside, it's to look further ahead, toward the Torino meeting. There I hope to see a solution to another potential problem, namely a lack of both standards and traffic work on application level services. The traffic fraternity has an opportunity to move from its traditional role analyzing existing systems to a new role, encouraging ISDN services' development by providing supporting forecasting and design technology in advance of implementation. This leads to the statements of a three-element "circular" applications introduction problem.

To properly plan - in fact to encourage - the evolution and expansion of pubblic and private networks for the growth of ISDN services it is necessary to forecast which services will be introduced, what traffic levels each service will attain and what individual traffic characteristics each will have. Predicting the successes of newly introduced services is a difficult task; estimating their characteristics in a real environment is even more daunting. The composite results of these exercises will govern the development direction of networks; the accuracy of these predictions will determine the ease or difficulty with which networks evolve; the flexibility of network designs ("robustness") will affect the scenario and success of ISDN services offerings.

Thus far most attention by the telecommunications community --administrations and network providers (service offerers) and their suppliers (both equipment and new services) -- has been directed toward the structure on which ISDN communications and services will be transported. Via hypothesized scenarios various traffic groupings and their characteristics have been studied. These have been largely transport-oriented, of necessity because initial design standards were needed urgently and because information has not been available upon which to base applications-related considerations.

Although there have not been major advances in predicting application's development, it is becoming increasingly inconvenient to defer decisions on standards as this is delaying provision of facilities for new services introduction. The result appears to be a (classical?) three-elements chicken-and-egg situation with:

. potential users waiting for services and unwilling to invest in terminal equipment capable of utilizing ISDN facilities until the services are available;

. administrations waiting for standards, services definitions and traffic-load development to guarantee revenue before investing in equipment for offering services (exception: French PTT);

. manufacturers waiting for that elusive "market window" before investing in the development and production of terminal and related equipment.

Meanwhile, all three groups await decisions (economic, entrepreneurial, political) on the specific siting of services: at network nodes, exterior to the network, or at the users' premises.

The problem areas just outlined are compounded by delays resulting from the uncertainties of broadband ISDN in two important aspects, namely, currently competing realizations and increasing questioning of broadband ISDN's commercial economics as adequate traffic loads seem less likely, due to rapid advances in compression techniques and the worldwide progress of CATV installations.

The traffic fraternity can help to resolve these problems and assist in making decisions on implementation directions; it could thus speed the offering of application level services, that big "S" in ISDN. I see the fraternity now able to affect ISDN's development and implementation directions, rather than being constrained to its traditional role of analyzing systems (again traditionally after their implementation). Additionally traffic work needs to put new (and unaccustomed) emphasis on economics (costs, revenues!!, market and services development). I'll look forward to reading these papers in Torino.

TRAFFIC ENGINEERING for ISDN Design and Planning
M. Bonatti and M. Decina (Editors)
Elsevier Science Publishers B.V. (North-Holland)
© IAC, 1988

EVOLVING NETWORK ARCHITECTURE AND TECHNOLOGY FOR ISDN

Maurizio Decina

Politecnico di Milano/Italtel

Milan, Italy

Some oustandindg aspects of the ISDN evolution are briefly reviewed; these are: the emerging <u>fast</u> <u>switching</u> techniques; the <u>intelligent</u> <u>network</u> features and services; the need to serve both <u>business</u> <u>and</u> <u>residential</u> users according to a market-driven deployment strategy.

INTRODUCTION

The ISDN represents the evolution of the <u>common</u> <u>carrier</u> telecommunication networks. Today we can characterize the <u>ISDN</u> by means of the following five attributes:

A) <u>end-to-end</u> <u>digital</u> <u>connectivity</u>;

B) <u>integrated</u> <u>services</u> <u>access</u>, for voice, data and image applications;

C) a reduced set of <u>world-wide</u> <u>standard</u> <u>interfaces</u>;

D) <u>intelligent</u> <u>network</u> <u>services</u>: these are the special services to meet the need of business users and to allow <u>customer</u> <u>control</u> on the network resources;

E) <u>enhanced</u> <u>network</u> <u>services</u>; these are network services beyond information transport, such as protocol mediation and database access for videotex applications.

In early stages the <u>narrowband</u> ISDN will be implemented by users/network interfaces using TDM mixtures of B and D-channels at the 144 kbit/s basic access and 1.5/2 Mbit/s primary access rates.

In later stages, the <u>wideband</u> ISDN is going to be realized by user/network interfaces at a rate that should be world-wide unique at around 150 Mbit/s (we support 149.760 Mbit/s). This user/network interface rate should meet by <u>octet</u> <u>interleaving</u> the multiplexing needs of 1.5 and 2 Mbit/s channels, as well as of 32, 45 and 140 Mbit/s channels. New switching techniques will be used in the evolving ISDN over the entire 150 Mbit/s bandwith or over portions of it, e.g. 45 and 32 Mbit/s.

Below we briefly treat a number of topics of outstanding importance in the ISDN evolution; these are:

  - the new switching techniques;
  - the network intelligence;
  - the special services and the ISDN.

SWITCHING TECHNIQUES

Fig.1 shows the spectrum of basic switching techniques pointing out the statistical switching ones: fast circuit and fast packet. These techniques aim at the realization of high capacity packet switches (several G bit/s of throughput) with less than 1 ms delay for multimedia applications. The power of statistical switching is shown by figures 2 and 3, where Fig. 2 illustrates characteristics of present switches in terms of port and "crosspoint" bandwidth, and of connection rate per "crosspoint". Fig. 3 shows what can be accomplished by "fast" switching.

An implementation of a fast packet switching fabric is given in Fig. 4, where a simple Banyan network with 3 stages is drawn. When the two-by-two switches have no buffer, then the fabric realizes fast circuit switching.

Research is being conducted on fast switching prototypes aiming at the implementation of port bandwidths of 32, 45 and 150 Mbit/s. A switch with thousand DS.3 ports will offer a throughput of more than 20 Gbit/s !

NETWORK INTELLIGENCE

Fig. 5 shows the current architecture of the intelligent ISDN, evolving from narrowband:

  - 64 kbit/s circuits and multirate;
  - 64 kbit/s X.25 packets;
  - 64 kbit/s and 1.5/2 Mbit/s leased channels for special
    services;

to wideband:

  - wideband circuits and channels (32/45 up to 150 Mbit/s);
  - wideband packets (fast packets over links at 32/45 up to 150
    Mbit/s).

The network intelligence is obtained through two network facilities:

  - operations support, to cater also for customer interactions;
  - signalling network and service data bases.

Intelligent network services include:

  - the network-wide Centrex;
  - the 800 service and its enhanced versions;

- the Private Virtual Network (PVN) service.

These services are realized by using the SS No. 7 interface to a service data base where customer data are stored and updated under customer control via operations support. The interaction of the service node on a call-by-call basis allows to route dynamically each call in order to provide the desired customer feature. The PVN service, for example, implements multiple private virtual networks on a call-by-call basis via the common carrier network infrastructures.

The scenario depicted in Fig. 5 finally makes clear that the ISDN Reference Protocol Model is multidimensional, as foreseen by the model of Fig. 6. Signalling is a full protocol layers process with specific application processes (e.g.the 800 service). Management is ubiquitous to allow operation support and customer control. It can use both signalling and information transport protocols and facilities. Moreover in the vision of Fig 6 it appears that users information can be processed within the network up to Layer 7, e.g. for protocol mediation, data base access and messaging.

Figs. 7 and 8 convey the intelligent network message in form of the "onion" scheme commonly used by computer people. In particular Fig. 8 illustrates the concept of customer control by forecasting future user programming domains over network resources and features.

The writer's message though, in front of Figs. 7 and 8 concerns the network evolution process that maybe will change technologies of transport (e.g. fast switching instead of switching), but will likely continue to use most of the already deployed upper onion skin layers (i.e. the application software). For reasons of continuity and cost, the intelligent network concept will force to software reuse for operation, administration, maintenance, service node features, etc.

SPECIAL SERVICES AND ISDN

It is today understood that the ISDN uses, and will likely use in the future, hybrid switching techniques: i.e. circuit and packet switching.

This concept is applied to both narrowband and wideband ISDN approaches. In the wideband network, circuit switching is used for voice, bulk data and motion video, while packet switching applies to voice as well, data and high speed imaging. Both techniques should operate on channels at up to hundreds of Mbit/s.

In an hybrid switching environment the degree of control capabilities for flexible bandwidth allocation is of great importance. Fig. 9 illustrates the problem with reference to a TDM frame format used on wideband hybrid channels. A field of the time frame ($\emptyset$) is devoted to OSI Layer 1 features. These are the TDM transmission formats to be used on optical facilities to allow proper maintenance and operation features such as: add-drop capabilities, span and network supervisory channels, protection switching and cross-connect switching. This format is required also in cases of fully packetized networks and is very attractive for special services provision.

The other fields include signalling (A), circuit switched TDM channels (B), and packet switched message-interleaved channels (C). Signalling can be used to set up both "physical" and "virtual" circuits in the B and C fields, as well as to move the boundary. In an alternative approach the A field is empty, while the signalling channel is virtual and embedded in the C field. This high speed signalling channel controls both virtual circuits in C and physical circuits in B, as well as boundary movements. While the former alternative shall be used in the early wideband ISDN stages, the latter alternative is going to be used in the evolving ISDN.

Fig. 10 shows two TDM frame formats to be used at the access interfaces of the wideband hybrid network. In the example, fixed boundary is used between circuit and packet resources. The first format applies at 600 Mbit/s with four chunks at 150 Mbit/s each: 3 wideband circuit switched channels and one fast packet data link. In addition the format incorporates at least two B-channels and one D-channel at 64 kbit/s each, for reasons of continuity and compatibility with narrowband ISDN terminals and switches. In this case, the D-channel is used for circuit switching of all circuit switched channels. It remains to be evaluated the D-channel capability to support at such slow speed (64 kbit/s) setting up and tear down of virtual circuits in the fast packet channel (150 Mbit/s). The second frame format in Fig. 10 shows similar criteria applied at an 150 Mbit/s interface where the four chunks are at 32 Mbit/s each. In the North American environment the 150 Mbit/s pipe can be partitioned into three chunks at 45 Mbit/s each.

It should be noted that in Fig. 10 there is no Layer 1 overhead included in the TDM frames (see Fig. 9). This overhead must be present and it can indeed be used to provide flexible routing of the circuit switched channels and of the packet switched channels to the proper serving switching offices as shown in Fig. 11.

A network deployment strategy is indeed proposed in Fig. 11. The business community is first served by a flexible "slow switched" Layer 1 network composed by fiber loops and feeders and by fiber DACSs (digital access and cross connect systems) also referred as "fiber hubs". Switching on demand via the fiber hubs provide for special services dedicated facilities to multiple business communities. This implementation stage can be realized in the short-term. Fiber hubs are then used to route 1.5/2 Mbit/s or 32/45/150 Mbit/s chunks towards "real time" switching equipment, according to the market demand for such applications. In Fig. 11 we have assumed, as an example: a narrowband ISDN switch (for residential and business users); a wideband circuit switch (for entertainment video switching) and a wideband packet switch (for business users). The Layer 1 TDM format proposed for such a strategy is similar to the Bellcore's SONET proposal and it applies to both user-network interfaces and intra-network interfaces, but it operates at the basic rate of 150 Mbit/s (149.760 Mbit/s) and it uses octet interleaving.

CONCLUSIONS

We have shortly commented some driving forces of the ISDN evolution from narrowband to wideband.

High speed switching in both circuit and packet modes is the

necessary mechanism to satisfy most emerging service requirements;
dynamic bandwidth allocation and the network control techniques
are the challenges in the design of large wideband networks loaded
by unknown service input traffic profiles.

Network intelligence is going to dominate the evolving network
architecture, regardless the specific transport mechanisms that
will gradually be deployed.

Market driven requirements of cost vs performance for various
service applications should ultimately dominate the selection of
the equipment and the network deployment strategy. Business needs
and residential needs should be carefully evaluated in particular
for the choice of the services that should economically justify
the large investments needed for the wideband network deployment.

Switching Techniques

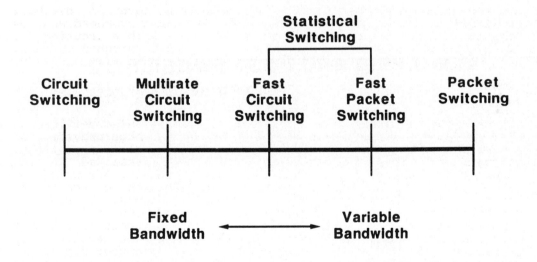

FIGURE 1

Switching and Fast Switching 1

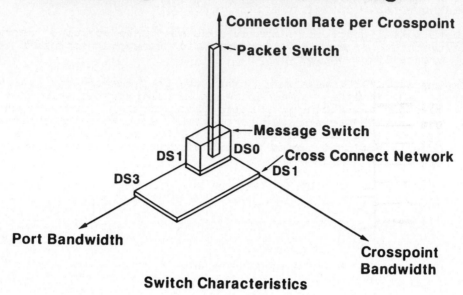

FIGURE 2

Switching and Fast Switching 2

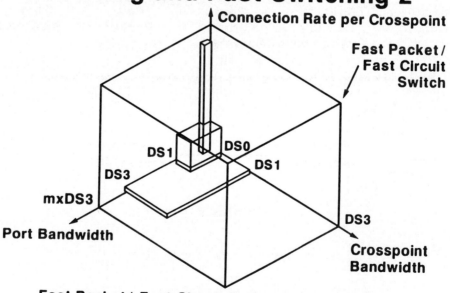

FIGURE 3

Fast Packet Switching Fabrics

- **Unbuffered / Buffered Banyans**
  - **High-Throughput / Low-Delay**
  - **Suitable for Integration**

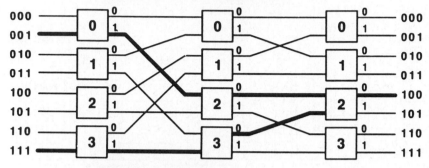

- **Critical Issues**
  - **Internal Links Speed**
  - **Broadcasting Capability**
  - **Fault Tolerance**

FIGURE 4

Intelligent ISDN Layout

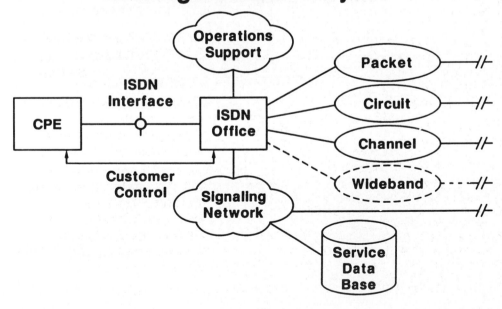

FIGURE 5

M. Decina

OSI Extension to ISDN
ISDN Protocol Reference Model

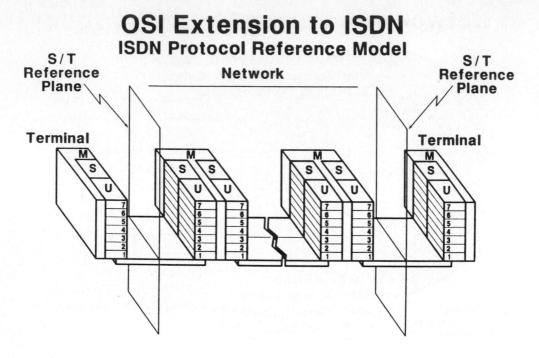

FIGURE 6

Intelligent Network Logical Architecture

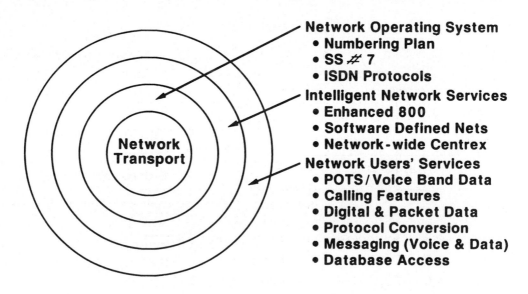

FIGURE 7

Network Functional Structure (2000)

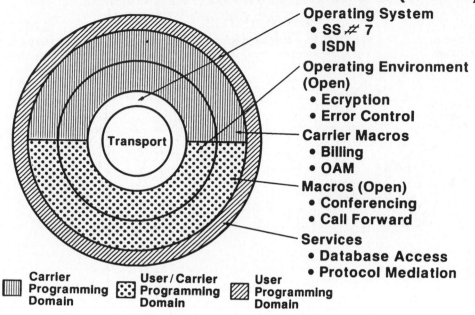

Operating System
- SS ≠ 7
- ISDN

Operating Environment (Open)
- Ecryption
- Error Control

Carrier Macros
- Billing
- OAM

Macros (Open)
- Conferencing
- Call Forward

Services
- Database Access
- Protocol Mediation

Carrier Programming Domain

User / Carrier Programming Domain

User Programming Domain

FIGURE 8

Bandwidth Allocation Control

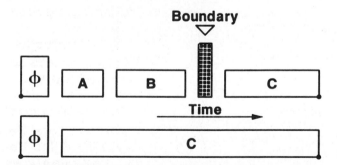

Boundary

φ | A | B | C

Time

φ | C

- φ - **Delimitation & Housekeeping Information**
- A - **Signaling & Control Information**
- B - **Circuit-Switched Information**
- C - **Packet-Switched Information**

FIGURE 9

M. Decina

Wideband Hybrid Network
Double-Star
Access TDM Frame Layout

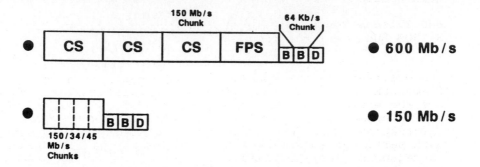

FIGURE 10

Metropolitan Area Fiber Network
Deployment Strategy

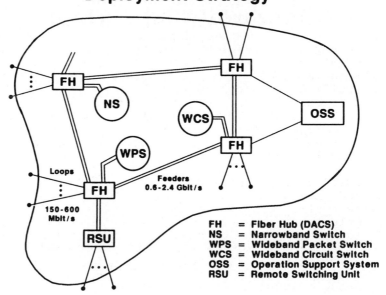

FH = Fiber Hub (DACS)
NS = Narrowband Switch
WPS = Wideband Packet Switch
WCS = Wideband Circuit Switch
OSS = Operation Support System
RSU = Remote Switching Unit

FIGURE 11

TRAFFIC ENGINEERING for ISDN Design and Planning
M. Bonatti and M. Decina (Editors)
Elsevier Science Publishers B.V. (North-Holland)
© IAC, 1988

CCITT AND ISDN TRAFFIC ENGINEERING

Géza GOSZTONY

BHG Telecom Works, Development Institute, P.O.Box 2
H-1509 Budapest, Hungary

The multiservice environment of ISDNs requires a general
framework for service quality characterization which covers the aspects of users and service providers. Since
CCITT Recommendations refer mainly to networks carrying
international traffic, present work concentrates on network performance issues. A possible framework is based
on measurable primary parameters and on secondary parameters which reflect the collective effect of the former.
Recommendations on ISDN traffic engineering can not be
restricted to GOS parameter definitions and monitoring
but have to include methods to describe traffic in the
user, control and management planes and should also find
a solution for proper determination of reference conditions.

MAIN STATEMENTS: Quality parameter framework and traffic
engineering methodology of CCITT improves design and evaluation of telecommunication services.

INTRODUCTION

ISDN traffic engineering work in CCITT was started in 1985. The
first review of results and problems was presented in the 4th ITC
Seminar /Brussels, 1986/ [LEGA 86]. The objectives, methods and
results of CCITT traffic engineering work have been several times
reviewed in Teletraffic Congresses and will not be dealt with here
[GOSZ 85]. CCITT as an international body responsible for stan-
dard-like Recommendations referring to telecommunications is primarily interested in network aspects and the results it requires
are of practical nature.

The basic CCITT concepts of ISDN have already been completed for
some time and they seemed to be stable enough to start detailed
ISDN service quality studies in the 1985-88 study period. The work
going on reflects the present, single-service oriented structure
of CCITT Study Groups with much parallel work and some misunderstandings. Therefore it would be a rather hopeless undertaking to
summarize all service quality related or only the grade of service
(GOS) related activities which have a bearing on future ISDN traffic engineering.

This paper will thus concentrate on two basic problems: (1) the
framework of ISDN service quality evaluation and (2) the scope of
ISDN traffic engineering Recommendations. If necessary some basic
considerations will also be presented since well clarified starting points are required in these areas.

The ideas offered are those of the author and are not necessarily identical to the views of CCITT Study Groups involved in relevant studies.

1. ISDN TRAFFIC ENGINEERING

1.1. Worldwide

It has been recognized several years ago that traffic engineering in the multiservice environment of future ISDNs will bring an incredible amount of work to be done. New technologies and/or new services require the introduction of many new GOS (grade of service) parameters and relevant studies should be performed in many cases within a short time and with a poor or even without any knowledge on traffic characteristics and user behaviour. Very often mixed traffic will be offered to resources and therefore the traditional models of traffic engineering may not be valid [KATZ 83], [PAND 84]. A rather limited survey on problems in this field to be solved by CCITT has also been presented [GOSZ 85].

The obvious progress in ISDN traffic engineering is indicated by several review type papers summarizing the most important aspects of ISDN way of thinking and the modelling of new services [KÜHN 86], presenting a structured approach using the OSI seven layer framework [REIS 86], trying to find a general way of describing the traffic handling process by combining graphical SDL (Specification and Description Language) type and MSC (Message Sequence Chart) type presentations into Event Flow Diagrams [BONA 86]. The necessity to reconsider the concept of traffic has also been recognized e.g. by analyzing the steps of transformation from user information transfer demand to traffic [GONZ 85] or by defining a new type reference traffic for design purposes [BERR 86].

1.2. Within CCITT

Telephone traffic engineering has a long tradition in CCITT. In the E.5xx Series of Recommendations almost all necessary aspects (GOS parameters and values, determination of reference traffic, carried traffic - offered traffic transformation, traffic measurement methodologies, forecasting, dimensioning methods, etc.) are covered to some extent, mainly from the operational point of view. Design GOS parameters for digital exchanges appear in Recommendations Q.504 and Q.514 (in preparation)[GOSZ 85]. For data traffic engineering GOS parameters can be found in the X.13x and X.14x Series of Recommendations. QOS (Quality of Service) aspects of the network services of (CCITT) OSI, including GOS parameters, appear in Rec. X.213. Work directed to draft new Recommendations and to improve existing ones is going on in all the above fields.

Besides these traditional activities ISDN oriented traffic engineering work has also begun. Three main streams can be identified. (a) QOS and performance aspects of ISDN in general are adressed by Study Group XVIII. These considerations include GOS. The same type of work is going on in Study Group II but the approach is somewhat different. (b) ISDN traffic engineering is covered in the E.7xx Series of Rec.s to be prepared by Study Group II. (c) The work in (a) and (b) has a major impact on new and modified Rec.s for dedicated networks and/or non-integrated services, mainly from the methodological point od view. This refers to Study Groups II, VII and XI.

The traditional single-service oriented structure of CCITT constitutes an extra problem in solving QOS and GOS problems. The first step to arrive at a common understanding has been done recently. (Joint coordination meeting on quality of service and performance issues of CCITT Study Group II, VII, XV and XVIII experts, Geneva, 1987. March.)

Important, not yet solved problems of the three areas mentioned appear below in some detail.

2. THE FRAMEWORK OF QUALITY PARAMETERS

GOS is one aspect of service quality and its characteristic parameters belong to the set of QOS parameters. In the multiservice environment of future ISDNs a practical framework of these parameters is an important and necessary tool for design and operation. Some general remarks on the interpretation and structure of service quality parameters are followed by a short summary of present, still discussed CCITT approaches.

2.1. The user-provider relativity

In very general terms service can be defined as: work or duty done for someone or something. Someone or something is the user of the service and should be interpreted in the broadest possible manner. The demand of the user is satisfied by the service offered by the provider. Thus user and provider have a relationship which is expressed by the service. User and provider are relative categories which exist only related to a given service. Restricting our considerations to ISDN we can find many user - service - provider triplets. Examples are: application service, teleservice, bearer service, Nth OSI layer service,D channel service.

As a consequence of the relativity mentioned above the same entity (in a wide sense) can be a user in one relation and a provider in the other. E.g. a provider of enhanced teleservices may be a user of bearer services offered by an other provider, etc. A more detailed presentation of this situation and its consequences is also possible [BONA 87].

2.2. Hierarchy of functions and items

The service appears as a set of functions offered by the provider. The functions are performed by physical and logical components, assemblies, units, subsystems, equipments, etc., which in general are regarded as items if they can be considered individually. There is an evident hierarchy both in HW (hardware) and SW (software) items, since a higher level item is normally composed from lower level items. There is a long chain from components (as ICs or macros) to a complete ISDN network for example.

In a similar way a function of the service offered by a given item (a provider) is normally an organized set of functions performed by lower level items. If a lower level function is not performed properly the performance of the upper level function may degrade.

The hierarchy of functions and items may but does not necessarily correspond to an alternating user - provider chain (for the former case see OSI layer services). During the traffic engineering of a complex system one is necessarily confronted to the hierarchy of functions (services) and items (servers).

2.3. Quality parameters

The service may be performed in a better or worse way i.e. with a certain quality. To be able to judge whether the functions of a service are performed appropriately quality parameters are defined and values or ranges as objectives are allotted to them. If the objectives are met the service performance is satisfactory. The complexity of the service determines the number of parameters required.

The user and the provider may have different aspects for the evaluation and therefore in most cases two correlated sets of quality parameters exist for the same service. The user e.g. is only interested in the access delay between two network access points, the provider has to design the network and may therefore define additional parameters influencing or constituting the access delay.

Studies may concentrate on a subset of service quality parameters, e.g. GOS parameters and neglect others. It may cause serious confusions however if the perspective of the whole picture becomes lost.

From the above considerations one can conclude that quality parameters should be arranged in a way to take into account the user - - provider relativity and the hierarchy of service functions mentioned.

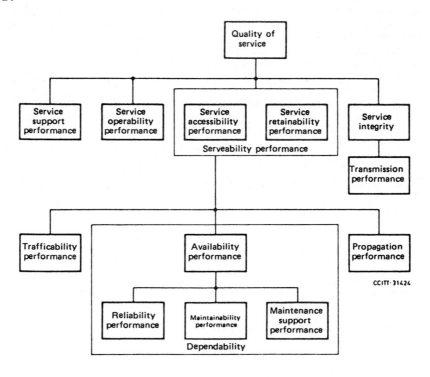

FIGURE 2.1

Performance concepts of Rec. G.106

2.4 A possible CCITT approach

At present two different frameworks exist in CCITT to arrange service quality concepts and parameters. One can be found in Rec.G.106 [CCIT 85a],[STRA 85], the other is still in preparation [CCIT 86a]. In spite of some earlier misunderstandings now it seems to be clear that the two frameworks are complementary. Instead of presenting a comparison an attempt of harmonization follows including also the results of the joint coordination meeting already mentioned.

2.4.1 Background

The first framework was prepared with a background based mainly on the telephone service, but intended to be used for all telecommunication services, see Fig.2.1. The dependability block is function performance oriented and therefore very general. This can be seen from the definition of availability:

- the ability of an item to be in a state to perform a required function at a given instant of time or at any instant of time within a given time interval, assuming that the external resources, if required, are provided.

G.106 adopts a structured approach and attempts to take all factors into account which contribute to the quality of service (QOS). The definition of QOS reads as follows:

- the collective effect of service performances which determine the degree of satisfaction of a user of the service.

GOS parameters belong to the trafficability block, traffic engineering calculations normally assume that considered resources do perform the required functions i.e. are available (are in up state). A delay caused by a properly dimensioned group of resources may be out of range if some resources get into a down state because of a HW or SW failure. In this case serveability will not be satisfactory due to the combined result of the lower levels.

The second framework is an attempt to continue the attribute oriented description, now in the field of ISDN servic quality. In Rec.s I.211, I.212 and I.340 a service quality attribute is already included for bearer services, teleservices and connection types, respectively [CCIT 85c]. Considerations at present are mainly directed to connection types and the collective term network performance is used for service quality. The second framework has already been used to update X.13x Recommendations.

Present studies of this framework refer to a part of the bearer service, which, from the technical point of view, can be accessed and is offered at the S/T interface (Fig.2.2), but the service itself is broader than network capabilities alone. A bearer service user may also be interested in the service support given by the provider, etc.

2.4.2 The primary and secondary parameter concept

Primary service quality parameters
- can directly be determined
- by observation of reference events related to the service
- at exactly defined boundaries of services e.g. access interfaces , networks or network components
- in significant or monitor points.

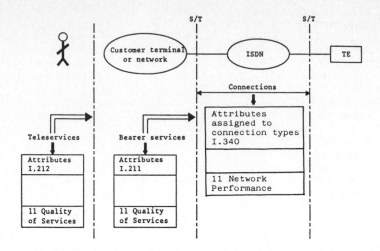

FIGURE 2.2

General scope of service quality [CCIT 86a]

E.g. in the case of packet switched service a packet level reference event occurs when a packet crossing a section boundary changes
the state of the packet level interface. For an entry event the
crossing of the first bit of the address field, for an exit event
the crossing of the last bit of the closing flag of the respective
frames should be considered as time of occurence. Fig.2.3 gives an
example, for further details see [CCIT 86b]. Delays can be determined by measuring time intervals between corresponding events,
loss is manifested by a missing event, etc.

Primary parameters are associated with values (limits, ranges) as
objectives. By comparing observed values with corresponding thresholds one can check if objectives have been met.

A secondary service quality parameter

   - is related to a set of primary parameters
   - reflecting the collective effect of them, and
   - has a two state (binary) character.

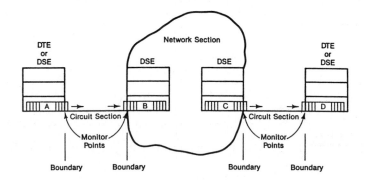

Packet Exit Events for Packets A and C
Packet Entry Events for Packets B and D

FIGURE 2.3

Example packet level reference events [CCIT 86b]

Secondary parameters describe performance based on events which
are defined as occuring when the value of a primary parameter
crosses a corresponding threshold (becomes out of range). These derived events identify the transition between the good (acceptable)
and wrong (unacceptable) states. Several secondary parameters may
be allotted to the totality of primary parameters belonging to the
service. Secondary parameters may be joined to form a more general
secondary parameter.

The traffic handling performance of a complex system (e.g. telephone exchange) can only be characterized with several GOS parameters. The performance is acceptable if the GOS vector consisting of
the parameters as components is inside that part of the GOS space
which is determined by the GOS parameter thresholds [GOSZ 84].

2.4.3 User and provider type parameters

As an example let us consider the parameters which can be defined
to characterize the network capabilities of bearer services. The
two type of parameters should be distinguished because of their
different purposes and applications. The difference between the
users' and providers' aspect is illustrated in Table 2.1.

TABLE 2.1
Aspects for the selection of user and provider
oriented bearer service quality parameters

user	provider
Bearer-service attributes oriented	Connection attributes oriented
Focus on user perceived effects	Focus on network planning, de-velopment, (design), operation and maintenance
Refers to the quality between bearer service access points	Refers to end-to-end or network component capabilities

User and provider type parameters may be identical or correlated.
The correlation is service and parameter specific. In Fig.2.4

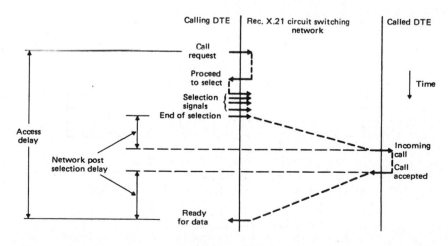

FIGURE 2.4
Relationship between access delay (X.140) and network
post selection delay (X.130) [CCIT 85b]

access delay is a user-oriented while network post selection delay
is a provider-oriented parameter.

In selecting parameters for the purpose of the provider the principles below apply:
- define compatible parameters to facilitate performance planning
- allocate performance objectives among network portions fairly
  and reasonably,
- impose only essential constraints on network internal designs.

Comparing bearer service parameters to teleservice parameters (both
for users and providers) the difference will be in the additional
aspects which cover the service quality requirements of user terminals and/or networks at the S/T interface (Fig.2.2).

2.4.4 Classification of primary parameters

For the classification of primary quality parameters a function/
criterion matrix seems to be appropriate. Fig. 2.5 presents an example with user-oriented parameters of Rec.X.140 [CCIT 86a], which
refer to datanetwork capabilities. The same or a similar presentation may be used in many cases. (XFR stands for transfer.)

	SPEED	ACCURACY	REFUSAL
ACCESS	– Access delay	– Incorrect access prob.	– Access denial prob.
USER INFO XFR	– User info XFR delay – User info XFR rate	– User info misdelivery prob. – Extra user info delivery prob. – User info error prob.	– User info loss prob.
DISENGA-GEMENT	– Diseng. delay	– Disengagement denial probability	

FIGURE 2.5

Rec.X.140 parameters in matrix format [CCIT 86a]

The matrix presentation refers explicitly to a single level of
functions. From the practical point of view it has many advantages.

2.4.5 Framework for secondary parameters

In the overall scheme of Rec.G.106 (Fig.2.1) the performance concepts can be regarded as secondary parameters in the sense of Para
2.4.2. (The corresponding primary parameters seem to be the measures of Rec.G.106, not detailed here.) One can easily follow the
grouping of secondary parameters up to the top, where the highest
level concept: QOS can be found. QOS is intended to include all aspects of service evaluation. QOS should be interpreted as a secondary parameter representing the effect of all primary parameters.

The existing scheme of Rec.G.106 may easily be modified to cover
the functional aspects of the mentioned matrix by appropriate secondary parameters referring to the rows of the matrix. See Fig.2.6,
terms are provisional. The network performance block should replace
the accessibility, retainability and integrity blocks, transmission

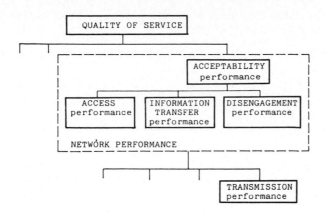

FIGURE 2.6

Function-oriented framework of secondary parameters

performance should be input to this block. It should be emphasized,
however, that the network performance term refers strictly to
bearer services, see the comments in Para 2.4.3.

For future applications, taking also the mentioned hierarchy of
service functions and items into account, one has to clarify how
the observability of primary parameters should be understood in
general. Remaining in the area of teleservices and bearer services
this seems to cause no difficulties.

2.5 Beyond the basic framework

The basic framework of service quality parameters is a tool both
for the user and for the provider. It may support the design and/or
the evaluation of the service by proper classification of relevant
concepts and parameters. Furthermore it is very important for CCITT
to facilitate the preparation of well understandable and unambiguous
Recommendations for this area.

This tool in its form presented above is, however not sufficient to
give a detailed picture for adequate interpretation of many details
of service quality problems. Methods like that in [BONA 86] may
form a solution. A concentrated but still managable layout to describe the several phases of a call together with relevant quality
parameters can be found in Rec.G.107 [CCIT 85d]. This modelling
approach has been extended to different services [CCIT 86c]. In
CCITT there is no general agreement yet about these methods.

3. ISDN RELATED GOS STUDIES

Study Group II started systematic studies on ISDN traffic engineering in 1985. Problems from the past having not yet been solved
even for telephony and new problems of the multiservice environment have both impact on relevant work.

3.1. Old problems

For a long time the time consistent busy hour (TCBH) concept was
the only method for defining reference traffic for GOS value determination. In the draft new text of Rec. E.500, still under discussion, the average daily peak hour (ADPH) and the fixed daily

measurement period (FDMP) concepts appear as alternatives.Detailed
measurements show that for telephony the reference traffic values
derived by these methods differ to some extent [CCIT 86c]. Which
should or can be chosen for non-telephone traffic or traffic mixes?

Unsuccessful call attempts provoke call repetition which has a non
negligible effect on the determination of offered traffic. A possible solution has been arrived at in Rec. E.501, but only for the
most simple arrangement. Repetition, even as a service feature will
survive for the ISDN era.

There is no decision in CCITT whether day-to-day busy hour traffic
variations should be taken into account. Let A be the random variable representing the busy hour traffic and let B(A)be a congestion function (probability of loss, delay, etc.). For convex congestion functions the relationship below is valid

$$B\{M(A)\} \leq M\{B(A)\}$$

Further if B(A) is continuous, non decreasing, bounded and B(0)=0
and B(A)>0 if A>0 are fulfilled

$$M(A)M\{B(A)\} \leq M\{A \cdot B(A)\}$$

holds [KASH 82]. At present the B{M(A)} approach appears in Recommendations. - M($\cdot$) stands for the expectance. Should this practice
be followed in the future?

It has always been a problem whether dimensioning models and methods should be included in Recommendations. This is a continuous
temptation for experts, yes and no both have advantages and drawbacks. Which answer should be given for ISDN?

3.2. Recent problems

This part is based mainly on discussions in and results of the
Study Group II Expert Group on ISDN traffic engineering. It is
however not an attempt to give a complete review of this work.

3.2.1. Traffic in ISDN

The various needs for information transfer of ISDN users are expressed to the network as a traffic demand. This demand generates
call attempts and traffic flows which can be observed at significant points within the network.

The process of how to determine the traffic which may be offered
to a given group of resources or may be measured at a given significant point can be seen in Fig.3.1. The multiservice environment is taken into account by those teleservice and bearer service
attributes which have an effect on the traffic. User demand attributes could cover aspects as
 - call intent arrival models
 - holding time distributions
 - call handling in case of congestion (loss, repetition, waiting,
   etc.)

For methods of how to transform information transfer demands into
traffic see [GONZ 86].

User, control and management plane should be understood according

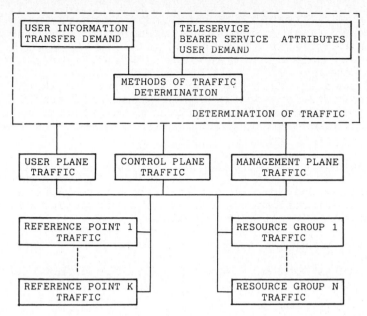

FIGURE 3.1

Traffic determination process in ISDN environment

to Rec.I.320 [CCITT 85c]. In significant points and at the input of resource groups a traffic-plane-mix may appear, see e.g. the D channel.

Further aspects, not yet mentioned, as user group (business, residence, profession, etc.) and call-outcome-mix (successful and unsuccessful for different reasons) have also to be taken into account.

In systems with packet switching or fast circuit switching a call can not be characterized by the holding time alone. A possible set of necessary parameters (random variables) is:

- call holding time,
- number of info-spurts (e.g. active periods) per call,
- number of bits per info-spurt,
- number of bits per packet.

In addition to the mean value the distributions will very likely also be required, since insensitivity results refer to loss systems only [IVER 85].

In a given significant point the parameters (random variables) below are sufficient to fully characterize the traffic:

a. number of - call attempts
            - simultaneously held ~ physical connections
                                  ~ data links
                                  ~ virtual circuits
b. throughput in - bits per second
               - packets per second

All the above parameters should be understood as mean values for a reference period (busy hour?).

For dimensioning purposes, additionally, reference conditions will also be necessary in a similar but much more complex way as call-

mixes are derived e.g. for SPC control SW dimensioning purposes.
Without these type assumptions the traffic determination process
of Fig.3.1 doesn't work.

3.2.2 GOS parameters

The QOS framework discussed earlier is appropriate to accommodate
GOS parameters to be used for CCITT. However in practice there will
be a three level parameter structure as follows:

- end-to-end user parameters,
- end-to-end parameter elements,
- technical performance or design elements.

End-to-end parameters consist of elements directly contributing to
them. Design elements refer to implementation specific resources,
their aggregate effect determines values in the two levels above.
Fig.3.2 gives an example. Times t1 to t6 representing delay parameter elements are related to the following layer 3 signalling
events:

t1 : from SETUP(calling side) or INFO (calling side)that
     contains enough information to set up a call to
     SETUP (called side),
t2 : from ALERT (called side)to ALERT (calling side),
t3 : from CONN (called side) to CONN (calling side),
t4 : from DISC (clearing side) to REL (clearing side),
t5 : from DISC (clearing side) to DISC (cleared side),
t6 : from SETUP (calling side) to SETUP ACK (calling side)
     (only in case of overlap sending).

service	elements / delay perceived by a user		delay GOS parameters for ISDN circuit switched connection						other possible elements		
									time spent in TE/TA		layer 1/2 activation time
			t1	t2	t3	t4	t5	t6	calling/ clearing	called/ cleared	
telephony	dial tone delay							x	x		x
	post dialling delay	case 1	x	x					x	x	x
		case 2	x						x	x	x
		case 3	x		x				x	x	x
X.21 data	post selection delay		x		x				x	x	
	clear request delay					x			x		
	clear indication delay						X.21 bis		x	x	

FIGURE 3.2

Relationship between delay GOS parameter elements for ISDN
switched connection and the end-to-end delays perceived
by a user

The delays perceived by the telephony user should be interpreted
as follows: (a) dial tone delay refers to the case of overlap sending; (b) in case 1 and case 2 the ringing tone is provided by the
calling TE and by the terminating local exchange, respectively;
(c) case 3 assumes an automatic answering terminal [YOKO 87].

A minimum set of ISDN network GOS parameters could be the following. New packet mode with CCS (common channel signalling) is assumed [PAND 87] :

```
                    - pre-selection delay,
                    - post-selection delay,
                    - answer signal delay,
                    - probability of congestion (blocking) ,
           and additionally for data:
                    - network transit delay,
                    - network clear indication delay.
```

3.2.3 Significant points

Significant (reference, monitor) points are points in the network
where traffic and GOS parameters should be related. Traffic and
primary GOS parameters will be measurable at significant points,
see also Para 2.4.2 and the example in Fig.2.3. Whether the dimensioning of design elements mentioned above will require the introduction of "virtual" significant points e.g. similarly as SAPs
(Service Access Point) in OSI, is for further study.

3.3 Recommendations

For data networks a framework for GOS (network performance) parameters already exists, see Fig.3.3. In Rec. X.140 the relationship
between the three parameter types is elaborated in detail. Reference traffic, GOS and traffic monitoring have not been covered yet
[CCIT 85b], [CCIT 86b].

	type of parameter			
	network performance		user perceived	OSI network service
delay	X.130	X.135^x	X.140	X.213
blocking	X.131	X.136^x		
reference events		X.134$^+$	x amended in the 1985-88 period	
XFR mode	circuit switched	packet switched	+ new	

FIGURE 3.3

GOS parameter framework for data networks

The proposed structure of ISDN traffic engineering Recommendations
appears below. Titles are provisional, + indicates completion by
1988.

  General

    + E.700 - Structure of the E.700 Series Recommendations
    + E.701 - Reference connections, significant points for ISDN
              traffic engineering

 ISDN traffic requirements

    + E.710 - ISDN traffic requirements overview
    + E.711 - User demand characteristics
    + E.712 - Reference models for control plane traffic
    + E.713 - Reference models for user plane traffic

 Grade of service and dimensioning models

    + E.720 - GOS concepts
    + E.721 - GOS parameters
    + E.722 - D-channel dimensioning model

Traffic administration and operation

```
E.730 - General considerations
E.731 - Measurement of traffic
E.732 - Forecasting
E.733 - GOS monitoring
```

CONCLUSION

CCITT serves the interests of intenational telecommunications and
its Recommendations refer to those areas where regulation is required. Although the dividing line of regulated and non regulated
telecommunication services is still discussed, service quality aspects will play an important role in the future too. ISDN service
quality framework and ISDN traffic engineering related activities
form only a small part of all work to be done. The success of this
CCITT standardization rests with the studies performed by teletraffic experts whatever organization they belong. They constitute the
basis, and their permanent help is indispensable to achieve results
everybody can be satisfied with.

ACKNOWLEDGEMENTS

Valuable suggestions and considerable help was given during the preparation of this paper by the colleagues of the author and especially by Ms.M. Ágostházi. The author is very indebted for them.

The permission of BHG Telecommunication Works to publish this paper
is highly acknowledged.

REFERENCES

[BERR 86] Berry,L.T.M.: Traffic base definitions for planning and
           dimensioning of integrated services networks - 4.ITC Seminar
           (ISDN traffic issues), Brussels, 1986.

[BONA 86] Bonatti,M., Roveri,A.: A traffic model for design choice
           of ISDN system architectures - 4.ITC Seminar (ISDN traffic
           issues), Brussels, 1986.

[BONA 87] Bonatti,M. Roveri,A.: Personal communication

[CCIT 85a] CCITT Recommendation: Concepts, terms and definitions re-
           lated to availability and reliability studies - Red Book,
           Fasc.III.1.,G.106., ITU, Geneva, 1985.

[CCIT 85b] CCITT Recommendation: General quality of service parame-
           ters for communication via public data networks - Red Book,
           Fasc.VIII.4., X.140., ITU, Geneva, 1985.

[CCIT 85c] CCITT Recommendations: Series I, Integrated Services Di-
           gital Network - Red Book, Fasc.III.5., ITU, Geneva, 1985.

[CCIT 85d] CCITT Recommendation: General considerations and model
           of a basic telephone call - Red Book, Fasc.III.1., G.107.,
           ITU, Geneva, 1985.

[CCIT 86a] CCITT Working Party XVIII/6: Meeting report - COM XVIII-
           R 24 B , 1986.

[CCIT 86b] CCITT Working Party VII/1: Meeting report - COM VII-R 16,
           1986.

[CCIT 86c] CCITT Working Party II/4: Meeting report - COM II-R 19,
           1986.

[GONZ 85] Gonzales Soto,O.: On traffic modelling and characterization of ISDN users - Data communication in the ISDN era, Proc., Perry,Y. ed., Elsevier Science Publ. B.V. (North Holland), 1985. pp.127-140.

[GONZ 86] Gonzales Soto,O., Medina,M.: Modelling and characterization of ISDN traffic - 4.ITC Seminar (ISDN traffic issues), Brussels, 1986.

[GOSZ 84] Gosztony,G.: From congestion to grade of service parameters - ITU Workshop on traffic engineering and forecasting, Athens, 1984. Doc.B.6.

[GOSZ 85] Gosztony,G.: The next step for CCITT: ISDN traffic engineering - 11.ITC, Kyoto, 1985. Paper 6.3.1, p.1-8.

[IVER 85] Iversen,V.B.: A generalization of the classical teletraffic theory - 11.ITC, Kyoto, 1985. Paper 1.4.5, p.1-7.

[KASH 82] Kashper,A., Rocklin,S.M., Szelag,C.R.: Effects of day-to-day load variation on trunk group blocking - BSTJ, 61.1982. 2. pp.123-135.

[KATZ 83] Katz,S.: Introduction of new network services - 10.ITC, Montreal, 1983. Paper 1.1.1, p.1-12.

[KÜHN 86] Kühn,P.: Modelling of new services in computer and communication networks - Computer networking and performance evaluation, Proc., Hasegawa,T. ed., Elsevier Science Publ. B.V. (North Holland) , 1986. pp.283-303.

[LEGA 86] Le Gall,P.: CCITT studies on ISDN traffic engineering - 4.ITC Seminar (ISDN traffic issues) , Brussels, 1986.

[PAND 84] Pandya,R.M., Robinson,W.R.: New services and their impact on traffic engineering - Telecom.J., 51.1984.June, pp.327-331.

[PAND 87] Pandya,R.M.: Personal communication.

[REIS 86] Reiser,M.: Communication system models embedded in the OSI-reference model, a survey - Computer networking and performance evaluation, Proc., Hasegava,T. ed., Elsevier Science Publ. B.V. (North Holland) , 1986. pp.85-111.

[STRA 85] Strandberg,K.: CCITT quality of service concepts applied to telecommunication service planning - ICC 85, Chicago, 1985.

[YOKO 87] Yokoi,T.: Personal communication.

TRAFFIC ENGINEERING for ISDN Design and Planning
M. Bonatti and M. Decina (Editors)
Elsevier Science Publishers B.V. (North-Holland)
© IAC, 1988

TRAFFIC ENGINEERING FOR ISDN DESIGN AND PLANNING

Paul J. Kuehn

Institute of Communications Switching and Data Technics
The University of Stuttgart
Seidenstrasse 36, 7000 Stuttgart 1, FRG

The introduction of new Integrated Services Digital Networks (ISDN)
poses a variety of new questions on performance modelling and traffic
engineering. The paper addresses the development of new networks and
services and the classical issues and methods of performance evaluation and traffic engineering. It is argued that these methods are no
longer sufficient for future networks. To characaterize the dimension
of the new questions we first derive a number of 'generic' traffic
models. The solution of these generic models forms the base for a
proper system analysis and traffic engineering of integrated services
networks and their control. The paper concludes with a survey of open
questions of traffic engineering for future ISDN's.

Main Statements: ISDN poses a variety of new questions on performance
modelling and traffic engineering. Their solution will be most important for the design, engineering and operation of the ISDN in future.

1. DEVELOPMENT OF COMMUNICATION NETWORKS AND SERVICES

Communication networks of the past have developed individually and were characterized by one dominating service as, e.g., voice telephony, telex or data
transmission. Through the advances of digital transmission, microcomputer control and software technology future communication networks will be able to
support a wide spectrum of services. Bases for these developments are cheap
VLSI hardware components for call processing, signal processing, switching and
storage, high-speed digital transmission, efficient high-level languages, and
the international standardization of services and protocols. For the latter,
the ISO Basic Reference Model for Open Systems Interconnection has greatly
enhanced the development of ISDN.

1.1 Physical Structure and ISDN-Capabilities

Fig. 1 shows the basic structure of the public ISDN and its major capabilities. The main aspects are:

a) Multiple terminal configuration on the customer premises comprizing

- Terminal Equipment (TE 1) with ISDN compatibility for voice, text, etc.

- Terminal Equipment (TE 2) not compatible to ISDN with Terminal Adpata-
  tion (TA) for protocol conversion

- Connection of Local Area Networks (LAN) through Gateways (GY)

- Free connectivity through a local bus system and an ISDN-socket

b) Unified Network Access (Basic Access) through

- Usage of the existing subscriber loop

- Network Termination (NT) as the end point of the public network

- Exchange Termination (ET) as the interface between the subscriber
  access and the switching exchange

- Provisioning of 2 B-channels (information channels) with 64 kbps FDX each for circuit switched connections or (optionally) packet access

- Provisioning of 1 D-channel with 16 kbps FDX for signalling (s), user packet (p) and teleaction (t) data; s-, p-, and t-connection management is transparent to the NT and subject to the D-channel protocol between TE(TA,GY) and ET (levels 2 and 3).

- Extended Network Access through the introduction of multiplexors (Basic Access Multiplexor) and concentrators in the subscriber area; both are connected with the switching exchange through PCM 30/32 transmission facilities (not shown in Fig. 1).

c) Multiple ISDN Capabilities within the ISDN through

- Circuit Switched (CS) B-channels

- CS H-channels of higher bandwidths (H_0: 384 kbps, H_{11} : 1536 kbps, H_{12} : 1920 kbps,...)

- Non-Switched B- and H-channels

- A uniform signalling network based on the common signalling channel concept of CCITT No.7

- Packed Switched (PS) facilities either by providing access to a separate PS-network or by integration of PS-services into the ISDN.

d) Provisioning of facilities for information storage, information processing and interworking with other networks through

- Data Bases for information (voice, data, text,...) storage and retrieval

- Hosts for Information Processing (server functions as, e.g., protocol conversion)

- Gateways (GY) for interconnection of ISDN and non-ISDN networks.

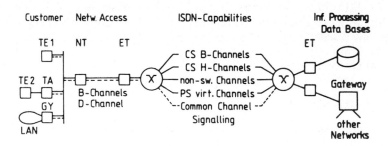

FIGURE 1
The ISDN Network Concept

1.2 ISDN-SERVICE CONCEPT

A "Service" comprises all technical, operational and legal aspects for a particular type of communication between users or between users and the provider of a public network. Within the ISDN various types of services are distinguished:

a) Bearer Services
   Bearer Services provide the circuit or packet switched transport of information between two terminal-network interfaces irrespective of the compatibility of the terminals. A typical example of these services are
   switched or non-switched 64 kbps (B-) channels for text, data and graphic
   applications.

b) Standard Services

   Standard Services provide the transport of information between two terminals with assurance of compatibility. The functionality comprises all
   7 layers. Typical representatives are:

   - ISDN Telephone
   - ISDN Teletex
   - ISDN Telefax
   - ISDN Textfax.

   Again, these services are based on switched B-channels with 64 kbps.

c) Higher Services

   Higher Services generally use centralized storage and processing capabilities of the ISDN. Typical examples of such services are

   - ISDN Videotex
   - ISDN Voice, Text and Fax Mail
   - Protocol conversion.

d) Services on the D-channel

   The D-channel basically carries signalling information (s-data). These
   data require only a small part of the available 16 kbps capacity so that
   low rate user packet data (p-data) may be transferred additionally over
   virtual connections or telemetric data (t-data) over permanent virtual
   connections.

e) Supplementary Service Attributes

   Additionally to the basic service attributes of the standard services the
   users may optionally subscribe for further service attributes as, e.g.,

   - abbreviated dialling
   - automatic repetition of calls in case of blocking
   - inward dialling into PBXes
   - automatic call back
   - call redirection
   - conferencing
   - reverse charging, etc.

1.3 Protocol Architecture

The exchange of information between users, application programs or any particular level entities is controlled by a set of rules subjected to a protocol
definition. Based on the layered protocol architecture of the ISO/CCITT OSI
Basic Reference Model CCITT has developed a generalized model for ISDN protocols. Whereas for packetized communication control and user information are
combined in the respective PDU's, circuit switched communication with separate
signalling channels and networks needs a multidimensional approach where different Protocol Planes are distinguished for User, Control and System Management information.

The multiple plane protocol architecture is illustrated in Fig. 2 for a CS-
connection through an ISDN with D-channel signalling for the network access
and No.7 common channel signalling network for network-internal signalling.

The relevant standards of CCITT are defined in the I-series for ISDN, particularly I 431, I 441 and I 451 for levels 1, 2 and 3 of the D-channel protocol, and in the No.7 Signalling System. Both, the D-channel and No.7 signalling protocols have been developed for their particular purposes, the control of the network access and network-internal control. Therefore, they differ considerably and an interworking is necessary at the origination and destination exchanges.

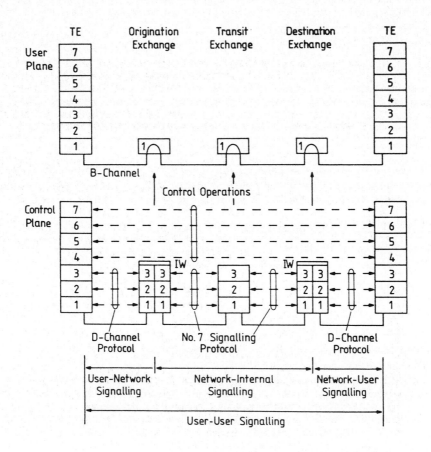

FIGURE 2
ISDN Protocol Architecture. Example: CS-Connection

2. NETWORK PERFORMANCE EVALUATION

2.1 Modelling

Modelling networking performance is essential to evaluate design alternatives and to dimension networking resources to meet throughput and grade of service requirements. Network models can be rather complex consisting of quite heterogeneous components, as

- SERVERS
- QUEUES
- RESOURCE MANAGEMENT
- PROTOCOLS
- TRAFFIC SOURCES.

These components are abstract representations of physical, logical and statistical entities of real systems. SERVER components represent the occupation of a processor or transmission channel for a particular task or call. The component QUEUE may refer to a well organized list of service requests or to a physical buffer for the intermediate storage of data units. RESOURCE MANAGEMENT consists of all strategical properties of computer or networking operating systems through which physical resources are temporarily assigned to requests or users. PROTOCOLS refer to the definition of the functional behavior of real systems with respect to basic services as connection establishment, exchange of data units, error recovery, routing, etc. TRAFFIC SOURCES, finally, characterize the dynamic load to the network including the statistical properties, user or subscriber behavior of human or nonhuman users of particular services.

The phenomenon of traffic generally refers to the system dynamics resulting from the interworking of all of these entities. Since most of the network resources are shared by a large number of independently acting users, bottlenecks may occur resulting in grade of service degradation as losses, blocking, delays or even malfunction.Performance evaluation aims at the experimental or theoretical analysis of the system model with respect to throughput and grade of service figures. These procedures are the basis of network planning and network management procedures to design and to operate networks according to a prescribed grade of service (GOS) under given load figures.

2.2 History of Performance Evaluation

Performance Evaluation of Communication Networks and Systems has a long tradition and reaches more than 80 years back. Its cornerstones are:

- Birth and Death analysis of loss and delay systems
  (Erlang 1917, Engset 1918)

- Analysis of systems with general service times
  (Pollaczek 1930, Crommelin 1932)

- Imbedded Markov Chain analysis
  (Kendall 1953)

- Queues with general input and service processes
  (Lindley 1952)

- Output of queuing systems
  (Burke, Reich, Cohen 1956-1957)

- Queuing networks
  (Jackson 1954, Kleinrock 1964, BCMP 1975)

- Queuing network algorithms
  (Buzen 1972, Reiser/Kobayashi 1976)

- Cyclic queuing systems
  (Cooper, Cohen, Takagi, Boxma 1970-1986)

- Equivalent Random Traffic Theory
  (Bretschneider, Wilkinson, Riordan 1955-1956)

- Analysis of multi-stage switching networks
  (Jacobaeus 1952, Clos 1953, Kharkevich 1960, Lotze 1970)

- Discrete Time simulation techniques
  (Kosten 1948, Neovius 1955).

The methods of analysis cover a wide spectrum, as

- finite state birth and death equations
- integral equation relationships
- phase type representations
- LS and GF transforms and function theory representations
- product form solutions
- convolutional and mean value computational algorithms
- functional and/or statistical independence
- effective accessibility representations
- equivalent random traffic techniques
- decomposition and aggregation techniques
- diffusion and fluid approximations.

The rich field of solutions cannot adequately or exhaustively referred to in this context. Methods of this kind and their results have been successfully applied for network dimensioning and planning.

Performance Analysis has now reached a status with a well-based theoretical framework, a huge number of solutions of specific problems (in particular in Operations Research and Computer Science), a wide spectrum of approximate approaches, and application support by traffic theory tables, numerical procedures and analytical as well as simulation program tools.

2.3 New Challenges for Performance Evaluation

Through the introduction of loosely coupled computer systems interconnected by Local Area or Wide Area Networks (LAN, WAN), distributed end systems and ISDN, a large set of new performance issues has arisen, as

- multiple access to broad band media
- multiplexing of connections and data streams
- data flow control and error recovery
- overload control and adaptive routing
- traffic characteristics of new services
- integration of voice and data
- integration of circuit and packet switching.

The classical solutions of queuing and traffic theory are in general not directly applicable and have to be complemented accordingly. Typically, new problems are characterized by a rather high degree of complexity. Methods for splitting global models into smaller ones with less complexity must be developed to take care of the inter-dependence due to wide-spanning protocol control mechanisms.

2.4 Generic Models for Network Performance Evaluation

To characterize the network performance evaluation issues, elementary structures and mechanisms will be reviewed in the following. This review addresses the most popular models of the past, and especially a number of new basic problems of networks for service integration. The developed models cannot be described rigorously in this short review and should be considered as 'generic' in the sense of their basic purpose.

2.4.1 Switching Networks

Switching networks allow a temporarily switched CS-connection between one in-put terminal (inlet) and one output terminal (outlet). They can be constructed as single stage connecting arrays with full accessibility (Fig. 3a), limited accessibility (Fig. 3b) or multi-stage connecting arrays with conjugated switching or step-by-step switching (Fig. 3c). Further details refer to the structure of interconnections, the number of stages, the path hunting strategy and the traffic source submodel.

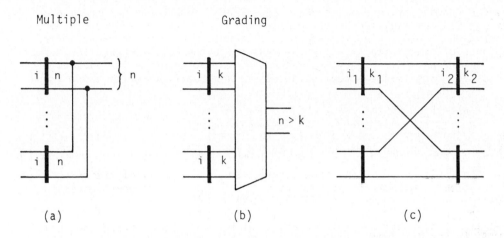

(a)   (b)   (c)

FIGURE 3
Basic Switching Network Structures

2.4.2 Network Models for CS-Traffic Routing

Alternate Routing aims at a simple and robust scheme to select routes within a partially meshed network dependent on the actual state of outgoing trunk groups. Fig. 4a shows the basic model of two primary trunk groups (PTG) and one secondary trunk group (STG). Traffics A_{11} and A_{12} are first offered to their PTG; if these PTG are fully occupied or if there is no access to an idle trunk, the traffic may overflow to the STG. Additionally, the STG may also be offered direct traffic A_2. The overflow changes the traffic characteristic into more "peakedness" which has to be taken into account for GOS calculations.

The signalling network capabilities of the future ISDN allows for more fle-xible choice of traffic paths according to global load conditions (adaptive routing). These problems are even more important as new networks are struc-tured less hierarchically. Generic models may be defined allowing for a finite number of routes within a prescribed origination-destination graph dependent on the availability of an idle origination-destination path.

2.4.3 Network Models for PS-Traffic Routing

In PS-networks the communication may be either connectionless (datagram,CL) or connectionoriented (virtual circuit,CO). In both cases, adaptive routing is applied aiming at criteria of the shortest expected origination-destination transfer time. Usually, each network node has some information on the actual network state which is periodically or aperiodically updated. There are no simple generic models; the complexity of the problem requires usually simula-tion techniques to evaluate the performance.

2.4.4 Network Models for CS Service Protection

Within hierarchical networks different traffic types share certain trunk
groups. As a classical example, the international inbound traffic shares the
downward trunk groups with the national traffic. In future services integrated
networks, traffics of various services and eventually different bandwidth or
importance may share the same trunk groups. To protect one traffic type
against the other, e.g., the inbound international traffic against national
traffic, various protection mechanisms have to be applied to meet specific
GOS-requirements.

In Fig. 4b two classical approaches are shown. The n trunks are divided into
two subgroups of n_1 and n_2 trunks, respectively, where the n_1 trunks are
exclusively reserved for traffic A_1 and the n_2 trunks are shared by both
traffics A_1 and A_2. Fig. 4c refers to a generalized solution where the acceptance of either traffic A_1 or A_2 depends on the actual occupation state
(x_1, x_2) of both traffic types. Methods of this category allow a bandwidth
allocation such that the individual GOS-criteria are met under given load.

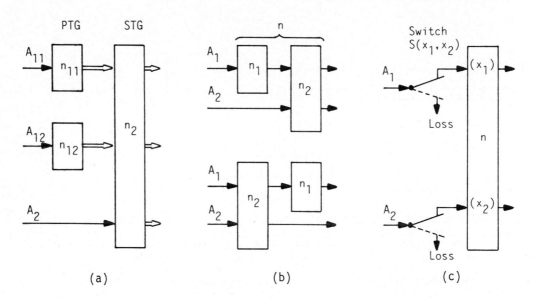

FIGURE 4
a) Overflow Model for Alternate Routing of CS-Connections
b) Service Protection Model by Subdivision of Trunk Groups
c) Service Protection Model by State-Dependent Acceptance Strategy

2.4.5 Variable Bandwidth Allocation

The required bandwidth of various services may vary considerably as, e.g., for

-   low speed data (program development, printing)   9.6 - 19.2 kbps
-   voice/telematic services   64 kbps
-   high resolution graphics   256 kbps
-   file transfer   1,000 - 10,000 kbps
-   video   64 - 140,000 kbps

Several of these services may share an individual trunk group of a CS-Network.
One solution of this problem is to assign single or multiple B-channels with
64 kbps each to these services. Fig. 5 shows the simplest model of a Time
Slotted Frame with several arrival streams for multi-slot connections.

For a proper management of multi-slot connections, extended models refer to

- switching networks with multi-slot connections

- subdivided frame structures with classes of connections, e.g., segments for 64 kbps, 384 kbps and 2.048 kbps

- path searching/channel allocation for multi-slot connections under the restriction of bit sequence integrity

- rearrangement of existing connections for purposes of concise packing of remaining multi-slot connections

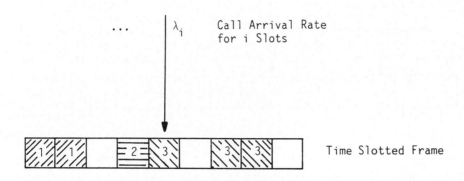

FIGURE 5
Basic Model for Multi-Slot CS-Connections

2.4.6 Advance Reservation

Within the broadband-type ISDN individual videophone connections, video conference connections, switched video program distribution and high speed point-to-point data transmission share the same broadband (optical fiber) channels. Teleconferences differ from individual communications with respect to

- predefined and reserved broadband connections between several teleconferencing studios

- much longer holding times.

Connection reservation schedules depend on various parameters, as

- arrival instant and advance time of reservation requests

- instant and duration of the requested connection

- bandwidth requirements

- sacrificing costs for advance channel blocking or delaying of reservation requests

- time discretization for scheduling algorithm.

Fig. 6 shows the principal model where call reservations and direct calls share a common time slotted transmission channel. The various reservation strategies can only be evaluated by simulation due to the model's complexity.

2.4.7 Single/Multi-Queue Delay Systems

Single/Multi-Queue, Single/Multi-Server delay systems are the most important basic models for applications, as

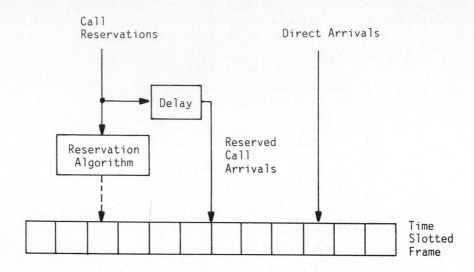

FIGURE 6
Basic Model for Bandwidth Management Including Advance Reservation

- call processing
- packet switching
- multiplexing of control/packet data streams.

Fig. 7 shows various basic models. In particular, requests of various types or originations may share one server; the server allocation may depend on prede-fined priorities (Fig. 7c) or on a cyclic polling mechanism (Fig. 7d). Polling models have a rather broad application reaching from data collection, packet multiplexing, processor scheduling to distributed multi-access of broadband media as in the case of Token-Passing for Local Area Networks (LAN). More so-phisticated Token allocation schemes may be based on Token Priorities and/or Timer devices to guarantee a timely Token issue for real-time or even synchro-nous communications applications (FDDI).

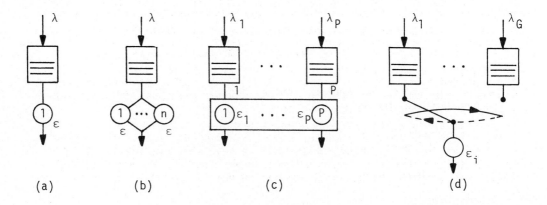

FIGURE 7
Single/Multi-Queue, Single/Multi-Server Delay Models

2.4.8 Packet Switching Nodes

New developments of high-capacity PS nodes direct to highly modularized structures. The modularization follows principles of partial function division and load sharing for purposes of a real-time efficient and protocol layer related implementation as well as load dependent extension, respectively. Fig. 8 shows a typical example of the new generation of high-capacity packet switches.

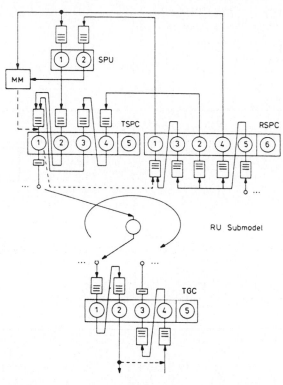

FIGURE 8
High Capacity Packet Switch Node Model

The model consists of peripheral processors (Terminator Group Controller TGC) handling a group of line/trunk terminating units and protocol functions up to layer 2. The number of TGC's may be extended according to the number of connected lines/trunks. At the more central side a variable number of Switching Processor Units SPU are responsible for routing of datagrams and virtual circuits as well as switching of packets (layer 3-functions). The number of SPU's depends on the PS capacity. SPU's and TGC's are interconnected through a high-speed Ring Unit bus system where the inbound and outbound traffic is additionally supported by specialized controllers RSPC and TSPC. All processor devices are of the multi-task types where the waiting requests are scheduled according to the specific task priorities.

The analysis of such models with up to several hundreds of processing modules, internal protocols and LAN-type interconnection schemes exceeds todays performance evaluation tools. The analysis is based on advanced decomposition and aggregation techniques.

2.4.9 CS/PS-Integration

Hybrid Switching systems are designed to support CS as well as PS. This leads to the problem how to assign channels/bandwidth to the various service requests.

Fig. 9 shows a very popular model for a broadband channel within a Local Area
Network. The synchronous frame is partitioned into a CS- and a PS-part with a
fixed or movable boundary in between. The CS-channels may be assigned by a
central device at connection establishment, whereas the PS-subchannel is assigned by a Token Passing protocol. If a packet transmission has not finished
at the frame boundary, it is interrupted at this time for the synchronous CS-
part. The CS-part is subdivided into basic channels; CS-connections are categorized into classes of bandwidth (multi-slot assignment).

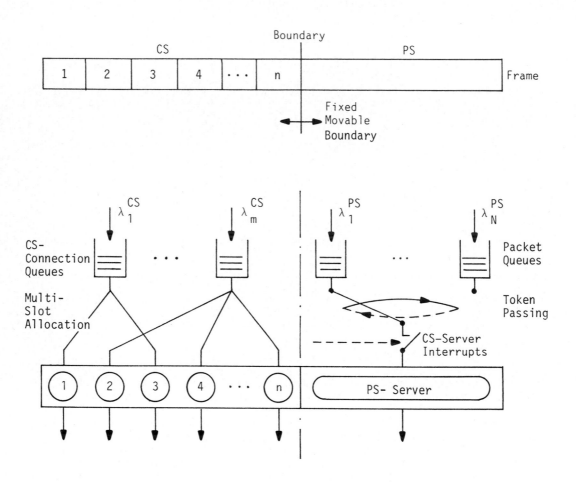

FIGURE 9
CS/PS-Integration by the Partitioned Frame Principle

Another class of hybrid switching systems bases on the Slotted Ring principle,
see Fig. 10. The ring system itself owns an inherent distributed ring buffer
which is subdivided into fixed size slots. Each slot may carry a CS-connection
of fixed bitrate or an individual data unit (packet). In case of a CS-connection, the slot is reserved for this connection at connection establishment,
whereas in case of PS, each slot is used individually depending on an idle
slot indication. The analysis of the PS-capability depends heavily on the origination-destination relation of individual PS-data units.

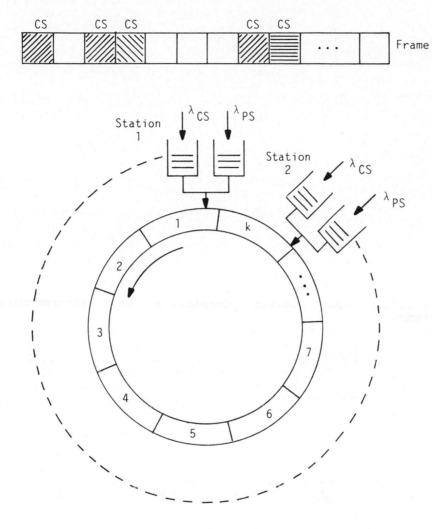

FIGURE 10
CS/PS-Integration by the Slotted Ring Principle

2.4.10 Fast Packet Switching (FPS)

New high speed VLSI circuitry, such as GaAs-Devices allow extremely fast operations which may be used for an all-packetized solution of all forms of communications. Real time, stream-like data flows as for voice or video communications do not require flow control and error recovery. Thus, such packets are just switched through. A packet may even be forwarded as soon as its destination link is known to save buffer space and delays. Such switching techniques are known as Fast Packet Switching (FPS) or Asynchronous Time Division (ATD).

Fig. 11 shows a generic model for FPS. Voice and data packets are multiplexed onto one channel. The packets are switched between different input and output channels by a parallel self-routing Banyan network consisting of elementary 2x2 switch fabrics. Delays may occur at the multiplexing devices and in front of the Binary Switching Network.

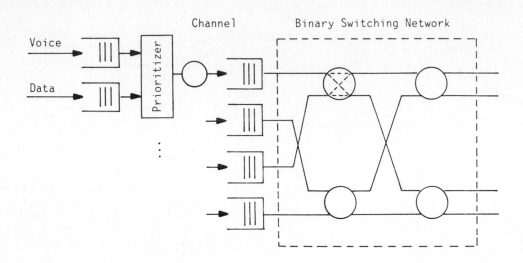

FIGURE 11
Basic Model for Fast Packet Switching

There are two principal types of delays: short delays to phase in simultaneously arriving packets and longer delays due to a temporary overload. In the
latter case, dynamic bit dropping for voice packets may be applied to reduce
these delays. The traffic performance depends also on the packet arrival
stream characteristics. To analyze whole FPS networks two more basic operations on packet data streams have to be treated: merging and splitting, see
Fig. 12.

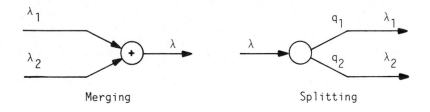

Merging   Splitting

FIGURE 12
Basic Operations for Packet Data Traffic Streams

2.4.11 Queuing Networks for Switching Control

Open or closed queuing networks, such as shown in Fig. 13a, form a powerful
means to model computer systems or packet networks and to estimate network
delays. Such models, however, are only rough approximations for real system
models. Basic models for switching system control fall outside the usual class
of queuing networks because of

- clock-type I/O for exchange of commands/responses between
  peripheral and central control

- prioritized processor scheduling

- branching processes, where, e.g., a command message is echoed by the CPU through several response messages with different destination, see Fig. 13b.

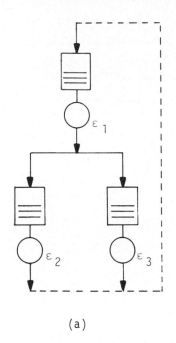

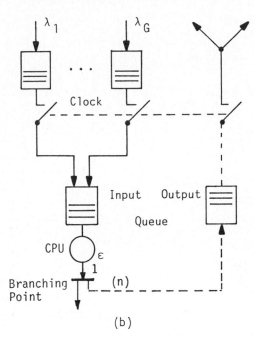

(a)   (b)

FIGURE 13
a) Open/Closed Model for Computer System or Packet Network
b) Switching System Control Model

2.4.12 Flow-and Congestion Control

Flow Control is used to adapt a slower data sink to a faster data source. Flow control uses various control schemes, such as source on/off-switching, throttling or window mechanisms. Such schemes are part of data transmission protocols. A simple example of a throttling flow control mechanism between remote source and sink models is shown in Fig. 14a. Dependent on the upcrossing (downcrossing) of level L1 (L2) of the sink arrival storage, a throttle (resume) command is sent upon which the source switches to the lower (higher) arrival rate λ_2 (λ_1). The total network delay has been modelled by a simple infinite server station.

Congestion Control aims at the overload protection of a centralized device or a whole switch. This is especially important for systems where human or non-human users repeat their calls in case of blocking: repeated call attempts lead to a high processing load with a low call completion rate which may finally result in a life-lock collapse. Ample control mechanisms have to be used which make sure that a call is accepted only when it can be completed almost sure; otherwise, calls should be blocked before they swamp the control with load of uncompleted calls, see Fig. 14b.

Both, flow and congestion control models have to be analyzed not only with respect to their static behavior but for their transient behavior in response on load variations.

2.4.13 Flow Controlled Virtual Connections

Handshake- or On/Off-protocols for flow control and error recovery lead to much overhead when the propagation delay increases. Therefore, sliding window protocols are used to maintain the throughput of such a connection. Window

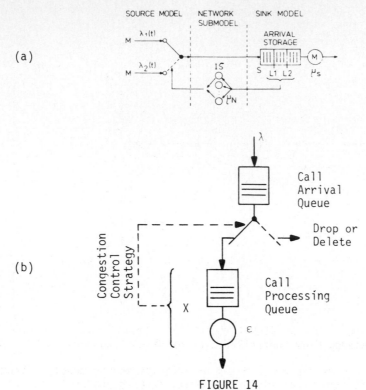

FIGURE 14
Models for Flow and Congestion Control
a)   Flow Control Model between Remote Source and Sink
b)   Congestion Control Model

flow control mechanisms can be found in almost all protocol layers for layer-specific connections between peer entities or even between entities of adjacent layers across the layered architecture.

Fig. 15 shows the generic model of a window flow controlled simplex connection between two layer (N)-entities. The Petri net symbol stands for the access mechanism: An (N)-Service Data Unit (SDU) from the upper layer is only accepted if the credit queue is nonempty (Y>0); each (N)-SDU is turned into an (N)-Protocol Data Unit (PDU) taking a credit with it from the credit queue. After reception, the (N)-SDU is extracted and passed to the upper layer; simultaneously an acknowledgement (N)-PDU is returned to the origin. Thus, there are always exactly W (window size) PDU's cycling around. This model allows the proper modelling of window flow control including acknowledging as well as transmission and propagation delays.

The simplex virtual connection of Fig. 15 can be extended to a full duplex (FDX) connection by using two separate flow control mechanisms for either direction. Note that both flow control mechanisms may use arbitrary window sizes, but share the same transmission channels, see Fig. 16.

Both models of Figs. 15 and 16 describe the already established virtual connection (VC). To establish the VC the connectionless service is used, i.e. individual datagram type packets are exchanged between both entities.

Both models are simplified; the simplification consists first of an aggregated behavior of the lower layers represented by simple channels. The parameters of these channel service times have to be found from a separate analysis, such that they are equivalent with respect to total throughput and transfer delay. There are several options to replace the lower layers: single server queues

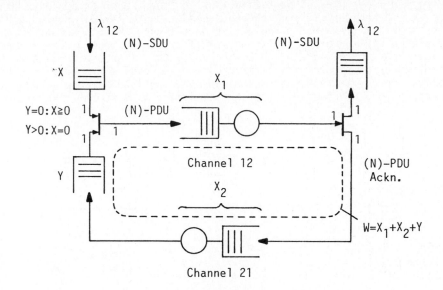

FIGURE 15
Model of a Window Flow Controlled Simplex Virtual Connection

with fixed or state-dependent service rates or infinite server models. Through this procedure, an iterative analysis of the multi-layered protocol architecture can be performed by successive aggregation, bottom-up.

Another simplification has been assumed by neglecting the (N)-entity processing times. There is no problem to extend the model to include these effects. Note, however, that these are implementation-dependent.

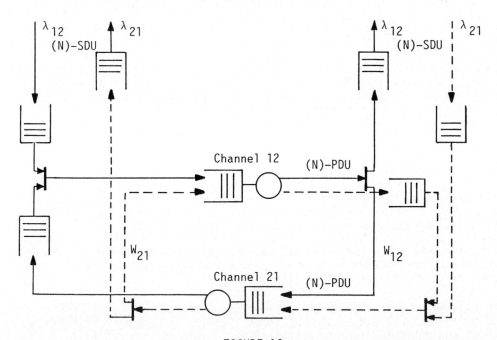

FIGURE 16
Model of a Window Flow Controlled FDX Virtual Connection

Finally, the models of Figs. 15 and 16 do not include the error process and error recovery mechanisms. In some cases as LANS's these may be dropped since their error probabilities are so small that performance is not measurably degraded. Within WAN's and particular on satellite links these processes have to be included. As in the case of HDLC link analyses, an erroneous data unit is rejected and error recovery is invoked upon a sequence error or a time-out. Analytically, these effects can be described by an inflated channel occupation time accounting for enforced idle and retransmission time in the case of an error.

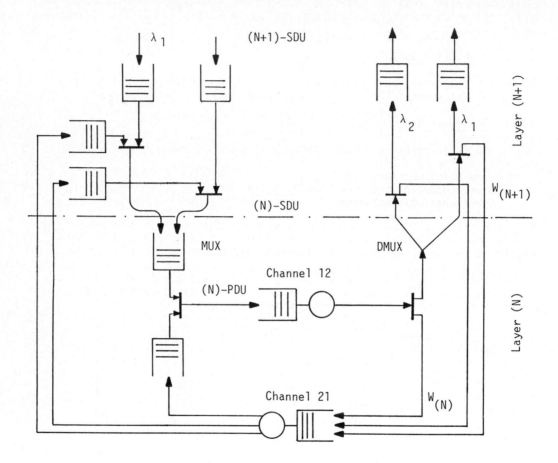

FIGURE 17
Connection Multiplexing (Example: Simplex Connections)

2.4.14 Connection Multiplexing

Several (N+1)-connections may be multiplexed onto one (N)-connection at the origination side and demultiplexed at the destination side. Fig. 17 shows the generic model where the (N+1)- as well as the (N)-connections are window flow controlled. Connection Multiplexing is a basic mechanism and can be found in various layers or network applications:

- Multiplexing of several LAP D-connections onto one Physical Link D-channel for ISDN subscriber access (here, the physical connection is not subjected to flow control)

- Multiplexing of several VC of X.25 layer 3 onto one Data Link LAP B-connection of X.25 layer 2

- Multiplexing of several Transport connections for different
  endsystem applications onto one Network Connection
- Multiplexing of several LLC-connections of layer 2b onto
  one MAC layer within Local Area Networks.

The analysis can be performed by replacing the whole layer (N)-submodel by an
aggregated delay station by which the individual (N+1)-connections fall apart.

Note that in Fig. 17 the acknowledgements of layer (N+1)-connections are
transmitted apart from the layer (N)-connection mechanism. There is no principal problem to transfer these acknowledgements within a FDX layer (N)-con-
nection, too.

2.4.15 Connection Splitting

The reverse operation to connection multiplexing is connection splitting by
which one (N+1)-connection is divided up into several (N)-connections.

2.4.16 Data Unit Management

In the ISO Basic Reference Model, three principal Data Unit Transformations
are defined, see Fig. 18:
- Segmenting/Reassembling
- Blocking/Deblocking
- Concatenation/Separation.

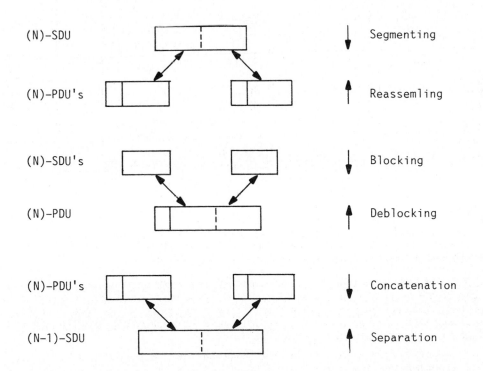

FIGURE 18
Data Unit Management

Data Unit Transformations are necessary when default block sizes of adjacent layers differ as, e.g., in LAN's and PS public data networks. Fig. 19 shows a generic processor model of a layer (N)-entity for Segmenting/Reassembling. Note that another new modelling element enters the stage: Assembly/Reassembly Queues. These queues buffer smaller data units until they can be combined for handover to the next process. Similar models are obtained for Blocking/De-blocking and Concatenation/Separation.

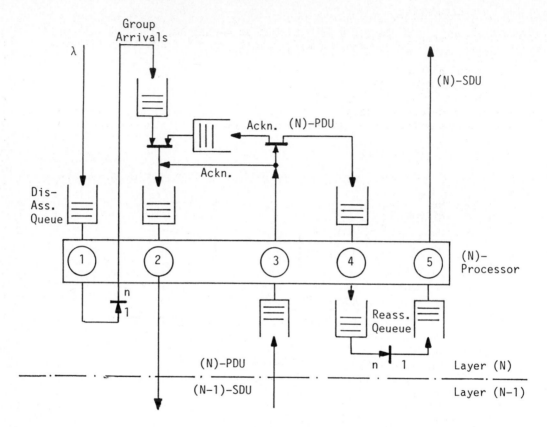

FIGURE 19
Data Unit Management: Segmenting/Reassembling

2.4.17 Network Call Control

To set up a network-wide CS-connection, ISDN uses a separate signalling network for interoffice signalling based on the CCITT Signalling System No.7. The analysis of such networks which are operated thoroughly in the PS-mode, leads to identical or similar basic models as introduced before.

The fast and reliable signalling unloads the information network from inband signalling overhead by approximately 10% of the total load. Besides its basic purpose as signalling vehicle for connection management, the signalling network forms also the basis for intelligent network management and feature support. Future ISDN's will be characterized by

- comparatively simple transport functions as the Bearer and Standard Services

- comparatively complex functions of Higher Services and Supplementary Services resting on network databases and network hosts allowing for feature support and even customer-defined network features.

To give just one example of such an application, Fig. 20 refers to a feature call handling: After initial call processing (phase 1), a Database Access Request is generated to look up or to provide the feature support. Call processing may proceed (phase 2) in parallel to the database access and can only be completed after the arrival of the Database Response (phase 3). This is another example for a model with a branching process and true parallel processing within communication networks.

2.4.18 Internetworking

Internetworking occurs between ISDN and LAN, PSTN, PSDN or between LAN and PSDN. Usually, such networks differ in various points as

- protocol hierarchy
- connection types (CO, CL)
- switching principles (PS, CS)
- protocol data unit sizes
- signalling methods (inband PS, outband CS)

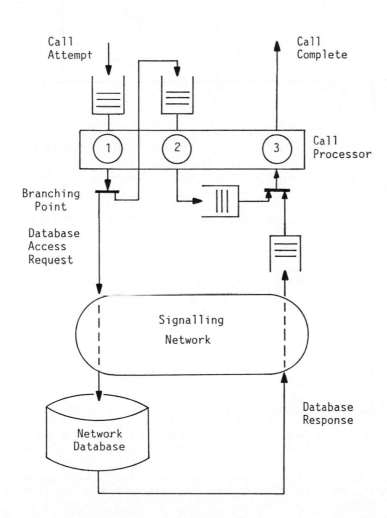

FIGURE 20
Feature Call Handling in ISDN Through Network Database Support

Models of the corresponding internetworking units as Bridges, Routers or Gateways reflect features as

- protocol layer of the relay function
- buffer structures for intermediate storage
- control procedures for transformations of connection types and data units
- flow control for back pressure functions, etc.

2.5. Source Traffic Models

For single service networks of the past, traffic has been modelled by a few parameters. Service integration leads to more complex traffic models with multiple parameters due to quite different service types, the separation of user information flow from control flow and due to variable bandwidth and throughput requirements. This may be illustrated by a few examples.

2.5.1 CS-Connections

Traffic source models for CS-calls for either service consist of

- Interarrival time distribution function
- Bandwidth requirement (number of B-channels)
- Holding time distribution function.

The simultaneous use of multiple services can be described by

- Joint probability of multi-service usage.

2.5.2 Connection Control

CS-connection set up/take downs are controlled in the ISDN using outband signalling through the D-channel. The source model for this channel consists of

- Requests for establishment of LAP D-connections for incoming/outgoing B-channel-connections
- Holding time of LAP D-connections (as holding time in 2.5.1)
- Signalling information arrival processes from TE to ET and vice versa within each established LAP D-Connection
- Frame length distribution
- Flow control parameter.

2.5.3 PS-Virtual Connection

Packet Switched Virtual Connections (VC) may be established through D- or B-channels in the ISDN. According to the inherent inband signalling method of PS, there is only one source model which consists of

- VC establishment requests
- VC holding time
- Data packet arrival process within an established VC
- Packet length distribution
- Throughput class requirement
- Flow Control parameter.

2.6 Advanced Methods for Performance Analysis

The new traffic issues cannot be treated completely by the well-established traffic theoretic methods. Advanced Techniques of Performance Analysis are necessary since the complexity of the related traffic models has been increased considerably through

- Multi-layered functionalities of the protocol architectures
- Extensive use of microprocessor equipment
- Wide-spanning dependencies through protocol relations
- Introduction of new services.

2.6.1 Advanced Simulation Techniques

Simulation allows the analysis of arbitrarily complex relationships. The increase of discrete time events and the extension of data structures pose the problem of storage and execution time limitations which limits in turn the sufficient gathering of statistical data for comparatively rare events. New approaches direct to

- Hybrid Simulation Techniques
- Aggregated Submodel Simulation Techniques
- Environment Simulation Techniques
- Parallel Simulation Techniques.

2.6.2 Advanced Analysis Techniques

Network planning requires efficient analytical methods and tools. Most of these methods are approximate and have to be validated by simulation. For analytical treatment a major problem is the reduction of the complexity. Basic Methods and approaches are

- Aggregation of subsystems
- Decomposition of complex systems into subsystems
- Timed Petri Net analysis techniques for cooperating processes
- Merging/splitting of nonrenewal point processes
- System analysis under correlated input processes
- Nonstationary process analyses
- Flow time distribution analyses.

3. TRAFFIC ENGINEERING

Traffic Engineering refers to a set of issues which can be described by

- Grade of Service (GOS) Definition
- Traffic Measurements and Forecasting
- Traffic Characterization
- Traffic Analysis Procedures
- Interaction between System/Network Architecture and GOS
- Network Planning
- Network Management.

3.1 Grade of Service Definition

GOS definitions are subjected to international standardization by CCITT. Typical GOS measures are

- Probability of blocking
- Probability of loss
- Probability of delay
- Mean and 95-percentiles of major delays as
    dial tone delay
    post dialling delay
    releasing delay.

Such definitions are principally valid for CS-connections of a single service. They have to be completed with respect to

- multiple services GOS
- GOS under overload/breakdown conditions.

For PS virtual connections similar GOS criteria hold as

- VC establishment delay
- Data packet delay
- GOS for services under negotiation, as achievable maximum throughput of a VC

- GOS for particular network accesses as D-channel or B-channel packet network access.

The various GOS-criteria have to be related to standardized load conditions. For ISDN services a reference customer load should be defined; this question is also related to the busy hour definition for ISDN.

3.2 Traffic Measurements and Forecasting

Traffic measurements are taken for several reasons

- Monitoring of user behavior
- Monitoring of network load
- Monitoring of GOS
- Validation of analysis and planning tools.

New questions of traffic measurements are focused at

- Change of user behavior with respect to new features
- User behavior and traffic values for newly introduced services or new applications
- Busy Hours of individual services
- GOS for new services and features.

Forecasting of traffic and service developments is particularly difficult, since they are highly dependent on user acceptance and the development of applications, terminal systems and networks.

3.3 Interaction between System/Network Architecture and GOS

The development of System and Network Architectures has been largely driven by standardization bodies. Since these bodies work in parallel and are only loose - ly coordinated, the whole architecture may not always fit to an application or to a real time and performance-efficient implementation. It can be expected that tailored but still OSI-compatible solutions will be implemented for special applications. Traffic Engineering may therefore give an important momentum on future network architectures and their implementation.

3.4 Network Planning and Network Management

Network planning addresses the problem how to structure and how to size network resources according to load, GOS and cost objective functions. This classical issue gets new dimensions in the light of new services and ISDN. Problems related hereto are:

- Objective function definition
- Fixing of planning parameters
- Development of dimensioning methods
- Definition of reference loads and reference busy hours
- Sensitivity of solutions with respect to changes of parameters
- Multi-parameter optimization
- Development of Network Management procedures and practices.

CONCLUSION

With the introduction of digital networks and service integration a major step will be reached into an information society. The evolution of public and private networks requires large amounts of capital investment. Traffic Engineering will form a major part in the development, planning and operation of new networks and services. To play this part responsibly and constructively, much work is still to be done to penetrate and to understand the issues and to support development, planning and operation accordingly. This paper has been written in this spirit. It was not possible to go into details and to evaluate the various approaches more deeply, but it is hoped nevertheless to have contributed to the classification of the issues.

TRAFFIC ENGINEERING for ISDN Design and Planning
M. Bonatti and M. Decina (Editors)
Elsevier Science Publishers B.V. (North-Holland)
© IAC, 1988

DISCUSSION

The discussion (comments, questions, answers) was concentrated on the following main topics:

1) Where and when hybrid switching will be more convenient?

2) Would the standardization activities be able to follow the technological progress and the systems spontaneous evolution?

3) Could the Traffic Engineering people influence the fast developping techniques driving the telecommunications evolution, and how?

4) Is the performance design possible without data and how can we have strategical planning without reliable network design?

5) How to cope with the growing telecommunications system complexity?

6) What will be the capital investments per subscriber for the first services installations in order to justify each ISDN phase in a deregulation environment?

Only a comment by M. Peyrade (CNET) was adressed to a specific topic considered in the presentation by M. Decina, namely: the permanent distinction between circuit switching and packet switching seems disregard completely the ATD switching.

M. Decina precised that he includes ATD switching in the "Statistical Switching" category, because ATD can provide both packet and circuit connections, as well as fast circuit or fast packet switching.

1 Convenience of hybrid switching.

P. de Ferra, observing a propensity towards hybrid switching (see figures 9 and 19 of Decina's paper) asked M. Decina about the convenience of the hybrid switching at any network level, for any service and at any time. There will be specific zones in a 3-dimensional map - having network levels, services and time frames as components - where the convenience exists and others where the convenience will not exist?

"The design of a single switching fabric (an "hybrid" one) able to handle very different types of service information (packet data and high definition broadcast TV at 100 Mbps) is a fascinating challenge and opportunity" - answered M. Decina - "However I don't believe that an industrial implementation of such a switch will soon became available for general use in telecommunications network. For broadband signals, I believe that we will experience the deployment of separate switching adjuncts to digital central offices, either in broadband circuit or in broadband packet technology".

2   ISDN and standardization

"The telecommunications technology progresses very fast, will CCITT
be able to go with the same speed in relevant standardizations?" was
the question by G. Gosztony to M. Decina that opened the discussion
on this topic.

M. Decina agreed that CCITT is becoming too slow in its standards
deliberations both in consideration of the fast moving technology
and in comparison with the high efficiency of the domestic US
standardization bodies as T1D1.

"The solution of this problem involves a general reorganization of
the CCITT structure and procedures so that the rithms of domestic
standardization activities could be better followed" - concluded
M. Decina.

The following discussion took also into consideration the gap
between the awareness of the standardization advantages and the
participation of the operating companies and of the manufacturers:
standardization is certainly not a prime company objective. The
rank of standardization as a company objective is, however, growing.

3   Influence of Traffic Engineering

The discussion on this topics was introduced by a question to
M. Decina by P. Kuehn.

"ISDN and other new network types are mainly driven by technological
development in hardware and in software" - commented P. Kuehn and
asked: "What role can teletraffic engineering play in this?   Is
teletraffic theory too slow to have an influence on these fast
developing techniques?"

This question was strengthened by G. Gosztony observing that the gap
between traffic engineering and new technologies seems becoming
wider nowadays, lessening the role of the traffic engineering also
in CCITT standardization.

M. Decina referred to his experience as Director of Central Research
Laboratories in Italtel: the group responsible of Network and
System Performance (a dozen people) contributed to the development
of Italtel main switching system, LINEA UT, not only doing the
performance analysis of alternatives proposed by the Switching
Division people or solving problems originated by them.

They cooperated actively in the definition phase, when the different
architectural and communication protocol alternatives were selected
and when the final choice was made. They were asked to continuously
monitoring that the traffic performances were maintained and
upgraded and that the new characteristics of the system would fit
well with the network evolution plans.

"The Teletraffic Engineers should emphasize their skills as system
engineers, being interested not only in the detailed assessment
analysis but in the global system design and evaluation.

Performance-costs tradeoffs will remain their kingdom but
architecture, protocols, modularities and growth need to be a
concern of fruitful cooperation with the designers".

S. Katz (AT&T Bell Laboratories) observed that, in the highly competitive environment that AT&T is confronting, there are more than 200 professionals at AT&T Bell Laboratories working on teletraffic tools and application studies. "These include: a Performance Analysis Workstation, used widely by systems designers to model new systems to investigate capacity and load-control strategies; switching systems analysis; traffic network planning; forecast and planning tools and applications for AT&T's Dynamic Non-Hierarchical Routing (DNHR); the Common Channel Signalling Network; International, Local Area and private voice/data networks. Teletraffic Network planners have recently influenced a major technology decision by AT&T on whether development of Wideband Packet Technology should proceed, by demonstrating its economic benefits and that we can engineer and manage this technology, without major service quality problems".

L. Gimpelson (Alcatel) mentioned the difficulties encountered by the national packet network in France few years ago because of the new Minitel users.

"In the next future, countries will become so dependent upon their ISDN networks that this Repair-After-Disaster scheme will no longer be acceptable. Since I made this statement in ITC11-Kyoto-1985, plans to put more and more vital services on national networks in less and less time have been developed.
As result, there is an increasing need to redefine the traffic fraternity's role toward anticipating problems and recommending solutions".

P. Kuehn (University of Stuttgart) agreed that often solutions are ready only after an intensive study of congestion problems experienced in the field and that a much more anticipation on critical congestions than before is required.

However the rationalization of the designs will remain a fundamental job for the teletraffic community: "The study of such problems gives a deeper insight into the interaction of system operation with traffic parameters. This can be used for proper system design. The real system must be observed through continuous measurements on the grade of service to meet customer requirements and to validate traffic engineering methods".

As far as Teletraffic Engineering contribution to standardization process is concerned, M. Decina agreed with G. Gosztony that it is traditionally late. The history of SG XI and SG XVIII work on traffic performances clearly confirms this situation. Some inconsistencies and some inadequacies in the GOS Recommandations could have been originated from that. However the situation must and could change. "Of course detailed analysis results will always be late: preliminary results are needed to strongly influence the standardization process at early stages when different system options are evaluated. Teletraffic engineers should therefore assume their full responsabilities in contributing to the service and system definition phases".

4 Performance Design Without Data

During the discussion on the previous topic, the lack of data characterizing the traffic offer as a B&D process, along with the lack of data on growth variables as significant as the number of the subscribers, the calling rate per subscriber and the interest matrix, was invoked as one of the main problems for an early impact of the teletraffic engineering on the ISDN Design and Planning.

Furthermore much more advanced system engineering results are needed to define implementation independent fundamental performance models.

M. Bonatti has commented this point arguing that:

- it is possible to define implementation independent fundamental performance models, extending Joel results;

- reliable traffic data can be invented and the risk of assuming them can be controlled if the problem to be solved is the first choice between largely different options. Morphological analysis (in particular Fisher discriminant analysis) and inverse statistics can be used.

(This topic was extensively discussed all over the Seminar, with reference to Robust Design Techniques, Scenario Forecasting and so on. The discussion served to reach more optimistic view on the future work).

5 Teletraffic and Growing Complexity of telecommunications systems.

Complexity has been invoked as the main problem Teletraffic Engineering cannot avoid and which originates the lack of preliminary but reliable results.

S. Katz, commenting this point, declared that "amidst the complexity of ISDN and modern technology, traffic problems are key issues and problems that lend themselves to simple ideas/principles/model approximations. The history of major teletraffic contributions has been marked by fundamental insights and concepts including: Equivalent Random Methods; techniques for modeling/engineering non-hierarchical networks; SPC capacity estimation; line load control; real time control of electronic switches; call gapping for signalling networks; trunk reservation; hard-to-reach code cancellation for network management".

"To my knowledge, we have never gotten into trouble when we studied a problem and applied a simplified model/action even though subsequent refinements were possible. We have experienced major problem when we overload a problem and had to react too late".

"The danger of the focus on complexity – he concluded – is that it does not lend to focus on what is important and meaningful.
We, as teletraffic professionals, must find important (simple) principles out of complex challenges, rather than celebrate the complexity".

G. Gosztony (BHG Telecom) agreed that basic traffic engineering methods and results are simple and robust although they refer to very complex systems. However, detailed analysis of complex structures can't be avoided since this background is needed to produce and to validate the "basic traffic engineering". Furthermore "the time of isolated traffic experts is over. Efficient work requires a structured team including problem oriented specialists and system oriented organizers. To arrive at essential

results, teams above a "critical size" are required. Structured
organization, size and time are essential".

"Complexity seems always to be the case at the beginning when we are
lacking in deeper insight into the system mechanics" – commented
P. Kuehn – "The study may reveal major system features which allow a
simplified but still accurate enough description". A close
cooperation with system designers is needed.

M. Decina and L. Gimpelson underlined the need of first solutions of
the complexity, based upon a new system engineering oriented
mentality of traffic engineers: no cooperation will be possible in
selecting alternatives and in choosing among them without such
contributions.

6 Capital investments per subscribers justifying ISDN development phases.

The discussion on this topic was originated by some of the
considerations presented by L. Gimpelson in his liaison statement
with the previous ITC seminar on ISDN and by the following comment
he made to M. Decina presentation:

"Based upon a study, requested by Belgian legislature following
discussions on massive fiber installation economics, four years ago
in Belgium, the capital investment per subscriber for CATV
installations was less than $100 (1987 US $). This figure is
significantly less than the one used by most studies attempting to
justify carrying entertainment video via broadband ISDN. At present
about 90% of Belgian households are connected to privately owned
commercial coaxial cable TV–FM distribution systems.

M. Decina presented an interesting figure, due to Snelling, on the
switching life cycle compression (see fig. 1).

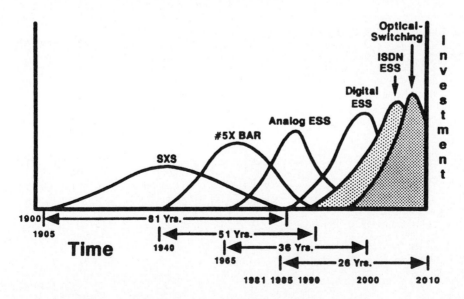

Fig. 1 Switching Life Cycle Compression
(Snelling's forecast)

TRAFFIC ENGINEERING for ISDN Design and Planning
M. Bonatti and M. Decina (Editors)
Elsevier Science Publishers B.V. (North-Holland)
© IAC, 1988

**TRAFFIC ENGINEERING TOMORROW:
BACK TO THE SYSTEM ENGINEERING?**

(Co-Chairman Comments to the Opening Session)

Mario Bonatti

ITALTEL, Italy

1. Contribution of Traffic Engineering to System Engineering.

At the beginning the Traffic Engineering was done by System Engineering people as part of their System Engineering activities.

The System Engineers have always been involved also in very detailed work at circuit design level, or at the interconnection design level, when this level was critical from the system engineering point of view. This fact has never originated a confusion between Hardware Design people, also at very high level of responsability, and System Engineering people, also at very low level of responsability. But, in a certain sense, the confusion was made for Traffic Engineering and this discipline became a special profession supporting the System Engineering activities but not admitted to the system definition phase.

Therefore we speak more about performance analysis than about performance design. And this is, in my opinion, the main reason of all the problems considered during the discussion. Performance analysis needs data. Performance analysis cannot be made without a very careful description of the system to be analysed. Performance analysis must solve the complexity.

Probably this is also the reason for considering the strategical planning and the service design as minor issues or not relevant/pertinent for Traffic Engineering. Actually, I think that the performance design is a part of the strategical planning as the discipline dealing with the cost-performance .vs. demand tradeoff over a long range period.

However, there have been in the past and there are now examples of productive and complete approaches: good concepts have been and are provided at the right moment as well as good decisions, good mathematics and good practice.

2. Network Evolution and Technology Evolution

The mutual influences and tradeoffs among high speed switching, network intelligence, optical technology, network deployement strategies and service deployement strategies could be modeled in order to have more precise guidelines for Traffic Engineering.

The influence of performability design, strategical planning, environmental analysis and need analysis on each of the previous components could reveal critical disciplinary problems to be solved at least at a rough system engineering level.

3. Standardization

A performance design reference framework is needed now (and not only a performance analysis or a dimensioning reference frame work).

Traffic characterization and performance parameters definition must be general enough to cover completely the ISDN spectrum and must avoid any detail that could require misleading approximations of the critical aspects and could produce wrong design choices.

Services, networks and systems attributes must be analyzed in order to decide their relevance for the performance design framework.

A reference architecture is needed to develop implementation independent models.

The impact of the social partners involved in the ISDN business in a competitive environment must be considered and a suitable definition of all the users involved must be recommended.

TRAFFIC ENGINEERING for ISDN Design and Planning
M. Bonatti and M. Decina (Editors)
Elsevier Science Publishers B.V. (North-Holland)
© IAC, 1988

SERVICE DEMAND AT THE TIME OF
ISDN INTRODUCTION

(Chairman Introduction to the Morning Session on Services)

Gerard Robin

ALCATEL, Belgium

The theory of teletraffic provides analytical methods or simulation tools to assist in the design of telecommunication systems and the implementation and dimensioning of the networks or of their components.

This theory has been applied so far to networks handling one type of traffic, usually for a well defined telecommunication service. Essential parameters are in this case well known, resulting from past experience, measurements in the field, or straightforward extrapolation of data accumulated during years of operation. Without reliable data, the best algorithms may well be useless.

Since there is no commercial ISDN service in operation at this time, with sufficient number of subscribers and stable tariff policy to provide a reliable basis of traffic data, an alternative is needed. The behaviour of telephone users in conventional networks is however well known, and important parameters such as calling rates, call duration have been measured since many years. It is possible to obtain some ISDN tentative data by assuming a migration of voice and data services to the ISDN. However this simple method must be used with caution, as ISDN will not offer the exact equivalent of the services existing on dedicated networks. Supplementary services will cover a much wider range of facilities. Combined services such as telephony with simultaneous facsimile transmission offer new possibilities. The higher bit rates available, 64 Kbit/s or even n x 64 Kbit/s may render practical services which would be too slow at the conventional rates ranging from 1.2 to 19.2 kbit/s.

Probably the most influential factor on the development of services will be the carriers' tariff policies, since very little is known of the elasticity of demand with respect to price. The only reference is the faster increase in long distance telephone traffic compared with local traffic. But this is also a result of a declining price trend or of other factors such as easier access to the service, fast automatic connection, etc...

The tutorial paper in this session, written by C. Marchetti, proposes a macroscopic study of telecommunication demand which, in the long term, should follow a very simple behaviour based on the ecological substitution model. The paper gives many historical examples taken from outside the telecommunication field. One can think that the development of telephony (invented in 1876) and the development of long distance, automatic telephony around 1925, also fit well the examples given, where Kondratieff cycles apply. It would be an interesting exercise to use the model for the introduction of ISDN.

The second paper by J.W. Roberts and A. Hoang Van examines a very new service offering, specific to the ISDN, multislot connections. Based on an analysis of the applications using such a service, it seems to be more suited to reserved connections than to on demand

establishment of connections. In such a case a dedicated network
could be more economic than an integrated one.

The third paper in the session, by O. Gonzalez Soto, considers the
complexity of planning a network carrying a whole range of services,
each having different characteristic parameters and possibly
competing with one another. In order to resolve this complexity, a
well known technique in structured analysis is proposed. Using an
unified multiservice characterization of traffic, the paper
describes the necessary steps of a planning study and gives results
obtained with a new computer modeling tool.

TRAFFIC ENGINEERING for ISDN Design and Planning
M. Bonatti and M. Decina (Editors)
Elsevier Science Publishers B.V. (North-Holland)
© IAC, 1988

DARWIN AND THE FUTURE OF ISDN

Cesare Marchetti

International Institute for Applied Systems Analysis
A-2361 Laxenburg, Austria

People who want to put new technology into practice always ask three questions: will it sell and, if so, how fast will the market grow and how large is the final demand likely to be? What I will show today is that such questions can *in principle* be answered, although many problems have to be solved each time we come to a particular case.

The basis for such a bold statement is that every system can be decomposed into competing sub-systems, and this competition can be described using a set of equations developed by Volterra and Lotka. These formulas, originally developed to describe the dynamics of ecological systems, where many species compete, appear extraordinarily apt to describe the dynamics of social affairs. Our confidence comes also from the fact we have worked out about 1000 practical cases, covering a very large spectrum of activities and system sizes.

The Volterra (1931) equations have not been solved in close form except for the (Malthusian) case of a species growing under a resource limitation and when one variety substitutes for another in a certain niche. For the general case one has to rely on numerical solutions (Nakicenovic, 1979).

The concept of "niche", although ambiguous and controversial, is central to the operation of our analysis. It corresponds well to the concept of "market", or of a possible ceiling. The total number of mushrooms in a wood is the "niche" for assessing the prowess of a mushroom picker.

The mathematics, as we see in the Appendix, are very simple. The tough problems in mapping a certain situation are more physical in nature, and common to the hard sciences. One has to find, basically by intuition, the parameters that count in the description of a certain system. Solving the second practical problem depends on luck: once a parameter has been spotted, one hopes that somebody for some reason kept statistics about that parameter, of good quality and over long periods of time.

The gist of the operation is that the way a system operated in the past contains essential information to describe its future. Furthermore, through hierarchical jumps in the analysis, one can speculate intelligently about systems not yet born – for example, fusion energy, still in the womb of today's "primary energy" system, and the "invention-innovation" system.

Let us now start with simple cases, transforming analogies from biology to business, to construct a set of working intuitions and analogies. Figures 1a-b give the simplest case of Malthusian population – a colony of bacteria growing in a bottle of nutrient, i.e., with limited resources available.

As the graphs show, the colony grows according to a logistic equation, saturating its environment in accordance with the resources available. We can take the final population as a measure of the

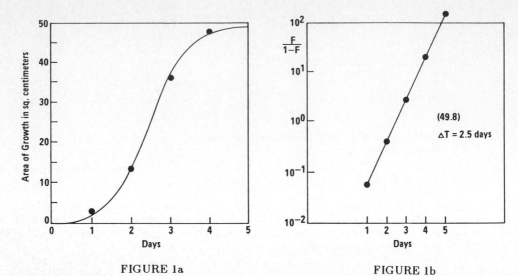

FIGURE 1a   FIGURE 1b

In Figure 1a, the size of a bacterial colony is reported versus time. By normalizing it to the final size of the population, we can express it as a fraction F of that population. We can represent then the logistic curve of Figure 1a in the form log F/1 - F, which is a straight line (Figure 1b). SOURCE: Lotka (1956).

size of the niche, and express the growth as a ratio between the population present and its remaining potential (F/1 - F). Ratios are usually more significant than actual values, but the formal reason for using them here is that log F/1 - F transforms a logistic in F in a straight line. I will use this Fisher and Pry (1970) transform most of the time.

Figure 2 shows the market penetration of mainframe computers in Japan. In this case the niche is not known *a priori*, but it can be calculated by best fit of the data. In this case, we deal with a "population" defined as the total number of mainframe computers installed.

We can also look at the growth of the car "population" (registered cars) in Italy (Figure 3) and observe that, in thirty years, it did follow a logistic equation with deviations of less than 0.5%, in

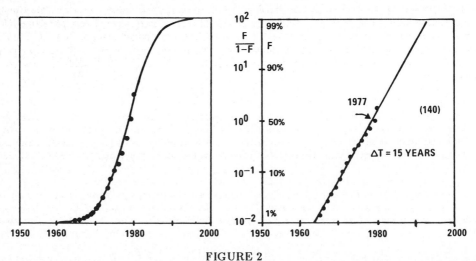

FIGURE 2

Here we mimic Figure 1 taking the number of installed mainframe computers in Japan. The "niche" is calculated by best fit of the partial data. SOURCE: Vacca (1986).

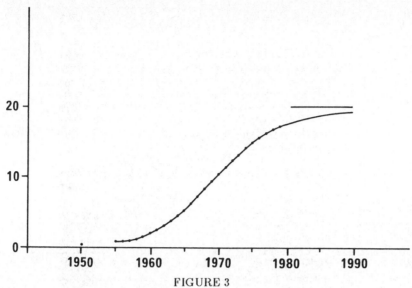

FIGURE 3

The "population" growth of registered cars in Italy shows insensitivity to external perturbations (e.g., the oil shock). A very general characteristic of growing population which I call "system homeostasis". SOURCE: Marchetti (1983).

spite of the many troubles that plagued cars during these years, not least the "oil crisis". Car sales tell another story, because car owners compensated for the higher running costs with savings in capital costs, that is, by delaying the purchase of a new car. But car population growth did stick to its original steady course. I will refer later on to this phenomenon as *homeostatic* (homeodynamic!) behavior of the system.

A very important footnote is that, to insure a good fit, the size of the niche should not change. For this reason, the single logistic analysis cannot be applied to the growth of human population because the *access technologies* that define the niche keep changing over time. Curiously, logistics were first applied to human populations by Verhulst (1845) during the last century, and Pearl (1924, 1925) obviously with mixed results. Another warning is about competitors more or less hidden in the niche, and subtracting resources.

The second case is that of a system growing under the control of a program which sets a peg to the growth. It has been observed in biology, where, e.g., a plant grows under genetic control, that the size often follows a logistic (Figure 4). This observation could be interpreted (assuming growth proportional to size, which is very natural) as growth regulated by a signal proportional to the difference between the actual size and the peg. Very simple regulatory engineering!

The interesting fact is that many more or less programmed infrastructures grow the same way – for example, telegraph lines in the United States (Figure 5) or railway networks in Italy (Figure 6). Incidentally, many of my examples refer to the USA because consistent, credible, and readable long-term statistics are so readily available there.

Before turning to more complicated cases, I would like to comment on the estimate procedure through fitting of the data to the size of the niche, i.e., of the market. If the data were absolutely precise and the system noiseless, one could get absolute precision at any time. The level of intrinsic noise in the system and that in the measurement basically determines how precise the forecast can be. An interesting analysis of the problem has been done by Debecker and Modis (1986).

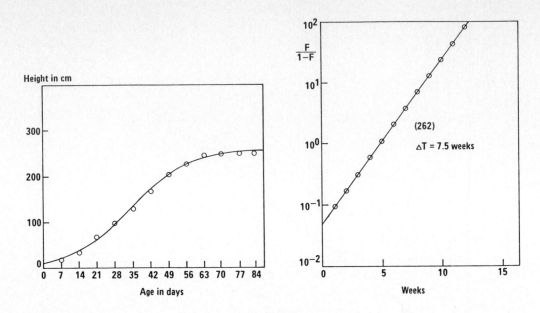

FIGURE 4

The growth of a sunflower (height) follows a neat logistic curve. One can see a plant as a population of cells, but the most probable cause is a simple regulatory system as outlined in the text.
DATA SOURCE: Lotka (1956) and Reed and Holland (1919).

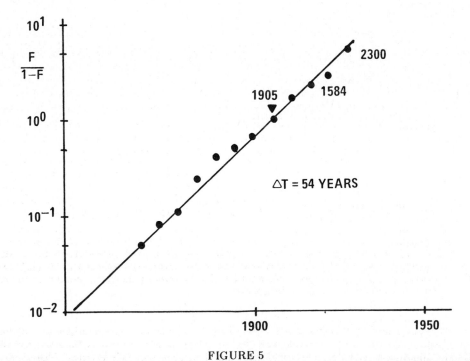

FIGURE 5

Length of wire for US telegraph lines. The 5-year time constant (time to go from 10% to 90% of
length) is quite characteristic for penetration of many technologies. SOURCE: Marchetti
(1986).

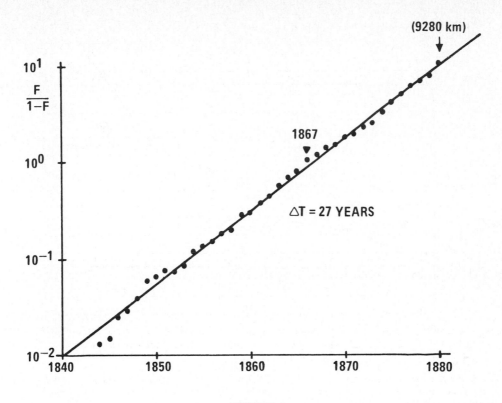

FIGURE 6

The first spurt of railway technology in Italy is here mapped in terms of track length. SOURCE: Marchetti (1986).

Less delicate are the cases of progressive substitution, e.g., by a mutant or by a new technology inside an already filled niche. If we are interested only in the share of the niche (market) taken by the competitors, then the absolute size of the niche can be forgotten and can be variable. An interesting case is the substitution of cars for horses in US personal transportation (Figures 7a-b) and of diesel for steam locomotives in the UK railways (Figure 8).

The most general and interesting case is that of multiple competition, where various generations of technology coexist and push each other in the same market . The case I will present first, and that was the first we treated using this model, is that of primary energy sources.

Wood, coal, oil, gas, and nuclear primary energy sources compete with each other, and their actual contribution in terms of tons of coal equivalent (tce) is reported in Figure 9, starting in 1860 at world level. The fitting of the data to a particular solution of the V-L equations was done with a computer package, and the result is reported in Figure 10, which reveals very interesting features of the global energy system. One is the great stability of the substitution process over very long periods of time. In fact, each energy source seems to enjoy a shelf-life, or holds its equation, interactively modified, for a full 100 years. Once the set of equations is anchored in a data base, we can in fact predict even 50 years ahead.

Figures 11a-c demonstrate this. Figure 11a gives the data base, i.e., market fractions of the various primary energies, wood, coal, oil, and gas, for the period 1900-1920. In Figure 11b, the equations are set using this data base. In Figure 11c the actual statistical data outside the 1900-1920 period are superimposed to check the predictive capacity of the equations forward and backward.

The results of the experiment are excellent for oil and coal, for which the 1970 market share (and the 1860) could be constructed with a 2% to 3% error. Natural gas fares less well because, at the

C. Marchetti

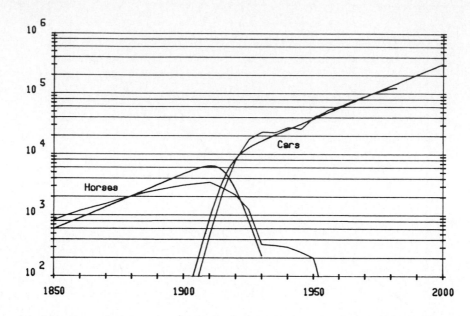

FIGURE 7a

The number of horses and cars in the USA. There is clearly a transition between 1900 and 1930, where practically all horses have been replaced by cars. SOURCE: Nakicenovic (1986a).

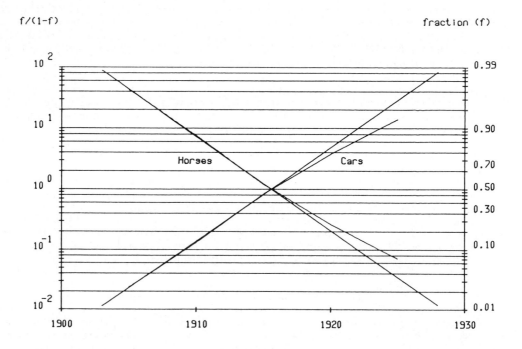

FIGURE 7b

Substitution of automobiles by horses in logistic terms. SOURCE: Nakicenovic (1986a).

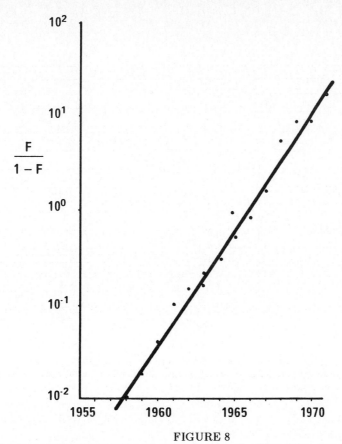

FIGURE 8

The substitution of diesels for steam locomotives in the UK. The complete substitution took about 30 years (time constant about 15 years).

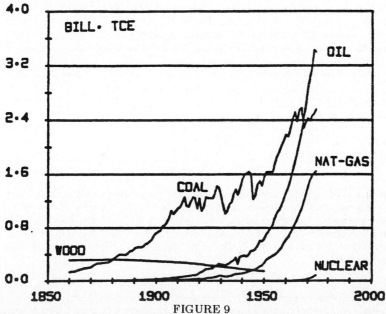

FIGURE 9

The general energy market can be decomposed into primary energies contributing to it. Their competition is the source of the dynamics. SOURCE: Marchetti and Nakicenovic (1979).

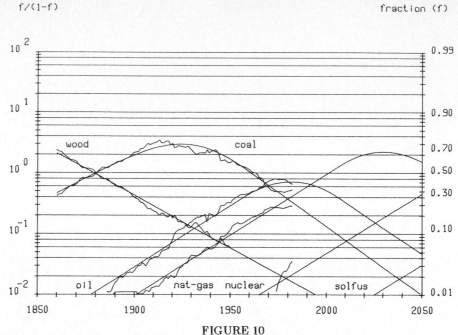

FIGURE 10

The data of Figure 9 are here fitted to a set of Volterra equation solutions. The stability of the substitution process over 100 years is really remarkable. SOURCE: Grübler and Nakicenovic (1987).

end of the fitting period (in 1920), it held only a 2% share of the market, and the penetration rates are usually not yet consolidated at that low level.

Figure 11 is a methodological landmark. It shows, once a system is properly mapped, that forecasting is possible even over a long period, naturally inside the characteristic time constant of the system. To go beyond that (e.g., to forecast the birth date of nuclear energy or fusion energy), one has to go to a meta level where time constants are longer. (The time constant is quantitatively defined as the time to go from 10% to 90% of the potential share.)

Just to enrich the zoo, Figure 12 reports the substitution sequence for sail, steam, and diesel (or gas turbine) propulsion of US commercial ships. Apart from the good fit, I would like to call your attention to the slow pace of substitution, much longer than the lifetime of ships themselves. What comes out from the many analyses we have done is that the innovation process is culturally controlled and has soft links to the level of investments. Even if it is just a new idea it may well take 50 years to penetrate.

Half a century ago Willis (1922) discovered empirically that under certain conditions biological systems behave the same way independently from abstraction in the level of conceptualization we use. Thus, for instance, a *species* produces *individuals* to fill a niche, but it can also produce mutants or *varieties* to fill a more articulated niche. *Families* produce species and *genera* families. The subsets are populations with the same statistical behavior, although with widely different time constants.

I have successfully applied this biological principle to the meta level of inventions and innovations, treating them as single objects generated at certain points in time. The original intention was to glimpse *when* a new primary energy is introduced in the market, and in particular when we might expect fusion to enjoy its window of opportunity.

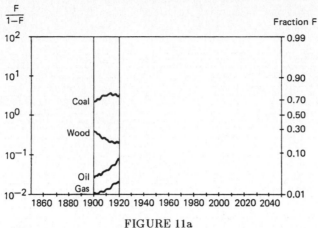

FIGURE 11a

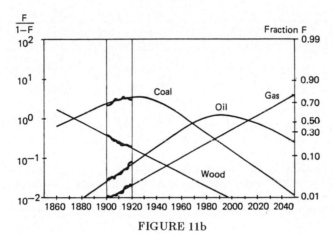

FIGURE 11b

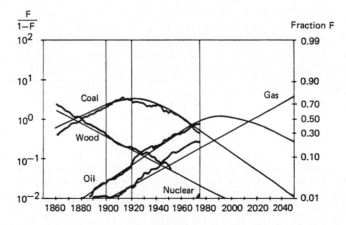

FIGURE 11c

The great stability in the dynamics of the competition is what makes such an analysis a precious tool for forecasting. An example is given here, where a 20-year data swath (1900-1920) constitutes the base (Figure 11a) on which the equations are set (Figure 11b) and then compared with actual statistics (Figure 11c). The forecast, which could have been made in 1920, is embarrassingly precise for coal and oil. The predicted growth of methane does not come out so well, because the penetration was still small at the end of the base period (about 2%). SOURCE: Marchetti and Nakicenovic (1979).

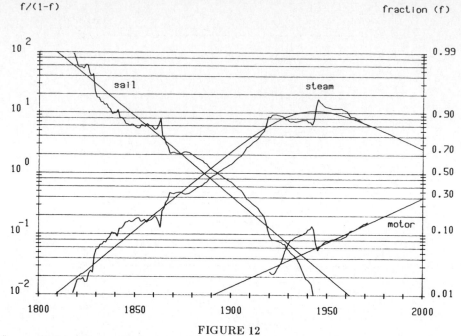

FIGURE 12

This "appendix" to Figure 10 suggests that things happen the same way, regardless of the field under study. SOURCE: Nakicenovic (1986b).

The data for basic inventions and innovations in the last couple of centuries were taken from Mensch (1975). An invention is dated by the birthday of a working prototype; an innovation, by the date of its first commercial sale. These very matter-of-fact definitions permit homogeneous dating for the whole process, which is the greatest merit of Mensch's analysis.

Mensch himself noted that innovations come basically in bunches, and so do inventions. In the period studied we have three bunches of inventions and three of innovations. I analyzed each bunch (Marchetti, 1981), with the hypothesis that, in Willis's spirit, each bunch would represent a population growing to fill its niche, i.e., the then-current demand for inventions or innovations. The results fit the expectations perfectly and are reported in abridged form in Figure 13. The lines with odd numbers represent invention waves; those with even numbers, the innovation waves. Inventions in line 1 go into innovation in line 2 and so on. One striking observation made by Mensch is that the order is respected (almost) in the two sets, i.e., first come first served, which can be very useful in forecasting *when* an invention will become commercially viable.

However, the analysis does not tell us *if* an innovation will succeed, because the analysis is made *a posteriori* and refers only to *winning ideas*, with no hint as to the scrap pile of losers. Looking at patent lists, we can estimate that the rate of success is on the order of 1% which, curiously, matches the successful mutation rate in biology.

This observation is very interesting philosophically because what emerges from our analysis is the obvious *determinism of the winners*. In other words, one cannot win a formula 1 race by driving zig-zag. Optimization, it is well known, robs the decision-making process of degrees of freedom. But we are always free to make mistakes!

We first put Figure 13 to use as shown in Figure 14. The innovation waves are mixed with the primary energy penetration spurts of Figure 10 to show that every wave has a new primary

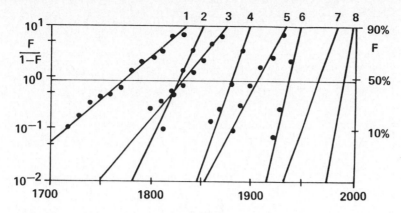

FIGURE 13

Populations of inventions (odd numbers) and innovations (even numbers) during the last 300 years. Each wave is analyzed for the cumulative number of inventions or innovations. Numbers 7 and 8 are calculated from the regularities, and constitute a forecast. For details of this approach, see Marchetti (1981).

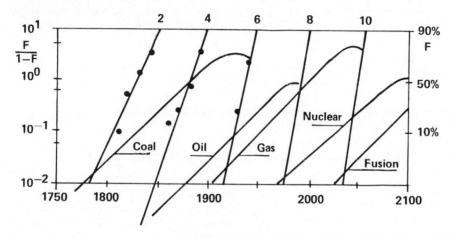

FIGURE 14

Innovation waves reveal a very deep pulse in the functioning of Western societies, and many events are tuned to them. The example reported shows that every wave has been associated with the introduction of a new primary energy. This makes possible a forecast for the introduction of nuclear fusion around 2025. SOURCE: Marchetti (1981).

energy associated with it. The fourth wave is calculated from the regularities of the first three, but the point of nuclear energy as initial challenge is real.

Another interesting observation is that the waves are equally spaced (by their center points) about 55 years apart. This implies a great pulsation that reappears in all sort of human affairs. Just to give an example, if the starts (opening of the first line) for subway networks are put together, we obtain three bunches, organized in populations and spanning a neat 55 years (Figure 15).

We can do the same thing with the general transportation infrastructure in the USA (Figure 16) by looking separately at canals, railways, paved roads, and airways. Each of them is part of a sequence, spaced about 55 years apart, and with intrinsic time constants for growth of the same

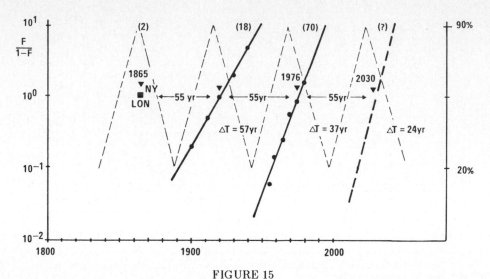

FIGURE 15

The cumulative numbers of *first line opening* for subways in world's cities are here analyzed in terms of population of networks. The dashed oscillation shows periods of booms and recession (Marchetti, 1986). The 2030 line is calculated from regularities.

US RAILROADS (3x10^5 MILES)
US PAVED ROADS (3.4x10^6 MILES)
US FEDERAL AIRWAYS (3.2x10^6 MILES)

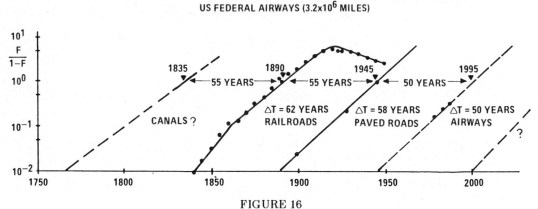

FIGURE 16

Successive waves of infrastructural construction are reported here using the concepts of Figures 5 and 6. The (virtual) saturation points are incorporated in the labels (for canals about 3×10^4 miles). The periodicity is about 55 years as usual. SOURCE: Marchetti (1986).

order of magnitude. We can also go to a meta level by merging all these transportation infrastructures, i.e., their cumulative length (Figure 17). First, we find that this sum, the infrastructure niche, can be well represented by a logistic. Second, we can express each separate infrastructure as a fraction of this total, as for the historic sources of energy, and we obtain a similar chart (Figure 18).

The interesting side of Figure 18 is that when a newcomer is started, we can calculate its progress since the beginning using the precalculated envelope (the infrastructure's logistic). We might also calculate when a newcomer (Maglev ?) has its opportunity window, if we can find regularities of the kind used for forecasting the entrance of new primary energy sources.

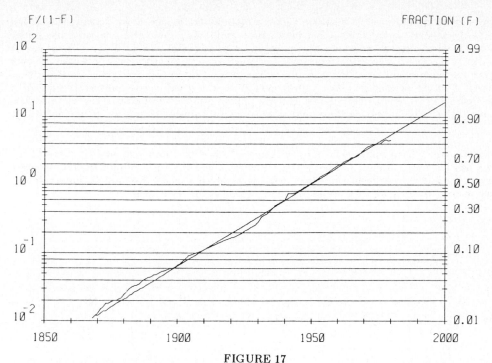

FIGURE 17

The sum of the length of all transport infrastructures reported in Figure 16 is here given in logistic form. Saturation occurs around 4.7×10^6 miles. This envelope permits us to look at the competition between modes, as in the case for energy. SOURCE: Grübler (1987).

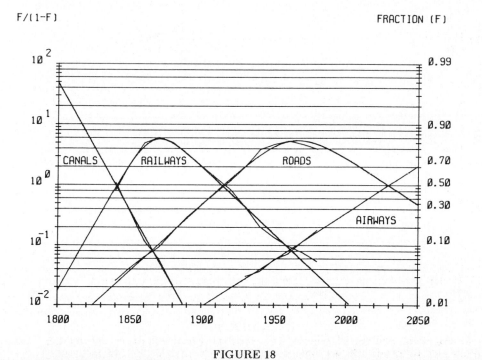

FIGURE 18

This chart by Nakicenovic (1987) shows transportation infrastructures in a competitive mode. The length for *airways* is the scheduled network. Curiously, the signs of decay for a certain system start appearing when it reaches the *relative* maximum penetration level.

This line of thinking might produce answers to some basic questions people in the ISDN are currently asking. Just to show that information traffic falls into the same patterns, I analyzed some cases of message transmission by letter, telegram, and telephone – the main competing modes in the past. The actual number of messages sent through the three channels (Figure 19) grows for Switzerland according to three logistic pulses (Figure 20), well shaped and correctly far apart. Also the market share for each mode follows the usual logistic pattern (Figure 21). We can repeat the exercise for Belgium (Figure 22) or other countries, but the picture does not change in principle, although the actual parameters are characteristic of the area under study.

In order to get hard numbers about something which is not born yet, one has to go to a meta level as I did show earlier. As the last charts show, a line of attack to solve the problem of ISDN services demand is outlined in Figures 16-22, to produce a model for total demand and a modal split in tune with Kondratiev cycles, including windows for newcomers.

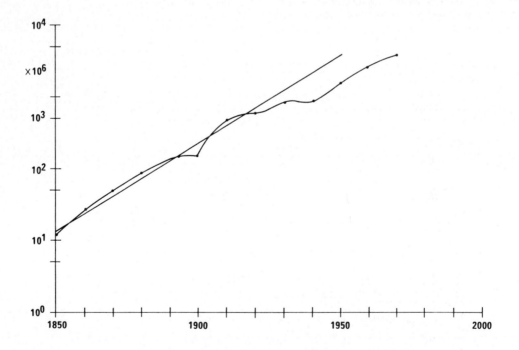

FIGURE 19

This is the total number of objects, i.e., message transmissions in Switzerland. Letters, telegrams, and telephone calls are lumped together. DATA SOURCE: Mitchell (1981).

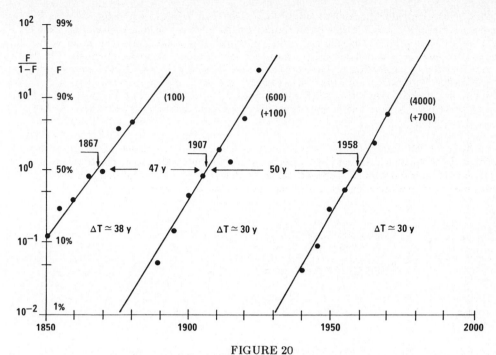

FIGURE 20

The data of Figure 19 can be neatly separated into three populations or pulses, holding respectively 100, 600, and 4000 (x 10^6) objects. DATA SOURCE: Mitchell (1981).

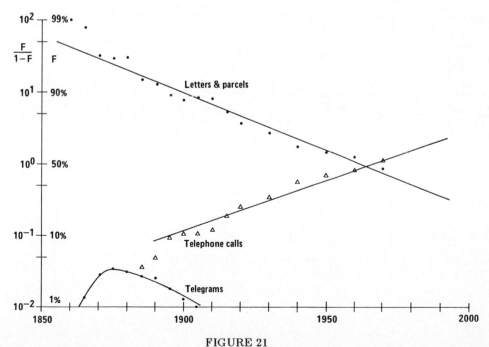

FIGURE 21

One can also analyze the data in an analogy with the primary energy sources of Figure 10, in terms of market-shares competition between letters, telegrams, and telephone calls. Telegrams never played a great role. DATA SOURCE: Mitchell (1981).

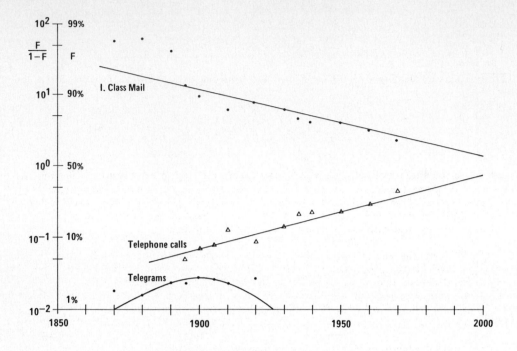

FIGURE 22
Just to show that the good quality of the result is not limited to the well-behaved patterns of Switzerland, I report the same analysis for Belgium. DATA SOURCE: Mitchell (1981).

APPENDIX

The equations for dealing with different cases are reducible to the general Volterra–Lotka equations

$$\frac{dN_i}{dt} = K_i N_i + \beta_i^{-1} \sum_{n}^{j=1} a_{ij} N_i N_j \quad , \tag{1}$$

where N_i is the number of individuals in species i, and a, β, and K are constants. The equation says a species grows (or decays) exponentially, but for the interactions with other species. A general treatment of these equations can be found in Montroll and Goel (1971) and Peschel and Mende (1986). Since closed solutions exist only for the case of one or two competitors, these treatments mainly deal with the general properties of the solutions.

In order to keep the analysis at a physically intuitive level, I use the original treatment of Verhulst (1845) for the population in a *niche* (Malthusian) and that of Haldane (1924) for the competition between two genes of different fitness. For the multiple competition, we have developed a computer package which works perfectly for actual cases (Marchetti and Nakicenovic, 1979), but whose identity with the Volterra equations is not fully proven (Nakicenovic, 1979).

Most of the results are presented using the coordinates for the linear transform of a logistic equation originally introduced by Fisher and Pry (1970).

The Malthusian Case

This modeling of the dynamics of population systems started with Verhulst in 1845, who quantified the Malthusian case. A physically very intuitive example is given by a population of bacteria growing in a bottle of broth. Bacteria can be seen as machinery to transform a set of chemicals in the broth into bacteria. The rate of this transformation, *coeteris paribus* (e.g., temperature), can be seen as proportional to the number of bacteria (the transforming machinery) and the concentration of the transformable chemicals.

Since all transformable chemicals will be transformed finally into bacterial bodies, to use homogeneous units one can measure broth chemicals in terms of bacterial bodies. So $N(t)$ is the number of bacteria at time t, and $\bar{N}$ is the amount of transformable chemicals at time 0, before multiplication starts. The Verhulst equation can then be written

$$\frac{dN}{dt} = aN(\bar{N} - N) \quad , \tag{2}$$

whose solution is

$$N(t) = \frac{\bar{N}}{1 - e^{-(at+b)}} \quad , \tag{3}$$

with b an integration constant, sometimes written as t_0, i.e., time at time 0; a is a rate constant which we assume to be independent of the size of the population. This means that there is no "proximity feedback". If we normalize to the final size of the system, $\bar{N}$, and explicate the linear expression, we can write equation (2) in the form suggested by Fisher and Pry (1970).

$$\log \frac{F}{1-F} = at + b \quad , \quad \text{where} \quad F = \frac{N}{\bar{N}} \quad . \tag{4}$$

Most of the charts are presented in this form. $\bar{N}$ is often called the *niche*, and the growth of a population is given as the fraction of the niche it fills. It is obvious that this analysis has been made with the assumption that *there are no competitors*. A single species grows to match the resources $(\bar{N})$ in a Malthusian fashion.

The fitting of empirical data requires calculation of the three parameters $\bar{N}$, a, and b, for which there are various recipes (Oliver, 1964; Blackman, 1972; Bossert, 1977). The problem is to choose the physically more significant representation and procedure.

I personally prefer to work with the Fisher and Pry transform, because it operates on *ratios* (e.g., of the size of two populations), and ratios seem to me more important than absolute values, both in biology and in social systems.

The calculation of $\bar{N}$ is usually of great interest, especially in economics. However, the value of $\bar{N}$ is very sensitive to the value of the data, i.e., to their errors, especially at the beginning of the growth. The problem of assessing the error on $\bar{N}$ has been studied by Debecker and Modis (1986), using numerical simulation.

The Malthusian logistic must be used with great precaution because it contains implicitly some important hypothesis:

- That there are no competitors in sight.
- That the size of a niche remains constant.
- That the species and its boundary conditions (e.g., temperature for the bacteria) stay the same.

The fact that in multiple competition the starts are always logistic may lead to the presumption that the system is Malthusian. When the transition period starts there is no way of patching up the logistic fit.

The fact that the niches keep changing, due to the introduction of new technologies, makes this treatment, generally speaking, unfit for dealing with the growth of human populations, a subject where Pearl (1924) first applied logistics. Since the treatment sometimes works and sometimes not, one can find much faith and disillusionment among demographers.

One-to-One Competition

The case was studied by Haldane for the penetration of a mutant or of a variety having some advantage in respect to the preexisting ones. These cases can be described quantitatively by saying that variety (1) has a reproductive advantage of k, over variety (2). Thus, for every generation the ratio of the number of individuals in the two varieties will be changed by $\dfrac{1}{(1-k)}$. If n is the number of generations, starting from $n = 0$, then we can write

$$\frac{N_1}{N_2} = \frac{R_0}{(1-k)^n} \quad , \quad \text{where} \quad R_0 = \frac{N_1}{N_2} \text{ at } t = 0 \tag{5}$$

If k is small, as it usually is in biology (typically 10^{-3}), we can write

$$\frac{N_1}{N_2} = \frac{R_0}{e^{kn}} \tag{6}$$

We are then formally back to square one, i.e., to the Malthusian case, except for the very favorable fact that we have an initial condition (R_0) instead of a final condition $(\bar{N})$. This means that in *relative terms* the evolution of the system is not sensitive to the size of the niche, a property that is extremely useful for forecasting in multiple competition cases. Since the generations can be assumed equally spaced, n is actually equivalent to time.

As for the biological case, it is difficult to prove that the "reproductive advantage" remains constant in time, especially when competition lasts for tens of years and the technology of the competitors keeps changing, not to speak of the social and organizational context. But the analysis of hundreds of cases shows that systems behave exactly *as if*.

Multiple Competition

Multiple competition is dealt using a computer package originally developed by Nakicenovic (1979). A simplified description says that all the competitors start in a logistic mode and phase out in a logistic mode. They undergo a transition from a logistic-in to a logistic-out during which they are calculated as "residuals", i.e., as the difference between the size of the niche and the sum of all the *ins* and *outs*. The details of the rules are be found in (Nakicenovic, 1979). This package has been used to treat about one hundred empirical cases, all of which always showed an excellent match with reality.

An attempt to link this kind of treatment to current views in economics has been made by Peterka (1977).

REFERENCES

Wade Blackman, Jr, A. (1972), A mathematical model for trend forecasts, *Technological Forecasting and Social Change, 3*:441-452).

Bossert, R.W. (1977), The logistic curve revived, programmed, and applied to electric utility forecasting, *Technological Forecasting and Social Change, 10*:357.

Debecker, A. and T. Modis (1986), *Determination of the Uncertainties in S-Curve Logistic Fits*. Geneva: Digital Equipment Corporation.

Fisher, J.C. and R.H. Pry (1970), A simple substitution model of technological change. *Technological Forecasting and Social Change 3*:75-88.

Grübler, A. (1987), Aufstieg und Fall von Infrastrukturen. *Technikergeschichte* (forthcoming).

Grübler, A. and N. Nakicenovic (1987), *The Dynamic Evolution of Methane Technologies*. Working Paper WP-87-02. Laxenburg, Austria: International Institute for Applied Systems Analysis.

Haldane, J.B.S. (1924), The mathematical theory of natural and artificial selection, *Transactions, Cambridge Philosophical Society, 23*:19-41.

Historical Statistics on the U.S. Colonial Times to 1970. Washington, DC: U.S. Department of Commerce (1975).

Lotka, A.J. (1956), *Elements of Mathematical Biology*. New York: Dover Publications, Inc.

Marchetti, C. (1981), *Society as a Learning System: Discovery, Invention and Innovation Cycles Revisited*. Research Report RR-81-29. Laxenburg, Austria: International Institute for Applied Systems Analysis.

Marchetti, C. (1983), The automobile in a system context: the past 80 years and the next 20 years. *Technological Forecasting and Social Change 23*:3-23.

Marchetti, C. (1986), Fifty-year pulsation in human affairs. *Futures 17*(3):376-88.

Marchetti, C. and N. Nakicenovic (1979), *The Dynamics of Energy Systems and the Logistic Substitution Model*. Research Report RR-79-13. Laxenburg, Austria: International Institute for Applied Systems Analysis.

Mensch, G. (1975), *Das technologische Patt*. Frankfurt: Umschau Verlag.

Mitchell, B.R. (1981), *European Historical Statistics, 1750-1975*. New York: Facts on File.

Montroll, E.W. and N.S. Goel (1971), On the Volterra and other nonlinear models of interacting populations, *Rev. Mod. Phys., 43*(2):231.

Nakicenovic, N. (1979), *Software Package for the Logistic Substitution Model*. Research Report RR-79-12. Laxenburg, Austria: International Institute for Applied Systems Analysis.

Nakicenovic, N. (1986a), The automobile road to technological change: diffusion of the automobile as a process of technological substitution. *Technological Forecasting and Social Change* *29*:309-340.

Nakicenovic, N. (1986b), *Patterns of Change: Technological Substitution and Long Waves in the United States*. Working Paper WP-86-13. Laxenburg, Austria: International Institute for Applied Systems Analysis.

Nakicenovic, N. (1987), *Transportation and Energy Systems in the U.S.* Working Paper WP-87-01. Laxenburg, Austria: International Institute for Applied Systems Analysis.

Oliver, F.R. (1964), Methods of estimating the logistic growth function, *Applied Statistics*, *13*:57-66.

Pearl, R. (1924), *Studies in Human Biology*. Baltimore: Williams and Wilkins Co.

Pearl, R. (1925), *The Biology of Population Growth*. New York: Alfred A. Knopf, Inc.

Peschel, M. and W. Mende (1986), *The Predator-Prey Model*. Springer Verlag: Berlin-Heidelberg-New York.

Peterka, V. (1977), *Macrodynamics of Technological Change – Market Penetration by New Technologies*. Research Report RR-77-22. Laxenburg, Austria: International Institute for Applied Systems Analysis.

Reed, H.S. and R.H. Holland (1919), *Proc. Natl. Acad. Sci. 5*:135-144.

Vacca, R. (1986), personal communication. Rome.

Verhulst, P.F. (1845), in *Nouveaux Memoires de l'Academie Royale des Sciences, des Lettres et des Beaux-Arts de Belgique 18*:1-38.

Volterra, V. (1931), *Lecon sur la Theorie Mathematique de la Lutte Pour la Vie*. Paris: Gauthier-Villars.

Willis, J.C. (1922), *Age and Area*. Cambridge: Cambridge University Press.

TRAFFIC ENGINEERING for ISDN Design and Planning
M. Bonatti and M. Decina (Editors)
Elsevier Science Publishers B.V. (North-Holland)
© IAC, 1988

CHARACTERISTICS OF SERVICES REQUIRING MULTI-SLOT
CONNECTIONS AND THEIR IMPACT ON ISDN DESIGN

J. W. ROBERTS and A. HOANG VAN

Centre National d'Etudes des Télécommunications
CNET/PAA/ATR
38-40 rue du Général Leclerc
92131 Issy les Moulineaux, France.

The impact of multi-slot traffic is examined through three aspects:
teleservice characteristics, bearer service options and teletraffic
issues. We distinguish, in particular, bearer services preserving time
slot sequence integrity, for services like videoconferencing, and
bearer services where data unit integrity can be maintained on
independently routed connections using a multilink protocol, suitable
for data transfer. Implied evaluation and network design questions are
examined through a survey of relevant literature for both demand and
reserved set up.

1. INTRODUCTION.

The emphasis of CCITT activity and national ISDN implementations is currently on
the integration of the telephone and essentially low speed packet switched data
and telematics services. Implementation of multi-slot, or n x 64 Kbps, services
is evoked but remains vague. There is however a growing need for transmission at
these rates for services such as videoconferencing and bulk data transfer which
is at present satisfied by leased lines and dedicated switched networks. The
provision of such services, through their particular performance requirements
and their influence on other services, could have a significant impact on ISDN
structure and operation. In this paper we provide a certain amount of
information which we hope will clarify the implied network design issues.

We examine the nature of the demand for multi-slot connections, discuss
constraints imposed by the provision of adapted bearer services and identify
some teletraffic problems which need to be solved to ensure their implementation
in the most cost effective way. Our attention is mainly directed to the
prospects for ISDN evolution in the near future, based on classical digital
switching technology with transmission at rates not exceeding 2 Mbps.

In section 2, we describe a number of teleservices requiring bit rates greater
than 64 Kbps and discuss their particular characteristics. We then present, in
section 3, the principal multi-slot bearer service alternatives, insisting on
the attributes which have a bearing on network traffic capacity. Sections 4 and
5 survey implied teletraffic issues for demand and reserved set up,
respectively, with extensive references to published work on the subject. In
section 6, our conclusion consists in a statement of what bearer services are,
in our opinion, best adapted to the considered teleservices and in a list of
multi-slot teletraffic problems which deserve further attention.

Note, finally, that the opinions expressed in this paper engage the
responsibility of the authors alone and should not be interpreted as the view of
the organisation to which they belong.

2. HIGH BIT RATE TELESERVICES

We identify a number of teleservices requiring high speed transmission, discuss their particular characteristics and performance requirements and attempt to gain some idea of their potential traffic volume. Rather than attempting an extensive description of each service we choose to highlight some significant differences with respect to the telephone service.

2.1 Considered services

We broadly classify services according to the type of information transmitted: bulk data, still pictures, moving pictures, hi-fi sound, multi-media.

By bulk data we mean the files of alphanumeric information traditionally handled by computers: data bases, programs, scientific calculations,... Required bit rate can be any within the considered range depending on the capabilities of terminal equipment. File sizes range from tens of kilo-octets for data exchanged between mainframes and intelligent work stations [1] to several hundred mega-octets when the content of an entire magnetic tape must be transferred.

Digitally coded still pictures must be transmitted at high speed in a number of applications ranging from computer aided design to consultation of image banks. The picture may be displayed on a screen (e.g. videotex) or result in a hard copy (e.g. facsimile). A still picture is typically coded in several hundreds of kilo-octets. Required transmission speed again depends on the capabilities of terminals but we may expect these to evolve to meet the ergonomic requirements of users: a photogragh can be displayed in 2 or 3 seconds at a transmission speed of 1 Mbps.

Moving pictures with relatively little movement can be transmitted with adequate quality at a speed less than 2 Mbps. This applies to the videoconference and videophone services: the former is a meeting service generally involving groups of people in two or more locations while the latter may be seen as an enhanced telephone service between two or exceptionally more individuals. Many different variants of the videoconference service have been identified [2]; in this paper we have in mind a simple implementation requiring bidirectional symmetric connections between two meeting rooms or between meeting rooms and a special equipment for multipoint conferences [3]. A videophone can transmit the image of the person speaking or, perhaps more usefully, display an object or document which is under discussion. The rate of 6×64 Kbps is a strong candidate for standardised videoconferencing while a person to person videophone can apparently make do with only 2×64 Kbps for picture and sound.

Hi-fi sound would be transmitted, for example, in an entertainment service giving users access to a central music library. A connection consisting of two 384 Kbps channels is required for stereo transmission (cf. CCITT Rec J41).

Finally, some teleservices make use of multi-media and therefore require more than one 64 Kbps connection. One example is audio-videotex used in remote learning programmes.

2.2 Traffic characteristics

The main features of ISDN architecture will continue for many years to be determined by the characteristics of the telephone service. Telephone traffic variations are well known. In particular, the network is dimensioned to meet grade of service conditions in a busy hour generally situated in mid morning. At other periods, and notably at night time, there is a lot of spare capacity which could be exploited by other services in an integrated network. Bulk data transfers for data base updates, for example, might naturally occur in these hours.

In the busy hour, telephone traffic is modelled as a stationary stochastic process characterised by a call arrival process (e.g. Poisson) and a service time distribution (mean around 3 minutes). Among multi-slot services, we believe that videoconferencing, in particular, will have traffic with quite different characteristics. Call arrivals will not be random but will be concentrated on a small number of preferred meeting start times and call durations will typically be of one or two hours.

The service time of bulk data transfer and still picture transmission is less an inherent characteristic than a result of terminal capabilities and network performance. Such traffic is more appropriately described through the distribution of the quantity of data to be transferred. Videotex or image bank consultation services naturally generate bursty traffic: short periods of high speed transmision interspersed by periods of inactivity during which the user views the displayed picture.

Telephone traffic per terminal is low, there is a large user population and any user has many potential correspondents; typically, 70% of traffic is between users in the same locality. It is these characteristics which largely determine the structure of the telecommunications network and notably explain the importance of the concentration and switching functions of its local part. The characteristics of multi-slot services might naturally lead to a quite different architecture. In [3], for example, it is argued that there is little advantage in local switching for videoconferences. The transfer of very large data files is likely to concerne only a small number of users with very specific needs.

2.3 Performance requirements

We distinguish performance requirements at call set up concerning service availability and performance requirements during the call concerning service transparency.

2.3.1 Availability.

Broadly speaking, telephone users require set up on demand with set up time not exceeding a few seconds; call blocking probability due to network congestion should not be more than a few percent [4].

Demand set up is not necessarily a requirement for all multi-slot services and, for videoconferencing in particular, users may prefer to guarantee successful set up by reserving their call in advance. Performance requirements concerning the success of a reservation request remain to be determined but it seems clear that the probability a booked meeting cannot take place because of congestion should be very low indeed (less than the probability of equipment failure, say).

Set up time should, as a rule of thumb, be roughly in proportion to the duration of the ensuing service. Thus, a set up time longer than that of the telephone is tolerable for an hour long videoconference while, on the other hand, a set up time greater than one second would be too long for high speed image consultation.

Call blocking probabilities should be small with respect to the probability of a call failing due to other causes (called terminal unavailable, equipment outages, ...). Note, however, that in the context of the ISDN, the provision of an automatic repeat attempt facility in the caller's terminal would give the user the impression of a system operating with delay. Appropriate limits for acceptable set up delay would have to be determined.

2.3 2 Transparency

Detailed service transparency requirements for speech are given in [4]. These principally express limits on constant and variable propagation times and specify bit error conditions which are subjectively tolerable.

Real time multi-slot services such as videoconference and videophone have similar requirements for undistorted communication whereas data and still pictures are by nature "elastic" with respect to transmission time. Bulk data transfer has an ultimate user requirement for error free transmission. This is achieved by the transfer protocol which detects and corrects any errors introduced by the link. The link error rate determines the effective throughput of the data connection and the tolerable limit is a complicated function of transmission speed and protocol parameters (cf. [5]). Digital link error performance requirements are specified in CCITT Rec G 821.

For multi-slot services, a particular requirement concerns the relationship between the information conveyed on different slots. If the bit stream generated by a teleservice is emitted sequentially in consecutive slots, the slot sequence itself constitutes a part of the transmitted information and must be preserved across the connection. This is known as the requirement to preserve time slot sequence integrity or TSSI. It is necessary for the videoconference service. Bulk data, on the other hand, can be transmitted without maintaining the slot sequence if an appropriate protocol is used (see section 3.3 below). A videophone service using one 64 Kbps link for voice and another for the image would not require a strict relationship between the corresponding slots although a difference in their propagation times should not be perceptible to users as a lack of synchronisation. This is also true of any multi-media service using a distinct link for each medium.

2.4 Traffic volume

Estimating demand for the considered services and the generated traffic volume is extremely speculative and little exists in the way of market research studies to aid our speculation. In this section we aim to identify at least the orders of magnitude of the respective traffic volumes.

It is first important to appreciate the enormous volume of digital information generated by the telephone service with speech coding at 64 Kbps. In one 3 minute call a telephone user generates the transfer of some 12 megabits of data in each transmission direction. By way of comparison, Tolstoy's "War and Peace", coded at 8 bits per character, is equivalent to the information volume exchanged in just 4 minutes of conversation. This comment illustrates the difficulty we have in imagining what sources of alphanumeric data can ever generate a significant amount of traffic compared with the telephone.

Bulk data transfer currently takes place mainly by physically transporting magnetic tapes and discs or by transmission over dedicated digital leased lines. There now also exist a number of satellite based networks offering switched high speed digital connections. In France, the TRANSFIX service currently provides several hundred leased lines at bit rates between 128 Kbps and 1 Mbps while the TRANSDYN service offers reserved and demand set up links using the satellite Telecom 1. The users of these services are banks and financial institutions, computer services companies, scientific research centres and manufacturing companies (cf. [6]).

The greatest demand for bulk data transfers comes from the scientific community: universities, nuclear research centres,... For instance, experiments using particle accelerators generate tens of thousands of mega-octets per day, part of which must be transmitted to various laboratories for processing, [6]. Clearly, however, this type of application only concerns a very limited number of potential users. The same is true for computer centre back up where data files must periodically be copied to a reserve machine capable of taking over a vital work load in the event of equipment failure.

In market research campaigns [7,8], many companies have expressed a file transfer requirement and they are becoming increasingly well equipped in information processing equipment. However, it should be borne in mind that most file transfers concern relatively small amounts of data for which the single slot rate of 64 Kbps is largely sufficient. For instance, a 5" floppy disc containing one mega-octet can be transmitted in only 2 minutes at 64 Kbps.

Considerably greater information flows would be generated by a generalisation of picture based services. Videoconferencing, in particular, is a potentially significant source of multi-slot traffic but, despite consistently optimistic forecasts, demand is still restricted to a very limited number of large companies. For instance, according to [9], only 20 or so Japanese companies currently use videoconference systems in the INS and growth trends show no sign of accelerating. The principal brake on development is certainly the high cost of providing this service. In France in 1986 the cost of codec and studio equipment was between 80 000 and 160 000 dollars with a call charge of 200 dollars per hour [6]. Videoconferencing is presently only cost effective as a substitute for travel when traffic is heavy (i.e. at least one meeting per day) and several people are spared from travelling at each meeting [9]. This explains why only very large companies are so far interested in this service. In a more favourable cost context, assuming some 500 studios used 50% of the time in the busy hour and transmitting at the rate of 384 Kbps, we would have a traffic equivalent to 750 telephone erlangs. This is to be compared with some 300 000 erlangs in the French intercity network.

The demand for a videophone service is largely unexplored. The choice of a transmission rate of 128 Kbps, compatible with the ISDN basic access, opens the potential market to include residential subscribers. Indeed, some see this service as being a major attraction in bringing customers to the ISDN. We personally remain somewhat sceptical of the value of transmitting a mediocre representation of the person speaking but recognise the advantage of being able to project a view of an object or document which is a subject of conversation.

The latter application of a videophone might also be satisfied by still picture services although their development is also likely to be restrained by the high cost of terminals (7000 to 15000 dollars according to [7]). In the light of the success of the French TELETEL alphamosaic videotex service, we see a strong potential market for services like photographic videotex and image bank consultation. However, their generalisation to residential subscribers depends on the availability of high speed access lines (greater than 144 Kbps) and is therefore unlikely to occur before the introduction of a future generation, video based ISDN. The same comment applies to hi-fi sound distribution which, in any case, only affects the local part of the network.

Facsimile traffic in the present network is growing rapidly and market research identifies a strong user requirement for higher speed and greater quality [7]. This need may, however, be satisfied by transmission at only 64Kbps (5 seconds to send an A4 page).

3. MULTI-SLOT BEARER SERVICES

To enable the provision of the above teleservices, the ISDN must offer a certain number of adapted bearer services. The choice of attributes for these bearer services can have important consequences on network structure and operation. In this section we present a number of possibilities currently under discussion, concentrating on the most significant aspects from a teletraffic point of view.

3.1 Information transfer rate and configuration

CCITT has so far standardised three multi-slot bearer service categories at bit rates of 384 Kbps, 1536 Kbps and 1920 Kbps (cf. Rec I 211). These are the bitrates of the HO, H11 and H12 access channels and correspond to 6, 24 and 30 slots per PCM frame, respectively. There is currently no agreement on other bit rates although there appears to be a growing concensus on the need for a 2 x 64 Kbps service compatible with the ISDN basic access.

In France, as in other countries, dedicated networks already offer multi-slot connections. The TRANSFIX service provides digital n x 64 Kbps leased lines with n taking the values 2, 4, 8, 16. The Telecom 1 satellite based TRANSDYN service provides demand set up for n = 2, 4, 6, 8, 12, 16, 18, 24, 30 and can establish reserved connections with any number of slots from 1 to 32.

Multi-slot bearer services can be bidirectional with the same bitrate in each direction as is customary for telephone connections. Alternatively, they can be unidirectional or bidirectional with diferent bit rates in each direction. We also distinguish point to point, multipoint and broadcast bearer services. In CCITT Rec I 211, only the bidirectional symmetric configuration is considered "essential".

3.2 Time Slot Sequence Integrity (TSSI)

The three bearer service categories defined in Rec I 211 are for "unrestricted digital information" and have the attribute "structural integrity at 8 KHz". According to the definitions in Rec I 130, these terms imply that the bearer services maintain TSSI. We have seen above that this corresponds to a performance requirement for some teleservices (e.g. videoconference).

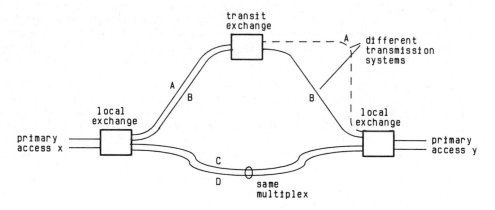

Figure 1. Different paths have different propagation times

Unfortunately, TSSI does not occur naturally in the integrated digital network. In Figure 1 we represent four 64 Kbps paths linking 4 slots of primary access x to 4 slots of primary access y. In general, all four paths have different propagation times: paths A and B are clearly longer than paths C and D; path A uses the same trunk groups as path B but is routed over different transmission systems with different propagation characteristics; paths C and D are identical from a transmission point of view but their propagation times differ due to switching delays in the local exchanges. Thus, if a multi-slot connection is established by combining n independently routed 64 Kbps channels, to ensure TSSI, the terminal equipments must compensate for the differences in propagation time by buffering the octets transmitted over the shortest paths.

In a perfectly synchronised network, and ignoring the possibility of channel failures, it would be sufficient to determine the delay to apply to each channel once and for all in an appropriately defined initialisation procedure. However, in a network where "slips" can occur due to imperfect synchronisation and where the physical path of any channel can change in mid-communication because of transmission system failures, it is necessary to continually monitor the channel transmission times to be able, at any moment, to adjust the respective resequencing delays.

A more straightforward technique for ensuring TSSI is to route all channels over the same transmission systems. In practice, this means choosing slots on the same primary PCM system as for paths C and D in Figure 1. These paths do rigourously keep the same difference in propagation time since both slips and transmission system changeovers affect each channel in exactly the same way. TSSI could thus be maintained relatively easily by applying the same fixed buffering throughout the communication. Furthermore, the need for buffering can generally be completely removed by an appropriate choice of paths through the switching network, as is illustrated below in the case of a single time switching stage.

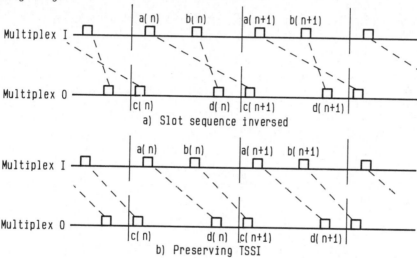

Figure 2. TSSI and time switch slot assignments

Figure 2 represents the operation of a time switch where incoming slots a and b must be switched to outgoing slots c and d. The switch is capable of copying the data in any slot on incoming multiplex I to any slot on outgoing multiplex O by storing the incoming octets in a buffer for up to 125 us: an octet is written to the buffer on arrival and read at the next occurence of the required outgoing slot. In Figure 2(a) where slot a is switched to slot c and slot b is switched to slot d, the time slot sequence is inversed whereas, in Figure 2(b), the assignment a to d and b to c maintains the octet sequence. In general, in switching n slots, it is always possible to assign outlets to inlets in such a way that TSSI is maintained although, as in Figure 2(b), the relative position of frame boundaries may change.

If the positions of frame boundaries must also be preserved, it is necessary to add a time switch to the communication path. Such a switch associated with the user's primary access could also place the incoming slots at specific positions corresponding, for example, to pre-designated H0 channels.

TSSI can also be maintained across an exchange by switching bit rate entities higher than 64 Kbps. Separate switching networks operating at, say, 384 Kbps and 1920 Kbps could be used for multi-slot calls.

3.3 Multilink protocol for data services

The alternative to the "8 KHz integrity" structure attribute is "service data unit integrity". In Rec I 211, this only applies to packet mode bearer services but, in our view, it may also be the appropriate attribute for multi-slot connections suitable for bulk data transfers. If data units are sent in parallel over n 64 Kbps channels there is no need to maintain TSSI. Correct data transfer can be accomplished using the multilink protocol (MLP) defined in CCITT Recommendations X 25 and X 75 and in ISO document DIS 7478.

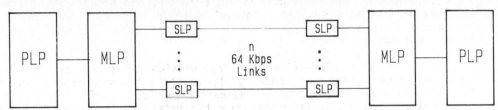

Figure 3. Multilink protocol operation

PLP - packet level protocol module   SLP - single link protocol module
MLP - multilink protocol module

A succinct description of this protocol is given in [10]. Its function is illustrated in Figure 3. Packets of data are supplied to the MLP by the packet level. The MLP adds a 2 octet header containing, notably, a multilink sequence number and dispatches the packet to one of n 64 Kbps channels. Each of these is controlled by a classical single link HDLC protocol. The transmitted frames thus have the structure shown in Figure 4.

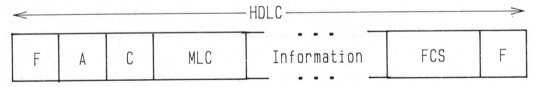

Figure 4. Multilink protocol frame format

F   flag   A,C   HDLC control variables
FCS frame check sequence   MLC   multilink control variables

At reception, the MLP receives error free packets (errors being corrected by the single link protocol) and has the task of putting them in sequence. In effect, their transmission time varies due to the different propagation times of the n channels and to the effect of retransmission of erroneous packets. Appropriate values for the size of the resequencing buffer and the protocol parameters for this application remain to be determined.

The establishment of such an independent path multi-slot bearer service would presumably be undertaken by the network following a single call by the user specifying the number of slots required n. The originating exchange would then create n independent calls to the destination user. It is necessary, in particular, to specify the course of action to be undertaken in case fewer than n paths are available. It would be a pity to block a data call in such circumstances since transmission could proceed using the above MLP with any number of channels established, albeit at a lower rate.

Complications might be avoided by leaving it to the user to set up his own multi-slot call by independently establishing a number of 64 Kbps unrestricted bearer services. This solution has the great advantage for the user of being immediately implementable in any network offering 64 Kbps connections. The value of n can vary during the communication as links become available or in case of link outages and, moreover, is no longer limited to 30 if the MLP and packet level protocols can support bit rates greater than 2 Mbps! There is, however, in the absence of any means of access control, an obvious danger for the network if this type of traffic were to develop.

Although the MLP is completely specified and is in use in packet switched networks, we are unaware of any implementation for bulk data transfer. Existing dedicated high speed digital networks do preserve TSSI and data is transmitted serially using HDLC-like single link protocols.

3.4 Packet mode bearer services

For certain teleservices involving the transmission of a series of still pictures (e.g. consultation of a catalogue), it could be more appropriate to use a packet mode rather than circuit mode bearer service. The information flow is very bursty (i.e. peak bit rate >> average bit rate) and the requirement for rapid response precludes the set up of a new circuit for each image. Such a service is, of course, beyond the capabilities of a first generation ISDN and would require an adapted technique such as asynchronous time division switching. The teletraffic problems arising in an implementation of this technique are discussed in [11].

3.5 Call set up

The communication establishment attribute has three possible values: demand, reserved and permanent which are defined in Rec. I 130 with reference to the time instants t0, t1, t2 and t3 depicted in Figure 5.

t0 = time at which request made   t2 = time at which call release is requested
t1 = time at which call is established   t3 = time at which call is cleared

Figure 5 Call establishment time instants

For a demand call, t0 and t1 and t2 and t3 are as close together as possible. This is the traditional set up mode for telephone calls.

A reserved call request occuring at t0 generally specifies both t1 and t2; optionally, t2 may not be fixed "a priori" corresponding to a call of undetermined duration.

A "permanent" connection is presumably distinguished by the fact that the interval t2-t1 is very much longer than in the case of demand or reserved calls although this is not specified in the I 130 definition.

In the French TRANSDYN service, communications can be reserved either on a call by call basis or periodically, the same connection being established at given times each day or each week. The latter notion is included in the CCITT definition of "semi-permanent connection" (Rec I 130). For TRANSDYN reserved connections, t1 and t2 must both be specified and can only take values which are an integral multiple of a 10 minute time unit. The notice interval t1-t0 can take any value up to 1 month.

4. DEMAND SET UP TRAFFIC MODELS

A considerable number of papers has been devoted to teletraffic models applicable to multi-slot traffic. In this section we provide an introduction to the problems posed by means of a rapid survey of this literature and indicate some areas needing further work.

4.1 The full availability group

Consider a group of C trunks (i.e. slots) serving M independent traffic streams. Stream i is characterised by a Poisson call arrival process of intensity λ_i, a service time of arbitrary distribution of mean h_i and a requirement for d_i trunks throughout this service time. If a stream i call arrives when fewer than d_i trunks are idle it is lost.

Early studies of this system are reported in [12], [13], [14] and [15]. Let $P(k_1...k_M)$ be the probability distribution of the numbers of calls present of each stream. Then P has the product form:

$$(1) \qquad P(k_1...k_M) = \prod_{i=1}^{M} a_i^{k_i} / k_i! \; . \; P(0...0)$$

where $a_i = \lambda_i h_i$ and $P(0...0)$ is given by a normalising condition.

We also have a product form if stream i arrival rate depends on the number of stream i calls present as, for example, in the case of finite source traffic, [13,14]. Kaufman [16] and Roberts [17] showed that (1) is independent of the service time distribution. The papers [16,17] also exhibit a simple recurrrence relation satisfied by the distribution of the total number of busy trunks. Let this distribution be $Q(n)$. We have,

$$(2) \qquad nQ(n) = \sum_i a_i d_i Q(n-d_i).$$

A more general form of (2), valid for state dependent arrivals of the form $\lambda_i(k_i) = \alpha_i + \beta_i k_i$, was given by Delbrouck, [18].

The stream i blocking probability B_i is given by

$$(3) \qquad B_i = \sum_{n \geqslant C-d_i+1} Q(n) \; .$$

The behaviour of B_i under varying traffic conditions was studied by Gimpelson [12] and, more recently by Johnson, [19]. It is shown, in particular, that the B_i are not necessarily strictly increasing functions of offered traffic intensity but can oscillate between local maxima and minima occuring at specific intensities determined by the relative values of C and slot requirements d_i.

Despite this local behaviour, it was noted by Roberts [20] that roughly the same distribution $Q(n)$ is obtained for different traffic mixes having in common the same mean $M = \sum a_i d_i$ and variance $V = \sum a_i d_i^2$. This makes it possible to approximate $Q(n)$ by matching the moments of a simpler distribution. Fiche et al [21] and Lindberger [22] suggest 2 moment approximations similar to the well known Hayward formula for overflow traffic, multi-slot traffic being essentially "peaky" (i.e. V>M).

4.2 Restricted availability

It is clear from (3) that, in the full availability system, blocking probabilities increase with the number of trunks required. To improve the performance of wideband calls and, more generally, to provide a mesure of service protection for all streams, it is possible to add stream access restrictions. Katschner and Scheller [23] identify two types of restriction: "class limitation" where the number of calls present of a given stream cannot exceed certain limits and "sum limitation" where stream access is stopped when the overall number of busy trunks passes a given threshold.

For the former type of restrictions, state probabilities $P(k_1...k_M)$ still have the product form (1). This form is, in fact, preserved for a much wider class of access restrictions, as shown by Aein [24] and Kaufman [16]. However, blocking calculations are now complex. Efficient algorithms have been proposed by Barberis and Brignolo [25] and by Kraimeche and Schwartz [26]. The latter papers also address the problem of optimising the values of stream restriction parameters to maximise trunk utilisation or to meet specified stream grade of service standards.

If all streams must meet the same blocking standards, the easiest and, perhaps, best access restriction is sum limitation with the same threshold (equal to capacity minus the greatest slot requirement d_i) applied to all streams, [20,23]. Sum limitation is also referred to as trunk or priority reservation. The product form no longer applies and exact performance results can only be obtained by numerically solving the state equations of an appropriately defined Markov chain, [23]. A simple approximation proposed in [20] gives good results when all streams have the same mean holding time. Lindberger [22] suggests an alternative approach which takes account of different stream holding times.

4.3 Path choice restrictions

We have seen in section 3 that certain bearer service implementations can impose restrictions on the trunks which can be used to set up multi-slot calls. Enomoto and Miyamoto [13] consider the case where multi-slot calls must occupy adjacent slots: they numerically solve exact state equations for small systems (C=4) and suggest an approximation applicable to larger capacities for a random slot hunting strategy. The hunting strategy has a profound effect on traffic capacities since this determines the likelyhood that idle trunks occupy adjacent slots.

Katschner and Scheller [23] and Ramaswami and Rao [27] look at the effect of imposing a limited choice of fixed groups of trunks for carrying multi-slot calls. In [23] different hunting strategies are compared: approximate blocking calculations are proposed for sequential hunting (all calls test trunks in the same fixed order and busy the first idle trunk or group of trunks found). In [27] a "call packing" strategy, whereby single slot calls are placed in the most heavily loaded available multi-slot group, is compared with the full availability group allowing flexible allocation. The authors consider the practically interesting case of a 24-slot primary ISDN access carrying a mixture of B and HO channels. They demonstrate that blocking for HO channels can typically be doubled by imposing fixed slot allocations.

A less strict path choice restriction is to require all slots of a multi-slot call to be in the same primary multiplex. This is necessary for bearer services providing connections with TSSI (see section 3.2). The effect on performance has been studied by Lutton and Roberts [28] and Conradt and Buchheister [29]. In [28] approximate calculations and simulations are used to compare sequential and random hunting strategies: while random hunting can have a drastic effect on trunk group capacities, the use of sequential hunting gives results which are close to those for a full availability group. Sequential hunting is shown in [29] to be practically equivalent to more complicated strategies, including call packing.

4.4 Resource sharing

The above mentioned studies show the importance of having adapted trunk selection strategies in switching nodes if we wish to implement bearer services with TSSI on shared trunk groups. An alternative very simple way to ensure that all slots of a multi-slot call are in the same multiplex is to create a distinct trunk group for each bit rate to be switched. This possibility demands more or less trunks than a shared group depending on the hunting strategy employed. In particular, it is no doubt preferable to use separate trunk groups if switching node operation is equivalent to random hunting.

In the literature, required capacities in "completely shared" (i.e. full availability) and "completely partitioned" (i.e. separate groups) groups of resources have been compared, [14], [19] and [30]. As a general statement, savings in required capacity due to resource sharing depend on the number of different streams and their bit rate requirement and traffic intensity: integration is most advantageous with many low intensity streams (see Table 2 in [19]); the difference in capacity tends to disappear as traffic volume increases. It has recently been pointed out by Katayama et al [33], in analysing a related system, that separate trunk groups can require fewer trunks than a shared group if services with different bit rate have quite different grade of service requirements.

Johnson [19] points to the advantage of flexibility inherent in a completely shared system in a context of uncertain demand. Clearly, integration is particularly advantageous when different services have non-coincident busy hours.

4.5 Network blocking

A potential advantage of multi-slot bearer service implementations using independently selected single slots rather than slots in the same multiplex is that channels may be selected on all available network paths. In fact, it is shown in [28] that this advantage is negligible in a hierarchical network where multi-slot calls gain little advantage from first being offered to high usage groups which are typically of low capacity. Clearly, the same may not be true in non hierarchical networks employing dynamic routing where there is a wider choice of paths and trunk groups tend to be of similar capacity.

A recent study by Dziong and Roberts [32] proposes a method for computing end to end blocking in a network carrying multi-slot traffic based on a generalisation of the recurrence (2) to cover multiple resource groups. We note that mixtures of unidirectional and bidirectional services on the same trunk group leads to similar evaluation problems since the channels in each group constitute a distinct resource group [33].

Internal congestion in exchange switching networks handling multi-slot traffic is evaluated in [21], [34] and [35] adapting the methods traditionally used for telephone switching networks. These methods assume, in particular, that link occupancy states are symmetric (i.e. all occupancy states with a given number of busy links are equally probable). This assumption could be incompatible with the trunk selection strategies necessary for providing bearer services with TSSI on integated trunk groups (cf. section 4.3). Conradt and Buchheister [29] evaluate the effect of sequential hunting in a particular switch architecture and show that internal congestion increases dramatically compared to random hunting. This conclusion cannot however be generalised to all switch architectures. Murakami et al compare the efficiency of two system architectures with integrated and separated switching for streams with different bit rates [36]. As a general comment, it seems to us that there is a need for further studies in this area to clarify the teletraffic issues and design options for switching nodes handling multi-slot calls.

4.6 Delay systems

Delay working has been seen as an alternative method for compensating for the unequal treatment of multi-slot calls in full availability groups. Gimpelson [12] considers a system where wide band calls can wait while Yamaguchi and Akiyama [37] and Kraimeche and Schwartz [38] allow wideband calls to preempt narrow band calls which then join a queue. In a data communication system studied by Wollner [39], all calls can wait with head of the line priority given to wideband calls. All these analyses are limited to two traffic streams and numerical results are obtained by solving the state equations of an appropriately defined Markov chain.

Queues with customers requiring a variable number of servers have been studied by Green [40] assuming servers are seized simultaneously but released independently. This model is used by Mason et al [41] to approximate the performance of a multi-slot queue arising in a multipoint video service. The queue where servers are released simultaneously was considered by Brill and Green [42]. Service discipline is FIFO and the authors analyse waiting time distributions. The analysis is complex and is apparently only applicable for small systems. Kraimeche and Schwartz [43] extend the results in [42] but only provide analytical results for a 2 server system.

In the light of the complexity of an exact analysis, there is a clear need for robust approximations. Possible approaches are included in [44] and [20] but these only provide a partial solution. Queueing models are important for evaluating multi-slot traffic in the ISDN, if only to approximate the effect of rapid automatic repeat attempts.

4.7 Multilink protocol evaluation

We have suggested the multilink protocol as a convenient way of implementing bulk data transfer in the ISDN. It remains, however, to confirm the efficiency of the protocol by means of a performance evaluation. The protocol has previously been evaluated for bursty traffic in a packet switched network [10] and for bulk data transfer over satellite links [45].

Note, finally, that the ability of this protocol to work with a variable number of links requires a particular traffic model for evaluating trunk group blocking probabilities. In case of congestion a bulk data transfer could start using all available slots and increase its "holding" during the call as other slots are released. In this system call service time is a variable depending on the number of slots seized.

5. RESERVATION TRAFFIC

Performance evaluation and network dimensioning for services operating with reserved set up cannot be performed using classical teletraffic models. In this section we review a number of modelling approaches proposed in the literature and discuss some performance and network design issues.

5.1 Analytical models

To gain insight into the behaviour of reservation systems, and thereby to make the right service implementation choices, we would like to dispose of analytical models equivalent to the classical tools of queueing theory. Roberts and Liao [46] examined a number of possible approaches and identified as the main difficulty the need to study stochastic processes with two time parameters: the time a request is made and the time for which service is requested. An exact analysis of such processes proves extremely difficult if not impossible. Iisaku and Urano [47] suggest a number of approximations but neglect to test their validity on numerical examples.

Reservation systems generally operate on the basis of a time unit of, say, 10 minutes or one hour: call start times and durations must be integral multiples of this unit. In such systems, the second time parameter mentioned above concerns specific time units and, in certain modelling approaches, can be assimilated to a dimension of the service system resources. Resources available in a given day can then be represented by a vector $Z(j)$ giving the number of channels available at time unit j, for $j=1,...,J$, where J is the number of time units in one day.

A reservation process for such a set of resources was studied in an early paper by Luss [48]. A series of N requests is offered to this system, each request being characterised by its start time and duration and by the caller's willingness to accept an alternative period in case of congestion. If a call cannot be satisfied within the day it is assumed to be lost. With very general assumptions concerning the distribution of start times and durations and the users' response to congestion, Luss is able to derive performance measures, such as the proportion of lost calls, exactly by means of recursive formulae. The latter depend, however, on a detailed description of system state giving the number of channels reserved in each time unit. Exponential complexity limits analysis to very small systems ($J=6$, $Z<5$).

In a second paper [49], Luss proposes an approximate method applicable to larger capacities. The principal simplification is to assume uniform caller behaviour allowing system state to be described simply by the total number of busy time units. The probability a particular demand is blocked in a given state is estimated by combinatorial arguments. Results are close to those of the previous model in comparable traffic conditions.

An alternative approach is adopted by Liao [50]. He considers the long term behaviour of a reservation system where request instants constitute a stationary homogeneous arrival process; notice interval and requested duration have given distributions. The objective is to calculate conditional call blocking probabilities for given notice and duration. In [51], for such a system, assuming blocked requests are lost, it is shown that these probabilities can be estimated from an analysis of a related discrete time loss system with demand set up.

If congestion is negligible, reservation traffic can be modelled as a birth process. Liao and Roberts [3] propose such a model for dimensioning a videoconference network taking account of the effect on the request arrival process of a finite studio population.

5.2 Performance characteristics

The above models and, more readily, simulation have been used to study the performance of particular reservation systems. The parameters used to measure performance depend on the assumed traffic model and do not necessarily well reflect the users' appreciation of service quality in a real system. It remains to define grade of service parameters and their appropriate values for network dimensioning.

Simulation results reported by Kodaira and Kawashima [52] refer to a system where blocked customers accept a different start time within a specified period of that requested (e.g. up to 3 days). The results show that the proportion of lost calls decreases markedly as the users' delay tolerance increases: in a quoted example, 12% of calls cannot start within an hour of the requested start time, 1% are blocked within 1 day while less than 0.1% cannot be satisfied within 3 days. Unfortunately, the general applicability of this observation depends on the validity of assumptions about user behaviour which are not specified in [52] (e.g. is it assumed that users blocked at 10:00 a.m. will accept an alternative reservation in the lunch period ?).

It is stated in [52] that a general advantage of reservation compared to demand set up is that the former results in a higher resource occupancy and consequently allows services to be offered at lower tarifs. The truth of this statement seems to depend on the assumption that a reservation system can be dimensioned to a more severe blocking probability standard. This remains to be proved: in [46], Roberts and Liao suggest that user reaction to a high congestion probability might have the undesirable effect of obliging users to progressively lengthen their notice to maintain the same quality of service. Further, it is shown in [51] that the proportion of blocked calls in a reservation system without negotiation (i.e. no attempt to find an alternative service period) is practically the same as the proportion of blocked calls in a discrete time loss system with demand set up. Obliging calls to start and end at a limited number of possible instants does bring some improvement in resource occupancy but at the cost of requiring users to round up (or down) their requested duration.

Lastly, we note that the model of videoconference traffic studied in [3] leads to an optimal dedicated network structure in the form of a single node to which all studios are connected directly. This structure results more from an assumption of high studio utilisation (> 0.5 erlang) than from the particular model of a reservation process.

5.3 Resource sharing

We maintain that it is not reasonable in an ISDN to mix reservation and demand traffic on the same trunk groups. Reserved calls are taken into account when the reservation is made. If resources are allocated without restriction, the amount available for demand calls is variable with consequent grade of service fluctuations [46]. Note, moreover, that if there must always remain sufficient capacity for demand calls in a completely shared system, then reserved calls are never blocked, whatever the required grade of service standard. These comments apply equally to the subscriber's access and would imply, for instance, that a videoconference studio should have a dedicated access.

Similar difficulties may arise if a reserved set up teleservice with a generally long notice interval (e.g. videoconference) were to share a trunk group with another teleservice with short notice (e.g. data transfer). The former automatically receives first come first served priority whatever the grade of service requirement. Reservation does however give the network operator the advantage of being able to restrict access in time as well as in space. Time zones can be set aside for specific teleservices or for calls of specific characteristics (bit rate, duration,...) to achieve greater resource occupancy by, in particular, imposing non-coincidence of busy hours.

6. CONCLUSIONS

By way of conclusion we give our personal opinions, based on the preceding discussion, of how the considered teleservices are likely to be implemented in the ISDN and then identify a number of problem areas deserving the attention of teletraffic engineers.

6.1 Bearer services for teleservices.

While recognising that we are certainly not the best qualified to make predictions about ISDN evolution, we do not hesitate to do so in the hope of stimulating discussion.

High speed bulk data transfer can be accomplished with little or no modification to the integrated digital network by using a multilink protocol. There is no need to maintain any strict relationship between the different slots which can thus correspond to independently established 64 Kbps connections. These could be provided by a multi-slot bearer service offering "data unit integrity" or, alternatively, consist of a group of 64 Kbps bearer services set up under user control.

Videoconferencing, on the other hand, would need a multi-slot bearer service preserving time slot sequence integrity. This requirement cannot be met without significant modifications to existing digital exchanges. Furthermore, fundamentally different traffic characteristics, including the use of reserved set up, make it unsuitable to share trunk groups and, indeed, access channels with services like the telephone. The cost of a dedicated network could well be considerably less than the cost of providing this service in the ISDN.

The videophone service may or may not require a bearer service with TSSI, depending essentially on the bit rate used to code the image. A 64 Kbps coded image allows independent slot selection and seems to us the best prospect for an early introduction of this service.

A multi-slot facsimile service could use the same bearer service as bulk data transfer. We feel, however, that other still picture services, based on image consultation, generate a bursty traffic which is ill-suited to circuit switching. Their introduction will probably have to wait for a future generation ISDN with high speed user access and allowing fast packet switching.

Hi-fi sound transmission would require two 384 Kbps connections preserving TSSI but there is unlikely to be a significant demand for such a service before the general introduction of high speed access for residential users.

The demand for multi-media services remains vague. However, there should be little additional difficulty in providing each medium on an adapted bearer service. In particular, the ISDN could, at an early date, provide services requiring 2 or more independent 64 Kbps connections.

6.2 Open teletraffic problems.

Although there now exists a substantial literature on multi-slot traffic problems (many of which, according to the above predictions, will not arise before some future generation ISDN), we identify a number of subjects requiring further research.

Exchange architectures suitable for multi-slot switching may be closely guarded commercial secrets. We would, however, like to see more work on the teletraffic aspects of different design options.

While multi-slot loss systems are now fairly well understood, we still need simple but robust methods for evaluating delay systems. One important application of such models would be to approximate the effect of the rapid automatic repeat attempts which become possible in the ISDN.

We have proposed the multilink protocol for high speed data transfer without having previously verified its efficiency in the ISDN context. It is necessary to evaluate the throughput performance of this protocol and to determine appropriate parameter values. A secondary problem is the calculation of congestion probabilities in a trunk group carrying such traffic: a call is characterised by its maximum bit rate and the quantity of data to be transmitted.

Although reserved set up must be seen as an expeditive for most multi-slot services (which cannot be established on demand in the present network), it seems to be a necessary attribute for videoconferencing at least. There is a need for basic models giving insight into performance characteristics as well as for more pragmatic approaches for network design.

ACKNOWLEDGEMENT

The information presented in this paper owes much to contributions from many colleagues in the CNET and elsewhere. In particular, the content has greatly benefitted from the participation of one of the authors in the European COST 214 Action.

REFERENCES

[1] Marshall, W.T. and Morgan, S.P. Statistics of mixed data traffic on a local area network. Computer Networks and ISDN systems. Vol 10, N°3,4 1985 (and ITC 11)

[2] Sabri, S. and Praseda, B. Video conferencing systems. Proc IEEE. Vol 73, N°4, 1984.

[3] Liao, K. and Roberts, J.W. Videoconference traffic and network design. IEEE Trans Commun. Vol 35, N°3, 1987.

[4] Gruber, J.G. and Le, N.H. Performance requirements for integrated voice/ data networks. IEEE J SAC. Vol 1, N°6, 1983.

[5] Bux, W., Kummerle K. and Truong, H.L. Balanced HDLC procedures: a performance analysis. IEEE Trans Commun. Vol 28, N°11, 1980.

[6] Proceedings of the advanced telecommunications services users seminar (UTISAT). Paris 1986.

[7] Medium bit rate transmission. Market research study by BVA for French PTT. 1986.

[8] Potential impact of the 144 Kbps ISDN. Market research study by M2I for French PTT. 1986.

[9] Video communication. Report on Japanese developments prepared by Eurogestion for French PTT. 1986.

[10] Nishizono, T., Kanemaki, K. and Yano, J. Multilink protocol for packet switched networks. Review of the ECL. Vol 33, N°5, 1985.

[11] Boyer, P., Boyer, J., Louvion, J.R. and Romoeuf, L. Modelling the ATD transfer technique. 5th ITC Seminar, Lake Como, 1987.

[12] Gimpelson, L. Analysis of mixtures of wide and narrow band traffic. IEEE Trans Commun. Vol 13, N°3, 1965.

[13] Enomoto, O. and Miyamoto, H. An analysis of mixtures of multiple bandwidth traffic on time division switching networks. NEC Res and Devel. N°41, 1976.

[14] Fredrikson, G.F.W. Analysis of channel utilisation in traffic concentrators. IEEE Trans Commun. Vol 22, N°8, 1974.

[15] Frenkel, G. The grade of service in multiple access satellite communication systems with demand assignment. IEEE Trans Commun. Vol 22, N°10, 1974.

[16] Kaufman, J.S. Blocking in a shared resource environment. IEEE Trans Commun. Vol 29, N°10, 1981.

[17] Roberts, J.W. A service system with heterogeneous user requirements. In Pujolle, G. Performance of data communication systems and their applications. North-Holland, 1981.

[18] Delbrouck, L.E.N. On the steady state distribution in a service facility carrying mixtures of traffic with different peakedness factors and capacity requirements. IEEE Trans Commun. Vol 31, N°11, 1983.

[19] Johnson, S.A. A performance analysis of integrated communications systems. Br Telecom Technol J. Vol 3, N°4, 1985.

[20] Roberts, J.W. Teletraffic models for the Telecom 1 integrated services network. ITC 10, Montreal, 1985.

[21] Fiche, G., Le Gall, P. and Ricupero, S. Study of blocking for multislot connections in digital link systems. ITC 11, Kyoto, 1985.

[22] Lindberger, K. Blocking for multislot heterogeneous traffic offered with reservation to a trunk group. 5th ITC Seminar, Lake Como, 1987.

[23] Katscner, L. and Scheller, R. Probability of loss of data traffics with different bit rates hunting one common PCM channel. ITC 8, Melbourne, 1976.

[24] Aein, J.M. A multi user class blocked calls cleared demand access model. IEEE Trans Commun. Vol 26, N°3, 1978.

[25] Barberis, G. and Brignolo, R. Capacity allocation in a DAMA satellite system. Vol 30, N°7, 1982.

[26] Kraimeche, B. and Schwartz, M. Traffic access control strategies in integrated digital networks. IEEE Infocom '84, San Diego, 1984.

[27] Ramaswami, V. Rao, K.A. Flexible time slot assignment – a performance study for the integrated services digital network. ITC 11, Kyoto, 1985.

[28] Lutton, J.L. and Roberts, J.W. Traffic performance of multi-slot call routing strategies in an integrated services digital network. ISS'84, Florence, 1984.

[29] Conradt, J. and Buchheister A. Considerations on loss probabilities of multi-slot connections. ITC 11, Kyoto, 1985.

[30] Aein, J.M. and Kosovitch, O.S. Satellite capacity allocation. Proc of the IEEE. Vol. 65, N°3, 1977.

[31] Katayama, T., Sumita, S. and Inamori, H. Study on traffic design methods in integrated services networks. Review of the ECL. Vol 34, N°5, 1986.

[32] Dziong, Z. and Roberts, J.W. Congestion probabilities in an integrated services network. To be published.

[33] Ohara, K., Kimura, G. and Katayama, T. Traffic studies of loss systems for one way and two way calls. Review of the ECL. Vol 34, N°5, 1986.

[34] Akiyama, M., Yamaguchi, T. and Morita, T. Wide band and narrow band traffic integration on multistage time division switching networks. Trans IECE (Japan). Vol 58-A, N°12, 1975.

[35] Saito, T., Inose, H. and Hayashi, S. Evaluation of traffic carrying capability in one stage and two stage time division networks handling data with a variety of speed classes. ITC 9, Torremolinos, 1979.

[36] Murakami, K., Masafumi, K. and Shinji, A. Traffic design for time division wideband switching networks. ITC 11, Kyoto, 1985.

[37] Yamaguchi, T. and Akiyama, M. An integrated hybrid traffic switching system mixing preemptive wideband and waitable narrow band calls. Trans IECE (Japan). Vol 53-A, N°4, 1970.

[38] Kraimeche, B. and Schwartz, M. Analysis of traffic access control strategies in integrated service networks. IEEE Trans Commun. Vol 33, N° 10, 1985.

[39] Wollner, E. A queueing problem in data transmission. ITC 7, Stockholm, 1973.

[40] Green, L. A queueing system in which customers require a random number of servers. Opns Res. Vol 28, N°6, 1980.

[41] Mason, L.G., DeSerres, Y. and Meubus, C. Circuit-switched multipoint service performance models. ITC 11, Kyoto, 1985.

[42] Brill, P.H. and Green, L. Queues in which customers receive simultaneous service from a random number of servers: a system point approach. Management Sci. Vol 30, N°1, 1984.

[43] Kraimeche, B. and Schwartz, M. Bandwidth allocation strategies in wideband integrated networks. IEEE J on SAC. Vol 4, N°6, 1986.

[44] Burakowski, W. Approximate methods of multi-user-class system analysis. ITC 10, Montreal, 1983.

[45] Pujolle, G. and Spaniol, O. Throughput of a satellite channel communication. ITC 10, Montreal, 1983.

[46] Roberts, J.W. and Liao, K. Traffic models for telecommunications services with advance capacity reservation. Computer networks and ISDN systems. Vol 10, N°3, 1985 (and ITC 11).

[47] Iisaku, S. and Urano, Y. Performance analysis of integrated communication systems with heterogeneous traffic. ITC 11, Kyoto, 1985.

[48] Luss, H. A model for advanced reservations for intercity visual conferencing services. Opl Res Quarterly. Vol 28, N°2, 1977.

[49] Luss, H. A model for advanced reservations for large scale conferencing services. J of the Opl Res Soc. Vol 31, N°3, 1980.

[50] Liao, K. Modélisation de systèmes de télécommunications fonctionnant avec réservating. Doctoral theses, Ecole Nationale Supérieure des Télécommunications, Paris, 1986.

[51] Roberts, J.W. and Liao, K. A queueing model of an advanced reservation system with blocked requests lost. To be published.

[52] Kodaira, K. and Kawashima, K. Traffic studies related to the Japanese ISDN. 4th ITC Seminar, Brussels, 1986.

TRAFFIC ENGINEERING for ISDN Design and Planning
M. Bonatti and M. Decina (Editors)
Elsevier Science Publishers B.V. (North-Holland)
© IAC, 1988

PLANNING ISDN: A STRUCTURED VIEW AND KEY RESULTS

Oscar GONZALEZ SOTO

ALCATEL Standard Eléctrica S.A. Madrid, Spain

ABSTRACT

The high number of narrowband or broadband services and the alternatives expected in future communication networks, present a new set of complexities to the planners and designers. This paper addresses an overview of new problems, planning processes and sample results of integrated services network planning. First, new challenges and complexities are identified in the planning of multiservices and the provision of corresponding network resources. Second, a structured planning process is proposed to aid the definition of planning activities and their interrelationships in a complex environment. Finally, some of the results obtained in specific planning projects are given to illustrate the type of works required at the integrated environments.

MAIN STATEMENT

A structured planning approach is proposed to meet the new challenges of telecommunication networks.

1. INTRODUCTION

Increasing demand for telecommunication services of voice, text, data and image as well as the new capacities provided by the digital technologies lead to the Integrated Services Digital Network defined (1) as the most appropriate to take advantage of the new economies of scale.

Conventional network dimensioning procedures have proven to be efficient in reaching adequate equilibrium among existing services demand, quality of service and network resource provisioning. That success is one of the key items that allowed the implementation of today's extended networks.

In the new context with new service mixes and higher network resource capacities, there is a need to found the new economies of scale and equilibria to match user needs and technology capabilities. The degree of expansion of new services is to a great extent a function of the new techno-economic equilibria in the basic communications triangle formed by Service users - Network operators - Equipment/Service providers.

The planning function in a complex environment is more than ever viewed as a "decision-making" process that requires updating-extension of the classical procedures of network design and optimization. Due to the important increase in the number of alternatives offered and the high volume of investment, associated mainly with the broad-band environment, a pre-selection of the most adequate solutions is mandatory. This increases the importance and effort required for the strategic planning as well as for the iteration between strategical planning and specific planning as indicated in figure 1.

New factors and complexities that contribute to the need for new approaches are mainly due to:

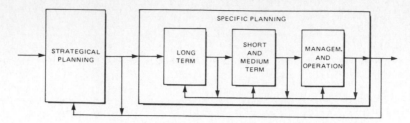

FIG. 1.- ITERATIVE PLANNING CYCLES

* Larger number of services to be analyzed belonging to different classes of interactive or distributed types.

* Larger number of parameters involved in the service and traffic characterization.

* Lack of historical data for new services and user behavior concerning these services.

* Important interrelations among variables in service and network modeling which imply modification of the assumptions for the degree of dependency within models and network sections.

* Quickly evolving technologies which modify resource capacities and capacity/cost ratios.

For the above listed new complexities, the natural starting point has been service definition and traffic characterization. Recent advances in the service definition area were carried out in the CCITT environment which showed important progress by the methodology based on service attributes (2). This approach allows a universal definition of services by eighteen attributes classified in three basic groups: Information transfer, Access, General.

In the area of traffic characterization, (3) proposes a unified multiservice characterization by relating information volume demand by the user, protocols and traffic demand. The Integrated Call Attempt unit is defined to represent service mixes at those network interfaces where the statistical large numbers law may be applied. (4) applies this characterization to a pilot study with evaluation of Integrated Call Attempts for narrowband services. (5) proposes traffic characteristics for the design of large PABXs with emphasis on the call completion degrees.

The fundamental problem of basic reference traffic definition is treated in (6) and (7) which brought up the need for new reference unit definition in multiclass networks. (7) also proposes a generalization of Traffic Reference Connection, Call Flow Diagram and Traffic Patterns. Statistical characterization and properties of flow mixes are addressed in (8) to (11) which analyze the properties of superpositions of different traffic classes and their impacts on resource dimensioning for both the loss and delay resources types.

This paper enlarges the observation scope for ISDN by considering new challenges in the planning of integrated networks with relation to the context of future networks and proposes in section 3 a structured approach to the ISDN planning activities and corresponding interrelations. A set of multiservice related results from applications to pilot studies of narrowband cases is provided at section 4 to illustrate new areas to be addressed by the Teletraffic community.

2. NEW CHALLENGES IN ISDN PLANNING

Most of networks related entities have applied planning models and activities to the existing dedicated networks. Required procedures are well ordered and explained by CCITT GAS contributions, (12) to (15).

When facing the short, medium and long term planning requirements and the associated investment decisions for new Telecommunication networks, a set of open problems obliges the review of classical planning procedures. Among the new challenges which force that review-updating, the following are emphasized in the service, technology and network areas:

2.1. Service related challenges

In the assumption of evolution towards a fully integrated network for all classes of narrowband and broadband services, the following issues have to be solved in relation to design and planning:

*   Service definition and grouping into classes from resource consumption and quality of service points of view.

*   Traffic characterization for each service and their mixes at the user side and at network interfaces.

*   Impact of network transfer modes on the relation between user and workload of network resources.

*   Evolution of user behavior and services according to the user learning process and to technological changes to both the terminals and the networks.

*   Service demand forecasting, cooperation for given applications, substitution and grouping in the user interface.

2.2. Technology related challenges

Fast evolving technology is expected to produce the largest impact on communication capabilities, resource sizes, quality of service and capacity/cost ratios. These items are fundamental inputs for strategic and long-term planning. The following issues are emphasized:

*   Technical evolution of transmission media (e.g. Fiber Optics, active optical components, connectors, etc.) which enlarges the margins of capacity and will lead to new transmission hierarchies.

*   New Network Transfer Modes being designed such as Synchronous Transfer Mode (STM) or Asynchronous Transfer Mode (ATM) for broadband applications, (16) to (19), which tend to a unified procedure to handle all service classes.

*   Coding and code compression techniques which increase end-to-end user capacities for a given bandwidth medium.

*   Software technique evolution which allows implementation of more intelligence in the operation of the network and an increase in functional flexibility.

*   Changes in cost structures which vary as a function of the communication mode and imply the need to update the cost assignment procedures to include in more detail the processing and software related costs.

2.3. Network related challenges

The communication network is influenced by all the forementioned factors and has, in addition, specific issues which require deep analysis and new operation procedures:

*   Network architecture, hierarchical levels, topology and node location for the target full integration case.

*   Evolution from today's dedicated networks towards the target, interworking among networks and transfer modes.

*   Traffic and workload characterization of the network resources as a function of mixes and transfer modes.

*   Evaluation of protocol behavior as an important component of the service-network interaction which impacts on the network interface capacities.

*   Dimensioning rules for individual network resources as a function of group size, service mix, resource assignment rules and specified quality of service per class.

*   Design criteria for the global integrated/hybrid network to take advantage of the new economies of scale.

*   Degree of intelligence in the network, which has to allocate resources either at the nodes or inter-nodes in a dynamic way and will interact with routing principles and sharing procedures.

These identified basic challenges configure the environment for Telecommunication network designers and planners. Most of them are problems today although initial analysis are being attempted. Planners need to foresee future networks, not existing ones, they have to rely on the most likely solutions and robust decisions derived from sensitivity analysis.

3. INTEGRATION PROFILES AND ECONOMIES OF SCALE

In order to have a comprehensive view of the evolution frame for networks and the integration scale, the following six dimensions fix the directions which have to be observed to plan evolution steps and integration degrees.

3.1 Dimensions in integration planning

a) Transmission integration degree: Which starts at fixed bandwidth assignment within the same physical resources and ranges up to dynamic resource assignment or even a unified one for each boundle.

b) Switching integration degree: varying from the circuit and packet mode treatment at the same node but with different modules up to the treatment by the same modules and evolution towards a unified procedure.

c) Service integration degree for either narrowband or broadband classes of the Interactive/Communicative type (including conversational, messaging and retrieval services) or Distribution type (with or without individual user control).

d) User class integration degree which represents the number of user categories with effective integration, either large-business, commercial or residential type which in turn have different levels of consumption in the communication activity.

e) Network integration degree for all the network types as a function of the extension, freezing or substitution policies applied to the plant already installed.

f) Geographical integration degree for a partial or full coverage of geographical areas as a function of the subscriber density, demand growth, revenue policy, etc.

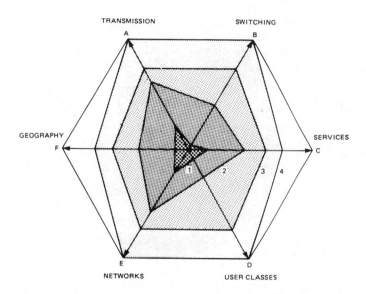

FIG. 2.- THE DIMENSIONS AND PROFILES FOR INTEGRATION

Figure 2 represents the six dimensions of the integration with a vertex associated with each concept and a growing degree of integration towards the periphery which may be considered as the assymptotic limit. Each combination of integration progress for every dimension provides a well defined integration step and a profile.

Profile 1 represents the actual starting point where some transmission resources are shared and the existing dedicated networks are interconnected to support services in a cooperative way.

Profile 2 correspond to the so-called minimum integration with a common subscriber access for narrowband services which implies a fundamental progress in the ISDN architecture.

Profile 3 indicates a medium integration scale which incorporates packet and circuit handling at the same nodes for high demand areas as well as the broad-band services by a standard interface. This step represents a major advance from the techno-economical point or view.

Profile 4 represents the high integration degree with a unified communication procedure which allows dynamic sharing of network resources according to user demand changes. This step is associated with the long-term ideal communication where capabilities are controlled by the user demand volume.

The multiple combinations of integration degrees and rhythms on each dimension as well as the coexistance of degrees in a network produce a series of intermediate steps which have to be carefully planned and quantified on techno-economical basis. The selection of the most appropriate profile for

evolution and the sound definition of transition strategies is in fact the
central job of the planner.

3.2 Economies of scale for integration

Capacity/cost ratios for the services demanded by the users will be a prime
driving force for the integration success at the above mentioned degrees. The
following economies of scale are presented as the main contributors to the
final cost per service:

*   Technological factor which increases capacity/cost ratios by means of new
    materials, VLSI designs, new coding techniques, signal processing and code
    compression among others.

*   Dimensioning factor due to the non-linearity of the functions and greater
    efficiency for larger groups. Packet switching mode and new transfer modes
    imply different dimensioning laws, non-linearity effects and modularity
    effects which need to be investigated. Greater security for larger group
    sizes in a multiservice network establishes a trade-off for the ultimate
    gain of this factor.

*   Service multiplexing factor. This is the most typical effect of integra-
    tion itself and allows resource sharing when various services with differ-
    ent busy periods are handled within a node or inter nodes as a function of
    the flow routing principles.

*   Fill-in degree for the transmission, switching and processing resources in
    a given time instant and through a given planning period. The impact of
    this factor on revenues is high with the new technologies which decrease
    marginal cost on the basis of larger capacity provisioning. Prime im-
    portance has to be devoted to installation scheduling plans as a function
    of demand growth.

*   Manufacturing volume factor for the network equipments. Complexity and
    high development cost for new systems imply a high sensitivity of the
    final cost to the number of manufactured units per type as compared with
    conventional solutions. The efficiency in reaching standards agreements
    has a paramount influence in this factor where it is essential to reach
    all the potential users.

First and last factors are the main responsibilities of technology developers
and coordinators of efforts towards the unification of standards. The remaining factors: Dimensioning, Multiplexing and Fill-in, concern mainly the Teletraffic community which has the responsibility to find adequate practical
methods to apply to in the envisaged networks.

4. A STRUCTURED APPROACH FOR THE ISDN PLANNING

In order to carry out the planning activities, subject to the forementioned
challenges, a structured planning methodology has been develop grounded on
the following principles:

1) Top-down identification of planning activities from the application per-
    spective to cover all the processes of a full planning cycle.

2) Structured interrelation among planning activities and data to allow the
    analysis of interdependences which may be different from one network
    alternative to another .

3) Hierarchical partition into different levels of detail according to the

type of planning: strategic or specific either for long term or short term.

4) Flexibility to incorporate different model complexities which interrelate data as technology and network integration evolve.

5) Selection of sub-sets of activities from the full set with strong dependencies when a partial planning problem is to be solved.

In order to organize the planning activities, the processes, data and their interrelations, basic ideas and experiences have been incorporated from structured design methods such as those proposed in (20) and (21). Following these principles, figure 3 represents the general planning activity with the corresponding external interfaces which are further split while maintaining the same basic module structure.

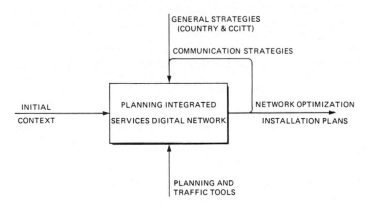

FIG. 3. STRUCTURED PLANNING ACTIVITY

* A left hand side arrow indicate input data such as network status, traffic measurement, element cost, etc.

* An upper side arrow represents control actions on the planning process by general policies or constraints such as service promotion, investment rate, technology availability, etc.

* A lower side arrow indicates the resource type supporting the activity execution such as data bases, analysis models, evaluation tools, etc.

* A right-hand side arrow gives the specific data, information, decision or plans obtained from a given process execution.

The feed-back of the communication strategies output on the control actions represents the impact of communications services availability on user behavior and the economy as well as the permanence of investment decisions already carried out on the following optimal solutions.

Both macroscopic activities and data sets are split with increasing degrees of detail up to the required modeling level (e.g. capacity allocation for a link, line module costing, service forecasting, etc).

4.1. Top-level planning process

The set of macroscopic planning activities, main interrelations and feed-back

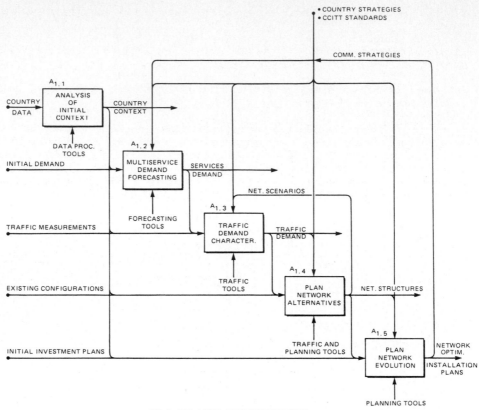

**FIG. 4.- TOP—LEVEL ACTIVITIES FOR THE
STRUCTURED PLANNING**

cycles to plan a Telecommunications network is summarized in figure 4. A brief description is given for each activity.

The full planning process implies the execution of all the activities maintaining the precedence relation, while a specific planning sub-problem may be solved by application of the subactivities which show higher interdependence.

The partition of activities to the following degree of detail is summarized in figures 5 to 9. This level of detail is applied both for strategic planning and long term planning, while short and medium term implementation planning require a further partition into activities with higher degrees of detail.

* Strategic planning is basically applied with the definition of typical reference cases representing a given country and later sensitivity analysis of uncertain parameters to obtain the impact of each factor and degree of robustness in the results.

* Long-term implementation planning and fundamental technical plans are applied with a full run through of the activities for all the network areas in a given country once the preselection of alternatives at strategic planning is completed.

A.1.1. Analysis of initial context: Collects and interrelates the existing data, at year 0, to be used for the telecommunication modeling and planning such as: population distribution, economical characterization, structure for existing voice and data networks, services offered, traffic measurements,

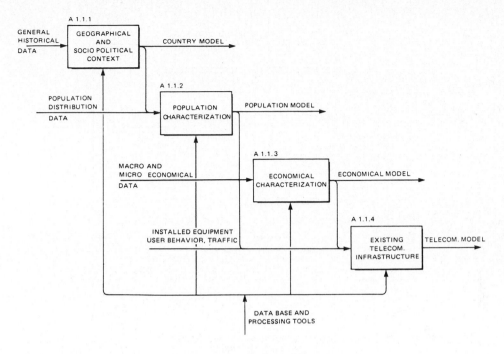

FIG. 5.- ANALYSIS OF INITIAL CONTEXT IN
STRUCTURED PLANNING

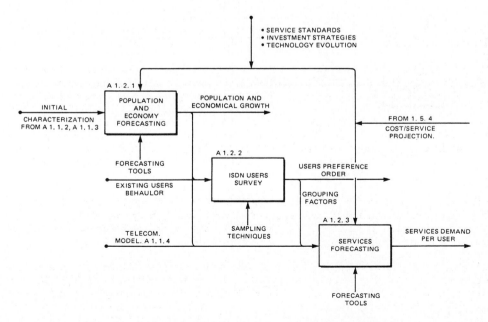

FIG. 6.- SERVICE FORECASTING IN STRUCTURED PLANNING

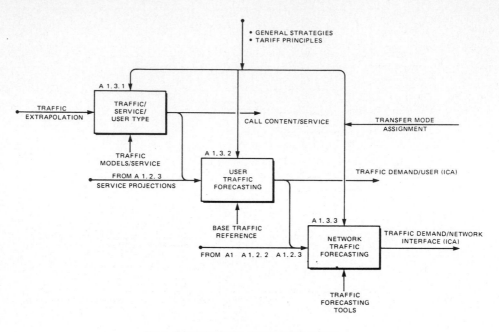

FIG. 7.- TRAFFIC DEMAND CHARACTERIZATION IN
STRUCTURED PLANNING

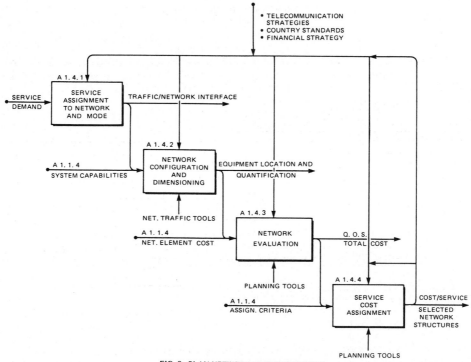

FIG. 8.- PLAN NETWORK ALTERNATIVES IN
STRUCTURED PLANNING

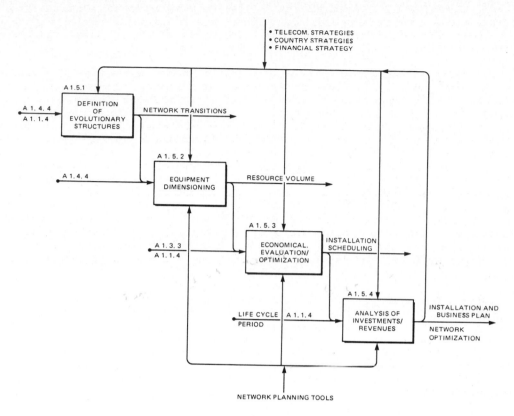

FIG. 9.- PLAN NETWORK EVOLUTION IN
STRUCTURED PLANNING

etc. This activity requires extension of the procedures being applied to voice networks by inclusion of all the services and networks, a deeper characterization of the population by activity sectors and investigation of the services information content.

A.1.2. Multiservice demand forecasting: Predicts demand growth at the planning period for each service and grouping of services per user as a function of service utility, expected cost and complexity. A procedure was developed to integrate forecasting of existing and new services through the interaction among country characterization in A.1.1, traffic characterization in A.1.3 and projection of cost per service in A.1.4. A tool (23) based on logistics was implemented to apply different adjusting procedures according to the knowledge of history per service and to derive service grouping at user interfaces. Once a reference case is obtained, sensitivity studies are done to the variation of uncertain parameters. A survey of methods to forecast new services is made at (22) which proposes a scenario technique.

A.1.3. Traffic demand characterization: Evaluates traffic demand for each service and service mixes based on previously projected services demand and traffic volume and characteristics per service. Many new models and measurements are required in this activity to account for the information traffic content of a call, arrival laws for calls and call information content, peakness factors, impact of transfer mode on the statistical characterization, etc. The traffic characterization for network interfaces of A.1.3 interacts with the selection of network alternatives at A.1.4 according to the associated transfer mode (e.g. packet versus circuit or ATM versus STM). An interaction cycle of both activities is required to obtain the impact of the alternatives. The parameter characterization and associated interrelations between information, protocol and traffic developed in (3) are applied in this activity.

A.1.4. Plan network alternatives: Designs, compares and optimizes network structures at a given time instant (cross-sectional). Different levels of detail for the network are considered, from the end-to-end reference network up to the full network area. Functions included in that activity comprise flow assignment, dimensioning and costing for different levels of integration. The alternatives for ISDN as well as the models which analyze previous functions are fundamentally different to the classical networks as pointed out in section 2. This activity determines the preselection of the most adequate alternative and is in fact the most extensively applied for strategic planning. The modeling of (24) and Cost Assignment to Telecommunication Services (CATS) tool of (25) were developed to evaluate integration alternatives for different degrees of integration and flow assignments within a network (different bandwith, system modularity, protocols, etc.). Further detailed application of subactivities imply a top-down demand assignment at network resources combined with the bottom-up provision of technology capacity and cost.

A.1.5. Plan network evolution: Analyzes the evolution path from the networks at year 0 up to the long term target network and moving through the previously selected alternatives by dynamic modeling. Network evolutions are analyzed here taking into account demand growth, required investments, technological transitions, interworking among networks and among transfer modes. Specific ISDN problems are the high number of paths, the analysis of interworking and the need to minimize technological transitions to reach integration effectively.

5. SOME RESULTS FROM APPLICATION STUDIES

Specific ISDN planning projects have been and are being carried out in which new concepts associated with integration are investigated. Examples of long term infrastructure planning, specific ISDN planning and prospectives for strategical planning in the evolution towards ISDN are given in (26), (27), (28).

In order to support these studies, a twofold approach is being followed: Firstly an extension of existing planning tools (29) is being carried out for those planning activities in which reusability of IDN developments is high. Secondly, new planning tools are being developed for those specific aspects of the integration which require new approaches and modeling like the tool CATS (25) for the evaluation and comparison of different degrees of integration and transfer mode options.

In following discusion, some examples of results obtained by the application of new tools in ISDN planning studies are given to illustrate the type of complexities and findings which are useful when addressing the previously mentioned planning challenges

5.1 Example of user multiservice demand

A structured multiservice forecast, following previously identified activities in A1.2 with the corresponding iteration with traffic characterization (A1.3) and evaluation of alternatives (A1.4.4) has been applied to the reference project (27). The ISDN survey on users and services placed special emphasis on modeling correlation among user categories, economic activity, stratification of consumption and service type preference. Figure 10 gives

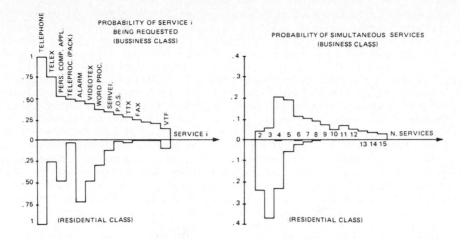

FIG. 10.- PROBABILITY OF SERVICE i BEING REQUESTED   FIG. 11.- PROBABILITY OF SERVICE AGGREGATION AT USER INTERFACE

the probability of a service (i) request by the business and residential user classes. Figure 11 provides the probability of service aggregation at the user interface for the business and residential user classes. Knowledge of the aggregation factor and the service mix distribution is particularly useful in dimensioning user access structures and planning subscriber loop media and subscriber premises network.

5.2 Examples from studies on alternatives

Several case studies were carried out on strategic planning and comparison of alternatives for different service assignments to communication modes. In particular, activities of A1.4 were applied to typical reference network cases with emphasis on the iteration with the remaining activities in the forecasting and traffic characterization areas.

Figure 12 provides an example of total costs and marginal costs (with optimum installation scheduling) for optical fiber links at different capacities. The

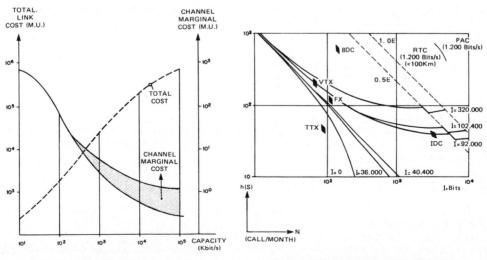

FIG. 12.- EVOLUTION OF TOTAL AND MARGINAL COSTS   FIG. 13.- PACKET VERSUS CIRCUIT THERESHOLD CURVES BASED ON TARIFFS (PROFILE 1)

large range of capacity and total cost variation produces high sensitivity to
the fill-in factor.

A tariff sensitivity analysis by application of the CATS was made for the
previously mentioned profile 1 (interconnected networks) to identify packet
versus circuit thereshold curves. Figure 13 shows these curves as a function
of service calling rate and holding time taking gross call information volume
"I" as a parameter. Narrowband services characterized at (3) are superposed
on this decision map, these are: Interactive Data Class (IDC) with I = 1.500
bits, Batch Data Class-Conversational (BDC) with I = 120.400, Videotex (VTX)
with I = 92.000, Teletex (TTX) with I = 36.000 and Facsimile (FAX) with I =
320.000. The optimum switching mode is derived for profile 1 from the tariff
point of view. For communication distances lower than 100 km, services
located below its thereshold curve, corresponding te the information volume
content "I", have cheaper charge by circuit mode, while those located in the
upper side have cheaper charge by packet mode.

Considering the reference profile 2 of a medium integration degree for narrowband services (all the nodes with packet and circuit capabilities), services
demand and projected costs for the year 1990, a set of results was obtained
by application of CATS to end-to-end networks with nominal load conditions
(25). Figure 14 gives relative cost/call/service referred to the basic telephone call when circuit and packet mode assignment is made. It clearly shows
the important sensitivity of cost to switching mode as well as the advantage
of relative cost prospective when applying service forecasting models.

Figure 15 provides sensitivity of packet versus circuit cost benefit according to the processing cost variation as a function of technological economies
of scale. It may be observed the robustness of preferred mode for the given
services except facsimile which required further analysis for an assignment
decision. These example cases are summarized for illustration purposes. A
wide number of cases has been analyzed and will be the subject of a future
publication.

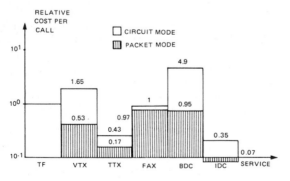

FIG. 14.- RELATIVE COST PER CALL PER SERVICE
IN A REFERENCE NETWORK OF PROFILE 2
(YEAR 1990)

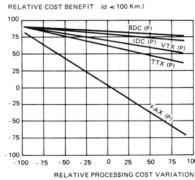

FIG. 15.- SENSITIVITY OF PREFERED MODE BENEFIT
TO PROCESSING COSTS (PROFILE 2)

6. CONCLUDING REMARKS

New challenges posed by the Telecommunication networks with service integration and new technologies were identified to aid the definition of design and
planning activities in practice.

A structured planning approach is proposed to guide strategic and specific planning activities and build new models and tools for the future integrated services environment.

Samples of multiservice related results of studies on narrowband services were given as an illustration of new findings and work areas in practical planning and decision-making.

In order to find equilibria among new economies of scale and quality of service offered to the user, the following research areas are fundamental:

- Investigation of system and network dimensioning functions for multiflow demands under sharing principles.

- Development of macroscopic models for strategic planning to interrelate economic and technical aspects of the network.

- Investigation of profiles for evolution of networks and transition strategies to optimize long-term investments.

Success in these areas will pave the way, without any doubt , to the wide availibility of new services and progress towarks the information society.

ACKNOWLEDGMENTS

I like to thank my colleagues of the Planning Department at the Research Center of Standard Eléctrica, S.A. and specially to J. Agusti and J.M. Silva for the constructive comments received.

REFERENCES

(1) CCITT. Red Book Vol III. I. series Recommendation Oct 1984
(2) CCITT. Red Book Vol III. Recommendation I:130. Oct. 1984
(3) O. González Soto. On traffic modeling and characterization of ISDN users. First international conference of data communications in the ISDN Era. IFIP. Tel-Aviv March 1985.
(4) M. Medina, R. Tudela, O. González Soto, T. Borja. Traffic characterization for ISDN planning studies. Specialist Seminar on ISDN traffic issues. ITC'86 Brussels.
(5) H. Hofstetter and D. Webber: Traffic models for large ISDN-PABX's. 11 th ITC. Kyoto 1985.
(6) L.T.M. Berry. Traffic Base definitions for planning and dimensioning Integrated Services Digital Networks. Specialist Seminar on ISDN traffic issues. ITC'86 Brussels.
(7) M. Bonatti, A. Roveri. A traffic model for design choice of ISDN system architectures. Specialist Seminar on ISDN traffic issues. ITC'86 Brussels
(8) J.M. Holtzman. Characteristics of superpositions of traffic streams. Specialist Seminar on ISDN traffic issues. ITC'86 Brussels.
(9) K. Sriram, W. Whitt: Characterizing superposition arrival processes in packet multiplexers for voice and data. GLOBECOM'85, New Orleans 1985
(10) G.F. Newell: Approximations for superposition arrival process in queues. Management Sc. Vol 30, 1984
(11) W. Whitt: Queues with superposition arrival processes in heavy traffic. Stochastic Processes and their Applications, Vol 21, 1986.
(12) GAS 3. General Network Planning. ITU Geneve 1983
(13) GAS 5 Part I. Factors influencing Telecommunication demand ITU Geneve 1982

(14)   GAS 5 Part II. Methods used for the long term forecasting of the internal Telecommunication demand and the necessary resources. ITU Geneve 1983

(15)   GAS 9 Economical and Technical aspects of the transition from analogue to digital Telecommunication Networks. ITU Geneve 1984.

(16)   P. Gonet, P. Adam, J.P. Condreuse: Asynchronous time division switching: The way to flexible broadband communications networks. Proc Int. Zurich Sem. on Digital Comm. Zurich 1986.

(17)   P. Gonet: Fast packet approach to integrated broadband networks. Computer Communications. 1986

(18)   De Prycker M., De Somer M.: An ATD broadband exchange with distributed control. CEPT Seminar Portugal 1987

(19)   De Prycker M. Bauwens J. The ATD concept: one universal bearer service. CEPT Seminar. Portugal 1987

(20)   Ross, D.T., Schumann, K.E.: Structured analysis for requirements definition. IEEE Transactions on Software Engineering, № 1, 1977

(21)   F. Vidondo, I. López, J.J. Girod.: GALILEO System Design Method, Electrical Communication. Vol 55, № 4, 1980

(22)   J.P. Dartois, M. Gruszecki, Demand forecasting for new Telecommunication services, 5th ITC Seminar. Traffic Engineering for ISDN Design and Planning, May 1987 Commo, Italy

(23)   J.M. Moral. Multiser: A Tool to Forecast Telecommunication Multiservices Demand. Int. Rep. 86-TR-82.09

(24)   O. González Soto, T. Borja: A step to ISDN Planning: From User Traffic to Service Cost Comparison 11 th ITC, 1980 Kyoto

(25)   J. Agustí, O. González Soto: Tool for ISDN Planning and the Analysis of Communication Alternatives Electrical Communication. 1987, Vol 61, № 1.

(26)   S.S. Choon, S.K. Lee, F. Casali, J.M. Silva: Planning the Evolution Towards the ISDN of the Seoul Telecommunication Network, NETWORKS 86, Innisbrook 1986

(27)   G. Uzcategui, B. Benaiges, O. González Soto, V. Navarro: Estudio de Planificación de una Red Digital de Servicios Integrados en Maracaibo. Internal Report

(28)   M. Medina, R. Tudela, J.M. Silva, O. González Soto: Protocol Aspects to be Considered in Planning the ISDN. ISS 87 Phoenix Arizona, March 1987

(29)   P.A. Caballero, F.J. de los Rios, F. Casali: Digital Network Planning. Electrical Communication 1985, Vol 57 № 1/2

TRAFFIC ENGINEERING for ISDN Design and Planning
M. Bonatti and M. Decina (Editors)
Elsevier Science Publishers B.V. (North-Holland)
© IAC, 1988

DISCUSSION

1 Darwin and the future of ISDN (C. Marchetti)

The discussion of the Tutorial Paper was centered on a few general aspects:

- the examples given by C. Marchetti all consider long time periods, 100 years or more, and macroscopic situations. On the other hand, the planning and traffic engineer in telecommunications looks at the microscopic level, and his time horizon is 10 or 15 years in broad studies and much less in specific applications. It seems that on that restricted scale, the substitution model is of limited use. In the case of ISDN, the observation of the initial period is not available and there is not sufficient data to establish a trend. Significant deviations from long term trends can occur and in cases where a few single values are obtained, it is very speculative to derive a trend;

- another aspect which came out of the discussion is the existence of regulatory constraints in the telecommunication world. Political events, administrative constraints, can significantly impact the evolutionary process. It was agreed that, if a deregulation trend is clearly visible, it may have effect in different countries at different times, and modify the near term predictions by a large factor.

In particular

C. Halgreen (Jutland Telephone Company) asked about the possibility of taking profit from the extended parallelism between the logistic growth of different technologies: from a statistical point of view, some knowledge of the growth rate will be very valuable in determining inflection points and saturation limits from data covering only the introduction of the new technologies.

The author answered confirming that in a class of fairly analogous innovations the time constant of penetration is similar: if one has the point of attack, the slope, i.e: the rate of penetration, is fairly well defined. This certainly helps determining the saturation point because one of the parameters to be found by fitting is eliminated (or its variance diminished).

G. Robin (Alcatel) asked if in the thousands cases analyzed by the author, he did find any exhibiting a significant departure from the model.

The author answered remembering the very interesting case of primary energy substitution in France. The "clocks" did stop for five years during German occupation in World War II. The curves become self-consistent by "cutting away" these five years.

Systems usually are resilient to perturbation because they react homeostatically. Sometimes the stress is too strong and they break down or substantially deviate from the original course, but even world wars do not usually change the long-term behavior of the system (as in primary energy substitution).

A. Jensen (chairman of IAC of ITC) remembered the Plessing observation that in Denmark the spread of telephone was composed of several logistic curves - first business group, then the middle class and then, with some delay, the workers, and asked if the author have observed a similar step-by-step development in other areas.

A two-step growth occurred for telephone subscribers in USA as clearly shown by the figure illustrated by the author in answering:

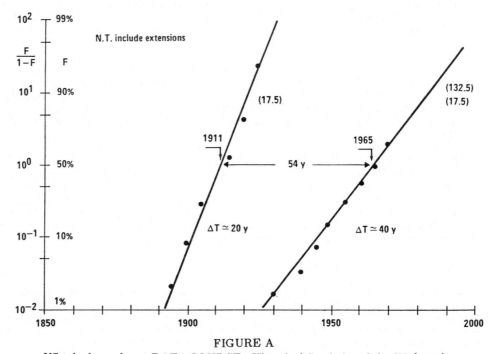

FIGURE A

US telephone data. DATA SOURCE: Historical Statistics of the US (1975).

However, the author affirmed that the Kondratiev long cycles have been the cause: the first step, in fact, ends approximately in 1940 and the second saturates in the 1990s, well in tune with the Kontradiev cycles.

R. Pandya (BNR) asked if the results of the model could be affected by socio-political systems of the countries concerned, e.g., countries where the economies are planned or certain sectors of technology are provided with special boosts by the governments.

For centrally planned countries like the Soviet Union, in the few cases the author could examine it, the situation is business as usual. For the countries where there is a government support to the development of technology, usually this has an influence at the beginning (market share <5%). Beyond that the system operates under its own steam, again producing business as usuall. The author did not analyze very specific areas of heavy government support to effect. But affirmed his skepticism. War itself does not accelerate technology!

P. Richards (BNR) reported about some applications of Fisher —Pry techniques to switching technologies at BNR. In general, the method appears to be as applicable to the switching industry as to the examples presented by the author. However digital doesn't appear as a separate technology and digital switches must be lumped into the more general category of stored program in order to fit the model.

The author confirmed that every object can be categorized at various levels of abstraction: an oak, a broad-leaved tree, a tree, a plant, a biological construct. The choice of the appropriate abstraction and indicators is a delicate one in view of the success of the modeling.

2 Characterization of services requiring multislot connections (J. Roberts)

C. Halgreen (Jutland Telephone Company) objected to prebooking as might be needed in a dedicated videoconference network, but not needed in an integrated network with the large capacity of an ISDN, that would allow finding the required resources within a few minutes.

The author answered that reservation is an inherent feature of the videoconference service. An integrated network would be optimized for the dominant services such as telephony and would be far from optimum for videoconferencing.

It should be noted that on the same subject K. Lindberger (Televerket) in the afternoon session had reached different conclusions. This divergence could be explained by different assumptions concerning the ratio of the multislot traffic to the single slot traffic.

It was also remarked that the evolution toward broadband ISDN with possible use of asynchronous transfer modes, offering bandwidth on demand, may eliminate the need for n x 64 Kbit/s services, in the longer term.

3 ISDN planning (O. Gonzales Soto)

B. Craignou (CNET) asked whether multiservice demand surveys have been actually performed using the method presented. The answer is positive: such a survey was carried out within the ITU pilot project for Venezuela. The author also clarified the meaning of "simultaneous" as referring to joint subscription to several services and not necessarily to the use at the same instant.

Several questions (F. Casali, FACE and B. Craignou, CNET) referred
to whether conventional planning tools could be used, or if specific
ones have to be developed. In fact both will be necessary, some
conventional tools and models need updating and new ones have to be
carried. In particular macroscopic tools for network screening
design alternatives are necessary.

S. Katz (AT&T - Bell Labs) suggested that to avoid the complexity of
multiple service, and since the ISDN user will request a high
quality of service, the teletraffic engineer should use simplicity
and conservatism in providing the facilities. This overdesign will
require higher investments but will reduce operating costs. The
author agreed with this proposal for the initial introduction, but
stated that as the data base grows, more accurate planning will
become practical and the initial cost penality will be reduced.

TRAFFIC ENGINEERING for ISDN Design and Planning
M. Bonatti and M. Decina (Editors)
Elsevier Science Publishers B.V. (North-Holland)
© IAC, 1988

SERVICE FORECASTING: A SIMPLE OR A COMPLEX TASK?

(Chairman Conclusions of the Morning Session on Services)

by Gerard Robin

ALCATEL, Belgium

It is pretty obvious that the forecasting of traffic demand in the heterogeneous case of an ISDN will be much more complex than the equivalent task for a dedicated network. However, a number of approaches can help reduce this complexity and provide useful results.

As digital networks only carry bit streams, it is essential to analyze the services and concentrate on the large flows rather than on the small tributaries (which may be nevertheless very important to the customer). Classical methods of modeling, extrapolation, and simulation are applicable and the concept of substitution —as presented in the Tutorial Paper— can be very useful during the introductory phase of ISDN.

One of the problems that will be encountered in the traffic engineering of switching systems is that switch elements may well be dedicated to different flows of traffic (64 Kbit/s multislot traffic, broadband traffic), so that the only integrated part of the network is the customer access. This situation may not exist anymore if ISDN evolves toward asynchronous, rather than synchronous transfer modes. This evolution would add a new degree of flexibility in planning as ATM is expected to provide bandwidth on demand, at least at call set up time, and perhaps dynamically during a call.

The rapid progress of technology and the diminishing cost of electronic and photonic techniques will undoubtedly modify current planning and modeling methods, allowing consideration of the network as a global resource available to all subscribers and placing therefore less emphasis on local and detailed optimization.

TRAFFIC ENGINEERING for ISDN Design and Planning
M. Bonatti and M. Decina (Editors)
Elsevier Science Publishers B.V. (North-Holland)
© IAC, 1988

KEY TRAFFIC ISSUES RELATING TO ISDN SERVICES

(Chairman Introduction to the Afternoon Session on Services)

David J. Songhurst

British Telecom, U.K.

Some of the most important ISDN service issues that affect planning are not normally considered by teletraffic engineers. These include the problem of identifying and quantifying new services, marketing, and competition. These factors add significantly to uncertainty over the future evolution of the network and the traffic demands placed upon it, and their influence should be borne in mind.

Three traffic issues, relating to ISDN services, are of particular importance:

- Forecasting the growth of new services, in an unstable environment and with inadequate base data.

- Traffic characterisation, for example quantifying parameters such as mean holding time and variability.

- Modelling the interaction between different types of traffic carried on a common network component.

These three issues were all addressed within the session. The main statements of the papers are given below:

J.M. Holtzman's paper analyses individual traffic streams in superposition in order to gain further insight into the use of peakedness and to support decisions on priority schemes and on integration .vs. segregation of traffic streams with different GOS targets. Some new techniques of analysis such as Markov modulated Poisson processes, Neuts matrix-geometric method and phase-type distributions are popularized.

K. Lindberger suggests approximations for the blocking probabilities for two individual traffic streams offered to a commun trunk group with a particular reservation discipline. The analysis of this simple case is useful in discussing the possible advantages of integration: an essential trunk saving is demonstrated in the analyzed case.

J.P. Dartois and M. Gruszecki offer a survey on the demand forecasting methodologies for new telecom services. The utility of classical forecasting techniques, of new or improved methods under study and of transferring techniques used outside the traditional ITC area of knowledge and practice, are examined. The policy issues and the introduction strategies adopted by the Administrations are decisive. A structured scenario technique is proposed that formalizes the decision making process of the main partners in the service telecommunication market. The success story of Teletel/Minitel in France is given as example.

V.A. Bolotin and J.G. Kappel discuss the factors considered in the subscriber traffic analysis and engineering in the new ISDN context, the needed modifications, upgradings and extensions. Group and day variability of subscriber traffic are generalized to several classes of service. In the section dedicated to the forecasting, the need of compounding elementary independent forecasting is underlined in order not to miss the "true" trend. Notes on call types, measurements, busy period analysis and GOS standards are also given.

J. Matsuda, T. Yokoi and K. Kawashima generalize the concept of reference traffic to multi-services systems. The paper examines the relationship between traffic mix variations and GOS. The measurements of these variations and the estimation of a "reference traffic" is also discussed. The approach is based upon GOS distributions, substituting the traditional "mean GOS" approach.

TRAFFIC ENGINEERING for ISDN Design and Planning
M. Bonatti and M. Decina (Editors)
Elsevier Science Publishers B.V. (North-Holland)
© IAC, 1988

EXAMINING INDIVIDUAL TRAFFIC STREAMS IN SUPERPOSITIONS

J. M. Holtzman

AT&T Bell Laboratories
Holmdel, New Jersey   07733, USA

ABSTRACT

The motivation for considering superposition processes in integrated services is that traffic streams will be combined. Moreover, in integrated services, heterogeneous traffic streams will be combined. It is thus important to understand the performance of the individual streams, which may experience different performance (blocking and/or delay) and which may be subject to different performance criteria. Understanding the performance of the individual streams can help in deciding whether FIFO is sufficient or whether a priority scheme is needed. Or, indeed, whether integration of different traffic types with different performance criteria is better than segregation.

We have two objectives, in addition to analyzing individual streams:

i.   To gain further insight into the use of peakedness.

ii. The popularization of some new techniques of analysis.

The first problem considered is concerned with clarifying the peakedness concept by examining the peakedness of individual streams as the number of thinned streams in a superposition increase. The next topic discussed concerns a $\Sigma GI_i/M/1$ queueing system, with non-homogeneous input renewal streams. We observe the result for the case of one input intensity approaching zero. This result helps to show the characteristics of the individual stream's delay.

We next turn to queueing systems with a finite waiting room in which case both loss and delay need to be calculated. Most integrated service congestion problems involve both loss and delay. Our motivation here is as much to make some relatively new results in queueing theory more popular with the teletraffic community as it is to solve a particular technical problem. That is, the technical problem under consideration, in addition to whatever practical importance it has, is used here as a vehicle for exposing methodology. New methodologies, these and others, will be needed to investigate the new congestion problems that will be encountered in integrated services. Although Poisson assumptions and peakedness will still have application, they will not be enough.

MAIN STATEMENT

Analysis of individual traffic streams in superpositions and, also, popularization of some new analysis techniques.

I. INTRODUCTION

Reference 1 discussed the characteristics of superpositions of traffic streams and methods to analyze them as inputs to service systems. This paper continues the discussion of superpositions but focuses more on the individual streams. (Stationarity of the streams is assumed throughout).

As discussed in [1], the motivation for considering superposition processes is that with integrated services, traffic streams will be combined. Moreover heterogeneous traffic streams will be combined.[1] For example, various types of data (including interactive and bulk), packetized voice, image and video need to be considered. It is thus important to understand the performance of the individual streams, which may experience different performance (blocking and/or delay) and which may be subject to different performance criteria. Understanding the performance of the individual streams can help in deciding whether FIFO is sufficient or whether a priority scheme is needed. Or, indeed, whether integration of different traffic types with different performance criteria is better than segregation. (For an example of integration giving worse performance, see [2]).

In Section II, we address the following question. Suppose we increase the number of independent streams in a superposition process while at the same time thinning each stream (to keep the superposition's intensity constant) and keeping the peakedness $z > 1$ of each stream fixed. The peakedness of the superpositions is fixed at $z > 1$; yet it seems that the superposition process convergence theorem says the superposition approaches Poisson ($z=1$). Is there a contradiction or a misunderstanding? This is an old question in teletraffic theory and the answer may be well known but I could not find it written down. The explanation clarifies the peakedness concept and the relationship between the individual steams and the superposition.

In Section III, we consider a simple approximation for obtaining the delays of individual streams in a $\Sigma GI_i/M/1$ queueing system. The objective is twofold. Firstly, the approximation might be used in some cases to actually calculate delays. Secondly, we can qualitatively examine the key factors affecting the delay of the individual streams.

In Section IV, we examine recent analyses of delay/loss systems — queueing systems with finite waiting room. We particularly emphasize one approach because it motivates discussion of some new matrix techniques in Section IV that are recommended to the teletraffic community.

Thus, we see that we have two objectives, in addition to analyzing individual streams:

   i.   To gain further insight into the use of peakedness and

   ii. The popularization of some new techniques of analysis.

This paper is *not* intended to be a survey of all the work in the field.

II. SUPERPOSITIONS OF PEAKED STREAMS

Consider a peaked traffic stream with mean M and peakedness $z > 1$. M is the (stationary) mean number of servers busy if the stream were offered to an infinite server group (independent exponential servers) with service rate μ and z is the variance-to-mean ratio of busy servers. Note that specifying M and z does not completely specify the traffic stream.

Now suppose we superpose n of these (mutually independent) streams keeping z fixed while keeping the total load fixed; hence each stream has mean M/n. It would seem that the convergence theorem to Poisson is satisfied, hence convergence to a superposition process with peakedness $z = 1$. Yet, for each n, the superposition process has peakedness $z > 1$. Is there a contradiction or a misunderstanding?

One of the problems is that situation described above is vague enough so that it is not clear what question is being asked. We have to be more specific. First, assume that each stream is renewal and orderly.[2] Now the key question is how the streams are thinned. If we linearly stretch the time scale of each stream then it is easily seen that as $n \to \infty$, $z \to 1$ (for a fixed mean service time). Thus, with what is probably the most natural method of thinning, the assumptions of the problem statement are not satisfied (the assumed invariance of z as n increases). Another way of thinning is by retaining each event with probability 1/n where n is the number of streams in the superposition process.[3] In this case, each thinned stream is asymptotically a Poisson process as $n \to \infty$. Thus $z \to 1$ and we are again not satisfying our assumed invariance of z as n increases.

Thus, let us instead specifically keep z fixed by imposing that constraint on a sequence of interrupted Poisson process, IPP's ([3]). For the two-moment match IPP,

$$\lambda = Mz(\mu) + 3z(\mu)(z(\mu)-1) \, , \tag{II-1}$$

$$\omega = \frac{M}{\lambda} \left(\frac{\lambda-M}{z(\mu)-1} -1 \right) \, , \tag{II-2}$$

$$\gamma = \left(\frac{\lambda}{M} -1 \right) \omega \, , \tag{II-3}$$

where λ is the rate of the Poisson process during the on-time of the IPP, γ^{-1} is the mean on-time, ω^{-1} is the mean off-time, and M and z are the mean and peakedness as defined previously. In (II-1) and (II-2), we show explicit dependence of z upon μ. Although this dependence is suppressed elsewhere in this section, we shall return to this dependence.

Now, let

$$M_n = \frac{m}{\mu n} \tag{II-4}$$

where m is the intensity of the original (unthinned) stream, μ^{-1} is the mean holding time on the ∞-server group. As $n \to \infty$, with $z > 1$ being kept constant,

$$\lambda \to 3z(z-1) \tag{II-5}$$

$$\omega^{-1} \to \frac{n\mu 3z(z-1)}{m(3z-1)} \tag{II-6}$$

$$\gamma^{-1} \to \frac{1}{3z-1} \tag{II-7}$$

The interpretation of (II-5) to (II-7) is as follows. As n, the number of thinned streams in the superposition process gets large, the mean on-time and the intensity of the Poisson process during the on-time approach constants and the mean off-time approaches linear growth. Now, one of the conditions for convergence of the superposition process to Poisson is that

$$\lim_{n \to \infty} \sum_{i=1}^{n} P \left\{ N_{ni}(t) \geq 2 \right\} = 0 \text{ for all } t > 0 \tag{II-8}$$

where $N_{ni}(t)$ is the number of points in [0, t] of one of the processes in the double sequence of independent stationary processes whose convergence is being investigated (see [4]; the result in [4] is repeated in [1]). The processes described by (II-5) - (II-7) do not satisfy (II-8). That is, the superpositions consist of a linearly growing number of IPP's, each of which has an (asymptotically) linear growth in mean off-times but with (asymptotically) constant on-time with (asymptotically) fixed λ. The net result is non-satisfaction of (II-8).

Let us recapitulate what we have done. It was recognized that the stated problem was not well posed and needed interpretation. The fuzzily stated problem dissolves when stated precisely. That is, the assumption underlying the question stated in the second paragraph of this section is the joint satisfaction of conditions for thinning, for keeping the peakedness fixed, and for the theorem of a convergence of superposition processes to Poisson. We showed in specific cases how one or another of the conditions are violated.

We considered three ways of thinning. The first two. stretching the time scale and retaining each event with probability 1/n, respectively, did not preserve the peakedness $z > 1$. To force the invariance of z, we used a sequence of IPP's (an unnatural method of thinning) and found that violated the conditions of theorem on convergence to Poisson. Yet another method of thinning is that considered in [5]. In [5], simple overflow processes with decreasing load and fixed peakedness are studied. See, in particular, Section IV of [5] for discussion of the increasing "bunchiness".

Also, note the dependence of the peakedness on the mean service time on the ∞-server group, μ^{-1}, which was used in discussion of the first method of thinning. This is normally implicit in classical trunking analysis where there is usually only one service time, assumed exponential. In fact, for orderly renewal processes, the peakedness is constant as a function of μ if and only if the arrival process is Poisson (see p. 19 of [6]). In integrated services, where there is more than one service time, this dependence on service time is important. The dependence on service time is made very explicit in [7] where peakedness is defined as a functional on service time distribution.

III. DELAYS OF INDIVIDUAL STREAMS

Consider a $\Sigma GI_i/M/1$ queueing system, with non-homogeneous input renewal streams. There are methods for analyzing the response of this system as experienced by an arbitrary arrival in the superposition process (see, e.g., [8] for approximation methods). To analyze the delay experienced by the individual streams, there are some exact results for specific cases (e.g., [9]) and some approximations (e.g., [10], [11]).

The result of [10] is for independent renewal processes offered to one exponential server. The interarrival time random variables are positive and non-lattice. First-come first-served discipline is assumed. Define for i = 1, 2.

$$\lambda_i = \textit{mean arrival rate of renewal process i}$$

$$\Phi_i = \textit{Laplace} - \textit{Stieltjes transform of the interarrival time distribution of renewal process i}$$

$$\mu^{-1} = \textit{mean service time}$$

$$\rho_i = \frac{\lambda_i}{\mu}$$

$$\rho = \rho_1 + \rho_2$$

$$D_i = \textit{approximation for mean delay experienced by } i-\textit{arrivals.}$$

It is assumed that $\rho < 1$.

The basic result of [10][4] is:

To solve the M

space is used.

corresponds to
corresponds to t
with 2 states, th

The infinitesmal

$$
\begin{array}{c|cc}
\underline{0} & Q-\Lambda & \\
\underline{1} & \mu I & Q \\
\underline{2} & & \\
\underline{c} & & \\
\underline{c+1} & & \\
\underline{c+k} & & \cdot
\end{array}
$$

where j denotes t

Once the stationa
interest can be
distributions of n
arrival and by an
arrival in any of
blocked) for any o

V. NEW MATRI

In reading [14],
MMPP/M/c/c+k q
Markov process f
generalizes it. Ge
methods expounde
universities. Furth
should help in spre
teletraffic researche

We limit our discu
There are widely
These generalizatio
algorithmic solution

As an example, co
textbooks (see, e.g
embedded Markov c

$$
D_1 = \mu^{-1} \left[\frac{\omega_1}{1-\omega_1} + \frac{\rho_{21}}{1-\omega_2} \right] \tag{III-1}
$$

$$
D_2 = \mu^{-1} \left[\frac{\omega_2}{1-\omega_2} + \frac{\rho_{12}}{1-\omega_1} \right] \tag{III-2}
$$

where

$$
\rho_{12} = \frac{\rho_1}{1-\rho_2} \tag{III-3}
$$

$$
\rho_{21} = \frac{\rho_2}{1-\rho_1} \tag{III-4}
$$

$$
\omega_1 = \Phi_1 \left[\mu(1-\rho_2)(1-\omega_1) \right] \tag{III-5}
$$

$$
\omega_2 = \Phi_2 \left[\mu(1-\rho_1)(1-\omega_2) \right] \tag{III-6}
$$

It is of interest to observe the result for the case of one input intensity approaching zero as a result of "linearly stretching" the stream (equivalent to changing the time scale).[5] If $\lambda_1 \to 0$, then

$$
D_1 \to \mu^{-1} \frac{\rho_2}{1-\omega_2} , \tag{III-7}
$$

which is the virtual waiting time (time average of waiting time) of the queue with only the second stream offered as input.[6] This is physically plausible because as the first stream gets thinner and thinner, each arrival approaches the case of an arbitrary point on the time axis.

The reason for pointing this out is to emphasize that the delay experienced by an individual stream depends not only on its burstiness and the burstiness of the superposition but also on the relative intensity. *In fact, when examining approximations for blocking or delay of individual streams, it is instructive to check for the case of one stream of very low intensity.*

Based on the above, we make the following heuristic observations:

(i) The individual stream contributes to the delay seen by an arbitrary arrival in the superposition process by contributing to the overall intensity and by affecting the variability of the superposition process.

(ii) The delay seen by arrivals in the individual stream can be thought of as having two contributions:

(a) the delay experienced by an arbitrary arrival in the superposition process, and

(b) a modification of (ii)a based on the mean and variability characteristics of the individual stream's interarrival time (through its distribution function).

Note that (ii)b depends on both the mean and variance and not just the coefficient of variation. In fact, as shown earlier, as the mean goes to the zero, the individual stream experience the time average of the delay — each arrival essentially appears to the queue as an arrival randomly placed in time.

IV. D

In Sect
There i
(the "p
to queι
be calc
queueir
technicε
whateve

Ref. 13
of a Pα
inputs c
an appr
Poisson
this app
queuein₂

We firsι
process.

the diffe

A is def
conditioι

where 0
obvious ≀

The inpu
Markov
MMPP/Ν
independ

An MM
according
generator
diagonal
rate of th

The IPP
between
variables
characterι

It is show
MMPP.
IPP's.

[3]   A. Kuczura, The Interrupted Poisson Process as an Overflow Process, *Bell System Technical J.*, Vol. 52, pp. 437-448 (1973).

[4]   E. Çinlar, Superposition of Point Processes in *Stochastic Point Processes*, ed. by P. A. W. Lewis, Wiley-Interscience, 1972.

[5]   P. J. Burke, The Limit of the Blocking as Offered Load Decreases with Fixed Peakedness, *Bell System Technical J.*, Vol. 61, No. 10, Part 1, pp. 2911-2916 (Dec. 1982).

[6]   C. E. M. Pearce, On the Peakedness of Primary and Secondary Processes, *Austral. Telecom Res.*, Vol. 12, No. 2, pp. 18-24 (1978).

[7]   A. E. Eckberg, Generalized Peakedness of Teletraffic Processes, *Proc. 10th Intl. Teletraffic Congress*, Paper 4.4.6.3, Montreal (June 1983).

[8]   W. Whitt, The Queueing Network Analyzer, *Bell System Technical J.*, Vol. 62, Part I, pp. 2779-2815 (1983).

[9]   A. Kuczura, Queues with Mixed Renewal and Poisson Inputs, *Bell System Technical J.*, Vol. 51, pp. 1305-1326 (1972).

[10] J. M. Holtzman, Mean Delays of Individual Streams into a Queue: The $\Sigma GI_i/M/1$ Queue, *Applied Probability — Computer Science: The Interface, Vol. 1*, Ed. by R. L. Disney and T. J. Ott (Proc. of January 1981 Conf.), Birkhauser, pp. 417-430 (1982).

[11] S. L. Albin, Delays for Customers from Different Arrival Streams to a Queue, *Management Science*, Vol. 32, No. 3, pp. 329-340 (March 1986).

[12] R. E. Strauch, When a Queue Looks the Same to an Arriving Customer as to an Observer, *Management Science*, Vol. 17, No. 3, pp. 140-141 (No. 1970).

[13] J. Matsumoto and Y. Wanatabe, Individual Traffic Characteristics of Queueing Systems with Multiple Poisson and Overflow Inputs, *IEEE Trans. on Comm.*, Vol. COM-33, No. 1, pp. 1-9 (1985).

[14] K. S. Meier-Hellstern, The Analysis of a Queue Arising in Overflow Models, to appear.

[15] K. S. Meier, *A Statistical Procedure for Fitting Markov-Modulated Poisson Processes*, Ph.D. Thesis, University of Delaware, December 1, 1984.

[16] M. F. Neuts, *Matrix - Geometric Solutions in Stochastic Models*, Johns-Hopkins University Press, 1981.

[17] D. M. Lucantoni and V. Ramaswami, book in preparation.

[18] D. Gross and C. M. Harris, *Fundamentals of Queueing Theory*, John Wiley and Sons, New York, 1974.

[19] H. Heffes and D. M. Lucantoni, A Markov Modulated Characterization of Packetized Voice and Data Traffic and Related Multiplexer Performance, *IEEE J. Selected Areas in Communications*, Vol. SAC-4, No. 6, pp. 856-868 (September 1986).

TRAFFIC ENGINEERING for ISDN Design and Planning
M. Bonatti and M. Decina (Editors)
Elsevier Science Publishers B.V. (North-Holland)
© IAC, 1988

151

BLOCKING FOR MULTI-SLOT HETEROGENOUS TRAFFIC STREAMS
OFFERED TO A TRUNK GROUP WITH RESERVATION

Karl Lindberger

Swedish Telecommunications Administration
Network Department S-123 86 FARSTA SWEDEN

ABSTRACT

For the discussion of possible advantages of an integration of
heterogenous circuit switched multi-slot traffic streams with
different band widths, peakedness factors and mean holding times, we
have suggested approximations for the blocking probabilities in a
particular problem. Two individual traffic streams are offered to a
common trunk group with a certain type of reservation where one of
those streams are blocked when there are less than a given number of
free trunks. This reservation makes it possible to change the ratio
of the two individual blocking probabilities in the direction to
what is demanded in the GOS. It appears that also the ratio of the
mean holding times of the two streams is an important parameter here.

Numerical examples are given, and for a typical application
including telephone and video call traffic the magnitude of the
trunk savings on a common trunk group due to integration can be
concluded. Consequences for the dimensioning of a whole network of
such a type are also discussed.

Main Statement: Essential trunk savings can be obtained by integration.

1.   INTRODUCTION

In the discussion of the network planning for services with higher bit rate
than 64 kbps (as for telephony) e.g. video call, the question of an integration of the traffic for such a service with telephone traffic is of great
interest. Different network solutions for such a new service are possible, a
dedicated circuit switched network or an integrated one based on either
circuit or packet switching. All these solutions have different advantages and
disadvantages with respect to simplicity, flexibility and savings in terms of
transmission, switching and processor capacity.

To be able to make the "best" choice one must answer a number of subquestions.
One such subquestion, which will be treated in this paper, is whether there
are any essential trunk savings by integration in the circuit switched case.
The number of traffic types to be integrated is in our study just two (for
simplicity). We shall consider a case of a one-slot type and a multi-slot type
of traffic. Several authors have studied similar problems also in connection
with integration of circuit switched data traffic streams of different bit
rates e.g. [1] - [7]. However, in order to be able to balance the two blocking
probabilities for the two traffic types when they are offered to a common
trunk group, we must also allow trunk reservation. In such a case it appears
that also the ratio of the mean holding times between the multi- and the one-
slot traffic types is an important parameter.

In section 2 we give the exact formulation of the problem. In section 3 we
suggest the approximations of the blocking probabilities in this problem and
we also give their explanation. Sections 4, 5 and 6 are studies of numerical

examples from different points of view. A comparison between similar cases but
with the mean holding time ratio as different as 1 and 20 is included. The
application in section 7 which we are particularly interested in, the one-slot
telephone traffic integrated with e.g. 6-slot (or 30-slot) video call traffic
gives us reason to assume that this ratio is rather 20 than 1.

We are also considering the consequences of this application in terms of
possible network savings. Even if we will refer to this particular application
in the paper, some conclusions can be used more generally.

2.   THE PROBLEM

Consider a trunk group with N trunks to which two traffic streams are offered,
one with calls needing 1 trunk and the other with calls needing any d trunks
(not necessarily consecutive ones) to be carried. The service times are
exponentially distributed with mean service times 1 and T respectively. A
certain number of trunk reservations R is determined i.e. the 1-slot calls are
blocked when there are at the most R free trunks and the d-slot traffic is
blocked when there are at the most d-1 free trunks. The arrival processes are
independent Poissonian or in the case of 1-slot traffic possibly peaked with
peakedness factor z_1 due to overflow arrangement for that traffic in the
network.

The total traffic offered to the trunk group is A and the proportion of 1-slot
traffic is p. Thus the call intensity for d-slot traffic is $(1-p)A/dT$.

The problem is to find approximations for the blocking probabilities B_1 and B_2
for the two traffic streams with 1- and d-slot traffic given the parameters
A, p, z_1, d, T, R and N.

What is new in this problem is that z_1 and T do not have to be 1.

Later we shall suggest an extension of the formulae for the case where also
the d-slot traffic has an individual peakedness factor $z_2 > 1$ due to overflow.

3.   THE APPROXIMATE BLOCKING PROBABILITIES

In this section we shall suggest approximations for blocking probabilities in
our problem. We shall also try to explain how they are constructed and discuss
for which values of the parameters they can be applied with reasonable
accuracy.

Define the following parameters

$$z = pz_1 + d(1-p)$$

$$E = E(\frac{N-z+1}{z}, \frac{A}{z}) \qquad ; \qquad Q = (N-z)/A$$

$$(d-R)/z = f_0 + f_1 \qquad ; \qquad R/z = r_0 + r_1$$

where f_0 and r_0 are the integer parts of the expressions respectively.

Furthermore we define

$$C_1 = Q^{R/z}\{\sum_{k=0}^{f_0-1} Q^k + f_1 Q^{f_0-(1-f_1)/2}\}$$

$$C_2 = \sum_{k=0}^{r_0-1} Q^k + r_1 Q^{r_0-(1-r_1)/2}$$

$$C_3 = \frac{1}{z} Q^{(2R-z+1)/2z}$$

$$C_4 = \frac{N - (R-1)/2}{A} (\frac{2pdT}{(1-p)(R+1)} + 1)/RQ^{(2d-R-1)/2z}$$

Now, when R > 0, the blocking probabilities for the two traffic streams with 1- and d-slot calls will be given by

$$B_1 = z_1 E(C_3 + C_2 - e^{-1/d} \frac{C_2 C_4 - C_3}{C_4 + 1 - e^{1/d}}) \tag{1}$$

$$B_2 = E(C_1 + C_2 - e^{-(d-R)/d} \frac{C_2 C_4 - C_3}{C_4 + 1 - e^{-1/d}}) \tag{2}$$

For cases with R = 0 the corresponding approximations are

$$B_1 = z_1 E C_3 \quad \text{and} \quad B_2 = E C_1$$

In the more general case, $z_2 > 1$, the peakedness of the total offered stream is

$$z = p z_1 + (1-p) z_2 d$$

and B_2 replaced by B_2/z_2 in (2), is then the only other suggested extension of (1) and (2).

However, when we now shall try to explain the approximations we shall assume that the two arrival processes are Poissonian, i.e. $z_1 = z_2 = 1$ to begin with.

The explanation of the approximation can now be done in three steps. At first we shall approximate the state probabilities of the unreserved system (R=0). If we also assume that z is an integer for simplicity, we can approximate the probability of the state set $\{N-z+1,...,N-1,N\}$ with

$$P_0(N-z+1),...,N) \approx E = E(\frac{N-z+1}{z}, \frac{A}{z}) \tag{3}$$

One could say that this approximation is Hayward-like with the following interpretation. In a corresponding infinite group with N as an arbitrary integer the probability of the state set above can, under certain conditions, be approximated by $\dfrac{z}{\sqrt{zA}}\ \phi\ (\dfrac{N-z+1-A}{\sqrt{zA}})$

or with similar expressions where N-z+1 is replaced by N or N-(z-1)/2

All these can be called normal approximations, and conditions for such are assumed. However, the first choice seems to be the best one for our particular application. Then the corresponding approximation in the finite case is just (3), if we accept approximations of the type

$$E(n,A) = \phi(\frac{n-A}{\sqrt{A}})/\ \sqrt{A}\ \Phi(\frac{n-A}{\sqrt{A}})$$

In the same spirit as (3) we also have the two approximations

$$P_0(N) \approx z^{-1}EQ^{-(z-1)/2z}\ \ ; \tag{4}$$

$$P_0(N-k) \approx P_0(N)Q^{k/z}\ \ \ (\text{for small } k) \tag{5}$$

since E represents the sum of z state probabilities.

The operations with Q in (4) and (5) are a type of geometrical interpolation.

In the unreserved system we also have the approximate relation

$$P_0(N-d-R+1,\ldots,N-d) = RQ^{(2d-R-1)/2z}P_0(N-R), \tag{6}$$

where the states on the left side are those from which the last R states can be reached in the corresponding reserved system.

Now as a second step in the approximation we note that in this reserved system there will be a new relation between the probabilities of the last R states, which can only be reached by a d-slot arrival, and those of the states "just before" e.g. the state N-R.

The intensity to the last R states is the arrival intensity of a d-slot call

i.e.   A(1-p)/dT

and the intensity from those states is approximately $(N-(R-1)/2)(\dfrac{2p}{R+1} + \dfrac{1-p}{dT})$

since the state N-(R-1)/2 can be regarded as a typical one among the last R ones and from that state there are (R+1)/2 steps down to the state N-R, unless the next step down is of size d. Note that the probability of such a d-slot departure from the last R states is here also dependent of T, the ratio of the mean service times.

From these observations we obtain the following approximate relation in the reserved system

$$P(N-R) = P(N-R+1,\ldots,N)\ C_4 \tag{7}$$

This new relation (7) implies that the probability of the last R states is reduced, in the reserved system, by

$$S = P_0(N-R+1,\ldots,N) - P(N-R+1,\ldots,N) \qquad (8)$$

A third step in the construction of the approximation is now to spread the reduction S over the other N-R states. However, a study of some exactly calculated examples (with $z_1=z_2=1$) shows that this can not be done proportionally to the P_0-distribution which would have been simple. Thus with those examples in mind we suggest the following form

$$P(N-R-k+1,\ldots,N-R) = P_0(N-R-k+1,\ldots,N-R) + (1-e^{-k/d})S \qquad (9)$$

i.e. the state N-R shall have the greatest proportion, $1-e^{-1/d}$, of the support from S. That something like this actually happens can be observed but of course the exact choice of expression and the exponent -k/d are a little difficult to explain in a concrete way.

As a consequence of the approximation in the unreserved system we also have

$$P_0(N-R) = EC_3 \qquad (10)$$

and

$$P_0(N-R+1,\ldots,N) = EC_2 \qquad (11)$$

Now by using the last five relations (7)-(11) and by putting k = 1 we obtain

$$S = E(C_2C_4-C_3)/(C_4+1-e^{-1/d}), \qquad (12)$$

when R > 0, and S = 0 when R = 0.

From (9) and (12) we get (1) and (2) for the case $z_1 = z_2 = 1$ by using our approximations of the probabilities of the particular states for which the two streams are blocked.

However, it is important to remember that this is an explanation of an approximation and not a proof of a theorem.

When the 1-slot (or even the d-slot) traffic has a peakedness factor $z_1 > 1(z_2>1)$ the total z will be changed but we still can use this Hayward-like approach since the Hayward model also works well to describe overflow-peaked traffic streams. The individual blocking probability for the 1-slot traffic is in this approximation model the probability of the states blocking that traffic multiplied by its peakedness factor z_1. This individual call/time congestion ratio can be well approximated by the peakedness factor for many typical cases in ordinary overflow theory with only 1-slot traffic streams, see e.g. [8], and thus we have suggested an extension of that use also to our method for this more general case.

So far we have roughly explained the approximations. Still it has to be pointed out that they are only meant to be used for certain typical cases with certain relations between the parameters. The limits between typical and untypical cases are not evident but here is a hint where the approximations are useful:

$N \geqslant 30$; $2 \leqslant d \leqslant 10$; $R < d$; $A < N$; $0.2 < p < 1$;

$z_1 \geqslant 1$; $0.001 \leqslant B_1, B_2 \leqslant 0.05$.

For essentially different cases one should be careful. Typical parameter combinations are given in the tables below.

If d is in the magnitude of 30 it seems that the approach of describing the variations of the total traffic stream with an average peakedness factor z doesn't always give the accuracy that is demanded.

When p = 0 only multiples of d are possible values for the distribution of the states but that fact is not taken into account in the approximation. Thus it should not be used when p is very close to 0.

Very small values of N compared to d is also a dangerous area for the approximation.

4.   A NUMERICAL EXAMPLE

We shall now study a typical example with $z_1 = 1$ for which we can compare the approximated values with exactly calculated results of the blocking probabilities. The example has the following parameter values

N = 94, A = 60, p = 0.6, z_1 = 1, d = 6, R = 0, 3, 5 and T = 1, 20.

In this example we have z = 3 and E = 0.0063.

Table 1			Blocking probabilities approx.	exact
R = 0		B_1	0.0018	0.0017
		B_2	0.0159	0.0150
R =3	T = 1	B_1	0.0057	0.0057
		B_2	0.0135	0.0130
	T = 20	B_1	0.0038	0.0038
		B_2	0.0121	0.0118
R = 5	T = 1	$B_1 = B_2$	0.0103	0.0100
	T = 20	$B_1 = B_2$	0.0059	0.0064

The most serious error is the case R = 5, T = 20 where the relative error is (0.593 - 0.638)/0.638 = - 7 %.

In terms of number of trunks at a GOS of B = 0.01 it means N = 90.5 instead of the exact value N = 91.0. However, this example should be used to illustrate the accuracy of the relations between the blocking probabilities for different R and T values. The accuracy of what E approximates may not be quite as good when (N, A, z) is far from (94, 60, 3). An error in this example in terms of N of ± 0.5 may in another example be 1 ± 0.5 for the different cases in it.

Note also that in the case T = 20 more total traffic is carried with R = 5 than with R = 0, since $\overline{B}_0$ = 0.00702, $\overline{B}_5$ = 0.00638

5. COMPARISON BETWEEN COMMON AND DEDICATED TRUNK GROUPS

We shall now give a number of examples where we compare the nearest N given $B_1 = B_2 \approx 0.01$ for a common trunk group where our formulae above are used and the corresponding N-value for the sum of two separate trunk groups dimensioned with Erlang or Hayward (in the case of $z_1=2$) methods. Since the examples are there to represent not only themselves but a number of similar cases in that area of the parameter room, we have chosen to dimension the separate 6-slot trunk group by the nearest integer to $6n_2+3$ and not by $6([n_2]+1)$ where n_2 is real valued such that $E(n_2,(1-p)A/6) = 0.01$.

By that we get rid of the extra variations caused by more or less luck in the roundings of the 6-slot trunk groups. In a few of our examples we shall also compare our approximate results with exact ones to indicate the magnitude of the errors in the approximations.

We shall explain one example. In all examples $d = 6$ and $B_1 = B_2 \approx 0.01$. For $A = 60$, $p = 0.5$, $z_1 = 1$ i.e. $R = 5$ we obtain with our formula $N = 97$ when $T = 1$ and $N = 92$ when $T = 20$. The corresponding exact results are $N = 97$ and $N = 93$ respectively i.e. our approximation is rather good here. The sum of the two dedicated trunk groups is $N_0 = 42 + 6 \cdot 10.8 + 3 = 110$ for both $T = 1$ and $T = 20$ and the savings $1 - N/110$ are 12 and 16 % respectively.

Table 2   Number of trunks for $B_1 = B_2 = 0.01$

d=6	p:prop. 1-slot traffic	N_1	N_{20}	N_0	$1-N_1/N_0$	$1-N_{20}/N_0$
A=30 z₁=1 R=5	0.90	51	50	60	0.15	0.17
	0.75	55	53	65	0.15	0.18
	0.50	60 (60)	56 (57)	69	0.13	0.19
	0.25	65	60	72	0.10	0.17
A=60 z₁=1 R=5	0.90	85	84	97	0.12	0.13
	0.75	90	87	103	0.13	0.16
	0.50	97 (97)	92 (93)	110	0.12	0.16
	0.25	103	97	112	0.08	0.13
A=60 z₁=2 R=3-4	0.90	92	91	103	0.11	0.12
	0.75	95	94	110	0.14	0.15
	0.50	100	98	116	0.14	0.16
	0.25	105	102	117	0.10	0.13
A=120 z₁=1 R=5	0.90	151	149	166	0.09	0.10
	0.75	157	153	175	0.10	0.13
	0.50	166 (166)	159 (160)	183	0.09	0.13
	0.25	175	165	187	0.06	0.12

6.   COMMENTS TO THE NUMERICAL RESULTS

The accuracy is rather good when d = 6. For the cases where we also have used an exact method we have obtained equal N_1-values when rounded to nearest integer and N_{20}-values which only are one unit lower with the approximative method than the exact one. However, when d > 10 e.g. d = 30 there are cases where the approximations are not very accurate and should not be used.

The change of z_1 from 1 to 2 does not change $N_0 - N_{20}$ or $N_0 - N_1$ (unless p < 0.5) very much i.e. the savings are not sensitive to the peakedness factor z_1. The fact that for each p-value $N_0 - N_{20}$ slowly increases and $(N_0-N_{20})/N_0$ slowly decreases as A runs from 30 over 60 to 120 gives us rather a good view of most of the interesting cases. Savings around 15 % are very typical when T = 20. There are always more savings if T = 20 than if T = 1.

Even though we have noted that our approximation is not always sufficiently accurate when d = 30, it is obvious that such cases could be interesting for comparison. Thus we have studied a few examples with the exact approach of the problem.

In all cases we have $B_1 = B_2 = 0.01$, $z_1 = 1$, d = 30, R = 29.

Table 3

A	p	N_1	N_{20}	N_0	$1-N_1/N_0$	$1-N_{20}/N_0$
60	0.50	174	165	185	0.06	0.11
120	0.25	273	269	291	0.06	0.08
120	0.50	255	242	275	0.07	0.12
240	0.25	437	421	456	0.04	0.08

As we can see there are some savings also when d=30 in particular when T=20. How important they are can be discussed by looking at the next table showing the additional trunks needed for the d-slot traffic for both the dedicated and the integrated cases, given an existing network for 1-slot traffic.

Let N_0'' be the d-slot trunks in N_0 and $A_1 = pA$, $A_2 = (1-p)A$

Table 4

A_1	A_2/d	N_0'' d = 30	$N_{20}-N_0$	N_1-N_0	N_0'' d = 6	$N_{20}-N_0$	N_1-N_0
30	1	143	-20	-11	29	-12	-10
60	2	200	-33	-20	40	-15	-13
30	3	249	-22	-18	50	-15	-12
60	6	381	-35	-19	76	-21	-15

We can see that even though 5 times as many trunks as in the case d = 6 is needed in the dedicated network when d = 30, we can only save twice as many by the integration when T = 20 and even less when T = 1. Thus in terms of percent of the total trunk group size the savings are essentially smaller when d = 30 than when d = 6 in the corresponding case. Note that the roundings are done as in section 5 i.e. N_0'' does not have to be a multiple of d.

7. POSSIBLE INTEGRATION SAVINGS IN A NETWORK

The main purpose of this paper is perhaps not the approximation method itself even though we have spent quite a lot of space trying to explain it. Certain modifications are of course always possible if one special quality e.g. simplicity, accuracy or generality should be regarded as more important than the others. However, the main reason for writing this paper is to answer some interesting questions concerning the advantages and disadvantages of integrating circuit switched traffic streams with different type of bandwidth.

To do so it was also important to have some tool to balance the individual blocking probabilities. One possibility is partial sharing policy as suggested in [9]. However, our choice here, which seems to give more carried traffic, particularly when $T = 20$, was to block one of the traffic streams when less than a certain number of trunks were free. With this complication of our loss system it was then evident that the blocking probabilities also were sensitive to the ratio of the mean service times, T. Since we only could find exact numerical results with great effort for a few special cases with Poissonian offered traffic streams, we found it necessary to suggest an approximation of the blocking probabilities including the parameters T and z_1, which can be said to be new in this paper. I think that the quality of the approximation in its present state is sufficient at least for the applications in this paper.

As a very typical possible application we have chosen the integration of telephone traffic (64 kbps) with that of a service we could call "video call", a video service without prebooking needing a bandwidth of 6 x 64 kbps. We are also assuming that it is possible, to a reasonable cost, to arrange the switching in a way that any 6 slots, not necessarily consecutive ones, are sufficient to carry such a video call. Today we have the service video-conferencing with prebooking, which needs 30 x 64 kbps per call but we know that it is now possible on 6 x 64 kbps to offer that particular picture quality, which in a way is accepted. We think that a less expensive video service without prebooking, which is used more informally, must be a demand.

The application is interesting because it concerns a great transmission volume, which is not the case with integrated circuit switched low bit rate data traffic streams of different types. That the ratio of the bandwidths is below 10 and that the traffic with lower bandwidth has a greater call intensity are also facts which make integration particularly suitable. Another possible application is of course videophone which would correspond to the case $d = 2$ (i.e. 2 x 64 kbps). For all these video services we have reason to believe the mean service time ratio, T, is rather of the magnitude 20 than near 1.

Now, how essential savings could this type of integration give in a realistic network? If the telephone network is of overflow type, then it is on the final choice trunk groups that the integration savings are of the interesting magnitude we have shown in our tables. If also the d-slot traffic network is of overflow type, then we need the extended version of our formulae including the parameter z_2. Thus by decomposition of our integrated network we have tools to dimension it as long as it does not include integrated high usage trunk groups. However, for simplicity let us assume that the telephone traffic has individual high usage trunk groups but their final choice trunk groups are integrated with the d-slot video traffic which has no overflow possibilities i.e. $z_2 = 1$.

With such an arrangement, what is the most typical case in Table 2? Well, it is always difficult to predict the traffic volume of a new service, but let us say that the case $A = 60$, $p = 0.75$, $z_1 = 2$ is typical. This means that to a final choice trunk group with 45 erlangs offered peaked telephone traffic is then also offered 2.5 video calls per busy hour with a mean holding time of 1 hour. I don't think this is an unrealistic size of the video call traffic at a time point when we have reached say 4000 (office) subscribers.

Now, we note that the savings are not very sensitive to some changes of the parameters. If z_1 is changed from 2 to 1 in our typical example the savings are still 16 trunks, if p is changed to 0.5 the savings are 18 and with a total A = 30 instead of 60 the savings for the corresponding p-values are around 12. Possibly it might be necessary to restrict the number of simultaneously carried video calls in order to avoid blocking periods for the telephone traffic, which are too much longer than in a dedicated network, but in most cases this is compensated in N with only one trunk. Thus it is not too much to say that an average saving on a trunk group is around 15 trunks or half a PCM-system.

However, talking in terms of PCM-systems or groups of 30 trunks the savings are not around 15 trunks on each integrated trunk group but rather uniformly distributed among the integers from 0 to 30 with an average of 15. Now, this last statement is only true if we compare with two dedicated trunk groups which have the possibility to share the last PCM-system in a fixed way. If we compare with the case of two totally separate trunk groups the additional savings are almost half a PCM-system due to double instead of single roundings to next multiple of 30. Thus we could say that the integration savings are almost 1 PCM-system per final choice trunk group in the telephone network. This could mean savings of the magnitude 500 PCM-systems in a network like the Swedish one.

Now, it is important to compare the costs of those trunk savings with the extra costs due to more complicated switching and processing e.g. to make sure that any 6 trunks (or at least any 6 trunks within the same PCM-system), not necessarily consecutive ones, can carry a video call.

My personal opinion is that for a considerable future time the costs and cost relations for PCM-systems (trunks), switching and processing will be such that with circuit switched integration of the type we have discussed, trunk savings will be larger than the extra costs due to more complicated switching and processing. I also think that the total savings will be of a magnitude which is economically interesting. An integration based on packet switching however will, in spite of the flexibility it offers, still cause too much extra costs for the high demand of processing capacity, at least if typical packets are rather small. Thus the ideas of this paper could be worth discussing.

REFERENCES

[1] Katzschner, L., Scheller, R., Probability of Loss of Data Traffics with Different Bit Rates Hunting One Common PCM Channel, Proc. 8th ITC Melbourne 1976.
[2] Lutton, J.L., Roberts, J.W., Traffic Performance of Multi-Slot Call Routing Strategies in an Integrated Service Digital Network, Proc. ISS84, Florence 1984.
[3] Roberts, J.W., Teletraffic Models for the Telecom 1 Integrated Services Network, Proc. 10th ITC, Montreal 1983.
[4] Kaufman, J., Blocking in a Shared Resource Environment, IEEE Trans Commun, Vol COM-29 No 10 (1981).
[5] Johnson, S.A., A Performance Analysis of Integrated Communications Systems, Br Telecom Technol. J. Vol 3 No 4 (1985).
[6] Conradt, J., Buchheister, A., Considerations on Loss Probability of Multi-Slot Connections, Proc. 11th ITC, Kyoto 1985.
[7] Fiche, G., Le Gall, P., Ricupero, S., Study of Blocking for Multislot Connections in Digital Link Systems, Proc. 11th ITC, Kyoto 1985.
[8] Lindberger, K., Simple Approximations of Overflow System Quantities for Additional Demands in the Optimization, Proc 10th ITC, Montreal 1983.
[9] Virtamo, J.T., Partial Sharing Access Control Policy in Switching Two Different Traffics in an Integrated Network, Techn. Research Centre of Finland (1986).

TRAFFIC ENGINEERING for ISDN Design and Planning
M. Bonatti and M. Decina (Editors)
Elsevier Science Publishers B.V. (North-Holland)
© IAC, 1988

DEMAND FORECASTING FOR NEW TELECOMMUNICATION SERVICES

J.-P. Dartois - CGE ALCATEL, Paris - France

M. Gruszecki - ALCATEL Bell Telephone, Antwerpen - Belgium

Abstract

Demand forecasting methodologies for new telecom services are at present being studied by researchers but very little has been published on the subject until now. This paper surveys the current situation concerning the utility of classical forecasting techniques for new services demand projection, new or improved methods under study and the transfer of useful techniques from outside the traditional ITC area of interest. In the absence of sufficient historical data needed to perform the forecast, the paper recommends the use of structured scenario alternatives as a planning and decision making support. The paper also states that demand projection for new services cannot be dissociated from the policy issue and the introduction strategy adopted by the Telecom Administration : a deliberate and convincing action can stimulate latent demand for a new service in a decisive way. A way to help the decision making process is to perform a structured analysis and assessment of forecasting uncertainties. This is described in the paper for the four main partners in the new services telecommunication market i.e. the Telecom Administrations, the manufacturers, the service providers and the users.

1. Introduction

Massive investments in modernizing and expanding the telecom networks of industrialized countries have been accompanied by a simultaneous rapid growth in traffic and hence in the Telecom Administrations* revenues. New telecom services, network digitalization, ISDN and broadband communication are promoted by the Administrations as a means of prolonging this fast growth once basic telephone demand has been satisfied, as will soon be the case in most industrialized countries. Likewise, the major telecom manufacturers are now in high gear as concerns the production capacities of modern digital equipment. The service providers, newcomers to the telecom market, are in a position to offer a large spectrum of new and attractive services. Last but not least, the users are becoming eager to discover and enjoy all the services offered, even if in most cases they are not fully aware of the nature of these services or of their need for them. In short, the time is ripe for major structural changes in telecommunications services. However, one important problem remains to be solved, namely the demand qualification and quantification for new telecom services. A question which is usually put to the telecom forecasting specialists.

Until the early 1970's, telecommunication forecasting was mostly concerned with telephone and telex services. Sufficient historical data (long time series) were available to perform forecasts using classical techniques. These techniques are at present well established and documented by extensive literature, including many excellent papers presented at the ITC Congresses, and supported by powerful informatic tools.

The situation for new or future services is quite different. Although demand forecasting is being studied by researchers, very little has been published to date. The methodologies used by the specialized consulting bureaus are usually kept confidential.

The difficulties arise from the following :

a) There is usually little or no historical data available.

b) The accelerating pace of technological innovation in computing and telecommunication has created a multitude of competing services. For instance, message communication may take the form of telex, facsimile, teletex, photo-videotex, etc.

* The term «Telecom Administration» is used in a broad sense : they are either government-controlled or operating in a «deregulated» environment.

c) The potential success of new telecom services is strongly influenced by the service introduction policy adopted by the Telecom Administrations.

d) The overall picture is very volatile, the forecasting must consider not only the sustained growth but also the possibility of failure for some of the competing services.

Demand forecasting which is more concerned with the identification of possible outcomes rather than with understanding what **is** or what **was** is expected to provide :

*   a systematic method to examine future developments and their interactions;

*   a context in which proposals can be evaluated for decision making;

*   if possible, advice about the optimum choice among possible alternatives.

The authors reviewed a large number of papers on forecasting to assess the utility of currently used methods and techniques for new telecom demand forecasting, including some from outside the traditional ITC interest area.

The classical forecasting techniques briefly discussed in the following section, can very roughly be subdivided into a) purely judgmental or intuitive approaches, b) explanatory methods such as causal or regression models, c) time series (extrapolative) methods, d) combinations of the above.

The scenario technique, usually classified among judgement methods, is discussed separately, since the structured scenario technique is viewed as a very interesting framework for using classical and new techniques supported by modern informatic tools.

2. Utility of classical methods for new telecom services forecasting

From the broad spectrum of available techniques, we have selected a few that are likely to be used for new services demand prognoses.

2.1. Judgement methods

Under the generic name of «Judgement Methods», the text books on forecasting usually consider such methods as Naive Extrapolation, Jury of Executive Opinion, Delphi Technique, Historical Analogy, etc. All these methods have one element in common, namely they rely heavily on the subjective judgement of the analysts rather than on quantitative models and methods.

Hogarth and Makridakis [1] performed an evaluation of the judgement methods, comparing initial forecasts in various branches of economy, business and finance with their outturn.

The conclusions of this evaluation are pessimistic. Long and medium range forecasts and planning based on judgement alone are notoriously inaccurate, they very often miss the turning points and compare badly even with results of simple quantitative models and methods. The judgement methods apparently lack the necessary discipline and structured approach and are vulnerable to subjective bias. These conclusions however, require a certain graduation : group judgement, e.g. Delphi panel, usually outperforms single person judgement; few exceptions have been observed.

To our knowledge such an evaluation has not been done for the telecom demand, as judgement methods were seldom used for telephone demand forecasting. In the absence of this evaluation, the judgement and intuitive methods should be used with the greatest care for new telecom services.

2.2. Market testing, User and Industrial Market Survey

Market testing is the usual way of compensating for the lack of sufficient historical data concerning new services or products. In its classical version, market testing / survey considers the responses of representative buyers (i.e. potential users of new services) to service offerings, tested and extrapolated to estimate the products future prospects.

In a recent article [12], a description is given of a sophisticated way of testing subscriber perceptions and preferences for new telecom services. In the first step, subscriber preferences for non-price features of new and existing services are quantified in order to identify market segments that value the same features.

The second step models how subscribers trade-off the valued features with the price of the service. This trade-off is then combined with the subscriber's monthly bills to produce an estimate of aggregate demand and is validated in a study of the demand for new digital data services. Finally, the third step involves tracking the actual demand for a new service after it has been deployed in order to quantify the uncertainty associated with the demand estimate obtained in step two.

If the quantification of uncertainty on the demand estimate cannot be obtained (e.g. because the service has not been deployed yet), the market testing results should be treated with great caution.

Example of Videotex market testing

In the early stages of videotex market testing, the reactions of potential residential users in several European and North American countries showed a very similar pattern. Residential users usually responded enthusiastically to the concept - the promise - of videotex, and then showed the same reluctance to spend more than 10 $ or so a month on terminals and access services. Trial users reacted in essentially the same way : they used the services heavily (free-of-charge) for the first months - often on accessing games - then their use of and interest in the service dropped significantly. If the service features that meet their personal needs (and can deliver tangible benefits in lifestyle improvement, enjoyment and cost saving) are not readily available at this stage, they abandon the service and even ask for the terminals to be removed (see e.g. [8]).

Data obtained with Industrial Market Survey are similar to those of consumer surveys but fewer, more knowledgeable industrial and Telecom Administrations subjects are sampled, resulting in a more informed evaluation.

2.3 Formal forecasting methods (time series)

Out of a considerable number of formal forecasting methods presently available, we have selected 5 major time series methods to present a summary and very brief comparison. The comparison in table 1 is based on the book written by Makridakis et. al. [18], which describes the results of a competition among 24 time series methods to determine their accuracy in handling 1001 and 111 different time series from various branches of economy, business, etc.

	Box-Jenkins	Single exponential smoothing	(Levandowski's) FORSYS	Bayesian model	Linear trend (regression fit)
Time span	Short term (Medium and long term in the framework of appropriate scenario alternatives)				
Inputs	Substantial data needed				Few
Mean absolute % error MAPE*	22	15	14	23	21
Number of times method was best or second best*	8	19	55	24	
Degree of complexity	High	Low	High	High	Low
Manual intervention required**	Yes	No	No	Yes	No

*   Results of the contest
**   In addition to running the computer program

Table 1   Comparison of 5 time series methods

The empirical study reported in [18] can be very helpful for selecting a formal method appropriate in a specific case depending on the time span of forecasting, type of data and required accuracy measures.

Model fitting and forecasting, beyond the existing data used to develop the model are different problems. Minimizing the model-fitting errors does not guarantee fewer errors in forecasting unless the assumption of constancy holds. This assumption is central in any statistical method and extremely important in forecasting : structural changes in data must not occur if the model-fitting results are to be accurately extrapolated beyond existing data.

In the take-off process of new telecom services we can expect structural shifts, changes of attitudes, policy interventions by the Telecom Administrations, etc. It is therefore very important that the formal methods for new services forecasting are used directly only in cases and in time horizons for which the constancy of data can be assumed and beyond this assumption in the framework of appropriate scenario alternatives. This is shown in table 1, indicating «short term» time span for the direct applicability of the different methods and «medium and long term» in combination with scenario alternatives.

Methods discussed in table 1 :

Box-Jenkins :

A complex and elegant forecasting method in which linear stochastic equations describe the behaviour of a time series. It assumes that the given series X_t is such that it can be reduced to stationarity by differencing a finite number of times d (d positive integer) so that $W_t = (1 - B)^d X_t$ is stationary. B is a back-shift operator on the index of the time series with $BX_t = X_{t-1}$, $B^2X_t = X_{t-2}$ and so on. W_t is a mixed autoregressive-moving average process :
$$(1 - \Phi_1 B - \Phi_2 B^2 - ..... - \Phi_p B^p) W_t = \Theta_0 + (1 - \Theta_1 B - \Theta_2 B^2 - ..... - \Theta_2 B^q) a_t$$
(a_t's are a sequence of identically distributed uncorrelated deviates referred to as «white noice»).

Combining the above relations yields the basic Box-Jenkins model for non-seasonal time series
$$(1 - \Phi_1 B - \Phi_2 B^2 - ..... - \Phi_p B^p) (1 - B)^d X_t = \Theta_0 + (1 - \Theta_1 B - \Theta_2 B^2 - ..... - \Theta_2 B^q) a_t,$$
which is said to represent an autoregressive integrated moving average process of order (p, d, q) denoted as ARIMA (p, d, q) [30].

Single exponential smoothing :

$$\text{Model fitting } \hat{X}_{t+1} = \alpha X_t + (1 - \alpha) \hat{X}_t$$

(α is choosen to minimize Σe^2, the mean square error, summing is over t from 1 to n − m).

$$\text{Forecasting } \hat{X}_{n-m+k} = \alpha X_{n-m} + (1 - \alpha) \hat{X}_{n-m+k-1}$$

FORSYS (Levandowski's) :

Forecasting system in which time series X_t is decomposed into trend M_t, seasonality S_t, influence of special actions Ψ_t, influence of independent exogenous variables E_t, $\mathcal{E}_t$ random noice.
$$X_t = f (M_t, S_t, \Psi_t, E_t, \mathcal{E}_t)$$
Predictions are obtained through a search among trend alternatives until one is found that minimizes the forecasting error [29].

Bayesian model :

Iterative forecasting starting with a subjectively specified prior for the mean level of the time series, the growth and seasonal factors. A new observation is used to update the priors and generate new forecasts [18].

Linear regression trend fitting :

Model fitting $\hat{X}_t = a + bt$
Forecasting $\hat{X}_{n-m+k} = a + b (n-m+k)$

2.4. Causal models

In the present context causal models refer to models, methods and relations which explicitly take into account proven economic, demographic or other variables to formulate mathematically (as is done in natural sciences) their effect on the demand for telecommunication services. A good example of causal models applied to telecommunications are the models of Böhm [4] developed for telephone main station demand and presented at several ITC congresses.

In this approach, telephone demand is disaggregated into homogeneous market segments (e.g. residential, business, etc.) and the behaviour of each sector is determined by empirical means, e.g. sample surveys and measurements. A well-known causal relation established by Böhm concerns the residential telephone demand. This relation links the disposable household income E and the average telephone penetration p

$$p = \int_0^\infty p(E)\, \varphi(E)\, dE$$

where $\varphi(E)dE$ is the proportion of households with an income between E and E + dE and p(E) penetration as a function of income E.

To our knowledge, no causal relations for new telecom services have been published to date. In our opinion it is of great importance that these relations are studied and established to improve the understanding of the success/failure mechanism for these services. For instance, considerable experience and history is available for the Videotex services. We believe that it should be possible to develop causal relations linking the demand and success of Videotex with the establishment of initial user base, availability of a large spectrum of services etc. (see the insert «The success story of Teletel/Minitel - Keys to success»).

3. Structured scenario technique

In its classical form, the scenario technique* considers smoothly unfolding narratives that describe an assumed future expressed through a sequence of time frames or snapshots. Khan and Wiener defined the scenarios as follows : «Scenarios are hypothetical sequences of events constructed for the purpose of focusing attention on causal processes and decision points. They answer two types of questions : a) How might some hypothetical situation arise, step by step ? b) What alternatives exist, for each actor, at each step, to prevent, divert or facilitate the process ?» [7].

In our approach we consider the scenario alternatives (as all forecasts) not as a «Knowledge base» but rather as a system of conjectures and anticipations which cannot in principle be fully justified, but which will be used as a working hypothesis as long as they can withstand tests and contradicting evidence. We will not claim that these scenarios are «true», «more or less certain» or even «probable». By creating scenarios we strive to enlarge our understanding of uncertainties, and create new - more realistic visions of the future.

Note that the classical scenarios, as all verbal theories, may be rich in contents and possess a high potential for describing in a vivid manner the possible alternatives, but they cannot be systematically analysed since no method for doing this is known at present.

The addition of a structuring and consistency checking mechanism, provides the scenario alternatives with a formal framework which defines precisely the considered events, time spans and quantification parameters. The formal part of the scenarios can therefore be analysed. Scenarios defined in this way can also be empirically tested as the considered services are deployed.

These structured scenarios are developed in three steps (see figure 1) :

a) First generation scenarios

The first generation scenarios are quantified narratives derived from expert opinions concerning specific new services, elicited from e.g. a Jury of Expert Opinion, Delphi panel, planning by the Telecom Administrations, results of Industrial Market Surveys, etc. [5].

These scenarios state the prevailing opinions of managers and experts concerning 1) the obvious and predetermined tendencies, 2) uncertainties for specific services, 3) inputs available (demographic, economical, existing telecom services data, etc.), 4) technological feasibility and assessment.

In emphasizing only the obvious issues and uncertainties, these scenarios often lead to simplistic and conflicting strategic solutions and are not useful for making decisions. The goal of these explanatory scenarios is not action but understanding. They are useful and intended as a starting point to ask better questions, understand the complexity of issues and prepare the decision scenarios. They also form the necessary link to second generation scenarios through which the managers can recognize their original opinions.

---

* Note that in fact all forecasting methods use some sort of scenario in an implicit (unconscious) or explicit form (for example a simple logistic function used for forecasting the service take-off assumes that the service will develop smoothly until reaching saturation and hence excludes the possibility of a non-success or failure).

b)   Second generation (decision) scenarios

The second generation scenarios are structured and quantified alternatives for decision making.

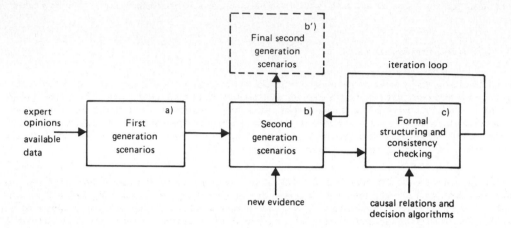

Fig. 1   Scenario generation process

The process shown above starts as follows :

1)   The first generation scenarios are transformed into the required format. All states, actions, events and consequences are represented in a parametrical way. The initial, intermediate and terminal states (time horizons) are indicated. If a narrative of the first generation scenario cannot be readily represented in a parametric form, it is transformed into quantified linguistic variables.

2)   The formal structure of second generation scenarios presents a framework in which a preliminary consistency check can be made : i.e. are all the required data available, if not - which new evidence is required, are there any contradictions within a specific alternative ?

3)   The quantification technique for each alternative is indicated.

4)   Input data and border conditions are specified (e.g. saturation value for the demand of a new service).

The above procedure is performed manually and provides the input for the iterative procedure using a specialised processor c). Each time new evidence comes in, the iteration loop is repeated. The final second generation scenarios are analysed and stored in b').

c)   Formal structuring, consistency checking and quantification processor

The above processor handles the alternatives one by one and comprises the following :

1)   Quantification tools (e.g. regression analysis program, time series processor, causal demand relations, etc.).

2)   Consistency checking mechanism (e.g. cross-impact analysis cf. section 5).

3)   Decision algorithms and causal relations between events (if available) comprised in an alternative. In the absence of such algorithms or relations, simple heuristic decision rules.

After analysis of each alternative, a comparison of alternatives is attempted, if the appropriate decision process can be defined.

The main effort in future studies will be directed towards testing and refinement of the scenario technique, namely building up the experience in construction, verification, consistency checking and practical application of scenarios for new services.

A practical example of Videotex introduction scenario has been presented at the seminar*.

---

*   A copy of the presentation can be obtained from the authors upon request.

4. The policy issue

The evolution of ISDN and new services in the foreseable future will largely depend on a complex set of relationships involving the Telecom Administration (bearer network providers), manufacturers, service providers and users (fig. 2).

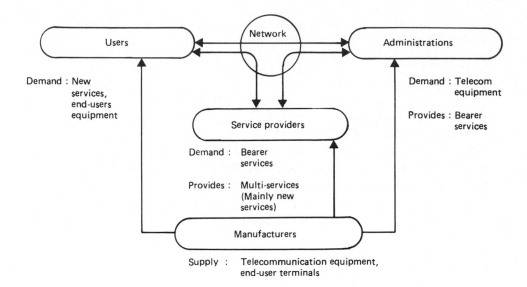

Fig. 2   Mayor players in the telecommunication market for new services

The decision making process in the telecom sector is at present characterised and complicated by the great fluidity of the socio-economic environment, rapid technological evolution in communication and computing (and their synergism) and uncertainties as concerns user demand [10].

An example of the decisive role of the policy issue is given in the insert «The success story of the French Teletel/Minitel».

The success story of Teletel/Minitel in France

By mid-86, the French public switched telephone network (PSTN) and thousands of Teleservice providers served about two million Teletel/Minitel subscribers, ten times as many as the worldwide total of all other networks. A success with both residential and business users, France's videotex is experiencing a rapid self-sustained market growth with a steady rise of the number of new users, per-terminal traffic and rapid increase of services offered to users.

Keys to success

a) *French Telecom Administration had enough faith in videotex to distribute cheap, easy to use terminals free-of-charge to users. In this way it quickly obtained a large user base, thus avoiding the situation prevalent in other countries in which service and bearer network providers hesitate to invest until there are enough users to guarantee profits, while potential users hesitate to acquire terminals until the services they need are available.*

b) *The Administration introduced «Kiosk-mode» charging. In this method, users pay for videotex calls on their ordinary telephone bills and the Telecom Administration hands over a proportion of the collected sums to remunerate the service providers. Therefore, there are no passwords, subscription fees or direct billing by the service providers, the public is usually apprehensive to accept.*

c) *Large spectrum of Teletel services offered to users : the Telecom Administration initiated the take-off and rapid increase of services by offering free-of-charge the electronic directory services EDS, a truly mass market on-line information service. Free distribution of the EDS has allowed millions of users to become familiar with Minitel and explore the world of videotex. As of June '86 there were some 3,000 on-line services receiving hundreds of thousands of calls every day.*

d) *The information retrieval via Teletel can be mastered by anybody with no need for special training.*

e) *User terminals are connected to the PSTN while most host computers (servers) are attached to the Transpac packet switched network with interfacing between the two networks assured by videotex gateways [11].*

In this way, a deliberate and convincing action by the Telecom Administration stimulated in a decisive way the demand for Teletel.

The French introduction policy of videotex is presently the only demonstration of how to solve the «critical mass» problem in the case of new telecom services. A clear lesson for forecasters is that demand projection for new services cannot be dissociated from the policy issue and introduction strategy adopted by the Administration.

The answers to some of the above questions and problems may be found by presenting uncertainties in a structured way and assessing these uncertainties.

The main uncertainties facing the four players in figure 2 are briefly reviewed as follows :

• Telecom Administration :
  - socio-economic environment and the budget which can be allocated to new services, ISDN and broadband communication;
  - acceptance of new services by the users;
  - technological developments and competition between services;
  - interconnectivity with external networks and standardisation of protocols;
  - tariff policy and charging strategy.

• Manufacturers and service providers (in addition to the above) face the following :
  - timing of the development cycle in accordance with the introduction policy for new services as adopted by the Administration;
  - prices and competition;
  - capacity to develop user-friendly terminal equipment and services;
  - technological breakthroughs.

• Users
  - capacity to cover all expenses related to the use of services;
  - ability to use the proposed services and terminal equipment easily and efficiently.

The presentation of uncertainties in a structured way may be obtained by using :

- structured scenario alternatives (cf. section 3);
- strategies for the implementation of new services, which spread the risks [27];
- traffic models for design choices of new system architectures, especially ISDN.
  M. Bonatti has presented a special study on this subject [13] during the previous ITC seminar held in Brussels in 1986.

Facing the above uncertainties and challenges implies that :

- telecom systems and networks are designed in such a way that errors in planning new services do not lead to major economic penalties, and that

- decisions concerning the implementations of switching systems and networks taken today constrain as little as possible the introduction of new services tomorrow.

The above objectives can only be attained by using «future safe» design that will allow ISDN, new value-added service modules and technological innovations to be introduced in a gradual way while retaining the fundamental architectures of digital switching systems and networks presently being installed (see e.g. [25, 26]).

Assessment of uncertainties and their consequences is an essential element in any purposeful planning and decision making. Demand forecasts for telecom services are usually followed up by checking their outturn, which can serve a posteriori for the assessment of the forecasting methods used and the actual forecast. Except for the above way of assessing a posteriori the uncertainty (and accuracy) of specific forecasting methods or just given forecasts, we usually do not have appropriate formal models according to which the probability of uncertain events could be computed. As a consequence, the assessment of uncertainties is often based on judgement of experts, assessment of forecasting methods and causal relations. This does not mean that no guidelines can be given on how to improve the assessment of the uncertainties process.

A number of remarkable studies have recently been published indicating how to perform forward or backward inferences, avoid biases, anchoring in the assessment of subjective probability distributions, misconceptions of regression, etc. [22], [23], [24]. These studies certainly deserve our full attention and are placed at the top of the list for further studies. One of the most urgent studies is the quantification of cost risks implied by overdimensioning the facilities and bearer network in case the actual demand for new services falls short of the forecast, and inversely the assessment of risk involved in underdimensioning the facilities i.e. grade of service degradation, loss of revenue, consequences of subscriber dissatisfaction, etc.

5.   Other methods

This section reviews a number of useful techniques which escaped the classifications of preceding sections.

5.1.   Cross-impact analysis

In its simplest form, cross-impact analysis is a procedure for probabilistic modelling an interdependent set of events and their impact on the forecast.

Given a subject whose future is to be explored and planned for, major potential occurrencies $O_1, O_2, ...O_i...$ which would make a substantial difference to its future are identified (see section 3.).

A cross-impact matrix (x_{ij}) containing estimates x_{ij} is constructed to indicate how one such occurrence O_i would affect the probability of any other occurrence O_j, in the set under consideration. The cross-impact model is a scenario alternative generator which in each run produces a scenario (a sequence of event occurrencies) that is plausible and consistent, given the probability and cross-impact effects among the events. The ability to add information that was not part of the prior information makes the interactive cross-impact model an open-ended technique for explanatory policy analysis. This capability is lacking in other analytical methods. The cross-impact analysis received considerable attention and was researched in the past few years, and is still surrounded by a certain controversy concerning the use of conditional probability and the Bayes theorem in the context of modelling the impact of future events. In cross-impact analysis, one is concerned about the probability that **a will** happen if **b happens** first. In classical probability, one asks for the probability that **a has** happened conditional on the fact that **b has** happened [19] [20].

We believe that this technique should be used in conjunction with the structured scenario technique and in this context it substantially improves the consistency of the forecasts. It does not remove the necessity of searching for causal relations governing the demand for new services.

5.2.   Growth and substitution patterns

Growth phenomena have been extensively studied in various fields of natural sciences such as biology, ecology and others. Logistic growth or Fisher-Pry functions have been successfully applied in many different cases to explain and predict among others the technological substitution. An original way of using the logistic model is discussed in a paper presented at this symposium [27]. Fisher and Pry [28] observed that once a substitution of the old service by the new one has progressed as far as a few percent, it usually proceeds to completion along a logistic curve $f/(1-f) = \exp(\alpha t + \beta)$, where t is a unit of time, α and β constants, f is the fractional market share of the new service and $1-f$ that of the old one.

The logistic and substitution functions may also provide simple and robust models for new telecom services forecasting. Here we consider a) representing substitution models for new telecom services covering both telecom and non-telecom services, the latter often providing a source of traffic for new services and b) growth models of existing services and diversion to new ones. Once established, these services may grow in a similar way to existing ones.

Fig. 3 shows a few typical growth patterns which could be of interest for new telecom services projection.

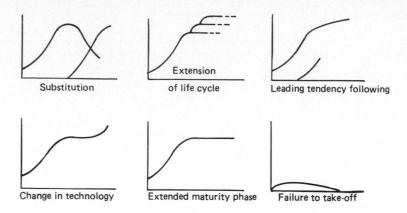

Fig. 3   Typical growth patterns

6.   Concluding remarks

In the preceding sections we expressed our belief that the time is ripe for major structural changes in the telecommunication services. The pace of progress and the way new services introduction will come about will largely depend on the introduction policy adopted by the concerned Telecom Administrations.

Knowing that uncertainty will be inherent in all forecasting and planning of new services, telecom systems and networks should be designed in such a way that errors in planning new services should not lead to major economic penalties.

The telecom manufacturers can promote the introduction of new services by delivering tolerant and «future safe» systems that will allow ISDN, new value-added service modules and technology innovations to be introduced in a gradual way while retaining the fundamental architecture of digital switching systems and networks presently being installed.

Demand forecasting for new telecom services should use structured and formal forecasting models in all cases in which the assumption of constancy of initial data holds, and beyond this assumption should use the framework of structured scenario technique.

7. REFERENCES AND BIBLIOGRAPHY

[1]   Hogarth R.M., Makridakis S.,
      «Forecasting and Planning : An Evaluation»
      Management Science, Vol. 27, No. 2, Febr. '81

[2]   Popper K.R.,
      «The Logic of Scientific Discovery»
      Hutchinson Publ. Co., London 1968

[3]   Martino J.P.,
      «Technological Forecasting for Decision
      Making»
      Elsevier Science Publ. Co., Amsterdam 1983

[4]   Böhm E. et al.,
      «Causal Models for Forecasting Telephone
      Services by Market Sectors»
      Proceedings of the 9th ITC, Torremolinos 1979

[5]   Wack P.,
      «Scenarios : Uncharted Waters Ahead»
      Harvard Business Review, Vol. 63, No. 5,
      Sept.-Oct. 1985

[6]   Naylor D.,
      «Scenarios for European Telecommunications»
      EURO VIII Conference, Lisbon 1986

[7]   Kahn H., Wiener A.,
      «The Year 2000»
      MacMillan, New York 1967

[8]   The Butler Cox Report Series
      «Videotex in Europe»
      Butler Cox & Partners Ltd., London, 1985

[9]   Eurodata Foundation
      «Data Communications in Europe
      1983-1991»

[10] Pernin J.-L., Schwartz A.Y.,
      «ISDN Evolution in France : An Existing
      All-Digital Plant Driven by the will to Innovate»
      Proceedings ISDN conference, June 1986,
      Online Intern., London-New York 1986

[11] Maury J.P.
      «Télétel au quotidien. Les choix du succès»
      Revue Française des Télécommunications,
      Juillet 1986

[12] Jennings D.L. et al.,
      «Techniques for Estimating Demand for New
      Services and Assessing Forecast Uncertainty»
      Proceedings IIIrd Intern. Network
      Planning Symposium «Networks 86»,
      «June 1 - 6, 1986, Innisbrook - Florida»

[13] Bonatti M. and Roveri A.,
      «A traffic Model for Design Choices of ISDN
      System Architectures»
      IVth ITC Specialists Seminar on ISDN Traffic
      Issues, Brussels,
      May 5 - 7, 1986

[14] Marchetti C.,
      «The Future»
      Seminar of the Italian Physical Society,
      Varenna, Italy, June-July 1986
      (see also document of the International
      Institute of Applied System Analysis,
      A-2361 Laxenbourg, Austria)

[15] Linstone H.A., Murray T.,
      «The Delphi Method : Techniques and
      Applications»
      Addison - Welsley, Reading, MA, 1975

[16] Makridakis S. et al.,
      «Forecasting : Methods and Applications»
      (2nd ed.)
      J. Willey & Sons, N.Y. 1983

[17] SAS Institute Inc.,
      «SAS/ETC User Guide 5th ed. and SAS User
      Guide : Statistics 5th ed.»
      SAS Inst. Inc., Cary, NC 2751-8000, 1984
      and 1985.

[18] Makridakis S., et. al.,
      «Forecasting Accuracy of Major Time Series
      Methods»
      J. Wiley, Chichester, 1984

[19] Helmer O.,
      «Reassessment of Cross-Impact Analysis»
      Futures, Oct. 1981

[20] Enzer S., Alter S.,
      «Cross-Impact Analysis and Classical Prob-
      ability»
      Futures, June 1978

[21] Enzer S.,
      «Interax - An Interactive Model for Studying
      Future Business Environments : Part I and II»
      Technological Forecasting and Social Change,
      Vol. 17, 1980

[22] Kahneman D. et. al. (eds.),
      «Judgement Under Uncertainty : Heuristics
      and Biases»
      Cambridge University Press, Cambridge,
      Mass., 1982

[23] Humphrey P., et. al. (eds.),
      «Analysing and Aiding Decision Process»
      North-Holland, Amsterdam, 1983

[24] Tversky A.,
      «Assessing Uncertainty»
      J. of Royal Statistical Society, n° 2, 1974

[25] Gimpelson L.A., Treves S.R.,
      «Telecommunication Networks Beyond ISDN
      Transport»
      Electrical Communication, vol. 59, n° 1/2,
      1985

[26] Gimpelson L.A.,
      «ISDN and value-added services in public and
      private networks»
      Proceedings of the 11th ITC Congress, Kyoto,
      1985

[27] Gonzalez Soto O.,
      «Planning ISDN : a structured view and key
      results»
      5th ITC Seminar, Lake Como, May 1987

[28] Fisher J.C., Pry R.,
      «A simple substitution model of technological
      change»
      Technological Forecasting and Social Change,
      vol. 3, 1971

[29] Lewandowski R.,
      «La prévision à Court Terme»
      Dunod, Paris, 1979

[30] Box E.P., Jenkins G.M.,
      «Time series analysis : forecasting and
      control»
      Holden-Day, San Francisco, 1976

TRAFFIC ENGINEERING for ISDN Design and Planning
M. Bonatti and M. Decina (Editors)
Elsevier Science Publishers B.V. (North-Holland)
© IAC, 1988

Subscriber Traffic in ISDN — The Key Questions

V.A. Bolotin, J.G. Kappel

Bell Communications Research, Red Bank, New Jersey, U.S.A.

In this paper we discuss some of the subscriber traffic analyses needed for pre-cutover and post-cutover engineering in ISDN. Specifically, subscriber traffic models important for circuit-switched facility provisioning are discussed.

A new model of subscriber traffic variability is described. The model reconciles different approaches to traffic variability among and within subscriber groups of limited size by extracting the "pure" group-to-group variability component from the combined group and day variation of subscriber line load.

Forecasting for traffic engineering of data communications services as part of the ISDN services is discussed. It is shown that attempts to forecast traffic on the basis of the total exchange data load (or data load per subscriber line) would lead to significant errors. Two major components, penetration of data services, and data traffic characteristics, should be forecast independently and then combined in the ISDN data traffic forecast.

Other open questions are discussed: data traffic call types, measurements, busy period analysis and potential service standard problems.

1. Problems of Subscriber Traffic Modeling in ISDN

1.1 Subscriber Traffic Data in Traditional Telephony

For traditional telephone networks with voice connections, most traffic engineering methods are well established. Factors that are considered in the subscriber traffic analysis and engineering are:

- Subscriber line usage and calling rate analysis for engineering including:
    - geographical area, class of service mix and time of day variability
    - day-to-day, group-to-group and year-to-year variability
    - forecasting
    - measurements
- Other topics, such as:
    - balancing load at the switch line group level
    - busy period analysis
    - grade of service standards

Methodologies for analysis of all these topics with respect to voice subscriber traffic are well developed in many countries. The topics from the above list have been discussed in various publications, most of the information being available in the proceedings of the ITC congresses. In the next section, we overview methodology problems for analysis of all these topics with respect to ISDN traffic.

1.2 ISDN Subscriber Traffic Analysis

The introduction of ISDN may be similar to the introduction of the touch-tone service in the USA, except for a scale factor. In the early years, primarily high usage subscribers will buy ISDN terminals. As the variety and usefulness of services provided over ISDN increases and terminal costs come down, more subscribers with normal traffic levels will buy the service. The average usage per ISDN line will decrease or level off over time, though of course not to the old exchange average usage, since the new services will stimulate more and varied types of traffic. Residential subscriber penetration will come later than business. Before we develop and accept practical engineering models for the ISDN networks we need to study the new types of traffic in detail.

For some years we will be observing ISDN traffic as a transient phenomenon with respect to specific characteristics (calling rate, usage, holding time) and to the total amount of traffic generated by ISDN subscribers. This will be a period of detailed studies of the new types of traffic and of engineering model development.

With respect to the geographical area, class of service mix and time of day shown in the list of factors in section 1.1, ISDN traffic may be measured and characterized the same way as voice traffic[1] and [2]. An emphasis here should be on the data component of subscriber traffic, and the analysis would be better if directed to the data traffic increment to the voice traffic component on B-channels. Possible changes in the stable pre-ISDN volume of the voice traffic might be observed, too.

In modern digital switches, relatively small ISDN line groups may be served by B-channel concentrators common to non-ISDN and ISDN line groups. Therefore a greater degree of imbalance than that for traditional traffic is to be expected. Even for traditional traffic, group-to-group variability and its relation to day-to-day variability has not been analyzed as a general phenomenon. We discuss this problem in section 2, where we demonstrate an approach that allows for quantitative separation of the day and group variability. In this discussion, analysis of traffic variability is applied mostly to line groups with effective load balancing. The methodology, however, is suitable for a generalized approach. It can be applied to cases of significant imbalance relevant both to voice line groups without load balancing but, especially, to ISDN line groups.

Section 3 emphasizes forecasting for traffic engineering of data communications services as part of ISDN services. It is shown that attempts to forecast traffic on the basis of the total exchange data load (or data load per subscriber line) would lead to serious underprovisioning or overprovisioning of ISDN switching equipment. Therefore two major components of the ISDN data traffic, penetration of data services, and data traffic characteristics, should be forecast independently and then combined in the ISDN data traffic forecast.

Section 4 contains a short discussion of some open questions in ISDN subscriber traffic analysis including measurements.

2. Group and Day Variability of Subscriber Traffic

2.1 Motivation

There exist different possible definitions of group-to-group variability, each intended to fit its own application. For instance, a group randomly chosen from the general subscriber line population will have its overall long-term average load - the average of the fixed hour load over all days of the year. In this case, group variability is the variability of this average among all groups. Limiting the set of days by, e.g., 60 weekdays of the average busy season (ABS) one obtains the ABS average. In this case, group variability would be defined as the variability of the ABS average load. It would be used to estimate how the quality of service characterized by the average ABS load differs from group to group and how bad this "average" service could be in groups with extremely large ABS load. Another definition would arise, if one is interested in group-to-group variability of the week's (5 day) average, or 10-day average, or 20-day average etc., which is relevant when once-a-week (two weeks', four weeks' etc.) load balancing is considered (see, e.g.,[3]). Neither of these definitions helps to describe the day-to-day variability of service quality within a single group, a characteristic important for line switching unit engineering.

In this section, a universal model is developed. The model makes it possible to reconcile different approaches to traffic variability among and within subscriber groups by extracting "pure" group-to-group variability component from the combined group and day variation of subscriber line load.

The load of subscriber line groups varies both from group to group and from day to day. Generally, the measured load has both variability components in it. To separate them from each other, one could increase the group size, thus asymptotically decreasing the group-to-group variability. On the other hand, one could perform a series of group-to-group variability studies with one day loads, thus eliminating the day-to-day variability. Hence it is natural to define the day-to-day variability as day-to-day distribution of the general population load average and to define the group-to-group variability as group-to-group distribution of one day (usually fixed hour) load. In terms of these definitions, the generally accepted notion of group-to-group variability as the variability of the ten-hour or fifteen-hour averages among groups of the same size is in fact a superposition of the two variability types.

2.2 Group-to-Group and Day-to-Day Variability

Let $L(y)$ be the c.d.f. of line usage Y, i.e., **the distribution of one-hour one-line load** in a given population of lines. For simplicity, we shall consider a case of one service class.

With respect to a n-line group load, an n-fold convolution of $L(y)$ with itself

$$G_n(y) = L^{n*}(y) \tag{2-1}$$

is the **group-to-group variation distribution.**

Consider a set of hours formed by the same hour of many days. Generally, **parameters of** $L(y)$ **are different for different days.** This is because the total one-hour load in the whole population of lines varies from day to day, so that at least the mean value of $L(y)$ varies from day to day. In general, the variance of $L(y)$ should vary from day to day, too. Being a convolution of $L(y)$, $G_n(y)$ **varies from day to day,** too. To distinguish these single day distributions from each other, we consider a family of distribution functions $L(x,y)$ or $G_n(x,y)$ depending on a parameter x. If this parameter is a random variable X, its c.d.f. $D(x)$ is a **day-to-day variation distribution.** In this paper, we assume that the random parameter x is the average total population line usage on a given day:

$$\int y \cdot dL(x,y) = x, \quad \int y \cdot dG_n(x,y) = n \cdot x .\tag{2-2}$$

2.3 Day-to-Day Variability of Subscriber Group Load

The c.d.f of the day-to-day variability of an n-line subscriber group load is

$$F_n(y) = \int G_n(x,y) \cdot dD(x) .\tag{2-3}$$

Its expected value $E(Y_n)$ is equal to $n \cdot E(X)$ where $E(X)$ is the expected value of the day-to-day variation c.d.f. $D(x)$. Its variance is

$$Var(Y_n) = E(Var(Y_n|X)) + Var(E(Y_n|X)) = E(Var(Y_n|X)) + Var(n \cdot X) .\tag{2-4}$$

Therefore for the day-to-day variability of the n-line group load Y_n

$$CV_{d,n}^2 = \frac{Var(Y_n)}{E^2(Y_n)} = \frac{E(Var(Y_n|X))}{n^2 E^2(X)} + \frac{Var(X)}{E^2(X)} = \frac{E(Var(Y_n|X))}{n^2 E^2(X)} + CV_{d,\infty}^2.\tag{2-5}$$

Here the second term, $CV_{d,\infty}$, characterizes the day-to-day variability for the total population of lines defined in section 2.3. The first term depends on how group-to-group variability changes from day to day, i.e. how $L(x,y)$ and $G_n(x,y)$ depend on x.

If the coefficient of variation is the same for all days, then it is not dependent on x and can be expressed as

$$CV_n = CV(Y_n|X) = \frac{\alpha}{\sqrt{n}} .\tag{2-6}$$

Therefore (see (2-2))

$$E(Var(Y_n|X)) = E(CV_n^2 \cdot E^2(Y_n|X)) = n\alpha^2 E(X^2) .\tag{2-7}$$

Formulae (2-5) and (2-7) lead to a clear-cut separation of the combined day-to-day and group-to-group variation into components:

$$CV_{d,n}^2 = CV_{d,\infty}^2 + CV_n^2 + CV_{d,\infty}^2 \cdot CV_n^2 .\tag{2-8}$$

For practical use, the negligible last term can be discarded.

There are indications that the variability of line unit load may deviate from the assumption (2-6). For example, on a day with a large total load, group loads may be relatively closer to each other than on a day with a small total load. In such a case, the coefficient of variation is larger for smaller X. Now CV_n is a variable dependent on X, and $Var(Y_n|X)$ in (2-4) and (2-5) needs to be described by a model. As an example, generalizing (2-6), we assume that

$$CV_n^2(X) = CV^2(Y_n|X) = \frac{1}{n}\left[\alpha^2 + \frac{\beta}{X}\right] . \tag{2-9}$$

$\beta=0$ corresponds to (2-6). Then

$$CV_{d,n}^2 = \frac{\alpha^2}{n} + \frac{\beta}{n \cdot \hat{E}(X)} + \left[1 + \frac{\alpha^2}{n}\right] \cdot CV_{d,\infty}^2 , \tag{2-10}$$

where $\hat{E}(X)$ is an estimate of the average (i.e. ABS) usage. The coefficients α and β should be estimated by values of $CV_n(X)$ measured on several days with different values of X.

A simpler approach, based on the same measured $CV_n(X)$ values, is a direct statistical estimation of $E(X)$ and $E(Var(Y_n|X))$ with the estimates applied to formula (2-5).

2.4 Model Testing

To quantify the proposed model of group-to-group and day-to-day variation one needs to estimate parameters of the distributions $L(y)$ and $D(x)$. Since $L(y)$ is not normally available, $G_n(y)$ for groups of lines may be used. A "uv"-size matrix containing measurements for u days on v line groups provides the necessary data. A sample computation for one month of data (18 weekdays) in 18 line groups (total 8214 lines) of one exchange rendered the following estimates: $CV_{d,\infty} = 0.054$, $CV_n = 0.092$, $CV_{d,n} = 0.108$, which agrees very well with formula (2-8).

2.5 Engineering Application

The most important use of this model is in estimating the expected peak period load of a line group of arbitrary size, for pre-cutover engineering of a large digital switch. Our major result is an engineering table - Table I - that is generic for High Day (HD) engineering of line load units. Given the HD capacity of a unit and a projected HD to Average Busy season (ABS) traffic load ratio for the exchange, the telephone company engineer directly obtains the correct HD/ABS ratio to be used for provisioning. The HD capacity is obtained from the supplier's load-service information and can be adjusted according to regional service requirements.

Table I. Line Load Unit HD/ABS Ratio						
Exchange HD/ABS Ratio for CCS	Unit HD Capacity (CCS)					
	200	500	1000	2000	5000	10000
1.0	1.39	1.23	1.16	1.11	1.07	1.05
1.1	1.41	1.26	1.19	1.15	1.12	1.11
1.2	1.45	1.31	1.26	1.23	1.21	1.21
1.3	1.51	1.39	1.35	1.32	1.31	1.30

The primary use of the model is improvement in digital switch line load unit engineering (see, e.g., [4]). A natural extension of this can be application of the model to load balancing[5].

2.6 Model Generalization

The model developed in section 2, describes one class of service and line groups that are subject to load-directed assignments for balancing. The most important extension of the model will take into account several classes of service within line groups balanced only according to class of service mix. This will be done within the scope of the basic approach.

This generalization is especially relevant to ISDN. Current introductions of ISDN service into digital switches can result in a combination of two very different types of line groups served by a common group of B-channel servers. The result is likely to be much larger values of CV_n with consequent larger adjustments in the HD/ABS ratios of Table I.

Further analysis of the total variability decomposition could be carried out in terms of higher moments. More detailed analysis based on the analytical approximation of the two basic distributions, $L(y)$ and $D(x)$ would provide more insight into the nature of subscriber traffic.

3. Forecasting

This section illustrates some problems specific to forecasting and traffic engineering for the data communications services that are an integral part of the ISDN services. It is shown that the application of standard trending and forecasting procedures directly to data terminal usage per subscriber line could result in significant errors.

Fig. 1 describes a hypothetical trend in penetration of data services into the population of subscriber telephone lines in an area. It is obvious that this penetration will be different for different classes of lines. In general, at least two classes should be considered, and the penetration for each class can be forecast by methods of demand analysis. In our hypothetical case, there are two classes - residential and business, and the trend curves are standard curves often used in forecasting methods.

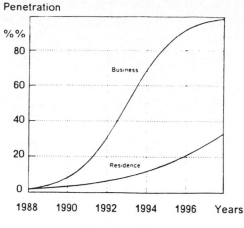

Fig. 1. Data Terminal Penetration vs. Time

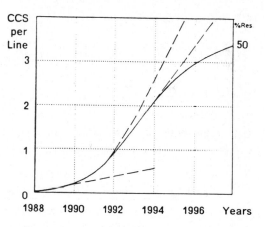

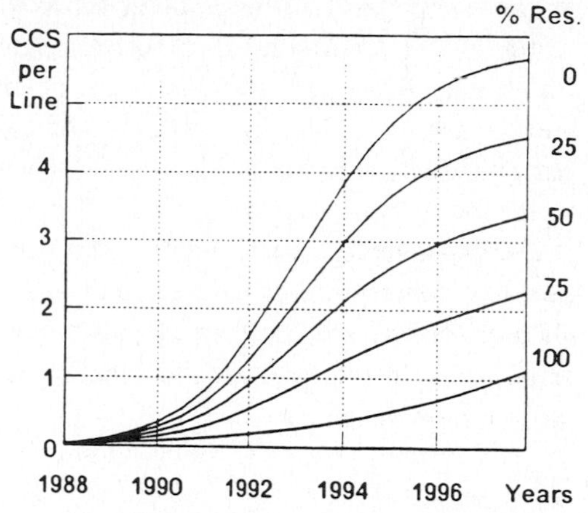

Fig. 3. Subscriber Line Data Usage vs. Time

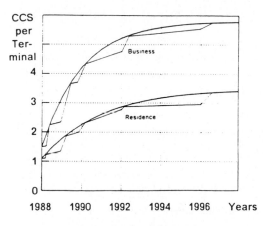

Fig. 2. Data Terminal Usage vs. Time

Fig. 4. Direct Data Usage per Line Forecast

The second major component of the subscriber ISDN traffic is data traffic per subscriber line. A hypothetical trend of the data load per line - terminal usage - is shown in Fig. 2. Jumps represent introduction of new services. For simplicity we show just a few jumps with the implication that each of these represents several introductions of new services. We expect that the general trend could be characterized by a smoothing curve as shown on the same chart, Fig. 2. The data usage needed for engineering is a result of combining the two primary components shown in Figures 1 and 2 by multiplying them. The result is data usage per line, and it is shown in Fig. 3.

One of the Fig. 3 curves is repeated in Fig. 4. This figure illustrates how forecasts of data usage per line (broken lines) based on the usage per line history miss the trend that results from the combined effect of the service penetration and traffic per terminal. For example, a forecast based on the initial years of service would probably underestimate data traffic significantly. On the other hand, the more advanced market of the following years would be overestimated because signs of saturation would be lost. This overestimation, and corresponding overprovisioning, would be sustained even later, as in the example of the third broken curve, notwithstanding the evidence that the trend subsides.

The complexity of the problem grows when other, equally important, factors listed in section 1.1 are considered. Uncertainty of estimates of new service penetration adds to the complexity of the problem. Both determining components of the total traffic (Figs. 1 and 2) are variables that could be forecast as functions of all of these factors, but the combined curve shown on Fig. 4 could not be.

Correspondingly, basic input data needed for forecasting ISDN data traffic should include: penetration of data services and data traffic characteristics broken down by line class of service, specific data on call types and traffic and line penetration changes as new services are introduced, and information related to various types of data traffic variability as described in section 1.1.

4. Some Major Open Questions

4.1 Notes on Call Types

For the purpose of analysis and, in particular, of forecasting total data traffic, subscriber traffic estimates could be obtained by an analysis of the traffic components separately for each type of ISDN call. An example of this approach was published in [6]. Table II illustrates the type of data to be used for subscriber traffic estimation with this methodology. Table II contains rough estimates for sample data call types. Each call type could potentially be carried on a circuit-switched B-channel, a packed-switched connection over a circuit-switched B-channel or a packet-switched D-channel.

Table II: ISDN Subscriber Traffic by Call Type				
Type of Call	Calls per Hour	Holding Time	Packets: Number/Size	
			From User	To User
Bulk data	1.0	1 min.	300/256	
Home information service	0.2	25 min.	1/20	6/256
Information retrieval	0.7	20 min.	1/20	8/256
Credit card verification	3.0	2 min.	1/64	1/64
Telebanking, business	0.7	30 min.	1/64	1/64
Telebanking, residential	0.1	5 min.	1/64	1/64

Obviously, the number of data call types is virtually unlimited. It may be impossible to combine them into meaningfully homogeneous groups. Therefore, it is doubtful that an analysis of data traffic by type of call would result in accurate estimates of the subscriber traffic. Rather, a relatively small number of ISDN subscriber classes of service properly identified would allow us to estimate data traffic by class of service suitable for exchange subscriber traffic estimation. This approach has proven to be successful in the analysis of voice traffic in the U.S.A. Bell operating companies [1].

4.2 Measurements

As discussed in sections 3 and 4.1, a relatively small number of ISDN subscriber classes need to be identified and used for traffic engineering and forecasting. It is important that operational and administrative personnel develop corresponding input data. For this purpose, individual subscriber special study measurements that can be made simultaneously for a large number of subscriber lines are highly desirable. New digital switches allow for such large scale measurements on individual subscriber lines. Such measurements should help to improve the quality of statistical data for ISDN traffic analysis and enable tracking of the build-up of ISDN traffic.

4.3 Busy Period Analysis

Extensive statistical analysis of the average busy season and highest day subscriber traffic discussed in [1] and [2] included estimation of subscriber traffic by class of service and by time of day. The estimates have been used in particular for predicting the busy hour position and possible change of it due to changes in the class of service mix. The data component of the subscriber traffic may also influence the position of the busy hour during the day. This phenomenon should be accounted for in the process of gradual development of the data traffic into a significant component of the total ISDN traffic.

4.4 An Example of an ISDN Service Standard Problem

Existing service standards for switching, e.g., those stated in the LATA Switching System Generic Requirements (LSSGR) for Bell operating companies in the U.S.A., need to be adjusted for ISDN services.

As an example, for lines served through ISDN access with a network-provided readiness signal (analogous to dial tone) a new component of access delay should be taken into consideration. This is the component that results from the recognition of the SETUP message.

For the ISDN access line with enbloc call origination another problem arises. The subscriber starts transmitting information notwithstanding potential delays in processing. Therefore the access delay within the switch would be perceived by the subscriber as post-dialing delay. Therefore the "post-dialing" delay standards should be revised in order to reflect this phenomenon.

REFERENCES

1. Bolotin, V.A., Kappel, J.G. *Bell System Traffic Usage by Class of Service.* Proc. 10th International Teletraffic Congress, Montreal, 2.4-1, 1983.

2. Bolotin, V.A. *Class of Service Analysis of Traffic Variations at Telephone Exchanges* Proc. 11th International Teletraffic Congress, Kyoto, 1986.

3. Hartman, M.G. *Customer Line Usage Studies.* Proc. 8ITC, Melbourne, Australia, 1976.

4. Friedman, K. *Precutover Extreme Value Engineering of a Local Digital Switch.* Proceedings of ITC-10, Montreal, 1983.

5. *Bell Laboratories Internal Correspondence.* 1981-82.

6. P.F. Pawlita, *Traffic Measurements in Data Networks. Recent Measurement Results, and Some Implications.* IEEE Trans. on Communications, Vol. Com-29, No. 4, April 1981.

TRAFFIC ENGINEERING for ISDN Design and Planning
M. Bonatti and M. Decina (Editors)
Elsevier Science Publishers B.V. (North-Holland)
© IAC, 1988

REFERENCE TRAFFIC FOR DIMENSIONING INTEGRATED SERVICES NETWORKS

Jun MATSUDA, Tadahiro YOKOI, and Konosuke KAWASHIMA

NTT Electrical Communications Laboratories
3-9-11 Midori-cho, Musashino-shi
Tokyo, 180 Japan

ABSTRACT Network resources are shared in Integrated Services
Networks by multi-class traffic streams having different
characteristics. This paper presents a generalized concept of
"reference traffic" for such systems. Based on this concept, the
dimensioning of multi-class traffic systems and the estimation of
"reference traffic" are discussed.

MAIN STATEMENT A generalized concept of reference traffic for
dimensioning multi-class traffic systems.

1. INTRODUCTION

Integrated Services Networks (ISNs) aim at greater convenience and economy
than dedicated communications networks by realizing various services such as
voice, data, facsimile and video in a common network. Network resources in
ISN would be shared by multi-class traffic streams having characteristics
which differ with respect to arrival/holding-time processes and service
disciplines. For such multi-class traffic systems, the grade of service (GOS)
is, in general, different for each traffic class, and the relationship between
the offered traffic mix and GOS is not as simple as for single-class traffic
systems. In addition, variations in the offered traffic are affected by the
interrelationship between traffic classes. These properties must be taken
into account in order to design and operate an efficient ISN.

Performance has been evaluated for various queueing systems with multi-class
traffic. There are, however, very few studies which take traffic variations
into account. Such consideration is indispensable for dimensioning ISNs which
handle real traffic. This paper examines the relationship between traffic mix
variations and GOS, and presents a generalized concept of "reference traffic"
which can serve as the basis for dimensioning multi-class traffic systems. In
addition, the measurement of traffic mix variations and the estimation of
"reference traffic" is also discussed.

2. DESIGN REQUIREMENTS

An approach based on the "mean" GOS has been presented by Berry [1]. In the
following, we would like to present an approach based on the "distribution" of
GOS. We assume that the GOS requirements are specified as:

> "the ratio of the number of days during which the GOS for a given time
> period within the day falls below a certain level L_k should be less than
> p_k for traffic class [k],"

rather than being specified simply by the mean GOS. We also refer to this
ratio briefly as "the ratio of the days with GOS inferior to a certain level"
hereinafter.

3. REFERENCE TRAFFIC

In this section, we present the concept of "reference traffic," i.e., a basis
for dimensioning which meets the GOS requirements described in Sec.2. Section
3.1 provides a brief description of the reference traffic used for
dimensioning single-class traffic systems for comparison with multi-class
traffic systems described in Sec.3.2.

3.1. Single-class traffic systems

The offered traffic varies not only from hour-to-hour within the day, but also
from day-to-day within the year for a given time period of the day. A yearly
distribution describing day-to-day variations in the offered traffic for a
time-consistent busy hour is shown in Fig.1.

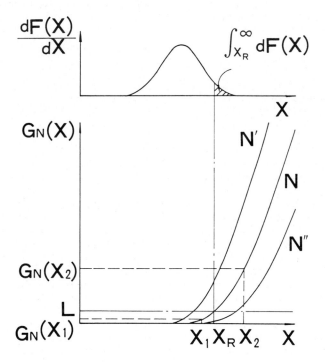

Fig. 1   A yearly distribution of offered traffic and reference traffic for
single-class traffic systems.

The relationship between offered traffic and GOS is also shown in Fig.1, given
the loss probability in the M/G/N/N loss system. It is noteworthy that the
GOS function $G_N(X)$ (X: offered traffic, N: the number of resources), e.g. the
Erlang loss formula in Fig.1, is generally monotonous. That is,

$$X_1 \leq X_2 \quad \Rightarrow \quad G_N(X_1) \leq G_N(X_2). \tag{1}$$

This implies that the ratio of the days with GOS inferior to $G_N(X_1)$ is less
than

$$\int_{X_1}^{\infty} dF(X), \tag{2}$$

where F(X) is a distribution function for day-to-day variations in the offered
traffic.

The GOS requirement for single class system is assumed to be specified as "the ratio of the number of days during which the GOS for a given time period within the day falls below a certain level L should be less than p." We can find a traffic level X_R for $F(X)$ such that

$$\int_{X_R}^{\infty} dF(X) = p. \tag{3}$$

If the number of resources, N, is dimensioned so that

$$G_N(X_R) \leq L, \tag{4}$$

then the ratio of the days with GOS inferior to $G_N(X_R)$ is guaranteed by (3) to be less than p. Therefore, from (4) it follows that the ratio of the days with GOS inferior to L is less than p. Namely, the GOS requirement is achieved by determining N so as to satisfy (4). X_R thus forms the basis of the traffic level for dimensioning single-class traffic systems and is called the reference traffic.

3.2. Multi-class traffic systems

For the sake of simplicity, the following describes the case having two traffic classes. The same arguments given below are also valid for cases having more than two traffic classes.

In general, a yearly distribution of the offered traffic mix (X,Y) for a given time period of the day is as shown in Fig.2, where X and Y are the offered traffic of class [1] and class [2], respectively. The significant difference between the multi-class traffic case and single-class traffic is that the (joint) distribution of the offered traffic mix (X,Y) can differ greatly depending on the correlation between the variations in offered traffic for each class even if the (marginal) distribution of the offered traffic is exactly the same with respect to each traffic class.

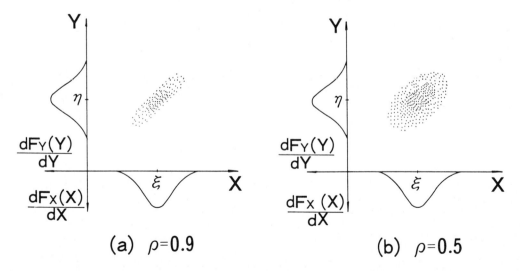

Fig. 2 Yearly distribution of an offered traffic mix.

On the other hand, the relationship between the offered traffic mix and GOS
has been analyzed for various queueing systems with multi-class traffic. The
notable points are

    - that the GOS is, in general, different for each traffic class,

and
    - that the relationship between the offered traffic mix and GOS is, in
      general, not as simple as for single-class traffic systems,

except for special cases, such as the $M_1, M_2 / G_1, G_2 / N / N$ loss system for which
the GOS (the loss probability in this case) is the same for each traffic
class. In this case, the GOS is given by the well-known Erlang loss formula,
$E_N(Z)$, where Z is $(X+Y)$, the sum of the offered traffic of each class.

In the following, we will consider the relationship between a yearly
distribution of the offered traffic mix and the dimensioning that meets the
GOS requirements mentioned in Sec.2, and present a concept of "reference
traffic" for multi-class traffic systems.

Let $G_N^{(k)}(X,Y)$ ((X,Y): offered traffic mix, N: the number of resources) denote
the GOS function corresponding to the GOS for traffic class [k] ($k=1,2$).
Plotting the points corresponding to the offered traffic mix (X,Y) for which

$$G_N^{(k)}(X,Y) = L_k, \tag{5}$$

we obtain a boundary curve represented by

$$B_N^{(k)}(X,Y) = 0 \tag{6}$$

as shown in Fig.3. Let $D_N^{(k)}$ denote the upper domain bounded by the curve
(6).

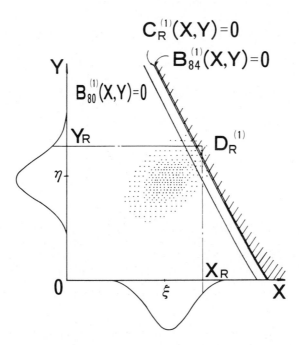

Fig. 3 Reference traffic for multi-class traffic systems.

Here, we assume that the GOS function is monotonous, that is,

$$X_1 \leq X_2, \quad Y_1 \leq Y_2 \quad \Rightarrow \quad G_N^{(k)}(X_1, Y_1) \leq G_N^{(k)}(X_2, Y_2). \qquad (7)$$

Then the ratio of the days with GOS for traffic class [k] inferior to the level L_k is less than

$$\int_{D_N^{(k)}} dF(X, Y), \qquad (8)$$

where $F(X,Y)$ is a (bivariate) distribution function for day-to-day variations in the offered traffic mix.

At this point, we will consider the curves which are (approximately) parallel to the boundary curves (6) and we represent each of those curves by

$$C^{(k)}(X, Y) = 0. \qquad (9)$$

Let $D^{(k)}$ denote the upper domain bounded by curve (9), the hatched area in Fig.3. Then the probability that the offered traffic mix is included in domain $D^{(k)}$ is given by

$$\int_{D^{(k)}} dF(X, Y). \qquad (10)$$

Given curve (9), we can find the (percentile) curve

$$C_R^{(k)}(X, Y) = 0 \qquad (11)$$

such that

$$\int_{D_R^{(k)}} dF(X, Y) = p_k. \qquad (12)$$

If the number of resources, N, is dimensioned so that boundary curve (6) is included in domain $D_R^{(k)}$, that is,

$$D_N^{(k)} \subseteq D_R^{(k)}, \qquad (13)$$

then

$$\int_{D_N^{(k)}} dF(X, Y) \leq \int_{D_R^{(k)}} dF(X, Y). \qquad (14)$$

The ratio of the days with GOS inferior to the level L_k is less than

$$\int_{D_N^{(k)}} dF(X, Y). \qquad (15)$$

Therefore, from (12) and (14) the ratio of the days with GOS inferior to the level L_k is less than p_k for traffic class [k]. Namely, curve (11) is a generalization of the concept "reference traffic" for multi-class traffic systems. We refer to this curve as the reference traffic curve.

4. EXAMPLE

A numerical example is given below to illustrate the ideas presented in Sec.3.2.

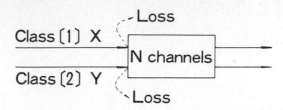

Fig. 4 Multi-class traffic system.

Here, we will consider the multi-class traffic system shown in Fig.4. Class [1] and class [2] calls are offered to a circuit group of size N. Calls for both classes describe a Poisson process. Class [1] calls occupy one channel, while class [2] calls occupy 6 channels. Class [1] calls are lost if all channels are occupied, while class [2] calls are lost if there are only less than 6 unoccupied channels in the system. Yearly distributions of offered traffic X (class [1]) and Y (class [2]) are assumed to obey $N(\xi, \sigma_1^2)$ and $N(\eta, \sigma_2^2)$, respectively, where $N(\mu, \sigma^2)$ denotes a normal distribution of mean μ and variance σ^2. Furthermore, let the correlation coefficient between X and Y be ρ. Namely the offered traffic mix (X,Y) obeys the bivariate normal distribution $N_2(\underline{\mu}, \Sigma)$ where

$$\underline{\mu} = (\xi, \eta) \tag{16}$$

$$\Sigma = \begin{pmatrix} \sigma_1^2 & \rho\sigma_1\sigma_2 \\ \rho\sigma_1\sigma_2 & \sigma_2^2 \end{pmatrix}. \tag{17}$$

Yearly distributions of the offered traffic mix are illustrated in Fig.2, where $\rho=0.9$ (Fig.2(a)) and $\rho=0.5$ (Fig.2(b)).

The GOS requirement is specified as "the ratio of the days with loss probability greater than 0.01 (for class [1] traffic) and 0.08 (for class [2] traffic) should be less than 5%." Figure 3 shows boundary curve (6) for N=80 and N=84 on which the loss probability for class [1] traffic is 0.01. The reference traffic curve (11) is also illustrated in Fig.3. The probability that the offered traffic mix is included in the upper domain bounded by curve (11) is 5%.

When the boundary curves are straight lines (at least in the area where the offered traffic mix is distributed) as in Fig.3, probabilities (8) and (10) can be easily calculated as follows:
Let a boundary curve be

$$aX + bY = c. \tag{18}$$

When (X,Y) obeys $N_2(\underline{\mu}, \Sigma)$, $z(=aX+bY)$ obeys $N(\zeta, \sigma^2)$,[2] where

$$\zeta = a\xi + b\eta \tag{19}$$

$$\sigma^2 = a^2\sigma_1^2 + 2ab\rho\sigma_1\sigma_2 + b^2\sigma_2^2. \tag{20}$$

Therefore, the probability that (X,Y) is included in the upper domain bounded by curve (18) is given by

$$\int_c^\infty (\sqrt{2\pi}\sigma)^{-1} \exp\{-(z-\zeta)^2/2\sigma^2\} \, dz. \tag{21}$$

The GOS requirement for class [1] traffic is satisfied by N_1=84. The number
of channels, N_2, by which the GOS requirement for class [2] traffic is
satisfied is similarly determined. Thus the size of circuit group is
dimensioned as $N=\max\{N_1,N_2\}$. If dimensioning is based on (X_R,Y_R) which are
the reference traffic of the individual traffic streams, more than N channels
would be needed.

Next we will study the relationship between the yearly distribution of the
offered traffic mix and GOS in greater detail. Figure 5 shows the
relationship between the correlation coefficient ρ and the ratio of the days
with loss probability greater than 0.01 for class [1] traffic. It is noted
that the ratio of the days with GOS inferior to the specified level varies
depending on ρ even if the number of channels is fixed. GOS becomes more
sensitive to ρ when the proportion of class [2] traffic becomes comparable to
class [1] traffic, as shown in Fig.5. This suggests that more attention
should be given to the value of ρ when the integrated service traffic has
grown rather than at an early stage when the newly integrated service traffic
is still small.

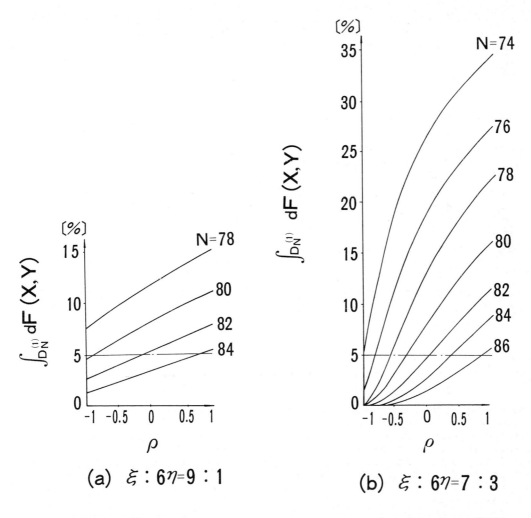

(a) $\xi : 6\eta = 9 : 1$

(b) $\xi : 6\eta = 7 : 3$

Fig. 5   Relationship between correlation coefficient ρ and the ratio of the
number of days during which the GOS falls below some specified level.

5. PARAMETER ESTIMATION OF YEARLY DISTRIBUTION

This section discusses the estimation of yearly distribution parameters for the offered traffic mix.

Let $U_1 = (x_1, y_1)$, $U_2 = (x_2\ y_2)$,..., $U_n = (x_n, y_n)$ be observations of traffic mix for n days. When these observations are independent,

$$\overline{U} = \frac{1}{n} \sum_{i=1}^{n} U_i \tag{22}$$

$$S = \sum_{i=1}^{n} (U_i - \overline{U})(U_i - \overline{U}) \tag{23}$$

are unbiased estimators for parameter μ and $(n-1)\Sigma$, respectively, where μ is the mean and Σ is the covariance matrix for a bivariate distribution. In other words, unbiased estimators of yearly distribution parameters for the offered traffic mix are given by

$$\hat{\xi} = \frac{1}{n} \sum_{i=1}^{n} x_i$$

$$\hat{\eta} = \frac{1}{n} \sum_{i=1}^{n} y_i$$

$$\hat{\sigma}_1^2 = \frac{1}{n-1} \sum_{i=1}^{n} (x_i - \hat{\xi})^2 \tag{24}$$

$$\hat{\sigma}_2^2 = \frac{1}{n-1} \sum_{i=1}^{n} (y_i - \hat{\eta})^2$$

$$\widehat{\rho\,\sigma_1\,\sigma_2} = \frac{1}{n-1} \sum_{i=1}^{n} (x_i - \hat{\xi})(y_i - \hat{\eta}).$$

Therefore, parameter ρ is estimated by

$$\hat{\rho} = \frac{\sum_{i=1}^{n} (x_i - \hat{\xi})(y_i - \hat{\eta})}{\{\sum_{i=1}^{n} (x_i - \hat{\xi})^2 \ \sum_{i=1}^{n} (y_i - \hat{\eta})^2\}^{1/2}} \ . \tag{25}$$

When the offered traffic mix obeys a bivariate normal distribution, the distribution of estimators (24),(25) are known [2], i.e., their accuracy can be evaluated.

The above discussion is based on the assumption that the offered traffic intensity can be observed for each class. In practice, however, it is not so easy to measure offered traffic intensity for a particular class of calls. Rather, it is easier to measure the number of calls in each class and the total carried traffic intensity. We have devised a method for indirectly estimating the individual offered traffic intensity from measurements of the number of calls in each class offered/carried and the total carried traffic intensity.

Although details of the method are not described here, a minimum square estimation is used assuming that the mean holding time for each class of traffic does not vary from day-to-day. Computer simulation shows that this method can estimate the offered traffic intensity in an individual class with practical accuracy if measurements are continued for 40 to 50 days. Furthermore, it is possible to obtain a more accurate estimate if the ratio of each class of calls varies widely from day-to-day. Field traffic data in telephone networks show that daily variation is small for the mean holding time but large for the ratio of calls for each destination[3]. This implies that the method presented here works well.

6. CONCLUSION

A generalized concept of "reference traffic" for dimensioning multi-class traffic system has been presented. This concept connects research on the performance evaluation of multi-class traffic systems with that on the dimensioning of Integrated Services Networks dealing with variations in the real traffic load.

Acknowledgement

The authors would like to thank the members of the Teletraffic Section and Hashida Research Section for their valuable discussion during the course of this work.

References

[1] Berry, L.T.M., Traffic Base Definitions for Planning and Dimensioning Integrated Services Networks, in: Brussels Specialist Seminar on ISDN Traffic Issues, May 1986.
[2] Rao, C. R., Linear Statistical Inference and Its Applications, 2nd edition, John Wiley & Sons, Inc. New York, 1973.
[3] Takemori, E., Usui, Y., and Matsuda, J., Field Data Analysis for Traffic Engineering, in: ITC 11, Kyoto, September 1985.

TRAFFIC ENGINEERING for ISDN Design and Planning
M. Bonatti and M. Decina (Editors)
Elsevier Science Publishers B.V. (North-Holland)
© IAC, 1988

STRUCTURAL RELATIONSHIPS IN AN ISDN BUSINESS

E. DE HERT*

ATEA
ATEALAAN, 2410 HERENTALS
BELGIUM

ABSTRACT

An identification methodology, based on a general systems approach using a layered structure of epistemological levels is discussed. Some experiences in the telecommunications business with the aid of the "Systems Approach Problem Solver", are described. Suggestions are made to apply such powerful methods in an ISDN environment.

MAIN STATEMENT

Structural relationships based on systems methodology can improve ISDN planning business.

1. INTRODUCTION

It is often impractible or even impossible to measure all relevant variables involved in complex processes. In an ISDN environment, the mix of call types from different user classes, looking for different teleservices, will have consequences on a broad range of switch- and networkparameters and related economical factors. Instead of dealing with the details of switch development and the network planning process with all kinds of implementation aspects, we look at those processes as a black box. This approach can be very instructive for traffic engineers and network planners. The result of their studies can in certain cases be compared with such high-level approaches, it even provides a gateway towards the macro-economic world [4]. About this last statement however, we are convinced that the traffic fraternity has to act as a "watching dog", in order to explain, or even correct certain relational behaviouristic results. This paper is a response to the request from the teletraffic community to find new ways and tools, which can be helpful.

---

* Is currently at EHSAL and ADECHO, Brussels, Belgium.

2. THE METHOD

The method used is a problem solving method, based on theories of Professor Klir from New York State University on systems methodology, complexity and reconstructability [2, 3]. The Systems Approach Problem Solver [1] was the software tool to tackle the problem. The method is searching and identifying relations between variables describing a specific system. It is important to note that the method is not restricted to search correlations between two variables, but three and multiple relations are simultaneously investigated too. Not only just relations between variables, but also between past, present and future values of the variables can be considered.

The systems methodology uses a hierarchy of epistemological types of systems. With the Systems Approach Problem Solver, we go through a series of transitions. Each transitions brings us on a higher system level and implies a higher degree of knowledge about the real world system.

On the lowest layer, level 0, we have the source system. It is defined by a set of variables, a set of potential values or states for each variable, and some way of describing the meaning of the variables and their values in terms of the associate attributes of the real world system under study. We distinguish two main types of variables, the so-called basic variables, related to the system itself, and the reference variable(s), which serve as a reference for the observed basic variables. Examples of these reference variables are time, individual machines, sites, or a combination.

If we add actual observations or measurements to the source system, we get the data system or epistemological level 1. The data system can be represented by a matrix, the rows are the basic variables and the columns represent possible states of the reference variable(s). An element of the matrix represents the state of the associated variable for that specific reference state. Relations between variables can be identified, because certain combinations of their states occur more often than others, in which case we are talking about "constraint". The number of observed states is mostly limited by a classification procedure, in order to reduce the number of possible states, and to get more constraint in the dataset.

The next higher level, level 2, is the behaviour system. Here we try to recognize reference parameter-invariant characterisation of the constraint among the basic variables. If we succeed, we can also generate basic variables within the reference variable set, if we want to, therefore, level 2 is also called the generative system. Relations are found using the concept of the mask. We are searching combinations of states at different reference points. This can be done by selecting a specific set of matrix elements in the data system. If we cover the rest, we just constructed a specific mask. This mask can now be shifted, so that the mask can be checked on each position for different reference parameter states. The amount of columns in the mask is defined as the depth of the mask. The selection of mask elements is done by looking for optimal behaviour. In order to evaluate all possible masks, we devide the basic variables in two groups. The generating group, or left hand variables gl, and the generated group or right hand variables gr. The behaviour is optimal if the measurements show that, with each combination of states of gl, we get only one combination of states of gr. In this case we get a deterministic result. If the number of sampling variables in the mask increases, or the depth of the mask increases, the probability to find deterministic behaviour will increase too, and we are still unsure about existing relations.

Level 3 tries to identify a structure and is called the structure system. This means a decomposition of the generative system in subsystems.

Level 4 is the metasystem, changes of systems defined on lower levels are allowed. The change is characterised by a reference parameter-invariant procedure.

Higher order metasystems and associated levels are also possible.

3. AN ISDN APPLICATION

The suggestion made in this section is based on some experiences with the SAPS system. We were faced with a typical switch- and associated network design problem. The mix of call types of a different nature has direct consequences on other parameters as e.g. processing-, transmission- and switching parameters. The processing capability turned out to be one of the most sensitive design elements, with heavy consequences on the switch development, and the network design and networkplanning activities. The identification of the influence of the individual call types based on practical measurements on different sites and on different points in time seemed to be an impossible mission. Multiple linear repressions gave unstable and unreasonable results. Nevertheless a solution was urgently required, since the network design and networkplanning scenarios looked seriously different, depending on the fact, which call types were more dominant than others. The SAPS system not only provided significantly more insight in the behaviour of the system, but even explained on level 3 what went wrong in the previous attempts. SAPS suggested, with the data available, not to try a split up between certain specific call types. The SAPS results told us, which call types were dominant and which types could be taken together, until more data becomes available.

New regression studies gave reasonable results. Doubtful measurement points were dropped. Omitting these doubtful measurement points satisfied the minimum value of the Fisher constant. Inversely the Fisher constant eliminated all doubtful cases. Stable and reasonable results came out. Based on these reliable results, the choice of a reasonable scenario could be made. From the previous experience it will be clear that the "preprocessing" work of systems such as SAPS will become increasingly important, as more and more user classes and teleservices appear. Since SAPS only "sees" data or behaviour, relations can be discovered with variables of a complete different nature: pure technical parameters, cost parameters, prices, income etc. The "intuition" of the manager can, at least partly, be supported by such robust methods.

4.   CONCLUSION

The hitherto abstract concepts and studies about systems methodology left the pure academic world and found their way towards practical applications and concrete projects. The discussed identification methodology has proven to be very useful in telecommunications and seems to become very promising in an ISDN planning business.

ACKNOWLEDGEMENTS

We should like to thank both ATEA, Herentals for allowing this study and Computing & Systems Consultants, Eindhoven for their logistic support in using and running the software.

REFERENCES

[1] Uyttenhove, H.J., Systems Approach Problem Solver: An Introduction and Guide. (Computing and Systems Consultants, Binghamton, N.Y. 81).

[2] Klir, G.J., Complexity: Some General Observations, Systems Research (Pergamon Press, 1985) Vol. 2 nr. 2, pp. 131-140.

[3] Klir, G.J. and Way, E.C., Reconstructability Analysis: Aims, Results, Open Problems, Systems Research (Pergamon Press, 1985) Vol. 2 nr. 2, pp. 141-163.

[4] De Hert E., Deregulation and Telecommunications, 18th Flemish Scientific Economic Congres, Report of the commission, in print (in Dutch).

TRAFFIC ENGINEERING for ISDN Design and Planning
M. Bonatti and M. Decina (Editors)
Elsevier Science Publishers B.V. (North-Holland)
© IAC, 1988

ISDN TRAFFIC CHARACTERIZATION AND FORECASTING

Beatriz CRAIGNOU

Centre National d'Etudes des Télécommunications
Division Architecture et Trafic dans les Réseaux
38/40 rue du Général Leclerc
92131 ISSY-LES-MOULINEAUX, France

This paper deals with some of the problems to be solved on ISDN
services demand and traffic forecasting. A quick survey about the
users and the services is made. An approach to determine accesses
and services demand is given as well as a possible method to calculate the load of various equipments. The uncertainty around these
forecasts is discussed.

Main statements : ISDN planning process and vulnerability to errors
in the prognosis.

1. INTRODUCTION

In order to implement ISDN and satisfy users needs in an efficient and
economic way, strategies for architectural capacities, services and access to
the network have to be elaborated based on services demand and type and amount
of traffic to be carried, that have then to be modelled and forecasted.

An ISDN provides a set of network capabilities which are defined by standardized protocols and functions and enable telecommunication services to be
offered to customers. Bearer services (circuit and packet modes) are characterized by their attributes ([1], I.211). Teleservices are characterized by the
same attributes as bearer services plus high layer attributes ([1], I.212). In
the same way, from the traffic point of view, user demand must be characterized by specific attributes (terminal distribution, teleservices traffic
demand, ...).

Interface structures to provide user access to the network, nB + D channels,
range between the basic access (n=2) and the primary access (n=23 or n=30).

The planning and dimensioning of resources used in the network will be made
depending on the bearer services and teleservices required to satisfy the
users demand. Forecasts have to take into account the number of accesses, the
number of terminals in the user installation and traffic characteristics of
teleservices. User needs of services and traffic per service may vary and be
explained and modelled according to socio-economic factors. So, for forecasting purposes, we have to distinguish categories of users and, for each
category, characterize the different types of traffic generated by the
services that are most likely to be used.

2. THE USERS

Implementations of the French ISDN pilot project RENAN [2] and of the required
infrastructure for the general ISDN have already started. It is expected that
in 1990 ISDN will cover the whole country.

RENAN and other field trials in the world give us some knowledge about users and services supply and demand.

According to the sector of their activities and then their needs for information transport, degree of computerized organization, present and envisaged telematic applications, revenues, etc, different segmentations of users may be done. As an exemple, for the around 25 millions of telephone main lines forecasted in France for 1992 the following segmentation is given in [3] :

Residential I (RI) : 90 % of main houses + secondary houses ; 19.3 million,
Residential II (RII) : 10 % of main houses + 75 % of professions with less
                       than 6 employees ; 3.75 million,
Small Business I (SBI) : 25 % of professions + businesses with less than 6
                       employees ; 1.5 million,
Small Business II (SBII) : Professions + businesses with 6 to 49 employees ;
                       600000,
Medium Business I (MBI) : Professions + businesses with 50 to 199 employees ;
                       55000,
Medium Business II (MBII) : Businesses with more than 200 employees and at
                       most 30 lines ; 8350,
Large Business (LB) : Businesses with more than 200 employees and more than 30
                       lines ; 2100.

In its starting phase ISDN will be of most interest for medium or large business users and will probably be concentrated in urban areas but, in the near future, users located in rural areas will ask for its sophisticated services and a rapid extension to all parts of the network will be necessary.

3. THE TELESERVICES

To ensure continuity, the ISDN will offer :
. teleservices available today using telephone or data networks : voice, teletex, facsimile, videotex, data transmission, teleaction, ...
. new teleservices that will probably need high speed or different channels simultaneous use : alphageometric or alphaphotographic videotex, audio-videotex, audiography, visiophony, ...

For all these teleservices, supplementary services will be available (some are already possible with intelligent terminals, others will require ISDN new signalling capabilities) : call forwarding, closed user group, direct dialling in, user-to-user signalling, call waiting, calling number identification or non-identification, credit card calling, conference call, three party service, call transfer, ...

Different papers give a characterization of most ISDN services (bit rate, traffic profiles, traffic volume, ...) and grade of service requirements (call set up time, permitted loss, call transmission delay, ...). Multi-slot traffic generated by services requiring high bit rates like bulk data, still and moving pictures, hi-fi sound, multi-media communications, is studied in [4].

As an example of combined services, structuring a 64 Kbit/s channel into (56+8) Kbit/s, text and graphic transmission may be associated to interconnect microcomputers with speech simultaneity.

4. DEMAND FORECASTS

In France as elsewhere, Delphi methods are applied to deduce ISDN services penetration. Without historical data about a service, the existing data for a similar service have to be taken as a pattern, assuming a certain improvement on transmission delays, user friendly dialogues, access facilities, terminal availability, competitive charges, etc.

To have an idea of who is going to ask for ISDN and for which services, inquiries among all user categories are realized. Although the answers are not always relevant since they are based on the relative usage of services proposed today, within a litle fuzzy charge policy and a lack of ISDN "social environment", we assume that user distributions will follow the expected patterns for leased lines, data networks, videotex, and so on. With time, new services proposed to the users may induce new requirements, their social environment and cultural background being influenced by the offer.

ISDN perception differs widely according to the type of enterprise.

LB and MBII user preoccupations deal with computerized architectures and optimization of voice communications. Their needs are mainly internal, between decentralized offices. For banks, ISDN will make easier internal and external voice and data communications, credit card processing,... Insurance companies, health organizations, newspapers, travel agencies, where large amounts of information are transmitted every day, will be among the first to ask for ISDN services such as quick text, image and data transfer.

MBI and SBII users centralize their needs in communication with customers, providers, data base access.

SBI, RII and RI users are mainly interested in data base access, microcomputer communication, audiovideotex and other facilities to make work at home more confortable.

Teleactions present great interest for almost all categories of users.

If the number and distribution of ISDN connections are based on the Minitel terminals installation plan (which is a rather optimistic approach) the ISDN user population will be more or less the following, in terms of user installations using $nB + D$ channels accesses $(2 \leqslant n \leqslant 30)$ [3] :

	1992	1997
RI	a few	a few
RII	150000	1098000
SBI	200000	904800
SBII	150000	444500
MBI	20000	43400
MBII	4200	7500
LB	1100	1900

which gives a little more than 525000 users in 1992 (around 2 % of telephone subscribers) and 2500000 in 1997 (around 10 % of telephone subscribers, assuming that in those years the number of subscribers will not increase very much).

A recent market research study for the French PTT estimates, for the horizon 92-93, a minimum of 150000 basic accesses and 10000 primary accesses. A parallel study estimates, for the same horizon, about 2.8 million terminals of all types, among which 1.8 million will be located in enterprises (750000 telephones on PABX). For the horizon 96-97, these estimates will a priori double and the market will not yet be saturated. Evaluation of the number of terminals is based on expected growth for telex, teletex, facsimile, microcomputers, minitels, telephone sets and on the transfer rate envisaged from PABX, private or public data networks to ISDN, for all categories of users.

More than the price, the inner quality of the services and their advantages from the user's point of view will in a sense define their potential market.

Plain ordinary telephone and telex services are precisely defined and may be judged unambiguously by the user. New services are complex and judgement is global, involving information transmission and processing. For instance, videotex demand depends on the quality of transmission (visualization time of a screen-page), the contents and organization of data bases and the performance of servers software ; demand on cabled network depends on TV-channels number and nature and associated possibilities like televideolibrary.

[5] gives curves and tables for different services demand forecasts and different categories of users. It is expected that voice will generate more than 70 % of the traffic and data services will probably double in 1990 the amount of this traffic today.

During its first 10 years, ISDN traffic in France is expected to increase at most by 5 % per year.

5. TRAFFIC FORECASTS

As dedicated networks (signalling, switched, packet, broadband) are concerned with the processing and transmission of calls, mainly in a minimum integration scheme [6], forecast must specify the amount of traffic that these networks have to deal with and particular requirements of involved equipment.

Traffic forecasts may be performed generalizing a method presented in [7].

Let us deal with the problem of dimensioning a specific part of the ISDN, e.g. inter-exchange transmission, basic accesses or processing capacity.

If we dispose of users number, categories and distribution, teleservices demand and traffic characteristics of teleservices, we may determine the input parameters for a traffic model and evaluate the load of various resources used by the network.

If an equivalence may be found between different traffic units (let us say millions of bits for some equipment), it is possible to aggregate the different ISDN traffic components to calculate the volume at every local exchange.

Up to 8 terminals of all types can be connected to a basic access. But a terminal, like a micro-computer, may have integrated functions and be used as a data base server, of for teletex, telex, facsimile, and so forth. For simplicity, we assume here that each terminal is associated with a unique service.

Let t_{ijh} represent the mean traffic in a certain period h of service j (among S services) per terminal installed in the premises of a user of category i (among C categories). Depending on the resource to be dimensioned, t_{ijh} may be given in erlangs (for trunks), bits (for packet channels) packets (for packet handling unit), signalling messages (for plan control or signalling), call processing time percentage (for the main control unit), ...

Let p_{ij} be the average number of terminals compatible with service j in the same installation and n_i the number of users of category i connected to the local exchange considered.

For the specific type of equipment we are considering, we define a constant α_j that describes the requirements of the equipment per call of service j. For instance, α_j may be the number of channels required by the service if transmission capacity is investigated. Then, the total load L_h for the equipment in the exchange is :

$$L_h = \sum_{i=1}^{C} \sum_{j=1}^{S} t_{ijh} \times p_{ij} \times n_i \times \alpha_j \qquad\qquad (*)$$

Then, present and forecasted data have to be provided concerning the users (categories and number), the services (number, type, bit rate, channels or specific requirements, busy hour), the terminals (average number per access per service), the traffic (mean values per terminal per service at its busy hour). Traffic is generally given in number of calls per hour ; the average call in number of pages or messages, bits per page or per message and characters per message ; call duration in seconds. These statistics allow the evaluation of the total number of calls/hour, packets/hour, voice, data and multiplexed data traffic in Erlangs, average voice call or data call duration, average packet size in bytes, particular load for an equipment, ... and the flows on signalling, switched, packet and wideband networks.

Even with very rough ideas about the constant α_j, it will turn out that certain services together will compose the most important part of the total load while the majority of the services can be neglected. For transmission, say, teletex and other low bit rate or low volume services may be negligible whereas videoconference and telephone traffic turn out to be critical services : videoconference because of the high α_j and telephone because of the high values of t_{ijh} or p_{ij}. Communication between computers, and then bulk data information transfer, seems to become one of the most critical services with very high t_{ijh}.

It could be even possible to neglect a service that is in itself of reasonable size if its busy hour occurs in a period where the other services vanish. So, to calculate the load, it is plausible to concentrate in the hourly period H where :

$$L_H = \max_h (L_h)$$

Concerning the uncertainty of forecasts, there is a main difference between ISDN an a set of dedicated networks. If dedicated networks have to be planned, they are planned under the uncertainty for each service in itself, the summands of (*), whereas for ISDN the uncertainty of planning becomes the uncertainty of the sum. This is particularly important since with a lot of emerging services it can be difficult to "guess" which service will be preferred by a user to meet certain communication needs. Will he use teletex or a general data network to send a report ? But, does it really matter which services are going to be selected or rejected or substituted by others ? As the different services are considered in one common sum it turns out that only the communication needs have to be forecasted and not the services selected to communicate.

Once the traffic volume per local exchange is calculated, the traffic by direction may be evaluated following patterns obtained by measurements on samples and the interworking networks considered. Then, the construction of initial matrices representing different traffics between exchanges at different geographical levels may be performed. Matrices will be projected, respecting the constraints of total traffic (de)composition patterns. The projected components may be compared to other projected values obtained for matrices limited to one or to a small set of services. The search to explain differences between these results certainly leads to more accurate forecasts.

6. CONCLUSION

The major impact of ISDN on transmission networks concerns bit rates choice. Otherwise, ISDN network strategy would be mainly located at switching or subscriber connection units.

In the starting phase there will be a low average density of ISDN users and services. Later, even if user needs evolve more slowly than techniques do, let us hope that a favourable modification of users behaviour will make ISDN popular. Nevertheless, a substantial logistic or even linear increase of traffic cannot be expected since in the later phase the sector covered will be more likely small business and residential subscribers fond of communicative micro-computers or seduced by facsimile, images banks, ... If telematic applications are to penetrate the residential mass market, equipment has to be highly standardized and inexpensive.

If the user does not mind about bit rates or other characteristics of bearer services, as long as his call succeeds within good quality requirements and at an acceptable price, the network will not make any difference between teleservices using the same support, that should then be charged in the same way.

For the planners, within an ISDN totally integrated, the competition between services will lose importance as they will share the same resources. So, the more integrated the network, the less vulnerable will it be to this competition and to determine which services are going to be used instead of others becomes less significant than to determine the amount of traffic carried by the network. Besides, in an advanced or totally integrated scheme the question of grade of service could be solved from the beginning if the highest requirement of bit rate is chosen to invest in transmission means. Here, again, economic considerations will weigh heavily. But, in such an integration scheme, it would be possible to allow weak marginal costs to the services requiring a low bit rate, since the peaks of these services would be attenuated, the loss probability being lower in respect to the total amount of traffic.

As the ISDN has to be competitive, and the trends of charges and terminal costs are supposed to go down, to calculate the demand we may assume that costs are low enough to make available any technically possible service and tariffs attractive enough to encourage every demand. Ignoring costs, demand forecasts will be rather optimistic but they may always be modulated when costs and charges policies will be officially adopted.

ACKNOWLEDGEMENTS

Progress in this work owes a lot to discussions on ISDN prognosis with some of my colleagues in the CNET and elsewhere.

REFERENCES

[1] Series I Recommendations. CCITT Red Book, Geneva, 1985.
[2] Etesse, L., RENAN : ISDN launching in France. ITU seminar on ISDN, Lisboa, 1986.
[3] Fiche, G., Le Palud, C. and Etesse, L., ISDN traffic assumptions and repercussions for the switching systems architectures. ISS, Phoenix, 1987.
[4] Roberts, J.W. and Hoang Van, A., Characteristics of services requiring multi-slot connections and their impact on ISDN design. 5th ITC seminar, Lake Como, 1987.
[5] CEPT/T/ELT - Estimates of the demand for new telecommunication services, 1986.
[6] Decina, M. and Rovery, A., ISDN, Architectures and Protocols. "Advanced Digital Communications and Signalling Processing". Prentice Hall, NJ, 1986.
[7] Aubin, F. and Craignou, B., Traffic forecasting with minimum data. ITC 11, Kyoto, 1985.

TRAFFIC ENGINEERING for ISDN Design and Planning
M. Bonatti and M. Decina (Editors)
Elsevier Science Publishers B.V. (North-Holland)
© IAC, 1988

DISCUSSION

1 Integration and trunk reservation

In answer to a question from D.J. Songhurst (British Telecom), K. Lindberger affirmed that the integration savings in terms of percent are greater when we have not just many but also small streams, which are particularly inefficient to carry in dedicated trunk groups.

The approximation presented at the seminar was meant to give some results for the principal discussion for and against integration, trunk reservation and so on.

To be used in a network optimisation program the method perhaps needs to be modified and generalised in some ways.

An extension from two to three streams could be done in a similar way but with about twice as many parameters and somewhat more complicated formulae.

In the case of many streams (eg. 10) a more general method is required.

2 Applications of Extreme Value Engineering for traffic administration of combined ISDN switches

In answer to a question by R. Pandya (BNR), V. Bolotin affirmed that the choice between TCBH (Time Consistent Busy Hour) and Extreme Value Engineering in dealing with ISDN traffic doesn't appear for the moment different from the choice in dealing with traditional (voice) traffic. Suitable engineering procedures to account for ISDN traffic require much more experience to be fully developed.

3 Standardisation of reference traffic by CCITT.

G. Gosztony (BHG Telecom and chairman of SGII of CCITT) asked for any possibility to standardise methods illustrated in Bolotin and Matsuda paper in order to take into account traffic variations on worlwide basis (an efficient procedure is still missing from CCITT Recommendations although this would be important for proper definition of reference traffics). "What are the traffic measurement requirements to use your method? Can these measurements be performed in countries with a moderate level of telecommunication development? Would you contribute to solve this problem in CCITT if a relevant question would be formulated for the next Study Period (1989-92?)".

Matsuda answered that his method can be applied to any multi-class traffic system for which some performance evaluation is available. However an extension to distributions other than normal-type needs further study. Traffic measurements do not require individual traffic densities but only total traffic density. In addition, the GOS is not so dependent on the correlation between integrated services traffic at an early stage when the newly integrated service traffic is still small.

Bolotin answered that the analysis of combined day and group traffic variability can be standardised on a worldwide basis, although an extension of this analysis to include cases of non-balanced traffic would be necessary. Measurement recommendations applicable to switching machines with different measurement capabilities should be developed too.

Both the authors declared their willingness to contribute to the CCITT standardisation work if a relevant question would be formulated.

4 Traffic forecasting: total volumes or volumes per service?

In answer to a comment by J. Seraj (Ericsson) about the need for forecasting traffic on a per service basis when the dimensioning of " call processing architecture" is required or cooperation with dedicated network is important, B. Craignou argued that only classes of services have to be considered.

B. Craignou proposes the following classification criteria:

- substitutibility of a service by another;

- usage of the same physical terminal for the services of the same class (if we distinguish virtual terminals associated with a unique service);

- nearly related busy periods;

- GOS, bitrate, or other technical requirements;

- and so on.

Then, according to the communication needs that could be satisfied by the service of a class, for every category of users, it would be possible to evaluate the traffic generated by the class. This traffic, and the particular requirements for the class, will be used to invest in (and dimension) transmission means and the necessary non-telecommunications infrastructure associated with the class of service (as server centres, databases, software ...).

However (see also the conclusions) the findings by V. Bolotin must be taken into account before concluding that it will be sufficient to forecast on a service class - user category basis.

TRAFFIC ENGINEERING for ISDN Design and Planning
M. Bonatti and M. Decina (Editors)
Elsevier Science Publishers B.V. (North-Holland)
© IAC, 1988

FORECASTING, TRAFFIC CHARACTERIZATION, INTERACTION EFFECTS OF INTEGRATION: SOME FINDINGS AND OPEN PROBLEMS

(Chairman Conclusions to the Afternoon Session on Services)

David J. Songhurst

British Telecom, U.K.

Forecasting

A properly structured approach should be used. For example, service penetration and usage per line should be forecast separately rather than forecasting total service traffic.

Where guesswork is necessary it should be formalised, e.g. by the use of structured scenario techniques. More than one technique should be used if possible.

The importance of company policy in stimulating demand should be recognised.

The possible impact of competition was not dealt with in this session.

Characterisation

We need to characterise between-day and between-group variability of customer traffic rates.

We also need to characterise the correlations between traffics of different service-types.

Detailed characterisation of multi-service traffic variability and correlations enables a generalised reference traffic to be defined so as to control joint blocking probabilily distributions within required limits.

Interaction

Stream superposition problems are studied by traffic engineers and by queueing theorists using different techniques. There should be more common awareness.

In order to realise the potential savings of integration we need to dimension using flexible approximation algorithms which can take account of the relevant factors (bandwidth, peakedness, mean holding times).

Further work is required to develop dimensioning methods of suitable generality and able to handle the integration of many traffic streams.

TRAFFIC ENGINEERING for ISDN Design and Planning
M. Bonatti and M. Decina (Editors)
Elsevier Science Publishers B.V. (North-Holland)
© IAC, 1988

ISDN: NEW CONTEXT AND NEW ISSUES FOR
NETWORK DESIGN AND PLANNING

(Chairman Introduction to the Morning Session on Networks)

Konosuke Kawashima

NTT, Japan

The traditional formulation of the network design problem for POTS needs to be revised in the ISDN context, not only because some of its steps (eg. traffic matrix forecasting) present problems, but also because some issues (eg: topology; routing, band assigment, flow control and congestion control patterns) can no more be considered as given, but must be considered as determined within a more complex design cycle.

Furthermore, both the optimization criteria and the GOS constraints need a new formulation; finally, internetworking issue must be introduced as a crucial one, in particular in connection with network planning.

Some of these topics were discussed in the two invited papers presented in the morning session. They were preceded by a tutorial given by L.F. Agnati on the "Emerging Complexity of the Brain".

Three main questions are central in the tutorial:

- could an interaction of two natural sciences, as neurophysiology and neurobiology, with artificial sciences be fruitful?

- will the present interaction with computer science and information theory be the only possible and will it be able to help the progress of the knowledge of the brain? The Nervous Central System is only a computational system?

- what could be the importance of the communication sciences (in particular of the switching sciences) for the progress of the brain knowledge?

To allow an answer to these questions, the following topics are presented:

- the main morphofunctional features of the neuronal networks;

- the evolutionary bases of the uniqueness of the human central nervous system (CNS);

- the wiring transmission and the volume transmission;

- the organization principles of the CNS;

- the plasticity of the CNS.

"ISDN Traffic Performance issues in an Evolving Network Environment" are discussed by P. Richards: network flexibility, new design

priority and advanced routing and control in the   future   integrated
transport systems are introduced.

G.R. Ash paper on "Traffic Network Routing, Control and   Design   for
ISDN Era" starts with a provocative sentence: there is no "N" in
the ISDN recommended until now; no network aspects are   present   in
the available ISDN concept.   The paper presented to the seminar
summarizes a contribution submitted to SG II and SG XVIII in   order
to start the Network Architecture work in CCITT.

TRAFFIC ENGINEERING for ISDN Design and Planning
M. Bonatti and M. Decina (Editors)
Elsevier Science Publishers B.V. (North-Holland)
© IAC, 1988

THE EMERGING COMPLEXITY OF THE BRAIN.
LIMITS OF BRAIN-COMPUTER ANALOGY

Luigi Francesco AGNATI, Michele ZOLI, Emilio MERLO PICH, Mirella
RUGGERI, Kjell FUXE*.

Institute of Human Physiology, University of Modena, via Campi 287,
41100, Modena; *Department of Histology, Karolinska Institutet,
Box 60400, S-104 01, Stockholm.

1. INTRODUCTION AND BASIC PROBLEMS.

From ancient times there has been the wish to construct a machine able to
simulate at least some brain functions. Thus, even if never scientifically
proven there are reports on the construction of skillful machines, such as the
"chess player" (Carroll 1975), which was able to win over Napoleon in a chess
game played in Schonbrunn in the 1809. However, even today, very few
performances of the central nervous system (CNS) have been attempted to be
emulated (see the artificial machines with logical skills -McCullum and Smith-;
with theorem proving skills -Gerlenter-; with playing skills -Moore, Strachey,
Samuel-; with learning skills; with decisional skills; with translation
skills).
Some aspects of the CNS have also been considered in the construction of
machines emulating biological performances (see self reproducing automata by
von Neumann and Walter, the Ross Ashby homeostate, the Kretz turtles...).
However, this approach has little to do with knowledge on how the CNS
functions. In the frame of these works as well as in the frame of the
"automata" theory (Church; von Neumann; Buchi, Elgot and Trauchtenbrot, Burks
and Wright; Copi; Elgot and Wright; Kleene; Meghill; Minski, see e.g., Gupta et
al. 1977) and in the "robot approach" phylosophy (Hull 1943, Craik 1966) the
CNS is considered as a "black box" and only the phenomenological description
of the brain operations is concerned.
More recently the progress in brain circuitry knowledge has given some
conceptual hints for the development of new kinds of computers for artificial
intelligence applications, using circuitry, morphologically and functionally,
copied from the brain (Stevens 1985).
Thus, it is possible to recognize three major aspects according to which
computer science, cybernetics and information theory can interact with our
knowledge of the brain function:
- to construct machines with single or aggregate performances similar to the
human brain (artificial intelligence program)
- to construct machines based on the knowledge of the brain circuitry (6th
generation computer program, Stevens 1985)
- on the basis of points a. and b., to reach a better understanding of how the
human brain functions (interpretational program, CNS modelling program)
These programs influence each other mutually and they establish a maze of
relationships. An example is given by the direct and indirect influence on the
neurophysiology and on the neurobiology of the information theory (following

Shannon), the cybernetics (following Wiener, von Neumann and Ashby) and the computer science (following von Neumann).

In particular two points of view seem to be important in neurophysiology: the computational point of view and the communicational point of view. The first has been prevalent in the past, the second is acquiring more and more importance.

The computational point of view focuses on the ability of transforming one type of input information into one type of output information, eventually through the cooperation of lower level computational units (LLCU). The LLCU exchange information among them to assure a fault-tolerant computation. The communications (switching and transmission) are no more than operational modalities.

The communicational point of view focuses on the ability of responding to a communication demand, instant by instant and over a development phase.

This framework can contribute to the progress of neurobiology with reference to the following open questions:

− Are all the cells of the CNS equivalent as far as the information handling, switching and transmission are concerned?

− Is it possible to recognize some kind of modular organization in the CNS?

− Which are the substrates for the information transfer to the CNS, within the CNS and from the CNS?

− Are there one or more codes for the messages in the CNS, and which are the "keys" of these codes?

− Are there one or more "logics" according to which the messages are elaborated, switched and transmitted in the CNS?

− How many of the capabilities of CNS depend on genetic (nature) versus epigenetic (nurture) influences?

Some aspects of these questions will be examined in the next paragraphs. As far as the last question is concerned, the issue is presently under a very ample debate (see e.g., Dawkins 1978, Changeux 1983), and will not be discussed in this presentation.

2. NEURONAL NETWORKS: MAIN MORPHOFUNCTIONAL FEATURES

The nervous networks are formed by neurons contacting each other in a chain-like manner. The typical neurons have the same morphologically defined regions (see fig.1), i.e., the cell body (also called pericaryon) and several fine arborizations originating from the cell body (the dendrites). The dendrites, together with the cell body, serve as the receptive apparatus of the neuron. A long tubular process which constitutes the conducting unit of the nerve cell is called the axon. The axon terminates with specialized endings, the axon terminals, which are part of the "synapses", i.e. of the sites where neurons communicate with each other. In fact, the synapse is formed by a pre-synaptic terminal which is separated from the post-synaptic receptive surface by a synaptic clet (Kandel 1985) (see fig.1). A neuron is morphologically a single cell in contact with hundreds of other neurons. Therefore, a nervous network may be considered as a set of neurons contacting each other via synapses.

The information flowing along the neuronal transmission line is coded both electrically and chemically. Nerve signals are transmitted at the axon membrane level as a fast all-or-none electrical phenomenon, the action potential, highly

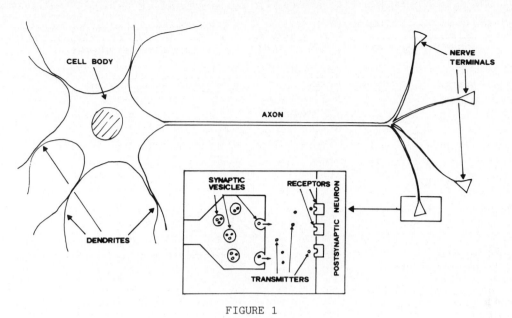

FIGURE 1

Schematic representation of the main morphofunctional features of a typical neuron.

effective in signalling over distance. At the synaptic endings the action potentials serve as a stimulus for the release of chemical substances (the neurotransmitters). The neurotransmitters diffuse across the synaptic cleft to the next cells and bind to specific membrane proteins (the receptors) which recognize and decode the chemical message carried by the neurotransmitters (see fig.1). In the post-synaptic membrane the neurotransmitter-receptor complex induces the formation of an electrotonic signal which may activate or inhibit the triggering of an action potential (ionotropic transmission, Mc Geer et al. 1977). Some neurotransmitter-receptor complexes can also induce metabolic changes in the post-synaptic cell (metabotropic transmission, Mc Geer et al. 1977). Specific receptors for the secreted neurotransmitters are present on the pre-synaptic terminal (also called autoreceptors). The activation of the autoreceptors produces a decrease of the neurotransmitter synthesis rate and/or of its release from the nerve terminal, constituting the closing branch of a negative feedback loop.

In the fifties, sir J. Eccles suggested, on the line of a hypothesis of Dale (1875-1968), that a neuron must contain only one type of neurotransmitter in all its terminals. Recent researches showed that a neuron may use more than one neurotramsmitter, and that several neuroactive chemical substances coexist in the same synapse (see book by Hokfelt et al. 1986). According to this evidence the presence of multiple parallel transmission lines of intra-synaptic communication at this level has been suggested (fig.2). Therefore, the synapse should be considered as a structure capable of complex information processing.

It is therefore possible to recognize multiple parallel transmission lines at the level of the synapse (Agnati et al. 1984). When these lines carry the same information the resulting redundancy may decrease the effect of the noise on the signal.

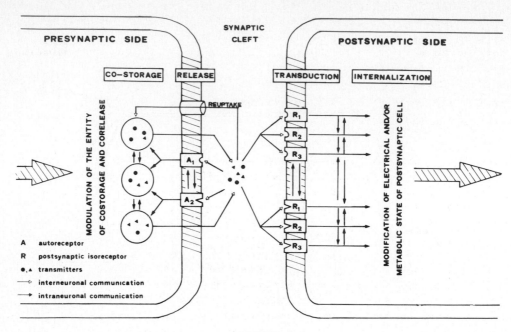

FIGURE 2

Schematic   representation   of   the   multiple   transmission   lines   and   their
interactions at pre- and post-synaptic level.

Another functional meaning of coexistence has been suggested in our laboratory
(Agnati et al. 1980, Fuxe and Agnati 1985, 1987). It has been shown that the
binding   between   a   neurotransmitter and its receptor at the post-synaptic site
may modulate the state of other adjacent receptors present in the membrane,
perhaps by means of allosteric interactions. Therefore, the total information
transfer from the presynaptic neuron and the possibility of the signal-to-error
ratio may be increased. Thus, the modulatory range of post-synaptic neuronal
activity is extremely enlarged.

2.1 The singularity of the neuron.

Not all the cells of the CNS are equivalent as far as the computation,
switching and transmission are concerned, since at least it is possible to
distinguish neurons from glial cells. However, we do not know if all the
neurons and all the glial cells are among them equivalent.
Actually, there are hints that each neuron may be unique (Changeux 1986) not
only   in   view of its set of inputs/outputs and recordings of past
electrochemical activity, but also in view of its "functional geometry". By
this term we want to point out how, "coetera paribus", the shape of a neuron,
in particular of its dendritic tree with its distribution of synaptic inputs,
can deeply affect its function (Shepherd 1979). Furthermore, the singularity of
each neuron is underlined by the evidence that the neuron itself may appear as
an aggregate of functional units represented by patches of macromolecular
complexes in its plasma membrane. Thus, local characteristics of the neuronal
membrane may differ from one site to another site, creating biochemical domains

sometimes endowed with different modalities in the handling of the electrochemical information. In fact, not only has it been reported that regional computation exists in distal dendritic trees (Graubard and Calvin 1979), but also that in the dendritic arborization of specific subclasses of neurons together with the classical electrotonic passive transmission there exists an all-or-none active transmission. For example, in cortical neurons remote dendritic inputs may act on ancillary trigger zones allowing the signal to be actively conducted to boost the final trigger zone in the axon.

2.2 The nature of brain signals and codes.

Presently we know that the CNS uses two types of substrates to transfer information: chemical and electrical signals. However, it should be noted that we cannot exclude the existence of other substrates for information transfer (e.g. magnetic signals).

Very little is fully established about the coding and the decoding of neurons. The best established neuronal code is the so called code of the "labelled lines": the activation of a particular set of neurons or fibers implies by itself some general features of the information carried in the neuronal message, such as e.g. the sensory modality and the site of the body surface to which it is referred.

Many "impulse" code formats have been proposed. As far as a single transmission line is concerned, a "frequency" code (based on the number of impulses per unitary time interval) and a "sequential order" code (based on the interval between the impulses) have been proposed. As far as a set of transmission lines is concerned, a "coincidence gating" code (based on the coincident or locked sequential pattern of activation or inhibition of a neuronal population by two or more transmission lines) and a "distributed" code (based on the profile of activity in a set of transmission lines) have been proposed (Mountcastle 1980a).

Much more hypothetical are the codes, called "nonimpulse" codes, which regulate the intercellular and intracellular communication based on local analogic signals, such as chemical and electrotonic signals. They will be discussed below in the frame of the new acquisition of knowledge on the chemical and electrical transmission in the CNS.

This aspect is also related to another area where our ignorance is pratically complete, i.e., the logic according to which these messages are elaborated in the CNS.

3. EVOLUTIONARY BASES OF THE UNIQUENESS OF THE HUMAN CENTRAL NERVOUS SYSTEM

As demonstrated by comparative studies, the basic elements constituting the CNS (class of cells, types of synaptic contacts, types of transmitter molecules etc.) are very similar in the different animal species, at least within the mammalians (see e.g., Changeux 1983). The uniqueness of human brain is probably due to a richer morphology of neurons, to the rise of microcircuits density and of the total number of nerve cells in the telencephalic areas. According to this evidence a model of brain functioning has been proposed (Agnati and Fuxe 1984a). It has been suggested that the progressive increase of the encephalization along phylogenesis is the result of two intertwiningly processes: the miniaturization of the circuits and the hierarchical

organization of the neural networks. In particular, the existence of the local circuits was described by Ramon y Cajal (1859-1934), at the beginning of the century. This author showed that the high density of local circuits may be considered the structural correlate of the integrative capability of the CNS, reaching their maximal density in the brain of the man. Recently, it has been demonstrated that the local circuits are formed by specialized parts of neurons in close contact with each other, which work as an integrative unit (Rakic 1979, Agnati et al. 1981). For example, reciprocal dendro-dendritic synapses constitute one type of such microcircuits (Shepherd 1978). Thus, local circuits are characterized by
- the high density of computational structures
- the potential for complex interactions
- the rapid processing of information
- the low energy expense.
Interactions between the different structures of the local circuit may be both electrical (graded local potentials) or chemical (synaptic release) (fig.3).

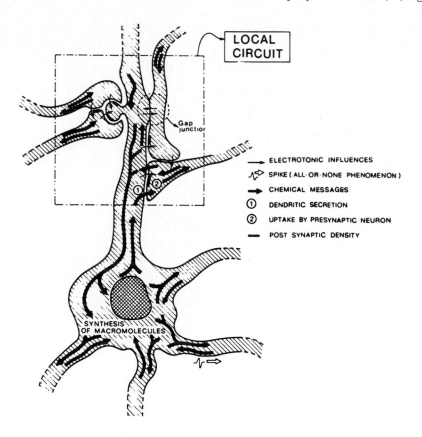

FIGURE 3

Schematic representation of the high synaptic density present in the local circuit.

As Metzler underlines (Metzler 1977) the use, at local circuit level, of graded potentials of low intensity requires high sensitivity, permitting discrimination which cannot be equaled by an all-or-none process, and endows them with the capability of explaining the analog nature of mental transformations.

This miniaturization process has similarities with the amazing increase of computational capabilities due to the miniaturization of the electronic components in the computers. On this basis, we proposed that the brain succeded into increasing its integrative activity by increasing the density of local circuits instead of the number of the networks, with an overall increase of the hierarchical levels (Agnati and Fuxe 1984a).

Cybernetics has shown that it is possible to project a system capable of extremely complex elaborations, using simple components, by increasing the number of hierarchical levels (Albus, 1981). Therefore, the fault tolerance of a system such as the CNS, built by elementary units characterized by simple computational functions and errors, is guaranteed by redundancy, vicarious potentiality and hierarchy. The heterogeneity of the elementary computational units allows a higher level of the fault tolerance of the computation compared with an equal number of homogeneous units (Winograd and Cowan 1963).

However, in order to cope with the complex tasks required by the adaptive behaviour, fault tolerance requires an increasing number of the elementary units of processing, leading to an increase
- of the size of the brain
- of the energy costs
- of the time wasting in signal transmission.
These disadvantages due to physical and chemical constraints are partially overcome by miniaturization. Therefore, information processing in the CNS takes place at the molecular level into local circuits, whose output can modulate neuronal networks of higher hierarchical level, which may affect brain areas which are anatomically distant but related to a defined function. On turn, these functional subsets interact with each other, being integrated into networks of maximal hierarchical level.

It is possible to conclude that the progressive superimposition of networks of higher hierarchical order gave to man the possibility to perform more and more complex mental operations, far from the "stimulus-response" paradigm, up to the appearance of the consciousness and the thought.

It is important to distinguish at least another kind of hierarchical organization present in the CNS (see fig.4). Together with a "computational hierarchy" as the one described above, an "architectonic hierarchy" is demonstrable in the CNS. In fact, lower centers and pathways (devoted to simpler tasks such as reflexes) and higher centers and pathways (devoted to more complex tasks such as, .g., integrated control of internal parameters) are both present, even if differently developed, in all vertebrate CNS. The two concepts are complementary since at each architectonic hierarchical level, a computational hierarchical organization can be recognized (see fig.4).

4. THE WIRING TRANSMISSION AND THE VOLUME TRANSMISSION: THE BRAIN GOES FAR AWAY FROM ANY COMPUTER.

It is clear that notwithstanding its complexity the neuronal network viewed as a set of neurons interacting by means of synaptic contacts is still amenable to a formal representation, which could use many suggestions from the computer world. However, this may not be the entire truth.

We have recently suggested the existence in the CNS of two types of

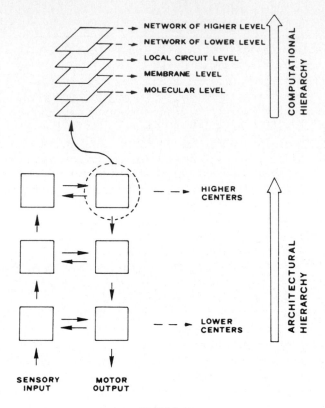

FIGURE 4

Schematic representation of the architectural and computational hierarchical organization of the CNS.

electrochemical transmission namely the wiring transmission (WT) and the volume transmission (VT) (Agnati et al. 1985, 1986a,b, Agnati et al. 1987a). The concepts are summarized in Tables 1 and 2. The WT is the classical type of electrochemical transmission, which rests on the physical substrate of the neuronal chain. The VT is a humoral type of electrochemical transmission. However, it does not only consist of chemical signals (such as paracrine and endocrine signals), diffusing in the extracellular fluid (ECF) to reach the appropriate receptors, but also of electrotonic signals, which operate in the ECF. In fact, the extracellular space of the brain may be considered as a collection of several interconnected restricted microenvironments. Thus, ion fluxes across cellular membranes can induce substantial local changes in the ion composition (Nicholson 1980). These ionic fluctuations in the ECF and the ionic fluxes from sources to sinks may represent signals for communication within and between local circuits, and, more generally, between CNS cells. In table 1 the possible role of glial cells and neurons in the WT and VT is summarized. In VT the glial cells control the ECF ion composition, the shaping of the ECF pathways (i.e. the communication channels between sources and sinks) for signal diffusion as well as the release, uptake, recognition and metabolism of humoral signals. Here again as for neuron structures there is the possibility of extremely complex "functional geometry" of ECF pathways. With regard to the function of neurons in VT they represent both the physical substrate and the main site of control of sources and sinks for electrotonic

		GLIA FUNCTIONS		NEURON FUNCTIONS	
		PHYSICAL	BIOCHEMICAL	PHYSICAL	BIOCHEMICAL
WIRING TRANSMISSION	ELECTRICAL SYNAPSE	SYNAPSE SEGREGATION	MODULATION OF COUPLING VIA ECF	LOCATION OF SYNAPSE	MODULATION OF COUPLING VIA ICF
	CHEMICAL SYNAPSE	SYNAPSE SEGREGATION	MODULATION OF SYNAPTIC CLEFT MICROENVIRONMENT	LOCATION OF SYNAPSE	CONTROL OF THE EFFICACY OF TRANSMISSION LINES AND THEIR INTERPLAY
VOLUME TRANSMISSION	ELECTROTONIC SIGNALS	SHAPING OF ECF PATHWAYS FOR SIGNAL DIFFUSION	CONTROL OF ECF ION COMPOSITION	LOCATION OF SOURCES AND SINKS FOR SIGNALS	CONTROL OF SOURCES AND SINKS FOR SIGNALS
	HUMORAL SIGNALS	SHAPING OF ECF PATHWAYS FOR SIGNAL DIFFUSION	RELEASE, UPTAKE AND METABOLISM OF SIGNALS	LOCATION OF SOURCES AND SINKS FOR SIGNALS	RELEASE, UPTAKE AND METABOLISM OF SIGNALS

TABLE 1

Main features of the morphofunctional roles of neurons and glial cells in the wiring and in the volume transmission (ICF=intracellular fluid).

	SPEED OF TRANSMISSION	DEGREE OF DIVERGENCE	SEGREGATION ("SAFETY OF THE TRANSMISSION)	PLASTICITY	PREFERENTIAL INFORMATION PROCESSING
"WIRING TRANSMISSION" NEURON LINKED ELECTRO-CHEMICAL TRANSMISSION	HIGH	LOW TO MODERATE	HIGH	LOW TO MODERATE	ELEMENTARY ELABORATION SHORT TERM ACTION
"VOLUME TRANSMISSION" HUMORAL ("OPEN") ELECTRO-CHEMICAL TRANSMISSION	LOW	HIGH TO VERY HIGH	LOW	HIGH TO VERY HIGH	HOLISTIC ELABORATION LONG TERM ACTION

TABLE 2

Schematic representation of the main features of the wiring and the volume transmission.

signals and of release, uptake and recognition for humoral signals. When we are focusing our attention on chemical signals in WT and VT it is possible to recognize some main differential features. Thus, as seen in table 2 the VT is characterized by a low speed and a long term action, a high degree of divergence and plasticity and a low safety of the transmission process. On the other hand, WT operates with a high speed and safety, and short term action, the divergency and plasticity being low. It seems clear that the integrative capability of the central and peripheral nervous system is increased by the presence of VT, which has different and very weak neuroanatomical constraints and which may affect the computing characteristics of the neuronal networks.

The description of the VT and WT can take advantage of the terminology of the communication science. The WT is based on a relatively limited number of transmission lines (the axons), which have a relatively high biological cost in terms of overall dimension and energy requirement. Thus, a rather high degree of switching is present in the neuronal networks, demonstrable as convergent and divergent pathways (see fig.5). Together with convergence and divergence, we can recognize in the CNS a certain number of dedicated lines, especially represented in the peripheral and central pathways of the sensory and motor systems.

The VT, on the contrary, faces completely different physical and energetical problems. In fact, the chemical transmission lines in a liquid volume are practically infinite and not expensive in biological terms: thus no switching is required (fig. 5). There is only a need of "biological traps", the receptors, which can recognize and transduce the signals (as in data flow computer architectures).

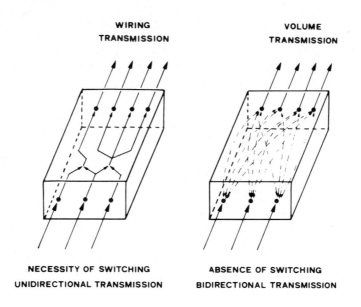

WIRING   **VOLUME**
TRANSMISSION   **TRANSMISSION**

NECESSITY OF SWITCHING   **ABSENCE OF SWITCHING**
UNIDIRECTIONAL TRANSMISSION   **BIDIRECTIONAL TRANSMISSION**

FIGURE 5

Schematic representation of some communicational features of the wiring and volume transmission. A high degree of switching is necessary for the wiring transmission, while no switching is required in the volume transmission. Furthermore, the volume transmission can be easily bidirectional, while the wiring transmission is usually unidirectional.

In order to understand the actions of humoral signals on the WT it is important to emphasize (see also above) that the synapse is now regarded as a highly complex electrometabolic integrative unit (see fig.2). It consists of multiple transmission lines (Agnati et al. 1984, Fuxe et al. 1984), which interact with one another at the pre- and post-synaptic membrane via intramembrane receptor-receptor interactions. Receptor-receptor interactions take place within the plane of the membrane (see Agnati et al. 1980, Fuxe and Agnati 1985, 1987), either directly or via interposed molecules. However, it should be considered that a "chemical message-receptor" complex can influence another receptor also via intracytoplasmatic mechanisms (Greengard 1987). Hence, short and long feedback loops among intramembrane macromolecular complexes (receptors, ion channels, ion pumps,...) can be recognized. In fig.6 the complexity of the integration is illustrated at the membrane level, where filtration and integration of the signals take place. The intracytoplasmatic

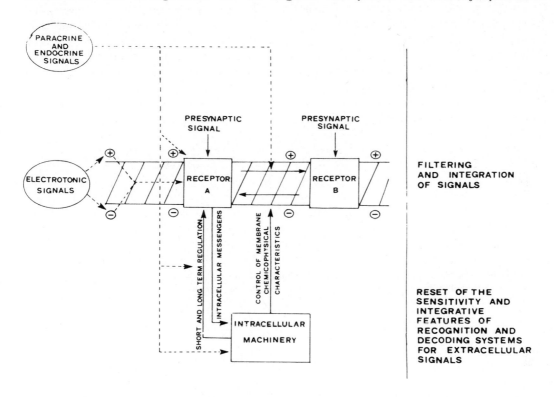

FIGURE 6

Possible interactions between volume transmission and wiring transmission at membrane as well as at intracellular levels.

mechanisms control the recognition sites and the decoding mechanisms in the membrane for ECF signals, in this way e.g. resetting the sensitivity in the integrative capability of the receptor mechanisms. Fig.6 illustrates also how hormonal and paracrine signals directly modulate the receptor characteristics or the receptor-receptor interactions in the membrane. The intracellular machinery and its short and long term regulation of the receptor mechanisms is also influenced, probably mainly via nuclear actions, at least as far as steroid and thyroid hormones are concerned (see book by Fuxe et al. 1981). The electrotonic signals in the VT control the membrane polarization, in this way influencing the opening or closure of ionic channels. Changes in membrane polarization probably lead to allosteric changes in intramembrane proteins of the receptor complex and of ion pumps. In this way electrical information can be transformed into chemical information. Thus, the two "languages" of the brain, i.e.the electrical and chemical signals, can be rapidly interconverted and the information coded into these two modalities, effectively integrated.

4.1. Peripheral modulation of wiring transmission

It must be considered that there exists a blood brain barrier, so that the CNS will not receive a number of peripheral signals. However, there exist chemical and physical "windows", through which the brain receives and delivers messages. Chemical "windows" select the signals on the basis of the existence of facilitated or active transport mechanisms, etc. The physical "windows" are represented by brain areas devoid of the blood brain barrier such as the area postrema, the median eminence and the subfornical organ. Also the neuronal inputs through the peripheral nervous system represent a part of the physical window (Fuxe et al. 1987)

4.2. Peripheral modulation of volume transmission

It should be considered that steroid hormones and thyroid hormones, and also peptide hormones acting on receptors present in areas where the blood brain barrier is absent, can affect some neuronal structures and influence the release of signals in the CNS. Some chemical signals may affect the neuronal networks via the ventricular system and the ECF. It seems likely that the steroid and thyroid hormones may influence the uptake of messengers and trophic factors in glial cells (mainly glucocorticoids) and neurons as well as their release from glial cells and neurons. Thus, the release and the uptake of paracrine signals from neurons reaching a distant receptor population may be highly influenced by those hormones, which thus can profoundly influence VT in the nervous system.
It is also conceivable that the ECF pathways which are of substantial importance in VT may be influenced by hormones in view, e.g., of the ability of glucocorticoids to control astroglia functions (Fuxe et al. 1987).

5. ASPECTS OF THE ORGANIZATION PRINCIPLES OF THE CNS.

It seems as if the basic texture of some CNS structures is made up of elementary units. Thus, it can be surmised that in the CNS three main types of basic organization can be recognized:
-A. regions organized in nuclei and subnuclei, defined by means of morphometrical methods (cell number, size, density...) on the basis of classical neuroanatomy (neuronal cell groups) and/or on the basis of chemical neuroanatomical markers (transmitter-identified neuronal cell groups), such as biosynthetic enzymes, transmitters, cotransmitters (Agnati and Fuxe 1984b). The subgroups can represent a kind of modular organization very heterogeneous regarding to morphological as well as to functional characteristics. Conversely, inside of the subnuclei, some kind of repetitive arrangements at microcircuit level can be recognized (e.g., the microcircuits formed by the motoneuron and the inhibitory interneuron of Renshaw in the anterior horn of the spinal cord). It is possible to distinguish the "diffuse type" of nuclear organization such as the one of reticular formation, from the "compact" nuclear organization such as the one of the thalamus and the hypothalamus.
-B. regions containing definite compartments, identified on the basis of

chemical neuroanatomy. These compartments, called "structural" modules can be recognized in the striatum (the "striosomes") and in the median eminence (the "medianosomes). The striosomes are repetitive, heterogeneous (regarding to size and shape) structures present in specific subregions of the striatum. At median eminence level the structural modules can be subdivided in a lower level modular organization based on the local circuits of transmitter-identified nerve terminals regulating the secretion of one hypothalamic hormone.

-C. regions made up by repetitive neuronal arrangements with or without well defined boundaries, such as the cortical columns and the cerebellum, respectively. In particular the columns are repetitive sets of cells which form a vertical structure throughout a brain region. Each column is involved in the integration of specific inputs. They are homogeneous regarding to size and shape. This organization is present in the somatosensory, visual, motor and frontal association cortex (Mountcastle 1980b).

Other principles of organization such as somatotopy (i.e., the segregation of subset of neurons or axons in the nuclei or pathways, respectively, according to the body surface area to which they are connected) can be superimposed on this basic buildup of neuronal circuits. Genetic and epigenetic influences can exert their actions in the frame of these organizational principles.

In the following paragraphs we will develop the concept of the modular organization of the CNS in the frame of the WT and VT.

5.1. Modules of wiring transmission

The cortical columns were identified on the basis of functional criteria, e.g. the neurons of a column respond to the same sensory stimulus applied to a specific area of the skin. The columns have been shown to be modality specific and site specific and were subsequently demonstrated to have an anatomical correlate. Recently, by studies in chemical neuroanatomy it has been possible to obtain indications that the modular organization is not unique for the cerebral cortex but exists also in other brain areas such as the striatum and the median eminence (Olson et al. 1972, Graybiel 1984, Fuxe et al. 1980, 1986, Agnati et al. 1987).

We have recently introduced the concept that there exist "integrative" modules in the brain, formed in the interaction zones between various structural modules (Fuxe et al. 1986). The overlap zones between two, three or more structural modules correspond to integrative modules of higher and higher level (fig.7 and 8). Each integrative module, of any level, may have different spatial and temporal patterns of activity, resulting in a very ample spectrum of functional states. This may be considered the functional counterpart of the "module", which is basically defined by means of the criteria borrowed from the chemical neuroanatomy.

5.2. Modules of volume transmission

Recently by means of automatic image analysis we have also been able to discover the existence of islands of neurons that contain glucocorticoid receptor like immunoreactivity (GR LI) within the striatum and the nucleus accumbens. These results provide the first evidence for the existence, at least in parts of the CNS, of structural modules characterized on the basis of humoral inputs. GR LI islands have a rather uniform distribution and are different from the striatal modules of the wiring transmission mentioned above

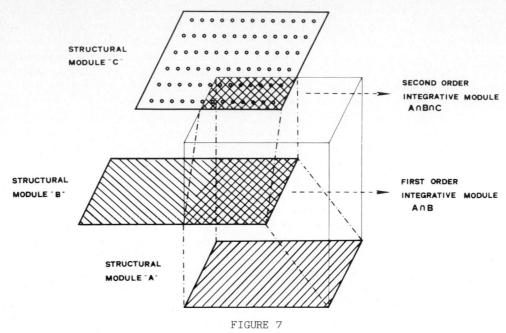

FIGURE 7

Schematic representation of the structural and the integrative modules of different orders. The integrative modules can be formalized by means of the set theory.

(see Zoli et al. 1987).

5.3. Functional aspects of the modular organization

One example of functional interaction between WT and VT modules is present in the local circuits formed by the various types of transmitter identified nerve terminals at median eminence level (Fuxe et al. 1986). In fact, at median eminence level (interface area between brain and endocrine system), the various types of transmitter identified nerve terminal networks are organized in compartments, the "structural" medianosomes, located in distinct parts of the median eminence forming rostrocaudal strips. In the overlap areas between different structural medianosomes (called "integrative" medianosomes) a modular arrangements made up by local circuits regulating the secretion of one hypothalamic hormone (called "hypothalamic hypophysiotropic hormones", HHH, e.g., releasing hormones) can be recognized. They have been called HHH modules (see fig.9). The HHH secreted by the median eminence controls the release of adenohypophyseal hormones. The differential activation of the various elements forming a HHH module results in a functional state, which will provide the appropriate output to control anterior pituitary hormone secretion. Receptors for various hypothalamic and hypophyseal hormones, such as thyreotropin releasing hormone and corticotropin releasing hormone, probably exist in various portions of the cell membranes of the nerve terminals constituting the local circuits of the medianosomes (Taylor and Burt 1982, De Souza et al. 1985). Thus, one important role of the hypothalamic and of the hypophyseal hormones is to modulate the activity of the median eminence local circuits, an

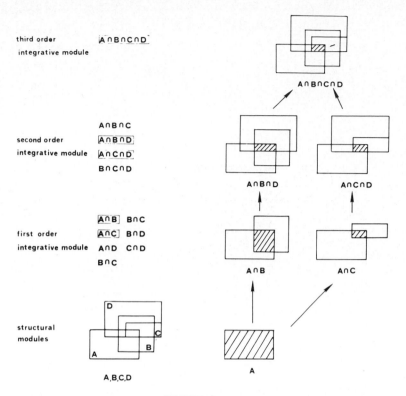

FIGURE 8

In the left panel the basic structural modules (A, B, C, D) and all the possible integrative modules of different orders are shown. The integrative modules represented in the right panel are within boxes.

In the right panel two possible sets of integrative modules are represented. The pathway on the far right shows how it is possible to obtain the same integrative module endowed with different integrative orders.

action which probably underies the ultra-short and short loop feed back action of the hypothalamic and of the hypophyseal hormones, respectively. From the above it becomes clear that one important site of action of hormones in the brain is the local circuit module, where the activated hormonal receptors of humoral modules interact with activated transmitter receptors of wiring modules to adjust the functional output.

6. PLASTICITY OF THE CNS

In the Hewitt's description of open "intelligent" systems, some features of the CNS could be recognized (Hewitt 1985). Open systems require a theory of computation in which

- I. processing might never halt
- II. processing may be required to provide output while still in operation
- III. processing can accept inputs from sources not anticipated when computation began.

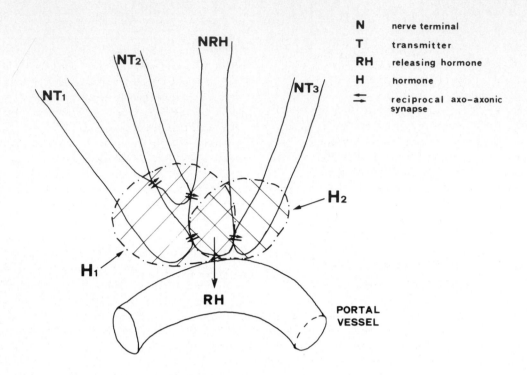

FIGURE 9

Schematic representation of a HHH module, organized around the terminal containing one hypothalamic hormone, e.g., a releasing hormone (RH). Different hormonal inputs can modulate the functional state of the HHH module. The RH itself can influence its secretion, representing the closing branch of the ultra-short feedback loop.

On the other hand, CNS has to be considered partially as a closed system, according to the fact that the result of its operational processes is the generation of a self-determined state (eigenbehavior, see Varela 1984). Asynchronous dynamic interactions with the environment based on the principles of commutativity, pluralism and accessibility (Hewitt 1985) are in balance with the operational closure of some CNS circuits in determining both the internal state and the management of information processing operations. Structural architectures which support such functions are the result of morphogenetic phenomena depending both on genetic and epigenetic influences (Changeux 1983). Thus, we can consider the CNS both as a closed system, regarding to its actual processing functions, and as an open system, regarding to the ontogenetic formation and continuous remodelling in the adult life of its circuitry.

The concept of plasticity of the nervous system refers to the capability of the neuronal substrate to continuously change either in the fetal and neonatal period or during the adult life in an adaptive fashion its processing characteristics. It is possible to distinguish a functional plasticity based on changes of the efficiency o the existing computational, switching and transmission elements from a structural plasticity based on changes of the number and morphological characteristics of the computational, switching and transmission elements. Functional and structural plasticity can be considered in the frame of the WT and/or the VT. We mention only some main aspects of this concept:

- WT functional plasticity: changes in the efficiency of synaptic transmission have been well characterized. For example, a decrease of the transmitter concentration in the synaptic cleft induces a compensatory increase in the density of post-synaptic receptors for that transmitter (phenomenon of the up-regulation). These plastic changes can take place also in response to signals coming from the VT (e.g., via receptor-receptor interactions).

- WT structural plasticity: cell growth and death and generation and degeneration of synaptic contacts take place during the morphogenesis. In the adult life, synapse turnover and/or remodelling of the cell geometry can be observed. These changes may be partly under the influences of VT signals such as gradients of energy (e.g., electrical fields) and/or of chemicals (e.g., trophic factors, i.e., informational molecules that can regulate the cellular survival and/or growth).

- VT functional plasticity: the chemical transmission of the VT type show the same plastic phenomena as the WT type. Furthermore, it should be considered that any change in the ECF volume and/or composition affects the efficiency of this type of transmission.

- VT structural plasticity: the structural plasticity of this type of transmission is very high. In fact, for example, the divergence of a chemical transmission , i.e. the number of targets, can be changed by simply inducing or preventing the appearance of receptor molecules for a message on the possible target cells. Furthermore, the glial cells can modify the shape of the ECF and hence the pathways connecting different computational elements.

One of the effects of plasticity in the adult life may be the optimization of the potential capability of processing of the CNS. This phenomenon may explain some improvements observed in the psychometric tests in the adult life and even during aging, in spite of the general decline of the chemico-physical substrate.

7. CONCLUSIONS

The extraordinary complexity of the CNS has been underlined. The following aspects have especially been considered:

1. the synapse is an integrative structure capable of highly sophisticated computational and communicational functions and is not simply a device to facilitate or to inhibit the firing of the postsynaptic cell

2. the neuronal networks are not the only chemico-physical substrate along which the information flows. The volume transmission must always be considered together with the wiring transmission

3. it seems possible that in the CNS some general principles of organization are present:

a. at molecular level there exist interactions among macromolecular complexes such as aggregates of receptors communicating via receptor-receptor interactions

b. at synaptic level there exist interactions among various synapses such as those in the local circuits

c. at micronetwork level there exist interactions among neurons and terminals such as those in the structural modules

d. at network level there exist interactions among pathways and neuronal nuclei involved in the control of a certain function.

4. it is also possible that during evolution two different trends have shaped the CNS : the hierarchical superimposition of more and more divergent networks, and the miniaturization of the elementary circuits.

The following topics have been discussed:

- the architecture of the CNS ad its component (neurons, modules, see ch.3 and 5)

- the effective use of the components of the CNS (see ch.2 and 4)

- adaptability, fault-tolerance and tolerance to environmental changes of the CNS (see ch.2 and 6)

- neuronal plasticity during development and adult life of the CNS (see ch.6)

In particular, the modelling power of the computational analogies in facing the emerging complexity of the brain has been examined. A possible role of switching in neuronal networks has been discussed with reference to the switching potentialities of the VT, which enhances the possibility of resources sharing in the CNS.

A multiple point of view on the CNS based on different relationships (hierarchies) among control, computation, communication and information will constitute a less limited approach than the computational point of view alone (see introduction).

ACKNOWLEDGMENTS

We thank dr. Mario Bonatti, for the useful discussions on computer and communication science.

REFERENCES

Agnati L.F. and Fuxe K., eds. (1984a) New concepts on the structure of the neural networks: the miniaturization and hierarchical organization of the central nervous system. Biosci. Rep., 4: 93-94.

Agnati L.F. and Fuxe K. (1984b) Computer assisted morphometry and microdensitometry of transmitter-identified neurons with special reference to the mesostriatal dopamine pathway. I. Methodological aspects. Acta Physiol. Scand., suppl. 532: 5-36.

Agnati L.F., Fuxe K., Zini I., Lenzi P., Hokfelt T. (1980) Aspects on receptor regulation and isoreceptor identification. Med. Biol., 58: 182-187.

Agnati L.F., Fuxe K., Ferri M., Benfenati F., Ogren S.-O. (1981) A new hypothesis on memory. A possible role of local circuits in the formation of the memory trace. Med. Biol., 59: 224-229.

Agnati L.F., Fuxe K., Battistini N., Zini I., Benfenati F., Merlo Pich E., Farabegoli C., Zoli M., Andersson K., Harfstrand A. (1984) Multiple transmission lines in central synapses and their interactions, In D. Kemali, P.V. Morozov and G. Toffano (Eds.) New research strategies in biological psychiatry, Biological psychiatry-New prospects vol. 3, John Libbey, London, pp. 58-71.

Agnati L.F., Fuxe K., Zoli M. (1985) Considerazioni sulle interazioni tra sistema nervoso centrale e sistema endocrino. Crescita, 14: 34-38.

Agnati L.F., Fuxe K., Zoli M., Merlo Pich E., Benfenati F., Zini I., Goldstein M. (1986a) Aspects on the information handling by the central nervous system: focus on cotransmission in the aged rat brain. In T. Hokfelt, K. Fuxe and B. Pernow (Eds.) Coexistence of neuronal messengers: a new principle in chemical transmission, Prog. Brain Res. vol. 68, Elsevier, Amsterdam, pp. 291-301

Agnati L.F., Fuxe K., Zoli M., Zini I., Toffano G., Ferraguti F. (1986b) A correlation analysis of the regional distribution of central enkephalin and B-endorphin immunoreactive terminals and of opiate receptors in adult and old male rats. Evidence for the existence of two main types of communication in the central nervous system: the volume transmission and the wiring transmission. Acta Physiol. Scand., 128: 201-207.

Agnati L.F., Fuxe K., Merlo Pich E., Zoli M., Zini I., Benfenati F., Harfstrand A., Goldstein M. (1987a) Aspects on the integrative capabilities of the central nervous system: evidence for volume transmission and its possible relevance for receptor-receptor interactions. In K. Fuxe and L.F. Agnati (Eds.) Receptor-receptor interactions. A new integrative mechanism, MacMillan Press, London, in press.

Agnati L.F., Fuxe K., Zoli M., Ferraguti F., Ouimet C., Walaas I., Hemmings H.C. Jr., Goldstein M., Greengard P. (1987b) Morphometrical analysis of tyrosine hydroxylase, enkephalin and DARPP-32 like immunoreactive profiles and their codistribution at three rostrocaudal levels of the rat neostriatum. Evidence for a complex islandic and striae organization. Neuroscience, submitted.

Albus J.S. (1981) Brains, behaviour and robotics, McGraw Hill, New York.

Carroll C.M. (1975) The great chess automaton, Dover Publ. Inc., New York.

Changeux J.-P. (1983) L'homme neuronal, Librairie Artheme Fayard, Paris.

Changeux J.-P. (1986) Coexistence of neuronal messengers and molecular selection. In T. Hokfelt, K. Fuxe and B. Pernow (Eds.) Coexistence of neuronal messengers: a new principle in chemical transmission, Progr. Brain Res. vol. 68, Elsevier, Amsterdam, pp. 373-403.

Craik K.J.W (1966) The mechanism of human action. In S.L. Sherwood (Ed.) The nature of psychology, Cambridge Un. Press, Cambridge.

Dawkins R.R. (1976) The selfish gene, Oxford Un. Press, Oxford.

De Souza E.B., Insel T.R., Perrin M.H., Rivier J., Vale W.S., Kuhar M.J. (1985) Corticotropin-releasing factor receptors are widely distributed within the rat central nervous system: an autoradiographic study. J. Neurosci., 5: 3189-3203.

Fuxe K. and Agnati L.F. (1985) Receptor-receptor interactions in the central nervous system. A new integrative mechanism in synapses. Med. Res. Rev., 5:

441–482.

Fuxe K. and Agnati L.F., eds. (1987) Receptor-receptor interactions. A new intramembrane integrative mechanism, MacMillan Press, London.

Fuxe K., Andersson K., Schwarcz R., Agnati L.F., Perez de la Mora M., Hokfelt T., Goldstein M., Ferland L., Possani L., Tapia R. (1979) Studies on different types of dopamine nerve terminals in the forebrain and their possible interactions with hormones and with neurons containing GABA, glutamate and opioid peptides, In L.J. Poirier, T.L. Sourkes and P.J. Bedard (Eds.) Advances in neurology vol. 24, Raven Press, New York, pp. 199–214.

Fuxe K., Gustafsson J.-A., Wetterberg L., eds. (1981) Steroid hormone regulation of the brain, Pergamon Press, Oxford.

Fuxe K., Agnati L.F., Andersson K., Martire M., Ogren S.-O., Giardino L., Battistini N., Grimaldi R., Farabegoli C., Harfstrand A., Toffano G. (1984) Receptor-receptor interactions in the central nervous system. Evidence for the existence of heterostatic synaptic mechanisms, In E.S. Vizi and K. Magyar (Eds.) Regulation of transmitter function: basic and clinical aspects, Akademia Kiado, Budapest, pp. 129–140.

Fuxe K., Andersson K., Harfstrand A., Agnati L.F., Eneroth P., Janson A.M., Vale W., Thorner M., Goldstein M. (1986) Medianosomes as integrative units in the external layer of the median eminence. Studies on GRF/catecholamine interactions in the hypothalamus of the male rat. Neurochem. Int., 9: 155–170.

Fuxe K., Agnati L.F., Hatfstrand A., Cintra A., Aronsson M., Zoli M., Gustafsson J.-A. (1987) Principles for the hormone regulation of wiring and volume transmission in the central nervous system. In Neuroendocrinology of mood, Current topics in neuroendocrinology vol.8, Springer-Verlag, Berlin-Heidelberg-New York, in press.

Graybiel A.M., Ragsdale C.W. (1983) Biochemical anatomy of the striatum, In P.C. Emson (Ed.) Chemical neuroanatomy, Raven Press, New York, pp. 427–504.

Graubard K. and Calvin W.H. (1979) Presynaptic dendrites: implications of sickeless synaptic transmission and dendritic geometry. In Schmitt F.O. and Worden F.G. (Eds.) The neurosciences: 4th study program, The MIT Press, Cambridge, Mass., pp. 317–331.

Greengard P. (1987) Receptor-receptor interactions mediated by protein phosphorylation. In K. Fuxe and L.F. Agnati (Eds.) Receptor-receptor interactions. A new intramembrane integrative mechanism, McMillan Press, London, pp. 444–453.

Gupta M.M., Saridis G.N., Gaines B.R., eds. (1977) Fuzzy automata and decision processes, North Holland, New York.

Hewitt C. (1985) The challenge of open systems. Byte, 10: 223–242.

Hokfelt T., Fuxe K., Pernow B., eds. (1986) Coexistence of neuronal messengers:

a new principle in chemical transmission, Prog. Brain Res. vol. 68, Elsevier, Amsterdam.

Hull C.L. (1943) Principles of behavior, Appleton-Century, New York.

Kandel E.R. (1985) Nerve cells and behavior, In E.R. Kandel and J.H. Schwartz (Eds.) Principles of neural science, 2nd ed., Elsevier, New York-Amsterdam, pp. 13-24.

Mc Geer P.Z., Eccles J., Mc Geer E.G. (1978) Molecular neurobiology of the mammalian brain, Plenum Press, New York.

Metzler J. (1977) Mental transformations. A top-down analysis. In J. Metzler (Ed.) Systems neuroscience, Academic Press, New York, pp. 1-24.

Mountcastle V.B. (1980a) Sensory receptors and neural encoding: introduction to sensory processes. In V.B. Mountcastle (Ed.) Medical physiology, 14th ed., vol. 1, The Mosby Company, Saint Louis, pp. 327-347.

Mountcastle V.B. (1980b) An organizing principle for cerebral function: the unit module and the distributed system. In G.M. Edelman and V.B. Mountcastle, The mindful brain, The MIT Press, Cambridge, Mass., pp. 7-50.

Nicholson C. (1980) Measurement of extracellular ions in the brain. Trends Neurosci., sept. 216-218.

Olsn L., Seiger A., Fuxe K. (1972) Heterogeneity of striatal and limbic dopamine innervation: highly fluorescent islands in developing and adult rats. Brain Res., 44: 283-288.

Rakic P. (1979) Genetic and epigenetic determinants of local neuronal circuits in the mammalian central nervous system. In F.O. Schmitt and F.G. Worden (Eds.) The neurosciences: 4th study program, The MIT Press, Cambridge, Mass., pp. 109-127.

Shepherd G.M. (1978) Microcircuits in the nervous system. Sci. Am., 238: 92-103.

Shepherd G.M. (1979) The synaptic organization of the brain, Oxford Un. Press, New York.

Stevens J.K. (1985) Reverse engineering the brain. Byte, 10: 286-299.

Taylor R.L. and Burt D.R. (1982) Species differencies in the brain regional distribution of receptor binding of thyrotropin-releasing hormone. J. Neurochem., 38: 1649-1656.

Varela F. (1980) Principles of biological autonomy, North-Holland, New York.

Winograd S. and Cowan J.D. (1963) Reliable computation in the presence of noise, The MIT Press, Cambridge, Mass., 1963.

Zoli M., Agnati L.F., Fuxe K., Zini I., Cintra A., Aronsson M., Wikstrom A.-C., Gustafsson J.-A. (1987) Evidence for the existence of a humoral mosaic organization in the dorsal striatum and nucleus accumbens of the male rat: studies on glucocorticoid receptor immunoreactive nerve cells. Brain Res., submitted.

TRAFFIC ENGINEERING for ISDN Design and Planning
M. Bonatti and M. Decina (Editors)
Elsevier Science Publishers B.V. (North-Holland)
© IAC, 1988

ISDN TRAFFIC PERFORMANCE ISSUES IN AN EVOLVING NETWORK ENVIRONMENT

Philip RICHARDS

BNR
Ottawa, Canada

Abstract

This paper provides a teletraffic perspective on four aspects of the
future ISDN environment: network flexibility, network design for
survivability, design for real-time performance, and advanced routing and control in future integrated transport. Each of these
aspects is illustrated through a performance modeling example.

Main statements

The network technologies and architectures associated with ISDN are
challenging us to develop new teletraffic methods and to apply them
in new ways.

1. BACKGROUND AND OBJECTIVE

ISDN will have major effects on the ways in which we characterize teletraffic
demand and teletraffic performance, with consequent implications for network
design and operations. However, while considering these ISDN-related changes,
it is important to keep in mind the broader technological, operational, and
architectural environment in which ISDN will function.

This paper is a proposal to open up some of these broader, ISDN-environment
issues from a teletraffic perspective. The sections that follow will introduce:

• network flexibility as a means of simplifying ISDN demand forecasting,

• new design priorities, which include
  - design for survivable networks,
  - design for real-time performance in switching components, and

• advanced routing and control in the future integrated transport systems
  that will support ISDN core evolution.

The intent of the paper is to share with the international teletraffic community our view of the broader network evolution challenges that will be inseparable from ISDN. Four examples are presented, based on ongoing modeling work
being carried out in BNR, to illustrate each major point. The purpose in each
case will be to state the motivation behind and objective of the work
involved, and provide a limited view of the results. Future papers will
address each area in greater detail including theoretical under pinnings,
modeling approach, and a fuller description and analysis of the results.

2. FORECASTING VERSUS FLEXIBILITY

The "integrated" in ISDN refers initially to access standards and supporting
access technology, but the ISDN vision also calls for evolution to integrated
core transport and to integrated transport operations. From a teletraffic
point of view, the implication is that all user demands -- from low intensity
D-channel signaling and data, to long holding-time wideband connections --
must be reduced to a single set of forecastable parameters that can be fed
into the telephone company's integrated forecasting, provisioning, and servicing system. As well as the multiplicity of traffic types, this integrated
system may also have to work to a multiplicity of traffic grades of service.
The challenge is to handle, or simplify, the resultant multidimensional
complexity.

Today's voice networks may be characterized as static (fixed circuit and traffic routings) in a stable, homogeneous traffic environment.

In contrast, ISDN will have to support heterogeneous, volatile traffic
demands. One approach is to develop the necessarily complex forecasting
systems that can handle volatile, heterogeneous demands. While this may be
possible, an easier alternative is to examine our assumptions about the
network itself. Does it have to be static, or can we build it to be responsive to changes in its traffic environment?

There are two, well-known approaches. One is dynamic traffic routing [1],
which directs the traffic flows in real-time to match the instantaneous condition of the logical trunking network. The other is dynamic reconfiguration of
circuits [2], which reconfigures the logical transport resources in near-real-
time to match shifting demand patterns. The technologies to implement both
kinds of control are available in terms of dynamic network controllers,
stored-program switching machines, and digital cross connects.

The net result of either kind of dynamic control is better resource sharing
than is possible in a static network. Resource sharing implies effective
aggregation of equipment units. This means that the traffic engineer can rely
on the laws of large numbers to simplify forecasting systems and lengthen
provisioning intervals. Frequent manual circuit rearrangements (trunk servicing) could eventually be made redundant by dynamic control.

The example that follows assumes a scenario where logical circuits in the core
can be assigned on demand and within minutes to any network (public or
private) that requests them. The relevant demand parameter from a core forecasting and provisioning viewpoint is therefore no longer traffic but
circuits. The example looks at the transport resource management situation
when circuits are the basic unit of demand.

Example: Transport Resource Management

In this example we model the network as a set of point-to-point circuits
routed over a grid of physical facilities. To provide a likely ISDN environment, let us assume a digital, fiber, metropolitan network. For simplicity,
all circuit demands will be modeled in units of 64 kbits bandwidth, with a
modularity of 24 circuits. The provisionable units of capacity are therefore
1.5 mbit channels.

Let us now consider the transport resource management problem from the point
of view of the network manager. It is his responsibility to ensure that
adequate capacity is in place to satisfy the expected demand for circuits over
some provisioning time interval T. The pool of resources (inventory) at his
disposal consists of transport capacity in units of 1.5 mbits or 24 logical

circuits. The network manager's problem is to satisfy three conflicting requirements, which are listed below.

- Grade of service: This may be expressed as a Probability of Delayed Order (PDO), where a "delayed order" is a circuit request that could not be immediately satisfied from the available pool of transport resources.

- Inventory costs: The unused capacity, or percent margin M, represents inefficiency in resource utilization.

- Operational costs: It is desirable to keep the provisioning interval T reasonably long, because of the operational overhead involved in ordering and provisioning the units of 1.5 mbit capacity.

Obviously, the customer grade of service (PDO), the percent margin M, and the provisioning interval T can be traded off against each other. Also, if given any two, we can in principle compute the third.

Having defined this simple version of the transport resource management problem, let us consider two other aspects of the situation: (a) the circuit demand model, and (b) the representation of differing degrees of network flexibility.

a) The circuit demand may arise from a combination of requests from the circuit-switched and packet-switched networks and directly from end-users' own private network requirements. In the ISDN era, it will be desirable to satisfy such demands rapidly (e.g. within minutes) since this will reduce or eliminate the need for fine-grained circuit and packet traffic forecasting systems, and provide excellent service to private networks. The technology to provide such rapid circuit assignment will be available in the form of intelligent multiplexers, digital cross connects, and network controllers. For maximum advantage to switched networks, some form of dynamic trunk assignment on switches would also be desirable.

The circuit demand model chosen for the example was a birth-death process. This kind of process is general in that it can accommodate nonstationary circuit "traffic", with long holding times. The model allows computation of growth (net population increase) and churn (birth/death activity) by looking at data for a past time interval, and then forecasting the expected circuit demand after a future time interval T.

b) Digital cross connects (DCS) provide the "tandem-switching" function. In our example, DCS 1/0 devices allow the logical 64 kbit circuits to be flexibly routed through the network. The flexibility parameter F for the network is the proportion of 1.5 mbit capacity with DCS 1/0 terminations. The greater the proportion, the greater the effective pooling of the 1.5 mbit transport resource.

The network shown in Figure 2.1 was modeled to quantify the trade-offs between grade of service (PDO), margin M, and provisioning interval T, for different values of the network flexibility parameter F. A sample of the results is shown in Figure 2.2. This particular bar chart quantifies the relationship between F and M for a given PDO and T.

This work is essential to the setting of performance standards and operational parameters for the core transport of ISDN services. It is also basic to the issues of cross-connect placement and to the architecture and dimensioning of cross-connect networks.

P. Richards

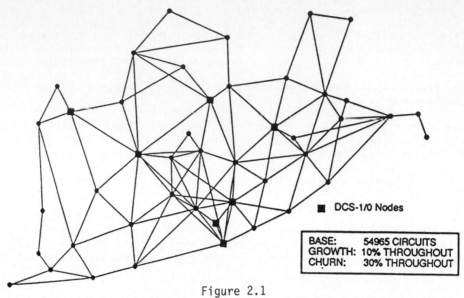

DCS-1/0 Nodes

BASE: 54965 CIRCUITS
GROWTH: 10% THROUGHOUT
CHURN: 30% THROUGHOUT

Figure 2.1
Test Network (Physical Layer)

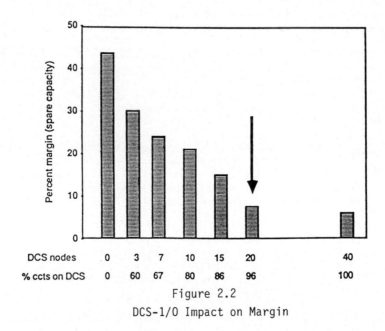

Figure 2.2
DCS-1/0 Impact on Margin

3. NEW DESIGN PRIORITIES: NETWORK SURVIVABILITY

The evolution to fiber-optic transmission systems facilitates the design of networks with much larger cross sections but lower physical connectivity than corresponding nonfiber designs. Simultaneously, the application of distributed processing architectures to digital switches is facilitating the introduction of very large switching components with termination and call-handling capacities in excess of 100,000 lines and 500,000 busy-hour calls/hour respectively.

In today's environment we design networks to meet specified traffic grades-of-service under nominal load conditions such as "Normal" or "High" loads. However, with larger equipment units to fail and the steeper load-service relationships of large cross-sections, there is a tendency towards network designs that perform very well under normal conditions but catastrophically under stress.

This means that our priorities must change, so that future ISDN grades-of-service will include traffic performance under prespecified stress conditions, as well as "nominal" load. Our work in this area on metropolitan and Canadian toll networks shows that effective survivability grades-of-service can and should be developed. These grades-of-service will then be key factors in driving new network design rules [3].

Example: Canadian toll network survivability model

The Canadian toll network of the early 1990's will have the fiber back-bone route shown in Figure 3.1, supplemented over most links by two microwave radio routes. Some route diversity therefore exists, and at the physical level the network design is heavily constrained. The emphasis of the performance modeling work is therefore to set circuit diversity and restoration objectives, and determine how large the fiber route can grow, relative to the radio routes, before failing to meet those objectives. The terms "route diversity", "circuit diversity", and "restoration" are defined more precisely in the text that follows.

A related, parallel effort is under way to specify the format and values of a survivability standard. The purpose of setting survivability standards is to ensure that, given a failure, the performance of the network will not degrade below a certain level. To ensure consistent service through time, the standard should be independent of network size, topology, or technology. However, to be practical, a survivability standard should be easily translatable into the network design and management objectives listed below.

• Maximum unit sizes to limit the magnitude of any single failure.

• Route diversity objectives to ensure physically diverse paths between nodes.

• Circuit diversity objectives to spread circuits over the physically diverse paths thereby diffusing the effects of a failure.

• Restoration objectives to ensure that spare capacity is available on physically diverse paths to accommodate some circuit rerouting after the failure has occurred.

An essential part of this work therefore involves computing the relationship between user-oriented performance parameters such as percentage blocking or lost traffic, and network-oriented parameters such as percentage lost capacity or lost trunks. For example, when a failure occurs, some of the traffic on the network is exposed to abnormally high blocking levels because some trunks

have been lost and not fully restored. Suppose a survivability standard were
to set limits on the amount of traffic which may potentially be exposed to
high blocking. It would then be necessary to be able to compute the number of
trunks which could be lost without exceeding the standard.

Our preliminary work in this area investigated the relationship between average network blocking and net lost capacity as a result of a partially-restored
failure. Figure 3.2 shows a scatter plot of the relationship between average
blocking and net lost capacity, for the various simulation runs that were
carried out for the Canadian toll network study described above. The simulation points cover node failures, link failures, and different sizes of
network representing different study years. The model assumed a realistic
level of circuit diversity, dynamic traffic routing [1], and a user reattempt
behaviour with a probability of 0.75.

By considering lost capacity in a full-grouped network, with high-efficiency
trunks, no diversity, and a reattempt probability also of 0.75, it was possible to derive an analytical relationship shown by the solid curve. As an
upper bound to the simulation points, the curve provides a safe and simple way
to translate between user-oriented and network-oriented objectives.

We are currently extending this analytical technique to deal with blocking
exposures (instead of average blocking) and to allow for circuit diversity.

Further steps include the definition of a preliminary survivability standard
for the Canadian toll network, and the application of that standard in setting
practical, consistent, circuit diversity and restoration objectives for the
planned transmission facilities. These in turn will define the point in time
when the physical, route diversity is inadequate, necessitating new physical
routes, or new technology, or both.

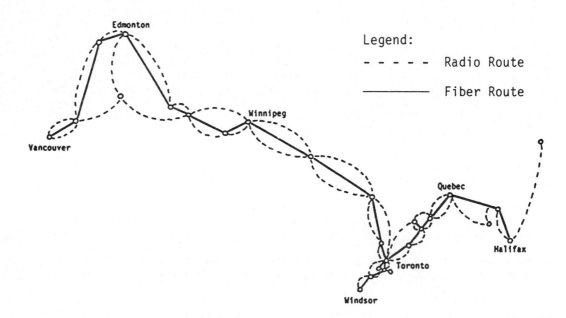

Figure 3.1
Canadian Long-Distance Network Model

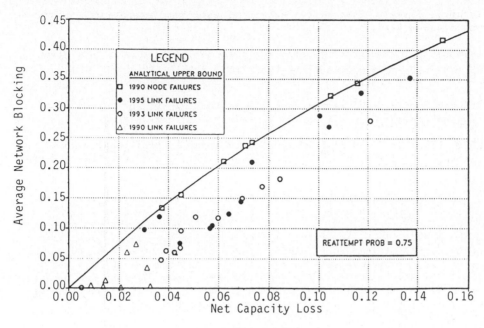

Figure 3.2

Analytical Upper Bound With Node and Link Failure
Simulation Results for Canadian Toll Network

4. NEW DESIGN PRIORITIES: DESIGN FOR REAL-TIME PERFORMANCE

Two major forces are at work in future-generation switching components.
First, increasing functionality, in part due to ISDN, is increasing the functional complexity of the machine and the processing power needed to run it.
Second, new processing engines and multiprocessor, distributed architectures
promise to be the solution. However, the telecommunications industry currently lacks the performance-oriented design methods to map increasing
functionality onto increasingly distributed processing power... in an orderly,
evolutionary manner, without compromising real-time performance.

Functional mapping onto distributed computing engines to achieve good real-
time performance follows two fundamental steps. First, the functions must be
mapped onto processors so that functional coupling and interprocessor communications are minimized and functional concurrency maximized. Second, within
each processor, functions must be mapped onto tasks so that the intertask
queueing delays, queue lengths, etc., are minimized. To assist the designer
in achieving these goals, we are developing a set of real-time design guidelines. The purpose is to shorten the design cycle by helping designers
produce efficient designs at the first iteration. Application of the guidelines would not be a substitute for the more formal real-time analysis and
capacity characterization that takes place once a design is firm.

As a first step at developing real-time design guidelines, we are examining
the trade-offs in the partitioning and prioritizing of tasks running on one
processor. The example that follows illustrates the approach to date, and
indicates the practical potential of such work.

Example: Multitasking, single processor case study

The early design stages of a digital switching component ideally call on two
sets of considerations:

a) the sequence of events and related logic in the processing of a single
    call, based on the disciplines of telecommunications engineering and
    computer science, and

b) the ensemble effects of many such calls contending for the resources of
    the system based on the discipline of teletraffic engineering.

The considerations in (a) will produce a design that is functionally sound;
the additional considerations in (b) are essential for good real-time performance.

All good real-time system designers make at least an intuitive allowance for
(b) when formulating a new architecture. However, there are some subtleties
which are evident from queueing theory but which are not necessarily evident
from common-sense. It is, therefore, appropriate for teletraffic specialists
to have some input into the early design stages of a new product or component.
One practical way to achieve this is by providing the designer with a set of
fairly general design guidelines for real-time performance, which can be used
at the designer's discretion. The case study that follows shows how an apparently good initial design of a switching system component was improved by
applying a simple set of real-time guidelines.

Figure 4.1.1 shows the initial configuration of four tasks running on a
processor in the peripheral module of a digital switch. Tasks A and B handle
peripheral-side and control-side messaging, respectively. Task C is a low-
occupancy call-processing task. Task D has both a message-handling, and a
low-level call-processing function. The relative task priorities are shown on
the diagram, where 1 indicates the highest priority.

Figure 4.1.2 shows a configuration revised for improved real-time performance.
The main changes involve: task A now handling all incoming messaging, from
both peripheral side and control side. Task B similarly handles all outgoing
messaging. Task C has had its priority increased. Task D's original two
functions have been re-assigned to two tasks, D1 and D2, with low and high
priorities.

Both the initial and revised configurations were tested in a detailed system
simulator. The load-service curves from the simulation runs are shown in
Figure 4.2, using dial-tone delay as the performance metric. The revised
configuration has led to a capacity improvement of 20 percent.

The design guidelines that were used to generate the revised configuration are
simple, and general enough to be applied in most practical digital switching
applications. The main principles are listed below.

• Messages should flow from lower priority to higher priority tasks.

• Low occupancy tasks should run at high priority, and high occupancy tasks
   at lower priority.

• Tasks of equal priority should be combined to reduce task wake-up overhead.

The first two points have a theoretical basis in queueing theory; the third is
common sense.

We are currently extending this work to cover a wide range of real-time design situations, including multiprocessor environments. In particular, the implementation of ISDN functional signaling is a timely and appropriate area for this kind of real-time design consideration.

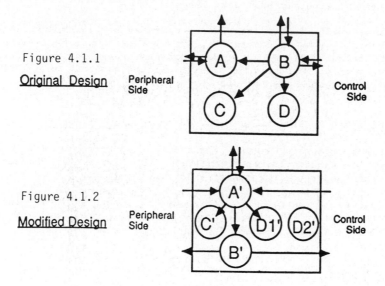

Figure 4.1.1

Original Design

Figure 4.1.2

Modified Design

Figure 4.1

Design for Real Time Case Study

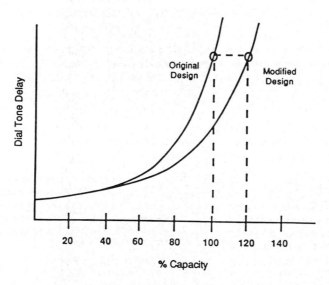

Figure 4.2

Design for Real Time Case Study Results

5. ROUTING AND CONTROL IN FUTURE-GENERATION NETWORKS

There exist a number of proposals for future-generation network technologies
to support the core network evolution of ISDN. These include fast packet
switching [4], burst switching [5], and fast circuit switching. So far, the
industry-wide analysis and debate on these alternatives has concentrated on
technological and architectural comparisons.

However, there are also important issues relating to teletraffic performance
including control, stability, capacity, and dimensioning. For example, our
work on fast circuit switching includes design of network-wide "overload
controls" with very fast response times to ensure stability and throughput
under stress conditions of overload or failure [6].

Example: Advanced Routing and Control of Integrated Transport

This performance modeling example is based on an exploratory design proposal
for a future, integrated transport network. The key network characteristics
from a routing and control perspective are listed below.

- Source routing by means of a message header, providing local, rapid set-up
  of individual calls, packets, or control messages (reaction time in the
  millisecond range).

- Network-wide control and allocation of allowable routes, based on header-
  table updates, with a time constant in the seconds/minutes range.

- Survivability as the governing principle of the network design, leading to
  two further properties:

  - a "logical dual-plane" design consisting of primary routes and back up
    secondary routes over separate physical paths, and

  - control messages given priority over user messages in the event of fail-
    ure or congestion to ensure stable degradation under adverse conditions.

These control principles were built into a network simulator, which was used
to test the design intent under extreme conditions of overload and failure on
a metropolitan-size test network. Two types of runs were carried out to
investigate:

a) the protective effect of the local, source-routing control, and

b) the restorative effect of the network recovery algorithm in re-assigning
    routes to restore throughput in a safe, stable manner.

The local control (a) has the capability of shifting the route between a
particular source-destination pair from a normal state (primary route) to an
unprotected state (secondary route), and finally to a disabled state (no
routes available to user-traffic). The trigger for the shifts is congestion
on the route, detected by message loss. The shifts are not applied to control
messages unless a link is cut completely.

The network recovery algorithm (b) bases its route assignments on trunk occu-
pancies, and communicates the updated routing tables back to the source nodes
by means of the high-priority control messages.

A state diagram indicating the domains and roles of the protective and restorative controls for a particular source-destination pair is shown in Figure 5.1.

Figure 5.2 shows the results of one of the simulation runs used to investigate the protective, local controls. The light, solid line is the offered load profile through time, representing a massive 600 percent overload. The heavy, solid curve shows the carried load. The black circles indicate times at which local control performs its protective action by shifting routes. The dotted line shows nondisabled load offered by those source-destination pairs not in a disabled state.

Figure 5.3 is the corresponding run, with the network recovery controls in operation. The clear circles represent times at which disabled source-destination pairs are selectively re-enabled with usable routes to restore throughput.

These results show the effectiveness of the local, protective control in preventing the loss of control messages by effectively preventing new user traffic from accessing the affected links in the network. The network-wide, restorative controls do not compromise this protection, yet they manage to maintain throughput at close to the maximum level sustainable by the network's capacity.

The experience gained through this particular modeling exercise is currently being applied in the comparison and design of advanced routing and control systems for future transport technologies.

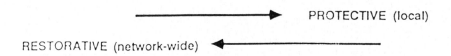

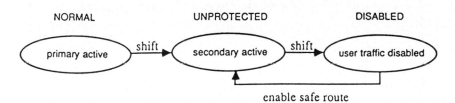

Figure 5.1

State Diagram for Protective and Restorative Controls

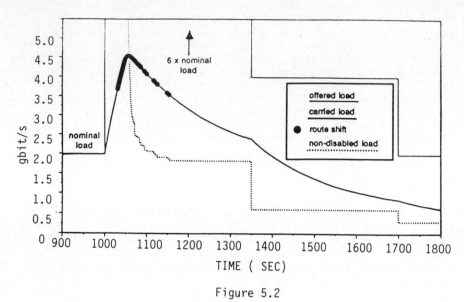

Figure 5.2

Throughput - Protective Controls Only

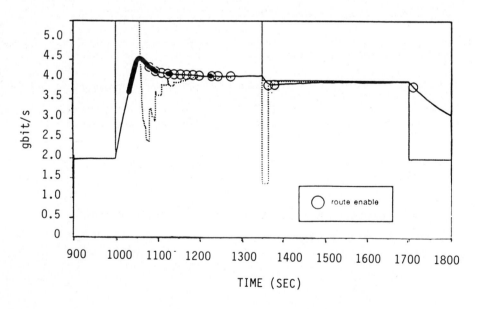

Figure 5.3

Throughput - Protective and Restorative Controls

6. SUMMARY

Traffic performance in ISDN cannot be taken out of the technological and architectural context within which ISDN will function. Fiber optics, distributed processing, and dynamic transport are not specific to ISDN, yet they are basic elements in the strategies of major equipment manufacturers (e.g. in Northern Telecom's Dynamic Network Architecture). These elements will therefore be as much a part of the eventual ISDN reality as 2B+D.

The modeling examples described in this paper cover four areas that, up to now, have not primarily been associated either with ISDN or teletraffic. However, they all represent fertile ground for the application of teletraffic techniques and are shaping up as major issues in the future ISDN environment.

It is hoped that the brief glimpse into each area provided by this paper will stimulate a broadening and diversification of teletraffic applications, as we enter the ISDN era.

ACKNOWLEDGEMENTS

I would like to thank the colleagues in my department who provided me with material for the examples and diagrams.

REFERENCES

1. W.H.Cameron et al, "Dynamic Routing for Intercity Telephone Networks", ITC10, Montreal, 1983.

2. P.Richards and R.Pandya, "Towards Dynamic Network Control", National Communications Forum, Chicago, 1985.

3. E.Roohy-Laleh and N. Ross, "Network Design for Survivability: Procedure and Case Study in a Dynamic Network Architecture", ICC Record, June 1986.

4. J.Turner and L.Wyatt, "A Packet Network Architecture for Integrated Services", Globecom'83.

5. E.Haselton, "New Switching Concept Integrates Voice and Data Bursts", Globecom'84.

6. G.J.Fitzpatrick, "Structurally Stable Control of an Extensive Fast Circuit-Switched Network", to be presented at INFOCOM'87, San Francisco, April 1987.

TRAFFIC ENGINEERING for ISDN Design and Planning
M. Bonatti and M. Decina (Editors)
Elsevier Science Publishers B.V. (North-Holland)
© IAC, 1988

Traffic Network Routing, Control, and Design for the ISDN Era

Gerald R. Ash

AT&T Bell Laboratories
Holmdel, New Jersey

ABSTRACT

Future ISDN switched digital services networks will provide a multiplicity of services on integrated transport networks. Switching nodes, interconnected by a flexible transmission network, provide connections for voice, data, and wideband services. These connections are distinguished by estimated resource requirements, traffic characteristics, and design performance objectives. This paper provides integrated network design methods, bandwidth allocation strategies, traffic/routing control plans, and traffic administration procedures for these multiservice integrated networks. The design procedure determines the routing and bandwidth capacity required to satisfy all service demands simultaneously on an integrated network. Each service demand meets its blocking and other performance objectives. Bandwidth allocation procedures manage network bandwidth according to a virtual trunk concept in which limits are placed on the number of connections for each service category. The traffic/routing control plan provides common channel signaling (CCS) call set-up of the logical connections, and network resource management based on near real-time traffic data. A dynamic routing strategy is used which includes real-time control of routing patterns. The network design methods are illustrated for example switched digital services networks.

MAIN STATEMENTS: "Provides network design algorithms, traffic/routing control plans, bandwidth allocation strategies, and traffic administration procedures for multiservice integrated networks"

1. INTRODUCTION

It is well recognized that there is actually no "N" in ISDN; that is there is no network aspect within the present ISDN concept. This present concept, as defined by the CCITT interface standards, says nothing about how the transport network between the ISDN interface points should be configured — only that it must transport the services defined by the interface standard. The likelihood is, however, that the ISDN transport network will evolve to a multiservice integrated network; in the case of the AT&T network, integration of switched digital services will occur in the initial ISDN implementation. In this paper we describe traffic engineering methods for integrated voice, data, and wideband services networks. These methods apply to multiservice circuit-switched networks, and can be extended to multiservice packet-switched networks. The initial application for these methods is for ISDN switched digital services networks, which represent multiservice circuit-switched applications.

The traffic engineering methods described in this paper anticipate network evolution toward multiservice integrated networks, and provide a framework for their design and optimization. These methods extend dynamic, nonhierarchical routing (DNHR) design and control concepts into these multiservice networks, and, as such, provide a framework for achieving the integrated network design of the future. A CCITT contribution entitled "Integrated Network Routing and Design" has recently been submitted to CCITT study Groups II and XVIII; the contribution summarizes the routing, control, and design techniques described in this paper.

We present a traffic engineering plan for these integrated networks, which includes design, routing, bandwidth allocation, traffic/routing control, and traffic administration. With these traffic engineering methods we can simultaneously meet performance objectives for voice, data and wideband services. Traffic engineering takes into account all the normal daily activities, including routing, bandwidth allocation, and congestion control, which are used to control systematic traffic variations and expected day-to-day variations. Traffic engineering excludes, however, network management activities associated with nonsystematic network overloads and network failures. Our approach is to characterize all service demands in common units: that is, by the mean, variance, and day-to-day variation of both the number of circuits and bandwidth per circuit demanded for each service type. We provide integrated network design methods that extend the design methods in operation for dynamic routing [1]. These integrated design methods incorporate a network bandwidth allocation procedure to allocate bandwidth to the various service types so they can meet their performance objectives. We describe how these integrated network designs could be controlled and administered in actual network operation. Traffic/routing control functions include call set up, real-time routing, network bandwidth allocation, link bandwidth allocation, and congestion control. Traffic administration includes data collection, forecasting, servicing, and routing administration.

2. REVIEW OF DNHR CONCEPTS FOR TELEPHONY

DNHR brings three principal changes to the network plan, which include a new network configuration, a new routing technique, and a new way of operating and designing the network. The DNHR network has only one class of switching system, and end-offices home on DNHR tandem offices by way of exchange access networks. The DNHR portion of the AT&T intercity network currently consists of 4ESS™ switches interconnected by the CCS network. Dynamic routing rules are used between pairs of DNHR switches, and conventional hierarchical routing rules are used between all other pairs of AT&T switches. These hierarchical switching systems home directly on DNHR switches.

The dynamic routing method illustrated in Figure 1, called "two-link dynamic routing with crankback," capitalizes on two factors: selection of minimum cost paths, as given by the DNHR unified algorithm (UA) design, between originating and terminating switches, and design of optimal, time-varying routing patterns to achieve minimum cost trunking by capitalizing on noncoincident network busy periods. We achieve the dynamic, or time

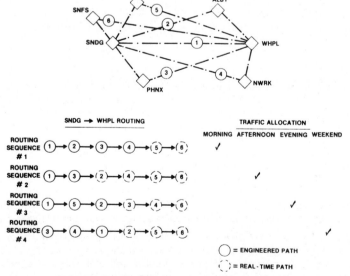

FIGURE 1 TWO-LINK DYNAMIC ROUTING WITH CRANKBACK

varying, nature of the routing scheme by varying the route choices with time. The routes, which consist of different sequences of paths, are designed to satisfy a node-to-node blocking requirement. Each path consists of one or, at most, two links or trunk groups in tandem. Paths used for routes in different time periods need not be the same. In Figure 1, the originating switch at San Diego (SNDG) retains control over a dynamically routed call until it is either completed to its destination at White Plains (WHPL) or blocked. The control of a call overflowing the second leg of a two-link connection (for instance, the ALBY-WHPL link of the SNDG-ALBY-WHPL path in routing sequence #1) is returned to the originating switch (SNDG) for possible further alternate routing. Control is returned when the via switch (ALBY in the example) sends a CCS crankback signal to the originating switch. Initially, 15 DNHR time periods are being used to divide up the hours of an average business day and weekend into contiguous routing intervals called load-set periods (LSPs). The real-time, traffic-sensitive component of DNHR uses "real-time" paths for possible completion of calls that overflow the "engineered" paths (see Figure 1). The engineered paths are designed to provide the objective blocking performance. The real-time paths, which are also determined by the UA embedded in the central forecasting system, can be used only if the number of idle trunks in a group is greater than a specified number of trunks--the reservation level--before the connection is made. This prevents calls that normally use a trunk group from being swamped by real-time routed calls.

The third principal change brought about by DNHR is the way the network is designed and operated. Several operations systems provide centralized functions such as switch planning, data collection, trunk forecasting, trunk servicing, routing administration, and network management. An overview of the operations systems used to support DNHR is given in Reference 2. Embedded within the forecasting and servicing systems is the UA, which simultaneously determines the trunking and routing for the entire DNHR network [2].

3. MULTISERVICE INTEGRATED NETWORK TRAFFIC ENGINEERING MODEL

Figure 2 illustrates the multiservice integrated network model we use for our traffic engineering methods. We have illustrated two fundamental service types which are

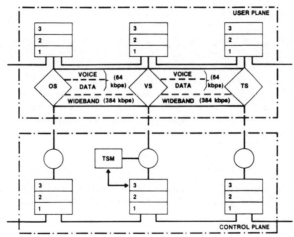

FIGURE 2 MULTISERVICE INTEGRATED NETWORK TRAFFIC ENGINEERING MODEL

distinguished by their traffic characteristics, bandwidth requirements, and design performance objectives. These service types include a) 64 kbps circuit mode connections, and b) 384 kbps circuit mode connections. The concept can readily be extended to other service types, such as 1536 kbps circuit mode connections and virtual circuit packet mode connections. Our multiservice integrated traffic engineering model considers bandwidth allocation and routing procedures. We discuss these topics first, and then we discuss the design procedures for multiservice integrated networks.

3.1 Overview of Bandwidth Allocation and Routing Procedures

In the bandwidth allocation strategy service demands are converted to elements of bandwidth or virtual trunks (VTs). There are two levels of bandwidth allocation that are accounted for in our network design method:

1) network bandwidth allocation: when virtual trunk connections are requested, a routing procedure is used to determine on which network path there exists sufficient bandwidth for the service; if no such path exists the connection is blocked.

2) link bandwidth allocation: a maximum number of virtual trunk connections, and hence a maximum allowed bandwidth, is allowed for each service type on each link; a link bandwidth allocation procedure is also used to ensure that a minimum allotted bandwidth is assured for each service type.

In the network bandwidth allocation strategy virtual connections (VCs) are converted to VTs by the equivalence

$$VT_{ik_h} = \frac{LBW_{ik}^h}{r_i} \tag{1}$$

where

LBW_{ik}^h = bandwidth allocated to service type i on link k in hour h

VT_{ik}^h = number of virtual trunks or maximum number of VCs for service type i on link k in hour h

r_i = average bandwidth per VC for service type i.

The quantity LBW_{ik}^h is determined in network design, as described below. The quantity r_i is known for each service type for purposes of network design. With the size of each virtual trunk subgroup (VTSG) determined, the routing strategy, which is a dynamic routing strategy, is used to set up switched virtual connections over these VTSGs. This call set up procedure for calls on virtual connections in ISDN is very similar to call set up on trunk connections in telephony, and uses two-link DNHR with crankback as described in Section 2. A real-time routing procedure is used to adjust the routing patterns in real time according to network traffic conditions. The call set up procedure is described in more detail in the next section.

3.2 Traffic/Routing Control Functions

Traffic/routing control functions include call set up, real-time routing, network bandwidth allocation, and link bandwidth allocation. These functions are now discussed.

3.2.1 Call Set Up

A CCS call set up procedure is used to establish virtual connections. Call set ups for virtual trunk connections build on DNHR logic [2], and these procedures are described here in detail. Each service type has a dynamic routing pattern which is used to select an idle VT path, as follows:

1) the originating switch (OS) translates the customer specified information including dialed digits and service type using a local data base or a centralized data base (where necessary) to determine the terminating switch (TS),

2) the OS selects the OS-TS routing sequences from the OS memory based on the TS and service type,

3) each switch defines a VTSG for each service type: each VTSG has a maximum number of VTs which has been initially determined in the network design but is adjusted in the link bandwidth allocation procedure described below,

4) VTs associated with these VTSGs are treated in the same way as trunks are treated in the OS, i.e., a resource counter in the OS keeps a count of idle VTs or total calls in progress as they are set up or disconnected, for each service type on each link,

5) in CCS call set up, the OS uses two-link DNHR path selection for VT paths (e.g., first select an idle VT on the first link of the first path choice by decrementing the idle-VT counter for that service type; then attempt to select an idle VT on the second link of the first path choice; if the second link VTs are all busy, crank back, and try the next path choice in a similar manner, etc.); this procedure provides OS control of every call in setting up VT paths, and

6) the existing real-time DNHR routing procedure [2] is used and node-to-node traffic data are collected for each service type; as an optional future enhancement, an extension of the DNHR real-time routing procedure could be used which employs a trunk status map (TSM) [3], to adjust routing patterns in real-time, according to network traffic conditions.

3.2.2 Network Bandwidth Allocation and Real-time Routing

The function performed continuously in network bandwidth allocation is the assignment of virtual trunks to calls with the use of the dynamic routing procedure described above. The real-time routing concept [2] uses the existing DNHR real-time routing procedure, as described above, or, as a possible future enhancement, could involve having each switch send status update messages, to the TSM, every few seconds of the number of idle VTs in each VTSG. With this enhancement, status messages would be sent only when the status of a VTSG had changed. In return, the TSM periodically would send ordered routing sequences to be used by the OSs to perform call set ups until the next update is received in a few seconds. These routing sequences would be determined by the TSM in real-time using the TSM dynamic routing strategy described in Reference 3. Separate routing sequences would be generated for each service type. Congestion control measures would be implemented by the TSM using a real-time routing procedure; these congestion control measures are described in Reference 3. A number of open issues require further investigation if the TSM were to be implemented. This extension of the routing method to TSM is not required, but could be considered as a means to achieve additional network flexibility.

3.2.3 Link Bandwidth Allocation

The above network bandwidth allocation strategy allocates the network bandwidth to all services in a systematic, equitable fashion. We also use a link bandwidth management strategy to ensure that the link bandwidth used by each service type on each link does not exceed the capacity allocated to it unless there is unused capacity from other services. The link bandwidth allocation is initially determined in network design, but is adjusted in the network control procedure described below.

The link bandwidth allocation procedure is used to control bandwidth utilization on links. This link bandwidth allocation procedure groups VTs of a like nature, that is, for each service type, onto separate VTSGs. As discussed above, there is a VTSG defined for each service type on each link. Each VTSG has a maximum and minimum allowed bandwidth limit. The maximum limit is controlled through the maximum number of VTs. The minimum bandwidth limit is controlled through adjustment of bandwidth control parameters used by the OS, which in effect reserve a minimum number of VTs for the service type. This procedure allows for both dedicated and shared bandwidth for each service type, which is necessary for efficient use of link bandwidth. Within the initial AT&T switched digital network the maximum number of VTs for a given service type equals the number of VTs that can be provided by the dedicated bandwidth plus the number of VTs that can be provided by the shared bandwidth. The minimum number of VTs equals the number of VTs that can be provided only by the dedicated bandwidth. These bandwidth limits are determined from the design link bandwidth LBW_{ik}^h, which is periodically updated through use of a method that is now explained.

The allowed bandwidth for each service type on each link is adjusted periodically (e.g., every 5 minutes). This update time interval will be the subject of future network simulation studies. An average spare capacity on the link is computed based on the difference between the total link bandwidth available $TLBW_k$ and the average link bandwidth in use $\overline{TLBW_k^h}$ in hour h:

$$SPAREBW_k^h = TLBW_k - \overline{TLBW_k^h}$$

The spare capacity is then allocated to the service types in proportion to their average bandwidth usage $\overline{LBW}_{ik}^h$ on each link k in each hour h.

$$SPAREBW_{ik}^h = SPAREBW_k^h \; \frac{\overline{LBW}_{ik}^h}{\sum\limits_{i=1}^{2} \overline{LBW}_{ik}^h}$$

This additional bandwidth is added to the design link bandwidth LBW_{ik}^h and the new minimum and maximum VTs and bandwidth control parameters associated with the service type are used to update the minimum and maximum allowed bandwidth on the VTSG. A longer term (e.g., 1-week) analysis is performed to determine if spare capacity exists for all hours over an average business day. If it does, the design link bandwidth LBW_{ik}^h for each service type is increased by an amount given by

$$SPAREBW_{ik} = \min_{h} \left[SPAREBW_k^h \right] \; \frac{\sum\limits_{h} \left[\overline{LBW}_{ik}^h \right]}{\sum\limits_{h} \left[\sum\limits_{i=1}^{2} \overline{LBW}_{ik}^h \right]}$$

These new design link bandwidth values are used to change the minimum and maximum VTs and bandwidth control parameters, as above.

3.3 Multiservice Integrated Network Design Procedure

3.3.1 Overview

Inputs to the integrated network design consist of the OS-TS traffic, blocking, and service quality objectives for each service type. The design methods determine the routing patterns and minimum cost network for all service types given these traffic inputs and the blocking and service quality constraints.

The design procedure simultaneously determines the routing and link capacities between all OS-TS pairs in the network. The objective is to minimize the global network cost while providing an objective OS-TS blocking and service quality levels between all OS-TS pairs in all LSPs. The steps of the design algorithm are illustrated in Figure 3; the design algorithm is an iterative procedure consisting of an Initialization module, a Select Routing module, a Dimension Network module, and an Update Optimal Link Blockings module. Since there is

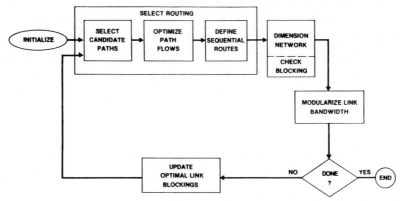

FIGURE 3 UNIFIED ALGORITHM DESIGN METHOD FOR INTEGRATED NETWORKS

a nonlinear relationship among the routing, capacity, and link blocking variables in the network optimization process, we solve for the routing, capacity, and link blocking variables iteratively. In this way the solution of the very large nonlinear optimization problem is decoupled into the solution of a large linear program (for the optimal routing), the solution of a large number of small nonlinear programs (for the optimal link blockings), and the solution of a large set of simultaneous nonlinear equations (for the optimal link bandwidth capacities).

Input parameters to the design algorithm include link cost, OS-TS offered load, and maximum OS-TS blocking level. The Initialization step estimates the optimal link blockings for each link in the network. Within the Select Routing and the Dimension Network modules, the current estimates of the optimal link blockings are held fixed. The Select Routing module determines the optimal routes for each design LSP by executing the three steps shown within the Select Routing block in Figure 3. The optimal routing is then provided to the Dimension Network, Check Blocking, and Modularize Link Bandwidth steps, which determine the number of trunks and modular bandwidth required on each link to meet the same optimal link blocking objectives assumed in the Select Routing step. Once the links have been sized, the cost of the network is evaluated and compared to that of the last iteration. If the network cost is still decreasing, the Update Optimal Link Blockings module computes new estimates of the optimal link blockings. The new link objectives are fed to the Select Routing module which again selects optimal routing, and so on.

3.3.2 Steps of the Design Procedure

Each of the service types has the following loads as input to the design process:

VC Traffic Load (erlangs):   by average business day and weekend hour h for each node pair; mean, variance, and level of day-to-day variation are used.

Bandwidth per VC (kbps):   by single stationary value for each service type; bandwidth allocated per VC $= r_i$, as defined in Equation (1).

Our notation for the average virtual connection traffic loads is VC_{ij}^h, where $h = 1,H$, $j = 1,K$, and $i = 1,2$ designate loads in hour h for node pair j associated with the two categories of VC traffic. $NNBW_{ij}^h = VC_{ij}^h \times r_i$ is used to denote the total bandwidth in hour h for node pair j associated with traffic for service type i $(i = 1,2)$. The notation VT_{ik}^h is used to denote the virtual trunk requirement for service type i on link k in hour h. Virtual trunk requirements are determined in the design procedure.

Steps in the UA design procedure shown in Figure 3 are the same as described in Reference 1, except for the following additions:

Select Routing

This step is unchanged except that the spare VC capacity determined in the Modularize Link Bandwidth step, described below, is used to set the existing link capacity variables in the heuristic optimization method used in the Optimize Path Flows step. This spare VC capacity is also considered in the shortest path selection procedure incorporated in the Select Candidate Paths step. These spare VC capacity variables in general are a function of the design hour h.

Dimension Network

This step is modified to size the virtual trunk capacity of each link to the optimal link blocking objective in each design hour (side hours as well as busy hour). This step therefore creates a variable VT_{ik}^h requirement for service type i on link k in hour h.

Modularize Link Bandwidth

This step rounds the virtual trunk group sizes on each link k so as to obtain a modular link bandwidth. The procedure first determines the total, non-modular link bandwidth requirement, $TLBW_k$, that satisfies the "background" load for other services on the link plus the requirements for the service type i currently being sized for. The rounding procedure subtracts, on each successive UA iteration, .6 DS1, .4 DS1, .2 DS1, and 0 DS1 , where DS1 equals the modular bandwidth size, from the total required link bandwidth (non-modular), with the background load as a lower bound, and rounds the result up to the nearest DS1 multiple to obtain the modular $TLBW_k$. That is

$$TLBW_k = \left\lceil \frac{\max\left[BGL_{ik}^h, \max_h\left(BGL_{ik}^h + LBW_{ik}^h\right) - f \times 1544\right]}{1544} \right\rceil \times 1544$$

where

$f = 0.6$ (first iteration), 0.4 (second iteration), 0.2 (third iteration), 0 (fourth and subsequent iterations).

$BGL_{ik}^h =$ background load on link k in hour h from other services considered up to this point (an expression is given below for BGL_{ik}^h).

$LBW_{ik}^h =$ bandwidth required for service type i on link k in hour h $\left(LBW_{ik}^h = VT_{ik}^h \times r_i\right)$.

$r_i =$ bandwidth per VC for service type i.

The link bandwidth will thus monotonically increase to an optimal modular value. Spare bandwidth from the rounding procedure is then used to compute spare VC flow capacity on each link k in each design hour h, as follows:

$$SPAREVC_{ik}^h = \left(TLBW_k - BGL_{ik}^h\right) \times 1/r_i$$

The spare VC capacity is used to set the existing link capacity variables in the select routing step. The initial routing of VC flows in iteration 1 of the heuristic optimization method used in the Optimize Path Flows step is the same routing used in the Modularize Link Bandwidth step.

Update Optimal Link Blockings

The Update Optimal Link Blockings procedure is unchanged except that the SPAREVC capacity, as computed above, is ignored in this computation. That is, the nonmodular VT_{ik}^h values are used for purposes of determining the optimal link blockings.

We now describe how the above steps are used to size the multiservice integrated network for all service types:

1) Order the virtual connection demands by decreasing total network bandwidth requirement in the network busy hour, i.e., from largest to smallest of $\max_h \sum_j NNBW_{ij}^h = \max_h \sum_j VC_{ij}^h \times r_i$; call these service types i_1, i_2.

2) For each service type i_n, n = 1,2 run the UA illustrated in Figure 3 to determine the VC flow on each link k in hour h, $VC_{i_nk}^h$. Use the modular bandwidth engineering procedure described above to modularize the total link bandwidth with

$$BGL_{i_nk}^h = \sum_{m=1}^{n-1} VT_{i_mk}^h \times r_{i_m}/\rho_{i_m}.$$

Note that the summation is defined to be zero when n = 1. $VT_{i_nk}^h$ is sized to the objective link blocking in all hours, as described above. The sizing procedure for the VT requirements considers mean, variance, and day-to-day variation of each virtual connection demand for each service type as in the current UA for telephony.

3) Compute spare VC flows on each link k for the next service type i_{n+1} to be engineered:

$$SPAREVC^h_{i_{n+1}k} = \left(TLBW_k - BGL^h_{i_nk} - LBW^h_{i_nk}\right) \times 1/r_{i_{n+1}}$$

Use these spare VC flows to initialize the existing link capacity variables in the Select Routing Step of the UA, and return to Step 2 for service type i_{n+1}.

These steps yield a) the number of VTs required for each service type, by hour, for each link, b) the design link bandwidth requirement for each VTSG associated with each service type, by hour, for each link, and c) the routing, by hour, for each service type.

4. MULTISERVICE INTEGRATED NETWORK TRAFFIC ADMINISTRATION

Traffic administration functions in the integrated network include data collection, forecasting, servicing, and routing administration. We envision these administration functions being performed by a centralized network control system (CNCS), illustrated in Figure 4. The

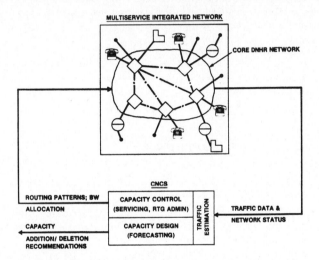

FIGURE 4 MULTISERVICE INTEGRATED NETWORK TRAFFIC ADMINISTRATION

objective of the data collection function is to collect load and performance data by service type. Load data includes calls per second, bits per second, and simultaneous virtual connections for each service type; performance data includes VT and VC blocking by service type. The forecasting function provides a multiyear forecast of capacity/routing requirements for the integrated network. This function, which is implemented in CNCS, determines trunk group sizes, link capacities, and routing within the integrated network. In order to forecast capacity and routing requirements for the integrated network, CNCS uses the node-to-node traffic data gathered from the OSs for each service type. This data is used to drive the load forecasting and sizing processes in the CNCS. The servicing function is to a) monitor the service being provided in the integrated network, and b) plan and schedule all capacity/routing changes that may be necessary to maintain objective network performance. Network service is monitored by direct measurement of network performance parameters, as provided by the data measurements specified above. When measured performance is below design objectives, the servicing module in CNCS is run to generate capacity and routing changes to restore objective service. The routing changes generated by the CNCS are automatically implemented into the switches' routing data bases through a routing assignment function in the CNCS. See References [2,4,5,6] for additional details on traffic administration.

5. INITIAL APPLICATION OF THE MULTISERVICE INTEGRATED NETWORK MODEL

Network design models and results are now briefly summarized for ISDN switched digital services networks. A full scale design of a switched digital network model was performed for the projected 64 kbps traffic and 384 kbps traffic. This integrated network model corresponds to the initial AT&T ISDN switched digital network. Given the initial projection for the 384 kbps traffic, we found that it was economical to combine the 384 kbps traffic with the 64 kbps traffic, and that the 384 kbps traffic could be carried on the network required for the 64 kbps traffic with virtually no increase in cost. If separate non-integrated networks were required for the 64 kbps traffic and the 384 kbps traffic, we found that the total cost of the separate networks would substantially exceed the cost of the integrated network. A future paper will discuss further details of design examples for multiservice integrated networks.

6. CONCLUSION

We have presented techniques for traffic engineering of multiservice integrated networks, which include network design methods, bandwidth allocation strategies, traffic/routing control plans, and traffic administration procedures. These methods extend DNHR design and control concepts to multiservice integrated networks. As such these methods provide the advantages of DNHR in reduced network investment, improved customer service, increased network flexibility, and standardized network operations support, and also provide a framework for the integrated network design of the future.

ACKNOWLEDGEMENT

I wish to thank B. M. Blake of AT&T Bell Laboratories for the initial implementation of the multiservice integrated network design methods and for the results on the multiservice network design reported in the paper.

REFERENCES

[1] Ash, G. R., Cardwell, R. H., Murray, R. P., "Design and Optimization of Networks with Dynamic Routing," BSTJ, Vol. 60, No. 8, October, 1981.

[2] Ash, G. R., Kafker, A. H., Krishnan, K. R., "Intercity Dynamic Routing Architecture and Feasibility," Proceedings of the Tenth International Teletraffic Congress, Montreal, Canada, June, 1983.

[3] Ash, G. R., "Use of a Trunk Status Map for Real-time DNHR," Proceedings of the Eleventh International Teletraffic Congress, Kyoto, Japan, September, 1985.

[4] Haenschke, D. G., Kettler, D. A., Oberer, E., "DNHR: A New SPC/CCIS Network Management Challenge," Proceedings of the Tenth International Teletraffic Congress, Montreal, Canada, June, 1983.

[5] David, A. J., Farber, N., "The Switch Planning System for the Dynamic Nonhierarchical Routing Network," Proceedings of the Tenth International Teletraffic Congress, Montreal, Canada, June, 1983.

[6] Ash, G. R., "Part III: Dynamic Nonhierarchical Routing," Proceedings of the ITU Seminar on Intelligent Routing Strategies Including Network Management Aspects, Zruc, Czechoslovakia, April, 1986.

TRAFFIC ENGINEERING for ISDN Design and Planning
M. Bonatti and M. Decina (Editors)
Elsevier Science Publishers B.V. (North-Holland)
© IAC, 1988

DISCUSSION

1 Analogies between Neuronal Networks and Integrated Telecommunication Networks.

O. Gonzales Soto commented Agnati's explanation that the difference between human and other mammals being is due to a differentation in the assignment of the functions to the layers of the nervous system (seen, since S.R. Cajal, as a hierarchical layered architecture of neuronal networks): the comparison between different network architectures from the point of view of the degree of intelligence they can support (or allow or express or promote) could constitute an useful occasion of crossfertilization between neurophisiology, artificial intelligence and telecommunication system engineering with great impact on, and great contribution opportunities for, network planning and design activities. Remembering the findings of S.R. Cajal on the neuronal interconnection evolution through the human life and the human evolution, Gonzales Soto asked if there is also the opportunity of fruitful analogies between the topological development of the neuronal nets and the one of the telecommunication networks.

L. Agnati remembered that S.R. Cajal stressed the importance of the microcircuits (aggregates of specialized parts of neurons in close contact with each other) for the appearance of higher integrative capabilities of the nervous system. However, detailed quantitative ontogenetic and phylogenetic studies to correlate this morphological aspect to the higher functions are still lacking. Agnati informed that the research team to which he belongs is working on the hypothesis that besides microcircuits made up by synaptic contacts, also other microcircuits, such as molecular interactions at the membrane level, should be active. These circuits could be organized according to hierarchical principles, which should be investigated both by means of ontogenetic and phylogenetic studies and by means of lesioning agents selective for the different types of circuits. The possibile analogies with communication networks could be useful, at least in exploring hypothesis, but much more detailed neurobiological knowledge seems necessary to keep it as operative or conclusive.

2 Quantitative Approach to Neuronal Networks.

O. Gonzales Soto, referring to the seven hierarchical levels of the nervous network and to the wired and volume types of communication, asked if there is any model of the information interexchange at each of the levels or at least any estimate of the information interchange volumes (e.g.:Mbit) and flow rate (e.g.:Mbps) that could help to analyze similarites with communication networks.

L. Agnati informed that only for simple cases there have been some attempts to formalize the wiring transmission (WT) (e.g. for single transmission lines - see: Griffith J.S. " Mathematical Neurobiology " Academic Press, London, 1971). A quantitative model of the volume transmission (VT) and of the cooperation between VT and WT will be one of the main future jobs with possible cooperation between neurobiology and communication system theory.

3 Forecasting of Uncertain Traffics.

D.J. Songhurst remembered that Network Planning must offer :

- Basic capacity allocation for the forecasted traffics,

- Contingencies for traffic variabilities within predictable (and forecasted) ranges,

- Contingencies for unpredictable events,

and asked comments by P. Richards and G.R. Ash on the relative importance of these planning objectives in the transition to ISDN and during its development.

Following P. Richards, the relative importance of the three objectives must be a function of the network provider's business objectives in a competitive environment. However, in most cases the "contingencies for unpredictable events" are becoming relatively more important, because a single event (e.g. a fiber link failure) affects many more subscribers simultaneously than in the past. This is a result of technological change (fiber, large digital switches) and related topological changes (networks with fewer but larger nodes and links and, therefore, with lower physical connectivity).

Following G.R. Ash, the network design should incorporate robust design methods yielding network architectures and network designs that are insensitive to the forecast errors. Such design methods must avoid underprovisioning for expected traffic variability and unpredictable events with as high a probability as possible. Flexible routing can be used in such robust design methods to minimize trunk augmentation and churn under the load uncertainties. Simplified design procedures are appropriate for the design step. For network administration and control, however, the objective is to maximize network throughput under existing load patterns, and high importance can be assigned to achieving the best quality solution possible, even if it is complex. Since load uncertainties are increasing with increased competition, increasing new services, and volatile calling patterns, increased emphasis is being placed on the administrative/control problem of routing optimization for traffic variability.

4 Network Survivability Design

4.1 Cost .vs. User Perceived QOS

S. Katz commented P. Richard's paper about service continuity issues, arguing that in a competitive environment, such as prevalent in the USA, designing a network for service continuity under failure needs to be examined so that the cost of this "insurance policy" is modest—due to robust design, and the gain can be stated in terms of customer-perceived service quality. How are these issues relevant to planning the Canadian Toll network?.

The trade-off between cost and customer-perceived service quality is central to, and explicit in the Canadian Toll network survivability standardization effort, answered P. Richards. A quantitative linkage between customer-perceived blocking under link failure conditions, and network oriented measures such as diversity and restoration has been provided. By adopting a standard that blocking shall not exceed x% on any trunk group affected by a link failure, Telecom Canada can place itself in a position to provide consistent performance to the customer independently on region, timeframe, or network technology deployment. Fixing a particular value for "x" is a question of business judgement (value of customer satisfaction versus cost of network diversity/restoration procedures and associated capacity requirements).

4.2 Failure Models

H. Heffes and J. Meyer asked P. Richards on the failure model used in the Canadian Survivability study : statistically independent node failures or correlated failures that may result for all nodes in a geographical area or for all nodes corresponding to a system release (resulting in a "random geographic spread")?.

P. Richards precised that the study of fiber link failures in the Telecom Canada Network (example # 2 in the paper) was limited to single failures. In this study every link in the network has been failed independently and non-cumulatively. In the advanced routing and control example (#4), the simulated network was subjected to massive overloads and multiple failures, in various combinations. These were basically diagnostic tests to see how well the control mechanisms stood up to very adverse conditions. In all the cases, the controls behaved in a stable, predictable manner, maintaining network throughput at or near the maximum possible level.

5 Link Calculation for Non-Hierarchical Network Design

R. Scherer asked G.R. Ash about the calculation of the links in a non-hierarchical network with very complex overflow schemes as the one proposed in the paper.

G.R. Ash answered that peakedness and day-to-day variation are used in the link calculations for the multiservice network engineering. A two-moments model based on the equivalent random technique is used as peakedness model and an equivalent load method is used to model day-to-day variations to account for the increased blocking which arises from the daily variation of load. Past studies have shown that if peakedness and day-to-day variations were not considered in the design, the network would be undersized and service would be degraded.

6 Computing Time for Determining Routing Algorithm

H.L. Hartmann commented fig.3 in Ash's paper asking how much CPU
time is needed for path selections and flow allocations for a large
network on a reference computer.   Knowledge based heuristics on
preferred starting topologies or other enhancements will be helpful
in order to reduce the computation time?.

"Two applications of the Unified Algorithm are relevant to the
question" – answered G.R. Ash. "First, a network design problem for
a full-scale network, which may typically involve up to 100 nodes
and 15 load-set-periods, can be solved in about one hour of CPU time
on an IBM 3081 mainframe computer. A network servicing problem in
which only one load-set-period needs to be considered at any given
time, requires a CPU time about one-fifteenth as great as the 15
period problem.   AT&T is currently investigating the use of
parallel/vector processors and simplified algorithms to further
reduce the run time".

ROUTING AND FAULT–TOLERANCE: TWO KEY ISSUES IN FUTURE NETWORK DESIGN AND PLANNING

(Chairman Comments to the Morning Session on Networks)

Konosuke Kawashima

NTT, Japan

The progress of the Optical Technologies and their impact on the local distribution technologies and on the nodal technologies, as well as the emergence of Network Intelligence constitute the context in which decide if a better understanding of how the human brain functions could be useful for the design of new Telecommunication Networks and new Switching Systems.

Few more points are added here to the considerations emerged during the discussion:

The synapse appears as a structure capable of very complex information processing: could a group of synapses merge and select information, acting as a switching machine?

The progressive hierachization of the neuronal networks, and the miniaturization of the circuits seem support the integrative capacities and the adaptability of the Central Nervous Systems in a fault tolerant way (see also Albus – 1981, and Winograd Cowan – 1963). Could the same techniques be useful in designing new Telecommunication Network Architectures?

"A rather high degree of switching is present in the neuronal networks, demonstrable as convergent and divergent pathways" in order to optimize the very expensive transmission lines (the axons) supporting the "wired communication (WC)" (a better terms for the telecommunication people that "wiring transmission" in neurophysiology). The "volume communication (VC)" chemically supported, needs "biological traps", the receptors, as in a broadcasting system (see also commmunication in data flow computers architectures). The interplay of WC and VC in routing information through the central nervous system and through the brain seen as a massively parallel computer (see also C. Stanfill on the set–up of the more convenient communication patterns for a specific computation), could represent a very productive analogy in inventing Telecommunication Network Architectures and Communication Protocols and distributing (and upgrading) the Network Intelligence.

Finally plasticity seems have something to do with Network Strategical Planning. "Plastic" networks would be much more easy objects for the strategical planning.

The way to a cooperation between Telecommunication System Engineering and Neurophysiology – Neurobiology seems however very hard; the first results cannot be forecasted in short times.
Once started, the business appears, however, very promising.

Richards and Ash contributions are self-speaking for Telecommunication System Engineering and Traffic people. Both offer matter of deep considerations and their harmonization could be taken as a first reference to be further completed and upgraded.

In particular, we would like to quote the following topics from Richard's paper:

- Analysis of the network responsivness to the changes in its traffic environment

  . dynamic traffic routing

  . dynamic network reconfiguration

  and criteria to evaluate the network responsivness

  . tradeoff between a single GOS parameter, an inventory costs parameter and an operational costs parameter.

- Network Design and Management Objectives for Network Fault-Tolerance

  . upper bounds for modules sizes

  . route diversity

  . circuits diversity

  . restoration,

and the following topics from Ash's paper:

- Multiservice Integrated Network Design Procedure determining the routing patterns and optimal bandwidth allocation for all service types and the optimal transport network, given the traffic inputs for each service and the GOS constraints,

- Multiservice Integrated Network Traffic Administration including data collection, forecasting, servicing and routing administration by a Centralized Network Control System.

TRAFFIC ENGINEERING for ISDN Design and Planning
M. Bonatti and M. Decina (Editors)
Elsevier Science Publishers B.V. (North-Holland)
© IAC, 1988

261

NETWORK EVOLUTION AND BEYOND

(Chairman Introduction to the Afternoon Session on Network)

Raj Pandya

BNR, Canada

Till very recently the major application of the telecommunications network was to provide a point-to-point, circuit-switched connection for simple telephony or message traffic. However, in recent years the scope and variety of communications services has seen a phenomenal growth. The challenge for the network designers and planners of today is not only to anticipate the nature and impact of future communication services but to evolve the communication network to support these services efficiently and economically.

The efficiency and economy in the network of the future will stem from new switching and transport architectures as well as from more efficient methods of controlling the traffic flows and logical circuit configurations in the network. Efficient operation of the network through proper Grade of Service measurement and tracking will also play a significant role.

Some of these topics were covered in the tutorial and the papers presented at the Seminar and the follow up discussions. The contents of the papers and the main focus of the discussions are summarized below:

The tutorial paper by Turner on Multipoint Communication Networks addresses future switching technologies to support multipoint communications, connection management, routing strategies and congestion control procedures for such networks.

Ackerley's paper describes a model for estimating and tracking the overall (end-to-end) grade of service for potential ISDN applications.

Kashper proposes Dynamic Nonhierarchical Routing (DNHR) type call setup and routing rules for multiservice applications in international circuit- switched networks. It also provides a mathematical formulation of the bandwidth allocation and dimensioning problem for such networks.

The paper by Watanabe discusses the cost impacts of dynamic routing on international ISDNs, taking into account the traffic profiles of mixed voice and message traffic on international circuits.

Eklundh's paper identifies some potential teletraffic issues that need to be addressed for implementing ISDN-type services and signalling protocols on cellular mobile systems.

TRAFFIC ENGINEERING for ISDN Design and Planning
M. Bonatti and M. Decina (Editors)
Elsevier Science Publishers B.V. (North-Holland)
© IAC, 1988

The Challenge of Multipoint Communication

Jonathan S. Turner

Abstract

The design of flexible communications systems, supporting a wide range of applications is the principal challenge facing the communications industry today. This paper focuses on the problem of multipoint communication, suitable for supporting such applications as entertainment video distribution, voice/video teleconferencing and LAN interconnection. We review the key issues involved in the design of multipoint communication networks, including switching system architecture, connection management, multipoint routing and congestion control. We conclude that flexible multipoint communications networks are technically feasible given current technology, and while there are many research issues requiring further study, it appears likely the cost of such networks may be only marginally higher than that of comparable point-to-point networks.

1. Introduction

The last decade has seen a tremendous growth in interest in flexible communications networks, capable of handling a wide range of different applications. Commercially, attention is currently focused on the Integrated Services Digital Network (ISDN), which represents a modest first step towards the goal of more flexible networks. Meanwhile, researchers around the world are exploring a variety of techniques that offer the potential of supporting a much wider range of applications, and equally important, may prove to be adaptable to the anticipated technology changes, that so often seem to render communications systems obsolete before they can be widely deployed.

The focus of most research efforts to date has been on techniques that can provide point-to-point connections at a variety of different rates. The spectrum of techniques studied have included multirate circuit switching at one end of the spectrum to fast circuit and fast packet switching at the other end. Hybrid techniques that combine conventional circuit and packet switching techniques have also been extensively studied. These techniques raise new issues in several areas of network design, including switching system design, connection management (or call processing), routing and overload control. While these issues are by no means fully understood, there is at least a growing recognition of the nature of the problems and approaches to solving them.

Jonathan S. Turner is an Associate Professor of Computer Science at Washington University, St. Louis, MO 63130. This work supported by grants from Bell Communications Research, Italtel SIT, NEC and the National Science Foundation (ECS 8600947).

This paper addresses the topic of networks for general multipoint communication. This is a natural extension of research on flexible point-to-point networks, and while it has received less serious attention to date, it promises to become a major thrust for new developments.

The motivation for multipoint communication comes from the recognition that there is a wide class of applications that requires it. The most obvious one is the distribution of entertainment programs, either audio or video. Several research organizations have organized programs designed around hybrid networks in which such "distributive services" are handled by a separate circuit-switched network. While such systems can effectively handle a few well-understood services, they provide little flexibility for supporting new services, since they can typically support only a few discrete channel rates and since they typically support only "one-to-many" connections, rather than general multipoint connections with multiple transmitters.

While the broadcast services such as entertainment video are obvious, there are many other services for which multipoint communication is important. A few of these are listed below.

- *Wire services*. News services like the Associated Press and Reuters distribute news reports from their bureaus to newspapers and radio stations throughout the world. A general multipoint connection would allow efficient transmission of this information from a moderate number of sources to a much larger number of receivers.

- *Multi-person conferences*. These services are currently handled by routing through a central point. They could be provided for efficiently and flexibly using a general multipoint connection.

- *Video lecture*. An important special case of a multi-person conference is a video lecture in which one speaker addresses a large audience, with provision for audience members to ask questions. Such a service could play an important role in education if it could be provided conveniently and inexpensively.

- *LAN interconnection*. Most large companies have local computer networks such as Ethernet at multiple locations. An extremely attractive service for them would be a multipoint connection that makes their geographically distributed LANs appear like one large network. Such a service would allow them to treat local and remote computers uniformly, allowing them to take advantage of the large base of networking software developed for LANs. The networking model offered by a multipoint-LAN is an attractive one for distributed operating systems and database applications. The extension of this model to geographically distributed networks would be very popular.

These examples indicate the possible range of services that multipoint connections can support. There is a much larger number of potential services that might become attractive if a flexible and economical multipoint connection capability were widely deployed.

If we accept the desirability of flexible multipoint communication as a goal, we are next faced with the question of whether or not such a capability is technically feasible and economically viable. While there remains a variety of challenging research problems, we contend that the answer to that question is yes. In section 2, several switching techniques that can be used to support flexible multipoint connections are reviewed. In section 3–5, research issues in connection management, routing and congestion control are discussed, key problems are identified and some potential solutions proposed. The reader should note that while the issues are discussed in the context of fast packet switching, most of the same issues arise in any network that provides multirate and multipoint communication.

2. Switching Techniques

In the last five or six years, several experimental switching system designs have been proposed that can support multirate communication in a flexible fashion. Several of these systems have been extended to support multipoint communication as well. Three such systems are discussed; the Starlite system originally developed by Alan Huang and Scott Knauer at AT&T Bell Labs and currently being developed further by a group at Bell Communications Research, the switching matrix for the Prelude experimental wide band switching system, developed by Coudreuse et. al. at CNET in France and the Broadcast Packet Switch being developed by this author at Washington University.

2.1. Starlite

Starlite is the name given to an experimental switching system developed by Alan Huang and Scott Knauer at AT&T Bell Labs [10,11,12]. The Starlite architecture was motivated by the observation that sorting networks, can be used to construct rearrangably non-blocking switching fabrics with distributed control. This observation was first put forward by Batcher [1] in 1968 in his seminal paper describing his *bitonic sorter* that sorts a set of n numbers using a network of approximately $(n/4)(\log n)^2$ simple comparison elements. For circuit switching applications, this observation leads to switching networks that are non-blocking, operationally very simple and eminently suited to VLSI implementation. To accommodate packet switching, mechanisms are needed to resolve contention between packets that arrive concurrently and are destined for the same output port. Multipoint communication requires additional mechanisms for packet replication. Huang and Knauer's contribution was the development of inexpensive VLSI implementations of Batcher's sorting network and the invention of a variety of supplementary networks which support packet switching and multipoint communication when used in concert with the sorting network.

While Huang and Knauer made no serious attempt to develop complete systems, they did develop a variety of useful tools that can be used for the construction of such systems and suggested ways in which they could be used. Figure 1 shows one possible implementation of a packet switch supporting multipoint communication. Packets arriving on external links enter a set of *Packet Processors* at left, which perform some address translation. For point-to-point packets this results in a destination PP number being placed in the packet header. This is used to guide the packet to the appropriate outgoing link.

For the moment, we will ignore the initial sort and copy networks at the top left and concentrate on what happens to packets when they enter the main sorting network at the middle of the figure. This network sorts packets in increasing order of their destination addresses, meaning that when the packets exit the sorting network, all packets with same destination address occupy a contiguous set of output links. The filters at the exit of the sorting network mark all but one packet destined for a particular address, by comparing the destination addresses of packets on adjacent links; if a packet has the same destination address as the packet on the next lower link, its *wait bit* is set. Packets for which the wait bit is zero are forwarded to the routing network at right which routes them to the proper outgoing links. Packets with the wait bit set are sent to one of a set of delay elements, which delays them for approximately one packet time, after which they are recirculated through the sorting network. It's useful to extend this basic scheme by adding a second field to each packet which records the number of times a packet has recirculated. By having the main sorting network use this field as a secondary sort key,

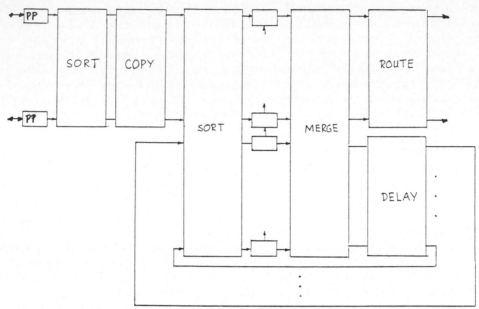

Figure 1: Starlite Switch Fabric

we can also order packets by their age, giving older packets priority over newer ones. This ensures that packets are transmitted in the same order in which they were received. If the network supports n external links and the main sort and merge networks have m input and output ports, up to $m - n$ packets may be recirculating at any time. Packets may be lost if during a cycle, more than $m - n$ packets have their delay bits set. The value of m is selected based on statistical considerations, to yield an acceptably low probability of packet loss.

We now turn to the issue of packet replication. The network is designed around the notion of a coordinated copy between source and destinations. That is, the source and the destinations must synchronize when a packet is to be copied. When the source PP sends a packet into the network, the destination PPs simultaneously send *blank packets* containing their address plus the address of the source in the headers. The initial sorting network sorts these packets on the source addresses, which places the original packet and associated blank packets on a contiguous set of links, upon exit from the sorting network. The copy network then copies the information from the source packets to each of the blank packets, a relatively straightforward process, given the sorted arrangement. When these packets enter the main sorting network, they are routed using destination addresses in the same way as point-to-point packets.

The Starlite system has some very attractive properties. The basic switch elements making up the various networks are simple and have a regular interconnection pattern, which makes the design of high speed VLSI implementations quite straightforward. The network is non-blocking and has a latency of only one bit time per stage of switching. It maintains packet sequencing, so that packets are received in the same order in which they are transmitted. The sharing of buffering across the switch fabric, rather than dedicated it to individual links provides more predictable performance in the face of statistical fluctuations in traffic.

The synchronization required for copying is a drawback of this approach, when used

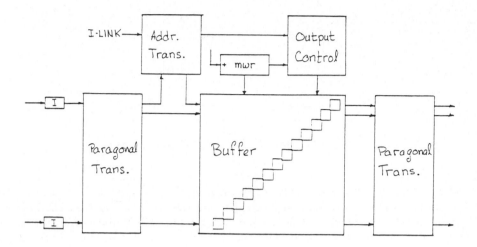

Figure 2: Prelude Switch Fabric

in a general packet switching environment. Some form of arbitration is required at the front end to schedule packets that must be copied, and while such a mechanism is probably feasible, no detailed proposal has been put forward. Also, while the switch elements are very simple, their interconnection is topologically complex relative to some competing proposals. Finally, the dimensioning of the main sort and merge networks is problematical; it appears likely that to achieve satisfactory performance in a general packet switching environment, these networks must have at least four to eight times as many inputs as there are external links. Nevertheless, the Starlite approach is a very promising one, and is a convincing demonstration of the power of a few simple ideas.

2.2. Prelude

The Prelude project began at CNET in France in the early eighties, with the objective of creating a flexible switching system that could provide point-to-point and multipoint communication at speeds up to a few hundred megabits per second [4,5,7]. It is based on a particularly simple form of fast packet switching referred to as *asynchronous time division multiplexing*, and uses a novel high speed switch fabric.

The basic structure of the Prelude switch fabric is shown in Figure 2. Packets enter at the transmission interfaces at left, which perform framing and synchronization functions. The packets are then passed through a rotative switch which transforms each packet to a so-called parallel-diagonal format (*paragonal*) in which each packet is distributed across the outputs of the rotative switch, with the first byte of each packet on the first output, the second byte on the second output, and so forth. This transformation places the headers of all packets on the first output of the switch, where they can all be processed by a centralized address translator. The address translator modifies the channel number in the header of the packet and then the modified packet is stored in a central buffer memory, still in the paragonal format. At the same time, the address translator passes

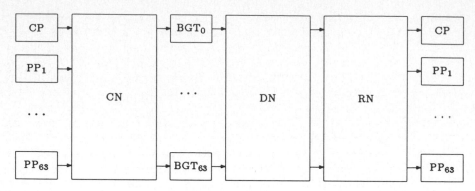

Figure 3: Broadcast Packet Switch Fabric

to the output control circuit, a bit vector defining which outputs are to receive copies of the packet. The output circuit stores the address at which the packet header was written in queues associated with the selected outputs. This information is used later to retrieve the packet from the central buffer. There is an output process that examines these queues in a cyclic fashion, initiating a new packet retrieval on each clock cycle. Broadcast is accomplished simply by reading the packet from the buffer once for each output that requires a copy. Note that these reads need not all take place during one packet cycle. Finally, a second rotative switch transforms the packets from the paragonal format back to the normal format so that they can be output on their respective links.

This design has several attractive features. The basic elements are simple; the rotative switches can be implemented as barrel shifters, requiring about $n \log n$ gates, the address translator and buffer are essentially just random access memories with a modest amount of control circuitry, and the output control consists of a fairly simple and regular collection of queues and address registers. As with Starlite it maintains packet sequencing and provides a single shared buffer rather than per line buffers. It is, on the whole simpler than the Starlite fabric and handles multipoint communication in a more satisfactory way.

The main drawback of this approach is its dependence on high speed memories, particularly in the central buffer. It must be possible to access this memory twice per clock time, once for reading and once for writing. There does not appear to be any architectural way to reduce the required memory cycle time for individual memory chips since the memory read-out process can access the memory chips in random order. Another drawback is that since channel translation takes place before packets are replicated, all the downstream copies of a multipoint packet carry the same channel number. This places operational restrictions on the assignment of channel numbers, that may be problematical, depending on the number of channels and multipoint connections. It is most troubling for general multipoint connections in which there are several transmitters. It appears that either all the links involved in such a connection must use the same channel number, or there must be a different channel number for every incoming port that can be the source of the packet. The latter solution requires that the downstream switches treat all those channel numbers similarly.

2.3. Broadcast Packet Switch

The Broadcast Packet Switch, proposed by Turner [26] is a switch fabric based on buffered binary routing networks. It is topologically simple and well-suited to VLSI implementation. The overall structure is shown in Figure 3. The system consists of a set of *Packet Processors* which interface to the external links and provide all per-packet protocol processing, a *Connection Processor* which sets up and maintains multipoint connections, and a switch fabric consisting of a *Copy Network*, a set of *Broadcast and Group Translators*, a *Distribution Network* and a *Routing Network*.

Packets enter one of the Packet Processors at left, where an address translation is performed. For point-to-point packets this yields an outgoing link number and an outgoing channel number. These are placed in the header of the packet, which then passes through the CN, one of the BGTs and the DN, following some arbitrary path. When the packet reaches the RN, it is routed using the outgoing link number. The RN is a conventional binary routing network with sufficient storage at each node to store a small number of complete packets. When the packet reaches the outgoing PP, the extra header information added at the incoming PP is stripped off and the packet is transmitted on the outgoing link. The role of the DN is to randomly distribute packets it receives across its outputs. This prevents congestion that can otherwise occur in the RN when subjected to traffic patterns with strong "communities-of-interest."

When a packet belonging to a multipoint connection is received at an incoming PP, it undergoes a similar translation process, but the information added to the packet header is different. It consists of two fields, a *Fanout* field which specifies the number of outgoing links which are to receive copies of the packet, and a *Broadcast Channel Number*, used by the BGTs. The CN replicates multipoint packets using the fanout field to guide its decisions. At each switch element where replication is performed, the fanout fields of the two copies are modified (essentially by halving the original fanout), so that a short time after the original packet enters the CN, the appropriate number of copies appears at its outputs. The BGTs then perform a translation similar to that done in the PPs, using the broadcast channel number in the copies to index a table, yielding a set of outgoing link and logical channel numbers. These are added to the packet header and used to guide the copies to the proper outgoing links.

This design is well-suited to implementation in a medium speed, high density technology like CMOS. While the individual switch elements are more complex than those in the Starlite and Prelude matrices, the topological complexity is very low, and the required speeds are relatively low. The only large memories are in the PPs and BGTs, and these need be accessed only once per packet cycle, permitting the use of high density memories with relatively long cycle times. While the switch elements are more complex than those in the the Starlite and Prelude fabric, this complexity has little impact on cost or performance.

The design does have some drawbacks. Unlike the Starlite and Prelude designs, the primary buffering is in the PPs, leading to less predictable performance in the presence of highly irregular traffic patterns. While the addition of some shared buffering is feasible, no detailed study of such an arrangement has yet been made. More seriously perhaps, is the fact that the system does not guarantee that packets are received in the same order as they are sent. While it is possible to modify the design to provide such a guarantee, the required changes impose operational constraints and degrade performance sufficiently to raise doubts about the merits of such changes. A more detailed analysis of these questions is required.

While none of the three switch fabrics reviewed above clearly dominates the others, all three represent technically feasible and economically viable solutions to the problem

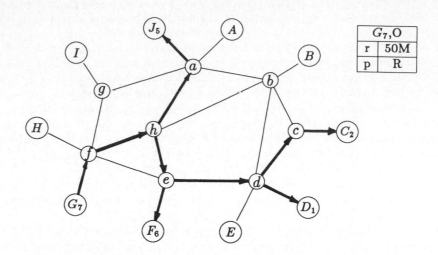

$G_7,$O	
r	50M
p	R

Figure 4: One-to-Many Connection

of flexible multipoint connections in a packet switched network. This observation makes
it clear that the fundamental issue of switching system architecture can be solved in
a variety of different ways. While there is a variety of other issues that remain to be
resolved, this provides reason for being confident that the goal of a network providing
flexible multipoint communication is attainable and worth pursuing.

3. Connection Management

Connection management refers to the collection of algorithms, data structures and protocols used to create and maintain connections among users. In conventional networks,
connections join two endpoints. In multipoint networks, connections may join an arbitrary number of endpoints. Several types of connections appear to be useful, including
point-to-point connections and simple broadcast connections having one transmitter and
many receivers. Connections in which all participants can both transmit and receive are
also useful, for conferencing and LAN interconnect applications among others.

As one considers applications of multipoint communication, one soon realizes that
what is needed is a general multipoint connection capability that realizes point-to-point,
broadcast and conference connections as special cases. This section briefly describes one
approach to connection management, that provides a flexible way of defining multipoint
connections supporting a wide variety of applications and which has the potential for
being effectively implemented in large networks.

We start by describing a simple one-way broadcast connection, illustrated in Figure 4.
The connection has a single transmitter G and receivers C, D, F and J. The subscripts
in the diagram represent the channel numbers that the various terminals use to identify
this particular connection among the set of connections present on the access links. The
internal nodes in the diagram represent switching systems and at various points the
stream of packets originating at G is replicated and forwarded to the appropriate points.
The connection induces a tree in the network, in much the same way that a point-to-point
connection induces a path in a conventional network. The table in the upper right-hand

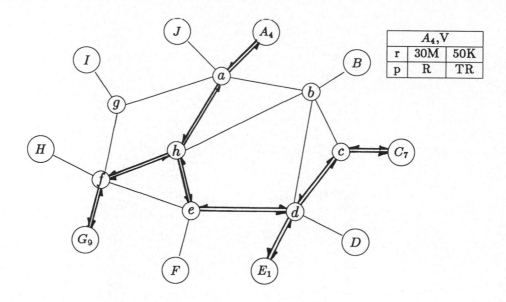

A_4,V		
r	30M	50K
p	R	TR

Figure 5: Connection for Video Lecture

corner of the diagram summarizes some global information describing this connection. The G_7 at the top is the *connection identifier*, which is a globally unique name identifying this connection and distinguishing it from all other connections in the network; the motivation for having a connection identifier will be explained below. One simple way of providing such an identifier is to use the address of the *owner* of the connection together with an integer distinguishing this connection from others that the owner may also be participating in. The owner of the connection is just that terminal that is responsible for the connection and controls access to it. This scheme has been used in the example, implying that G is the owner, as well as the only transmitter in the connection. The 50M, denotes a *rate specification* of 50 megabits per second. In a real network, a more complex rate specification is required, allowing specification of peak rate, average rate and some measure of "burstiness," but for the moment, we will ignore this issue. Each endpoint participating in the connection can have *transmit-only* permission, *receive-only* permission or *transmit/receive* permission. The permission concept provides the basic mechanisms needed to allow the specification of general multipoint connections, that can be tailored to different applications. The network uses the permission information to allocate resources, (primarily link bandwidth) appropriately. The R at the bottom of the table defines the *default permission* to be receive-only, meaning that whenever an endpoint is added to the connection it is initially assigned receive-only permission; this can of course be changed by the owner if some other permission is required.

The example illustrates a connection that might be appropriate for distributing an entertainment video signal. To establish such a connection, G would send a control message to the network, describing the type of connection required. At that point it could begin transmitting on the connection, but initially there would be no one to receive the signal. Endpoints can be added to the connection in one of two ways. First G, as the owner, can send a message to the network asking that a particular endpoint be added. In response, the network would send a *connection invitation* to the specified endpoint

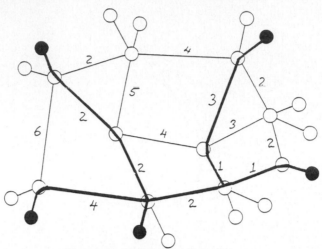

Figure 6: Multipoint Routing

and if the endpoint agrees (by exchange of control messages) to join the connection, the network would find an appropriate path and allocate the necessary resources to include the new endpoint in the connection. For entertainment video signals, a more appropriate way of adding an endpoint is at the endpoint's request. That is, an endpoint could send a control message to the network, requesting that it be added to a specified connection. To make such a request, the endpoint must specify the appropriate connection identifier. For entertainment video signals, this information would typically be widely available and could be built into terminal equipment, or programmed in, as appropriate. In response to such a request, the network would first search for the nearest place that the specified connection is available and attempt to add the new endpoint by creating a branch at that point.

Addition of new endpoints from "outside" the connection raises the need for some form of authorization. In the example, the O at the top of the figure specifies that this connection is *open*, meaning that anyone who wishes to join the connection may do so without explicit authorization from the owner. This would probably be the appropriate specification for a commercial video broadcast. Other options include *closed*, meaning that no one can join from outside and *verify*, meaning that outsiders may join, but only after getting explicit permission from the owner.

This example has illustrated the essential notions of the multipoint connection mechanism. A point-to-point connection for voice communication can be readily described using these mechanisms. In that case, the rate specification might be 50 kilobits per second rather than 50 megabits, the default permission would be TR, for transmit/receive and the outside access specification would be C (closed). Notice that in neither example, is there any need for the switching systems supporting the connection to have detailed knowledge of the connection, such as whether the signals carried are voice or video. Such information is required in the terminals and possibly network interface equipment (depending on the desired form of access), but is not needed anywhere in the core of the network. This *application-ignorance* is important for maintaining the flexible nature of the network. By keeping that information from the network core, we ensure that changes in the applications cannot affect the network's operation in any fundamental way.

Figure 5 gives an example of a more complicated connection requiring two related but **separate channels within a single connection. This connection is intended for use in a**

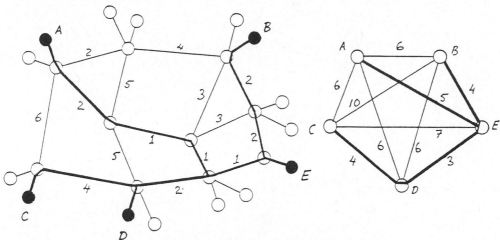

Figure 7: Minimum Spanning Tree Heuristic

video lecture situation. It includes a downstream channel from A to C, E and G, which has a rate of 30 megabits per second and a default permission of receive-only. It also has a second channel, which can be used for upstream audio, allowing the audience members to direct questions to the speaker. It has its own rate and default permissions specified. The network allocates link bandwidth separately for the two channels, but routes them through the same set of switches, for convenience in handling addition of new endpoints. The concept of multiple channels within a connection, is an important extension of the basic multipoint connection mechanism that can be useful in more complex applications.

4. Routing of Multipoint Connections

Routing connections in point-to-point networks is typically treated as a shortest path problem in a graph. Nodes represent switching systems, edges represent links and the edge lengths represent the costs associated with using a link. At the time a connection is established, one attempts to find the shortest available path connecting the desired pair of endpoints.

Routing a multipoint connection is comparable. Instead of the shortest path, one is interested in the shortest subtree of the network containing a given set of endpoints. This subtree may contain *transit nodes*, not in the specified set of endpoints. An example of a multipoint connection is given in Figure 6. The selection of transit nodes makes the problem more difficult than point-to-point routing. In fact, finding the shortest subtree connecting a set of points is a classical problem in graph theory (the Steiner tree problem) and is known to be NP-complete. This means that the existence of efficient algorithms for finding the optimal route is unlikely. Consequently, one is forced to turn to algorithms that may produce sub-optimal solutions, but which can be expected to work acceptably well in practice.

It turns out that for the Steiner tree problem, there are several known approximation algorithms that provide a good starting point for work on multipoint routing. The best known algorithm is called the *minimum spanning tree heuristic* or MST. It has been shown that the solutions produced by MST have a cost that is never more than twice optimal, and experimental results show that it is typically within five percent of optimal.

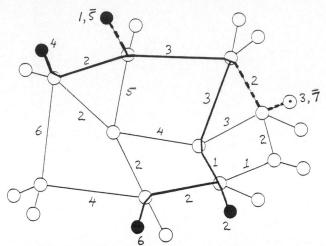

Figure 8: Routing Dynamic Connections

An example of the MST heuristic is given in Figure 7. Our objective is to find a subtree connecting nodes A, B, C, D and E. The first step is to construct another graph the *induced graph* containing just the nodes to be connected. All pairs of nodes in the induced graph are connected by an edge, with cost equal to the length of the shortest path in the original graph, connecting that pair. So for example, the length of the edge from A to E in the induced graph is 5 because the shortest path from A to E in the original graph has length 5. The second step in the algorithm is to find a minimum spanning tree in the induced graph; that is a shortest subtree that includes all the nodes in the induced graph. This can be done efficiently using well-known algorithms. For the example, the minimum spanning tree has a cost of 16, as indicated in the figure. Finally, the edges of the minimum spanning tree are mapped back onto paths in the original graph, giving the solution shown, which has a cost of 15. Note that this solution exceeds the cost of an optimal solution by one. The MST heuristic can be applied directly to routing of static multipoint connections, in which the identity of all endpoints is known in advance and in networks where centralized routing is feasible. Distributed implementations are also possible, but have yet to be developed. In any case, MST provides a useful measurement tool that can be used for comparison with other algorithms.

We now turn to the dynamic version of multipoint routing in which endpoints join and leave the connection over an extended period of time. Perhaps the simplest algorithm for this problem is to add a new endpoint to a connection, by using the shortest path from that endpoint to some node that is already in the connection. Similarly, one drops an endpoint, by simply removing that portion of the connection that serves only that endpoint. This simple *greedy algorithm* is illustrated in Figure 8. The numbers next to the solid nodes represent a sequence of events. Unbarred integers denote joining the connection and barred integers denote leaving the connection. So in the example, the connection initially consists of nodes B and D, joined later by nodes C and A (in that order). Then, node B leaves the connection, node E joins and node C leaves. Note that the algorithm can produce solutions that are far from optimal; in the example, the final arrangement could be reduced by 5 units. Experimental results have shown it to perform reasonably well, producing connections having costs that are typically within 30% of the cost of MST. One attractive feature of the algorithm is that it works incrementally, modifying the connection by addition or deletion, rather than making more complex

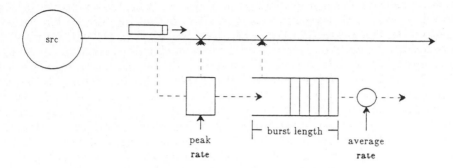

Figure 9: Simple Bandwidth Enforcement Mechanism

rearrangements. This mode of operation, while limiting the performance, may well be the only practical way to go.

5. Congestion Control

A principal advantage of packet switched networks is their ability to dynamically allocate bandwidth to the users who need it at a particular instant. Since networks are subject to rapid statistical variations in demand, care must be taken to ensure acceptable performance under conditions of peak loading. An effective congestion control system requires several specific methods, each acting on a different time scale. In connection-oriented packet networks, long term overloads can be prevented by the allocation of bandwidth to connections and the refusal of new connections unless the needed bandwidth is available. This means that the network must provide a mechanism for users to specify their bandwidth needs and an indication of the burstiness of their transmissions, and must enforce limits to prevent users from exceeding their allocations. Short term demand variations are handled by buffering within the network. To limit delay variability and keep memory buffer memory sizes at a reasonable level, the amount of buffering at each link should probably be limited to about 1 ms worth. For 100 Mb/s links this translates to about 100 Kb of memory.

When a user establishes a connection, he must provide a *rate specification* that in some sense describes the traffic characteristics of the connection. It must include the connection's *peak rate*, its *average rate* and some measure of how bursty it is. The network must be able to use the rate specification to determine what portion of each link's capacity should be allocated to the connection. In addition, the network must have a straightforward way of ensuring that the user does not exceed the allocation. One simple mechanism can be viewed as a *pseudo-buffer*, positioned at the edge of the network (this is sometimes called the "leaky bucket" method). Whenever a user sends a packet over a connection, the length of the pseudo-buffer at the network boundary is increased by one. So long as this doesn't cause the pseudo-buffer to overflow, the packet simply passes over the connection; if the pseudo-buffer does overflow, the packet is discarded (an alternative strategy is to buffer the packet and flow control the user). This idea is illustrated in Figure 9. The pseudo-buffer accepts packets at a certain maximum rate (the connection's peak rate), is drained at a constant rate (the connection's average rate) and has a maximum length (the connection's maximum burst length). These three parameters may all be specified by the user, allowing him in effect, to specify the characteristics of a kind of *virtual private link* to be associated with the connection. The network uses these parameters to determine a *bandwidth allocation* for the connection. The bandwidth allocation is selected to ensure acceptable performance (measured primarily in terms of packet loss rate) for all connections sharing links with the given connection. In general, the bandwidth allocation will lie somewhere between the peak and average rates. If the burst length and/or the peak rate are small, the bandwidth allocation can be close to the average length. If the burst length is long (meaning comparable in size to the link buffers) and the the peak rate is high (meaning comparable to the link rates), the bandwidth allocation may have to be close to the peak rate to ensure acceptable performance.

While bandwidth allocation and enforcement can limit long term congestion, other methods are needed to cope with congestion of intermediate duration. One class of methods, uses feedback to the sources. The feedback is triggered at the point where congestion occurs. Those connections contributing to the congestion are requested to reduce their rate of transmission, allowing the congestion time to clear up. In a high speed packet network, these methods appear of limited value, due to the time scales involved. Such feedback mechanisms may require 100 ms to take effect, but link buffers can fill and overflow in just a few milliseconds. For switching systems designed around shared buffers, such feedback mechanisms may be useful (since it takes longer for a large, shared buffer to overflow), but systems designed around per link buffers will likely find them of little value.

One promising method for coping with the shorter term overloads is the introduction of packet priorities. During high demand periods, the network can preferentially discard low priority packets. If half the packets on a specific FOL have low priority, that FOL can tolerate peak periods of arbitrary duration without losing any high priority packets. Priorities can be used to advantage for signals containing large amounts of redundant information. For example, video signals can be transmitted with the high order bits of each pixel carried in high priority packets and the low order bits carried in low priority packets. Occasional loss of low priority packets would probably be imperceptible. Periods of a few seconds during which many low priority packets are lost, are likely to be perceptible, but only mildly annoying to the viewer. Similar methods have been used very effectively for packet transmission of voice signals.

The above discussion applies to point-to-point connections and multipoint connections with a single transmitter. In these cases, it is straightforward to provide the bandwidth enforcement function entirely at the edge of the network. Connections with two or more transmitters and three or more receivers raise new issues, because in this case it becomes possible for packet streams from different transmitters to converge with one another inside the network, creating loads larger than are permitted at the boundary.

When one considers applications involving multiple transmitters, it becomes evident that in many cases, while there are many *potential transmitters* there is only one or a few *concurrent transmitters*. This suggests that the connection description should be augmented to include a specification of the number of concurrent transmitters. Given this information, the network can allocate sufficient bandwidth to support the specified number. It then of course, must ensure that this number is not exceeded.

There are several possible approaches to this last problem. If one wishes to control the problem entirely at the network boundary, one can apply the pseudo-buffer idea; the required change is that the length of the pseudo-buffer is incremented for every packet entering and leaving at a given boundary point. Doing this at all boundary points allows one to prevent long term congestion. The problem of course, is that the enforcement mechanism comes into play only after the congestion has occurred, when it can no longer do any good. One can modify the basic mechanism so that it "punishes" users who exceed their allocation, but this does not seem fully satisfactory.

Another approach is to have some explicit contention mechanism. The most obvious possibility is to require that each active transmitter hold a special packet called a *token* before being allowed to transmit. A connection may have several tokens, passed among the set of potential transmitters. The key drawback here is that it appears to require a mechanism for reliable token transmission, adding considerable complication to both the network and its use.

A third approach is the brute force one. Perform bandwidth enforcement throughout the network rather than just at the boundary. A bandwidth enforcer for several hundred channels is simple enough to implement on a single custom integrated circuit. The main constraint on chip area is the memory to store the information needed to simulate the pseudo-buffers for each channel. We have estimated that between 16 and 24 bytes per channel are required. Using the larger value of 24 bytes, we find that 256 channels can be handled by a chip with 50 Kbits of on-chip memory. This may be sufficient, even for links capable of carrying a much larger number of channels, since enforcement for low speed connections need be done only at the boundary. The added cost, while significant is not excessive.

6. Conclusions

This is an exciting period in the development of communications systems. Rapid improvements in technology now make it possible to implement flexible communications systems supporting a remarkably wide range of applications. The key challenge is to design systems that do not constrain that range unnecessarily and which allow predicted technology advances to be incorporated in such a way as to further extend the range.

We have discussed the problem of multipoint communication from several different angles, reviewing the problems of switching system architecture, connection management, routing and congestion control. While we by no means have a full understanding of all these issues, the nature of the problems is becoming apparent and there is good reason to be believe that viable solutions can be developed.

Acknowledgements. This work has been supported by the National Science Foundation and the Washington University Consortium for Research on Advanced Communications Systems, whose members include Bell Communications Research, Italtel SIT and NEC. I gratefully acknowledge their generous support. I particularly wish to thank Gil Devey and Steve Wolf of NSF, Eric Nussbaum and Neil Haller of Bell Communications Research, Maurizio Dècina and Anna Robrock of Italtel and Akihiro Kitamura and Noboru Suzuki of NEC. This paper describes work done collaboratively with several graduate students at Washington University. In particular, Kurt Haserodt, now at AT&T Bell Laboratories worked with me on connection management, Buddy Waxman is currently addressing the multipoint routing problem and Shahid Akhtar, the congestion control problem.

References

[1] Batcher, K. E. "Sorting Networks and Their Applications," *Proceedings of the Spring Joint Computer Conference*, 1968, 307–314.

[2] Beckner, M. W., T. T. Lee, S. E. Minzer. "A Protocol and Prototype for Broadband Subscriber Access to ISDNs," *International Switching Symposium*, 3/87.

[3] Bubenik, Richard and Jonathan S. Turner. "Performance of a Broadcast Packet Switch." Washington University Computer Science Department, WUCS-86-10, 6/3/86.

[4] Coudreuse, J. P. and M. Servel. "Asynchronous Time-Division Techniques: An Experimental Packet Network Integrating Videocommunication," *Proceedings of the International Switching Symposium*, 1984.

[5] Dieudonne, M. and M. Quinquis. "Switching Techniques Review for Asynchronous Time Division Multiplexing," *International Switching Symposium*, 3/87.

[6] Giorcelli, S., C. Demichelis, G. Giandonato and R. Melen. "Experimenting with Fast Packet Switching Techniques in First Generation ISDN Environment," *International Switching Symposium*, 3/87.

[7] Gonet, P., P. Adam, J. P. Coudreuse. "Asynchronous Time-Division Switching: the Way to Flexible Broadband Communication Networks," *Proceedings of the International Zurich Seminar on Digital Communication*, 3/86, 141–148.

[8] Hayward, G., L. Linnell, D. Mahoney and L. Smoot. "A Broadband Local Access System Using Emerging Technology Components," *International Switching Symposium*, 3/87.

[9] Hoberecht William L. "A Layered Network Protocol for Packet Voice and Data Integration," *IEEE Journal on Selected Areas in Communications*, vol. SAC-1, no. 6, 12/83, 1006–1013.

[10] Huang, Alan and Scott Knauer. "Starlite: a Wideband Digital Switch," *Proceedings of Globecom 84*, 12/84, 121–125.

[11] Huang, Alan. "Distributed Prioritized Concentrator," U.S. Patent 4,472,801, 1984.

[12] Huang, Alan and Scott Knauer. "Wideband Digital Switching Network," U.S. Patent 4,542,497, 1985.

[13] Jenq, Yih-Chyun. "Performance Analysis of a Packet Switch Based on a Single-Buffered Banyan Network," *IEEE Journal on Selected Areas in Communications*, vol. SAC-1, no. 6, 12/83, 1014–1021.

[14] Lea, Chin-tau. "The Load-Sharing Banyan Network," *IEEE Transactions on Computers*, 12/86.

[15] Karol, M. J., M. G. Hluchyj and S. P. Morgan. "Input vs. Output Queueing on a Space-Division Packet Switch," *Proceedings of Globecom*, 12/86.

[16] Kulzer, John J. and Warren A. Montgomery. "Statistical Switching Architectures for Future Services," *Proceedings of the International Switching Symposium*, 5/84.

[17] Montgomery, Warren A. "Techniques for Packet Voice Synchronization," *IEEE Journal on Selected Areas in Communications*, vol. SAC-1, no. 6, 12/83, 1022–1028.

[18] Muise, R. W., T. J. Schonfeld and G. H. Zimmerman III. "Experiments in Wideband Packet Technology," *Proceedings of the International Zurich Seminar on Digital Communication*, 3/86, 135–139.

[19] Rettberg, R., C. Wyman, D. Hunt, M. Hoffman, P. Carvey, B. Hyde, W. Clark and M. Kraley. "Development of a Voice Funnel System: Design Report," Bolt Beranek and Newman, Report No. 4098, 8/79.

[20] Richards, Gaylord and Frank K. Hwang. "A Two Stage Rearrangeable Broadcast Switching Network," *IEEE Transactions on Communications*, 10/85.

[21] Sincoskie, W. D. "Transparent Interconnection of Broadcast Networks," *Proceedings of the International Zurich Seminar on Digital Communication*, 3/86, 131–134.

[22] Staehler, R. E., J. J. Mansell, E. Messerli, G. W. R. Luderer, A. K. Vaidya. "Wideband Packet Technology for Switching Systems," *International Switching Symposium*, 3/87.

[23] Takeuchi, Takao, Hiroshi Suzuki, Shin-ichiro Hayano, Hiroki Niwa and Takehiko Yamaguchi. "An Experimental Synchronous Composite Packet Switching System," *Proceedings of the International Zurich Seminar on Digital Communication*, 3/86, 149–153.

[24] Turner, Jonathan S. and Leonard F. Wyatt. "A Packet Network Architecture for Integrated Services," *Proceedings of Globecom 83*, 11/83, 45–50.

[25] Turner, Jonathan S. "Fast Packet Switching System," United States Patent #4,494,230, 1/15/85.

[26] Turner, Jonathan S. "Design of a Broadcast Packet Network," *Proceedings of Infocom*, 4/86.

[27] Turner, Jonathan S. "New Directions in Communications," *IEEE Communications Magazine*, 10/86.

[28] Turner, Jonathan S. "Design of an Integrated Services *Packet* Network," *IEEE Journal on Selected Areas in Communications*, 11/86.

[29] Yeh, Y. S., M. G. Hluchyj and A. S. Acampora. "The Knockout Switch: a Simple Modular Architecture for High Performance Packet Switching," *International Switching Symposium*, 3/87.

TRAFFIC ENGINEERING for ISDN Design and Planning
M. Bonatti and M. Decina (Editors)
Elsevier Science Publishers B.V. (North-Holland)
© IAC, 1988

THE STUDY OF NETWORK PERFORMANCE IN RELATION TO ISDN

R G Ackerley, N W Macfadyen, D J Songhurst

Performance Engineering Division, British Telecom Research Laboratories, Martlesham Heath, Ipswich, IP5 7RE, UK

Models of overall grade-of-service performance have been developed, with application to British Telecom digital main and local networks. The models allow the effects of many traffic, network, and planning characteristics to be quantified. Results are presented for a reference model network, and the typically low mean blockings with high variability are contrasted with the problems of dimensioning multi-service networks.

MAIN STATEMENT

End-to-end grade-of-service distributions across a digital network must be quantified in order to achieve a rational dimensioning policy, particularly in a multi-service environment.

1   INTRODUCTION

The problems of dimensioning multiservice networks are highly complex and are being intensively studied. The presence of variable bit-rate traffic, or of capacity allocation in units of variable size, means that relatively complex multivariate grade-of-service (GOS) requirements have to be specified, rather than the simple single-figure end-to-end or link congestion values to which present telephony networks are dimensioned.

ISDN users are likely to have sophisticated and demanding service requirements. The problem therefore arises of how to ensure that the GOS which they receive from the network as a whole meets their expectations (which may be very different from those of the typical present telephony user), while at the same time avoiding the large-scale and costly provision of unnecessary new equipment.

It is not clear indeed that the concept of sizing any network, whether large or small, to a single set of notional design-date traffic values is necessarily always either appropriate or optimal. This is especially true in the UK and USA, in the new environment of liberalisation and competition between carriers, and is likely to be increasingly true elsewhere. In a commercial environment, a balance must be struck between the convenience of the customer and the economics, that is to say, the profitability to the operating company - and to do this in a defensible and satisfactory manner we must not confine ourselves to the study of the grade-of-service at any particular instant of time with idealised fixed sets of variables, but rather study how the overall end-to-end grade-of-service (OGOS), as seen by the customer, actually does behave. And in order to allow the appropriate balance between the interests of the consumer and the provider, this must be done not only with reference to the 'worst-case' scenario (in some suitably defined sense) as seen by the customer, but also with reference to the overall long-term average behaviour which is the principal determinant of the network costs. It is, for instance, not reasonable to size on the assumption of simultaneous network-wide design-date if the reality in practice is that equipment is always installed early, and frequently a good deal early, so that construction staff can be kept uniformly busy throughout the year.

Nor indeed is it reasonable to insist upon highly-accurate dimensioning to detailed target values when it is impossible or too costly to acquire the necessary data. These are not mere technical reservations - they are fundamental considerations which should lie at the heart of any genuine network dimensioning and operating policy. Their relevance in the future is likely to increase rather than decrease, as the hardware cost of digital transmission and switching equipment continues to fall in real terms, and the modularity with which equipment is provided continues to grow.

The Performance Engineering Division of British Telecom is therefore constructing a detailed quantitative model of OGOS which will allow the study of the actual implications which all these effects have for grade-of-service and network cost. The function of the model is to quantify the network performance over an extended period (for example one year) in terms of the distribution of GOS values experienced by customers of a particular type. This statistical model allows the study of hypothetical network structures, routing strategies and dimensioning methods, in terms of their effects on the OGOS distribution experienced by customers. It is necessarily analytic because by the nature of any model which produces distributions of grade-of-service for different traffic streams in a large network, it is impracticable to use simulation.

The model is at present restricted to circuit group congestion in circuit-switched networks. It does not represent congestion within exchanges or the effects of network management actions, since in a digital environment these effects would be significant only in exceptional circumstances which require separate analysis. The model represents on-demand call set-up, and permanent or semi-permanent connections, but it does not treat call reservation facilities.

The specific application to ISDN lies in the ability to analyse the OGOS performance of different types of traffic, and in particular to investigate the use of priority systems such as trunk reservation for controlling relative service levels [1]. In the longer term the OGOS methodology should be applied to multiple bit-rate networks. Section 5 of this paper provides some further discussion of heterogeneous traffic, while the remainder of the paper describes the application of the model to a large national digital network.

The use of statistical models to relate provisioning procedures to blocking distributions has largely been pioneered by AT&T in particular Franks et al [2], Neal [3], and Elsinger & Pack [4]. Horn [5] has also drawn attention to the need for this approach in order to ensure that dimensioning practices are sensibly related to realistic measures of network performance. The models developed by British Telecom are aimed at the objectives identified by Horn, but the methods are less purely analytical than those described by AT&T. Instead we have made substantial use of numerical methods in order to include all relevant factors and their impact on end-to-end GOS.

2   MODEL DESCRIPTION

2.1   Link Planning or End-to-end Planning?

There are two fundamentally different cases to consider, which require very different types of model. This distinction depends on the nature of the dimensioning process adopted by the operating company: that is, whether the network is engineered on a link-by-link or end-to-end basis. In the former case, traffics are recorded and forecast on each link in the network individually, and each of these is sized and provided according to its own definite criteria without reference to the remainder of the network; whereas in an end-to-end dimensioned network, by contrast, it is the end-to-end traffic streams which are the fundamental planning entities, and the transmission links are sized together so that every traffic stream shall meet its own defined grade-of-service.

This rather obvious distinction actually requires the construction of two quite different models, for in the one case the stream GOS can be calculated by starting from the quasi-independent link GOS values, whereas in the other the link GOS values are only determined once the stream GOS values are known - which means that the network must be solved as a whole, in practice by iterative methods. We have therefore constructed models to represent each of these categories separately.

In this paper we shall confine our attention to the link-engineered model, which is of greater relevance to large-scale country-wide networks. True end-to-end dimensioning of a network is not in practice feasible when there are several hundred thousand traffic streams involved: indeed, our own studies have shown that even networks as small as 50 nodes can cause severe problems with iterative algorithms and serious, systematic discrepancies between the numerical results of different analytic models.

2.2   Model Parameters and Assumptions

The link-engineered model takes into account, inter alia, the effects of

- Network structure and routing strategies
- Service protection
- Day-to-day traffic variability
- The measurement and forecasting process
- Growth
- Dimensioning methods
- Provisioning practices
- Excess-capacity (private-circuit) usage
- Overloads
- Transmission failures

Given suitable data defining daily traffic profiles on each circuit group it is possible to analyse OGOS performance for different times of day, but we shall here restrict attention to the simpler model of a network-wide busy-period (for example a period of one hour or longer during the morning).

The assumptions upon which the model is based include in particular:

- Stationarity of traffic within the busy-period
- Poisson offered traffic flows - the effects of repeat attempts are not modelled
- Statistical independence of GOS on different links
- Product-form traffic distributions.

The last assumption here needs some explanation. In order to derive a distribution over call attempts - that is, over customers - the congestion figures must be traffic-weighted before assembly. There are statistical difficulties involved here which cannot be resolved within the context of a model which does not contain a detailed geographical representation of the network involved, and must be validated instead by comparison with the actual state of affairs. This validation has been performed for a variety of different structures, and agreement has been excellent.

2.3   Model Structure

The structure of the model is as follows:

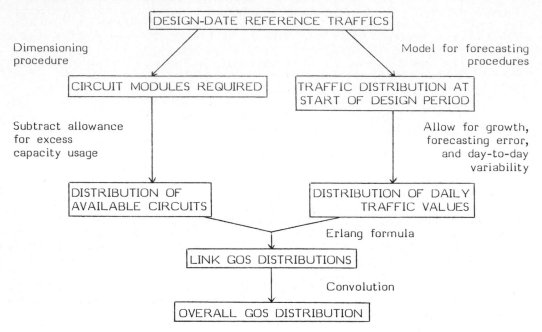

The starting point is the set of forecast design-date traffic values to which circuit groups are dimensioned.   In practice it is sufficient to use a small subset of link traffic values (no more than 15) provided that these are chosen to represent the full range of link traffic sizes present in the network and that they are appropriately weighted.   Moving down the left branch of the diagram we next dimension each link using the standard operational dimensioning procedures and allowing for modularity of equipment provision.   Finally we make allowance for excess capacity usage, reflecting the fact that excess capacity on circuit groups may be used for private circuits or semi-permanent connections.   A probabilistic model is used for this allowance, so that we obtain, for each design-date link traffic value, a distribution representing the number of circuits actually available for carrying traffic on that link.

Moving down the right branch of the diagram we construct, from each forecast traffic value, a distribution representing the traffic at the start of the considered design period.   This requires models of the operational measurement and forecasting procedures used.   This distribution is then converted into a distribution of traffic throughout the design period, using factors such as growth rate, forecasting error and day-to-day variability.

We now have, for each nominal link size, distributions representing actual daily busy-period traffics and available circuits.   These are brought together to give link GOS distributions.   This step requires repeated calculation of Erlang-type formulae, for which assembler-coded versions of efficient algorithms are used [6].

The final step is to compute the end-to-end OGOS distribution as a weighted sum of convolutions of link GOS distributions, over all the different path-types allowed by the routing strategy.   This convolution approach assumes that GOS values on successive links can be added to give the end-to-end GOS (which is a good approximation when GOS values are not too high - see [7]), and that link GOS distributions are statistically independent.   The latter assumption is believed to be reasonable, but it could be invalidated by, for example, the occurrence of frequent network-wide traffic overloads, or high growth rates combined with simultaneous design-dates for many different circuit groups.

A further facility in the model is to provide 'expected worst-case' distributions, representing performance experienced over the worst routes through the network and at the worst times in the design cycle.

The methodology that has been briefly summarised above will be presented in more detail at ITC12.

3   REFERENCE MODEL

3.1   Network Structure

The overall grade of service distributions obtained from the model have been found to be dependent on the network structure and routing scheme employed.   In order to investigate effects other than these the following two tier hierarchical reference network was used to produce all the results quoted in this paper.   It comprises a trunk network, consisting of 20 trunk exchanges (T) fully interconnected by bothway trunk links, and 400 local exchanges (L) each of which is connected to the trunk network by a single access link.

Fixed routing using the path comprising the fewest links is employed, although the effects of alternative routing have been investigated and will be reported at ITC12. Thus there are two types of possible path through the network:

(i)   L - T - L
(ii)   L - T - T - L

3.2   Link Size Profiles

The following sample consisting of 14 links is used for the trunk links:

Traffic:	100	150	200	250	300	350	400	450	550	600	800
Weighting:	5	10	16	20	24	26	25	24	18	13	5

Traffic:	1000	1200	1500
Weighting:	2	1	1

The following sample consisting of 15 links is used for the access links:

Traffic:	100	200	300	400	450	500	550	600	700	750	800
Weighting:	12	14	18	27	35	45	49	51	50	47	35

Traffic:	900	1000	1200	1500
Weighting:	10	4	2	1

The proportions of each type of path are therefore as follows:

L - T - T - L   64%
L - T - L   36%

3.3   Traffic Measurement and Forecasting

The network is link engineered and the reference traffic used to dimension the links is the Assessed Representative Traffic (ART).   This is a BT procedure defined by the mean of the highest pair of 12 traffic values, each of which is the mean of the busy hour working-day traffic values for the route over one week in a particular month. The model can use other reference traffics (for example, that recommended in CCITT Recommendation E500).

The forecast growth rate used is 7% per annum. The achieved growth rate varies from route to route and is taken to be Normally distributed with mean 7% and standard deviation 1%.

3.4   Dimensioning

Link dimensioning is performed according to the nominal design date traffic. Three criteria are used as follows:

(i)   At the nominal traffic level, link blocking must not exceed the nominal grade of service.

(ii)   At 10% overload, link blocking must not exceed 2.5 times the nominal grade of service.

(iii)   At 20% overload, link blocking must not exceed 6.25 times the nominal grade of service.

The Erlang 'B' formula is used to calculate link blocking. A modularity of 30 circuits is employed throughout.

3.5   Provisioning

Links are augmented annually and enough capacity is provided at each augmentation to satisfy the above dimensioning criteria for the following year. All links are augmented independently in time except when considering the worst-case scenario.

3.6   Traffic Variability

The model of day-to-day route traffic variability is taken from extensive studies lasting 5 years at a number of exchanges in the UK [8]. The variance, var(A), of the daily busy hour traffic level, A, is given by

$$var(A) = kA + \lambda A^2$$

where $k = 0.133$
and $\lambda = 0.00083$

The second term here represents a 'social effect' which causes high correlations between parcels of traffic, and hence increases the variance of large streams. Mean traffic levels on Mondays are taken to be 7% higher than on the remaining weekdays.

4   RESULTS

Some preliminary results from the model are given below. More extensive results will be presented at ITC12.

4.1   OGOS Distribution

Figure 1 shows the OGOS distribution found on a Monday when access links and trunk links are both dimensioned to a design GOS of 2%. If the blocking on all links was equal to this design GOS then 2-link and 3-link calls would experience blockings of approximately 4% and 6% respectively. Therefore, with the proportions of 2-link and 3-link calls given in section 3.2, the equivalent end-to-end design GOS is 5.3% (0.36 x 4% + 0.64 x 6%). The OGOS distribution is displayed as a probability density function with a linear scale. Most of the probability is concentrated well below the equivalent end-to-end design GOS. The graph has a very long, thin tail that cannot be shown. The shape of this graph is quite typical.

Figure 2 shows the same distribution on a logarithmic scale. There is a well defined hump with a maximum at about 1.6%. Using this scale has the following advantages:

(i)   It is possible to span the entire range of GOS values of interest, with the unwanted resolution at high values removed, and information about the region of low GOS added.

(ii)   More of the graph's structure is revealed.

(iii)   The GOS scale corresponds more closely with the customer's perception of congestion - the difference between a GOS of 4% and 4.5% is perceived to be less significant than that between 0.5% and 1%.

When comparing OGOS distributions it is useful to examine certain percentiles of the cumulative distribution (typically the median, and the levels exceeded by 10%, 5% and 1% of the traffic). In this case, 10% of the Monday busy-hour traffic sees a GOS worse than 3.3% and only 2% sees a worse GOS than the end-to-end design GOS. For other weekdays, 10% sees a GOS worse than 0.6% and less than 0.01% sees a worse GOS than the end-to-end design GOS.

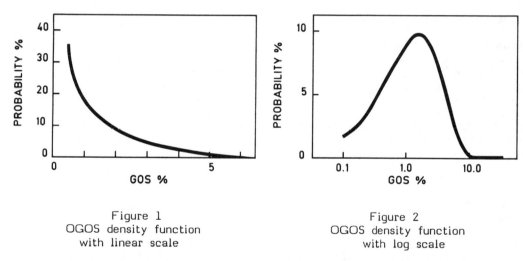

Figure 1
OGOS density function
with linear scale

Figure 2
OGOS density function
with log scale

4.2   Effect of Design GOS

Figure 3 shows how the percentiles of the OGOS distribution vary over the range of end-to-end design GOS values from 2% to 9%. The ratio of access-link to trunk-link design GOS has been kept constant at 1. Observe that even the 1% point is still below the end-to-end design GOS up to a value of 4%. Note that the 1, 5 and 10 percentiles increase rapidly with increasing design GOS above an end-to-end value of 3%.

4.3   Tradeoff Between Network Cost and OGOS Performance

Figure 4 shows how the 10% point of the OGOS distribution varies with network cost for three different access-link to trunk-link design GOS ratios. Network cost is measured here in thousands of 30-channel modules. For a (access:trunk) ratio of 1:4, the curve lies to the right. As this ratio is increased, the curve moves to the left until the ratio reaches 1:1. Above this ratio, the curve moves back to the right. The other percentiles behave in a similar way, so for this particular network the optimal design GOS ratio is 1:1. Note that network cost does not depend critically on the precise ratio chosen, nor on the precise target value of the 10% point of the

OGOS distribution.

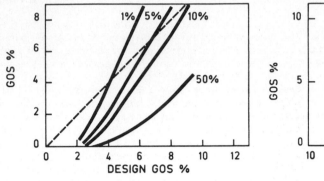 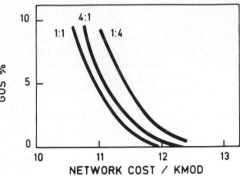

Figure 3
Variation with Design GOS

Figure 4
OGOS v. Cost Tradeoff

4.4   Worst Case Behaviour

It can be argued that, because a customer's perception of congestion is influenced unduly by periods of poor service, it is not only the OGOS distribution for the network which is important, but also the GOS distribution seen by traffic streams in the tail of the distribution.   The network considered has 400 local exchanges, and so there are almost 160,000 individual traffic streams.   The 'worst case' stream is chosen so that there are 20 streams which perform at least as badly.   For a network where all links are augmented at a common date, 10% of the time this worst case stream sees a GOS worse than 9%, and for over half of the time it sees a GOS worse than the end-to-end design GOS (c.f. section 5.1).

4.5   Sensitivity

From the above results it can be seen that the OGOS distribution is sensitive to the following factors:

> Overload
> End-to-end design GOS
> Design GOS ratio

Sensitivity studies have revealed that the OGOS distribution is sensitive to the following additional factors

> Network structure
> Route-size profiles
> Routing strategy
> Modularity of provision
> Overload protection
> Forecasting error

But, it is insensitive to the following:

> Traffic variability
> Growth rate (forecast correctly)
> Growth variance

The sensitivity to these factors increases rapidly with the end-to-end design GOS.

5   TREATMENT OF HETEROGENEOUS TRAFFIC

5.1   Peaky Daily Traffic Profile

Over short time intervals the ISDN call arrival process can be considered to be Poisson. The daily traffic profile is likely to have narrow predictable peaks, because many 2B + D users will be small offices and shops and might therefore be expected to make calls to some large data-base or other central facility to update records just before opening in the morning. The effect on non-ISDN traffic sharing the same digital network will depend on the magnitude and duration of these peaks and their position in relation to the non-ISDN traffic profile peaks. If the peaks are narrow enough they will have little effect on non-ISDN traffic, because it is reasonable to expect a non-ISDN customer to smooth his demand over a longer period. Therefore, a shorter busy period should be used for measuring ISDN traffic than for non-ISDN traffic. The application of trunk reservation could ensure that ISDN traffic has priority during these peaks, if desired. The model can be used to investigate such effects.

5.2   Multiple Channel Calls

With the introduction of a '2B + D' ISDN service it is likely that some services will require two 64 kbit/s channels for the duration of their calls. An example of such a service is slow-scan viewphone. Such calls will experience a poorer grade of service, because, to be set-up, they require at least 2 free channels to be available. Also these calls will worsen the grade of service experienced by calls requiring one channel. The magnitude of this effect can easily be calculated for the case of a single link using the usual multi-dimensional Erlang 'B' formula (see, for example, [1]). Table 1 shows the blocking experienced by calls of both types, in the range of interest 0.1% to 1%, as the number of channels (N) on the link is increased for total offered traffic (A), 100E and 500E and for proportions (p) of 2 channel calls 0% and 11%. The error ratio shows the factor by which the blocking would be under-estimated if the Erlang 'B' formula were to be used (with the same channel traffic).

A	N	Blocking %						
		1 channel calls			2 channel calls			
		p=0%	p=11%	error ratio	p=0.5%	error ratio	p=11%	error ratio
20	30	0.846	1.12	1.32	2.15	2.54	2.69	3.18
	33	0.204	0.346	1.70	0.558	2.74	0.868	4.25
	36	0.0381	0.0877	2.30	0.112	2.94	0.229	6.01
	38	0.0108	0.0316	2.93	0.0335	3.10	0.0848	7.85
100	117	0.979	1.14	1.16	2.14	2.19	2.44	2.49
	123	0.310	0.431	1.39	0.704	2.27	0.943	3.04
	128	0.0968	0.164	1.69	0.228	2.36	0.364	3.76
	134	0.0187	0.0420	2.25	0.0459	2.45	0.0955	5.11
500	527	0.954	1.00	1.05	1.97	2.06	2.05	2.15
	539	0.406	0.482	1.19	0.853	2.10	0.995	2.45
	554	0.102	0.151	1.48	0.220	2.16	0.315	3.09
	566	0.0258	0.0478	1.85	0.0571	2.21	0.101	3.91

Table 1
The Effect of Multiple Channel Calls

The error ratio for both types of calls decreases

(i)   as the number of channels decreases (for constant offered channel traffic and proportion of 2 channel calls),

(ii)   as the proportion of 2 channel calls decreases (for constant offered channel traffic and number of channels), and

(iii)   as the total offered channel traffic increases (for constant blocking and proportion of 2 channel calls).

Note that the blocking experienced by 1 channel traffic approaches $E(N,A)$ and the blocking experienced by 2 channel traffic approaches $(1 + N/A)E(N,A)$ as the proportion of 2 channel traffic approaches 0 (for constant offered channel traffic and number of channels), where $E(N,A)$ is the Erlang 'B' formula.

For the purposes of calculating the OGOS distribution these effects are relatively small in the region of interest especially for 1 channel traffic, and therefore only the total traffic offered to a link need be considered. Note that if the second channel is required after a delay (for example, when making a telephony call and then sending some data during the call) the effects will be reduced further.

5.3   Unequal Holding Time Calls and Trunk Reservation

It is possible to provide ISDN calls with a better grade of service than non-ISDN calls being carried on the same network by the use of Trunk Reservation. If a trunk reservation parameter, r, is applied to a traffic stream offered to a link then a call from this stream will not be set up if there are r or less free circuits. This provides a better grade of service on the link for the other streams. Trunk Reservation is more usually applied to overflow traffic in networks with automatic alternative routing [9], but the technique is also useful here. For the case of ISDN and non-ISDN calls offered to a single link and having the same mean holding times the blocking probabilities are given by the usual formula (see [10], for example).

However, it is likely that the mean holding times for ISDN and non-ISDN calls will differ significantly. In such a case the birth and death equations for the system are two dimensional. The effect of differing mean holding times has been investigated [11] by solving a truncated subset of these equations using QNAP [12]. Some specimen results are shown in Table 2 for the following values of the input parameters:

(i)   Proportion of ISDN traffic = 20%

(ii)   ISDN to non-ISDN holding time ratio (h_1/h_2) = 0.25 and 1.0

(iii)   Trunk reservation parameters (r) = 1 and 2

(iv)   Number of channels (N) = 30 and 120.

N	r	A	Blocking %					
			ISDN			Non-ISDN		
			$h_2=4h_1$	$h_2=h_1$	error ratio	$h_2=4h_1$	$h_2=h_1$	error ratio
30	1	15.7	0.0198	0.00865	2.28	0.0991	0.0913	1.09
		17.8	0.103	0.0461	2.23	0.469	0.434	1.09
		19.1	0.231	0.105	2.20	0.998	0.930	1.07
		22.4	1.02	0.487	2.09	3.93	3.75	1.05
	2	14.9	0.00411	0.000801	5.13	0.0971	0.0873	1.11
		18.2	0.0584	0.0121	4.83	1.00	0.906	1.10
		19.1	0.100	0.0212	4.72	1.59	1.45	1.10
		25.2	1.01	0.249	4.06	10.7	10.3	1.04
120	1	91.0	0.0259	0.0112	2.31	0.0954	0.0845	1.13
		96.0	0.105	0.0464	2.26	0.373	0.336	1.11
		100.5	0.285	0.129	2.21	0.983	0.900	1.09
		108.5	1.00	0.478	2.09	3.29	3.12	1.05
	2	90.0	0.00885	0.00163	5.43	0.0995	0.0833	1.19
		99.0	0.0966	0.0190	5.08	0.947	0.823	1.15
		99.5	0.107	0.0211	5.07	1.04	0.907	1.15
		116.0	1.00	0.231	4.33	7.98	7.57	1.05

Table 2
The Effect of Unequal Holding Times

The error ratio, which is the factor by which the blocking probabilities are in error if it is assumed that both call types have equal mean holding times,

- (i)   increases with the trunk reservation parameter used
- (ii)   increases as the ISDN to non-ISDN mean holding time ratio decreases
- (iii)   increases with the proportion of ISDN traffic
- (iv)   decreases slightly as the offered traffic increases (for a constant number of channels)
- (v)   increases slightly with the number of channels (for constant blocking or offered traffic per channel)

Note that the magnitude of these effects is tiny for non-ISDN traffic (the factor is approximately 1 throughout the range of parameters considered), and that the factor is exactly 1 for the following limiting cases:

- (i)   ISDN to non-ISDN mean holding time ratio = 1 (by definition)
- (ii)   Proportion of ISDN traffic = 0%
- (iii)   Trunk reservation parameter = 0

Again, for OGOS purposes these differences can be ignored, especially for non-ISDN calls, and it can be assumed, therefore, that the mean holding times of ISDN and non-ISDN calls are equal.

5.4   Multi-service Networks

As has already been mentioned the present study has been restricted to investigating the overall performance of circuit switched networks, although many of its conclusions are also likely to apply to multi-service networks. In [1], complete sharing and fixed boundary multi-service systems are compared. It was found that the complete sharing system is tolerant of variations in traffic mix and overload, and has a bandwidth advantage. High bit rate services experience a poorer grade of service than low bit rate services, but trunk reservation can be used to control the relative grades of service and, indeed, equalise them if required.

6   CONCLUSIONS

(i)   It is fundamentally impossible for the OGOS distribution to be concentrated around the design GOS value.   Therefore, a network cannot be operated with universally acceptable congestion levels and little spare capacity.

(ii)   Actual congestion levels bear virtually no resemblance at all to nominal design date targets.

(iii)   GOS requirements for each service should be of the form:

Not more than x% of traffic overall should see an end-to-end GOS worse than y% during the busy period, and

the median worst-case congestion should be no worse than z%.

(iv)   The accuracy required of traffic measurements, forecasts and end-to-end blocking calculations for different services should be assessed with reference to the variability inherent in OGOS distributions.

ACKNOWLEDGEMENTS

Acknowledgement is made to the Director of Research of British Telecom for permission to publish this paper.

REFERENCES

[1]   S A Johnson, 'A performance analysis of integrated communications systems', British Telecom Technology Journal, Vol 3 No 4, October 1985, pp 36-45

[2]   R L Franks, H Heffes, J M Holtzman, S Horing, 'A model relating measurement and forecast errors to the provisioning of direct final trunk groups', ITC8 paper 133, 1976

[3]   S R Neal, 'Blocking distributions for trunk network administration', Bell System Technical Journal, Vol 59, July 1980, pp 829-844.

[4]   D A Elsinger, C D Pack, 'Analytical models of a BOC trunk provisioning process', ITC11 paper 2.4A.3, 1985.

[5]   R W Horn, 'End-to-end connection probability - the next major engineering issue?', ITC9 paper 627, 1979.

[6]   R F Farmer, I Kaufman, 'On the numerical evaluation of some basic traffic formulae', Networks, Vol 8, No 2, pp 153-186, 1978

[7]   C Harvey, C R Hills, 'Determining grades of service in a network', ITC9 paper 626, 1979

[8]   A C Cole, 'A study of traffic flow in relation to CCITT recommendations for the measurement of telephone traffic flow, call attempts and seizures', ITC10 paper 1.4-7NR, 1983

[9]   D J Songhurst, 'Protection against traffic overload in hierarchical networks employing alternative routing', 1st Network Planning Symposium paper iX.3, 1980

[10]   J M Akinpelu, 'The overload performance of engineered networks with non hierarchical and hierarchical routing', ITC10 paper 3.2-4R, 1983.

[11]   M Azmoodeh & D Everitt, 'Congestion probabilities for a trunk reservation system with unequal mean holding times', BT/E&P/R15 Internal Memorandum TM85/54, 1985.

[12]   D Potier, 'New users' introduction to QNAP2', INRIA Technical Report No.40.

TRAFFIC ENGINEERING for ISDN Design and Planning
M. Bonatti and M. Decina (Editors)
Elsevier Science Publishers B.V. (North-Holland)
© IAC, 1988

Bandwidth Allocation and Network Dimensioning for International Multiservice Networks

Arik N. Kashper

AT&T Bell Laboratories
Crawfords Corner Road
Holmdel, New Jersey, 07733
USA

ABSTRACT

This paper proposes a design methodology for international ISDNs based on Dynamic Nonhierarchical Routing (DNHR) call set-up and routing rules. This approach results in full-access international networks and allows us to solve the international ISDN dimensioning problem by considering the bilateral network as a single digital pipe. This paper also describes how to calculate blocking probabilities for different traffic types and outlines a heuristic algorithm that addresses the bandwidth allocation problem in the ISDN environment.

Main Statement

Design and routing for international ISDNs based on full-access engineering principles are proposed.

1. Introduction

This paper proposes an approach to the design of emerging international multiservice networks. These networks will permit digital connectivity between the nations and provide for a variety of international voice, data and wideband services with different traffic characteristics, bit rates and performance objectives.

We argue that robustness of the network design to variations in traffic demands and flexibility of the network routing should be the prime objectives of the international ISDN engineering philosophy. To satisfy these objectives, we extend the Dynamic Nonhierarchical Routing (DNHR) type call set-up and routing rules for national ISDNs introduced in [1] and propose the evolution to full-access international multiservice networks. We also present a mathematical formulation and a heuristic solution of bandwidth allocation and sizing problems for this full-access international ISDN.

2. Evolution of Transmission Technology

In the early 1990s, international networks will evolve from the present analog, individual service configurations to international ISDNs with integrated access and customer control capabilities. The introduction of ISDNs between the United States and Europe and the United States and the Orient will be based on the planned deployment of sophisticated digital transmission and switching technologies, the most important of which is undersea optical fiber cables.

In 1988, the first transatlantic optical fiber cable, TAT-8, will become operational. Initially, it will connect the East Coast of the United States to France and the United Kingdom. The other European countries will access the cable via land extension lines. TAT-8 will have a capacity of 7,560 64 kb/s Minimum Assignable Units of Ownership* (7,560 MAUOs). The implementation of the new Digital

---

* A Minimum Assignable Unit of Ownership is in excess of 64 kb/s, but 64 kb/s is available to the network for information transport.

Circuit Multiplication System (DCMS) technology, which combines digital speech interpolation with Adaptive Differential Pulse Code Modulation (ADPCM) techniques, will translate the TAT-8 capacity into 37.800 64 kb/s virtual voice circuits. Then, intercontinental fiber optical cables will extend to the Pacific, first connecting California to Hawaii, and then proceeding to Guam, Japan and Philippines.

The introduction of these transmission facilities will permit end-to-end digital connectivity and will make international ISDN service offerings both feasible and economically attractive. It will also allow international network providers to accommodate a multiplicity of services (equivalently, random demands for bandwidth usage with different intensities, message lengths and bit rates) on a single, integrated network.

3. Traffic Engineering Principles

The deployment of international ISDN requires a resolution of various facility compatibility challenges and poses unique problems to teletraffic engineers. Facing a variety of ISDN services and traffic types that currently lack adequate traffic descriptions, teletraffic engineers have to decide how to evolve network management, forecasting and servicing practices to the ISDN era. The lack of historical traffic data on emerging services prevents us from testing the applicability of classical voice-based rules and algorithms. It suggests, however, that an "ideal" ISDN design should be impervious to service mixtures and traffic types. In addition, it dictates that international network providers must have the ability to adapt to rapid changes of various traffic levels. Thus, robustness of the network design and flexibility of the network routing are two cornerstones of the ISDN engineering philosophy.

4. International ISDN: Full-Access Engineering

In a companion paper entitled "Traffic Network Routing, Control and Design for the ISDN Era," G. R. Ash [1] describes traffic engineering methods for an integrated circuit-switched national network that provides voice, data and wideband services. We apply similar principles to the problem of engineering international multiservice networks. In particular, in Section 4.1 we introduce Dynamic Nonhierarchical Routing (DNHR) type call set-up and routing rules that result in full-access international ISDN. Consequently, we can approximate international ISDN needs between two nations by considering the bilateral network as a single digital pipe. Clearly, the full-access policy satisfies our robustness and routing flexibility objectives. In addition, it simplifies bandwidth allocation and dimensioning problems.

For the sake of simplicity, we concentrate on the problem of designing an international multiservice network between two nations. It is well known, however, that international dynamic routing is especially attractive when used to design networks among three or more countries located in different time zones [5]. Our approach, described in detail in Section 4.1, can be generalized to handle these situations.

Currently, there are no plans for integrating international circuit-switched and packet-switched networks. Thus, in this paper we concentrate on circuit-switched international multiservice networks. We would like to note, however, that similar network design ideas may also prove useful in the design and optimization of international packet networks.

4.1 Realization of Full Access

First, we assume that an international ISDN and a national ISDN are owned and operated by the same administration, and the integration of transmission and switching facilities is technologically feasible. To combine national and international ISDN economically, we need to extend a call set-up procedure introduced in [1] for establishing virtual trunk connections. In particular, international service requests introduced at the originating national switch require a special treatment. We can still capitalize on DNHR type call processing principles, including originating call control, common channel signaling and crankback capabilities. However, in contrast with [1], we define three-link paths and permit multiple entry and exit points for international service requests.

That is, to establish virtual trunk connections, the Originating Switch (OS) in the national network translates the customer-specified international destination and service type to determine the ordered list of national International Gateway (IG) switch and terminating Foreign Country (FC) international gateway switch pairs. As in conventional DNHR, for a given OS-IG pair and service type, there is a data base that specifies one or two-link routing sequences in the national network. The union of these national and international routing sequences defines the trunk or virtual circuit routing between the OS and the foreign country for a given service type.

Alternatively, if we assume that an international and national ISDNs cannot be combined, then the international requests can be processed at international gateways following two-link conventional DNHR or real-time adaptive routing rules. In this case, international gateways become originating and transit DNHR switches, and foreign gateways play the role of terminating switches. In contrast to the combined national/international ISDN design, this approach requires the existence of a dedicated network between international gateways to carry international traffic. In both cases, however, nonhierarchical routing principles allow us to minimize the amount of international network capacity required to achieve the desired grade of service. Based on our numerical experience, non-hierarchical bilateral networks between the United States and foreign countries are significantly cheaper (2% - 9%) than conventional hierarchical networks with the same throughput.

In general, under full access scenario, all connection possibilities to the foreign country $(IG_l - FC_J)$ will be examined and, therefore, we can approach the problem of engineering the international ISDN as the problem of allocating bandwidth of a single network resource. The simplification that we just made reduces the complexity of the original problem and allows us to use circuit access control methods introduced in [3].

5. Bandwidth Allocation and Network Dimensioning

We consider the problem of finding a minimal bandwidth resource that can accommodate k types of service requests with given arrival rates, λ_l, service rates, μ_l, and information bit rates (number of time slots required), b_l. It is assumed that traffic streams are independent Poisson processes. Because of our single digital pipe approximation, we assume that request for service is rejected if it requires more bandwidth than is currently available (for this service type) on *all* IG_l-FC_J connections.

It has been observed that if no bandwidth allocation strategy is employed and complete sharing of a bandwidth resource is allowed, then the resulting network may have undesirable performance characteristics [2]. First, network resources may not be efficiently utilized in terms of the total throughput. Second, different traffic types may experience uneven blocking probabilities. Typically, lower bit rate traffic streams tend to have better grades of service than higher bit rates traffic streams.

To optimize network performance (or to achieve specified grades of service for different traffic types), similar types can be grouped into subsets or clusters. Then, the total bandwidth should be allocated between these clusters to obtain required performance characteristics, to the extent possible.

5.1 Mathematical Formulation

In the development to follow, we assume that k traffic types are grouped into M non-overlapping clusters and that for each cluster there is a bandwidth limit, F_m, where F_m is less than the total resource capacity, F. Following [3], under these assumptions the state of the network at equilibrium can be described by a vector $\mathbf{n} = (n_1, ..., n_k)$, where n_l is the number of service requests in progress of type i. Then, the state probabilities can be found by the product form solution

$$P(\mathbf{n}) = \left(\prod_{l=1}^{k} \rho_l^{n_l}/n_l! \right) \Big/ \sum_{\mathbf{n}} \prod_{l=1}^{k} \rho_l^{n_l}/n_l! \ , \tag{1}$$

where $\rho_l = \lambda_l/\mu_l$ and the sum is taken over all admissible system states; that is, the total bandwidth usage and the cluster bandwidth usage should be less than F and F_m, respectively. Mathematically, admissible states are described by

$$W = \{\mathbf{n} \mid \sum_{l=1}^{k} n_l b_l \leq F \text{ and } \sum_{l} n_l b_l \leq F_m, \text{ for } m=1,...,M\} \ , \tag{2}$$

where the second sum is taken over all i that belong to m−th cluster, and b_i specifies the bandwidth unit requirement for i−s traffic type.

To calculate two major performance characteristics, the average system throughput and blocking probabilities for each service type, we need to introduce auxiliary functions $G(j,m)$ and $G_m(j)$

$$G(j,m) = \sum_n \prod_{l=1}^{k} \rho_l^{n_l}/n_l! , \quad \begin{matrix} j=0, & ..., F, \\ m=1, & ...,M \end{matrix} \qquad (3)$$

where the sum is taken over all states admissible in the first m clusters and such that $n \cdot b = j$, and

$$G_m(j) = \sum_n \prod_l \rho_l^{n_l}/n_l! ; \qquad (4)$$

where the sum is taken over all states admissible in m−th cluster with the total bandwidth usage equal to j.

Then, as shown in [3], functions $G(j,m)$ and $G_m(j)$ can be computed recursively and the performance characteristics of interest can be expressed by

$$E = \sum_{i=0}^{F} iG(i,M) / \sum_{j=0}^{F} G(j,M) \qquad (5)$$

and

$$P_i = \sum_{j=0}^{b_i-1} [G(F-j,M) + G_m(F_m-j)A_j] / \sum_{j=0}^{F} G(j,M) , \qquad (6)$$

where

$$A_j = \sum_{n=0}^{N_j} G(n,M-1) \text{ and } N_j = F-F_m-b_i+j .$$

The first quantity, E, defines the average system throughput. The second quantity, P_i, gives an expression for the blocking probability of traffic type i. Without loss of generality, in (6) we assume that this traffic type belongs to m−th cluster.

5.2 Dimensioning Heuristic

We note that for a given description of service demands, λ_1, μ_1, b_l and specified grades of service, B_l, there is an optimal partition of K service types into M clusters, and there is an optimal vector of bandwidth restrictions, F_1, $\cdots F_M$. Finding the best clustering and bandwidth allocation (restriction) policy is a computationally difficult combinatorial optimization problem. An initial numerical experience reported in the literature indicates, however, that "sensible" clustering arrangements which typically group traffic types with similar bit rates, blocking requirements and holding times result in consistent performance levels. Therefore, we assume that M non-overlapping groups of service types have been identified by numerical experimentation and the remaining problem is to determine bandwidth limits F_1, F_2, $\cdots$,F_M and the total capacity, F.

This problem can be addressed by the following heuristic:

Step 1. Set $F_1 = F_2 = \cdots = F_M = F$

Step 2. Find F such that for all service types the desired grade of service is achieved; that is,

$$P_m \leq B_m \ . \tag{7}$$

Step 3. Find cluster m with the maximum difference in the desired blocking level, B_m, and calculated blocking level, P_m.

Step 4. Reduce F_m by $k\Delta_m$, where k is an integer, to find pairs (F_m, F) for which conditions (7) are satisfied and F is minimized.

Step 5. Update old values F_m and F, where F_m is set to the lowest limit corresponding to F and return to Step 3.

The algorithm terminates when the reduction in any bandwidth level, F_m, leads to the violation of (7). The output of this procedure specifies the total bandwidth requirement F and the sequence of bandwidth controls F_1, $\cdots F_M$. The specific distribution of bandwidth requirements for each IG-FC connection remains to be made, based on the current international network topology and gateway switch capacity considerations.

5.3 Bandwidth Allocation Alternatives

This approach to bandwidth allocation, based on restricted access control ideas, provides one possible way for solving the multiservice network dimensioning problem. In addition to this approach, the problem of maximizing throughput and providing specified grade of service for each service class can be addressed by applying classical split circuit group or trunk reservation principles. The first approach splits the total bandwidth into M+1 parts, F_0, F_1,...F_M. The capacity F_0 is shared by all service types and the capacities F_m are dedicated to corresponding clusters. In contrast to the restricted bandwidth allocation principle, in this case, $F_1+F_2+...+F_M<F$. The second approach (trunk reservation) is also defined in terms of the vector F_1,...F_M, where F_m specifies that a request for service (cluster m) is rejected if there is only F_m or fewer bandwidth units of capacity left. The question which control strategy is the most practical in the ISDN era remains open and provides an interesting topic for further research.

[1]   G. R. Ash, "Traffic Network Routing, Control and Design for the ISDN Era," this volume, invited paper presented at the 5th ITC Seminar on Traffic Engineering for ISDN, Lake Como, Italy, May, 1987.

[2]   J. S. Kaufman, "Blocking in a Shared Resource Environment," IEEE Transactions on Communications, COM-29, No. 10, October, 1981.

[3]   B. Kraimeche and M. Schwartz, "Circuit Access Control Strategies in Integrated Digital Networks," Proceedings of the INFOCOM '84, San Francisco, California, April, 1984.

[4]   M. Schwartz and B. Kraimeche, "An Analytic Control Model for an Integrated Node," INFOCOM '83, San Diego, April, 1983.

[5]   Y. Watanabe, J. Matsumoto and H. Mori, "Design and Performance Evaluation of International Telephone Networks with Dynamic Routing," Proceedings of 11th ITC, Kyoto, Japan, 4.3A-3, 1985.

TRAFFIC ENGINEERING for ISDN Design and Planning
M. Bonatti and M. Decina (Editors)
Elsevier Science Publishers B.V. (North-Holland)
© IAC, 1988

DYNAMIC ROUTING SCHEMES FOR INTERNATIONAL ISDNs

Yu WATANABE and Hiromichi MORI

Kokusai Denshin Denwa Co., Ltd. (KDD)
2-1-23, Nakameguro Meguro-ku, Tokyo 153,
Japan

Along with the advance in network digitalization and development of new service capabilities, international telecommunication networks are evolving toward global ISDNs, in which new routing techniques such as dynamic routing will become implementable for more efficient and cost effective networks. In this paper, 24-hour traffic demand profiles for international ISDN traffic streams are studied, and a simple network dimensioning method with dynamic routing corresponding to the traffic profiles is presented. Based upon numerical results, the effects of service integration and a dynamic routing scheme in network cost savings are discussed and it is concluded that major improvement of network utilization and remarkable network cost savings are attainable by the use of this dynamic routing scheme in international ISDNs.

MAIN STATEMENT

24-hour traffic demand profiles in international ISDNs are studied, and the effects of service integration and a dynamic routing scheme in network cost savings are discussed.

1. INTRODUCTION

Due to the remarkable progress of stored program controlled (SPC) exchanges and common channel signalling systems, highly advanced and sophisticated network control techniques, which enable delicate traffic control responsive to network status, will become available in future ISDNs. Accordingly, network resource utilization and network reliability will be improved with these advanced network control techniques. The dynamic routing scheme is considered to be one of the advanced network control techniques and many studies on design methods and the performance evaluation of telephone networks with dynamic routing have been published [1]-[3].

In networks with dynamic routing, network resource utilizations are improved using time varying routing patterns which are determined according to the variation of the traffic volume in each part of networks. In the international networks, traffic demands among countries change in profiles according to time differences, causing traffic busy hours to appear at different time periods for each pair of originating and destination countries. Hence, the dynamic routing scheme to realize effective use of the idle capacities of the lightly loaded part of the network in busy hour traffic will improve the network resource utilization.

The authors have already studied dynamic routing schemes in international public switched telephone networks (PSTNs) [3]. In the course of the study, the cost savings attained by dynamic routing schemes were estimated based on the profiles of the voice traffic. Results showed that the use of the dynamic routing scheme in international PSTNs is very advantageous.

However, in the present international PSTN, the percentage of non-voice traffic (e.g. facsimile traffic) in total traffic has been increasing. The demand profiles of voice and non-voice traffic are different and therefore, in the near future, it can be supposed that the traffic profiles in the international PSTN will not be able to be restricts to those of voice traffic.

In ISDNs, non-voice services (e.g. data, facsimile and video signal communications) are integrated with voice services and the occupancy rate of non-voice traffic in the total traffic will increase. Those voice and non-voice services share physically common network resources. As a result of shared network resources, network resource utilization will be improved. Furthermore, in the international ISDNs, with the integration of voice and non-voice service traffic, the traffic profiles are deformed and large cost savings in network resources are expected through the use of the dynamic routing. Hence, in the international ISDNs, the network resource utilization can be improved not only merely by the integration of the services but also by the traffic profile changes. These improvements can realize considerable cost savings in international ISDNs.

However, to realize such cost efficient ISDNs under the dynamic routing scheme, the following issues remain:

i)   network design methods,
ii) network performance evaluation methods and
iii) cost effective network evolution plans.

In this paper, traffic demand profiles for the international ISDN are considered. Then, a simple design method for networks with dynamic routing is described. Numerical results for simple example networks are given to illustrate expected cost savings attained by the use of dynamic routing in the international ISDN.

2. TRAFFIC DEMAND PROFILES IN THE INTERNATIONAL ISDN

The demand profiles of voice traffic have already become evident through the studies on the actual telephone traffic in the present international PSTN. The formulas and the numerical tables to calculate hourly traffic demand as a function of the time difference are given in the References [4] and [5].

The profiles of voice traffic in the present international PSTN are characterized by the statistical manner of the subscribers in that international telephone call intents occur on working time (e.g. business hours) for both calling and called parties, even if the calling and called subscribers belong to the two different time zones. Therefore, concentrations of the traffic to a short time period and sharpened peak of the traffic demand profiles are found for the traffic between two countries with a short overlapping of working times.

On the other hand, for non-voice services such as data, facsimile and video signal communications, traffic demand profiles are characterized by the features of individual services and therefore the traffic profiles in future ISDNs will be diverse. However, in this paper, it is assumed that the traffic profiles of non-voice services in early ISDN stages will be similar to those of the non-voice traffic in the present PSTN.

According to the studies on the characteristics of the non-voice traffic shown in the Reference [6], it was shown that the profiles of non-voice traffic in present PSTN are closely approximated by the profiles of the international telex traffic. Therefore, in this paper, the profiles of international telex traffic are used to represent the profiles of non-voice traffic in international ISDNs.

The demand profiles of the international telex traffic streams are mainly determined by the working time of the country of the calling party, no matter what time it is in the country of the called party. It is because telex terminals can receive messages without the attendance of an operator (non-attendant mode operation). Non-voice calls in the international ISDN are considered to be communications between terminals which are operated in the non-attendant mode, at least on the receiving end. Hence, it is quite reasonable to assume that the profiles of non-voice traffic have features similar to those of telex traffic.

From the above considerations in non-voice traffic in future ISDNs, it is concluded that international ISDN traffic profiles can be approximated by the composition of traffic profiles of international telephone and telex. Figure 1 shows examples of international telephone and telex traffic profiles.

From figure 1, it is obvious that the characteristics of international ISDN traffic are quite different from those of the individual international telephone and telex traffic in hourly traffic demand profiles. The busy hour traffic of the telephone and telex mutually cover the non-busy hours of the others in the

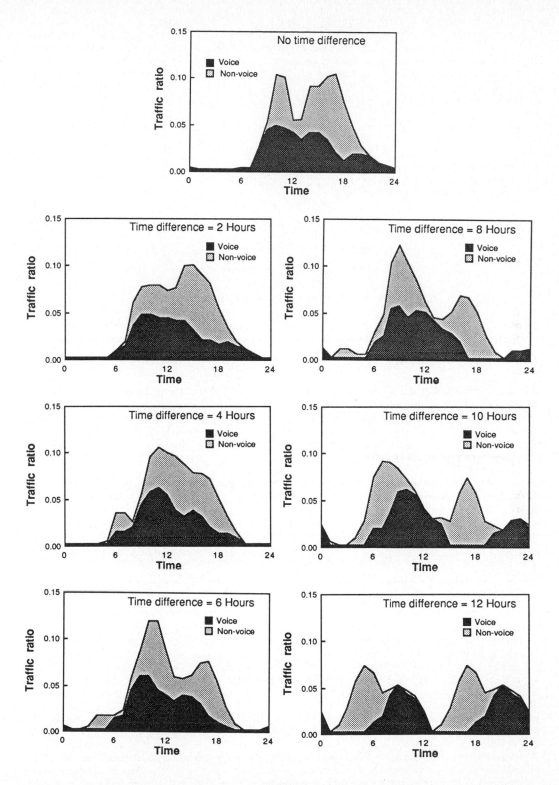

FIGURE 1

International telephone (voice) and telex (non-voice) traffic profiles

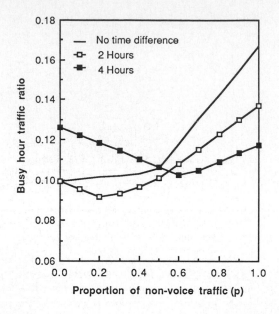

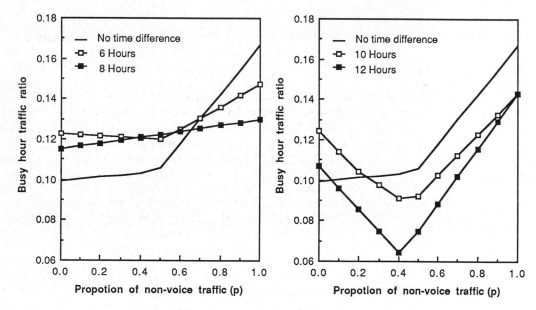

FIGURE 2
Busy hour traffic ratio

case that the time difference between the originating and destination countries results in inconsistency between telephone and telex busy hours.

Furthermore, the international ISDN traffic profiles are greatly changed not only by the time difference but also by the ratio of the mixture of voice and non-voice traffic. Hence, there exists an optimum ratio of voice and non-voice traffic where the ISDN traffic profiles become flatter compared with the individual profiles of voice and non-voice traffic. This contributes to the increase in network resource utilization during non-busy hours of each service.

As an index of the flatness of the traffic profile, busy hour traffic ratio, which is the ratio of traffic volume in the busy hour to the total whole day traffic volume, is considered. Figure 2 shows the busy hour traffic ratio, where x axis indicates the ratio of the non-voice traffic to the total traffic:

p = (Total 24-hour non-voice traffic volume) /
(Sum of the 24-hour voice and non-voice traffic volumes)   (1)

This figure shows following features of the international ISDN traffic profiles:

i) Where there is no time difference between originating and destination countries, the busy hour traffic ratio monotonously increases with the increase of the ratio of the non-voice traffic. This means that the traffic profile in the domestic network without regional time differences sharpens with the evolution of service integration.

ii) Where time differences between originating and destination countries exist, within a certain range of the non-voice traffic ratio, the busy hour traffic ratio tends to decrease with the increase of the ratio of non-voice traffic.

3. DESIGN METHOD OF INTERNATIONAL ISDN WITH DYNAMIC ROUTING

The dynamic routing schemes are categorized into the following two types:

i) Pre-planned time varying type where hourly routing patterns are determined according to the predicted hourly traffic demand between each originating destination countries pair.

ii) Network state dependent type where routing patterns are updated on a real time base taking account of congestion conditions of each circuit group.

In this paper, the dynamic routing scheme of the pre-planned time varying type is considered and a simple design method is presented in this section.

In general, telecommunications network design is composed of two optimization steps, namely, routing pattern optimization and circuit group size optimization. For the design of a network with pre-planned time varying dynamic routing, these two optimization steps are also necessary.

In the routing pattern optimization step for a network with dynamic routing, each hourly routing pattern is determined taking all hourly traffic demand into account, and accordingly the size of the optimization problem for routing patterns becomes larger than that of the fixed routing scheme. As an example of a solution method of this large optimization problem, the multi-commodity approach is studied in the Reference [1].

The next optimization step is circuit group size dimensioning, in which circuit group sizes are determined for given hourly offered traffic volumes and grade of service requirements. The circuit group size dimensioning problem, considering multi-hour traffic demand, can be formulated as a non-linear programming problem with many unknowns and a solution can be obtained numerically using a non-linear optimization algorithm [2].

In this paper, under the following assumptions, a simple algorithm is used for the design of ISDNs with dynamic routing:

i) A network is modeled by a set of nodes and links, which respectively represent a switching centers and circuit groups between them.

ii) Traffic demand between each originating and destination pair is considered to be the required traffic flow between nodes.

iii) A load sharing routing scheme is employed at every switching centers and offered traffic can be distributed among the direct path and the indirect paths according to given proportions.

iv) The required circuit group size is proportional to the traffic flow volume on the link, which means that the required grade of services can be guaranteed with constant circuit group utilizations.

Under these assumptions, multi-commodity flow problems are solved to minimize total link cost. With assumption iii), the routing patterns are directly determined from the flow pattern obtained as a solution of this multi-commodity flow problem. Furthermore, with assumption iv) the circuit group sizes can be easily obtained from the total traffic flow volume on the link.

We employ the following notations.

- Indexes

$k = 1,2, ... , K$: index of originating and destination node pair,
$i = 1,2, ... , I_k$: index for route of the k-th node pair,
$l = 1,2, ... , L$: index of link,
$t = 1,2, ... , 24$: index of time period.

- Constants

c_l : per circuit cost of link l,
d_{kt} : traffic demand of node pair k in time period t,
a_{iktl} : $= 1$ (in the case that i-th route of the demand pair k in time period t contain the link l),
$= 0$ (otherwise).

- Variables

y_{ikt} : traffic flow volume of k-th demand pair on i-th route in time period t,
x_l : upperbound of the total traffic flow volume on link l.

Using these notations, the multi-commodity flow problem to minimize total network cost is formulated as follows:

$$\min z = \Sigma_l \, c_l \, x_l, \tag{2}$$

subject to

$$x_l \geqq \Sigma_{k,i} \, a_{iktl} \, y_{ikt}, \tag{3}$$

$$\Sigma_i \, y_{ikt} = d_{kt}, \tag{4}$$

$$x_l, \, y_{ikt} \geqq 0. \tag{5}$$

The value x_l obtained from a solution of the linear programming problem given in the equations (2)-(5) is the link capacity required to meet all 24-hour traffic flow demands.

4. NUMERICAL EXAMPLES

In this section, design results of various example international ISDNs are described. Traffic demand profiles considered in section 2 and the design method described in section 3 are employed for the calculations. As in the Reference [1], the direct path and indirect paths with a tandem switching center are assumed to be used to carry the offered traffic.

To estimate cost savings and network resource utilization improvements attained by service integration and use of the dynamic routing scheme separately, example networks are designed for the following three conditions:

i) Sep_Dir : Voice and non-voice traffic are *separated* and the both are carried by dedicated networks using the *direct* routing scheme.

ii) Int_Dir : Voice and non-voice traffic are *integrated* and the mixed traffic is carried by a network using the *direct* routing scheme.

iii) Int_Dyn : Voice and non-voice traffic are *integrated* and the mixed traffic is carried by a network using the *dynamic* routing scheme.

First, a 3-node example network between Japan, a north American country and a European country is considered. The busy hour traffic volume between the north American and European countries and between Japan and the European country is assumed to be 5.0 and 0.4, respectively, in condition that the volume between Japan and the north American country is set to unity. The ratio of non-voice traffic p, which is defined in the equation (1), is taken to be the same for the traffic between every node pair, and the circuit costs of all links are assumed to be the same.

Figure 3 shows the relation between the non-voice traffic ratio and the total network cost. In this figure, the network costs of Int_Dir and Int_Dyn are expressed in values relative to that of Sep_Dir. This figure accounts for the following features of service integration and dynamic routing:

i)   The network cost of Int_Dir is less than that of Sep_Dir. This means that network cost is reduced by service integration. The cost saving effect of service integration is maximum around $p = 0.3$ in this example.

ii) By the use of dynamic routing, further savings in network cost are obtained. Differences between plots for Int_Dir and Int_Dyn indicate cost saving realized through the use of dynamic routing. In this example, the cost saving through the dynamic routing is maximum around $p = 0.4$.

iii) The cost saving attained by the both service integration and use of the dynamic routing is maximum around p = 0.4, where network cost is reduced about 20%.

iv) In the cases of $p = 0.0$ and $p = 1.0$, which means that only voice or non-voice traffic exist, cost savings are obtained by the use of dynamic routing. The cost saving at $p = 0.0$ is greater than that at $p = 1.0$. Because non-voice traffic busy hour are approximately coincide no matter what time it is in the destination country, and therefore the alternate paths do not have sufficient capacity to carry busy hour traffic.

The cost saving through the use of dynamic routing is attained if the alternate routings of busy hour traffic can fill the non-busy hours of the other routes and the resultant traffic profiles become flatter. In this example, we assume that the circuit costs of all links are the same and therefore the degree of the network utilization improvements, which are shown in the Figure 4, is identical to network cost savings. Where the network utilization ρ is defined as follows:

$$\rho = A/B \qquad\qquad\qquad (5)$$

where

A: Sum of the traffic volumes which are carried by all links in the network in a day and

B: (Sum of the link capacities of the network) × 24.

As the next example, a 4-node example network between Japan, a north American country, a European country and an Oceanic country is considered. Figures 5 and 6 show the cost savings and the network utilization improvements respectively. The degrees of the cost savings and the network utilization improvements for this example are greater than those for the 3-node network. The reason for this is that the increase of the number of nodes in the network diversifies the combinations of the time difference between originating and destination countries, and the chances for alternate routing using idle capacity increases.

As the last example, a relatively large international network with dynamic routing is designed. Eight nations in the network are selected according to the estimated future traffic volume from/to Japan. In this example, circuit group costs are assumed to be proportional to the geographical distances between the countries. Figures 7 and 8 show the cost savings and the network utilization improvements respectively. The degrees of the cost savings and the network utilization improvements for this example are greater than those for the 3- and 4-node examples. The cost savings and network utilization improvements attained by the both service integration and dynamic routing is maximum around $p = 0.4$, where network cost is reduced about 35%. Since in this example, circuit group costs are

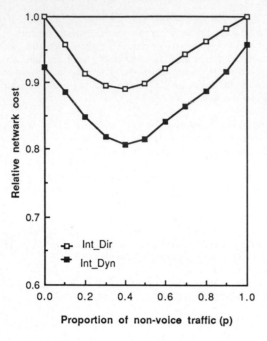

FIGURE 3
Total network cost of 3-node example network

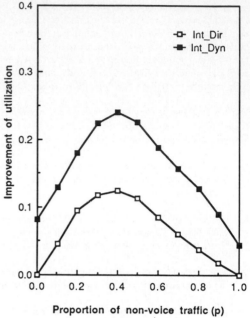

FIGURE 4
Network utilization improvement of 3-node
example network

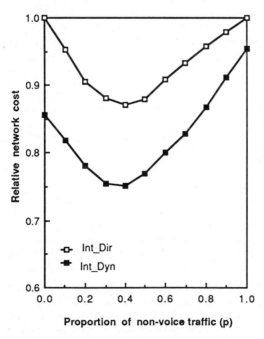

FIGURE 5
Total network cost of 4-node example network

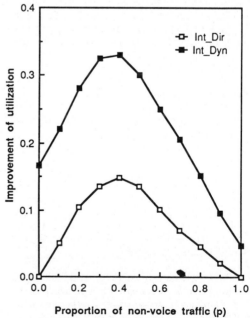

FIGURE 6
Network utilization improvement of 4-node
example network

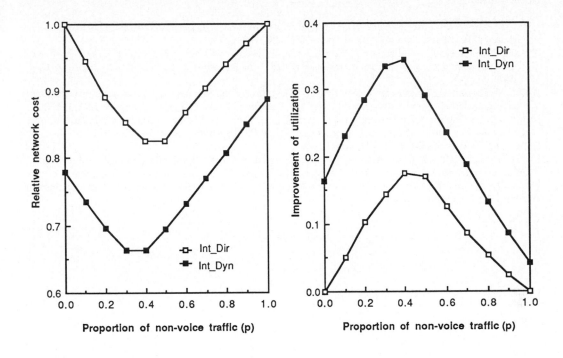

FIGURE 7
Total network cost of 8-node example network

FIGURE 8
Network utilization improvement of 8-node
example network

assumed to be proportional to the geographical distances and optimizations are made to minimize network cost, the degrees of the network utilization improvements are smaller than the degrees of the cost savings.

5. CONCLUSIONS

The traffic profiles of the international ISDN traffic demand were considered based on the measurement of the profiles of voice and non-voice traffic in the present international PSTN. The results show that international ISDN traffic demand profiles are different from individual voice and non-voice traffic profiles and that the international ISDN traffic profiles can be approximately modeled by the composition of traffic profiles of international telephone and telex.

A simple network design algorithm based on the multi-commodity approach was shown, and the design results for model international ISDNs indicate the potential for significant network cost savings and network utilization improvement through service integration and use of the dynamic routing scheme. The degree of the network cost savings and network utilization improvement increases with the increase of the number of the countries in the network, this means that the wide-spread use of the dynamic routing scheme in international ISDNs is very advantageous.

ACKNOWLEDGEMENTS

The authors wish to acknowledge the continued guidance of Drs. T. Muratani and K. Ono of KDD Research and Development Laboratories, and also wish to express their gratitude to Mr. Y. Ikeda and the members of the Switching Systems Laboratory. The authors would like to thank their colleague Mr. T. Oda for valuable contribution to this work.

REFERENCES

[1] G. R. Ash, R. H. Cardwell and R. P. Murry, "Design and optimization of networks with dynamic routing," Bell Syst. Tech. J., Vol. 60, pp. 1787-1820, 1981

[2] M. Pioro and B. Wallström, "Multihour optimization of non-hierarchical circuit switched communication network with sequential routing," Proceedings of 11th ITC, Kyoto, Japan, 4.4A-3, 1985

[3] Y. Watanabe, J. Matsumoto and H. Mori, "Design and performance evaluation of international telephone networks with dynamic routing," Proceedings of 11th ITC, Kyoto, Japan, 4.3A-3, 1985

[4] T. Ohta, "Network efficiency and network planning considering telecommunication traffic influenced by time difference," Proceedings of 7th ITC, Stockholm, Sweden, 425, 1973

[5] CCITT Recommendation E. 523, 1984

[6] K. Ohno, T. Hirose and M. Kojima, "Characteristics of non-voice application over the international public switched telephone network," Proceedings of 11th ITC, Kyoto, Japan, 3.2B-4, 1985

[7] N. Hattori and K. Yamada, "Traffic characteristics of the international telex calls," Proceedings of 7th ITC, Stockholm, Sweden, 443, 1973

TRAFFIC ENGINEERING for ISDN Design and Planning
M. Bonatti and M. Decina (Editors)
Elsevier Science Publishers B.V. (North-Holland)
© IAC, 1988

TELETRAFFIC ISSUES IN A MOBILE ISDN

Berth EKLUNDH and Bengt STAVENOW

Ericsson, S-223 70 LUND, Sweden

Mobile communications are among the fastest growing areas of telecommunications. A second generation of mobile communication systems
is under way, which should provide an increased traffic handling
capacity and an enhanced functionality, while incorporating the
basic ISDN functions. This paper discusses, in general terms, the
design of such a mobile system, identifies some interesting teletraffic issues and presents preliminary results. The topics that are
briefly covered are channel allocation schemes, protocol performance, and the design of a random multiple access system.

Main Statements - Identification and penetration of a number of
teletraffic issues in an ISDN-compatible digital mobile telecommunications system.

1.   INTRODUCTION

Change is very rapid in the communications business. Some years ago, few new
about mobile communications; today mobile telephony is among the fastest growing areas of the telecommunications industry. Mobile telecommunication of today are virtually identical to mobile telephony.

At the same time as the use of mobile telephony is exploding in many areas of
the world, change is also coming in other parts of the telephone network. The
demand for new services and integrated access has brought about the concept of
ISDN, by means of which a more universal and versatile network could be envisaged. ISDN is, from the users' perspective, an all-in-one digital network,
capable of transmitting user data and signalling transparently over the network. There seems to be no major technological problems connected with the
introduction of ISDN, and an evolution of ISDN, broadband ISDN, operating with
several hundreds of megabits/s in the user access, is already being discussed.

The tremendous growth of mobile telephony and the demand for new services are
calling for a second generation of mobile communications systems, which at the
same time are able of offering service to an increased number of mobile
communications users and to enhance the functionality of the current mobile
networks. A new system should consequently have an increased traffic handling
capacity, while incorporating the basic ISDN functions.

A move towards such a network is severely hampered by the fact that the available radio spectrum, which is necessary for the transmission of data between
the mobile user and the fixed network, is very limited. System design will
therefore be a delicate matter, and great care has to be taken in order to
design a flexible, efficient and versatile network.

The need for a standardised, pan-European mobile telephone network was early
recognised by the CEPT. A special study group, CEPT/GSM, was formed and given
the task of specifying a new mobile communications system. Work within
CEPT/GSM is currently under way, and it is yet unknown what the final

suggestion will look like. It is possible, however, to outline some common
system features and in general terms discuss the effects of different system
designs.

This contribution will deal with some teletraffic aspects of the design of a
new, ISDN-compatible mobile network. Below, an ad hoc system description is
given. The description covers only parts, which are relevant from a teletraffic point of view. After the general system description, some interesting
design issues and their impact on system performance are discussed.

2.   GENERAL SYSTEM DESCRIPTION

One of the main features of ISDN is the possibility of out of band signalling.
In an ISDN this feature is accomplished through the use of a time division
user access, which in its basic form handles 144 kbits/s user data (2B+D).

In a mobile environment such data rates cannot be offered if the same or
better system capacity, compared with the current analogue systems, should be
accomplished. It is therefore necessary to design a system which uses much
lower transmission rates, while maintaining the basic ISDN functionality and
out of band signalling.

One prerequisite for the success of a new digital mobile system is the availability of a wide variety of terminals, ranging from cheap and simple port-
ables, capable of transmitting voice conversations, to advanced equipment with
full ISDN functionality. For this to be feasible and affordable, it is likely
that out of band signalling has to be performed by means of a time division
multiplex.

Once the basic decision concerning the structure of the access system has been
made, there are a number of related issues to be addressed. Some of these are:

- If full ISDN compatibility cannot be achieved, in what respect should ISDN
  be limited in order to make the new digital system competitive in comparison
  with the present analogue system?

- How should the out-of-band signalling facility be arranged?

- The new system is expected to offer a higher spectrum efficiency, a higher
  voice traffic handling capacity and more flexible system solutions. How
  should these goals be accomplished and how big are the effects?

- ISDN, as it is specified in the I-recommendations, implies a certain collection of protocols at the three lower layers of the OSI model. To what extent
  is it feasible and practical to use these protocols in a mobile network, and
  what will be the effects of an attempt to adapt the protocols to a mobile
  environment?

There are a number of factors that influence the answers to the questions
above. One has already been mentioned: the scarcity of available radio spectrum. A second important factor is the error performance of the transmission
between the base station and the mobile terminal. In a fixed environment,
error performance is relatively good with error rates in the range 1E-5 to
1E-7 in most cases. These error rates facilitate efficient use of HDLC-like
protocols such as LAPD and LAPB. In the mobile environment error performance
will not be as good as in the fixed environment, if realistic system solutions
are considered.

A B-channel in an ISDN uses 64 kbits/s for transmitting PCM coded voice information and other circuit switched user data. If the voice traffic capacity of

a mobile network should be kept high, it is not possible to use 64 kbits/s for transmission of voice information. By using more efficient encoding techniques it should be possible to reduce the required transmission rate to 16 or 8 kbits/s. But even in such a case there will not be room for more than one B-channel, and this channel will have very limited capacity for transmission of user data other than voice, since the bad error performance will require heavy encoding of the information flow.

In an ISDN, a basic interface is permanently allocated to each subscriber. In a mobile environment, this is of course out of the question, at least concerning the B-channels, which evidently have to be allocated on a demand basis. Considering a D-channel of 16 kbit/s, a permanent allocation is not justifiable either, since utilisation of the D-channel is estimated to be far too low. If a permanent allocation of D-channel capacity is not feasible, two options are at hand: allocation of a dedicated D-channel at connection set up time, and random sharing among all mobile terminals of a common D-channel resource. The first option involves a random component too, since a dedicated D-channel has to be demanded in one way or another.

It is therefore obvious that D-channel signalling will involve transmission over a random access channel, irrespective of whether a dedicated D-channel is alloted or not. Transmission over error prone random access channels from equipments that are unable to listen and talk at the same time is a difficult protocol issue and the performance of various alternatives will be treated in a separate section below.

As stated above, protocols in the CCITT I-recommendations are designed for an environment that differs from the one encountered in a mobile environment. Considering the layer 3 protocol, much of the functionality can be kept, but the protocol should be extended with procedures and messages to handle mobile specific functions, such as the hand-over function, channel assignment procedures, and so on. It is especially the layer 2 protocol, usually referred to as LAPD, which may suffer from the increased error rate and uncertainty of the transmission. Results from an investigation of a modified LAPD protocol are presented below and discussed in the context of a mobile application.

For obvious reasons, the ISDN layer 1 protocol cannot be used on the radio channel in a mobile network, and a new protocol has to be designed. The major influence of this protocol on higher layers will be the basic slot structure that has to be used due to synchronisation and multiplexing demands.

3.   EXAMPLES OF TELETRAFFIC ISSUES AND PRELIMINARY RESULTS

3.1   Description of a Hypothetical Digital Mobile System

As discussed above, there are a number of factors influencing the final choice of system design. Although arguments for flexibility and ISDN compatibility are of great importance, the most essential requirement in a mobile system must be that the system should be optimized to carry a traffic mix, where the larger part is voice traffic.

Without entering a detailed argumentation, the following main characteristics of a narrow-band FD/TDMA digital mobile system are outlined [1]:

- The total available radio spectrum for digital mobile services is frequency divided into a number of 300 kHz wide radio frequencies.

- On each radio frequency a time division multiplex scheme, providing 10 slots per TDMA frame, is adopted. The duration of a TDMA frame is 8 ms.

- The system parameters given above yield that with a system bandwidth of 2 x
  24 MHz, the total number of duplex channels will be about 800.

- Every time slot corresponds to a channel with a gross bitrate of 34 kbit/s,
  which is capable of comprising one of the following two types of channels:
  1/ a Bm-channel, with a net bitrate of 16 kbit/s for speech coding, multi-
     plexed with a Dm-channel, with a net rate of 2 kbit/s at the link layer
     (uncoded)
  2/ a transparent Bm/Dm-channel, with a net bitrate of about 25 kbits/s at
     the link layer (uncoded)

- The available channels can be used in two different ways, either as dedicated channels, which are allocated to a user on demand basis and can be any
  of the channel types listed above, or as a number of common control channels
  (CCCH), which are common Dm-channels shared among cell sites and mobile terminals throughout the system.

- Results from speech quality tests with speech coders operating at 16 kbits/s
  show that the speech quality is acceptable at a bit error rate of 1 percent
  or lower. Taking also the effects of different signal processing methods and
  traffic handling methods into account, the minimum re-use pattern in a digital system will be about 7 cells, which is quite a gain compared with an
  analogue system, in which a 21 cell re-use pattern is used for small cells.

3.2   Performance of a HDLC-like protocol in a Mobile Environment

As described in the previous section, a dedicated channel used for data information transfer is formed by an allocated time slot, which is repeated once
every 8 ms on a regular basis. Considering the system parameters given above,
the number of bits in each slot available at the data link layer will be about
200 bits.

Since the frame delimitation function is provided at the physical layer, some
slight modifications of the LAPD protocol are assumed. Some of these are:

- Each time slot contains a complete data link frame or a data link sub-frame,
  if the network protocol data unit has to be divided into several data link
  protocol data units.

- A data link frame or sub-frame transmitted in a layer 1 slot corresponds
  functionally to a LAPD frame, with regard to sequence control, error detection and flow control.

It is a well-known fact in the area of mobile radio communications that bit
errors on a radio channel are not independent, but occur in bursts. Considering the hypothetical system, this shows to be a great advantage, since otherwise it would have been impossible to obtain an acceptable throughput with an
average bitrate of up to 1 percent. Results from simulations of the TDMA
scheme show, when a plausible model for bit errors on the radio channel is
applied, that the probability for a data link frame to be erroneous is approximately a factor ten larger than the average bit error rate. In some
cases, the probability for an erroneous frame was measured to be as large as
several tens of percent. Furthermore, successive data link frames of a connection are almost independent, due to the multiplexing structure.

The modified version of LAPD has been studied in the mobile environment discussed in the previous paragraph. Results regarding maximal throughput and
delays in a symmetrical load situation have been obtained for single frame
operation and multiple frame operation.

In single frame operation, the performance is very sensitive to the value of the timer controlling the maximum time between transmission of command frames and the reception of the corresponding response or acknowledgement frames. Furthermore, the maximal throughput is limited by the fact that acknowledgement frames occupy an entire layer 1 time slot.

The multiple frame operation shows to be more robust and rather insensitive to the value of the timer. An acceptable throughput is achievable, even in cases of a high probability for data link frame errors, if steps are taken in the implementation to carry as many acknowledgements as possible piggybacked.

3.3   Channel Allocation Principles and System Capacity

In this section different channel assignment schemes are discussed and some results regarding the system capacity in the different cases are presented.

Traditionally, channel assignment is based on the principle referred to as fixed assignment. In the assumed digital system, a plausible fixed cell layout should be based on a 9 cell re-use pattern, to enable the use of corner il-luminated cells. The number of channels per cell will accordingly be about 89, and the traffic handling capacity is readily given by the Erlang-B formula.

A number of additional functions, to enhance the capacity achieved by the fixed assignment technique, have been proposed. These functions take advantage of the fact that in reality there is always overlap regions in the cell pattern, in which a mobile station can choose to be bound to any of a number of cell sites. Among the functions that have been investigated are the Directed Retry function [2] and the Load Sharing function [3], which both in-crease the traffic capacity to a large extent. On the other hand, these types of functions, as well as the algorithms discussed below, are characterized by an increased amount of hand-overs. In the analogue systems, this is a dis-advantage, because the hand-over function is performed in-band, but in an ISDN-compatible system the hand-over function can be handled without the two subscribers noticing it.

Another class of assignment techniques is the hybrid channel assignment scheme, in which some channels are partitioned among the cells according to the fixed scheme, while others are kept in a common pool and may be allocated to a cell dynamically on demand basis. For realistic cell patterns the performance of a hybrid scheme has to be studied by means of simulation.

At low load levels the hybrid channel assignment scheme performs better than the fixed channel assignment scheme, but at higher load levels the algorithm is unable to re-use the dynamic channels as densely as possible. Thorough in-vestigations have shown [4,5], that the hybrid channel assignment scheme could be an attractive solution, if the number of channels per cell is rather low, say up to 20, and the channel re-use pattern is large. For a larger number of channels and smaller re-use patterns, the gain is considerably smaller, pri-marily due to the increased trunking efficiency.

Furthermore, in this latter case, which corresponds to the case studied in this paper, the hybrid assignment scheme has a great drawback. At high load levels the system easily enters a semi stable state. In this state some cells have allocated nearly all the dynamic channels or are the only cells which may allocate the dynamic channels. The reason for this effect is elaborated in [6], which also discusses the technique presented in the next paragraph.

In a system with re-use partition [7], a cell layout with a combined 3/9 cell re-use pattern can be adopted. In such a system, mobile terminals that are close to the cell site are primarily allocated channels in the 3 cell re-use

pattern, while the channels in the 9 cell re-use pattern may be used within
the whole cell area. Considering the required radio signal quality, it can be
shown [8], that the channels in the 3 cell re-use pattern can be used in approximately half the cell area.

Re-use partition can be studied analytically [9], and the channels in a cell
may be modelled by a simple grading. To increase channel utilization and/or
reduce blocking, rearranging of calls from the 9 cell re-use pattern to the 3
cell re-use pattern is recommended. Another positive effect of rearranging is
that the blocking experienced by the two classes of mobile terminals, close to
and far from the cell site, will become more equal. Still, however, blocking
for mobile terminals close to the cell site will always be smaller than for
mobile terminals farther away. To overcome this, service protection on a small
number of channels in the 9 cell re-use pattern can be adopted. The blocking
probabilities can hereby be equalized.

Finally, it is worth mentioning the adaptive channel allocation algorithm. In
a digital system, a cell layout with a 3 cell re-use pattern with adaptive
channel allocation is a possible solution. It is however likely that an adaptive scheme does not increase traffic capacity significantly, but there are
other weighty reasons, as discussed in [1].

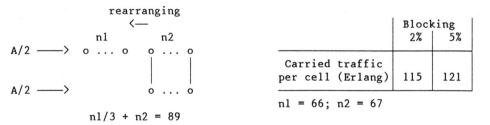

i/ Fixed Channel Assignment		Blocking	
		2%	5%
89	Carried traffic		
A ——> o o o ... o	per cell (Erlang)	77	84

ii/ Hybrid Channel Assignment		Blocking	
		2%	5%
80 9 dyn.ch./cell	Carried traffic		
A ——> o o ... o o ... o	per cell (Erlang)	82	86

iii/ Re-use Partition

		Blocking	
rearranging		2%	5%
<—			
n1 n2	Carried traffic		
A/2 ——> o ... o o ... o	per cell (Erlang)	115	121
A/2 ——> o ... o			

n1/3 + n2 = 89   n1 = 66; n2 = 67

Figure 1. Models and Comparative Results

3.4   Information Transfer on CCCH

The aim of this section is to discuss the problems arising in connection with
the random access channel, which henceforth will be referred to as common
control channel (CCCH). As discussed previously, such a channel has to exist
in the system, independent of system design. To limit the discussion, it is
assumed that the main purpose of the CCCH is to carry two types of signalling

sequences at the network layer: short signalling sequences that are not associated with a Bm-channel connection, for instance the location updating procedure, and the signalling sequences required to allocate a dedicated channel.

There are various aspects to be considered regarding the information transfer
on a CCCH. Unlike the information transfer on dedicated channels, communications are not performed in a point-to-point mode, but on a channel shared by
mobile terminals bound to the same cell site. Some signalling messages, such
as paging messages, are transmitted by the cell site in a broadcast mode,
while other messages, originating at the mobile stations, are transmitted in a
Random Multiple Access (RMA) mode.

Before penetrating the topic in more detail, the following general presumptions must be emphasized:

- It is assumed, in the hypothetical mobile system, that a mobile terminal is
  not able to transmit a layer 1 time slot and receive another slot
  simultaneously.

- A mobile terminal receives and interprets information transmitted by the
  cell site to which it is bound (in some cases a number of cell sites), but
  does not react on messages from other mobile terminals.

- A network protocol data unit may be partitioned into a variable number of
  data link frames dependent on the size of the network PDU.

Considering the required signalling capacity, a rough, approximative analysis
reveals that it is plausible that the CCCH bound to a cell site consists of a
single channel. Thus, if it is assumed that one frequency-pair is reserved
globally, this can be time division multiplexed among about 10 cell sites, see
figure 2. An advantage by using a single frequency-pair is that, being in
stand-by mode, a mobile terminal can be tuned to a predefined frequency, and
is able to react on messages transmitted by a number of cell sites.

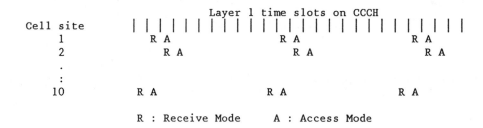

Figure 2. Multiplexing Scheme on CCCH.

As stated above, the CCCH is in no way an error-free channel. Furthermore,
some of the layer 1 slots generated by the mobile terminals are transmitted in
a Random Multiple Access (RMA) environment. Thus, the lower layer protocols
have to handle 'ordinary' bit errors caused by, for instance, fading phenomenon, as well as corrupted frames due to simultaneous transmissions from
different mobile terminals.

Three different types of signalling sub-sequences can be recognized at the
network layer, as depicted in figure 3.

It is likely that most sub-sequences will be of the type referred to as cell
site controlled. In this case, the REQ-message is transmitted by a cell site

and destined to a mobile terminal temporarily bound to that particular site. A
reasonable protocol would be that other terminals bound to the same site receive the message as well, and those that receive the message correctly are
silent during the time slot in which the ACK-response is presumed to be returned.

There are several reasons why a mobile terminal would be unable to comply with
such a reservation protocol. First, there is a rather high probability that a
message will be discarded due to bit errors. Secondly, the length of the
ACK-response, in number of data link layer frames, is not fixed, which introduces an additional uncertainty. Referring to the problem of Hidden Terminals
[10], it seems doubtful, if a reservation protocol will provide a capacity
which is significantly higher than an ordinary RMA protocol, which in this
case corresponds to a slotted ALOHA protocol. In the following paragraphs, the
discussion will therefore be limited to the slotted ALOHA case.

In the other two sub-sequences, referred to as mobile originated and cell site
originated, the messages originated from the mobile terminals are transmitted
in a RMA context according to the slotted ALOHA protocol. The cell site originated sequence, where the PAGE-message is transmitted by several cell sites,
is used when the system is unaware of the exact location of the addressed
mobile terminal.

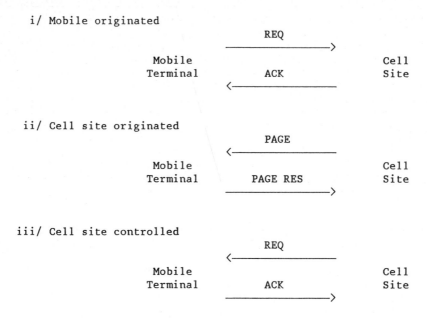

Figure 3. Basic Signalling Sequences on CCCH.

Since there are a number of tough problems associated with an acknowledged
operation at the data link layer on the CCCH, it is assumed that information
transfer is performed in unacknowledged mode. This results in that a message
at the network layer is received correctly, only if all the data link frames,
of which the message consists, are received without errors.

Taking all these presumptions into consideration, a suitable model is the
slotted ALOHA protocol with variable message length. Extending the basic
slotted ALOHA analysis for an infinite population of users [10], the following
system of equations may be defined

$$s_i = g_i e^{-(\sum_1^n g_j)iT} (1-P_f)^i \qquad\qquad i=1,\ldots,n$$

where

>   T : the duration of a layer 1 time slot
> P_f : the probability of a data link frame to be erroneous

The i:th equation defines the input rate (or the throughput rate) of messages occupying i layer 1 time slots (s_i) as a function of the corresponding channel traffic rates (g_i).

Given the input rates (s_i, i=1,...,n) the system of equations is solved readily by substitutions and iterations.

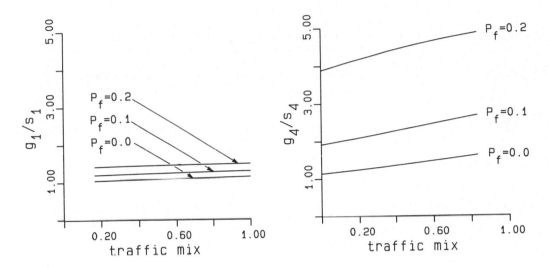

Figure 4. Example of Numerical Results from a slotted ALOHA system with variable message lengths.

There are a number of interesting characteristics that may be extracted from the numerical results. If, for instance, the offered traffic is fixed, i.e. $\sum_1 s_i i$ = constant, the channel performance as a function of the traffic mix may be illustrated. The results shown in figure 4 correspond to a case where the input consists of messages occupying one and four time slots, respectively, and where the channel, in absence of bit errors, is loaded to approximately one third of its maximum capacity. Figure 4 illustrates the number of trans-missions of the two types of messages as a function of the traffic mix. The values on the x-axes represent the ratio of the traffic offered by messages occupying one time slot to the traffic offered by all messages.

4.   CONCLUSIONS

The design of an ISDN-compatible digital mobile telecommunications system is a delicate task. In this paper some basic teletraffic problems are identified and each problem is discussed briefly. The survey, which by no means claims to be complete, shows that there are a great variety of problems, ranging from traditional teletraffic topics to the performance of novel datacommunication protocols. Each problem will be covered in more detail in coming papers, which also will include more exhaustive presentations of methods and results.

REFERENCES

[1] J Uddenfeldt, B Persson, "A Digital FD/TDMA System for a New Generation Cellular Radio", DMR-conference, Sweden, 14-16 October, 1986.

[2] B Eklundh, "Chanel Utilization and Blocking Probability in a Cellular Mobile Telephone System with Directed Retry", IEEE Trans. on Comm., April 1986.

[3] B Eklundh, J Karlsson, "Load Sharing in a Cellular Mobile Telephone System – Blocking Probabilities and Channel Utilization", ISS'87, Phoenix, 1987.

[4] T J Kahwa and N D Georganas, "A Hybrid Channel Assignment Scheme in Large-Scale Cellular-Structured Mobile Communication Systems", IEEE Trans. on Comm, Vol COM-26, No 4, April 1978, pp. 432-438.

[5] L Ahlberg, "Channel Allocation Principles in Mobile Communication Systems", (in swedish) NTS-conference, Denmark, 26-28 August, 1986.

[6] K Saellberg, B Stavenow, and B Eklundh, "Hybrid Channel Assignment and Re-use Partition in a Cellular Digital Mobile Telephone System", to be presented at IEEE VTC'87, June 1-3, 1987.

[7] S W Halpern, "Re-use partitioning in Cellular Systems", Proc. of IEEE Veh. Techn. Conf. 1983, pp.322-327.

[8] J-E Stjernvall, "Calculation of Capacity and Co-Channel Interference in a Cellular System", DMR-conference, Espoo, Finland, 5-7 February, 1985.

[9] L Reneby, "Rearranging of Calls in Telecommunication Systems", CODEN: LUTEDX(TETS-7085)/1-16/(1984) & Local 6, Lund Inst. of Tech., Sweden.

[10] L Kleinrock, "Queueing Systems, Volume II: Computer Applications", Wiley 1976.

TRAFFIC ENGINEERING for ISDN Design and Planning
M. Bonatti and M. Decina (Editors)
Elsevier Science Publishers B.V. (North-Holland)
© IAC, 1988

ON THE DIMENSIONING OF TRUNK GROUPS IN THE ISDN

Ruth Kleinewillinghöfer-Kopp and Eckart Wollner

Research Institute of the Deutsche Bundespost,
Darmstadt, F.R.G.

Trunk groups which are offered various services requiring
different bandwidths (multi-slot connections) are modelled
by loss systems offered a superposition of batched arrival
processes. In order to balance the blocking probabilities
of the traffic types, occupation restrictions are introduced to the service system. Three methods are examined
including the widely discussed trunk reservation. One of
the occupation restriction methods presented in this paper
leads to a service system in which, in contrast to the
model with trunk reservation, the steady-state probabilities are insensitive to the service time distributions and
are in product form.

MAIN STATEMENTS: A model of a service system with occupation
restriction is given which has the insensitivity property.
This property is not valid if trunk reservation is used.

1. INTRODUCTION

In future, numerous telecommunication services showing different
stochastic features and bandwidths shall be handled via a uniform
network, the ISDN. Basic principles including the problem of integration on the subscriber loop have been discussed extensively in
recent years and have been treated in relevant CCITT recommendations.

Current ISDN plans assume a network model which is based on a fixed
(basic) channel size of 64 kbit/s and a combination of packet switching and circuit switching methods with the switching systems (the
trunk groups) operating as loss systems in the case of circuit-
switched services. However, there are still no final regulations
governing the handling of the various services in this network. The
integration of circuit-switched services which require different
bandwidths i.e. which require various numbers of channels simultaneously (multi-slot connections), calls for a decision in favour of
one of the two basic options:

A. Depending on the stochastic features and the bandwidth needed,
   the types of traffic (services) are carried <u>separately</u> over
   different trunk groups.

B. The traffic is carried over <u>common</u> trunk groups.

In the case of strategy A. each trunk group is offered only one
traffic type which requires $g \in N$ channels simultaneously. Such processes can be modelled by processes with batched arrivals in constant batch sizes g. Assuming a Poisson arrival process (M) and a
recurrent service process (GI), the trunk group with S channels
represents a loss system of (Kendall-) type $M^g/GI/S/0$. This is the

well known Erlang model, which for g=1, forms the basis of the methods used for dimensioning a telephone network. As the steady-
state probabilities (blocking formula, etc.) and the characteristics of the overflow traffic are similar for g=1 and for g>1, the
dimensioning rules developed for telephone traffic, i.e. for g=1,
remain to be extended to the case g>1.

In the case of strategy B. the arriving point process can be understood as a superposition of say $Q \varepsilon N$ different flow (traffic) types.
Analogous to the Erlang model we assume each flow i, i=1,...,Q, to
be a Poisson process (M_i) with batched arrivals of size g_i and recurrent service processes GI_i ($\vec{GI}:=(GI_1,...,GI_Q)$). This leads to the
service system $\sum_{i=1}^{Q} M_i^{g_i}/\vec{GI}/S/0$ which is called in the following model (B.0).

It is well known that if two flows i and j with same characteristics but with $g_i > g_j$ are handled via a common trunk group, flow i
will occur greater losses than flow j. The consequences are different blocking probabilities, which also means that flows needing
greater bandwidths are mostly carried via the final route if an alternative routing scheme is given. It is currently being discussed
to solve these problems by means of trunk reservation. But if trunk
reservation is introduced to the system (B.0), a new model (B.1) is
given in which in general the insensitivity property is not valid
and no product form solution for the steady-state probabilities can
be derived, not even if the service times are exponentially distributed ([2]).

An interesting question is if there are, besides trunk reservation,
any other possibilities setting up an occupation restriction leading to service systems with nicer properties. This paper offers two
other methods discussed in the models (B.2) and (B.3). In model
(B.3) the steady-state probabilities are in product form and are
insensitive to the service time distributions, and the probabilities for the number of servers (channels) occupied can be calculated by a recursion formula.

2. THE MODELS

The basis for our models with occupation restriction is the service
system (B.0) which itself is based on the following assumptions:

(1) $Q \varepsilon N$ independent Poisson arrival processes (M_i, i=1,...,Q)
(2)   recurrent service processes (GI_i, i=1,...,Q)
(3)   loss system with $S \varepsilon N$ identical servers
(4)   batched arrivals (constant batch sizes g_i, i=1,...,Q)
(5)   batch services with "whole batch acceptance", i.e. either all
      members in an arriving batch are served simultaneously or all
      members in the batch are rejected.
(6)   random selection of idle servers (channels)

and on the blocking condition:

(7)   an arriving batch of flow i, i=1,...,Q, is rejected from the
      system if and only if less than g_i of the S servers are idle.

This model is discussed in [3] where it is proved:

Properties of model (B.0): The steady-state probabilities for the
number of batches of each flow i, i=1,...,Q, in the system are insensitive to the service time distributions. Furthermore, by these
probabilities which are in product form the steady-state probabilities for the number of servers occupied can be determined recursively.

2.1. MODEL (B.1)

Definition: A loss system of type (B.0) is called model (B.1) if the following condition is fulfilled:

An arriving batch of flow i, i=1,...,Q, is rejected from the system if $R1_i \in N \cup \{0\}$ servers are already occupied or if less than g_i servers are idle.

Both criteria for rejection (blocking) can be combined if $R1_i \leq S-g_i+1$ $\forall$ i=1,...,Q, is chosen. If $R1_i = S-g_i+1$ $\forall$ i=1,...,Q, the resulting model is (B.0), the service system to which no further occupation restriction is introduced.

Properties of model (B.1): In general, the steady-state probabilities for the number of batches in the system are not insensitive to the service time distributions and are not in product form.

This result is proved in [2]. In the special case $\sum_{i=1}^{Q} M_i^g/M/S/0;R1$ in which all traffic flows require the same bandwidth $g=:g_i$ $\forall$ i=1,...,Q, and have an exponentially distributed service time with the same mean $1/\mu=:1/\mu_i$ $\forall$ i=1,...,Q, the steady-state probability P_{ng} of ng servers being occupied is given by (see [2]):

$$P_{ng} = P_0 \cdot \frac{1}{n!} \cdot \prod_{k=1}^{n} A(k) \qquad \forall n = 1,\ldots,[S/g]$$

where

$$A(k) := \sum_{i=1}^{Q} A_i \cdot h((k-1)g,i) \qquad ; \qquad A_i := \lambda_i/\mu_i \quad \forall i = 1,\ldots,Q$$

$$h(j,i) = \begin{cases} 1 & \text{if} \quad j < R1_i \\ 0 & \text{otherwise} \end{cases} \qquad \forall j = 0,\ldots,S \; ; \; i = 1,\ldots,Q \; .$$

In more general cases (for example with exponentially distributed service times, different or equal bandwidth and/or different or equal mean service times), for computing the probabilities of n servers being occupied, the system of balance equations in the steady state needs to be solved separately for each selection of the vector R1.

2.2. MODEL (B.2)

Definition: A loss system of type (B.0) is called model (B.2) if the following condition is fulfilled:

The S servers are divided into Q+1 subsets $R2_k$, k=0,...,Q, of size d(k) (d(0)+...+d(Q) = S). Each arriving batch of flow i, i=1,...,Q, is first offered to $R2_0$. If no occupation can be established (less than g_i idle servers), the batch is offered (overflows) to $R2_i$. If still no occupation can be made (less than g_i idle servers in $R2_i$) the batch is rejected.

Properties of model (B.2): In general, the steady-state probabilities for the number of the batches in the system are not insensitive to the service time distributions and are not in product form.

This result is also proved in [2]. As in model (B.1), no general formulae for the probabilities can be derived. By setting $R2_0 = 0$ it is easily seen that this model covers the situation given in case A.

2.3. MODEL (B.3)

<u>Definition:</u> A loss system of type (B.0) is called model (B.3) if
the following condition is fulfilled:

An arriving batch of flow i, i=1,...,Q, is rejected from the
system if $R3_i \in N\cup\{0\}$ batches of flow i are already in service or if less than g_i servers are idle.

Again both rejection criteria can, without loss of generality, be
combined by choosing $0 \leq R3_i \leq [S/g_i]$ ∀ i=1,...,Q. In /2/ the
following is proved:

<u>Properties of model (B.3):</u>

a) The steady-state probabilities for the number of batches of each
   flow i, i=1,...,Q, in the system are in product form and are insensitive to the service time distributions.

b) For the probability P_n that n servers (channels) are occupied
   the following recursion formula holds:

$$P_n = \frac{1}{n} \cdot \sum_{\substack{i=1 \\ g_i \leq n}}^{Q} g_i \cdot A_i \cdot (P_{n-g_i} - T(R3_i,i,n-g_i)) \qquad \forall\ n = 1,...,S$$

where $A_i := \lambda_i/\mu_i$ ∀ i=1,...,Q, and T is defined by

$$T(k,i,j) := Pr \left\{ \begin{array}{l} \text{(exactly) k batches of flow i are in the system} \\ \text{and (exactly) j servers are occupied} \end{array} \right\}$$

From the probabilities T the individual loss probabilities for each
flow i, i=1,...,Q, can be derived.

3. FINAL REMARKS

The decision on how to handle the various services in the ISDN depends on theoretical and practical aspects. The present paper dealt
with theoretical concepts by analyzing the properties of the associated models as regards whether or not general solution formulae
can be derived. Since such formulae are needed for the dimensioning
of the trunk groups the respective results are also of practical
use. Of course, from the practical point of view, a numerical comparison of the individual blocking probabilities etc. in the different models is of further interest. This will be published in a
forthcoming paper.

REFERENCES

/1/ Gnedenko, B.W. and König, D., Handbuch der Bedienungstheorie
     I and II. Akademie-Verlag Berlin 1984.
/2/ Kleinewillinghöfer-Kopp, R., Bedienungssysteme mit poisson-
     schen Gruppenankünften und Belegungsbeschränkungen. Forschungs-
     institut der DBP 032 TB 23, 1986.
/3/ Mills, R.C., Models of stochastic service systems with
     batched arrivals. Diss., Columbia University, 1980.

TRAFFIC ENGINEERING for ISDN Design and Planning
M. Bonatti and M. Decina (Editors)
Elsevier Science Publishers B.V. (North-Holland)
© IAC, 1988

Impact of ISDN on Planning Efforts for Private Data Networks in the United States

Mary A. Johnston

Telecommunications Consulting Group
BBN Communications Corporation
50 Moulton Street
Cambridge, Massachusetts   USA   02238

Abstract: Sophisticated users of telecommunications in the United States remain unconvinced regarding the merits of ISDN ,due to large investments in private wide area network and Local Area Network technologies.   Successful deployment of ISDN must provide for interconnection to private   facilities.

Main Statement: Acceptance of ISDN by American users is still in doubt.

Initial Standards Efforts Geared to Needs of Public Carriers

Despite the fact that the initial ISDN planning and trial efforts have focussed on common carrier uses and services, large telecommunications users in the United States may first take widespread advantage of ISDN functionality in the premises environment.   Due to the fragmentation of the American telecommunications market resulting from deregulation of customer premises equipment (CPE) in 1983 and the breakup of AT&T in 1984, demonstrations of effective ISDN environments have been difficult to construct.   Regional Company trials have focussed on local access issues and have done little more than replicate digital services already available to American telecommunications users through the CCIS signaling networks.   Furthermore, lack of tariffs have made it impossible for users to conduct serious cost/benefits analyzes.

Instances of wide areas ISDNs, connecting multiple central offices across multiple local access and transport areas (LATAs), are not due to the US market until 1988.   Furthermore, firm international standards for interconnection to private networks, particularly private packet networks, remain unavailable.   Unlike Europe, where telecommunications users must depend heavily on public carrier offerings, the most sophisticated American users, such as the

Defense Department or the largest corporations, already have multi-
million dollar commitments to private voice and data networks.
Consequently, American users remain unconvinced that investment
in ISDN-based technologies will greatly improved their
telecommunications environments.

Users Consider ISDN for Premises Environments

As part of an ongoing ISDN feasibility study for the Defense Data
Network [1], the BBN Telecommunications Consulting Group, has
identified premises equipment as a new pressure point for planners
facing ISDN decisions. Among both government and private network
users, we have noted widespread consideration of ISDN as the focal
point for next generation private network architectures. The US
Army and Air Force are being particularly influenced by ISDN as they
design their next generation base communications plans. [2]

The critical CPE investment decision for these organizations
focuses on tradeoffs between continued investment in Local Area
Networks (LANS) to meet campus or base-wide data needs vs. delay
of investment until ISDN-Private Branch Exchanges (PBXs) become
commercially available. Work at BBN indicates that a hybrid
environment, relying on existing LAN technology and the emerging
FDDI (Fiber Distributed Data Interface) standards for high data rate
applications, combined with ISDN-PBXs for 64Kbps and under
requirements, may be the most cost effective solution. Of course,
development of standards for interconnection of LANs to ISDNs will
be critical to the success of this type of architecture.

User organizations facing this type of decision are often attempting
to forecast the future of technology in an effort to avoid investment
in technologies which will soon be rendered obsolete.
Unfortunately, given the speed of technological development this
goal is generally impossible to attain. Commercial users often solve
this problem through the use of rapid depreciation schedules which
permit them to change out older equipment every 3 to 7 years.
However, government users are usually not given such a luxury.
Hence, while many commercial users are now investing in LANs,
betting that ISDN equipment will not be ready for close to five
years, the government groups feel strong pressure to make a one-
time commitment for the next 10 to 20 years. Their best guess at
this time is leaning towards ISDN solutions.

Table 1 below highlights the decision factors by which these
planners weigh commitment to one or another technology.
Commercial users generally implement a decision within a year of
making it while widespread government investment follows a much
longer time schedule, often lagging commercial users by two to

three years. As can be seen, the biggest questions remains, how quickly will suitable standards for support of private networks, particularly private packet networks evolve.

Table 1: Premises Tradeoffs: ISDN vs. LANS

	ISDN	LANS
Standards orientation to date:	voice oriented	data oriented
Market drivers:	vendors	users
Time for support of private data nets:	1992	current
Geographic support:	wide area	premises
Wiring:	Twisted Pair	special media
Evolution:	Slow	Rapid
Data Rates:	64 Kbps	Multi-megabit

Highly Competitive Markets Place Unique Demands on ISDN

American users of telecommunications products and services have grown used to shouldering much of the burden for management of their private networks. Since the AT&T divestiture most large corporations have invested heavily in personnel and in private facilities. Desire to gain insulation from wide swings in tariffed rates (such as the hugh increases to hit short haul private lines in recent years), combined with the goal of gaining control over corporate communications resources so as to use them to compete in the firm's business areas, have all led to the development of highly entrenched private networks. It is unlikely ISDN will replace these private facilities and organizations.

The simple fact that the common carriers will subscribe to ISDN principles is not enough to ensure that users in competitive markets will rapidly embrace the technology as well. Efforts to implement ISDNs in the public networks must work closely with the demands of the private networks, if these organizations are to be expected to purchase advanced services, often called intelligent network services in the US. Most private networks are already capable of maintaining internal numbering plans, supporting least cost routing, and are developing methods for dynamic reconfiguration of bandwidth. The next phase of ISDN standards development must seriously consider interworking with private networks if these users are to retain any significant interest in public services.

Many users remember the X.121 Data Network Numbering experience, which virtually ignored private data networks. Similar treatment of private networks in the ISDN environment will be proof enough to users in competitive markets that ISDN is not for them. These users know that they can build their own networks, write their own software, and install competing technologies if the public carrier services are not compatible with the demands of their private networks. The success with which ISDN penetrates the premises arena will be a strong indication of how well it will fare among the ranks of private network users.

References:

[1] ISDN Trial Recommendation for the Defense Data Network, Mary A. Johnston, September 1986. BBN Communications Report Number 6321. Prepared for the Defense Communications Agency.

[2] Premises Technology Study, James G. Herman Project Manager and Editor, December 1986. BBN Communications Report Number 6417. Prepared for the Defense Communications Agency.

TRAFFIC ENGINEERING for ISDN Design and Planning
M. Bonatti and M. Decina (Editors)
Elsevier Science Publishers B.V. (North-Holland)
© IAC, 1988

DISCUSSION

1 Multipoint Communication (J.S.Turner)

1.1 Error Correction Procedures

The error correction procedures are not discussed in the paper - observed R.A. Skoog (AT&T Bell Laboratories) - How will be implemented any error correction procedures at the network edges for multipoint connections? Does that mean that multipoint connections will be considered only for applications not requiring error corrections (e.g. audio and video)?

J.S. Turner agreed that error correction is a complicate problem in a multipoint communication context "If the packet loss rate for a single link is under 10.E-06 one can handle multipoint connections with about 10.E+04 endpoints using sequence numbers and negative acknowledgements (with these values, one would expect about one packet in 100 to be re-transmitted)" - commented J.S. Turner - "When the connection becomes larger than this, one must partition things into multiple levels to keep the retransmission traffic from becoming too large".

1.2 Flow and Congestion Control

In answer to a question by M. Gerla (UCLA) on Flow and Congestion Control on Banyan Networks, J.S. Turner precised that there is a hardware flow control mechanism within the Switch Fabric to prevent buffer overflows. The packet processors have larger buffer which, therefore, are not protected by any explicit flow control mechanism.

R. Pandya (BNR) asked how could multiple transmitters be controlled in the proposed multipoint connections system.

"A definitive answer cannot yet be given, also if an hard work is in progress on that" - answered J.S. Turner - "some per node mechanisms appear to be required, but they can be fairly simple".

1.3 Multipoint Services With Reservation.

P. Richards asked two questions referring to multipoint services with reservation (such as multimedia teleconference).

Firstly, referring to a statement by J. Roberts (CNET) during the morning session on services (services with reservation are best provided on separate networks), he asked how could this statement be rationalized with a philosophy of providing a single, multipurpose transport resource.

Secondly, what will be the requirements (and the effects) of the reservation on the congestion control?

While it may be appropriate to reserve a portion of network
resources for reservation – type services, J.S. Turner could not
see any reason to segregate the network. The advantage of a single
network – he commented – is of course that one can easily shift the
proportion of network resources among different connection types.

2 Overall Grade of Service Models (R.G. Ackerley).

The evolution of the grade of service as a stochastic process,
allowing the estimate of figures such as: probability that the
system is performing in a specific way, e.g. is blocking t–more
minutes, has not been considered by the authors – precised R.G.
Ackerley in answer to a question by C. Rasmussen (Copenhagen
Telecom).

3 Dynamic Routing (A.N. Kashper, Y. Watanabe)

3.1 Different routing disciplines for wideband and narrowband traffic.

In answer to a question by L.G. Mason (INRS Telecommunications)
asking on the advantages and disadvantages of adopting different
routing disciplines for wideband and narrow band traffic, the
authors felt that such differentiation is not necessary, because the
use of alternate overflow routing is not considered.

In particular A.N. Kashper precised that in his approach traffic
flow patterns are optimized to minimize network cost. Therefore,
solutions obtained after optimization are flow patterns for mixed
traffic streams. Routing patterns for each traffic stream are
determined according to the traffic flow pattern, and circuit group
sizes are dimensioned. The routing pattern between a node pair is
assumed to be the same and circuit group sizes required are assumed
to be proportional to the offered traffic volume, no matter what
band–width traffic is offered.

However – commented A.N.Kashper – peakedness of wide–band overflow
traffic is considered to be extremely high and utilization of
alternate routes which carry wide–band overflow traffic will
decrease. Hence, more detailed study on alternative routing of
multiple band–width traffic is needed for strict circuit group
dimensioning.

4 Mobile ISDN (B.Ecklundh)

The implementation of ISDN services on Mobile Systems is still
in its exploratory stage and most of the discussion represented an
attempt to understand the basic approach and the limitations imposed
by the radio channel.

Furthermore, M. Falleni (Telettra) asked about which types of data
services have been envisaged in the experiment and B. Ecklund
mentioned primarily low speed data services such as alarm and
surveillance, but also document transfer, ordering and simple
messaging.

Finally, commenting a question by C. Halgreen (Jutland Telecom) about the use of the Dm – channels for user-to-user signalling of bursty traffic, B. Ecklundh declared that, even if the Dm-channels has been used, such a solution seems controversial: actually "a single common channel would be advantageous from a signalling point of view, since the mobiles in that case would always know which channel to use for receiving calls. But, a single common channel could probably not handle any user p-data, since it would be saturated with signalling information. Users could be directed to a common Dm-channel, but problems arise when a random access protocol should be implemented over a very error prone channel which uses a HDLC-like protocol on layer two".

TRAFFIC ENGINEERING for ISDN Design and Planning
M. Bonatti and M. Decina (Editors)
Elsevier Science Publishers B.V. (North-Holland)
© IAC, 1988

NETWORK EVOLUTION AND BEYOND

(Chairman   Conclusion to the Afternoon Session on Network)

Raj Pandya

BNR, Canada

There is an increasing requirement for flexible and robust network
design to alleviate uncertainty of demand forecasting for future
ISDN services. Suitable metrics for such network attributes as
flexibility, survivability and robustness are needed.

Though the current ISDN specification calls for integration at the
access level only, numerous studies are underway to assess the
traffic performance and design impacts of integration at the network
level, i.e. multiservice networks.

A few papers that addressed data services on ISDN and interworking
of ISDNs with existing voice and data networks would have broadened
the perspective of the network sessions.

A close and continued interaction is needed between the teletraffic
research community and the groups involved in developing ISDN
interworking requirements, signalling protocols and performance
specifications.   This is necessary to ensure that the teletraffic
community continues to provide pragmatic solutions to mainstream
ISDN issues.

TRAFFIC ENGINEERING for ISDN Design and Planning
M. Bonatti and M. Decina (Editors)
Elsevier Science Publishers B.V. (North-Holland)
© IAC, 1988

WILL FAULT-TOLERANCE BECOME
A KEY ISSUE FOR ISDN DESIGN AND PLANNING?

(Introduction to the Tutorial on Performability Design)

M. Bonatti

ITALTEL, Italy

Traffic and reliability are traditionally considered separately in planning and in designing Telecommunication network and systems, because of the difference of scale between the two underlying stochastic processes and of the difficulty to deal with performance concepts influenced by their interaction.

The same doesn't happen in Computer Science, because in some very important computer applications the dependence of the users on the system is crucial and thus the fault-tolerance is very critical.

In Telecommunication, the fault-tolerance issue impacts with a much more complicated system and because of the pervasiveness of the POTS and the very high reliability targets required to the accesses, the nodes and the links, the subscribers don't perceive critical dependencies on traditional designs.

However, economy of scale of the designs and of the plans could take profit considering fault-tolerance targets as tradeoff.

The frequently mentioned and still vague concept of robustness could also be better defined taking into account fault-tolerance theory.

Finally, performability (and not only performance) design guidelines could become very important in a Multiservice Environment such as ISDN in which some critical communications instances could require fault-tolerance targets typical of some computer applications.

The paper by J. Meyer explains the Performability Theory and anticipates some possible applications to the ISDN network and system analysis.

The discussions walked through all these topics, confirming their relevance and concluded that integrated performability design and planning guidelines will be very important for ISDN. The need of further considering, both in planning and in design, the robustness to forecasting uncertainties was further underlined.

TRAFFIC ENGINEERING for ISDN Design and Planning
M. Bonatti and M. Decina (Editors)
Elsevier Science Publishers B.V. (North-Holland)
© IAC, 1988

Performability Evaluation: Techniques and Tools

J. F. Meyer

Computing Research Laboratory
Electrical Engineering and Computer Science Department
The University of Michigan
Ann Arbor, MI 48109, USA

Abstract

Integrated services digital networks have a number of characteristics which complicate their evaluation. In particular, since they are likely to exhibit degradable performance, the concept of performability can provide more refined assessments of their ability to perform under fault and error conditions. This paper reviews the foundations of model-based performability evaluation, and discusses various techniques and tools which have been developed for this purpose.

1 Introduction

Integrated services digital networks (ISDNs) are representative of a growing class of distributed real-time systems which present new and challenging evaluation problems. As compared to systems of a more centralized and dedicated nature, one of the complicating factors is greater diversity in the services demanded from the system. This increases the complexity of workload (traffic) conditions and, in the case of model-based evaluations, the difficulties encountered in workload modeling. Specifically, when contrasting the evaluation needs of ISDNs with those of conventional telephone networks, this may be a dominating factor.

Other complications are due to the physical distribution of processing resources and to real-time constraints on system performance. These typically result in high degrees of parallelism and in requirements on the times that certain processes can be initiated or completed. Because of requirements concerning dependability (i.e., reliability or availability; see [1]) as well as performance, such systems frequently employ fault tolerance techniques which further complicate the evaluation process. Finally, due to a combination of these factors, system performance is typically "degradable", i.e., between the extremes of non-degraded performance and failure, the system can perform at intermediate levels which provide varying degrees of benefit to the user.

Generally, when evaluating a system, one seeks to relate and quantify aspects of what the system is and does with respect to what the system is required to be and do. Moreover, since what a system does (e.g., how well it performs) depends on what it is (e.g., how its resources are altered by faults), both need to be addressed in the evaluation process. This is often accomplished by treating *performance* and *dependability* as separate issues, under the assumption that a system either performs as expected (delivers its expected service) or fails. In such cases, performance can be identified with "failure-free performance" and dependability means "the ability to perform successfully". On the other hand, if a system is degradable (i.e, its performance is degradable; see above), these distinctions preclude the evaluation of its ability to perform at levels other than success and failure. What is called for instead are truly unified performance-dependability evaluations which, in our terminology, quantify a system's *performability* [2,3].

The intent of this paper is to review the foundations of performability evaluation and to discuss techniques and tools which have been developed for its implementation. More specifically, our remarks concern evaluations which are model-based, i.e., the dynamics of a system and its environment are represented by a "base model" which, relative to a designated "performance variable", supports evaluation of the system's "ability to perform". The types of models considered in this context include analytic models, simulation models, and, generally, hybrid models that incorporate both analysis and simulation. Section 2 reviews the general framework for this methodology which, although conceived explicitly for model-based evaluations, can likewise serve as a conceptual framework for experimental evaluations of performability (those obtained via measurements of actual systems). Techniques for the construction and solution of performability models are surveyed in Section 3. The concluding section discusses software tools which implement such techniques.

2 Performability

A general framework for model-based performability evaluation was first introduced in 1978 [2], with a somewhat more refined description appearing in 1980 [3]. This framework grew from some ideas concerning "partial success" which had been formulated (but not openly published) a number of years before [4], and from a notion of "computation-based reliability" which was examined in the mid-1970s [5,6]. It was also motivated by the recognition, inherent in work done at that time by Borgerson and Freitas [7], that degradable systems required special attention with regard to the kind of measures and models that might be used in their evaluation.

The application aim, at the outset, was the evaluation of ultra-reliable aircraft control computers being developed for the U.S. Space Agency (NASA) by both SRI International [8] and the C.S. Draper Laboratory [9]. One intended feature of these systems was an ability to shed workload (beginning with the least critical tasks) if a loss of computing resources, due to faults, demanded it. Accordingly, these systems could provide varying degrees of service over a specified period of use (e.g., the duration of a flight of the aircraft) and, hence, exhibited the type of degradable performance we wished to accommodate.

Prior to settling on the concepts and terminology introduced in [2], we initially viewed the unification of performance and reliability (or, in more recent terms, performance and dependability) as a measure of system "effectiveness" [10,11], where its formulation depended on an intermediate association of "worth" (utility, reward, benefit) with each possible level of accomplishment. (This view was consistent with the definition proposed in [4] but differed with respect to lower-level details.) However, as the desired amount of generality became clearer, we decided (in late 1976) that performance-reliability aspects of effectiveness should be separated from the worths that one might associate with their outcomes. The resulting concept was more refined and, consequently, could still be employed in higher-level, worth-oriented evaluations of system effectiveness. In words, it measured a system's "ability to perform" (as quantified by probabilities), whence the term "performability" which we adopted a short time later.

In more formal terms, performability and its associated concepts are defined as follows [2,3]. Let S denote the system in question where, generally, S is interpreted as including not only a system, per se, but also relevant aspects of its environment (e.g., workload, external sources of faults, etc.). Then the *performance* of S over a specified *utilization period* T is a random variable Y taking values in a set A. Elements of A are the *accomplishment levels* (performance outcomes) to be distinguished in the evaluation process. The *performability* of S is the probability measure $Perf$ (denoted p_S in [2,3]) induced by Y where, for any measurable set B of accomplishment levels $(B \subseteq A)$,

$$Perf(B) = \text{ the probability that } S \text{ performs at a level in } B.$$

Solution of performability is based on an underlying stochastic process X, called a *base model* of S, which represents the dynamics of the system's structure, internal state, and environment during utilization. By its definition, the base model must also "support" the solution of $Perf$ in the sense that, for any any accomplishment set B of interest, $Perf(B)$ can be formulated in terms of X. This is insured via the notion of a *capability function* which maps trajectories of X into values of Y (i.e., levels of accomplishment). A base model X together with a performance variable Y is a *performability model* of S.

The concept of performability is thus quite general and, with experience gained by ourselves and others over the past 10 years (see below), we've found that most any combined performance-dependability measure can be expressed (via an appropriate reformulation, when necessary) as a performability measure. Moreover, depending on the choice of base model X and performance variable Y, performability models can be specialized to serve as performance models (of the usual type) and models for dependability evaluation (reliability models, availability models). For example, if the structure of a computing system S is presumed to be fixed and correct (i.e., the base model X represents changes only in the system's internal state and environment) and, for a designated utilization period $T = [0, t]$, we let Y be the average throughput rate during $[0, t]$, i.e.,

$$Y = \frac{\text{number of jobs processed during } [0, t]}{t}$$

then (X, Y) is a (strict) performance model. At the other extreme, suppose the states of X are representative of structure only, and are classified as either "operational" (if the system is operational for that structure) or "nonoperational". If, further, we take Y to be variable

$$Y = \begin{cases} 1 & \text{if } X \text{ is an operational state throughout } [0,t], \\ 0 & \text{else} \end{cases}$$

then (X, Y) is a reliability model and $Perf(\{1\})$ expresses the the traditional concept of reliability (i.e., the probability that the system is operational throughout its utilization).

In the development of techniques and tools for model-based performability evaluation (as reviewed in the sections that follow), we recognized the importance of such specializations, i.e., we wanted the methods to be useful and efficient for more traditional evaluations of both performance and dependability. At the same time, we wanted to insure that they could apply as well to the type of truly unified measures that are captured by the general notion of performability.

The need for such measures has likewise been recognized by others who, with various approaches, have contributed to the basic literature on this subject. This includes studies by Beaudry ([12,13]; performance-related reliability measures), Losq ([14]; degradable systems composed of degradable resources), Troy ([15]; efficiency evaluation), Gay and Ketelsen([16]; performance evaluation of degradable systems), Mine and Hatayama ([17]; job-related reliability), De Souza ([18]; benefit analysis of fault tolerance), Castillo and Siewiorek ([19,20]; performance-reliability models for computing systems), Chou and Abraham ([21]; performance-availability models of shared resource multiprocessors). Osaki and Nishio ([22]; reliability of information), Beyaert, Florin, Lonc, and Natkin ([23]; dependability evaluation using stochastic Petri nets), Huslende ([24,25]; combined performance-reliability evaluation for degradable systems), Arlat and Laprie ([26]; performance-related dependability evaluation), Munarin ([27]; performance/reliability analysis of gracefully degrading systems), and Krishna and Shin ([28]; performance measures for multiprocessor controllers).

3   Techniques

In general terms, model-based performability evaluation is a two-step procedure involving 1) construction of a performability model for the system and measure in question, and 2) evaluation of the measure via solution of the model. More precisely, performability model *construction* (Step 1) consists of identifying a performance variable Y (corresponding to the desired measure) and determining a base model X that represents the system plus its environment. In many cases, as discussed below, construction of X may invoke lower-level models, e.g., graphical models, which are useful in deriving appropriate process characterizations. Performability model *solution* (Step 2) is a procedure which produces performability values $Perf(B)$ for accomplishment sets B that are of interest to the user. Generally, knowledge of the probability distribution function (PDF) of Y suffices to determine such values. Accordingly, we regard a performability model as (fully) "solved" once the PDF of Y is determined. Solution of a PDF can be obtained through a closed-form solution (expressed as a function of base model and performance variable parameters) or a numerical solution (approximated for a finite number of values via analysis or simulation).

3.1   Model Construction

When the system to be evaluated is relatively simple, a performability model (X, Y) can often be constructed directly. That is to say, once the performance variable Y is identified, X can either be characterized directly in analytic terms (e.g., by a generator matrix in the case of a continuous-time Markov process) or be represented directly by a computer program which can simulate its behavior. However, most realistic systems are not in this category, calling for more sophisticated means of model construction. A useful approach in the latter regard is to view the construction of X as a procedure which moves step by step through a hierarchy of models.

When system performance can be quantified in terms of a relatively small number of accomplishment levels (possible values of Y), it is possible to consider each level individually and move top down through a model hierarchy which has X at the bottom. In this case, construction of performability models exploits a well known property of discrete random variables which, in the terminology of the modeling framework, says the following. Since Y is discrete, the set A of possible accomplishment levels is countable and, hence, the probability distribution

$$\{P[Y = a]|a \in A\}$$

suffices to determine the performability of S. Accordingly, in the case of a model of this type, the performability of S can be alternatively defined as the function $Perf : A \to [0, 1]$ where, for $a \in A$,

$$Perf(a) = P[Y = a].$$

If we assume further that A is finite then performability is likewise finite, i.e., the values of $Perf$ can be tabulated.

The base model part (the stochastic process X) of a model of this type represents a sufficiently detailed probabilistic description of changes in a system's structure (due to faults and fault recovery), internal state, and environment to permit solution of the performability values $Perf(a)$. It is constructed by first decomposing the utilization period $[0, t]$ into a finite number of consecutive time periods called *phases*. For each phase, a system's intraphase behavior is represented by a continuous-time, finite-state stochastic process which is typically a time-homogeneous Markov process. Different phases, however, may be modeled by different processes, subject to constraints which permit the determination of (conditional) interphase transition probabilities. Combination of these processes results in a *phased model* [29] which constitutes the base model X. Relative to a specified performance variable Y, X is required to "support" Y in the sense that the end-of-phase samples of X uniquely determine the value of Y.

Performability evaluations of this type can thus be viewed as generalizations of "phased mission" reliability evaluations (see [30,31,32], for example). Techniques used to construct and solve such models are likewise more general and complex, due in part to the less restricted nature of phased base models. A more challenging property of these models, however, is due to the general manner in which the base model X relates to the performance variable Y via a capability function [2,3]. Relative to a given level of accomplishment, the end-of-phase samples of X can be *functionally dependent* [33], e.g., knowing that $Y = a$, knowledge of the state of X at the end of phase i can contribute to knowledge of the state of X at the end of some other phase j. In contrast, assumptions made in the construction of phased mission reliability models (see [32], for example) are such that, with respect to the accomplishment level "success," the phases must be functionally independent (as established in [33], Theorem 6).

More recent work has focused on a bottom-up approach, where a lower-level network model is used to represent the system structure and environment. In this case, the base model is at the top of the hierarchy and can support performance variables which are either discrete or continuous. Moreover, this approach is more naturally suited to the construction of performability models which can capture the properties identified in our introductory remarks, namely parallelism, timeliness, fault tolerance, and degradable performance. These network-level models are referred to as *stochastic activity networks* (SANs) [34,35] and, informally, they can be viewed as models which generalize stochastic Petri nets [36,37] and incorporate certain features of queueing models. Moreover, our experience to date indicates that they are indeed well suited to the modeling of systems having the properties cited above.

Structurally, SANs have primitives consisting of *activities, places, input gates, and output gates*. Activities ("transitions" in Petri net terminology) are of two types, *timed* and *instantaneous*. Timed activities represent activities of the modeled system whose durations impact the system's ability to perform. Instantaneous activities, on the other hand, represent system activities which, relative to the performance variable in question, complete in a negligible amount of time. Cases associated with activities permit the realization of two types of spatial uncertainty. Uncertainty about which activities are enabled in a certain state is realized by cases associated with intervening instantaneous activities. Uncertainty about the next state assumed upon completion of a timed activity is realized by cases associated with that activity. Places are as in Petri nets. Gates were introduced to permit greater flexibility in defining enabling and completion rules.

The stochastic nature of the nets is realized by associating an activity time distribution function with each timed activity and a probability distribution with each set of cases. Generally, both distributions can depend on the global marking of the network. A *reactivation function* [35] is also associated with each timed activity. This function specifies, for each marking, a set of *reactivation markings*. Informally, given that an activity is activated in a specific marking, the activity is *reactivated* whenever any marking in the set of reactivation markings is reached. This provides a mechanism for restarting activities that have been activated, either with the same or different distribution. This decision is made on a per activity basis (based on the reactivation function), and is not a net-wide execution policy.

Others have likewise examined the use of stochastic extensions of Petri nets for performance and/or reliability evaluation. Notable is the work of Behr *et al.* ([38]; Evaluation Nets), Chiola ([39]; Generalized Stochastic Petri Nets), Cumani ([40]; Stochastic Petri nets with phase type distributions), Dugan *et al.* ([41]; Extended Stochastic Petri Nets), Godbersen and Meyer ([42]; Function Nets), Marsan *et al.* ([43]; Generalized Stochastic Petri Nets), Molloy ([37,44]; Timed Petri Nets), Natkin ([36]; Timed Petri Nets), and Törn ([45]; Simulation Nets).

To assist the process of describing SAN behavior, a higher-level class of models was defined. These models, referred to as *stochastic activity systems* (SASs) [35], provide a natural state-level representation of stochastic activity networks. This representation is achieved by constructing the SAS *realized* by a SAN. SASs thus provide useful intermediate representations which can be regarded as probabilistic extensions of Keller's "named transition systems" [46,47]. The state of a SAS corresponds to a stable marking of the underlying SAN; a name on a transition (between states) is the name of the activity whose completion caused that transition. (Note that, because activities have "cases", the same name may be associated with several transitions from a given SAS state.) Since activity names are retained, SASs permit the study of "activity-marking" behavior.

Several choices are possible for a higher-level, stochastic process representation of the system that will serve as the base model component of a performability model. One type of SAS behavior that can be studied is the stochastic "marking behavior." Formally, the stochastic *marking behavior* of a SAS is a stochastic process $\{X_t \mid t \geq t_0\}$, where X_t is the marking (of the corresponding SAN) at time t, given that the SAN is in its initial marking at time $t = t_0$. In this case, the reachable stable markings of the SAN form the state-space of the process. When information regarding activity completions as well as markings is desired, the "activity-marking behavior" [48] of the SAS can be studied. This notion of behavior makes use of a more detailed notion of state, the "am-state". Informally, each am-state is a pair (a, q) where the first component is the most recently completed activity and the second component is the current SAS state. The initial state of the SAS is then represented by an am-state $(\triangledown, q_0)$, where $\triangledown$ is a fictitious activity that completes at $t = 0$, bringing the SAN into its initial marking q_0.

With the preceding notion of state, we are able to define a stochastic process such that its state trajectories capture successive alternations between activity completions and resulting stable markings. Informally, then, the am-behavior captures both the sequence of am-states that are reached during an execution of a SAN and the times of activity completions during the execution. For a formal definition of the am-behavior of a SAS, see [48]. While this notion of behavior can conceptually support an extremely large class of performance variables, solution of this stochastic process is typically difficult, due to the large state-spaces that result from realistic network-level models. Accordingly, our most recent work [49] has resulted in construction methods that produce higher-level (less detailed) models which support more restricted classes of variables. These methods make use of knowledge regarding both the performance variable and structure of the network, and can lead to considerable reductions in the size of a base model.

3.2 Model Solution

Solution of performability models depends both on the variables of interest and characteristics of the underlying base model. For base models constructed using the top-down elaboration technique described in the previous section, solution of a performability value $Perf(a)$ is, conceptually, a two-step procedure:

1. Determine the set U_a of all base model state trajectories (as characterized by their end-of-phase samples) that correspond, via the capability function, to $Y = a$.

2. Using knowledge of X, determine the probability of the trajectory set U_a. This probability is the value of $Perf(a)$.

Execution of step 1) exploits the hierarchy used to establish the base model elaboration and, employing matrix representations of trajectory sets and an accompanying matrix calculus, proceeds, in a top-down manner, to determine a suitable representation of U_a (see [3,50]). An important feature of this method is the ability to account for functional dependencies in the process of determining U_a. As a consequence, U_a is ultimately represented as a union of disjoint "Cartesian" trajectory sets. Other approaches require such dependencies to be recognized, manually, during the process of model construction (see [51] for a detailed assessment of these differences).

Step 2) is performed by first calculating the probability of each of the Cartesian subsets determined in step 1), using formulas described in [29,52] and developed for this purpose. Since these subsets are disjoint, the sum of these probabilities yields the desired solution.

Results of performability evaluations using this technique are reported in a number of papers and technical reports [50,51,52,53,54,55,56]. These include a relatively comprehensive performability evaluation of the SIFT computer [54,55], where SIFT's computational environment is a transoceanic flight of an advanced commercial aircraft. Performability, in this case, is quantified in terms of five accomplishment levels, ranging from a "perfect" flight to loss of the aircraft. Generally, these techniques are best suited to performability evaluations where the user (of the evaluation results) is interested in whether a system satisfies certain "bottom line" performability requirements.

Another interesting class of solution methods are those which have been developed for performability models that incorporate the notion of a "reward model." Informally, a reward model is constructed by associating rewards with the behavior of the process under study. The most typical way of doing this has been to define a function r from the set of states to the nonnegative real numbers, where $r(q)$ is interpreted as the rate at which reward is accumulated in state q. If such rates are the only contributions to total reward, we refer to such reward models as "rate-based". More generally, rewards (in this case termed "bonuses") can also be associated with state transitions. A natural performance variable, in this context, is the reward Y_t accumulated during some utilization period $[0, t]$.

For such models, and specifically for semi-Markov base models with rate and bonus rewards, Howard [57] derived solutions of the expected reward $E[Y_t]$. However (as noted by Howard), the complexity of this formulation limits its use to theoretical interpretation in all but the simplest cases. Techniques for obtaining a full solution of performability (i.e., the PDF of Y_t) were developed in [58] for a special class of degradable system models. These results included a closed-form solution of performability for a specific dual-processor example. We later extended this work [59] to provide a solution, albeit computationally expensive, for the performability of systems which are acyclic and nonrecoverable [60] and the reward structure is rate-based. An algorithmic time-domain solution for the distribution of Y_t was developed by Goyal and Tantawi [61] for acyclic rate-based models.

Solution of reward models using transform techniques has also been investigated. In particular, Donatiello and Iyer [62] provided a closed-form time-domain solution using transform techniques with a rate-based reward structure, thus generalizing the technique we described in [58]. Iyer *et al.* [63] later extended this work to obtain a solution in the transform domain for Markov models and an explicit computational formula for each moment of Y_t. Kulkarni *et al.* [64] obtained a similar transform solution, but considered models where some transitions cause the loss of all accumulated reward. They also obtained solutions for the distribution of Y_t for non-trivial repairable systems by numerical inversion of the transform solution. Most recently, Ciciani and Grassi have derived a closed-form solution for general acyclic Markov reward models [65].

Many general techniques may also be useful as performability solution methods. These include general solution methods for stochastic processes (e.g. [66]), solution by simulation (e.g. [67,68,69]), and numerical methods for linear systems (e.g. [70]).

4 Tools

Most of the model construction and solution techniques surveyed above require machine implementation to be practically applied. Both the complexity of the construction procedures and the typical sizes of resulting base models make this a necessity. For example, in the case of the top-down construction and solution techniques described earlier, this need motivated the development of METAPHOR [50]. Tools have also been developed, to one extent or another, for each of the stochastic extensions to Petri Nets referred to in the previous section. In particular, such tools include an extensive software package, called METASAN [71], which has been developed specifically for the construction and solution of SAN-based performability models. This package was designed and implemented at the Industrial Technology Institute in Ann Arbor, Michigan.

METASAN was written using UNIX tools (C, Yacc, Lex, and Csh) and contains some 37,000 lines of source code. Models consist of two parts: a description of the structure of the net, and a description of the desired performance variables and solution method to be used in the evaluation process. Solution options include analytical techniques (applicable under certain well defined conditions) as well as both terminating and steady-state simulation.

At the highest level, one interacts with METASAN through a menu structure. This menu permits access to the two basic files that make up a METASAN model: a structure file and an experiment file. The structure file is a direct translation of the SAN into a textual form that can be accepted by the package. Specification of the performance variable(s) and solution algorithm is done via the experiment file. Model construction consists of describing the structure of the system to be modeled using the editor, compiling the description, describing the experiment file, and compiling the experiment file. The result of these actions is a machine understandable description (a collection of C data structures and procedures) of the system to be modeled and the desired performance variables. By then selecting the model solution option, this machine readable description is bound to the correct solution module and is executed.

The SAN description language, *Sanscript*, permits a SAN to be specified in a textual form understandable to the (SAN) compiler. Sanscript also permits easy specification of complex enabling predicates, activity time functions, reactivation functions, and gate functions. At a high-level, a Sanscript description consists of four parts: a header, local variable declarations, definition of all the primitives used, and a specification of all functions values and interconnections associated with each primitive. A host of activity time distribution types are available, representing all service distributions normally used in evaluation. An activity time distribution of "inst" is used to denote an instantaneous activity. Complex activity time distribution parameters, case distributions, gate predicates and functions, and reactivation functions may be specified using the "*MARK*" function and a few lines of C code. Here the notation "*MARK(place)*" refers to the current marking of place "*place*". Many stochastic activity networks contain numerous similar subnetworks (e.g., nodes in a computer network) that are replicated many times. Construction of these subnetworks directly in Sanscript would be tedious. To simplify such constructions, we provide a macro-preprocessor for METASAN. This preprocessor allows one to define subnetworks once in a parameterized manner, and then construct a specific subnetwork via a single macro call. After the specification of the SAN in Sanscript is complete, it is passed to the SAN compiler and translated into an internal form understandable by the solution modules. The SAN compiler is written in Yacc (yet another compiler compiler), Lex, and C.

The experiment file permits a great deal of versatility in the definition of performance variables. Unlike many modeling packages which limit evaluations to a few pre-defined variables (e.g. queue length, server utilization), METASAN permits the specification of complex user-defined performance variables. Performance variables specified for solution by simulation are based on the notion of a *path*. Informally, a path is a sequence of marking, activity, case triples which define a possible behavior on the net. Events such as initiations of paths, completions of paths, and traversals of paths are then naturally defined. Definition of these events make it possible to estimate a variety of time related characteristics of path sets. All conventional performance variables plus a wide class of un-conventional variables can be represented in this framework.

Specification of variables to be solved via an analytic solver is done by writing them in terms of terms of possible "solution vectors" for a given solution method. For example, a solution vector produced by the steady-state state occupancy solver is the probability of being in a state (or, for ergodic systems, the fraction of time spent in that state) in the long run. Solution vectors for the transient solver are the state occupancy probabilities at specific times. Variables that are expressed directly in terms of these solution vectors are called *basic variables*. Basic variables can then be used, together with constants, to construct *derived variables*. Finally, a report section specifies which variables are to be reported.

A variety of analytic solvers are implemented in the package. Steady-state state occupancy probabilities are obtained either by Gaussian elimination or by Gauss-Seidel iteration, depending on the size of the state-space and convergence characteristics of the particular model. Reward model solution techniques are also implemented. In the case of Markov reward models, a variation on a technique proposed by Goyal and Tantawi [61] is used. Solution for the state occupancy probabilities at a specific time for Markov stochastic activity systems is accomplished using a randomization technique proposed by Gross and Miller [72,73].

Conditions exist when solution of the base model via analytic means becomes intractable. This can occur, for example, when complex reactivation functions are specified, activity time distributions are general, the desired performance variables are sufficiently complex, or the state space is extremely large. In this case, a simulation solver may be used. Both the terminating and steady-state simulation solvers are based on a discrete-event next-event time advance simulator core. Currently, two methods for confidence interval estimation are supported. The first is an iterative method based on the replication approach, and is used for terminating simulations. Using this method, one specifies the relative precision and level of confidence desired as part of the experiment file input. The second method is used for steady-state simulations and is an iterative batching procedure, where the user must specify the length of initial transient, batch size, relative precision desired, and level of confidence desired.

Experience with the use of METASAN at the Industrial Technology Institute and the University of Michigan has shown that it is applicable to a variety of distributed real-time systems. In particular, such applications have included computer-communication networks, multiprocessor systems, and automated manufacturing systems. As suggested at the outset, ISDNs are likewise representative of such systems. Hence, although performability studies of specific ISDN architectures have yet to be undertaken, we believe that tools such as METASAN will be required for this purpose.

References

[1] J.C. Laprie, "Dependable computing and fault tolerance: Concepts and terminology," in *Proc. 1985 Int. Conf. on Fault-Tolerant Computing,* Ann Arbor, MI, June 1985, pp. 2-11.

[2] J.F. Meyer, "On evaluating the performability of degradable computing systems," in *Proc. 1978 Int. Symp. on Fault-Tolerant Computing,* Toulouse, France, June 1978, pp. 44-49.

[3] J.F. Meyer, "On evaluating the performability of degradable computing systems," *IEEE Trans. on Comput.,* vol. C-22, pp. 720-731, Aug. 1980.

[4] J.F. Meyer, "A definition of system reliability," Tech. Summary No. 3341-66-1, Jet Propulsion Laboratory, February 1966.

[5] J.F. Meyer, "Computation-based reliability analysis," in *Proc. 1975 Int. Symp. on Fault-Tolerant Computing,* Paris, June 1975, pp. 223.

[6] J.F. Meyer, "Computation-based reliability analysis," *IEEE Trans. on Comput.,* vol. 25, no. 6, pp. 578-584, June 1976.

[7] B.R. Borgerson and R.F. Freitas, "A reliability model for gracefully degrading and standby-sparing systems," *IEEE Trans. Comput.,* vol. C-24, pp. 517-525, May 1975.

[8] J.H. Wensley *et al.,* "SIFT: Design and analysis of a fault-tolerant computer for aircraft control," *Proc. of the IEEE,* vol. 66, pp. 1240-1255, Oct. 1978.

[9] A.L. Hopkins *et al.,* "FTMP–A highly reliable fault-tolerant multiprocess for aircraft", vol. 66, pp. 1221-1239, Oct. 1978.

[10] J.F. Meyer, "An approach to evaluating the effectiveness of computing systems," in *Proc. 1976 Conf. on Information Sciences and Systems,* The Johns Hopkins Univ., Baltimore, MD, April 1976, pp. 376-383.

[11] J.F. Meyer, "A model hierarchy for evaluating the effectiveness of computing systems," in *Proc. 3rd National Reliability Symp.,* Perros-Guirec, France, Sept. 1976, pp. 539-555.

[12] M.D. Beaudry, "Performance related reliability measures for computing systems," in *Proc. 1977 Int. Symp. on Fault-Tolerant Computing,* Los Angeles, CA, June 1977, pp. 16-21.

[13] M.D. Beaudry, "Performance-related reliability measures for computing systems," *IEEE Trans. Computers,* vol. c-27, pp. 540-547, June 1978.

[14] J. Losq, "Effects of failures on gracefully degradable systems," in *Proc. 1977 Int. Symp. on Fault-Tolerant Computing,* Los Angeles, CA, June 1977, pp. 29-34.

[15] R. Troy, "Dynamic reconfiguration: An algorithm and its efficiency evaluation," in *Proc. 1977 Int. Symp. on Fault-Tolerant Computing,* Los Angeles, CA, June 1977.

[16] F.A. Gay, and M.L. Ketelsen, "Performance evaluation of gracefully degrading systems," in *Proc. 1979 Int. Symp. on Fault-Tolerant Computing,* Madison, WI, June 1979, pp. 51-58.

[17] H. Mine and K. Hatayama, "Performance related reliability measures for computing systems," in *Proc. 1979 Int. Symp. on Fault-Tolerant Computing,* Madison, WI, June 1979, pp. 59-62.

[18] J.M. De Souza, "A unified method for the benefit analysis of fault-tolerance," in *Proc. 1980 Int. Symp. on Fault-Tolerant Computing,* Kyoto, Japan, Oct. 1980, pp. 201-203.

[19] X. Castillo and D.P. Siewiorek, "A performance reliability model for computing systems," in *Proc. 1980 Int. Symp. on Fault-Tolerant Computing,* Kyoto, Japan, Oct. 1980, pp. 187-192.

[20] X. Castillo and D.P. Siewiorek, "Workload, performance, and reliability of digital computing systems," in *Proc. 1981 Int. Symp. on Fault-Tolerant Computing,* Portland, ME, June 1981, pp. 84-89.

[21] T.C.K. Chou and J.A. Abraham, "Performance/availability model of shared resource multiprocessors," *IEEE Trans. Reliability,* vol. R-29, no. 1, pp. 70-76, April 1980.

[22] S. Osaki and T. Nishio, "Reliability evaluation of some fault-tolerant computer architectures," in *Lecture Notes in Computer Science.* Berlin, Germany: Springer-Verlag, 1980.

[23] B. Beyaert, G. Florin, P. Lonc, and S. Natkin, "Evaluation of computer system dependability using stochastic Petri nets," in *Proc. 1981 11th Int. Symp. on Fault-Tolerant Computing,* Portland, ME, June 1981, pp. 66-71.

[24] E. Huslende, "A Combined evaluation of performance and reliability for degradable systems," in *Proc. ACM/SIGMETRICS Conf. on Meas. and Modeling of Computing Syst.,* Las Vegas, Nevada, Sept. 1981, pp. 157-164.

[25] E. Huslende, "Optimal/cost reliability allocation in communication networks," in *Proc. 1983 Int. Symp. on Fault-Tolerant Computing,* Milano, Italy, June 1983, pp. 348-355.

[26] J. Arlat and J.C. Laprie, "Performance-related dependability evaluation of supercomputer systems," in *Proc. 1983 Int. Symp. on Fault-Tolerant Computing,* Milano, Italy, June 1983, pp. 276-283.

[27] J.A. Munarin, "Dynamic workload model for performance/reliability analysis of gracefully degrading systems," in *Proc. 1983, Int. Symp. on Fault-Tolerant Computing,* Milano, Italy, June 1983, pp. 290-295.

[28] C.M. Krishna and K.G. Shin, "Performance measures for multiprocessor controllers," in *Performance '83*. A.K. Agrawala and S.K. Tripathi, (eds), Amsterdam: North Holland, 1983, pp. 229-250.

[29] L.T. Wu and J.F. Meyer, "Phased models for evaluating the performability of computing systems," in *Proc. of the 1979 John Hopkins Conf. on Information Sciences and Systems,* Baltimore, MD, March 1979, pp. 426-431.

[30] H.S. Winokur, Jr., and L.J. Goldstein, "Analysis of mission-oriented systems," *IEEE Trans. Reliability,* vol. R-18, no. 4, pp. 144-148, Nov. 1969.

[31] J.L. Bricker, "A unified method for analyzing mission reliability for fault tolerant computer systems," *IEEE Trans. Reliability,* vol. R-22, no. 2, pp. 72-77, June 1973.

[32] J.D. Esary and H. Ziehms, "Reliability analysis of phased missions," in *Reliability and Fault Tree Analysis.* Philadelphia, PA:SIAM, 1975, pp. 213-236.

[33] R.A. Ballance and J.F. Meyer, "Functional dependence and its application to system evaluation," in *Proc. 1978 John Hopkins Conf. on Info. Sci. and Syst.,* Baltimore, MD, March 1978, pp. 280-285.

[34] A. Movaghar, "Performability modeling with stochastic activity networks," CRL-TR-8-85, Computing Research Laboratory, University of Michigan, Ann Arbor, Sept. 1985.

[35] J. F. Meyer, A. Movaghar and W. H. Sanders, "Stochastic activity networks: Structure, behavior, and application", in *Proc. Int. Workshop on Timed Petri Nets*, Torino, Italy, July 1986, pp. 106-115.

[36] S. Natkin, "Reseaux de Petri Stochastiques", Thèse de Docteur-Ingénieur, CNAM-PARIS, June 1980.

[37] M. K. Molloy, "Performance analysis using stochastic Petri nets", *IEEE Trans. Comput.*, vol. C-31, pp. 913-917, Sept. 1982.

[38] J.P. Behr, N. Dahmen, J. Muller, and H. Rodenbeck, "Graphical modeling with FOR-CASD," in *Computer Applications in Production and Engineering,* North-Holland Publishing Company, 1983, pp. 61-630.

[39] G. Chiola, "A software package of the analysis of generalized stochastic Petri net models," in *Proc. Int. Workshop on Timed Petri Nets,* Torino, Italy, July 1-3, 1985, pp. 136-143.

[40] A. Cumani, " ESP - A package of the evaluation of stochastic Petri nets with phase-type distributed transition times," in *Proc. Int. Workshop on Timed Petri Nets,* Torino, Italy, July 1-3, 1985, pp. 144-151.

[41] J. B. Dugan, K. S. Trivedi, R. M. Geist and V. F. Nicola, "Extended stochastic Petri nets: Applications and analysis," in *Performance 84*, North-Holland, 1984, pp. 507-519.

[42] H.P. Godberson and B.E. Meyer, "Function nets as a tool for the simulation of information systems," in *Proceedings of the Summer Computer Simulation Conference,* Seattle, WA, August 25-27, 1980.

[43] M. A. Marsan, G. Balbo and G. Conte, "A class of generalized stochastic Petri nets for performance evaluation of multiprocessor systems," *ACM Trans. on Computer Systems*, vol. 2, no. 2, pp. 93-122, May 1984.

[44] M.K. Molloy, "Discrete time stochastic Petri nets," *IEEE Transactions of Software Engineering*, vol. SE-11, no.4, pp. 417-423, April 1985.

[45] A. A. Törn, "Simulation nets, a simulation modeling and validation tool," *Simulation*, vol. 45, no. 2, pp. 71-75, Aug. 1985.

[46] R. M. Keller, "Vector replacement systems: A formalism for modeling asynchronous systems," *Computer Science Lab Rpt. No. 117*, Princeton Univ., Dec. 1972.

[47] R. M. Keller, "Formal verification of parallel programs", *CACM*, vol. 19, pp. 371-384, July 1976.

[48] W. H. Sanders and J. F. Meyer, "Performability evaluation of distributed systems using stochastic activity networks," *Proc. Int. Workshop on Petri Nets and Performance Models* (to be presented), Madison, WI, August 1987.

[49] W.H. Sanders and J.F. Meyer, "Variable driven construction methods for stochastic activity networks," *Proc. of the Second International Workshop on Applied Mathematics and Performance/Reliability Models of Computer/Communication Systems*, Rome, Italy, May 1987.

[50] D.G. Furchtgott, "Performability models and solutions," Tech. Report CRL-TR-8-84, University of Michigan, Ann Arbor, MI, Jan. 1984.

[51] E.F. Hitt, M.S. Bridgman and A.C. Robinson, "Comparative analysis of techniques for evaluating the effectiveness of aircraft computing systems," *NASA Contractor Report 159358*, Battelle Columbus Laboratories, Columbus, OH, April 1981.

[52] L.T. Wu, "Models for evaluating the performability of degradable computing systems," Tech. Report CRL-TR-7-82, University of Michigan, Ann Arbor, MI, June 1982.

[53] D.G. Furchtgott, J.F. Meyer, "Performability evaluation of fault-tolerant multiprocessors," in *1978 Government Micro-circuit Applications Conf. Digest of Papers*, Monterey, CA, Nov. 1978, pp. 362-365.

[54] J.F. Meyer, D.G. Furchtgott, L.T. Wu, "Performability evaluation of the SIFT computer," in *Proc. 1979 Int. Symp on Fault-Tolerant Computing*, Madison, WI, June 1979, pp. 43-50.

[55] J.F. Meyer, D.G. Furchtgott, L.T. Wu, "Performability evaluation of the SIFT computer," *IEEE Trans. Comput.*, vol. C-22, pp. 501-509, June 1980.

[56] J.F. Meyer and L.T. Wu, "Evaluation of computing systems using functionals of a Markov Process," in *Proc. 14th Annu. Hawaii Int. Conf. on Syst. Sci.*, Honolulu, HI, Jan. 1981, pp. 74-83.

[57] R. A. Howard, *Dynamic Probabilistic Systems, Vol. II: Semi-Markov and Decision Processes,* NY: Wiley, 1971.

[58] J.F. Meyer, "Closed-form solutions of performability," in *Proc. 1981 Int. Symp. on Fault-Tolerant Computing,* Portland, ME, June 1981, pp. 66-71.

[59] D.G. Furchtgott and J.F. Meyer, "A performability solution method for degradable, nonrepairable systems," *IEEE Trans. Comput.,* vol. C-33, June 1984.

[60] L.T. Wu, "Operational models for the evaluation of degradable computing systems," in *ACM/SIGMETRICS Conf. on Measurement and Modeling of Computer Systems,* Seattle, WA, Aug. 1982, pp. 179-185.

[61] A. Goyal and A.N. Tantawi, "Evaluation of performability for degradable computer systems," IBM Res. Report RC10529 (Revised), Dec. 1984.

[62] L. Donatiello and B.R. Iyer, "Analysis of a composite performance reliability measure for fault tolerant systems," IBM Res. Report RC10325, Jan. 1984.

[63] B. R. Iyer, L. Donatiello and P. Heidelberger, "Analysis of performability for stochastic models of fault-tolerant systems," *IEEE Trans. on Comp.,* vol. C-35, no. 10, pp. 902-907, Oct. 1986.

[64] V.G. Kulkarni, V.F. Nicola, R.M. Smith, and K.S. Trivedi, "Numerical evaluation of performability measures and job completion time in repairable fault-tolerant systems " in *Proc. of the 16th Int. symp. on Fault-Tolerant Computing,* Vienna, Austria, July 1986, pp. 252-257.

[65] B. Ciciani and V. Grassi, "Performability Evaluation of Fault-Tolerant Satellite Systems," in *IEEE Transactions on Communications,* April 1987.

[66] E. Cinlar, *Introduction to Stochastic Processes.* Englewood Cliffs, N.J.: Prentice-Hall, 1975.

[67] A.M. Law, and W.D. Kelton, *Simulation modeling and analysis.* NY:McGraw-Hill, 1982.

[68] S.S. Lavenberg, *Computer Performance Modeling Handbook.* New York, NY: Academic Press, 1983.

[69] B.P. Zeigler, *Theory of Modelling and Simulation.* NY: Wiley, 1976.

[70] G.H. Golub, "Matrix Computiations." Baltimore, MD: John Hopkins University Press, 1983.

[71] W. H. Sanders and J. F. Meyer, "METASAN: A performability evaluation tool based on stochastic activity networks," in *Proc. ACM-IEEE Comp. Soc. 1986 Fall Joint Comp. Conf.,* Dallas, TX, Nov. 1986.

[72] D. Gross and D.R. Miller, "The randomization technique as a modeling tool and solution procedure for transient Markov processes," *Operations Research,* vol. 32, no. 2, pp. 343-361, March-April 1984.

[73] D.R. Miller, "Reliability calculation using randomization for Markovian fault-tolerant computing systems," in *Proc. 1983 Int. Symp. Fault-Tolerant Computing,* Milano, Italy, June 1983, pp. 284-289.

TRAFFIC ENGINEERING for ISDN Design and Planning
M. Bonatti and M. Decina (Editors)
Elsevier Science Publishers B.V. (North-Holland)
© IAC, 1988

ISDN SYSTEMS – MODELING AND ANALYSIS

(Chairman Introduction on the Morning Session on Systems)

Harry Heffes

AT&T Bell Labs, USA

Teletraffic engineers and researchers are faced with increasing
challenges in modeling and analyzing ISDN systems, where questions
relating to the performance of access, network and switch
architectures need to be addressed. Complicating the task is the
ISDN traffic environment which is characterized by a large diversity
of call types with uncertainties in their associated traffic
characteristics and resource requirements. The traffic environment
is further influenced by the network and switch control
architectures (e.g. congestion and flow control) which need to be
taken into account when evaluating system performance. This
sometimes requires models which yield transient behavior of the
congestion control response. In some cases, evaluating, either
analytically or even from simulations, system performance measures
of interest is a difficult task. For example, in broadband systems,
where extremely low probability tails of end-to-end delay
distributions may be of interest, accurate models are needed for
performance prediction.

The papers presented in the morning session on systems address some
of the above issues, while other issues, e.g., control issues, are
more directly addressed in the afternoon session. Specifically the
morning session consists of three invited papers dealing with
diverse communication issues such as: communication architectures
for parallel computers, performance of the basic rate ISDN D-channel
offered a diversity of traffic types, and modelling of an
experimental integrated broadband communication network.

The first paper is a tutorial, by C. Stanfill of Thinking Machines
Corporation, on the communication architecture in the Connection
Machine ^{TM} System. Before getting to the specifics of the
Connection Machine System, a parallel computer with over 65,000
processors, various types of communication patterns, of algorithms
and program behavior characteristics are illustrated. For example,
communication patterns such as localized patterns, arising in
computer vision (e.g., line detectors), and fan-in fan-out patterns,
which need to be supported by the architecture, are discussed. In
addition, the impact of program behavior characteristics, such as
the degree of coupling of activities on the various processors, on
the communication need (e.g., bursty communication needs arising
from a tightly coupled application) is discussed. After reviewing
various interconnect topologies (e.g., busses, crossbars, Clos
networks, rings, fat trees, omega networks, hypercubes) and their
asymptotic behaviour with respect to the number of processors, some
specifics of the Connection Machine System (e.g., hypercube
architecture, routing, buffering, etc.) are given.
Non-communication-related programming issues and real-time control
issues are not presented in the paper. In the discussion, issues
such as real-time control, networking, multitasking and reliability

are addressed.

The second paper, by J. Seraj of Ericsson Telecom, on the impact of service mixtures on the ISDN D-channel performance, presents a simulation study of the basic access D-channel, offered a wide variety of traffic types resulting from a wide variety of services and subscriber models. Based on a simulation study, which included user-to-user traffic and various types of low priority data traffic, it is concluded that for a properly controlled network, signalling delays were acceptable. Delays experienced by various categories of low priority data traffic are also presented. The results do not include the effects of software processing times. The importance of including processing times when analyzing signaling delays is addressed in the comments by P.J. Kuehn, as well as in the paper by R.A. Skoog presented in the afternoon session on Systems. In addition, R.A. Skoog concludes that there is ample D-channel capacity, for both the basic and primary rate access, to handle call setups for B-channels and to carry significant amounts of user-to-user information, without appreciable signaling delays.

The third paper by P. Boyer, et. al. of CNET, read by J.R. Louvion, presents queueing models for various aspects of an experimental integrated broadband communication network, called PRELUDE, which uses the Asynchronous Time-Division (ATD) transfer technique. The models are intended to address the problems of dimensioning the switch control queues and depacketizer queues, as well as the engineering of the depacketizer delay parameters (so-called extra waiting times) to avoid depacketizer starvation. The last item requires an analysis for the end-to-end delay distribution. Using a 30-node asynchronous circuit model and simplifying independence assumptions, estimates of the required depacketizer delay parameters, as well as queue capacities are obtained. Many of the questions posed to the authors related to the accuracy of the simplifying assumptions. Control issues, such as congestion control, are not addressed and are considered to be off-line functions.

TRAFFIC ENGINEERING for ISDN Design and Planning
M. Bonatti and M. Decina (Editors)
Elsevier Science Publishers B.V. (North-Holland)
© IAC, 1988

Communications Architecture in the Connection Machine™ System

Craig Stanfill

Thinking Machines Corporation
245 First Street
Cambridge, Massachusetts, 01242
USA

To build computers which are fundamentally more powerful than those currently available, it is necessary to build systems incorporating large numbers of processors. At this point, communications architecture becomes the dominant problem facing the machine designer, for if the processors cannot communicate they cannot cooperate in solving a problem. Many different architectures have been proposed, but most scale poorly, so that the number of processors they can support is limited either by interconnect bandwidth or by escalating hardware costs. Other architectures scale well, but are limited to specialized applications. However, the family of architectures including omega networks, hypercubes, and fat–trees scales well both in terms of hardware required and in terms of communications time. One such architecture, the hypercube, was chosen as the basis of a new parallel computer, the Connection Machine System.

Main Statement Communications architecture is a dominant issue in computer architecture.

1. Computer Architecture as Communications Architecture

The recent revolution in micro–electronics has opened up an opportunity to build computers which are many times more powerful than their predecessors. By linking together tens of thousands of inexpensive microprocessors, it is possible to build machines which can perform over 10^9 operations per second, compared with the 10^7 which is typical of large uniprocessor machines. The key to realizing this potential lies in building a communication system which allows information to be transferred from one processor to another. For this reason, communications architecture has become an inseparable part of computer architecture.

When electronic computers were developed in the 40's and 50's, the bulk of the system cost was in the central processing unit and primary storage. The transfer of information between the two was accomplished by running a modest number of wires (the *memory bus*) from one part of the machine to another. In each computational cycle, the processor may read a value from memory or write a value to memory. This is the well known von Neumann architecture.

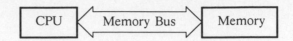

The von Neumann Architecture

When trying to build more powerful computers, the simple memory bus becomes a fundamental limitation. Suppose the single CPU in the von Neumann machine is replaced with four CPUs:

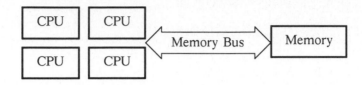

A Four–Processor von Neumann Machine

The resulting four-processor machine is fundamentally no more powerful than the single-processor machine because, although the processing component of the system is now four times more powerful, the communications component has not changed. A possible remedy to this problem is using four busses and four memories.

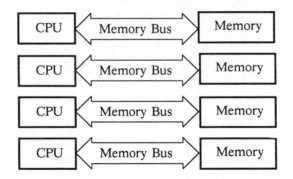

Adding Busses and Memories

This design has four times the computational power of the original von Neumann machine, but is no longer a single machine. In order to cooperate in performing a computation, the CPUs must be able to communicate not only with their own memories but among themselves. When such a communication system has been added, the result is no longer a von Neumann machine, but something completely new: a parallel computer. The architecture of communications systems is therefore an important issue in the design of parallel computers.

2. Requirements for a Communications Architecture

Instantaneous communications with infinite bandwidth among arbitrary sets of processors is obviously desirable and, just as obviously, impossible. This section will discuss the key tradeoffs which must be made in the communications architecture and how various compromises are likely to affect overall system utility. This discussion will be based on work by Hillis [1].

2.1. Communication Patterns

The first step is to characterize the communication patterns of the algorithms to be run on a parallel computer. Relevant features include locality, regularity, fan in, and fan out. Note that this discussion pertains to patterns of data movement for abstract algorithms, and not to any particular communication architecture. Any of the algorithms discussed below could be run on a serial von Neumann computer, or on a variety of parallel machines.

Many algorithms have highly localized communication patterns: if the problem is embedded in a two- or three-dimensional grid, then a given computation will only need to access data in a small region of the grid. Algorithms for computer vision, such as line detectors, are particularly likely to exhibit this sort of behavior. For example, if an image is represented as a grid of dots (pixels), lines may be detected by finding all dark pixels which have exactly two dark neighbors.

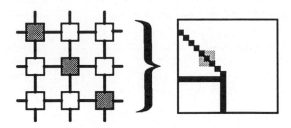

Local Communications on a Grid

Many algorithms generate very regular communication patterns, even if that communication is not strictly local. A good example is an algorithm which finds the total of a set of numbers represented as a binary tree. In this algorithm, there are two types of structures: *leaves,* which contain numbers, and *nodes,* which can refer to either two leaves or to two other nodes. To total up the values of the leaves, the nodes of the tree repeatedly ask each of their two children for their total, until the process terminates at the root of the tree.

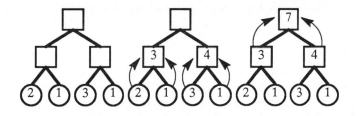

Regular Communications

In the general case, an algorithm may exhibit neither local nor regular communication patterns. For example, the components making up a silicon chip can be connected in an arbitrary pattern. To simulate the behavior of such a chip, a computer must allow information such as voltage and current to be moved around in arbitrary patterns. The difficulty of implementing a communications subsystem which can handle these arbitrary patterns is the primary reason why the widespread use of parallel computers has been slow in coming.

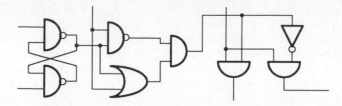

A Problem with Arbitrary Connectivity

Communications patterns can also differ in the number of destinations to receive a given message (fan–out) and the number of destinations attempting to send a message the same place (fan–in). The simplest case is when both fan–in and fan–out are 1 (i.e. one–to–one). The most difficult case is when fan–in and fan–out are both high (i.e. each sender is broadcasting to many destinations, and each receiver gets many incoming messages. An example of this is a neural network simulation, where an individual neuron has a large number (several hunderds) of inputs and outputs.

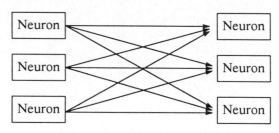

Combined Fan–in and Fan–out

In summary, algorithms can be characterized by their communications pattern. Some algorithms use only local communications, while other communicate in very regular patterns. In many cases, however, an algorithm will require the unrestricted flow of information between different structures taking part in the computation. Further complicating the situation, communications are not always one–to–one; there are many cases where the pattern is many–to–one (fan–out), one–to–many (fan–in), or even many–to–many (combined fan–in and fan–out). If the communications architecture of a parallel computer does not efficiently support all these modes of communication, the system's usefulness may be sharply limited.

2.2. Program Behavior

A single communications task is not an isolated episode, but part of a larger computation. The way in which these tasks are linked together into programs affects the load which is placed on the communications subsystem. One variable is the degree of coupling and sparseness: the uniformity of the communications needs throughout the system, and the proportion of the processors needing communications services at any moment. A second variable is the size of the packets which need to be moved around, whether they are short messages or sustained bursts of information. Finally, the degree to which the communications pattern is dynamic affects system performance; if a pattern remains uniform throughout a long computation, then the cost of an expensive setup phase may have negligible effect overall, whereas with a highly dynamic pattern setup costs may dominate the computation.

One important aspect of a parallel computation is the degree to which the actions taking place in the various processors is coupled. In a tightly coupled computation, all processors will be performing the same action at the same time. Periods of high communications activity will alternate with periods when the communications system is inactive. Furthermore, no processor will be able to proceed until every message in the communications pattern has reached its destination. In this situation the time required to perform a communications task, from start to finish, is the primary measure of system performance. In a loosely coupled system, the various processors will be performing dissimilar activities, so that communication and computation will overlap. Here the most relevant measure of system performance is the total effective bandwidth of the system.

Compute	Communicate		Compute
Compute	Communicate		Compute
Compute	Communicate		Compute
Compute	Communicate		Compute

Compute	Communicate		Compute
Communicate		Compute	
Compute	Communicate		
Communicate	Compute		Compute

Tight vs Loose Coupling

Another important aspect of a computation is sparseness: the proportion of processors trying to communicate at a given time. A communications system which is adequate when only 10% of the processors are trying to communicate may be woefully inadequate when the load approaches 100%; if a communications system is not carefully designed, putting too many messages into it at once may cause a traffic jam to develop, so that the movement of information comes nearly to a halt.

A third important characteristic of a computation is the size of the information packets being exchanged. If packets are large, then it is sensible to establish a complete path from sender to receiver before transmitting the data. The machine would then have a *circuit switching* architecture. However, if the packets are small, then it is sensible to send the data in a series of short jumps, buffering it at intermediate points. This yields a *packet switching* scheme. Using a circuit switching system with short messages may be inefficient because bandwidth may be wasted while waiting to establish the circuit. On the other hand, using packet switching with long messages may result in inefficiency if the messages are longer than the size of the intermediate buffers, which would necessitate breaking the message into several smaller units.

Finally, there is a distinction between a static communication pattern and a dynamic one. Establishing a communication pattern may involve significant setup time. If the pattern is unchanging, then this setup time does not matter very much. If, on the other hand, the pattern changes from one communications phase to the next, then setup time becomes a significant issue.

In short, the behavior of a program over time significantly affects the performance of the communications system of a parallel computer. If the various computations are strongly coupled, then the time to completion for a communications pattern (rather than bandwidth) is the best measure of performance. If every processor tries to communicate simultaneously, there is a danger of a traffic jam. If the size of the packets is small, then a circuit switching network may suffer from excessive overhead in establishing connections. Finally, if the communication pattern is highly dynamic, then a system requiring a high setup cost will be inefficient.

3. Communications Systems

Over the years, many different ways of combining processors, memories, and communications systems have been suggested or tried. Some methods work quite well for modest numbers of processors, but become impractical as the number of processors climbs into the thousands. This section will discuss some of these methods and point out their relative strengths and weaknesses. Of particular interest is how the cost building the system and the time needed to deliver a set of messages grows as the number of processors (N) increases.

This discussion is based on work by Hillis [1]. For a review of communications topologies, see Broomel and Heath [2], Thompson [3], or Benes [4]. For a taxonomy of parallel architectures, see Schwartz [5]

3.1. Shared vs Local Memory

There are two general ways of using a communications system in a parallel computer. The first is to interpose it between the CPU and the memories. In this case, the computer's memory will accessible to all processors, and the system will have a *shared memory* architecture.

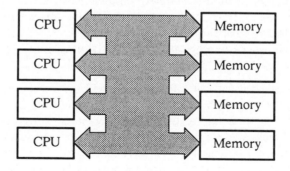

A Shared Memory Computer

It is also possible to use a communications system for direct communications between CPUs, yielding a *local memory* architecture. The main difference between the two styles of machine is that in a shared memory computer, data flows in only one direction during one communications activity (from the CPU to the memory, or vice–versa), while in a local memory computer data may enter or exit the communications system through any port.

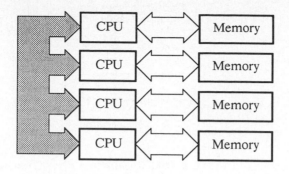

A Local Memory Computer

3.2. Shared Busses

One simple communications architecture is a single communications bus which is shared by all processors. This scheme suffers from several major problems. First, the bandwidth of the bus limits the total communications activity of the system. One way of compensating for this is by increasing the bandwidth of the bus. If the size of the packets is large (e.g. several hundred bits), then this can be done by making the bus wider. Another strategy is to use a higher level of technology in the bus than in the processors; it might then be possible to couple processors with a cycle time of 100 nanoseconds with a bus having a cycle time of 10 nanoseconds. This strategy suffers because the cost of building faster and faster busses escalates out of control; and in any event there is a limit to how fast a bus may be built. A second limitation with a shared bus is the time needed to arbitrate access to the bus; the speed of light places fundamental limits on how quickly ownership of the bus can be changed. A third limitation stems from the electrical fan-out of the bus; as the number of processors tapping into the bus increases, difficulties arise in supplying sufficient energy to drive all the taps.

In summary, a shared bus limits the total amount of information that can be exchanged (due to bandwidth restrictions) as well as the total number of messages that can be exchanged (due to arbitration restrictions). This limits the usefulness of shared busses to architectures with relatively small numbers of processors.

For a discussion of a bus structured machines, see Davidson [6] (AMP-1*).

3.3. Crossbars

The simplest way of constructing a communications system is to connect every node to every other node, producing what is called a crossbar switch. A crossbar has certain advantages: communications time is independent of the number of processors, and it does not matter how many processors are simultaneously trying to communicate. In addition, if several connections out of a node are simultaneously active, then it is possible to implement fan-out in an efficient manner (this gives no help, however, in handling fan-in). The disadvantage of a crossbar is that the number of connections increases as the square of the number of processors: a 1000 processor machine would need 1,000,000 connections. This makes crossbars useful only for relatively small machines (up to a hundred processors or so). For a discussion of some crossbar machines, see Buehrer [7] (EMPRESS) or Trujillos [8] (Multimicrocomputer).

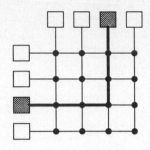

A 4x4 Crossbar

3.4. Clos Networks

If connections are one–to–one, then multi–layer networks with many of the same properties as a crossbar can be constructed with far fewer switches. These are called *Clos* networks. For example, a 5 layer Clos network with 1000 inputs requires only 146,300 switches, as opposed to 1,000,000 for a full crossbar. Nevertheless, costs still grow so fast as to preclude their use in machines with large numbers of processors. Clos networks are described by Benes [4]

3.5. Rings

A ring network consists of a set of communications nodes arranged in a circle. At regular intervals, each node transmits information to the node to its right, and receives information from the node to its left. The nodes then examine the messages, and remove those which have reached their destination. Rings suffer from the same bandwidth limitations as shared busses, as a finite amount of information that can be moved from one station to the next on any cycle. Arbitration and electrical fan–out problems do not arise, but in their place are latency problems: the time needed to deliver a message is proportional to the number of nodes in the network. Again, this architecture is not feasible for large numbers of processors. For a discussion of the ZMOB, a 256 processor machine using a ring network, see Rieger [9].

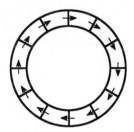

A 12 node Ring Network

3.6. Grids

It is also possible to structure a machine as a two dimensional grid. Such a machine has several advantages. First, it is easily laid out on two dimensional boards and chips. Second, it allows very fast local communications. Third, it scales indefinitely: it is practical to build a grid machine of nearly unlimited size. The disadvantage of a grid structure is that communications between non–adjacent processors may have to pass through a large number of intermediate processors; this limits the applicability of grid machines to algorithms using only local communications. For a discussion some actual grid machines, see Slotnick [10] (ILLIAC IV), Batcher [11] (STARAN) or Batcher [12] (MPP).

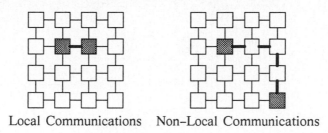

Local Communications   Non–Local Communications

A 16 Processor Grid

3.7. Trees

The simplest topology that supports non–local communications for machines of arbitrary size is the tree. Trees have the advantage that for a machine with N processors, the distance between two nodes is never more than $\log_2 N$, and the cost grows linearly in N. In addition, it supports some of the most common regular communications patterns quite well. The disadvantage is that the root of the tree is a communications bottleneck. Furthermore, in the worst case every message in the system must pass through the root, and for an average random pattern half the messages will pass through it. This limits the applicability of tree machines to algorithms with one of a few regular communications patterns. For discussions of tree machines, see Shaw [13] (NON–VON) or Stolfo [14] (DADO).

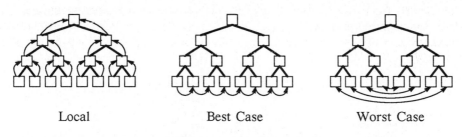

Local   Best Case   Worst Case

15 Node Binary Tree

3.8. Fat Trees

The problem of root congestion in tree machines may be remedied by adding extra communications paths at the higher levels of the tree. For example, the first and second levels might be connected by single wires, the second and third levels by double wires, the third and fourth by quadruple wires, and so forth. All computation takes place at the leaves of the tree. The interior nodes switch signals between the various channels connecting to it. One advantage of fat trees is that, by varying the number of wires at each level, a family of architectures suitable for a variety of different applications can be generated. If the total number of wires at each level is kept constant (i.e. level N has 2^N wires), then the total cost of the network will be $N \log_2 N$, and the average time for a random one–to–one communications pattern will be $\log_2 N$. Both these numbers grow slowly enough to allow the construction of fat–tree machines with tens of thousands, even millions, of processing elements. Leiserson [15] proves that fat trees are universal, in the sense that a fat tree can simulate any physically buildable machine with no more than a $\log_2 N$ factor slowdown.

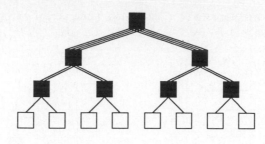

A Fat Tree

3.9. Omega Networks

An omega network (or shuffle exchange or perfect shuffle) is a multi-layer switching network such that layer k allows signals to either propagate straight through or to be swapped with a signal 2^k wires away. As was the case with fat trees, the hardware cost grows as $N \log_2 N$ in the number of processors, and the communications time is $\log^2 N$. One property of the omega network is that it has a bipartite topology: messages go from a set of input ports to a disjoint set of output ports. This makes butterflies well suited to shared memory architectures, where memories may be placed at the bottom of the switch and processors at the top. Another feature of an omega network is that there is exactly one path between any input node and any output node. This simplifies the routing of messages through the network. There are, however, patterns where a traffic jam develops and routing takes much more time. One remedy to this problem is to send messages via a randomly chosen intermediate processor, converting the problem to one with two random routings. Another remedy is to add additional data paths to allow for alternative routes. For discussions of some machines using omega networks, see Bolt Beranek and Newman Inc. [16], Rettberg and Thomas [17] (Butterfly™), or Schwartz [18] (Ultracomputer). For a demonstration of the equivalence of many omega-like networks, see Parker [19] or Snir [20].

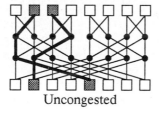
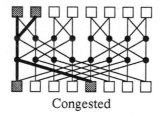

Uncongested   Congested

A 3-layer Omega Network

3.10. Hypercubes

A hypercube (or N-cube) is a topology in which each of 2^k nodes is connected to k other nodes (the details of how this connection takes place are easier illustrated, below, than described). As with an omega network, a machine with N processors requires on the order of $N \log_2 N$ components to construct, and has $\log^2 N$ communication time. Its other properties are somewhat different. First, it has a uniform topology, in that messages may be both received and sent by one node in a single cycle. For this reason, hypercubes are particularly useful in local memory machines. Second, there are many routes connecting any pair of nodes. This leads to added flexibility in avoiding congestion and traffic jams, provided the routing algorithm is able to take advantage of this added flexibility. It should be noted that in a hypercube, there are N wires coming out of each node. In order to completely use this available communications bandwidth, it is therefore desirable to put approximately N processors at each node. This also facilitates the use of the redundant data paths by allowing up to N messages to converge on a single node. For a discussion of a machines based on hypercubes, see Hillis [1] (Connection Machine^{TM} System).

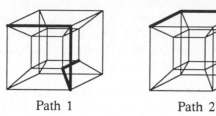

Path 1   Path 2

A 4–Cube, showing two independent paths

3.11. Summary

A parallel computer requires a communications network to move information between its processors. Some communications architectures, such as shared busses and ring networks, have limited bandwidth, placing a strict ceiling on the number of processors which they can support. Others, such as crossbars and Clos networks, have communication times which remains essentially constant as the size of the machine grows, but costs which grow so fast that they are economically infeasible for large numbers of processors. Grid and tree machines can be build to arbitrary sizes, but their topology limits the communications patterns they can efficiently execute to either local or certain regular patterns. Fat trees, butterflies, and hypercubes are a good compromise between escalating cost and deteriorating performance; their cost per processor grows as $N \log_2 N$ in the number of processors, and their communication time increases as $\log_2 N$. This allows fat–tree, omega network, and hypercube machines of arbitrary size to be constructed. The choice between these architectures is governed by engineering and board layout concerns (e.g. compactness, uniformity, and ease of wiring) which are beyond the scope of this paper.

4. Architecture of the Connection Machine^{TM} System

The previous section described the various interconnect topologies available to the computer architect. This section will describe how one such topology — the hypercube — was used as the basis of the Connection Machine^{TM} System. The explanation will include a discussion of factors governing the construction of the nodes, the routing of messages, and some problems associated with fan–in and fan–out. Programming issues will not be discussed except as they impact on communications issues.

4.1. Communications Architecture

The primary design constraint on the Connection Machine System was that it have several orders of magnitude more computational power than a conventional machine. This immediately ruled out any sort of von Neumann machine, as well as parallel architectures (such as shared bus, ring, and cross bar) which are infeasible for large numbers of processors. An additional constraint was that it handle non–local and non–regular communications patterns. This ruled out grid and tree machines, leaving the choice between omega networks and hypercubes (design of the Connection Machine predates Leiserson's work on fat trees). Eventually, the hypercube was chosen.

A full explanation of why the hypercube was chosen over the omega network is beyond the scope of this discussion, but a few notes are in order. First, a hypercube has redundant data paths. This, it was felt, would reduce delays in routing due to contention for wires. Second, a hypercube has only computational nodes, rather than a mixture of computational and switching nodes; this reduces the number of different component types In addition, it makes the computational facilities of the individual processors available to assist in the routing of messages. Finally, every node in a hypercube is topologically equivalent; this means that only one type of node, and one type of board to carry those nodes, is ever needed. Based on economic and engineering limits, a hypercube with 4096 (2^{12}) nodes was chosen.

There are advantages to placing more than one processor at each node of a hypercube. First, for the regular patterns alluded to above, it is optimal to have one processor attached to each wire of a node. Second, for non-regular patterns, doubling the number of processors at each node causes the communications time to increase by a factor of less than two. This effect is due to the efficient utilization of the interconnecting wires. A hypercube has sufficient bandwidth to route messages in $\log_2 N$ time. However, because it is impossible to keep all wires busy all the time, the actual communication time is $\log^2 N$. Putting several processors at each wire and queuing messages waiting to use the wire increases the utilization of the system's raw bandwidth. Partly on the basis of these considerations, each node was given 16 processors. This gives a total of 65,536 (2^{16}) processors.

4.2. The Router

Each node is contained in a single chip, which contains the 16 processors, the hypercube node, and connections to 12 wires. The processors' local memory is located elsewhere. The router performs 5 functions: *injecting*, *routing*, *buffering*, *referring*, and *delivering*. Injecting is removing a message from a processor and placing it in the hypercube network. Routing is switching a message to a wire. Buffering is temporarily storing a message when a wire is being used. Referring is sending a message over a random wire when buffer space is exhausted. Delivering is removing a message which has reached its destination out of·the hypercube system and placing it in a processor.

It is possible to assign binary numbers to the node of a hypercube in such a way that the numbers assigned to two nodes differ by exactly one bit if and only if they are connected by an edge. Furthermore, every dimension of the hypercube corresponds to a bit position in the address. In the figure below, the left–right dimension corresponds to the rightmost bit, the in–out dimension corresponds to the middle bit, and the up–down dimension corresponds to the leftmost bit. This yields the routing algorithm for the Connection Machine System. First, for every message, find the *relative address* by taking the exclusive–OR of the addresses of the sending and receiving processors. Second, send the message over *any* unused wire corresponding to a 1 in the relative address. If no such wire can be found, put the message in a buffer. If no buffer is available, send the message over any free wire. Third, whenever a message crosses a wire, the corresponding bit in the relative address is inverted. Finally, when the relative address contains all 0's, the message has reached its destination.

```
        110        111
  100      101
    |        |       |
    |    010     011
  000        001
```

Numbering of Nodes on a 3–Cube

This scheme works quite well for one–to–one communications patterns, so that a pattern of 65,536 32–bit messages can be routed in 800 microseconds. A modification of this scheme suggested by Blelloch [21] allows patterns with fan–in and fan–out to be routed in approximately twice the basic message cycle time. For fan–out, this is done by using a fast ($\log_2 N$ time) algorithm to make an appropriate number of copies of each message, then using the routing algorithm shown above the deliver the copies. For fan–in, the above process is inverted. The two may be used together to implement combined fan–in and fan–out. The only disadvantage of Blelloch's methods is that they require a substantial amount of time (16 milliseconds) to set up, and are thus poorly suited to applications with highly dynamic communications patterns having fan–in or fan–out. The implications of these techniques have been investigated by Hillis and Steele [22].

5. Summary

In summary, computer architecture has become, in large measure, communications architecture. This is because the only way to build computers which are fundamentally more powerful than those currently available is to use thousands or tens of thousands of processing elements. At this point, communications rather than computation becomes the primary preoccupation of the computer architect. Many communications schemes have been suggested. Some of these are unsuitable for large architectures, either because their bandwidth does not increase quickly enough or because their cost escalates too quickly. Other communications schemes are indefinitely scalable, but are limited to specialized applications by restrictions on the sorts of message patterns they can support. Finally, there is a group of schemes, including fat trees, omega networks, and hypercubes, that are indefinitely scalable, both in terms of their cost and the time needed to deliver a set of messages.

One such scheme, the hypercube, was chosen as the basis of the Connection Machine System. The communications system it contains supports 65,536 processors, can transmit 65,536 messages in 800 microseconds, and can be adapted to patterns with high degrees of fan–in and fan–out. The result is the state–of–the–art in computer communications architecture.

References

[1]   Hillis, D., *The Connection Machine*, (MIT Press, Cambridge Massachusetts, 1986).

[2]   Broomel, G., and Heath, J.R., "Classification Categories and Historical Development of Circuit Switching Topologies," *Computing Surveys* 15 (2) (1983) pp 95–133.

[3]   Thompson, C., "Generalized Connection Networks for Parallel Processor Intercommunication," *IEEE transactions on Computers*, C–27 (12) (1978).

[4] Benes, V. E., *Mathematical Theory of Connecting Networks and Telephone Traffic* (Academic Press, 1965).

[5] Schwartz, J., "A Taxonomic Table of Parallel Computers, Based on 55 Designs," Courant Institute, New York University (1983).

[6] Davidson, E., "A Multiple Stream Microprocessor Prototype System: AMP–1*," Coordinated Science Laboratory, University of Illinois, Urbana, IL, and *IEEE* (1980).

[7] Buehrer, R. E., et al, "The ETH–Multiprocessor EMPRESS: A Dynamically Configurable MIMD System," *IEEE Transactions on Computers* C–31 (11) (1982) pp 1035–1044.

[8] Trujillo, V., "System Architecture of a Reconfigurable Multimicroprocessor Research System," *1982 International Conference on Parallel Processing* (1982).

[9] Rieger, C., "ZMOB: A Mob of 256 Cooperative Z80A–Based Microcomputers," Computer Science Tech. Rep. Series TR–852, University of Maryland, College Park, MD, (1979).

[10] Slotnick, D. L, et al., "The ILLIAC IV Computer," *IEEE Transactions on Computers* C–17 (8) (1978) pp 746–757.

[11] Batcher, K. E., "STARAN Parallel Processor System Hardware," *AFIPS Conf. Proc.* 43 (1974) pp 405–410.

[12] Batcher, K. E., "Design of a Massively Parallel Processor," *IEEE Transactions on Computers, C–29* (9) (1980).

[13] Shaw, D.E., "The NON–VON Supercomputer," Department of Computer Science, Columbia University (1982).

[14] Stolfo, S., and Shaw, D., "DADO: A Tree–Structured Machine Architecture for Production Systems," Department of Computer Science, Columbia University (1982).

[15] Leiserson, C.E., "FAT–TREES: Universal Networks for Hardware–Efficient Supercomputing," *1985 International Conference on Parallel Processing,* IEEE Computer Society (August 1985).

[16] Bolt Beranek and Newman Inc., "Development of a Butterfly Multiprocessor Test Bed," Report 5872, Quarterly Technical Report No. 1 (1985).

[17] Rettberg, R., and Thomas, R., "Contention Is No Obstacle to Shared–Memory Multiprocessing," *Communications of the ACM,* 9 (12) (December 1986) pp 1202–1212.

[18] Schwartz, J., "Ultracomputers," *ACM Transactions on Programming Languages and Systems* 2 (4) (1980) pp 484–521.

[19] Parker, D., "Notes on Shuffle/Exchange–Type Switching Networks," *IEEE Transactions on Computers* C–29 (3) (1980) pp 213–222.

[20] Snir, M., "Comments on Lens and Hypertrees — or the Perfect–Shuffle Again," Ultracomputer Note 38, Computer Science Department, New York University (1982).

[21] Blelloch, G., "Parallel prefix versus concurrent memory access," Technical Report, Thinking Machines Corporation, Cambridge MA (June 1986).

[22] Hillis, D., and Steele, G., "Data Parallel Algorithms," *Communications of the ACM,* 29 (12) (December 1986) pp 1170–1183.

TRAFFIC ENGINEERING for ISDN Design and Planning
M. Bonatti and M. Decina (Editors)
Elsevier Science Publishers B.V. (North-Holland)
© IAC, 1988

367

The Impact of Service Mixtures on the ISDN D-channel Performance

Jila Seraj

TELEFONAKTIEBOLAGET LM ERICSSON, Ericsson Telecom
S-126 25 STOCKHOLM, Sweden
Telex: 14910 ERICS, Telephone: +46 8 7194371

Abstract

In this paper a study of the Basic Access D-channel is presented. The study is based on computer simulations and results in recommendations concerning the appropriate services to be carried on the D-channel. Memory requirements in the ET (Exchange Terminal) for a number of subscribers and concentration of the data flow on the D-channels onto a 64 kb/s data link are also disscussed.

Main Statement   The signalling delay caused by the ISDN Basic access D-channel capacity is acceptable if proper flow control is applied.

1 Introduction

The demand for telecommunications services has increased dramatically during the last decade, and forecasts show the same tendency in a near future. The ISDN Access will be used for these services. This necessitates an investigation to iden- tify the possible capacity bottlenecks for the subscriber access.

An ISDN subscriber will probably try to utilize the offered access capacity as much as possible, and at the same time expects better quality of service than in the pre-ISDN. To provide a good quality of service requires a well functioning signalling network which is both reliable and cause a minimum of delay.

Different subscriber access structures are defined by CCITT, but the author be- leives that the evolution of ISDN will begin with the introduction of the Basic Access (2B+D) and the primary rate access (30B+D or 23B+D).

D-channel is primarily intended to carry signalling information for the B-chan- nels, but may also be used to carry teleaction informations and packet switched data. Thus the D-channel is a part of the signalling plane in ISDN and therefore its capability of carrying signalling information of great importance.

In this paper only the Basic Access D-channel is studied. In chapter 2 the Basic Access structure and signalling procedures are presented breifly. In chapter 3 a simulation study of the Basic Access D-channel is presented. Results are examined in detail in chapter 4.

2 The Basic Access

The ISDN Basic Access consists of two 64 kb/s B-channels and one 16 kb/s D-channel. Up to eight terminals could be connected to a Basic Access. The two B-channels may be used in both circuit switched and packet switched mode, but the D-channel uses a frame orineted layered protocol.

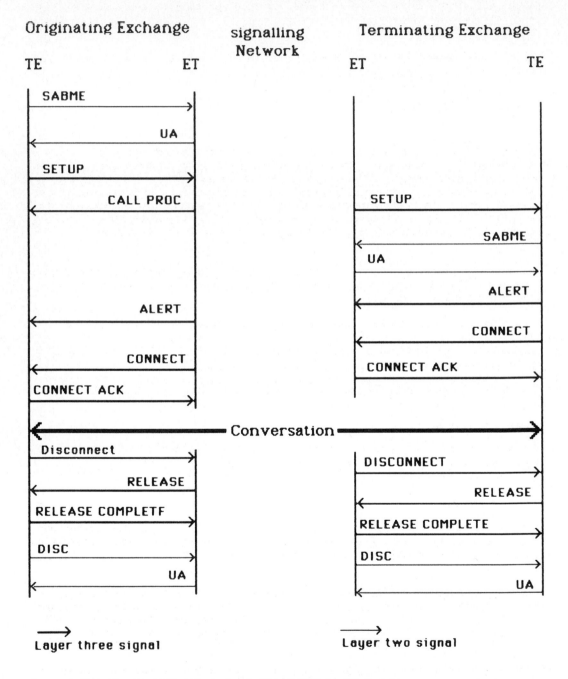

Figure 1 Signalling Procedure for a simple Circuit Switched Call.

There are two types of frames: signal frames and data frames. Signal frames have higher priority than data frames when accessing the D-channel, but they cannot interrupt an ongoing transmission of a data frame.

In the direction subscriber to exchange the Round Robin scheduling method is applied within each priority class, but in the other direction there is no such resource allocation method. The D-channel protocol provides a flow control based on gliding window (layer two function).

The maximum length of the information field within a D-channel frame is 260 octets

2.1   SIGNALLING PROCEDURES

To establish a call on the B- or D-channel, a virtual signalling connection on the D-channel is necessary (layer two procedures). The layer three signalling procedure begins when the layer two signalling connection is established. When a call is finished the virtual signalling connection on the D-channel will be released. Figure one gives an example of signalling procedure for a simple circuit switched call. The interested reader is encouraged to study the CCITT red book volume III for a complete list of signals and signalling procedures.

In addition to the ordinary circuit switched and packet switched data connections, an ISDN subscriber may send USER-TO-USER signals. There are three ways to send USER-TO-USER signals:

* As a part of layer three signals during a call setup or release procedures.

* By layer three USERINFO signals during the active state of a circuit switched connection.

* By an independent USER-TO-USER signalling connection.

3 Simulation Study

The aim of this simulation study is to analyse the D-channel capacity and to identify possible bottlenecks.

3.1   OBJECTIVES

This study has four objectives: to analyse signal delay, data delay, memory requirements and concentration of the D-channel data traffic on a 64 Kb/s common data link.

3.1.1   SIGNAL DELAY

The signalling delay requirements defined in Rec Q.514 by CCITT include rather complex signalling procedures on the D-channel (e g sending dial tone requires at least two signals in each direction), and processing in TE (Terminal Equipment), ET (Exchange Terminal) and the exchange itself. It is important to meet these requirements, and therefore we have assumed that not more than 1 % of the signals should wait longer than 50 ms for transmission on the D-channel.

3.1.2 DATA DELAY

Two major types of data services are recognizable: those with a person waiting
for the response and those without. If there is no person waiting, there is normally no reason for requiring a short response time. But if a person tries to
carry on a conversation, a response time delay longer than five seconds will
disturb him.

In this study we adapt a rule of thumb saying that the transmission delay of
question plus response packets should not be longer than 10 % of the total response time. Therefore, delays for a data service are accepted if the sum of
transmission time and waiting time to be transmitted is less than 500 ms in 99 %
of the cases.

3.2   ASSUMPTIONS

The following assumptions are made for this study:

3.2.1   CONFIGURATION

Figure 2 shows the configuration of the simulated system.

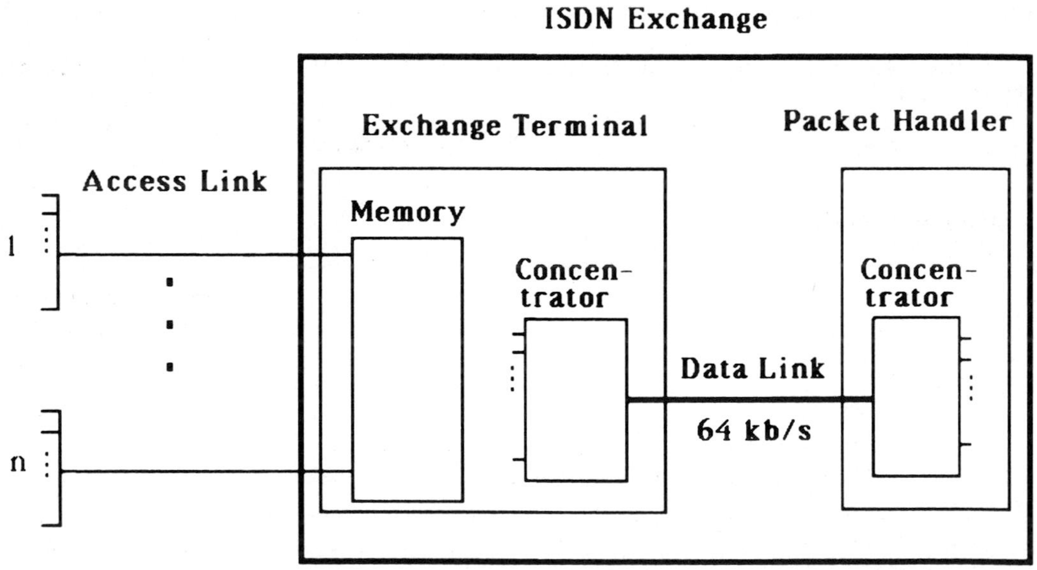

Figure 2 Configuration of the Simulated system.

* A number of ISDN Basic Accesses are connected to an ET.

* Frames to and from the D-channels are stored in a common memory.

* Only one TE answers an incoming call SETUP signal.

* Call control procedures on the D-channel follows the available CCITT recommendations when this study started.

* Window size for data frames is eight.

* Two cases of window sizes for signal frames are studied: window sizes one and eight.

* No signal has been longer than 130 octets in the simulations.

* Data packets on the D-channel are multiplexed to a common 64 Kb/s data link. It is assumed that each subscriber has a unique port in the multiplexor. Only one frame is transmitted from each port at a time (5) and then the multiplexor scans the next port (non-exhaustive cyclic protocol, in the sequel called Round Robin). The same is true of the opposite direction.

* No software processing time is assumed, neither in the ET nor in the TE.

* No fault situation is taken into account.

3.2.2   TRAFFIC MODEL

ISDN services can be roughly classified into the following types according to their traffic characteristics:

  Voice.
  Message transfer.
  Data transaction.
  Information retrieval.
  Interactive data dialog.
  File transfer.
  Teletex.
  Facsimile.

Telephones will be used in about the same way as today. The major difference will be the new facilities and functions added to the telephones and exchanges: automatic reattempt, waiting call etc. These features will result in a higher signalling volume than today. The access to two B-channels makes it possible to have two simultaneous telephone calls to/from an ISDN Basic Access.

Message transfer service employs USER-TO-USER signalling which carries messages between subscribers either in connection with a circuit switched call on a B-channel or independently. The message transfer service is attractive to subscribers and will probably be widely used (if not restricted by flow control or high price) and will replace some telephone calls and teletex messages.

The traffic values used in this study are based on measurements and forecasts (3, 4, 6) and the range of values used is presented in figure 3.

Service	Number of sessions per hour	Mean Batch length in octets		Mean number of batches per sessions
		TE -> ET	ET -> TE	
Voice	9-30			
Message Transfer	8-50	32-256	32-256	1
Data Trans-action	20-60	35	35	2
Information retreival	1.2-32	20-40	200-400	2-20
Interactive data	1.6	850	600	50
Teletex	1-5	500-10000	200-10000	1
File Transfer	1-2			

Figure 3 The Traffic Model.

3.2.3   SUBSCRIBER MODEL

To make a complete model of the traffic on the D-channel we have to know what services are used in the Basic Access and on which channel; in other words we must have a subscriber model.

A closer look at the forecasting reports (5,6,7) suggests 5 major categories of non-residential subscribers with service mixtures presented in figure 4.

The author does not claim that these five categories contain all possible subscriber categories or service mixtures but believes that the most utilized services and the most common telecommunication needs, in a not too far future, are taken into account.

The Swedish equivalent of these subscriber categories could for instance be a post office, an insurance company, a travel agency, a small business site, and a large business site respectively.

Cate-gory	Voice	Message transfer	Data trans-action	Informa-tion retrie-val	Inter-active Data Dialogue	Teletex	File transfer
1	9	8	60	1.2		3	1
		100	35	40		1000	
		100	35	400		1000	
		1	2	10		1	
2	30	8		32		4.8	1
		100		20		1500	
		100		400		1500	
		1		2		1	
3	15	20	20	21		5	
		256	35	20		500	
		256	35	200		200	
		1	2	5		1	
4	14	8		1.6	1.6	1.5	
		256		30	850	2400	
		256		200	600	2400	
		1		20	50	1	
5	17	8		1.6	1.6	1.5	2
		256		20	850	10 000	
		256		200	600	10 000	
		1		5	50	1	

Please read values at each box as

Number of busy hour call attempts
Mean batch length sent from TE
Mean batch length sent from ET
Number of batches per call

Figure 4 The Subscriber Model.

3.3   RESULTS

In the first five simulations all services except voice and file transfer uti-lized the D-channel. It was expected to be the worst case. Results from each simulation were compared with the delay requirements. If any simulation result did not fulfil the delay requirements, we tried to find out what factors caused the delay by changing traffic parameters and service mixtures of that category.

The most important function of the D-channel is to carry signalling information. Therefore we started by monitoring the signal delay for each category.

3.3.1   SIGNAL DELAY

Our simulations did not show considerable signal delay when window size one was applied. In the case of window size 8, excessive signal delay occurred for categories 3-5 (see figure 5). The D-channel load in the ET -> TE direction (see figure 6) was lower for category 3 than for catagory 2. Thus, differences in the D-channel load could not explain differences in the signal delay and further study seemed to be necessary.

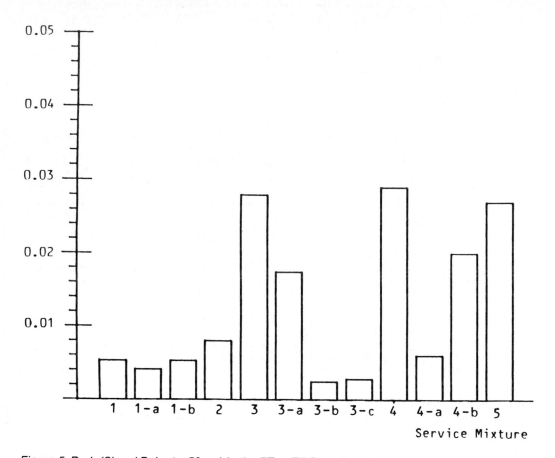

Figure 5 Prob (Signal Delay > 50 ms) in the ET → TE Direction. Window size = 8.

To analyse the reasons for the delay when using window size 8 the following experience was made. We defined a new service mixture, 3-a, which was identical with category 3 but with 50 message transfers per hour and 100 octets mean length equal to the mean length for categories 1 and 2 and containing the same amount of information as category 3. This change resulted in a shorter signal delay in the ET -> TE direction, but still not satisfactory.

To see whether it was the data traffic on the D-channel which caused this problem, service mixture 3-b was defined, being identical with category 3 but without message transfer. This service mixture resulted in a satisfactory signal delay, which shows that the data traffic on the D-channel alone does not cause excessive signal delay.

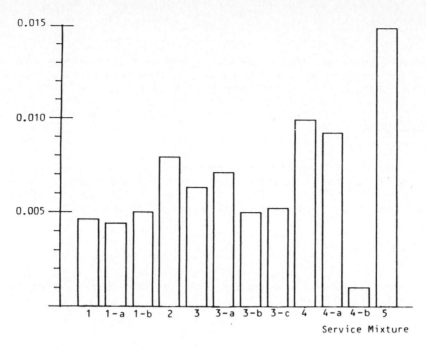

Figure 6 D-channel Load in the ET → TE Direction.

To see whether message transfer service could be added without resulting in long signal delays, service mixture 3-c was defined. It was identical with category 3 but with the mean message length reduced from 256 to 32 octets. This service mixture, too, resulted in acceptable signal delays.

These experiments indicate that the signal delay is more sensitive to message transfer service than to data services, and that both message length and the number of messages influence the signal delay.

It is interesting to point out that signal traffic was not disturbed at all in the TE -> ET direction. The reason is the Round Robin resource allocation method in the TE -> ET direction which does not allow any terminal to send more than one signal (or data) frame before giving all the other terminals a chance to send their signal (or data) frames. In the other direction, when window size 8 is applied, practically no flow control exists and therefore a signal has to wait for all other signals that have arrived before it.

These results are summarized in the following:

* When the D-channel is used for pure signalling, the signal delays are acceptable.

* Data traffic on the D-channel does not influence the signal delay in a dramatic way because data frames have lower priority than signal frames.

* An effective flow control in the ET -> TE direction is strongly recommended.

* In the absence of an appropriate flow control, message transfer service may cause considerable signal delays if the messages are long (longer than one frame) or numerous (more than 20 per hour).

3.3.2 DATA DELAY

The next step in our simulation study was to analyse the data delay. The window size for packet frames is assumed to be 8. Due to differences in the traffic characteristics, each service will be considered separately.

– DATA TRANSACTION

This service consists of two short messages (about 35 octets each) in either direction. None of our simulations has shown any considerable delay for this service, even when used quite often (60 calls per hour). This again indicates that very short frames do not experience long delays on the D-channel.

– INFORMATION RETRIEVAL

Data delay for this service was negligible in the TE -> ET direction; therefore no diagrams of these values are presented.

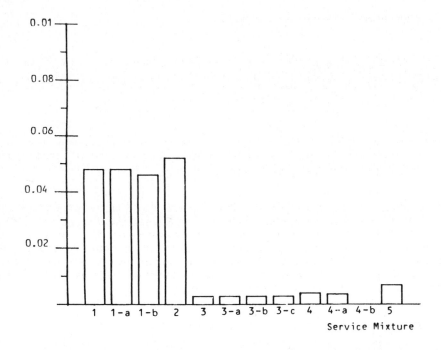

Figure 7 Prob (Data Delay > 500 ms) in the ET → TE direction, Infornmation Retreival Service.

In the ET -> TE direction, categories 3,4 and 5 do not show any problems while categories 1 and 2 do (see figure 7). A look at figure 6 does not suggest any strict relationship between the load on the D-channel and the delay experienced. To see whether the long teletex batches caused this problem, service mixture 1-a was defined which differs from category 1 only in having teletex on the B-channel. This resulted in slightly shorter delay values but still not satisfactory. Therefore service mixture 1-b was defined, almost identical with 1-a, but with the data transaction service using the B-channel. Delays were reduced but still not satisfactory. These experiments indicate that if the mean batch length is shorter than a D-channel frame the delays are acceptable but not otherwise. A long batch has longer transmission time and risks being interrupted by signal frames.

- INTERACTIVE DATA

Delay values were not satisfactory in any direction. The reason is that the transmission speed on the D-channel is not high enough for the batch lengths of this service.

- FILE TRANSFER and TELETEX

These services do not require an immediate response and therefore the delay is of little or no interest.

3.3.3   MEMORY REQUIREMENTS

The memory usage gives an indication of the processing need in the ET (to separate signal and data frames, protocol handling for layer 2 and 3 etc). Figures 8 and 9 show, for 30 Basic Accesses, the mean and max memory usage during the simulations in the absence of software processing delay.

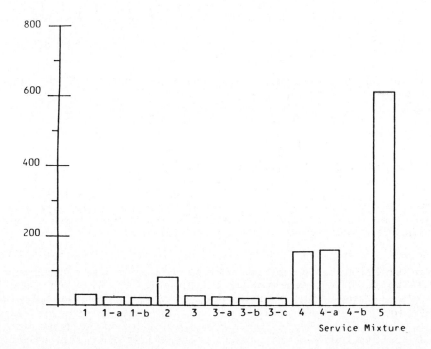

Figure 8 Mean Memory Usage in the Absence of Processing Delay. 30 Basic Accesses.

It follows easily that the memory usage is high when services with large data batches (1 Kbyte or larger) are included. This suggests that restrictions on the batch sizes sent over the D-channel should be applied.

It should be noticed that there is no linear relationship between the load on the D-channel and the memory usage. It seems that the batch sizes have a greater influence on the memory requirements.

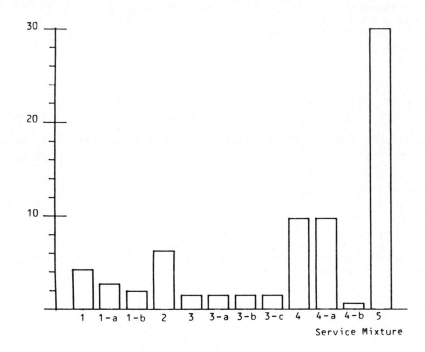

Figure 9 Max Memory Usage Measured During the Simulations in kbytes. 30 Basic Accesses. No Processing Delay.

3.3.4   CONCENTRATION of D-CHANNEL DATA TRAFFIC

When concentrating data taffic on a 64 kb/s common data link for a number of subscribers (see fig 2) one could expect that a high grade of concentration might cause long delays when accessing the common data link.

The number of Basic Accesses concentrated on the common data link is varied from 30 to 120. We accept delays caused by concentration on the common data link if the sum of all transmission times and waiting times to be transmitted does not exceed 500 ms in 99% of the cases.

For Data Transaction service no considerable delay is noted, which once more indicates the good performance of services with very short batches.

Interactive Data service was not interesting from this point of view because the delay experienced on the D-channel is not acceptable.

Information Retreival service has almost accptable delay for service mixture 3 for up to 120 Accesses (see figure 10).

The major difference between service mixture 3 and service mixtures 4 and 5 is the batch length of the services involved. This indicates once more the disadvantage of sending bulks of data on the D-channel. More investigations are required, however.

In a realistic situation, when processing times are added to the delays, the delay experienced by each service will increase steeper than shown in figure 10.

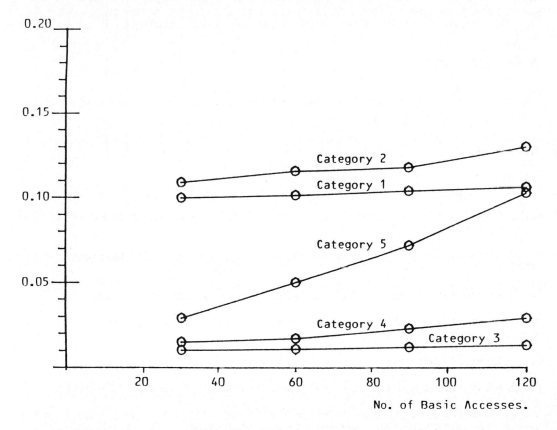

Figure 10 Prob (Data Delay from PH to TE > 500 ms). Information Retreival Service.

4 Conclusion

Results from this study indicate that:

* Signal delays are acceptable in the absence of message transfer service.

* In the absence of flow control the message transfer service may cause signal delays in the ET -> TE direction if this service is used frequently (more than 20 times per hour) or the message lengths are long (exceeding 100 octets on average), but the same is not true of the opposite direction. This difference is due to the Round Robin resource allocation.

* Data services with short batches (about one D-channel frame length) do not experience unacceptable delays.

* Data services with large batches are not suited for utilizing the D-channel, for three reasons:

  - Because they experience long delays.
  - Because the processing need in the ET will increase.
  - Because they will delay others when concentrating on a common data link.

It should be noted that these results are valid under assumptions made in this study. Changes in the protocol and/or traffic parameters may change the results. However, the author believes that the main ideas presented in this paper will be valid. The interested reader is encouraged to check with other papers (8,9,10) which consider different question about the D-channel capacity.

Acknowledgement

I wish to thank my collegue Mr. Hebert Vitureira for his programming efforts and fruitful discussions.

References

[1.] CCITT Red book VIII

[2.] L-Å Selin, U Thune, "ISDN System Trials, Experiences, System Implications and Ongoing Activities". ISSLS 1984.

[3.] L Larsson et al, "User Demand and Implementation of New Services". ISSLS 1984

[4.] H Hofstetter, D Weber, "Traffic Models for Large ISDN PABXs". ITC 11.

[5.] L-Å Selin,H Limdqvist "New Services and their Capacity Requirements for Digital Subscriber Line". ISSLS 82

[6.] J Seraj, "Subscriber Model for ISDN Services". Not yet published.

[7.] Swedish Tele Administration "Datakommunikation i västeuropa 1979-1987"

[8.] W. Fischer, E.-H Goeldner "Performance of the ISDN User-network Interface for Signalling and Packetized User-data Transfer". ISS 87

[9.] W. Fischer, E.-H. Goeldner, W. Berner "Performance of the ISDN D-channel Protocol, A Simulation Study". ICCC 8

[10.] P. Le Gall "Modelling ISDN Traffic for D-channel Access" CCITT contribution COMII-36.

TRAFFIC ENGINEERING for ISDN Design and Planning
M. Bonatti and M. Decina (Editors)
Elsevier Science Publishers B.V. (North-Holland)
© IAC, 1988

Modelling the ATD transfer technique

P. BOYER, J. BOYER, J-R. LOUVION, L. ROMOEUF

CNET LAA/SLC/EVP - BP 40 - 22301 LANNION CEDEX - France

Telephone 33.96.05.37.07
Telex   730963F
Area of interest : performance design.

French PTT Lab CNET-LANNION has introduced a new promising transfer technique for IBCN's, the evaluation of which challenges queueing theory.

Abstract

The evolution towards the Integrated Broadband Communication Network is undertaken by several countries.

In France, system designers of CNET in Lannion have assembled an experimental IBCN called PRELUDE based upon a 4.5 Gbps switching matrix and a new and promising transfer mode called the Asynchronous Time-Division technique.

During the project, performance evaluation studies have been carried through, aiming to validate the ATD concepts and to dimension the switching matrix.

This paper reviews the IBCN lab experiments in the world, with operational characteristics ; ATD concepts are detailed and the most important features of IBCN modelling are given.

Finally, the network dimensioning is carried through giving packet size, buffers length, loss probabilities and waiting times.

Introduction

In IBCN context, arise a lot of new services, the constraints of which cannot be handled by presently available transfer techniques : mechanisms implemented in data networks (X25, ...) are too complex for real-time or high bitrate services, synchronous circuit switching cannot handle optimally sporadic flows, dedicated networks are clearly not flexible.

System designers have to cope with highly different bitrates, continuous or sporadic information flows ; to make it harder, let us say that most of new services characteristics are yet unknown.

As a transfer technique, Asynchronous Time-Division mechanisms prove to be able to take up the challenge of network flexibility - PRELUDE experiment | GAC 86 |.

As ATD technique is new, the need for dimensioning the systems and validating both technical and technological options is of crucial importance ; even more involved traffic phenomena differ significantly from plain telephony : both arrival processes - periodic flows with random phasing, geometric flows - and service processes - cyclic server with positive change over times, deterministic service time - yield new models which are a challenge for queueing theory as quantities to evaluate are tiny probabilities or percentiles.

This paper briefly gives some insight on the main features of the ATD transfer technique and describes the mechanisms ensuring the PRELUDE network time-transparency ; then it details the modelling work and related queueing models ; finally the network time-transparency evaluation is performed, dimensioning both mechanisms and systems.

I

The new transfer mode

The main objective of the new ISDN standards has been to integrate from the subscriber point of view, the access to two different networks : telephone and data switched networks.

But new services are steadily emerging in our communicating societies ; it is already now obvious that some services will present requirements which are not well met by these ISDN networks ; here are three examples :

i) coming from data users, the need for large file transfer could require high transfer rates (1 to 10 Mbps) during very short periods of time.

ii) services using still pictures are likely to have a wide range of applications for professional as well as for residential uses ; typically they need bursts of data (some hundred of kbps) during short times (half a second) with random delay between bursts.

iii) High-Quality sound and digital moving pictures will need transfer from a few 64 kbps to some 20 Mbps even 100 Mbps for High-Definition TV.

Would a single network be able to cope with so different types of signals ?

I.1 - the Integrated Broadband Communication Network

If possible, the integration of all services in a same communication network would be an attractive solution ; but faced to unavoidable - and somewhat unforesee a-ble - evolutions of services, techniques and technologies, the network must provide a high flexibility.

As an emphasis, let us note that the known wideband services at this time -TV, HDTV, High-Quality sound, still pictures, data base access, computer communications, fast file transfer - produce either steady, sporadic or various bitrates ranging from 1 kbps up to 100 Mbps.

Research on IBCN has been undertaken by many countries :

Belgium : Bell Telephone Manufacturing (ITT, then ANV) is working on a 684 Mbps switching exchange with self-routing packets | PrS 87 |.

Italy : CSELT is carrying evaluation of advanced switching techniques based upon label-addressing, fast cut-through approach, short fixed-length, self-routing packets, Banyan networks | MGP 86 |.

France : French PTT Lab, CNET has assembled an experimental network PRELUDE including 280 Mbps time-slotted multiplexes and 4.5 Gbps ATD switches, carrying 16-bytes voice, data and picture packets along virtual circuits | GAC 86 |.

Great Britain : British Telecom has assembled in 1984 a 15 Mbps multiservices slotted ring | FaA 85 | and is now working on a 140 Mbps ATD switch based upon ORWELL ring protocol | Gal 86 |.

Japan : NEC is working on an experimental system called Synchronous Composite Packet Switching using a 200 Mbps switch for voice, data and still picture | TSH 86 |.

USA : to our knowledge, US Labs are rather working on ISDN than genuine IBCN: their experiments carry mainly voice and data. We have quoted:

GTE Labs have planned to work on variable length, self-routing voice and data bursts carried by 1.5 Mbps T1-links and switched by a 786 Mbps ring | Ams 83 |.

ATT Bell Labs have assembled an experimental wideband packet network based upon self-routing 74-bytes packets, 8 Mbps Banyan switch and 1.5 Mbps high-speed links carrying statistically multiplexed data and 32 kbps voice | MSZ 86 |.

I.2 - the ATD transfer technique

Several options have been investigated for a full integration of the switching functions : cut-through fast packet switching | MSZ 86 | and Asynchronous Time-Division Technique | Cou 83 |, | PrB 87 |.

ATD switching takes place between circuit switching and packet switching; it may be called label switching.

It may be defined with these four following features :

i) From the circuit point of view it keeps fixed and small size of the information blocks (15 to 30 bytes), extreme simplicity of the exchange protocols, reduced to simple hardware multiplexing schemes ; flow, traffic and error controls are higher level and end-to-end functions.

ii) From the packet point of view it keeps the explicit identification of the channel the information block belongs to, using a label in a small header (1 to 3 bytes).
Although labelling causes overhead, it increases the transmission efficiency : indeed, it allows :

. full sharing of the multiplex bitrate between all the sources - without any allocation scheme.

. statistical multiplexing of variable bitrate sources.

iii) ATD switching uses virtual circuit mode for all connections.

iv) Full integration: no distinction is made between different services; equivalently, services are independent of the transfer network.

Implementation of these ATD concepts has been the aim of PRELUDE experiment | GAC 86 |, now working in CNET Laboratory in Lannion. PRELUDE will be detailed in the following chapter. References | PrS 87 |, | Gal 86 | are also relevant of ATD and they concern experiments very close to PRELUDE.

I.3 - ATD concepts and OSI layer protocols

For teletraffic engineers working on X25-like packet networks, the most astonishing feature of ATD technique is certainly the rejection of any protocol outside of the network layers (1 to 3).

Finally, ATD technique provides end-to-end transparent switched logical links at level 1.

Transfers which need a better quality will then require additional specific functions located in the terminals and selected at the set-up of the call.

I.3.a error-detection and correction protocols

Error-detecting or correcting protocols are too complex to remain realistic at very high bitrates.

Furthermore, these mechanisms are highly dependent upon the type of signal they are supposed to protect ; but all packets look alike within the network.

Anyway, these controls are likely to introduce useless complexity : an end-to-end recovery mechanism is far more efficient than a packet-oriented one, and high-security communications will use their own additional protocols.

I.3.b load and flow control

The classical flow control mechanisms are no more suitable to high speed networks that have real-time constraints to meet for a part of the information flows they carry : these mechanisms are too complex to remain realistic at very high bitrates.

The backward reaction towards the source when a congestion occurs somewhere in the network would probably have a delayed effect, that is likely to come too late.

Load control mechanism must belong to an "off-line" level ; with respect to the traffic characteristics of a communication to be set up, the load control mechanism verifies if the network has enough resources to carry the new communication.

The source must abide by its "contract" - the declared traffic characteristics - and it is the goal of the flow control mechanism implemented in the terminal equipment ; the source will suffer no other bounds at the packet level.

II

PRELUDE and IBCN context

According to the ATD concepts defined upwards, CNET experiment has two main features :

i) flexibility : digital information is organized in 15-bytes packets which are inserted - with an extra byte for labelling - on the next free time slot of a multiplex ; this enables the network to be fed with various and sporadic bitrates.

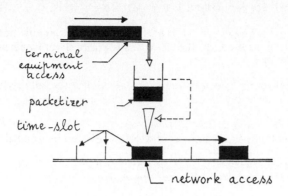

Network access in PRELUDE | Cou 83 |
Figure 1

ii) simplicity : transfer mechanisms have been simplified as much as possible so as to be able to cope with the very high throughput needed by future videocommunication networks. As a result, functions that were previously performed inside the network have been removed up to the periphery : the information transfer network ensures neither flow-control nor error-control nor error-recovery concerning the information itself.

Comparing with "classical" networks which manage the quality of each communication all along the network - in each node - PRELUDE separates the network itself (switching and transmission functions) from the periphery (terminal adaptation which have to manage the quality of transfer).

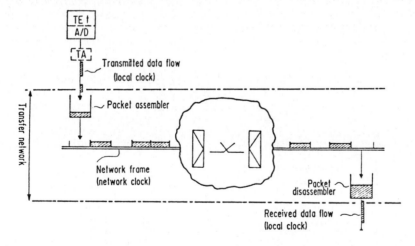

network/application independence | GAC 86 |
Figure 2

II.1 - terminal adaptation

The digital information emitted by a source has been considerably modified when arriving at the receiving terminal so that this one cannot handle it without any processing :

i) scattering the information into packets partially destroys its semantic structure.

ii) multiplexing packets at the access and successive switching nodes introduces transfer delay variations.

iii) the independence between the clocks of the network and any application means that the receiving terminal is not given any information on the transmitting clock frequency.

iv) losses of packet may occur in the outgoing stage of the switching nodes.

Network transparency means data-flow restructuring ; this is performed by a synchronizing stage at the receiving side : the depacketizer, the functions of which are :

- smoothing the propagation delay variations through a buffer queue ;

- restructuring the signal with the help of synchronizing patterns inserted by the transmitting side adaptator ;

- correcting if necessary that receiver clock frequency, using these synchronizing patterns and again a buffer memory.

II.2 – switching in PRELUDE

The PRELUDE switching matrix handles 16 incoming and 16 outgoing 280 Mbps multiplexes for a total 4.5 Gbps switching capacity.

Arriving packets on a multiplex are queued in the corresponding buffer cyclically polled one at a time, every $\theta = 28$ ns ; the information block is directly stored in a common "paragonal" memory and separated from the labels which are multiplexed from the 16 inputs towards the switching control unit.

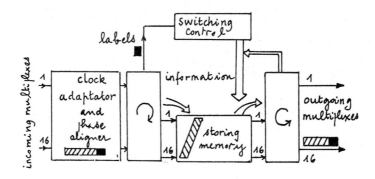

PRELUDE switching matrix symbolic structure | TSC 84 |
Figure 3

That control unit consists of a routing memory and 16 queues dedicated one to each outgoing multiplex. The routing memory analyses the label ; it delivers :

i) the translated label which is stored in the buffer memory.

ii) a signal to activate the control queue (or the control queues when broadcast is needed) corresponding to the outgoing multiplex(es) to which the packet has to be sent. The storage address of the packet is queued there.

To transmit packets further on the outgoing multiplexes these 16 control queues are cyclically polled, one at a time, every θ = 28 ns.

II.3 - characteristics of the main known services

An ATD network is able to handle any type of communication ; it transfers various bitrate flows either continuous or sporadic :

Data transfer, teleprocessing, still pictures communications produce sporadic bitrate flows ;

Telephony, high-quality sound and video broadcasting produce continuous bitrate flows.

For any service, the semantics of the emitted bitrate flow consist in data and time-organisation and so are the terms of transparency constraints.

The severity of these constraints depends upon the sensibility of the receiver to semantic alteration :

kind of service	sensibility of the receiver to	
	data alteration	time-organization alteration
data transfer	high	low
Telephony	low	moderate
High-Quality sound	moderate	extremely high
video	low	moderate

In this paper, we study the flow time-organization alterations implied by ATD transfer technique and mechanisms - implemented in the receiving side - to retrieve the original time-organization in order to ensure network time-transparency.

III

Models for performance evaluation

Proving the technical and technological feasibility of a complete network based upon such mechanisms has been the aim of PRELUDE experimentation. It was however important to add to it a careful study of the traffic behaviour of such a queueing network. The reasons for modelling it, were :

- the problems of dimensioning the receiver smoothing queue and designing the smoothing algorithm, both depending on the expected propagation delay variations.

- the problem of dimensioning the switching matrix buffer memory and queues, and of evaluating the residual packet loss rate due to saturation of the queues.

Because the ATD transfer technique is based mainly upon multiplexing and packet switching, models have been yielded of a multiplexor and a switching node ; let us add a model of a virtual circuit involving 30 switching nodes corresponding to the transfer of information emitted by a national-scale videocommunication.

Let us mention at this point a relevant paper by TURNER and WYATT |TuW 83| answering the same questions concerning an integrated voice and data network; our contribution lies mainly in more sophisticated modelling.

III.1 - arrival processes

Two kinds of traffic are carried by an IBCN network ; some are sporadic flows of information* (presently data transfer, teleprocessing) corresponding to low bitrates - about 1 kbps ; others are continuous flows ($T\varphi$: telephony, TV : video and HQ : high-quality sound broadcasting) with bitrates from 64 kbps ($T\varphi$) up to 64 Mbps (TV) emitted by steady sources.

In this context of services, sporadic flows may be neglected because the corresponding offered load is negligible.

For any communication, a terminal equipment delivers a digital information stream which is gathered into 16-bytes packets (including a 1-byte label) by a packetizer : a packet is delivered every $T_{T\varphi}$ (resp. T_{TV}, T_{HQ}) seconds.

The bitrates characteristics of these services are listed below :

	bitrate	packets/s	period
TV	64 Mbps	$5.6\ 10^5$	1.8 μs
HQ	2.8 Mbps	$2.4\ 10^4$	41 μs
$T\varphi$	64 kbps	546	1.8 ms

* we do no involve here still pictures communications for which work is still in progress.

Packets from different sources are inserted on the outgoing multiplex into the next free time-slot.

Because sources are independent, and the beginning of any communication is unknown, the arrival process in the multiplexor is the superposition of periodic processes with random phasing.

The switching unit is completely synchronized ; as a consequence, packets may enter the unit only every internal elementary time θ , one at a time.

We assume balanced offered load conditions on the 16 incoming multiplexes for the traffic re-emitted by one control queue.

Then, sampling the arrivals dedicated to one control queue, we assume that the probability p that an arrival takes place at any elementary time is constant and that successive arrivals are independent from each other ; these assumptions give auspicious conditions to observe largest packet transfer delay fluctuations.

Hence, the arrival process in a control queue of a switching unit is geometric with parameter p and time-slot duration θ .

III.2 - service processes

All the packets have the same size (16 bytes) and all the multiplexes have the same throughput (280 Mbps) ; so each packet needs a constant duration Δ = 450 ns to be (re-)emitted.

In a multiplexer, the service consists of emitting the packet on a multiplex ; it will be chosen deterministic with value Δ .

In a switching node, control queues are being cyclically explored : a packet entering an empty queue will wait for the cyclic grant before re-emission ; the duration of the cycle is Δ . This leads us to a walking-type server A with null service duration.

III.3 - queueing models for the ATD transfer technique

Modelling a multiplexor yields a $D_1 + ... + D_n$ / D / 1 queueing model with different periods T_i - periodic flows with random phasing and one deterministic server ; in the special case of identical periods - when multiplexed communications are of the same type - this model is renamed nD/D/1 and has been completely investigated | Gra 84 |, | BDGP 84 | ; otherwise numerical simulations have been run.

Modelling a control queue of a switching node yields a Geo/D/1/n, or Geo/A/1/n queueing model, depending on whether we neglect the cyclic grant or not ; let us note that these models are discrete - time queueing systems allowing simultaneous arrival and departure in any internal elementary time - all the papers we know dealing with discrete time queueing do not allow this still actual behaviour, the Geo/D/1 and Geo/D/1/n models have been recently fully investigated | GLB 86 |, the waiting time distribution in the Geo/A/1 queue is simply related to its equivalent in the corresponding Geo/D/1 queue | GeI 80 |.

The end-to-end asynchronous circuit is modelled by a network of thirty queues in series with intermediate geometric arrivals ; transfer delays along the circuit have been studied using simulation runs and analytical approximations.

IV

PRELUDE dimensioning for transparency

Successive packets of a same communication carried through an empty network experience the same transfer delay D ; as a matter of fact, this delay depends only on the successive constant shifts between an incoming multiplex frame and the clock of the corresponding switching-matrix ; when several communications have to share the transmission capacity of a single multiplex, successive packets experience queueing in the control queues of successive switching-matrixes; for a given matrix, the waiting times are different for successive packets : various services are involved in the traffic carried by the network and they give birth to periodic packet flows with different periods.

Hence, these packets do not experience the same transfer delay along the asynchronous circuit.

For a receiving terminal waiting for a continuous digital stream, network transparency means uninterrupted activity of the depacketizer during the whole time of the communication : if the arrival of the (n+1)st packet takes place after the release of the nth packet, how does the depacketizer manage to feed the receiving terminal ? That is the CLAC phenomenon - or depacketizer starvation - which has to be avoided:

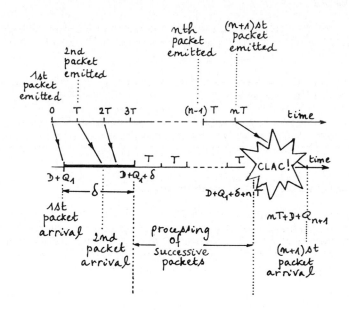

the depacketizer starvation
Figure 4

In the PRELUDE experiment, the processing of the first packet of each communication only will be delayed by the depacketizer during an extra waiting-time δ ;

Let Q_n, $n \geq 1$ be the cumulative waiting time in control queues experienced by the n-th packet and assume that the communication produces a T-periodic packet flow.

The (n+1)st packet arrives at epoch $(nT + D + Q_{n+1})$; if we assume that the depacketizer works without interruption, the processing of the n-th packet ends at epoch $(D + Q_1 + \delta + nT)$.

If we want to avoid an idle period of the depacketizer, the condition on δ is the following :

$$Q_{n+1} - Q_1 \leq \delta$$

As cumulative waiting times can be very large, there exists no practical value of δ such that this inequality holds for each $n \geq 1$; nevertheless, δ can be chosen in such a way that this inequality holds for almost all $n \geq 1$:

We consider Q_n, $n \geq 1$ as different values of a random variable Q ; δ is chosen as the $(1-10^{-9})$-percentile of $\overline{Q}$ distribution :

$$P (Q > \delta) = 10^{-9}$$

We have studied the cumulative distribution function of Q under severe load conditions.

IV.1 - evaluating the extra-waiting time

Let us consider a national-scale communication which is carried through an asynchronous circuit connecting 30 switching matrixes ; we assume that every multiplex carried load is 0.9 with balanced traffic conditions.

The asynchronous circuit can be modelled by a network of 30 queues FQ_i in series (figure 5) with intermediate arrival packet flows φ_i corresponding to the activity of the network beside the tagged communication.

φ_i flows are supposed to be geometric of constant rate λ_G : each θ second a φ_i -packet arrives in FQ_i with constant probability $p = \lambda_G \cdot \theta$ (here $\theta = 28$ ns).

As soon as served in FQ_i queue, a φ_i-packet is removed from the asynchronous circuit, and a tagged-packet enters the FQ_{i+1} queue.

The service in FQ_i queue is fictitious : the packet only receives the authorization to be re-emitted towards FQ_{i+1} ; the service duration is null ; after service completion, the "walking-type" server is unavailable during Δ (here $\Delta = 450$ ns), due to the cyclic polling of other control queues in the switching matrix control part.

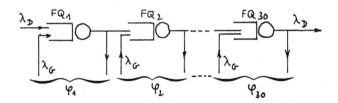

A queueing model for the asynchronous circuit
Figure 5

The distribution of successive packets cumulated waiting times is not available from queueing theory ; we have used several ways globally giving a consistent point of view.

IV.1.a the central limit approximation

Using the central limit theorem certainly is the simplest but also crudest way to obtain some results ; let us assume that the successive waiting times W_i of any tagged packet arriving in FQ_i queue $1 \leq i \leq 30$, are independent and identically distributed random variables with mean EW_q and variance var W_q.

Consider Q as the sum $W_1 + ... + W_{30}$. It approaches therefore a normal distribution with mean m = 30 EW_q and variance σ^2 = 30 var W_q.

FQ_i control queues are supposed to be large enough so that packet losses are negligible (see IV.3 below).

EW_q and var W_q are the mean and variance of the queueing time in a Geo/A/1 model (see III.3 above); let EW'_q and var W'_q be the mean and variance of the queueing time in a Geo/D/1 ; they are given explicit formulae in a recent paper | GLB 86 |; applying results in a paper by Gelenbe and Iasnogorodski | GeI 80 |, we obtain:

$$EW_q = EW'_q + \frac{\Delta}{2}$$
$$Var\ W_q = var\ W'_q + \frac{\Delta^2}{12}$$

Let ρ = 0.9 be the carried load of any multiplex ; remind that Δ = 0.45 μs, numerical values follow :

$$EW_q = 4.72\ \Delta = 2.12\ \mu s$$

$$Var\ W_q = 20.61\ \Delta^2 = 4.17\ (\mu s)^2$$

so that:

$$m = 141.6\ \Delta = 63.7\ \mu s$$
$$\sigma = 24.86\ \Delta = 11.19\ \mu s$$

The evaluation of δ - $(1-10^{-9})$-percentile of a Gaussian law - is straight forward :

$$\delta = m + 6\ \sigma = 290.8\ \Delta = 131\ \mu s$$

Remarks :

1 - in an actual asynchronous circuit, it is difficult to say whether the successive waiting times in FQ_i's control queues of a tagged packet would be independent or not; our model assumes independence, enforcing the normal approximation.

2 - the server's walking type has little effect when ρ = 0.9 : it represents 10 % of the value of EW_q and 0.4 % of the value of var W_q.

3 - this evaluation - based upon the values of EW_q and var W_q - involves measurements performed over all the packets processed by a control queue.

If one wants to study a special type of communication, measurements must be performed only over all tagged packets ; then the control queue must be modelled as a D + Geo/A/1 queue but analytical results - at least EW_q and var W_q - are not yet available at present time ; then we have used simulation runs.

IV.1.b simulation of the transfer of a tagged communication

The tagged communication is T-periodic with constant rate λ_D, depending on the type of the communication :

$$T_{TV} = 2 \ \mu s \qquad \lambda_{TV} = 64 \ \text{Mbps} \qquad \lambda_G = 188 \ \text{Mbps}$$

$$T_{HQ} = 46 \ \mu s \qquad \lambda_{HQ} = 2.8 \ \text{Mbps} \qquad \lambda_G = 249.2 \ \text{Mbps}$$

During the simulation run, 10^7 tagged packet transfer delay measurements have been performed ; they can be considered as different values of a random variable Q_{TV} (resp. Q_{HQ}).

Q_{TV} and Q_{HQ} do not have the same cdf, that will be explained further on :

i) up to a $(1-10-5)$-percentile, the obtained distribution of $(Q_{TV})^{1/4}$ looks like a Gaussian distribution with mean m = 2.64 $(\mu s)^{1/4}$ and standard deviation $\sigma = 0.08 \ (\mu s)^{1/4}$.

As the extra-waiting time δ_{TV} is the $(1-10^{-9})$-percentile of this cdf, extrapolation gives

$$\delta_{TV} = (m + 6 \sigma)^4 = 97 \ \mu s.$$

ii) up to a $(1-10^{-5})$-percentile, the obtained distribution of $(Q_{HQ})^{1/3}$ looks like a gaussian distribution with mean m = 3.88 $(\mu s)^{1/3}$ and standard deviation $\sigma = 0.23 \ (\mu s)^{1/3}$; hence

$$\delta_{HQ} = (m + 6 \sigma)^3 = 148 \ \mu s$$

Geometric flow ω_i introduces randomness on the queueing time of tagged packets in FQ_i queue ; higher is the rate λ_D, lower is the rate λ_G and weaker the effect introduced ; this explains why Q_{HQ} values are more scattered than Q_{TV} ones.

IV.1.c very small bitrate approximation

Direct reasoning leads to the asymptotic cumulative distribution function of the transfer delay of packets of a low-rate $T\omega$ communication at 64 kbps.

As the interarrival of two successive $T\omega$ - packets is very long - compared to the traffic activity of ω_i flows - each $T\omega$ - packet finds every control queue i in a stationnary state with local arrival ω_i ; as a consequence its successive waiting times are identically distributed.

Moreover they are independent : as a matter of fact, ω_i flows are independent and do not interact.

At this point, one can use the central limit approximation, but we are given information on the distribution of these waiting times : as the offered load of each control queue is high ($\rho = 0.9$), we neglect the server's walking type and we use the KINGMAN approximation for waiting times in a GI/GI/1 queue which asserts that they can be considered exponentially distributed.

Hence, the transfer delay of a $T\varphi$-packet is the sum of 30 independent, exponentially distributed random variables, the distribution and percentiles of which are well-known; finally, we obtain:

$$\delta T_\varphi = 159 \,\mu s$$

As $T\varphi$ is a very low-rate communication, the random effects introduced by ω_i flows are as big as possible ; δT_φ may then be considered as the highest value of extra-waiting time δ.

IV.2 - which capacity for the depacketizer queue ?

In the worst case, the random part of the transfer delay of the first packet of a newly set-up communication is δ.

Its depacketizing will begin at epoch $D + 2\delta$: as D is a common time-shift, only $2\delta/T$ packets may have joined the depacketizer queue, at this time.

According to this worst case, the depacketizer must accept

$$N = 1 + 2\delta/T \text{ packets.}$$

The maximum value of N is obtained for a TV communication ; we have $T_{TV} = 2\,\mu s$, $\delta T_{TV} = 97\,\mu s$, thus N = 98 packets.

We note that N remains unchanged for different homothetic networks ; if the multiplex runs two times lower and the source rate emits two times slower, T and δ are both two times greater.

IV.3 - dimensioning the switching matrix control queues

A newly set-up communication on PRELUDE is given a transmission capacity on each multiplex of the virtual circuit : a loss of packet may occur only in a switching node ; in such a node, a loss may occur only if a control queue in the outgoing stage is full.
As incoming buffers are cyclically polled with a positive changeover time $\theta = 28$ ns, arrivals in a control queue take place at epochs $k\theta$ with k integer.

Let us consider the traffic dedicated to one control queue ; we assume that the outgoing multiplex load ρ is due, with balanced conditions, to all incoming multi-plexes.

This assumption gives auspicious conditions for bursty packet arrivals and losses.

We assume that the packet arrival process is geometric with parameter $\theta = 28$ ns and p = $\rho/16$: a packet may arrive at epoch $k\theta$ independently of all other preceding arrivals with probability p.

We consider moderate to severe load conditions ($\rho > 0.7$) ; hence, a few packets only find the control queue empty and wait for the cyclic server ; as a slightly optimistic approximation the server "walking-type" has been neglected.

The service offered in a control queue is the re-emission on the outgoing multiplex, the duration of which is $\Delta = 450$ ns.

Let K be the capacity of the control queue.

In terms of queueing theory, the behaviour of the control queue is described by a Geo/D/1/K model ; it has been recently investigated | GLB 86 | ; explicit formulae give the probability distribution function of the waiting time and the state probabilities, particularly the probability of saturation (i.e. loss probability as arrivals are geometric).

With respect to the values of K we obtain the following variations of the loss function of the offered load (Figure 6).

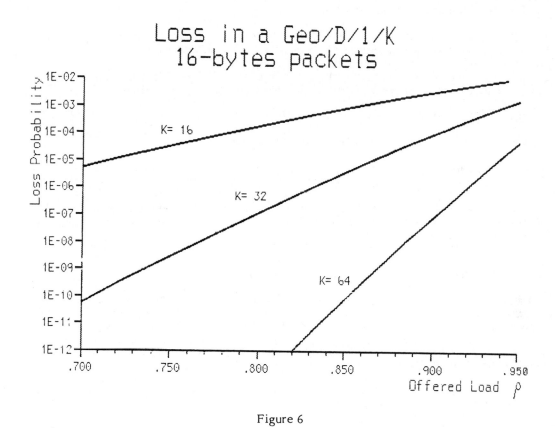

Figure 6

Packet loss must be a negligible phenomenon ; system designers have to dimension the control queue so that it may contain K = 64 storing addresses : while the outgoing multiplex load stays under 0.85, the loss probability remains smaller than 10^{-10}.

Remark :   ideally, the common "paragonal" memory (see II.2) must contain 16.K packets. The saturation of this buffer will occur iff all the 16 control queues are saturated, the probability of which is 10^{-160}.

If a tiny loss is tolerated, the actual size of this buffer would be five to ten times smaller :

Let n_k, $1 \leq k \leq 16$, be the number of storing addresses waiting in the i-th control queue at a given epoch ; the (n_k)'s variables are iid with known mean En_1 and variance $var(n_1)$ | GLB 86 |. The paragonal memory contains $n_1 + ... + n_{16}$ packets ;

Let M be the capacity of the paragonal memory ; assuming a loss probability 10^{-12} in the paragonal memory gives :

$$P(n_1 + ... + n_{16} > M) = 10^{-12}$$

Applying the central-limit theorem, the distribution of this sum is roughly Gaussian with mean $16\, En_1$ and variance $16\, var(n_1)$ so that :

$$M = 16\, En_1 + 7\sqrt{16\, var(n_1)}$$

For $\rho = 0.85$, $En_1 = 3.108$, $var(n_1) = 9.280$ and M = 136 packets (7.5 times smaller than the previous value 1024).

V

Influence of the packet size

It is known from Pollaczek-Kintchine formula that fixed-length packet is a better option than variable-length with respect to queueing performances - let us remind, for instance, that the average waiting time in an M/M/1 queue is twice than in a M/D/1 queue.

Moreover, fixed-length packets allow parallel processing in the ATD switch, increasing the switching capacity that can be expected from a given technology.

On the contrary, very few arguments tell in the favor of variable-length packets, this option being less and less defended in the offices of standards. Let us mention however flexibility : long packets are more convenient for large file transfers whereas short packets can meet real-time requirements (HQ sound for example).

Once decided that IBCN packets must have a fixed length, a question remains : what is the good length ?

The length depends on different parameters : the label size, the size of the useful information, the extra-waiting time and the depacketizer queue length at the receiving side, the memory needed for a given loss in a switching node.

In an ATD network, a virtual circuit can be modelled as a set of queues in series, the servers of which are the successive capacities of the multiplexes ; the service time - that is the reemission time - is proportional to the packet length.

Hence, the sojourn time in a control queue and the capacity of the memory associated to this queue increase linearly with the packet size.

Let us now consider the end-to-end asynchronous circuit.

If the packet size increases, so does the end-to-end delay ; hence, the extra-waiting time at the beginning of the communication and the capacity of the depacketizer memory are also increasing.

The study assumes that the useful information carried by a multiplex is constant and corresponds to a useful load ρ_u ; an extra load must be added for the label, which depends on the size of the label L_e and the size of the information block L_i.

The actual load on the multiplex is then :

$$\rho = \rho_u \left(1 + \frac{L_e}{L_i} \right)$$

The actual load on the multiplex has a strong influence on the traffic flow along the asynchronous circuit : if the load is high, the end-to-end transfer delays are very scattered and a high capacity is needed in the nodes and in the depacketizer.

The packet size and the actual load vary in opposite directions ; an optimal size of the asynchronous packet is then foreseeable.

In the case of a narrow-band network, ROBIEUX has derived a similar result pointing out an optimal packet size | Rob 81 |.

It will be noted that this optimal size is identical for all the quantities computed ; this phenomenon can be explained by the fixed length of the packets : the statistics for memory occupation and sojourn time are identical.

In the following, the size of the label L_e will be assumed constant for all the packets.

The optimal size of the packet decreases with the useful load ρ_u carried by the multiplex : for given useful load ρ_u and header size L_e ; there is a lower bound on L_i corresponding to an actual load $\rho = 1$. From the preceding formula, this bound on L_i increases with L_e or ρ_u and so does the optimal size of the packet, leading to longer packets.

In the following numerical applications, the label size L_e will be taken equal to 2 bytes, which allows the identification of 2 000 virtual channels with a systematic recovery of a single error.

V.1 - on the depacketizer algorithm

Two different cases will be considered : a TV high-bitrate communication (64 Mbps) and the limit case of a null bitrate communication (that is with a negligible bitrate compared with the output multiplex throughput).

V.1.a - null bitrate communication

Here is considered the boundary case of a communication with a bitrate very small compared to the throughput of the output multiplex ; the highest value for the extra-waiting time is then obtained, because the whole load carried by the multiplex is disturbing (cf § IV.1.c).

Figure 7 shows the variations of the extra-waiting time function of the information length L_i for different values of the load carried by the multiplex. The multiplex has a 280 Mbps throughput, but it is very easy - by a simple rule of three - to obtain results for another value.

A minimum value of the extra-waiting time can be observed, it corresponds to L_i = 23 bytes for ρ_u = 0.85 and to L_i = 16 bytes for ρ_u = 0.80.

Around this minimum, the behaviour is the following ; if L_i increases, the actual load ρ tends to the value ρ_u and the scattering of the end-to-end delay increases linearly with the packet size L (and so does the reemission duration) ; if L_i decreases, the actual load increases and tends to 1, and the scattering of the end-to-end delay also increases, though the reemission duration is linearly decreasing with the packet length.

V.1.b - 64 Mbps TV communication

The flow of a 64 Mbps TV communication on a 280 or 560 Mbps multiplex has been simulated ; 3 useful load conditions (ρ_u = 0.75, 0.80 and 0.85) have been considered (Figures 8 and 9).

The extra-waiting time associated to the beginning of the communication has a minimum which does not depend on the multiplex throughput but only on the useful load ρ_u : this minimum corresponds to an information block of L_i = 23 bytes for ρ_u = 0.85 and L_i = 16 bytes for ρ_u = 0.80.

V.2 - on the depacketizer queue length

Let us denote the extra-waiting time of the first packet of the communication by δ , the emission period of the source by T and the number of packets that have to be stored in the depacketizer by N ; then, from § IV.2, it can be written :

$$N = 1 + 2 \ \frac{\delta}{T}$$

Let us remind that this value is obtained in the worst case of the first packet experiencing the maximum end-to-end delay through the network.

The memory size associated in the depacketizer is then :

$$N (L_e + L_i)$$

The unfavourable case of a high-bitrate 32 Mbps video communication is considered.

Figure 10 shows the variation of the depacketizer queue length as a function of the information block size L_i : a minimum value of the   queue length   can be observed ; it corresponds to L_i = 23 bytes for ρ_u = 0.85 and L_i = 16 bytes for ρ_u = 0.80.

On the right-hand side of this minimum, when L_i increases, the extra-waiting time δ and the emission period T are both increasing linearly and their ratio δ /T becomes constant ; hence, the number of packets that have to be stored in the depacketizer becomes also constant and so the memory associated to this queue is linearly increasing with the packet size.

On the other side of the minimum, when L_i decreases, the actual load ρ tends to 1 ; the extra-waiting time is then increasing very fast and so is the depacketizer queue length and the memory associated to this queue.

V.3 - on the capacity of the COPRIN paragonal memory

Once the actual load carried by the outgoing multiplex is known, the number K of labels a control queue must accept is computed, so that the residual loss is less than 10^{-9} ; if the packet size is L bytes, the COPRIN common paragonal memory must then hold KL bytes per multiplex.

Figure 11 represents this memory as a function of the information block length L_i ; there exists also a minimum for L_i = 23 bytes with a useful load ρ_u = 0.85 and L_i = 16 bytes with ρ_u = 0.80.

On the right-hand side of this minimum, when L_i increases, the actual load carried by the multiplex tends to the lower boundary ρ_u, leading to a constant control queue length K, and then to a memory associated to this queue linearly increasing with the packet length.

On the other side, when L_i decreases, the actual load ρ tends to 1 ; the number K of labels in a control queue then increases very fast and so does the memory associated to this queue (even if the packet length is linearly decreasing).

Conclusion

Many laboratories, all around the world, are involved in studies on the Integrated Broadband Communication Network ; among them, the French PTT Lab CNET has introduced a new transfer mode called Asynchronous Time-Division technique.

This technique is very promising because the network is then able to manage very different bitrates : all the services, from the 64 Kbps voice to the 64 Mbps high-definition video, use only the capacity they need. Furthermore, this technique allows broadcasting and sporadic flow multiplexing.

In return, a terminal adaptation is needed in order to ensure time-transparency in most cases :

- the extra waiting time of the first packet of a TV communication (resp. HQ, T_φ) is 100 μs (resp. 150 μs, 160 μs) ; the depacketizer starvation then happens with a probability lower than 10^{-9}.

- the depacketizer queue length must be able to accept at least 98 packets.

- in a switching-matrix, each control queue contains up to 64 storing addresses ; hence, the packet-loss probability remains smaller than 10^{-10} up to an outgoing multiplex load level 0.85.

As far as packet length is concerned, an optimal value can be observed for performances and dimensioning of an Asynchronous Time-Division network : the optimal packet length L_i increases with the useful load ρ_u carried by the multiplex ; L_i = 23 bytes for ρ_u = 0.85 and L_i = 16 bytes for ρ_u = 0.80.

Around this optimal value, these quantities - extra-waiting time and queue lengths have a dissymetrical behaviour : on the left-hand side, they are increasing very fast when the information block length L_i decreases ; on the right-hand side, they are linearly increasing, when L_i increases.

The useful load is very difficult to be fully controlled ; it is then more secure to choose a packet length a little bit higher than the optimum, allowing the quantities involved to be less sensible to the useful load. With a useful load ρ_u = 0.80, this leads to 26-bytes packets (24 bytes for information and 2 for label) and with ρ_u = 0.85, 34-bytes packets (32 for information and 2 for label).

Acknowledgements

The authors are grateful to J.-P. COUDREUSE for valuable and helpful comments on an early draft of this work.

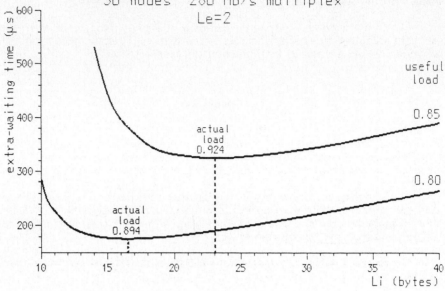

Figure 7

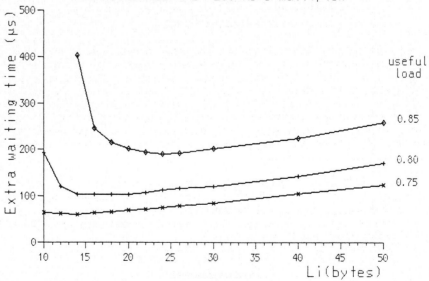

Figure 8

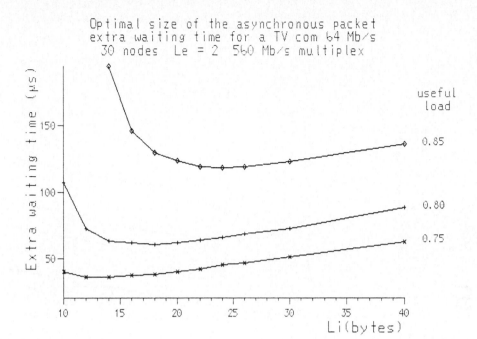

Figure 9

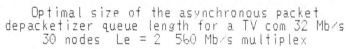

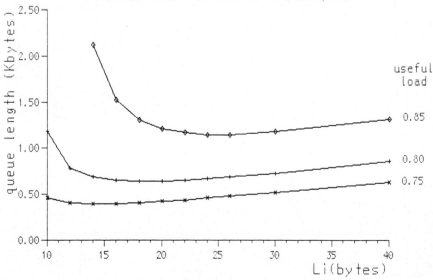

Figure 10

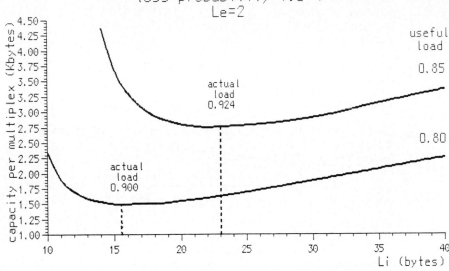

Figure 11

References

| Ams 83 | Burst switching - an Introduction.
S.R. Amstutz
IEEE Communications Magazine 11-1983

| BDGP 84 | The output process of the single server queue with periodic arrival process
and deterministic service time.
P. Boyer, A. Dupuis, A. Gravey, J-M. Pitié
Lecture Notes in Control and Information Science
Vol 60 Springer Verlag - 1984

| Cou 83 | Les réseaux temporels asynchrones: du transfert de données à l'image
animée.
J-P. Coudreuse
Echo des Recherches n°112 - Editions CNET 1983

| FaA 85 | ORWELL : a protocol for an integrated services local network.
R.M. Falconer - J.L. Adams
British Telecom Technol. Journal
Vol. 3 n°4 - 10-1985.

| GAC 86 | Asynchronous Time-Division switching: the way to flexible broadband
communication networks.
P. Gonet, P. Adam, J-P. Coudreuse
IEEE International Zurich Seminar on Digital Communications March 1986

| Gal 86 | A technique for implementing an Asynchronous Time-Division switch.
I.D. Gallagher
British Telecom Internal Memorandum.
TA2 86/26 TA 2.4.3. - 01-1986.

| Gel 80 | A queue with server of walking type.
E. Gelenbe, R. Iasnogorodski
Annales Institut H. Poincaré.
Vol. XVI n° 1 - 1980.

| GLB 86 | Files d'attente à temps discret : cas des files à processus d'arrivée
géométrique et serveur déterministe.
A. Gravey, J-R. Louvion, P. Boyer
Workshop on Computer Performance evaluation. INRIA Sophia-Antipolis -
1986.

| Gra 84 | Temps d'attente et nombre de clients dans une file nD/D/1.
A. Gravey
Annales de l'institut Henri Poincaré
Vol 20 n°1 - 1984

| MGP 86 | Advanced switching techniques for future telecommunication services.
R. Melen, E. Garetti, F. Perardi
ICC'86 - Toronto 1986.

| MSZ 86 | Digital communications experiments in wideband packet technology.
R.W. Muise, T.J. Schonfeld, G.H. Zimmerman
IEEE International Zurich Seminar on Digital Communications March 1986

| PrB 87 | The ATD concept : one universal bearer service.
              Martin De Prycker, Jan Bauwens
              CEPT-GSLB Seminar on broadband switching.
              Albufeira (Portugal) 01-1987.

| PrS 87 | An ATD broadband switching exchange with distributed control.
              M. De Prycker, M. De Somer
              CEPT-GSLB Seminar on broadband switching.
              Albufeira (Portugal) - January 1987.

| Rob 81 | Les délais de transmission dans un réseau numérique paroles/données à
              commutation de paquets.
              C. Robieux
              Revue technique Thomson-CSF
              Vol 13 n°3 09 - 1981

| TSC 84 | Asynchronous time-division techniques : an experimental packet network
              integrating videocommunication.
              A. Thomas, M. Servel, J-P. Coudreuse
              ISS'84 - Florence - Mai 1984.

| TSH 86 | An experimental Synchronous composite packet switching system.
              T. Takeuchi, H. Suzuki, S. Hayano, H. Niwa, T. Yamaguchi.
              IEEE International Zurich Seminar on Digital Communications March 1986

| TuW 83 | A packet network architecture from integrated services.
              J.S. Turner, L.F. Wyatt
              Globecom 83 - 12-1983 - paper 2-1-1

DISCUSSION

This section addresses the issues raised during the question and answer period. Related remarks, as well as more general comments on these papers, are offered in the chairman's concluding remarks.

1 The Connection Machine System (C. Stanfill – Thinking Machines).

The issues discussed here include reliability, networking, real-time control, support of multitasking and broadcasting, as well as applications.

1.1 Reliability.

R. Ackerley (British Telecom) asked about the reliability of the Connection Machine System, in view of the large number of processor connections.

C. Stanfill responded that, at the component level, a failure rate comparable to all large computers having about one square meter of silicon, is achieved. At the circuit level, he noted that the key to building a reliable computer is minimizing the number of single-point failure modes by the use of ECC protection on all circuits where possible.

1.2 Support of Broadcasting and Multitasking.

M. Gerla (UCLA) asked about the nature of this support.

C. Stanfill stated that support for one-to-many and many-to-one communications patterns is done by dynamically constructing Fan-In/Fan-Out trees. He also indicated that multitasking is not supported at the hardware level. Only one process at a time can be active. He noted that serial machines which also support one process at a time, implement multitasking in software by process switching and that a different class of parallel machines, the "Control-Level Parallel" machines, are based on true multitasking.

1.3 Applications.

H. Heffes (AT&T Bell Laboratories) asked about system applications and the suitability of the architecture for parallel simulation of telecommunication systems.

C. Stanfill commented on VLSI simulation and optimization, where each processor is given one VLSI device; on Information Retrieval, where each processor is given one document in a full text data base; and on Vision and Graphics where each processor is given one pixel. He also indicated that parallel simulation of telecommunication systems have not been implemented.

1.4 Control Issues.

P.J. Kuehn (University of Stuttgart) commented that "the distributed nature of communication networks requires more overall control, a "Network Operating System", which is reflected by rather complex hierarchical protocol architectures, protocol handlers, network database systems, network management and so forth. Highly parallel computers similarly need programming languages for parallel computing, operating systems, machine level control (e.g., bus arbitration, routers), etc." He asked C. Stanfill to comment on control issues for the parallel computer architecture.

C. Stanfill replied that in a telecommunications network, there is always a mix of traffic, various bandwidths and durations of messages. In addition, the bandwidths of individual communication links differ. Finally, the topology of the network is non-uniform. Because of this, problems of routing and bandwidth allocation arise which cannot easily be solved by local operations. This necessitates a network operating system to make such decisions. In contrast, a Connection Machine System deals with uniform message sizes at a given time. Also, the bandwidths of the links are uniform and the topology is completely regular. As a result, all routing and allocation decisions can be made on a local basis, so no network operating system is needed for these purposes. Other than this, the need for language compilers, file systems, and I/O monitors is as for any other computer.

1.5 Networking.

J. Meyer (University of Michigan) asked about the characteristics of the Connection Machine System relative to Input/Output and Networking (inteconnected Connection Machine Systems).

C. Stanfill answered that for each 8192 processors, there is an I/O port which can handle 32 Mbyte per second. For a 64K processor, the I/O bandwidth totals 256 Mbyte per second. Two I/O devices, a disk unit (the "data vault™") and a real-time graphic display, are currently available. It is also possible to build a jumper to connect two I/O ports, allowing two machines which are physically close to be networked. Non-local networking has yet to be explored, but obviously requires very powerful telecommunications.

1.6 Expansion.

B. Stavenow (Ericsson) commented that one of the most important characteristics of a telecommunications networks is that it should be possible to expand the network by adding additional nodes without having to rearrange the existing communication nodes. He asked about the properties of the Connection Machine System in this respect. He also asked about the number of nodes that have to be added to expand from an nD-hypercube to an (n+1)D-hypercube.

A Connection Machine Systems may be expanded by factors of 2, responded C. Stanfill. This is done by plugging in additional circuit boards and connecting them via ribbon cable. Machines with 2E+14, 2E+15, and 2E+16 processors are currently marketed.

Internally at Thinking Machines, machines with between 2E+9 and 2E+13 processors are sometimes operated. The number of processors is always a power of 2.

2 D-Channel Performance (J. Seraj, Ericsson)

P.J. Kuehn (University of Stuttgart) expressed his appreciation for the inclusion of service types and customer types in the performance analysis of the D-channel. In general, stated P.J. Kuehn, the D-channel signaling is not affected much by p-data D-channel load, and signaling does not load the D-channel significantly, at least in the case of basic accesses. Recent similar studies at the University of Stuttgart have shown that throughput and delay are affected by various factors which have to be carefully considered:

- Protocol processing at ET-side for many TEs handled by 1 ET.

- Number of TEs connected to one basic access for destinating calls (sequential set ups of LAPD-connections).

- Window-size choice affects throughput differently when system is channel- or processor-bound, see Seraj's Ref.(8).

- Bit error probabilities greater than 10E-4 drastically reduce the achievable throughput.

- Signaling message prioritization is usually only considered at protocol handlers. Therefore, p-data do in fact influence s-data when not carefully implemented.

3 ATD Transfer Technique (J.R. Louvion, CNET)

3.1 Upper Limit of Tandem ATD Switches.

G.R. Ash (AT&T Bell Laboratories) asked about the practical upper limit on the number of tandem ATD switches in one connection, assuming that the ATD method is used for network access as well as internal network transport, for:

  a) voice services, to meet build-out delay objectives and low-probability packet dropping objectives,

and

  b) data services (wideband and narrowband), to meet delay objectives and near-zero probability packet dropping objectives,

assuming that the network is not "over-engineered".

J.R. Louvion remarked that the average propagation delay through a COPRIN elementary switching matrix is less than 3 μs for a load lower than 0.95. For a five-stage switch, this mean delay remains lower than 15 μs. Hence, the end-to-end mean delay does not appear as a constraint on the number of nodes in an asynchronous circuit. On the other hand, the extra waiting time, which is the (10E-9) percentile of the end-to-end queueing delay, also depends upon the number of nodes in the end-to-end asynchronous circuit; but the relative difference between mean and (10E-9) percentile decreases with the number of nodes, as shown in the following table.

number of node	6	12	24
mean queueing delay (μs)	64	127	254
extra waiting time (μs)	160	254	386

The extra waiting time is then compatible with the constraints associated with the services.

3.2 Bandwidth Allocation.

L.G. Mason (INRS Telecommunications) asked about the Bandwidth Allocation scheme intended, in order to ensure that a particular service type receives the apppropriate end-to-end GOS objective.

"We think that, for steady communications, deterministic allocation schemes work quite well", answered J.R. Louvion, "For sporadic sources, statistical multiplexing must be used for transmission efficiency reasons. Work is still in progress".

3.3 Modeling Techniques and Assumptions.

3.3.1

L. Berry (University of Adelaide) commented that in multi-service networks the arrival processes may have a wide range of coefficients of variation and asked about the reason for assuming a geometric input in the model.

J.R. Louvion answered that the model assumes steady traffic sources emitting periodic packet flows. Such flows are superimposed on a discrete time basis. Two assumptions lay under the geometric assumption:

- any source delivers its packets on the same multiplex; hence, the different input multiplexes in any node may be considered independent,

- towards a given output multiplex, all the input multiplexes contribute equally.

3.3.2

H. Heffes (AT&T Bell Laboratories) and P.R. Richards (BNR) asked about depacketizer starvation.

The variability of the end-to-end delay is a critical factor in the determination of depacketizer starvation, commented H. Heffes. He noted that the analysis presented assumes independence of waiting times at the intermediate nodes, as well as balanced load conditions and geometric arrivals at intermediate nodes. He asked if the authors have studied and could comment on the effect of positive correlations of delays at successive nodes, and more bursty arrivals at intermediate nodes, on the probability of depacketizer starvation and on the choice of depacketizer delay parameters.

Successive waiting times of the same packet in successive nodes of an asynchronous circuit are dependent except for the case of the low rate communication, answered J.R. Louvion. Although the disturbing flows are independent at intermediate nodes, it may be seen that:

- successive waiting times of the same packet in the successive nodes are dependent,

- waiting times of successive packets in the same node are dependent.

This was the reason for undertaking an expensive simulation of the asynchronous circuit.
However, in the traffic studies no special arrival patterns have been considered because they could not be related to any actual situation.

P. Richards asked if the problem of depacketizer starvation implied a fundamental limit on the range of bit rates that could be simultaneously handled by an ATDM network (e.g., could a low bit rate data service be "starved" by simultaneous video communications?).

J.R. Louvion answered that even in the extremal case of a null bit rate communication, for which the whole load at any node is disturbing, the depacketizer extra waiting time is about 160 μs for a 280 Mbps multiplex.

3.3.3

J.M. Holtzman (AT&T Bell Laboratories) asked about the relationships between the solution of the $nD/D/1$ queueing model by A.E. Eckberg with the model of the multiplexer utilized by the authors.

The paper by Eckberg, answered J.R. Louvion, offers an algorithmic solution leading to the exact result for the delay in a $nD/D/1$. The paper by Gravey ["Temps d'attente et nombre de clients dans une file $nD/D/1$", Annales de l'Institut Henri Poincare', Vol. 20, No. 1, 1984] gives an explicit solution for both the number in the system and the delay. Apart from the specific interest in closed form expressions, this solution allows higher values of the number of input lines (up to 100).

In his paper, Eckberg published results for less than 20 lines which agree with those of Gravey's work.

3.3.4

In answer to a question by J. Seraj, observing that one approximation seems to be overestimating and the other underestimating the simulation results, J.R. Louvion responded that:

. the simulation takes into account the cyclic grant of re-emission and the discrete time arrival,

. the Geo/D/1/k model drops out the cyclic grant, which constitutes an optimistic approximation which is very accurate when the offered load is high,

. M/D/1/K model drops out the discrete time assumption giving origin to bursts of packets, and leads to pessimistic results with a poor accuracy for high load.

3.4 Label Switching

In answer to a question by M. Gerla, about how the switching matrix label switching time of 28 µsec was achieved, J.R. Louvion commented that ECL technology allows a 300 MHz clock frequency. In the PRELUDE experiment the label switching is only running at 35 MHz.

TRAFFIC ENGINEERING for ISDN Design and Planning
M. Bonatti and M. Decina (Editors)
Elsevier Science Publishers B.V. (North-Holland)
© IAC, 1988

THE CHALLENGE OF ISDN SYSTEM MODELING

(Chairman Comments on the Morning Session on Systems)

Harry Heffes

AT&T Bell Labs, USA

Modeling issues, related to the ATD transfer technique, were of
particular interest in this session. The challenges that remain
have to do with the development and validation of accurate models,
and/or performance bounds, for end-to-end delay distributions.
These models should include any significant dependence effects and
allow for general traffic processes, which can be related to the
various services provided by the network. A further challenge lies
in the integration of control and resource allocation strategies
into these models.

The broad range of communication issues treated in the session
papers generated much interest. Here we give some final
perspectives. On occasion, we will comment specifically on a
particular question and response, presented in the discussion.

The paper by Stanfill, while not directly related to ISDN Traffic
Engineering, Design and Planning, dealt with and raised issues of
interest to the teletraffic community. Topics such as
interconnection architectures, control, reliability, networking,
routing and buffering, traffic patterns resulting from different
types of applications, were touched on either directly by the paper
or indirectly via the discussion. There was particular interest in,
for example, control and assigment issues for general classes of
applications. Finally, teletraffic issues such as the size of
information packets, circuit vs. packet switching, and dynamic
communications needs, were also discussed.

The paper by Seraj dealt with the important problem of studying the
performance of the basic access D-Channel, offered traffic mixtures
resulting from different customer and service types. It is
generally agreed that, under the low signaling load, with proper
control, priority assignment, and implementation, the D-channel
signaling performance should be acceptable. This is supported by
comments by P.J. Kuehn and the paper by R.A. Skoog. They also
point out the importance of including processing times in the
analysis. Other important points are raised in the comments by P.J.
Kuehn and the discussion of processor scheduling in support of
signaling performance in R.A. Skoog's paper.

The paper on modeling of the ATD transfer technique generated many
questions dealing with modeling assumptions, allocation and control
of network resources, reference to earlier relevant work, as well as
other issues. Since the models presented for dimensioning the
switch control queues and the depacketizer queues, as well as for
engineering the depacketizer delay parameters, contain many
simplifying assumptions (e.g., independence of delays at
intermediate nodes, normality of end-to-end delays, etc., used in
build-out delay calculations), more extensive validation
experiments, than those reported, would be of interest. Important
control issues, which need further consideration, are the problems

of congestion control and resource allocation. The paper considers congestion control to be an off-line function and the allocation of bandwidth is raised in the question of L.G. Mason. We note that issues associated with the design of switch overload and congestion control strategies, in an ISDN environment are treated in the paper by A.E. Eckberg and P.E. Wirth. A final point worth noting has to do with the response to the question by J.M. Holtzman relating to the solution of the nD/D/1 multiplexer model. The algorithm specified in Eckberg '79 [A.E. Eckberg. Jr., "The Single Server Queue with Period Arrival Process and Deterministic Service Times", IEEE Transactions on Communications, Vol. Com.-27, No.3 March 1979, pp.556-562], yields a computationally efficient exact solution for the complementary waiting time distribution which is not limited to less than 20 lines (straightforward implementation utilizing standard double precision yelds exact computations for the waiting time distribution for numbers of lines in excess of 130). In Eckberg '82 [A.E. Eckberg. Jr., "Response Time Analysis for Pipelining Jobs in a Tree Network of Processors", Applied Probability – Computer Science – The Interface, Vol. I, R.L. Disney and T.J. Ott, Eds., Cambridge, MA, Birkhauser, 1982, pp.382-413], a closed form expression was given for the coefficients for which a recursive solution was given in Eckberg '79. Nevertheless [Gra'84] provides an alternate elegant solution for quantities of interest.

TRAFFIC ENGINEERING for ISDN Design and Planning
M. Bonatti and M. Decina (Editors)
Elsevier Science Publishers B.V. (North-Holland)
© IAC, 1988

OPTIMIZATION, ACCESS CONTROL AND RESOURCE ALLOCATION : CRUCIAL PROBLEMS IN DESIGNING ISDN ACCESSES AND SWITCHES

(Chairman Introduction to the Afternoon Session on System)

Jacques Labetoulle

CNET - France

The last technical session covered a wide range of topics, namely:

- Engineering of Common Signaling Networks,

- Robust ISDN Accesses,

- Multirate Switching Networks,

- Overload and Control Strategies for ISDN Switches,

- Engineering of LAPD Frame Relay Protocols,

- DASS1 Protocol Performance.

The lectures and the discussion revealed that a great effort is still needed for a better understanding of the behaviour of the access and switching part of ISDN. During the session it was noticed that these parts of future networks will be very costly, thus it will become crucial to optimize them and to control the access to the network.

Another reason of this effort comes from the still existing uncertainty on offered traffics. That means that the system must be able to adapt the resource allocation to the varying demands. This last topic was the subject of some major contributions to the session.

In particular:

The paper on Common Channel Signaling by R.A. Skoog offers considerations on the D-Channel and the CCS7 Network. The D-Channel capacity and the number of D-Channels that can be supported by a D-Channel processing module are considered. Referring to the CCS7 Network the maximum load that a signaling link can support is determined, engineering it for Steady State Conditions, for Transmission Errors and for Changeover Transients. Finally a Congestion Control procedure is analyzed in order to individuate critical characteristics of the flows offered to the signaling links.

The paper on Economical and Robust ISDN Access by N. Kim and C. Pack analyzes various ISDN access architectures when a Remote Terminal/Digital Loop Carrier System is considered relatively to the better tradeoff between various criteria, including facility utilization, GOS targets and sensitivity to forecast errors. A new robust access scheme is proposed.

G. Niestegge discusses Non-blocking Switching Networks for multichannel connections and introduces "Wide-sense" Non-blocking Arrangements and rearrangement procedures. Independent switching, parallel switching and non-blocking parallel switching of multichannel connections on a Two-Stage Reversed Switching Arrangement are considered. Three-Stage Reversed Switching are also shortly discussed.

A.E. Eckberg and P. Wirth discuss issues associated with designing the real-time traffic control architecture for a network of switches. The large number of call types in an ISDN, the need to support pre-ISDN and ISDN interfaces and call types, and the uncertainty in the ISDN call mixes are considered as stressing the importance of an effective network control architecture in providing robustness to varying network traffic conditions. The main factors influencing the switching technology and the chosen set of Performance Objectives in pre-ISDN and in ISDN environments are discussed. After a description of some possible components of a control architecture, with some comments on their effectivness, the authors propose some guidelines for designing a control architecture in a multiservice environment.

K.M. Rege and K.J. Chen, in their paper dealing with the engineering of LAPD Frame-Relay Protocols, present a model of LAPD based packet switching networks ignoring the control aspects such as call-set-up and tear-down. The model incorporate LAPD protocol's features which may have significant performance implications, including : dropping out-of-sequence frames, layer 2 timers, rejects, poll frames and responses to poll, frames loss because of buffer overflows, "stop-duration" control scheme. Three kinds of virtual circuits ("character interactive", "block interative" and "file transfer") generate the traffic patterns. The performance of the frame-relay and edge-terminated LAPD implementations without congestion control are compared and the performance of the frame-relay implementation with stop duration congestion control is discussed.

S.E. Swedan, D.G. Smith and J.L. Smith, in their paper dealing with the performance of the DASS1 protocol, examine an aspect of the retransmission procedure and discuss a method that can be used to improve the protocol performance. The performance is discussed in terms of maximum throughput, mean transfer time and total channel load. The effect of the gap period and the degradation due to one frame error are discussed.

TRAFFIC ENGINEERING for ISDN Design and Planning
M. Bonatti and M. Decina (Editors)
Elsevier Science Publishers B.V. (North-Holland)
© IAC, 1988

PERFORMANCE AND ENGINEERING OF COMMON CHANNEL SIGNALING NETWORKS SUPPORTING ISDN

R. A. Skoog

AT&T Bell Laboratories
Holmdel, New Jersey 07733 U.S.A.

With ISDN a broad range of signaling traffic will be carried, and this paper considers the effects of this traffic on the performance and engineering of signaling networks. We consider the performance and engineering issues for the D-channel and the common channel signaling network. For the D-channel we discuss the capacity and delay performance, and for the common channel signaling network we develop results for signaling link engineering and congestion control. A focus is placed on the effects of user-to-user information since it has the greatest potential for affecting message lengths and signaling performance.

1. INTRODUCTION

Common Channel Signaling (CCS) is an integral component of ISDN, and properly engineered CCS networks will be critical for the provision of ISDN services. ISDN services require out-of-band signaling all the way to the customer, where the signaling between the network Exchange Termination (ET) and the customer Terminal Equipment (TE) is over a D-channel using the CCITT Digital Access Signaling System[1]. In the network, signaling is provided by CCITT Signaling System No. 7 (CSS7)[2] for information flow and control between network signaling points. The first three levels of CSS7 make up the Message Transfer Part (MTP), which serves as the transport system for the reliable transfer of signaling messages between network signaling points. At the higher levels we consider the ISDN User Part (ISDN-UP), providing the exchange of call control information between switching systems, and the Transaction Capability (TC), providing for the exchange of non-circuit related data between signaling points.

Figure 1 illustrates a generic structure of ISDN access, and represents the distributed processing used in modern exchange systems. The access lines from the customer TE (either basic rate 2B+D or primary rate 23B+D) terminate on an Access Distribution Module, which separates the B- and D-channels, and the D-channels terminate on D-channel Processing Modules. The D-channel Processing Modules provide the functionality to terminate the Q.921/Q.931 protocol and interwork with call processing, the CSS7 signaling network and the packet data network.

In this paper we are concerned with the performance and engineering issues related to the D-channel and CSS7 signaling networks. One signaling capability of ISDN that has the potential for providing feature rich services is the transport of User-to-User Information (UUI) from customer TE to customer TE. UUI can significantly alter the characteristics of signaling traffic, and its potential effects must be understood if the signaling networks are to be properly engineered for ISDN services. In the next section we briefly consider the performance and engineering issues relating to the D-channel and the D-channel processing module. In Section 3 we consider the CSS7 signaling network performance and engineering issues related to transporting UUI. The potential effect of UUI is to increase the message lengths carried on the CSS7 network, and we examine what effect this could have on signaling link engineering and congestion control.

2. ACCESS CONSIDERATIONS

The major engineering considerations for the D-channel access are the D-channel capacity and the number of D-channels that can be supported by a D-channel processing module. The main

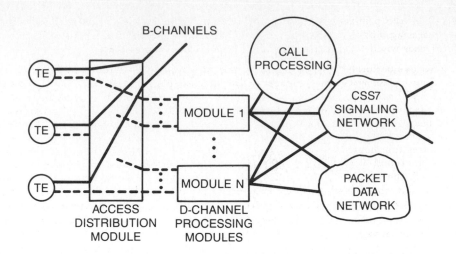

FIGURE 1   GENERIC STRUCTURE OF ISDN ACCESS

performance measures are delay and probability of overload. The major components of the delay in each direction are the queueing and transmission time on the D-channel and the processing time in the D-channel processing module.

2.1 D-Channel Capacity

The D-channel signaling traffic consists of signaling for B-channels, signaling to set up Temporary Signaling Connections (TSCs) for UUI, and the UUI on TSCs and Permanent Signaling Connections (PSCs). In addition the D-channel can carry packet data, but since signaling is given priority, the data traffic will not have a significant effect on signaling queueing delays. Therefore, from a signaling perspective, the D-channel capacity relates to the amount of signaling traffic the D-channel can support without having excessive queueing delays. Some simple calculations show that the D-channel signaling capacity is large, and therefore D-channel queueing delay should not be a major factor in access delay.

Consider the basic rate access and the signaling load resulting from B-channel signaling. There is a maximum of about 330 octets carried from ET to TE for each call set-up. The TE to ET load is about 10% less. If the maximum of 130 octets of UUI is included in all messages that can carry UUI, the maximum transfer per call is about 655 octets. Assume both B-channels are operating at 1 Erlang with a mean holding time of 4 minutes, which yields 15 calls per hour per B-channel. The resulting utilization on the 16 kb/s D-channel is about 0.14% without UUI and 0.27% with UUI. Thus, the load caused by B-channel call set-up is negligibly small, and significant signaling load could result only if there were large amounts of UUI sent on TSCs and PSCs.

For primary rate access the 64 kb/s D-channel can be used to signal for several primary rate lines, and thus the signaling load has the potential for being much greater. Using the above maximum load figures, the number of B-channels required to load the D-channel to 1% utilization is approximately 60 (2.5 primary rate lines) when no UUI is present and 30 when UUI is present. Thus, there is ample D-channel capacity to handle call set-up for B-channels and carry significant amounts of UUI without causing appreciable queueing delays.

2.2 The D-Channel Processing Module

Since D-channel queueing delays are not seen to be appreciable, the D-channel processing module will be the primary contributor to D-channel signaling delay and overload. Each D-channel processing module will service several D-channels, and the performance characteristics of this processor will determine the number of D-channels it can support.

The functions performed by the D-channel processing module, aside from Layer 1 functions, fall into three major functional blocks: Layer 2 multiplex procedures, Layer 2 data link procedures, and Layer 3 procedures. On receipt of a frame, the multiplex procedure checks for flags, does error detection, and if the frame is correct delivers it to the appropriate data link procedure based on the data link connection identifier. On frame transmission the multiplex procedure provides the data link layer contention resolution based on SAPI. The Layer 2 data link procedures functional block performs all the peer-to-peer Layer 2 functions. The Layer 3 procedures functional block does the Layer 3 message processing and provides the interfaces to call processing, the CSS7 network and the packet data network. We assume that the system is designed so that the Layer 2 multiplex procedures are not the bottleneck, and that the performance is limited by a single microprocessor providing the other two functional blocks for all D-channels terminating on the D-channel processing module. This microprocessor will be called the core processor.

The core processor must do a complex array of tasks, which vary for different types of messages received. Queueing models must be developed to adequately characterize this system. The design of scheduling algorithms will be critical to achieving satisfactory delay and overload performance. For example, a typical implementation might use interrupt processing to handle message processing, and the issue of priority must be addressed. To prevent packet data from affecting signaling delays, it would be desirable to give signaling priority in the core processor. It is also desirable to give priority to messages received from the network side, since in overload the traffic on the D-channels can be more quickly and effectively controlled. Scheduling will also play a role in overload control. An effective technique to handle overloads with interrupt processing is to switch to a clocked schedule when loads get too high. This reduces the effect of overheads in switching between different processes, and provides more available real time for message processing. Finally, an important area to address is how to engineer and balance loads on D-channel processing modules. These problems are similar to what is currently done for switching systems, and the existing body of knowledge should provide considerable insights into the signaling problem. The engineering criteria for signaling, however, should be more conservative than for switching, since the signaling portion of the network should not be a bottleneck.

3. CCS7 NETWORK CONSIDERATIONS

In this section we examine the signaling link engineering and congestion control performance in a CCS7 signaling network carrying ISDN traffic. The major effect that ISDN will have on the signaling network is that UUI will be transported either in ISDN-UP messages or as separate messages on TSCs and PSCs. Carrying UUI in the signaling network has the potential for increasing the message lengths, and this will affect both delay and congestion control performance. To achieve satisfactory delay performance, the signaling links may have to be engineered to operate at lower utilizations, decreasing the network efficiency. For congestion control, we find that larger message lengths increase the response time and the queue lengths reached while traffic is controlled. This results in larger congestion threshold levels, and thus the allowed delay of higher priority traffic during congestion must be increased.

In a previous paper[4] the delay performance of signaling links under steady state load was considered, and it was shown that the introduction of UUI without a limitation of maximum message length can cause a significant increase in the variance of delay at all link utilizations. Those results suggested that a limit on UUI message lengths would be desirable. In this section we examine signaling link delay performance from the point of view of determining the engineered load, and this involves looking at both steady state and transient conditions. In Reference[4] signaling network congestion control was analyzed to determine the effect of UUI. This section extends that analysis to give a more complete characterization of the congestion controls.

3.1 Signaling Link Engineering

Signaling networks provide the high availability required by providing diverse extra capacity to handle the load of any failed component. The amount of redundant capacity depends on the network architecture. We will assume the configuration used in North America, where a simple mating of Signal Transfer Points (STPs) is used, and in this configuration the links are engineered to handle twice their normal load. To determine the maximum load that a signaling link can support, two conditions must be considered. One is where the link is operating in steady state, and the other is where the transmission error rate becomes high enough to cause a signaling link changeover (CO).

3.1.1 Engineering for Steady State Conditions The approach used to engineer signaling links is to determine a maximum utilization, ρ_{max}, that the link should have when there are no failures in the network. To handle failures, the link should be able to support a utilization of $2\rho_{max}$. One approach to determining ρ_{max} is to establish upper bounds on the mean and 95% delay, where the delay is what would be seen at a random point in time during a random busy hour. Since the probability of having a failure in the network at a random point in time is small, the probability distribution for this delay is determined by the steady state behavior of the link with no failures, and thus when the link is operating at ρ_{max}. To prevent significant degradation in delay performance under failure conditions, delay objectives must also be established for signaling links operating at $2\rho_{max}$.

The delay objectives for the link operating at $2\rho_{max}$ could be stated as upper bounds on the mean and 95% delays, but this is not enough of a constraint. Simply looking at delay can lead to operating points that are on the steep portion of the delay *vs* utilization curve. Thus it is necessary to also impose an upper bound on the delay sensitivity. Let $Q(\rho)$ denote the mean queueing delay at utilization ρ. The objective that we impose on sensitivity is that for some upper bound, L, $\frac{dQ}{d\rho}(2\rho_{max}) \leqslant L$.

The choice for the engineered load ρ_{max} will be the minimum obtained from the criteria given above. Since $\rho_{max} < 0.5$, the delays at ρ_{max} lie on the flat portion of the delay curve, and consequently the delay criteria for ρ_{max} are not critical. As a result, the delay criteria for $2\rho_{max}$ are the ones that usually dominate and establish ρ_{max}, and this will be assumed here.

We use the following notation:

$$
\begin{aligned}
S &= \text{message service time (a random variable)} \\
\overline{S}, \overline{S^2} &= \text{first and second moments of } S \\
\overline{M} &= \text{mean message length} \\
\mu &= \text{message service rate} \\
\lambda &= \text{message arrival rate} \\
C &= \text{link speed (octets/sec)} \\
\rho &= \text{link utilization} \\
T_f &= \text{service time of fill-in signal units} \\
Q(\rho) &= \text{mean queueing delay at utilization } \rho
\end{aligned}
$$

To illustrate the effect of UUI on ρ_{max} we assume the message arrival process is Poisson, and thus the queueing delay is given by (see Q.706[2])

$$
Q(\rho) = \frac{T_f}{2} + \frac{\rho}{2(1-\rho)} \frac{\overline{S^2}}{\overline{S}} . \tag{1}
$$

A delay constraint requiring $Q(2\rho_{max}) \leqslant D$ gives

$$
\rho_{max} \leqslant \frac{D}{2D + \overline{S^2}/\overline{S}} , \tag{2}
$$

and the sensitivity constraint $\frac{dQ}{d\rho}(2\rho_{max}) \leqslant L$ gives

$$\rho_{max} \leqslant \frac{1}{2}\left[1 - \left[\frac{\overline{S^2}/\overline{S}}{2L}\right]^{\frac{1}{2}}\right].$$

(3)

Figure 2 illustrates the bounds on ρ_{max} given by (2) and (3) for D=15 ms and L=100 ms.

To put these results in perspective, we will look at some approximate traffic models. The model for signaling traffic without UUI is equal arrival rates of ISDN-UP messages and Transaction Capability (TC) messages with message lengths of 21 and 60 octets, respectively. For UUI included in ISDN-UP messages we consider having 40% of the messages carrying UUI. The amount of UUI is either 32 octets or 128 octets. For TSC or PSC UUI we assume that 20% of the message load is TSC/PSC UUI, and the message lengths are 128 or 256 octets. Table 1 gives the values for $\overline{S^2}/\overline{S}$ for the various combinations of these traffic patterns assuming 64 kb/s signaling links.

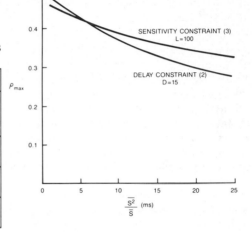

Table 1　Values of $\overline{S^2}/\overline{S}$ for Different Traffic Mixes

TSC/PSC UUI	ISDN-UP UUI		
	NO UUI	32 Octet	128 Octet
NO UUI	6.3	6.6	12
128 Octet	10.6	10.4	13.3
256 Octet	22	21.2	21.8

FIGURE 2　MAXIMUM LINK UTILIZATION ρ_{max} FROM DELAY CONSTRAINT (2) AND SENSITIVITY CONSTRAINT (3)

The effect of UUI on ρ_{max} can be significant with large message lengths. The worst case illustrated in Table 1 is 256 octet UUI on TSC/PSC, and it makes little difference whether UUI is also in the ISUP messages. Comparing this traffic mix with no UUI present shows that ρ_{max} would be reduced by about 19% if the sensitivity constraint (3) is used, and it would be reduced by about 30% if the delay constraint (2) is used. One conclusion that can be reached is that if UUI is to be permitted without limiting its message length, then the links will have to be engineered to lower utilizations.

3.1.2 Engineering for Transmission Errors and Changeover Transients When transmission errors occur, all messages sent after an errored message must be retransmitted. This causes the effective link utilization to be increased, and if the error rate is high enough it will have a significant effect on delay. CSS7 protects against serious degradation in performance by removing traffic from a link when its error rate becomes too high. This procedure is called a Changeover (CO). The decision to begin a CO is based on a "leaky bucket" counter. For each signal unit received in error a +1 count is recorded, and for each 256 signal units received a -1 count is recorded if the cumulative count is > 0. When the cumulative count reaches 64 a CO is started. The length of time it takes from the beginning of an error burst to the beginning of CO depends on the signal unit error rate, and at some error rates a sizable queue will build up before CO. The size of this queue build-up will depend on ρ and the message length distribution, and thus the CO transients must be considered in choosing ρ_{max}.

To analyze link behavior with transmission errors, we will use the concept of virtual service time introduced by Bux, Kummerle, and Truong[5]. Consider a message to be received in error. Since all messages sent after the considered message will be retransmitted, the service time of this message is the time it takes to send a copy of it that will be received without error. This service time is called the virtual service time. For the CSS7 protocol the virtual service time, S_v, can be modeled as $S_v = S + N(S + t_{ack})$, where the random variable N is the number of retransmissions and t_{ack} is the time to receive an acknowledgement after message transmission (twice the propagation time plus processing time at the far end). Let p_m denote the probability that a message is received in error. Then $Pr(N=n) = p_m^n(1 - p_m)$, and the expected value of S_v is

$$E[S_v] = \frac{\bar{S}}{1 - p_m} + t_{ack}\frac{p_m}{1 - p_m}. \tag{4}$$

The effective message service rate, μ_{eff}, is then

$$\mu_{eff} = \frac{1 - p_m}{1 + p_m \mu t_{ack}}\mu . \tag{5}$$

The queueing delay is given by (1) with $\bar{S}$ and $\bar{S^2}$ replaced by $\bar{S}_v$ and $\bar{S}_v^2$, respectively, and ρ replaced by $\rho_{eff} = \lambda/\mu_{eff}$.

The build-up in the link transmit queue during a CO event is illustrated in Figure 3. A noise burst begins at $t=0$ and a build-up to Q_{co} occurs while the "leaky bucket" fills to the threshold count of 64. At that time, t_{co}, a CO is started. Before traffic is diverted to alternate paths, a procedure is performed between the two ends of the link, and for a time interval, δ, all messages received will be queued. The expected queue length when traffic begins to be rerouted is therefore $\bar{Q}_{co} + \rho C\delta$. We assume that this queue is transferred quickly to an alternate link, and therefore messages arriving to the alternate link just after this transfer will see an expected queueing delay of $\bar{Q}_{co}/C + \rho\delta$. The link engineering criterion we will consider is limiting this expected delay to a value τ_{co} when the link that failed was operating at utilization ρ_{max}. The engineering criterion is therefore to have ρ_{max} satisfy

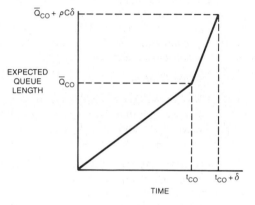

FIGURE 3   ILLUSTRATION OF QUEUE BUILD-UP BEFORE CHANGEOVER

$$\bar{Q}_{co}^{max}(\rho_{max}) + \rho_{max}C\delta \leqslant \tau_{co}C , \tag{6}$$

where $\bar{Q}_{co}^{max}(\rho) = \underset{p_m}{Max}[\bar{Q}_{co}(\rho)]$.

To examine this criterion, we determine $\bar{Q}_{co}^{max}(\rho)$. The maximum of $\bar{Q}_{co}$ will occur when $\rho_{eff} > 1$, and in this condition the link will quickly become fully utilized with message signal units (i.e., there will be no fill-in signal units). In this case the time for the "leaky bucket" count to reach 64, t_{co}, is approximated by $t_{co} \approx (64/\mu)/(p_m - 1/256)$. During this time the message throughput of the link is μ_{eff}, and $\bar{Q}_{co}$ can be approximated by[6]

$$\bar{Q}_{co} \approx (\lambda - \mu_{eff})t_{co}\bar{M}$$

$$= \left[\rho - \frac{1 - p_m}{1 + p_m\mu t_{ack}}\right]\left[\frac{64\bar{M}}{p_m - \frac{1}{256}}\right] . \tag{7}$$

Differentiating (7) with respect to p_m shows the maximum of $\bar{Q}_{co}$, $\bar{Q}_{co}^{max}$, occurs at the value of p_m satisfying the quadratic equation

$$p_m^2 - \frac{2(1 - \rho)}{1 + \rho\mu t_{ack}}p_m - \frac{1 - \rho - \frac{1 + \mu t_{ack}}{256}}{(1 + \rho\mu t_{ack})\mu t_{ack}} = 0. \tag{8}$$

Figure 4 illustrates the queue build-up at time $t_{co} + \delta$, $\bar{Q}_{co}^{max}(\rho) + \rho C\delta$, as a function of ρ for $\overline{M}$ ranging from 40 octets (no UUI) to 100 octets. Also shown is the application of the constraint (6) with τ_{co} = 375 ms. These results show that if (6) is the dominant constraint, then the message length can have a measurable effect on the engineered link capacity ρ_{max}. For the case illustrated, increasing the average message length from 40 to 100 octets decreases ρ_{max} by about 0.08.

In determining the signaling link engineered capacity, ρ_{max}, the delay constraints (2) and (3) and the CO transient constraint (6) must be considered, and the smallest value obtained for ρ_{max} will determine the link capacity. From the above results, no matter which constraint becomes dominant, the message length distribution will have a measurable effect.

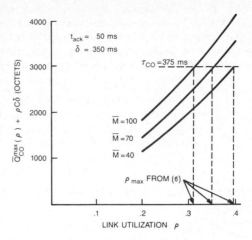

FIGURE 4 MAXIMUM OF EXPECTED QUEUE LENGTH DURING CHANGEOVER

3.2 Congestion Control

The CSS7 congestion control procedures were analyzed in Reference[4] to determine the effect of the message length distribution and how UUI could affect the network. In this section we will extend that analysis and provide a more complete characterization of the congestion control response.

3.2.1 Congestion Control Procedures

We consider the national option of CSS7 congestion control in which there are congestion access priorities. In this option of congestion control, there are $N+1$ $(0 \leqslant N \leqslant 3)$ levels of congestion access priority and N congestion onset thresholds T_n $(n=1,...,N)$. When the buffer occupancy exceeds a given congestion onset threshold, say n, the congestion status of the signaling link is set to n. When a message arrives to the link destined for signaling point (SP) X, its congestion priority is checked. If its congestion priority is $\geqslant n$, the message is transmitted normally. Otherwise a transfer-controlled (TFC) message is sent to the originating signaling point in response. The TFC gives the destination SP, X, of the received message and the congestion level, n, of the signaling link. The originating signaling point then stops sending messages of priority $\leqslant n-1$ to SP X. These actions continue until the transmit buffer occupancy drops to the congestion abatement threshold A_n. In addition, there is a corresponding discard threshold D_n, and while the transmit buffer occupancy exceeds this discard threshold all messages received with priority $\leqslant n-1$ are discarded. The congestion thresholds are chosen so that $A_n < T_n < D_n < T_{n+1}$. Methods for choosing congestion thresholds are described in Reference[6].

When a signaling point receives a TFC message, it starts a timer, T15 in Q.704,[2] and when this timer expires it sends a congestion test message to the destination given in the TFC message. At the same time it starts another timer, T16 in Q.704, and if a TFC is not received by the time T16 expires, the signaling point starts sending traffic to the concerned destination. If it receives a TFC for that destination, it starts timer T15 again and repeats the above procedure. Assuming T16 is set to be approximately equal to the time it takes to receive a TFC in response to a congestion test message, the length of time a signaling point will be under control from a TFC will be an integer multiple of the control time $t_c = T15 + T16$. Timer T15 should be set so that t_c is slightly larger than the time it takes to reach the abatement threshold. If it was much shorter, the congestion test messages would add to the signaling link traffic and prolong the congestion. If it was much larger, the link would be under utilized. One important application of an analysis of congestion control response is to properly set timer T15.

3.2.2 Analysis of Congestion Control Response

We consider a signaling link with transmit buffer occupancy at the first congestion threshold, T_1, at time $t=0$. The traffic to the link is assumed to consist of two independent Poisson streams. One stream consists of UUI messages, and these messages will be assumed to have congestion priority 0. This will be the controlled traffic, and its related parameters will have index $i=0$. The other traffic stream consists of ISDN-UP and TC messages, and these messages will be assumed to have congestion priority $\geqslant 1$. This traffic will not be controlled, and it will be indexed with $i=1$. The following notation will be used:

λ_i = message arrival rate for traffic stream i
M_i = average message length for traffic stream i
S_i = average service time for traffic stream $i = M_i/C$
ρ_i = link utilization from traffic stream $i = \lambda_i S_i$
N_t = transmit buffer occupancy at time t (octets)
$\overline{N}_t$ = the expected value of N_t
t_c = the control time $T15 + T16$ for the congestion test procedure

The traffic rate to the congested link is $\lambda_0 M_0 + \lambda_1 M_1$, and we assume the link is driven into congestion because this traffic rate is greater than the link speed C (i.e., $\rho_0 + \rho_1 > 1$). It is also assumed that $\rho_1 < 1$ so that after the UUI traffic has been completely removed the link will no longer be congested. To simplify the presentation, we assume that the time between sending a TFC and the resultant reduction in traffic at the congested link is negligible.

We first summarize the analysis in Reference[4]. The mean transmit buffer occupancy, $\overline{N}_t$, is determined to characterize the congestion control response time and transmit buffer transients. We assume there are K independent UUI source-destination pairs sending traffic to the congested link, each with message rate λ_0/K. Let X_t denote the number of UUI source-destination pairs that have been sent congestion notification in $(0,t]$. Its expected value is given by[4]

$$E[X_t] = K(1 - e^{-\lambda_0 t/K}) . \tag{9}$$

Let $\lambda_{0,t}$ denote the UUI message arrival rate at time t and τ_r the time to reach the abatement threshold A_1. Then, for $0 \leqslant t < \tau_r$, $\lambda_{0,t} = (\lambda_0/K)/(K - X_{t-\tau_0})$. $\overline{N}_t$ is given by[4]

$$\overline{N}_t = T_1 + M_0 \int_0^t E[\lambda_{0,\sigma}]d\sigma + M_1\lambda_1 t - Ct$$

$$= T_1 + M_0 \left[\lambda_0\tau_0 + K - Ke^{-\lambda_0(t-\tau_0)/K} \right] + M_1\lambda_1 t - Ct , \quad 0 \leqslant t < \tau_r \tag{10}$$

Figure 5 illustrates the behavior of $\overline{N}_t$. When the onset threshold T_1 is reached at $t = 0$, the controlled traffic begins to be removed. However, $\overline{N}_t$ continues to rise until time τ_1, which is easily found from (10) to be

$$\tau_1 = \psi_1 KS_0 ; \quad \psi_1 = \frac{1}{\rho_0}\ln\frac{\rho_0}{1-\rho_1} \tag{11}$$

and it reaches the level

$$\overline{N}_{\tau_1} = T_1 + \kappa_1 M_0 K ; \quad \kappa_1 = 1 - \frac{1-\rho_1}{\rho_0}\left[1 + \ln\frac{\rho_0}{1-\rho_1} \right] . \tag{12}$$

The time it takes for $\overline{N}_t$ to return to the onset threshold level T_1 is denoted by τ_2 and given by[4]

$$\tau_2 = \psi_2 KS_0 ; \quad \psi_2 = \xi/\rho_0 , \tag{13}$$

where ξ satisfies the equation $(1-e^{-\xi})/\xi = (1-\rho_1)/\rho_0$.

We now analyze the behavior of $\overline{N}_t$ after the abatement threshold A_1 is reached. As discussed above, if a source-destination pair went into control at time t, it will begin sending traffic after time it_c, where i is the smallest integer satisfying $\overline{N}_{t+it_c} < A_1$. Assume $\tau_r = kt_c$ for some integer k. The number of source-destination pairs to begin sending traffic by time $\tau_r + \delta$, denoted by Z_δ, is the sum of the number that went into control during the intervals $[0, \delta)$, $[t_c, t_c+\delta)$, ..., $[(k-1)t_c, (k-1)t_c+\delta)$. Using (9) it follows that the expected number to come under control in the interval $[jt_c, jt_c+\delta)$ is $Ke^{-\lambda_0 jt_c/K}(1 - e^{-\lambda_0\delta/K})$. Summing from $j = 1$ to k gives

$$\bar{Z}_\delta = K(1 - e^{-\lambda\phi/K})\frac{1 - e^{-\lambda\sigma_r/K}}{1 - e^{-\lambda\sigma_c/K}} \ . \tag{14}$$

Since $X_{\tau_r+\delta} = X_{\tau_r} - Z_\delta$, (9) and (14) give, for $0 \leqslant \delta < t_c$,

$$\bar{X}_{\tau_r+\delta} = K(1 - e^{-\lambda\sigma_r/K})\left[1 - \frac{1 - e^{-\lambda\phi/K}}{1 - e^{-\lambda\sigma_c/K}}\right] \ . \tag{15}$$

To determine $\bar{N}_{\tau_r+\delta}$ we note that $E[\lambda_{0,\,\tau_r+\delta}] = (\lambda_0/K)(K - \bar{X}_{\tau_r+\delta})$, and hence for $0 \leqslant \delta < t_c$

$$\bar{N}_{\tau_r+\delta} = A_1 + (M_1\lambda_1 - C)\delta + M_0\int_0^\delta E[\lambda_{0,\,\tau_r+\sigma}]d\sigma$$

$$= A_1 - \left[1 - \rho_1 - \rho_0(e^{-\lambda\sigma_r/K} + \zeta)\right]C\delta - \zeta KM_0(1 - e^{-\lambda\phi/K}) \ , \tag{16}$$

where $\zeta = (1 - e^{-\lambda\sigma_r/K})/(1 - e^{-\lambda\sigma_c/K})$. The minimum of $\bar{N}_{\tau_r+\delta}$ occurs at $\delta = \delta^*$ given by

$$\delta^* = \psi_3KS_0 \ ; \ \psi_3 = -\frac{1}{\rho_0}\ln\gamma \ , \tag{17}$$

where $\gamma = (\rho_0\zeta + \rho_1 - 1 + \rho_0e^{-\lambda\sigma_r/K}/(\rho_0\zeta)$ and $\bar{N}_{\tau_r+\delta^*}$ is given by

$$\bar{N}_{\tau_r+\delta^*} = A_1 - \kappa_2M_0K \ ; \ \kappa_2 = \zeta[1 - \gamma(1 - \ln\gamma)] \ . \tag{18}$$

The above relationships are illustrated in Figure 5. The amount that $\bar{N}_t$ goes above T_1 and below A_1 is proportional to M_0K, and thus the overall size of the congestion control response is scaled by M_0K. The times τ_1, τ_2 and δ^* are proportional to KS_0, and thus a major portion of the overall cycle time is scaled by KS_0. In setting the abatement threshold, it is desirable to make it high enough that the probability of the queue becoming empty is small. This will keep the link operating at maximum throughput. The separation between T_1 and A_1 is determined to keep the probability small that the link will enter congestion when the traffic load has fallen below $\rho = 1$[6]. Therefore, as K or M_0 increase, A_1 should be increased, which in turn causes T_1 and all the other thresholds to be increased. The result is that with larger message lengths, the average delays during congestion seen by the higher priority traffic will go up.

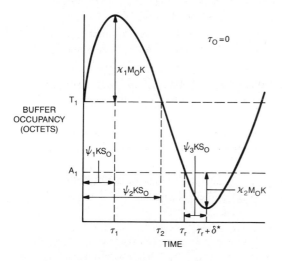

FIGURE 5   ILLUSTRATION OF BUFFER OCCUPANCY
DURING CONGESTION CONTROL

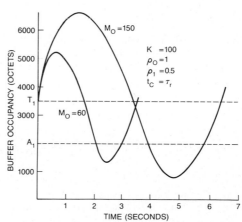

FIGURE 6   EXPECTED VALUE OF BUFFER OCCUPANCY, $\bar{N}_t$,
DURING CONGESTION CONTROL

Figure 6 illustrates these results for a case in which $k = 1$ (i.e., $t_c = \tau_r$). Two values for M_0 are considered. The smaller value, 60 octets, corresponds to TC traffic being controlled and no UUI present. The larger value, 150 octets, corresponds to UUI traffic being controlled. The scaling effects discussed above are apparent for both size and frequency. As discussed above, it is important to know the frequency of the response so that timer T15 can be set.

4. CONCLUSIONS

In this paper we have discussed the signaling performance and engineering issues related to ISDN for both the access and the CSS7 portion of the network. For the CSS7 portion of the network, we have described the signaling link engineering methodologies and developed results showing how the message length distribution can affect the engineered capacity. It was shown that if UUI introduces large messages into the network, then the maximum link utilization may have to be reduced by up to 30%. We also showed how link engineering must not only consider steady state queueing delays, but must also consider the transient behavior during signaling link changeover.

In analyzing congestion controls it is also found that message length can have a significant effect. The congestion control response was analyzed and found to be scaled in both magnitude and time by the mean message length of the controlled traffic and the number of source destination pairs contributing traffic. The result is that if larger message lengths are to be carried on the CSS7 network, then congestion thresholds will have to be increased, and consequently the delay experienced by higher priority traffic during congestion will increase. From the results obtained on signaling link delay behavior and CSS7 congestion controls, it appears reasonable to limit UUI message lengths. More study and understanding is needed to assess what restrictions on services a length limitation may have. However, it seems reasonable to begin service with a limitation that will assure the signaling network will provide a high level of performance for all users.

REFERENCES

1. CCITT Study Group XI, "Digital Access Signaling System, Red Book, Recommendation Q.920-Q.931," Volume VI, Fascicle VI.9, October, 1984.

2. CCITT Study Group XI, "Specifications of Signaling System No. 7, Red Book, Recommendations Q.701-Q.714 and Q.721-Q.795," Volume VI, Facicle VI.7, October, 1984.

4. A. R. Modarressi and R. A. Skoog, "Performance Considerations of Signaling Networks in an ISDN Environment," Proceedings of the Brussels Specialists Seminar on ISDN Traffic Issues, May, 1986.

5. W. Bux, K. Kummerle, and H. L. Truong, "Balanced HDLC Procedures: A Performance Analysis," IEEE Trans. on Communications, Vol. COM-28, No. 11, November, 1980, pp.1889-1898.

6. J. M. Akinpelu and R. A. Skoog, "Controlling Transients and Overloads in Common Channel Signaling Networks," Proceedings of ITC 11, Kyoto, September, 1985.

TRAFFIC ENGINEERING for ISDN Design and Planning
M. Bonatti and M. Decina (Editors)
Elsevier Science Publishers B.V. (North-Holland)
© IAC, 1988

SWITCH OVERLOAD AND FLOW CONTROL STRATEGIES IN AN ISDN ENVIRONMENT

A.E. ECKBERG and P.E. WIRTH

AT&T Bell Laboratories
Crawfords Corner Road
Holmdel, NJ   07733   USA

As the concepts of Integrated Services Digital Networks (ISDN) have evolved, numerous issues have been raised concerning the design and efficient operation of systems with ISDN capabilities. There are many architectural options in designing networks for both current and anticipated ISDN capabilities. This tutorial paper discusses issues associated with designing the real-time, traffic control architecture for the network of switches. The control objectives and control design issues are described and illustrated with generic architectural examples in order to develop a comprehensive philosophy and set of strategies that should underlie the design of an ISDN switch traffic control architecture.

Main Statement: Effective network overload control architectures in an ISDN environment allow the maximum usable capacity to be derived from the network resources.

1. INTRODUCTION

As the concept of Integrated Services Digital Networks (ISDN) has become a reality, numerous issues have been raised concerning the design and efficient operation of systems with ISDN capabilities. Much work has been and is being done in the standards arenas to define access arrangements and interfaces allowing ISDN terminal equipments to interface with ISDNs, and to provide effective internetworking between separate ISDNs [1]. However, standardization has not been imposed on the internals of an ISDN; consequently, developers and manufacturers of equipment and providers of services currently have many architectural options for ISDNs.

One of the factors complicating the design of an ISDN is the large number of call types that may coexist within it. A typical situation is for a network with ISDN capabilities to evolve from a pre-ISDN network, and thus network issues associated with the support of both ISDN and pre-ISDN interfaces and call types become important. Moreover, although all ISDN calls might be categorized as involving an ISDN "out-of-band" signaling arrangement extending to the end terminal, within this class there are likely to be a large number of diverse call characteristics, e.g.:
- circuit-switched calls;
- calls, not necessarily data-oriented, for which transport is effected via packet switching, possibly over a non-channelized interface;
- calls of different throughput classes, i.e., requiring different transmission rates, either packet- or circuit-switched (e.g., voice, data, image, video);
- multi-media calls (e.g., voice/data or voice/image), i.e., requiring simultaneous connections between pairs of end terminals;
- calls for which throughput requirements change within the call itself (i.e., variable-rate calls);
- calls associated with special enhanced features, either switch- or outside-vendor-provided, at call set-up or at random times within the call duration;
- calls supporting applications with different end-to-end service requirements, e.g., with respect to network call set-up completion or packet delays and/or throughputs.

In the above it is important to anticipate call types that future standards may require ISDNs to support. The wide spectrum of telecommunications capabilities and flexibility made possible through ISDN brings with it a large degree of uncertainty concerning which call types will be most prevalent and how greatly the traffic they generate will stress the network resources. This uncertainty may itself lead to the need for conservative traffic engineering of the network.

The architecture of a network can greatly influence the efficiency and effectiveness with which the network can be made to operate. One particularly important component of the overall network architecture, which helps address the traffic uncertainty issue mentioned above, is the network *traffic control architecture,* i.e., the system of automatic algorithms implemented within network components and control actions initiated either manually or automatically via operations systems, the purpose of which is to derive the maximum benefit from the existing network resources in handling whatever traffic arises. An effective network traffic control architecture should provide robustness to varying network traffic conditions so that the network and its resources can be efficiently engineered.

This paper is concerned with one element of the overall network traffic control architecture, namely the *real-time, traffic control architecture* of the network switches. The real-time control architecture of each network switch must manage the switch resources needed for call control and data transport, and in particular provide switch resource protection against traffic overloads in order to maintain a high level of throughput even when the switch and/or the network are stressed beyond their normal traffic-handling capacities. In addition, the switch control architecture may have as an objective the fair allocation of switch resources among the various end users [2]; this may be especially important during switch overloads. This switch control architecture encompasses switch overload controls that are needed to effectively deny or throttle new call setup requests at the switch based on the current and projected future utilizations of all switch resources [3,4,5], as well as switch flow and congestion control actions that are needed to manage the allocation and utilization of switch resources in real-time by calls currently in progress, especially for packet switched calls [6,7].

The number of issues associated with the real-time, automatic control architecture of a switch in an ISDN environment is enormous. For the purposes of this tutorial paper we draw attention to issues in the following two broad categories: *control objectives* and *control design.* These issues are illustrated with generic architectural examples in order to develop a comprehensive philosophy and set of strategies that should underly the design of an ISDN switch control architecture to accommodate both current and possible future ISDN capabilities.

2. OBJECTIVES INFLUENCING SWITCH CONTROL ARCHITECTURES

The first step in devising a strategy for a switch traffic control architecture is to establish the objectives that need to be achieved through use of such controls. Such objectives should capture the essential performance issues associated with the wide spectrum of services (both call management and call transport) that the switch may support. To draw attention to these performance issues, we first sketch out the evolution of switching technology through circuit switching, packet switching, integrated circuit and packet switching, and finally to the use of high speed VLSI technology to achieve maximum flexibility in integrating a wide variety of services via a uniform switching vehicle. We then summarize the most relevant performance objectives that result.

2.1 Evolution of Switching Technology, and Associated Performance Issues

Basic circuit switching, the core switching capability of most telecommunications networks, involves the establishment of a fixed bandwidth connection through a switch, or series of switches, which may then be used at 100% of its bandwidth for the duration of the call. Because no traffic-related performance issues are associated with a circuit-switched call once the connection has been established, traffic engineering attention is typically focused at performance issues that arise during the setup and tear-down phase of the call. These issues revolve around the ability of the switch to respond quickly to actions by the caller (influenced by the availability of switch processor real time), as well as the availability of switch resources that are needed during certain phases of the setup (i.e., service circuits) and switch resources that will be needed for the duration of the call (connectivity through the switch fabric). The connection bandwidth being requested may be one of a finite set of bandwidths (i.e., multi-rate switching), in which case the availability of switch fabric connectivity depends on the bandwidth being requested.

A variety of signaling delays during call setup and various post-dialing delay components, to which the caller may be sensitized by auditory cues, must be kept within carefully chosen design objectives in order for the switch to provide adequate performance. Excessive signaling delays are likely to result in abandonments and subsequent retries by impatient callers.

The original motivation of packet switching was to achieve improved transmission efficiency in the transport of data between two end users. Since the majority of data has "bursty" traffic characteristics, data transport over a circuit-switched network connection results in the network resources allocated for that connection being used for only a fraction of the duration of the connection. Packet switching attempts to achieve improved efficiency by utilizing network resources only when the need for such resources arises during the individual data bursts associated with an end-to-end data transaction. The packet switching technique involves segmenting each burst of data into a sequence of packets according to some packetizing algorithm, appending to each resulting packet a header of addressing and control information that specifies how the packet is to be transported through the network and how it is to be handled at the destination, and then transporting each packet through the network, usually as soon as it has been created. The packetizing and data-reassembling algorithms may be provided at the network interfaces, or may be performed in the end-user terminal equipments.

For most data applications, packet switching achieves improved transmission efficiency (although there is overhead due to the transport of packet headers in addition to the original data), but at the expense of real time resources that are now utilized to effect the transport of every packet through the network. Moreover, packet switching introduces an additional delay component to the end-to-end flow time of data: data may be detained at the originating end of a connection while a packet is being created; and once it has been created, a packet must make its way through a series of network switching nodes and transmission facilities, while experiencing individual queueing and transmission delays at each point along the way. Packets typically need to be buffered at network nodes along the connection, and during congestion buffers may be held longer and packets may need to be discarded in the network due to lack of buffers. Proper choices of packet sizes and speeds of network transmission facilities can reduce this additional delay component, and the likelihood of packet losses can be kept low with proper buffer sizing, but the existence of this delay and packet losses and their monotonically increasing behavior with increasing network loads are facts that must always be taken into consideration in the design of packet switching architectures.

The introduction of packet switching technology brings with it the new performance issue of variable, load-sensitive information transport delays and packet losses. Some services implemented via packet switching are viable only if end-to-end packet delays and losses can be kept within relatively small bounds with high probability; moreover, packet switching protocols often involve timers for detecting and responding to lost packets with retransmissions, and these timers may be triggered by excessively delayed packets. From the end-user's point of view, the key performance issue may be the attainable level of "goodput," the rate at which information can be transported across the network in a usable form. The level of "goodput" is typically determined by the rate at which the end-user sends information, the magnitude of packet delays and losses in the network, and the protocol actions taken by the destination user in reaction to late or missing transported information.

Packet switching services may also introduce performance issues associated with the setup of the connection. Communication via packet switching may be over a "virtual circuit," i.e., a two-way connection explicitly set up through the network by procedures involving a pair of end users and various network components and over which the end-users can then communicate with packets, or it may be "connectionless" in that no connection setup procedure is performed prior to the transport of information from one end-user to another. In addition, virtual circuits may be switched virtual circuits (SVCs), set up, and then later taken down, in real time for the interval of time over which the need for this connection exists; or, they may be permanent virtual circuits (PVCs), for which the setup is done administratively and which remain set up for long durations of time during which active periods of packet transport are typically interspersed with long periods of virtual circuit inactivity. The setup of an SVC will typically involve delays, while the setup request is handled by a sequence of nodes in the network, that are sensitive to network and switch loads. It is often the case that such setup delays must be kept within bounds, at all levels of loads, particularly because the setup request may have originated at an automated terminal which may be programmed to reattempt the setup at the expiration of a timer if the original request has not been responded to. While the important performance issue of call setup delay is associated with SVCs, SVCs afford the network with an important tactic for controlling load. That is, at high levels of load SVC setup requests can be denied, thereby protecting the network from experiencing additional loading due to packet transport. Such a control tactic is more limited for PVCs and connectionless packet services, which may present the network with packets for transport in a virtually uncontrolled way. Thus the issue of controlling network load caused by packet transport becomes an extremely important one.

While the performance issues associated with purely circuit-switched or packet-switched networks can be complex by themselves, these issues become more complex as networks integrate these two classes of services. Moreover, new technologies have resulted in packet switching techniques that are more hardware-based, and thus have much higher real time capacities for handling packets. These trends have resulted in packet switching being seriously considered for the transport mechanism for many non-data applications, e.g., voice, image, and low-speed video, since existing or soon-to-exist packet switching networks can achieve extremely low packet transport delays [8]. Within the context of a means for providing integrated services to end users, packet switching has the additional appeals of: (i) providing a unified transport mechanism for all services, and (ii) allowing each active service to achieve whatever instantaneous rate of information transport it requires. However, with these more flexible techniques for providing services come more complex control issues.

2.2 Summary of Performance Objectives

The essence of the above-described performance issues can be captured by establishing performance objectives for the following types of service parameters that influence the acceptability of performance from the end-user perspective:

   i. For services supported by circuit switching:
- signaling delays during call setup, especially
  - dial tone delay
  - post-dialing delay and various of its components
- service blocking

  ii. For services supported by packet switching:
- signaling delays during call setup, especially when automatic reattempt timers at terminals may be triggered
- end-to-end packet transport delays through the network, especially when
  - packet retransmission timers may be triggered
  - packet delays may affect the viability of reassembling an information stream at the destination network edge, as, e.g., with packetized voice or packetized video
- packet losses in the network due to lack of buffers
- level of information throughput that is attainable via packet transport
- service blocking for switched virtual circuits

From the network perspective these service parameters need to be transformed into performance objectives for each component in the system, providing a set of specific objectives to be met by each component for each call type. [9]

Within the context of meeting the specific performance objectives of each system component, the service provider has the additional objective of providing fair access to end users. Fair end user access refers to the ability of an end user to set up a call of some type and receive the same level of service as a different end user setting up a call of the same type. Differences may exist among the priorities placed on call set-ups of different types; however, the large variety of call types in an ISDN poses the challenge of how to allocate priorities.

The final objective of the service provider is to maximize the capacity of the system so that service can be provided to the end users as cheaply as possible.

2.3 Examples from Pre-ISDN Environment

2.3.1 Non-overload: In determining the control objectives for a switching component in a pre-ISDN circuit switching environment the major types of traffic to be considered are calls originating and terminating on lines and trunks. Certain performance objectives will be operative for each of these call types. These performance objectives can be used to properly allocate processing priorities to the different call types [10].

2.3.2 Overload: In an overload situation the basic objectives of the system are to
- *protect low priority work* so that essential audit and maintenance functions are periodically performed;
- *maintain good throughput in all processors* ensuring that as little thrashing as possible takes place;
- *prevent cascading of overload* so that an overload in one component does not cause an overload in another component;
- *give priority to calls on which work has already been expended* so as to maximize the useful end-to-end throughput.

Objectives for an overloaded system tend to be stated loosely and generically rather than providing specific delay requirements that are to be met when the load on the system exceeds the capacity. This means that there may be considerable flexibility in designing an overload control architecture.

2.4 Examples of Additional Considerations in ISDN Environment

2.4.1 Non-overload: Additional complexities exist in determining the basic control objectives in an ISDN environment due to the existence of the many more types of work that resources are required to handle. For example, both circuit and packet switching call control may be handled by the same processor. This same processor may also provide the transport function during the data transfer phase of a packet switched call as well as handling user-to-user Q.931 information messages. Since each processor is allocated a certain portion of the end-to-end user requirement to handle each of these call types, some priorities may need to be established so that messages with the tightest requirements can be handled at a higher priority. One difficulty that may be encountered in implementing such a priority system is that many message types may not be distinguishable without some processing. Thus a new objective for the control architecture must be to balance the real-time expended in prioritizing messages with the need to prioritize.

In an ISDN environment non-traditional schemes may need to be employed to meet strict delay requirements. This means that the mix of traffic could have a much larger influence on the ability of the system to meet the competing performance objectives than in a pre-ISDN environment. Thus the control objectives need to specify for which traffic mixes the performance objectives are to be met.

Although an ISDN environment does not necessitate a distributed switching architecture, the two frequently go hand-in-hand. A distributed architecture contributes to the complexity of setting the control objectives in that there may be many components involved in the handling of any particular message type. Thus the task of allocating the end-to-end performance requirements to the components of the system will be more complex.

2.4.2 Overload: In an ISDN environment the basic control objectives during overload remain similar to those in a pre-ISDN environment. It is to be expected that when a switch experiences an overload condition there will be some amount of service degradation. However, in an ISDN environment the multiplicity of call types and traffic mixes requires that relative grades of service must be defined. Since the switch is simultaneously handling call-processing functions of various types, it must allocate the switch resources among these functions. This allocation of resources affects the grades of service experienced by calls in various states. It may be that certain end-users have been allocated a high priority which should be maintained even during an overload. An associated situation is where a packet-switched call may have negotiated for a particular throughput, it must be decided whether this throughput must be provided in overload. It must be determined whether the degradation of the service provided to customers should be somewhat uniform across call types or whether some call types should be given a much higher grade of service at the expense of other call types.

Since in an ISDN environment the acceptance of a call request for either packet switching or circuit switching can commit the switch to an unknown amount of future work, another consideration in setting the control objectives for overload is at what rate new call requests should be accepted so that the future workload of the switching components is manageable. In the determination of this control objective it should be determined whether it is preferable for the switch to accept a large portion of the new call requests while providing substantially degraded service to calls that require continuing resource allocation, or to accept a smaller portion of new call requests while maintaining a higher grade of service for existing calls that require continuing resource allocation.

These considerations indicate that additional control objectives are required in an ISDN environment to quantify the basic service tradeoffs among calls in various states.

3. CONTROL ARCHITECTURES

An overload control strategy should be designed to meet the needs of the end users as just described. Some potential components of an overload control design require controlling call setups while others are within-call congestion, flow, and resource management controls. In this section we describe some of the possible components of a control architecture and provide some examples of their effectiveness.

3.1 Possible Components of Control Architectures

3.1.1 Conservative engineering: One simple method of "controlling" traffic so that sufficient resources are available at all times for all traffic types is to over-engineer the network resources so that it is nearly certain that congestion does not occur. If network resources are cheap enough and uncertainty in forecasting both the load and the burstiness of traffic are low enough, then this method can prove a very effective means for insuring that the control objectives described in the preceding section are met.

The traffic arriving at any of the components of the system can be characterized by the mean arrival rate and the burstiness. Both of these parameters are random variables and are subject to errors in forecasting. Normal traffic engineering is done by using delay objectives like those described in the preceding sections to determine the level of load which meets the delay criterion. In a circuit switching environment uncertainty in the mean load is experienced and should be considered in the development of a traffic engineering methodology [11]. In the ISDN environment the uncertainty in the mean and the burstiness must be accounted for in the engineering process (particularly if conservative engineering is used as the principal element of the control architecture).

In order to determine the degree to which the network must be over-engineered it is first necessary to have an understanding of the distributions of the mean and the burstiness that can be expected (See Figure 1). In order to ensure that the system almost surely does not experience congestion a burstiness associated with a small tail probability γ is selected (Curve B in Figure 1). This defines the load-delay curve which is operative in the given environment. The mean delay objective can then be used to define the load (for the chosen burstiness) that will achieve the mean delay objective. However, since the mean load should cause this delay objective to be exceeded only a small percentage of the time the actual mean load that is engineered to must be l^* [12].

In engineering an ISDN network procedures such as these should always be followed. However, if no other flow or congestion control components are used, then the values of κ and γ need to be set more conservatively. The degree of conservatism required in setting κ and γ depends on the effectiveness of the control architecture and the consequences to the system of experiencing an overload.

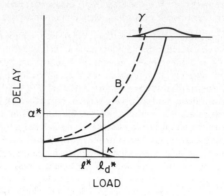

Figure 1. Conservative Engineering in an ISDN Environment. Engineer mean load l^* so that P[burstiness$>b_\gamma$]$=\gamma$ and P[mean load $>l_{d^*}$]$=\kappa$

3.1.2 Control of call requests: In a non-overload situation the primary objective of the control architecture is to balance the resource and real-time needs of the various call types so that the capacity of the system is as high as possible while meeting all performance objectives. The processor scheduling is the primary means for achieving this desired control. In a system in which the arrival time of call requests is recorded and there is no real time lost in classifying call types an "earliest due date" scheduling policy minimizes the lateness experienced by customers. This is not easily implementable in a real-time system. However, effective controls can be implemented through the establishment of a priority system. The priorities for a processor can be established by taking the allocated time for each processor, subtracting the processing time and prioritizing the residual allowed queueing times. A detailed analysis of the system is usually required to determine the scheduling that effects the most desirable results.

An often-used component of an overload control design is to deny new call set-ups according to established priorities. This can be an effective mechanism for overload control because it not only reduces the current workload, but also has an impact on the future workload. Such a control can be implemented in response to local conditions or in one processor as a result of overload control conditions occurring in another processor.

In an ISDN environment at call set-up it may be difficult to accurately predict the future switch resource demands that may be generated by a given call. Thus it may not be possible at the time of call setup to accurately determine the type of a given call. This may be of particular importance for packet-switched calls, for which real-time call transport capabilities must be continually provided by the switch throughout the call duration. Unfortunately, the "throughput class" of the call may be only a very rough indicator of the required switch resources and thus of the call type.

3.1.3 Throttling of user information packets: For packet-switched calls, switch resources continue to be required during the transport phase of the call. Key switch resources (e.g., bus and link bandwidths and packet buffers) are needed to effect packet transport, and thus schemes need to be devised for allocating these resources. In any switch which supports some services via packet switching, it is crucial that the switch have mechanisms for throttling the flow of packets. Priority assignments, load-shedding techniques, and load-throttling techniques are likely to be essential ingredients of a control architecture. These mechanisms are needed both to control overloads due to packet transport and to ensure adequate performance to all services which may be supported by a common packet multiplexing technique. Thus, it may also be necessary to selectively throttle different packet streams.

As an example, the contents of Q.931 information messages may range from critically important digit information for call completion to possibly low priority, non-critical data transfer. Thus in any control architecture it would be desirable to be able to selectively throttle user information packets at different levels of overload. However, this may be difficult since the message must be partially deciphered before it can be prioritized. It must be determined if so much real time is wasted in this process that it becomes counterproductive.

3.1.3.1 Protocol-provided protection: For packet-switched data, the windows and acknowledgements of existing protocols provide a throttling mechanism and thus some natural protection to the switch during overload. However, each of these mechanisms carries with it certain problems. For this reason new methods of control need to be investigated. These include end-to-end network windows, adaptive windows between the CPE and the network, the delaying of acknowledgements to the end users, reservation methods for high-resource calls and load-shedding and tradeoffs involving quality of service.

3.1.3.2 Bandwidth management: In contrast to the X.25 data service, for many services now being supported by packet switching, explicit flow controls that may be issued by the network and recognized by the end terminals to effect throttling at sources may not be applicable. Examples are services where circuits are emulated via packet switching, such as packetized voice, voice-band data, and video. Moreover, future packet-switched data services may be implemented without full network termination of transport protocols (e.g., LAPD Frame Relay, as described in [13]), and may rely instead on end-to-end flow control mechanisms. For such services, the need still exists to control packet transport loads placed on the switch and the network.

A technique that has been proposed is *bandwidth management,* which entails a system of controls by which end-users or groups of end-users negotiate a level of throughput with the network, where "throughput" denotes demands placed on the network for transport bandwidth and/or other key network resources. This throughput can be considered "guaranteed" by the network to the end-user; however, the end-user may exceed this guaranteed level of throughput. The network monitors the throughput demands in real-time, and discards packets associated with excessive demands if doing so is required to relieve switch or network congestion. Note that this differs from the situation with X.25 data service, where explicit access flow controls can be applied to terminals and where a major objective is to maintain data integrity within the network. Bandwidth management provides network protection from overloads due to packet sources that might otherwise be uncontrollable,[1] and also provides a fair control scheme, since it is based on negotiated throughputs. It also can be shown to result in less conservative engineering of the network, and it provides the end-users with a flexible framework within which some of their traffic can be sent "at risk" (i.e., that which exceeds the guaranteed throughput), but still with a high level of guaranteed delivery if the network is not experiencing congestion. Moreover, when used with data packet sources that employ end-to-end window-based protocols, during overload periods bandwidth management provides incentives for self-throttling by window adaptation procedures that may be run in the terminals themselves.[2]

3.2 Example

The following generic example has been constructed to provide further insights into the problem of designing a control architecture for an ISDN switching environment. We first describe the basic architecture of the system and the control objectives that need to be met. We next suggest a possible control architecture that could be implemented if conservative engineering proves to be too costly.

3.2.1 Basic Architecture: The Basic architecture of the hypothetical switching node is shown in Figure 2. In this architecture D and B channels have been split by the Line Interface Units and are attached to different processors. In order to simplify the example we have assumed that the Central Processing Unit (CP) handles only circuit switched control messages and packet switched call setup messages and that no packet switching is allowed on the D-channel. The Peripheral Processors (PP) handle packet switched control messages and data.

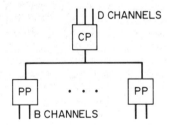

Figure 2. Basic Architecture

Table 1 contains the set of control objectives relevant to circuit and packet switching that need to be considered in designing the control architecture.

The preceding information indicates that the allowable queueing delay in the CP is 20 ms. for packet switched setups and 100 ms for circuit switched requests indicating that priority may appropriately be given to packet switched setups over circuit switched setups. However, the relative intrinsic value of circuit switched setups and packet switched setups should be considered in the final assignment of priorities.

---

1. Network protection is guaranteed only if the totality of negotiated bandwidths does not exceed the network capacity; however, exceeding the network capacity would be allowed if the full negotiated bandwidths were only rarely used. In this latter case, higher level controls would provide ultimate network protection.

2. Another strategy is for the network to send explicit "stop" commands to the terminals, as described in [13].

TABLE 1. Circuit and Packet Switching Objectives for a Switching Node (in msec)

	Call Setup (Circuit)		Call Setup (Packet)			Data Transfer	
	Total	CP	Total	PP	CP	Total	PP
Allocations	300	200	100	25 each	50	100	50 each
Processing Times		100		10 each	30		20

3.2.2 Possible control architecture: The following is an outline of a possible control architecture for this generic system for both non-overload and overload situations.

> Non-overload:
> PP: 1. Equal priorities given to packet switched setup and transport
>   2. Bandwidth management used to ensure fair customer access to resources
> CP: 1. Packet switched setup given higher priority than circuit switched setup
> Real-time Overload:
> PP: 1. Use bandwidth management to protect the network
>   2. Deny new call setups
> CP: 1. CP sends messages to the PPs carrying the CP overload status
>   2. Packet and circuit switched setups served by CP at appropriate priorities

3.2.3 Results for Bandwidth Management: Bandwidth management can be an especially effective control if coupled with procedures in the end-user terminals for self-throttling when a reduction in effective throughput (or "goodput"), due to discard by the network of excessive throughput demands, can be detected in the end-user terminals. To illustrate, we consider an example where an end-user is guaranteed a throughput of 4.0 packets/sec or 1024 octets/sec, whichever is more limiting. It is assumed that the end-user application is data-oriented and involves an end-to-end window-based protocol. Further, it is assumed that this application involves interactions between an end-user and a host computer which, if supported by unconstrained network throughputs, would stabilize at an end-user-to-host average throughput of 5.5 packets/sec. When network resources are lightly loaded, the end-user can achieve an increase in "goodput" by increasing the size of his end-to-end window, although the "goodput" never exceeds the 5.5 packets/sec level associated with unconstrained end-user-to-host interactions; this is depicted by the solid curve in Figure 3 below. However, when the network is congested, if the end-user utilizes a window size that results in an excessive throughput (i.e., beyond the guaranteed level of 4.0 packets/sec.), packets will be discarded, and the resulting end-to-end retransmissions (likely consisting of entire windows of packets, depending on the details of the end-to-end protocol) result in a "goodput" that begins to fall with increasing window size. This effect is depicted by the dashed curves in Figure 3, which represent possible "goodput" vs. window size relationships for both moderate and fairly extreme congestion scenarios. In the congested case the end-user's "goodput" is maximized if the end-to-end window can keep the throughput at or near the guaranteed level. Note that the end-to-end window size that yields the guaranteed throughput will depend on the round trip network delay, and thus will increase with increasing network congestion. It has been shown that simple window adaptation procedures triggered by retransmitted and successfully acknowledged packets, such as have been described in [14] and [15], can maximize the "goodput" attainable by the end-user over a wide range of network loading conditions, while maintaining fair allocation of network resources between end-users.[16]

3.2.4 Results for call setup denial at periphery The following call setup denial scheme was modeled for a system with objectives and architecture similar to those described in the preceding section.
1. The CP dynamically determines when the PPs should allow new call setups based on the number of queued setups.
2. Through coordination of the PP and CP, packets that would result in ineffective attempts due to long queueing time at the CP are dropped with minimal real-time cost and clear request is sent to the DTE.

The throughput characterization of the system and the impact of this coordination are shown in Figure 4. The results indicate that this type of control scheme can lead to excellent system performance under lightly loaded as well as heavily overloaded conditions [17].

4. CONCLUSIONS—GUIDELINES FOR DESIGNING A CONTROL ARCHITECTURE

From the foregoing it can be seen that the design of a control architecture in an ISDN environment involves art as well as science. Nonetheless it is apparent that certain procedures can be followed that will contribute to the design of a comprehensive, successful control strategy. These include:
1. Understand the control objectives of the system.
2. Understand the network architecture.
3. Determine the cost of conservatively engineering the network. If this is sufficiently low, then only a minimal effort needs to be made in designing the control architecture.
4. Determine the possible components of the control architecture.

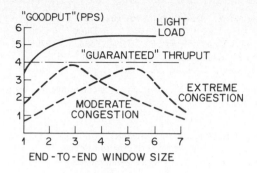

Figure 3. Goodput Attainable with Bandwidth Management vs. Window Size

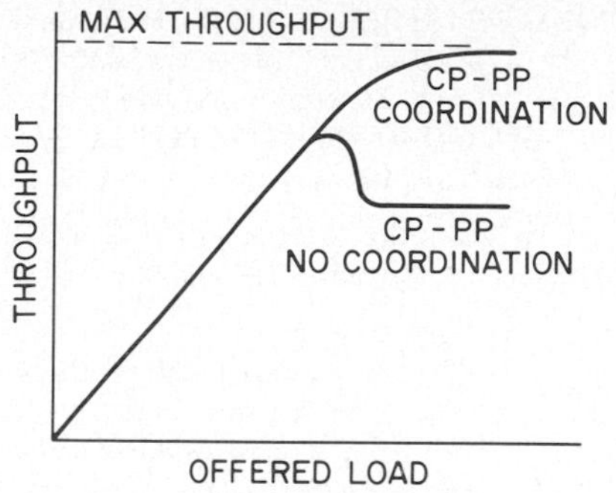

Figure 4. Throughput Characterization of Call Setup Denial Control Scheme

5. Develop a basic control architecture based on modeling and experience. This basic architecture should be designed so as to help the system meet as many of the control objectives as possible.

6. For each new call type that may be added to the system determine its relationship in the priority structures to the existing call types and appropriately adjust the control architecture.

This paper has attempted to outline many of the issues associated with designing comprehensive, elegant control architectures. Much work remains to be done both in understanding the performance of the control components and in understanding the total system performance once the control architecture has been designed.

5. ACKNOWLEDGEMENTS

We would like to thank the many people whose thoughts and discussions have contributed to the ideas in this paper. In particular we mention Gagan Choudhury, Haeng Koo, Daniel Luan, David Lucantoni, Nader Mehravari, and Kathleen Meier-Hellstern whose experiences in designing control architectures for real systems have helped us to more clearly define the significant issues.

REFERENCES

[1] CCITT ISDN Recommendations, Series I and Q.

[2] Yamamoto, M., et. al., "Delay Analysis of Window Controlled Network with Finite Input Buffer," ICC, 58.2.1, 1986.

[3] Doshi, B. T., Heffes, H., "Analysis of Overload Control Schemes for a Class of Distributed Switching Machines," ITC 10, 5.22 Montreal, 1983.

[4] Tran-Gia, P., "Subcall-Oriented Modelling of Overload Control in SPC Switched Systems," ITC 10, 5.21, Montreal, 1983.

[5] Manfield, D., Denis, B., Basu, K., and Rouleau, G., "Overload Control in a Hierarchical Switching System," ITC 11, 5.1B-4, Kyoto, 1985.

[6] Korner, U., "Congestion Control in Packet Switching Computer Communication Networks," ITC 10, 3.35, Montreal, 1983.

[7] Davis, M. E., and Pehlert, W. K., "Evaluation of No. 1 PSS Congestion Control Strategies," *Performance of Computer Communication Systems,* H. Ruding and W. Bux (editors), North-Holland, 1984, pp.449-461.

[8] R. W. Muise, T. J. Schonfeld, G. H. Zimmerman, "Digital Communications Experiments in Wideband Packet Technology," *Proc. of International Zurich Seminar on Digital Communication,* March, 1986, pp. 134-139.

[9] Paolucci, R. and Seitz, N. B., "A General Framework for Describing Quality of Service and Network Performance Standards in Digital Networks," ICC, 30.6.1, 1985.

[10] Bonatti, M., Barbuio, C., Cappellini, G., Padulosi, U., "Model for an Effective Definition of End-to-End GOS Parameters and for their Repartition in IDN Networks," ITC 11 4.2B-3, Kyoto, 1985.

[11] Coco, R., Farel, R. A., Potter, R. M., Wirth, P. E., "Relationships between Utilization Service and Forecast Uncertainty for Central Office Equipment," ITC 10 1.21, Montreal, 1983.

[12] Meier-Hellstern, K. S., Private communication.

[13] Rege, K. M. and Chen, K.-J., "A Performance Study of LAPD Frame-Relay Protocols for Packetized Data Transfer over ISDN Networks," to be presented at 5th ITC Seminar: Traffic Engineering for ISDN Design and Planning, 1987.

[14] Bux, W. and Grillo, D., "Flow Control in Local-Area Networks of Interconnected Token Rings," *IEEE Trans. Commun., COM-33,* pp. 1058-1066, Oct. 1985.

[15] Jain, R., "A Timeout-Based Congestion Control Scheme for Window Flow-Controlled Networks," *IEEE J. Selected Areas in Commun, SAC-4,* pp.1162-1167, Oct. 1986.

[16] Luan, D. T. and Lucantoni, D. M., Private communication.

[17] Choudhury, G. L., Private communication.

TRAFFIC ENGINEERING for ISDN Design and Planning
M. Bonatti and M. Decina (Editors)
Elsevier Science Publishers B.V. (North-Holland)
© IAC, 1988

AN ADAPTIVE CONCENTRATION SCHEME FOR ISDN ACCESS

Noshik Kim and Charles D. Pack

Bell Communications Research
331 Newman Springs Road
Red Bank, New Jersey 07701 U.S.A
(201) 758-2174

This paper analyzes the traffic characteristics of various ISDN access architectures when a Remote Terminal/Digital Loop Carrier system is considered. We propose a new architecture employing an adaptive concentration scheme. We indicate how this new technique should improve dramatically transmission facility utilization, while maintaining good traffic performance, and also provide the flexibility to accommodate highly uncertain ISDN demand fluctuations.

THE ADAPTIVE CONCENTRATION TECHNIQUE IMPROVES FACILITY UTILIZATION OVER THE STATIC CONCENTRATION SCHEME AT ITS BEST WITH TRAFFIC EFFICIENCY NEARLY THE SAME AS THE DEDICATED TDM ACCESS PROCEDURE.

1. INTRODUCTION

Although some aspects of ISDN have been standardized, there are many architectural and equipment alternatives that must be analyzed for flexibility and technical and economical feasibility, especially as the technology matures and customer migration intensifies. In this paper, we are particularly concerned with the efficiency, economy, robustness, and performance of various access schemes, ranging from dedicated to dynamically shared arrangements.

While we focus on a traffic engineering perspective of the access scheme, we recognize the need for a total system view, including the impacts on the cost and performance of the ISDN switch. This more complete view, with more careful tuning of system parameters and implementation considerations will be covered in future work.

1.1 Background

This paper models and analyzes the traffic characteristics of various ISDN access architectures when a Remote Terminal/Digital Loop Carrier system is considered. In particular, we focus on the "basic" access arrangement because the diversity of its user characteristics suggests opportunities for improving efficiency. Furthermore, at this time, the "primary" arrangement employs only a direct access connection, without multiplexing or concentration.

Several basic access architecture alternatives are considered from a traffic engineering aspect, including a new one employing an adaptive concentration scheme. We indicate how this new technique should improve dramatically transmission facility utilization, while maintaining good traffic performance, and provide flexibility to accommodate highly uncertain ISDN demand traffic. In the ISDN environment, voice and data from a user are transported to the network simultaneously through a single Digital Subscriber Loop (DSL). As a result, various services can be offered without providing additional circuits, whereas the existing loop architectures require roughly as many circuits as the number of services offered. This is, in fact, one of the strong driving forces toward ISDN because a great savings can be achieved on access provisioning while, at the same time, there is also an increase in the degrees of freedom in service provisioning. However, because ISDN demand necessitates a new, more complex and more integrated, switching architecture, there would be an additional investment in new switching facilities. Hence, a key issue in an ISDN economic study is whether or not the savings on access facilities, the efficiency and flexibility, and the additional revenue obtained by offering new "ISDN" services would be greater than any increase in costs for new switching equipment and support processes.

In this paper, we examine a family of ISDN access alternatives. We analyze them relative to various criteria, including facility utilization, blocking and delay. We show that previously analyzed procedures provide reasonably good performance, from a customer perspective, but may be wasteful of facility capacity and sensitive to forecast errors. Our new procedure should allow improved facility utilization and robustness while maintaining acceptable traffic performance levels.

1.2 ISDN Access Alternatives

1.2.1 Background

There are B, D, H0 and H11 channels provided to transport messages in ISDN. They transmit digital signals at rates of 64 kbps, 16 or 64 kbps, 384 kbps and 1536 kbps, respectively. ISDN currently plans to offer two kinds of user access: One is the "basic" access which has up to 2B+D. That is, a user can subscribe to D, B+D or 2B+D. The other is the "primary" access which has up to 23B+D with, possibly, some or all the channels being combined to form H0 or H11 channels. Note that the D channel for the primary access is an extended D channel which carries 64 kbps. (The basic access D channel is only 16 kbps.) The D channel is for signaling, packet data and telemetry. The B channel is primarily for circuit switching of voice and bulk data, although it is also possible for the end-users to subscribe to access to the packet switched network through B channels. The H0 and H11 channels are for channel switching of audio and video, i.e. digital signals with very high transmission rates.

As multiplexing techniques mature and transmission technologies improve in their transmission rates, e.g. using optical fiber, the Remote Terminal (RT) and Digital Loop Carrier (DLC) system seems to be a promising access architecture for integrated access in an ISDN environment, where message traffic from multiple end-users are mixed in the RT and transported to the central office (with the use of repeaters as needed). When the DS1 (Digital Signal Level 1: 1544 kbps) rate is used for the DLC, an RT would ordinarily be for "mixing" the basic access because the primary access user may already transmit at DS1 rates from the Customer Premises Equipment (CPE).

1.2.2 Improved Efficiency for Basic Access

A direct connection, employing a 2 wire or 4 wire metallic loop, would provide the simplest but, in most cases, a lightly utilized and perhaps costly linkage to the central office. Therefore, to take advantage of high speed technology, an RT/DLC may be considered.

In the standard arrangement, an RT/DLC system employs Time Division Multiplexing technique and transports traffic at the DS1 (1.544 mbps) rate to the central office. When an RT/DLC system with Time Division Multiplexing is used for ISDN basic access, a 2B+D subscription is normally assumed for all basic access users. It does not cause any blocking or delay (except propagation delay) during access, but the utilization of the RT/DLC facility can be very poor and, therefore, the system can be viewed as highly inefficient from an economics point of view. (i.e., it performs *pairgain* not *concentration*.)

To improve the efficiency of the DS1 system, an access concentration scheme has been proposed by others, especially for D channel packet traffic. A concentrator, in general, has a smaller output capacity than the total input capacity and a finite size buffer. Concentration would improve the facility usage of RT/DLC, but delay or even blocking may be incurred during the access, due to traffic burstiness. In general, for some period of time, a concentrated RT has a fixed output capacity for D channel traffic and for B channel traffic. Therefore, it is possible that D channel traffic experiences congestion while B channel traffic utilization of its allocated capacity is low.

To accommodate such time-varying and unpredictable B and D channel capacity requirements, a variable concentration output capacity can be considered for the basic access with an RT/DLC system. That is, based on the burstiness of incoming traffic, D channel concentration output capacity is adaptively adjusted, relative to the B channel allocation, so as not to cause a serious delay or blocking. The total capacity for B and D channel transmission remains fixed. In general, one can use a forecast or "real-time" information, along with adaptation logic, to update RT output allocation slowly or quickly, respectively. Hence, when a total DLC transmission rate is set at a constant, one should consider the traffic characteristics of D and B channel traffics, and their correlation, since they are to share a fixed DLC capacity, e.g. DS1 transmission rate.

1.2.3 Summary of Results

A traffic state space representation is used and several traffic performance indices are introduced and quantified for the ISDN basic access architecture alternatives. We describe the relative performance of the multiplexed access, the concentrated access, and our new adaptive access concentration scheme with a simple control strategy.

We show that an adaptive access concentration offers great transmission savings potential as well as robustness to forecast errors and demand volatility. In fact, an adaptive concentration scheme would be particularly useful when the DLC system is upgraded to a higher transmission rate, e.g. DS3, or for a Remote Switching Unit where a concentration is ordinarily performed for trunking efficiencies with large user populations.

Finally, the technique shows potential for an ISDN transition scheme where the relative inefficiency of non-ISDN customers, added as B or B+D at the RT, can be improved by adaptive concentration.

1.3 Outline of The Rest of Memo

In Chapter II, four basic access alternatives are investigated: the direct access, the time division multiplexing, the concentrated access, and the adaptive concentration scheme. When incoming traffic to the RT are assumed to be stochastic with known distribution functions, the access alternatives are compared by computing the following performance measures: the facility efficiency, the traffic efficiency, and the congestion probabilities on B channel and D channel traffics. When queueing is allowed for D channel traffic in the concentration cases, we compute the average queue length and the average delay for D channel traffic and the blocking probability for B channel traffic, using a computer simulation. In Chapter III, an adaptive concentration is analyzed further. Section III.1 explains system control objectives when congested or non-congested traffic states are encountered. Section III.2 illustrates congestion control alternatives that must be considered and proposes a specific strategy to resolve a contention between D channel traffic and B channel traffic. We use a simple congestion control strategy, but leave for further work the design of a more sophisticated algorithm. Our current strategy was modeled by a computer simulation to compute the numerical solutions of the performance parameters introduced in Chapter II. Chapter IV contains numerical results for each of access alternatives. Assumptions and parameter values applied during the computation are listed in Section IV.1. Section IV.2 shows actual computations from formulae as well as a computer simulation results. At the end, there is a comparison among the numerical solution results obtained for the various access alternatives. Chapter V summarizes the advantages, disadvantages and requirements for an adaptive concentration scheme for the ISDN basic access.

2. ACCESS ARCHITECTURE ALTERNATIVES

Access, in this paper, is defined as the transport of messages originating from the customer premises equipment (CPE) and destined for the central office (CO). Therefore, in this paper, the traffic system parameters are computed and compared only for access facilities themselves, and not for CPE or for switch and inter-office facilities. When a "universal" DLC (UDLC) is employed, the Central Office Terminal (COT) is assumed not to cause additional traffic congestion by itself. This is because, from the access traffic engineering point of view, the switch and trunk facilities are assumed to be infinitely fast and to have sufficient capacities. When an "integrated" DLC (IDLC) is employed, the COT is not even considered as part of the access facility. Hence, the key issue in the basic access architecture, which would influence the traffic characteristics, is whether or not an RT/DLC system is used and, if used, what type of traffic "mixing" is performed by the RT.

2.1 Direct Access

All of the dedicated primary access and basic access arrangements without "mixing" are in this category. Each provides an uninterrupted transport and the CO will receive the traffic in the exactly same way as the CPE has generated and transmitted it. Note that mB+D traffic is mixed at the CPE, not on the access facility.

However, the direct basic access has a physical limitation due to the maximum distance allowed for 2 wire and 4 wire metallic loops. Furthermore, it may not be the best access alternative when a relatively high or volatile demand growth is predicted. That is, there is a limit to the number of direct access subscribers in an area, such that the cost of implementing metallic loops would be less economical than the cost of an RT/DLC arrangement, for the same number of basic access subscribers. The concept is quite analogous to the wire centering or tandem location issues in switching.

Hence, the motivation for considering time division multiplexed access, as a way to reduce line haul without blocking, lies in the economics of the equipment and the distance between the users and the CO. Therefore, the decision as to whether to multiplex or not is an economic one. The "service" provided to the customer is the same and can be analyzed by the same performance measures. We will introduce such performance measures next.

2.2 Multiplexed Access

A previously studied method of mixing multiple 2B+D subscribers is to use time division multiplexing (TDM) at the RT to transport these dedicated time slots to the CO via DLC at the DS1 transmission rate. Although, in theory, 2B+D, B+D, or only D might be available to the basic access users, a fully multiplexed RT would probably assume all 2B+D's and provide the number of input plug-in's accordingly. If customers had complete choice in their subscription rates, the TDM and the COT would need constant reconfiguration to reassign time slots for maximum efficiency. Therefore, for our analysis we assume all 2B+D subscribers. Then,

$$m_0 = 2n_0 \qquad\qquad\qquad \text{(Eq II.2.1)}$$

where m_0 is the number of B channels and n_0 is the number of D channels plugged in the multiplexed RT. Figure II.1 shows the $X-Y$ plane for D and B channel traffic states assuming DS1 (1.544 mbps) total channel capacity, but with 8 kbps being used in maintenance and control, leaving 1.536 mbps capacity. Let:

> m = the number of offered B channels. $0 \le m \le m_0$
> n = the number of offered D channels. $0 \le n \le n_0$
> $X = 16000 \cdot n$ = offered D channel traffic in bps.
> $Y = 64000 \cdot m$ = offered B channel traffic in bps.
> r_x = the total bits/second allocated for D channels in DS1.
> r_y = the total bits/second allocated for B channels in DS1.
> R : the point (r_x , r_y)

For a fully time division multiplexing (TDM),

$$X + Y \le 1536000 \qquad\qquad\qquad \text{(Eq II.2.2)}$$

Hence, the point (X,Y) should be within the region of $(0,0)$-$(0,1536k)$-$(1536k,0)$. That is, an RT can fully multiplex the incoming B and D channel traffics, without a loss, when m and n take on values such that the point (X,Y) is located within the region. Note that, due to the requirement that usage be in multiples of 2B+D, the maximum of n_0 and m_0 is 10 and 20, respectively. Hence, $r_x = (16k)(10)$, $r_y = (64k)(20)$, and the point R does not touch the line $(0,1536k)$-$(1536k,0)$.

An RT with TDM allocates a time slot for each channel in a cyclic manner even when a signal is not present and, therefore, the DLC carries an empty time slot to the CO. In our terminology, this would result in a waste of facility usage. Hence, the *Facility Efficiency* can be defined and computed as:

$$\begin{aligned} \textit{Facility Efficiency} &= P[\textit{ A non-empty time slot is transmitted }] \qquad \text{(Eq II.2.3)}\\ &= \frac{E[X] + E[Y]}{1536000} \end{aligned}$$

Note that the Facility Efficiency is identical to the standard terminology of facility occupancy. An RT with TDM, however, will not cause any traffic congestion, neither blocking nor delay. Therefore, the *Traffic Efficiency* is defined and computed as:

$$\begin{aligned} \textit{Traffic Efficiency} &= P[\, X \le r_x,\, Y \le r_y \,] \qquad\qquad \text{(Eq II.2.4)}\\ &= 1.0 \end{aligned}$$

The *probability of Traffic Congestion on B channel*, U_B, is 0.

$$\begin{aligned} U_B &= P[\, Y > r_y \,] \qquad\qquad\qquad \text{(Eq II.2.5)}\\ &= 0.0 \end{aligned}$$

The *probability of Traffic Congestion on D channel*, U_D, is also 0.

$$\begin{aligned} U_D &= P[\, X > r_x \,] \qquad\qquad\qquad \text{(Eq II.2.6)}\\ &= 0.0 \end{aligned}$$

In analogy to the direct access architecture, the RT with TDM provides "direct" transportation from the RT to the CO. The difference, from traffic engineering's point of view, is just like the difference between many passenger cars and a big bus. Hence, the TDM access would be justified when the RT/DLC provision has an economic benefit over the provision of many metallic loops individually terminated at the CO. Therefore, one needs an economic measure, say of cost per kilo-bit, to choose between the direct and RT-with-TDM access arrangements.

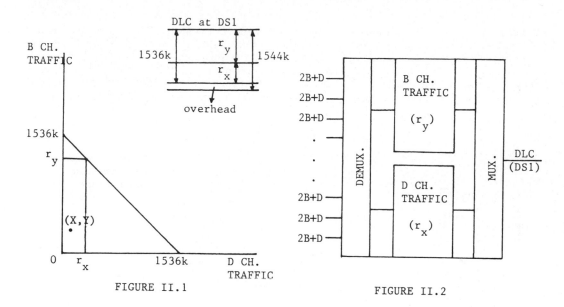

FIGURE II.1   FIGURE II.2

2.3 Concentrated Access

Recall that the TDM scheme assured no blocking or delay and, hence, might be expected to have low Facility Efficiency. (We will show this in Section IV.) Concentration techniques, sometimes called asynchronous multiplexing or statistical multiplexing, can be considered to improve the Facility Efficiency. That is, a concentrator takes data from active channels only, and the total number of B channels and D channels plugged in the RT can be increased, as long as there is some burstiness(randomness) to the demand traffics. In this scheme, there is neither a designated time slot, nor is there an empty time slot transmitted to the CO unless there is less incoming traffic than an output capacity. However, because the output capacity allocated to the B and to the D channel traffic is fixed, there will be some traffic congestion resulting in blocking, or in delay when queueing is allowed. Furthermore, there must be additional address information to identify the data source. This addressing overhead would, in fact, result in an additional burden to the RT/DLC system. Figure II.2 illustrates a simplified functional structure of an RT with concentration, wherein 1.472 mbps are dedicated to B channel output and 64 kbps for D channel output. Let m_1 be the number of B channels and n_1 be the number of D channels plugged in the concentrated RT. Then, in general,

$$m_1 \geq m_0 \qquad \text{(Eq II.3.1)}$$
$$n_1 \geq n_0 \qquad \text{(Eq II.3.2)}$$

Figure II.3 shows an example of such a case. The shaded areas, above and to the right of the dashed lines, show B and D channel congestion, respectively. Consistent with (Eq II.2.3), with congestion but not queueing, the Facility Efficiency would be computed as follows:

$$Facility\ Efficiency = P[\ A\ non\text{-}empty\ time\ slot\ is\ transmitted\ ] \qquad \text{(Eq II.3.3)}$$
$$= 1.0 - \frac{E[(r_x - X)^+] + E[(r_y - Y)^+]}{1536000}$$

where $(\cdot)^+ = \cdot$ if positive, and 0 else.

In general, an RT with concentration would have a higher value for the Facility Efficiency than would an RT with TDM. However, by design, it is expected that the RT with concentration has substantial traffic congestion, since the total input capacity is larger than the output capacity and the incoming traffics are bursty.

Assuming no queueing is applied, the Traffic Efficiency, as defined in (Eq II.2.4), would be:

$$\text{Traffic Efficiency} = P[\,X \leq r_x,\ Y \leq r_y\,] \tag{Eq II.3.4}$$

Separately, the Traffic Congestion probabilities on B channel traffic and D channel traffic are:

$$U_D = P[\,X > r_x\,] \tag{Eq II.3.5}$$
$$U_B = P[\,Y > r_y\,] \tag{Eq II.3.6}$$

In practice, when traffic congestion occurs, an incoming D channel traffic will be queued for processing, and some delay will occur. Furthermore, if the buffer size is not sufficient, the rest of incoming traffic, after buffer saturation, will be blocked. On the other hand, congested traffic on B channels will be blocked without queueing. In addition to the traffic performance parameters defined in this section, the blocking probability for B channel traffic congestion and the average queue length and delay for D channel traffic congestion will be computed by a computer simulation.

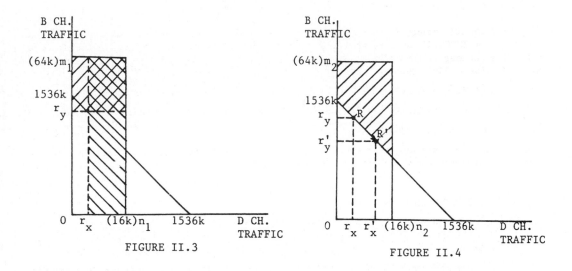

FIGURE II.3   FIGURE II.4

2.4 Adaptive Access Concentration

In the previous subsections, we described two access schemes that have outstanding performance but low Facility Efficiency and one that should improve Facility Efficiency with some service degradation. One problem with the latter concentration technique is the specification of the essentially fixed parameters that are part of system design. We address these deficiencies now.

When demand uncertainty or volatility is considered for the incoming traffic, the RT/DLC system dimensioning is not an easy task: e.g., the assumed number of plugged-in D and B channels, the D channel buffer size, etc. Furthermore, since a user is allowed to subscribe to either D, B+D, or 2B+D, the number of end-users will not have an unique correspondence to the number of incoming B and D channels.

Therefore, knowing that the traffic on B channels and D channels are bursty and varying with time, and that these traffics will share the finite capacity of DLC, we propose that the output capacity of the RT/DLC system be dynamically allocated, as needed. That is, the output capacity is automatically adjusted, based on the current state of B and D incoming traffic. In ISDN, no B channel will be processed until a call request via the D channel is accepted and a call set-up is completed. Hence, an "instructive" concentration can be performed in the RT for B channel transportation to the CO, meaning that the CO has instructed the RT to send the message. At the same time, the bursty incoming traffic on the D channel can be transported to the CO through "any" DLC capacity available and the CO will recognize this traffic as D channel packet traffic.

In summary, with this adaptive concentration technique, the B channel and D channel output capacities are fixed at any point in time, but that allocation can be adjusted (soon), depending on the current demands.

Let m_2 be the number of B channels and n_2 be the number of D channels plugged in the adaptively concentrated RT. In general,

$$m_2 \geq m_1 \geq m_0 \qquad \text{(Eq II.4.1)}$$
$$n_2 \geq n_1 \geq n_0 \qquad \text{(Eq II.4.2)}$$

Figure II.4 illustrates the $X - Y$ plane for an example of an adaptive concentration access scheme, assuming essentially no time delay for adaptation. The operation is described as follows:

Suppose the point R represents the current output capacity allocation, called "the operating point", hereafter. When the D channel traffic increases up to r_x', the operating point R moves to the new operating point, R', if in-progress traffic on the B channels is less than r_y. Without adaptation, these would have been D channel traffic congestion, as if essentially the RT with fixed concentration were applied. The Facility Efficiency would be computed as:

$$\text{Facility Efficiency} = 1.0 - \frac{E\left[(1536000 - X - Y)^+\right]}{1536000} \qquad \text{(Eq II.4.3)}$$

A generic control strategy will be described in Section III. When a "perfect" control method is assumed, an RT/DLC system can transport the incoming B and D channel traffic without congestion, as long as the traffic on B and D channel is mapped into any point within the region $(0,0)$-$(0,1536k)$-$\{1536k-(16k)(n_2)\}$ -$\{(16k)(n_2),0\}$ in Figure II.4. Then, the Traffic Efficiency is:

$$\text{Traffic Efficiency} = P\left[\, X + Y \leq 1536000 \,\right] \qquad \text{(Eq II.4.4)}$$

Hence, the joint probability of Traffic Congestion for B channel traffic and D channel traffic is:

$$U_{B,D} = 1.0 - \text{Traffic Efficiency} \qquad \text{(Eq II.4.5)}$$

Note that $U_{B,D}$ can not simply be factored into U_B and U_D, without a specific congestion control strategy. This will be further investigated in Section III.2.

3. ADAPTIVE ACCESS CONCENTRATION SCHEME

In this chapter, an adaptively controlled RT will be closely examined and described. The ultimate purpose of controlling the RT is to transport user messages through B and D channels to the CO via the DLC without serious traffic congestion in a highly efficient and, hence, cost-effective way.

Loosely speaking, this cost efficiency is obtained by having the RT combine onto one DS1 system as many end-users as possible without having unsatisfactory traffic performance. That is, we will achieve high Facility Efficiency, while keeping Traffic Efficiency high and Traffic Congestion low. We will illustrate these points later.

The following are key factors that will influence the design and implementation of this new adaptive access technique:

1) ISDN demand traffic arriving at the RT/DLC system is highly uncertain and may be inherently volatile. ISDN demand forecasting methods are in the preliminary stages, and will evolve as experience is obtained.

2) The combination of B channels and D channels plugged in an RT, as the traffic volume per channel, will vary from site to site.

3) Although the DLC transmission rate is currently set at DS1, it is expected to be upgraded, e.g. to DS3, eventually.

4) During the transition, POTS traffic and ISDN traffic will be mixed together at the RT and the balance between these traffics will not remain constant. That is, in the interim, POTS traffic will be converted to B or B+D and plugged in the RT, along with new ISDN traffic. The resultant combination of B and D channel traffic is truly unpredictable.

In summary, it would be convenient, if not essential, for the CO to have a central control over the RT/DLC system capacity allocation, rather than to individually update the RT's which will have already been deployed in the Carrier Serving Areas (CSA). Figure III.1 shows such a central control arrangement, which will be an integral part of the adaptive access architecture.

3.1 System Control Objectives

Consider an RT/DLC system. Let $X(k)$ be the total D channel offered traffic and $Y(k)$ be the total B channel offered traffic in bps at $t = kT$, where k is an integer and T is the fundamental system time unit.

Let $r_x(k)$ and $r_y(k)$ be the RT output capacities allocated at $t = kT$ for the D and B channel incoming traffic, respectively.

From the fact that DLC operates at the DS1 rate (minus overhead),

$$r_x(k) + r_y(k) = 1536000 \qquad \text{(Eq III.1.1)}$$

The necessary condition for non-congested traffic is:

$$X(k) + Y(k) \leq 1536000 \qquad \text{(Eq III.1.2)}$$

The sufficient condition for the non-congested traffic is:

$$X(k) \leq r_x(k) \qquad \text{(Eq III.1.3)}$$
$$Y(k) \leq r_y(k) \qquad \text{(Eq III.1.4)}$$

The (ideal) objective control for non-congested traffic is that $r_x(k)$ and $r_y(k)$ should be determined such that (Eq III.1.1), (Eq III.1.2), (Eq III.1.3), and (Eq III.1.4) are satisfied for all k. Note that $X(k)$ and $Y(k)$ are the random variables (demands) for D and B channel capacity, respectively.

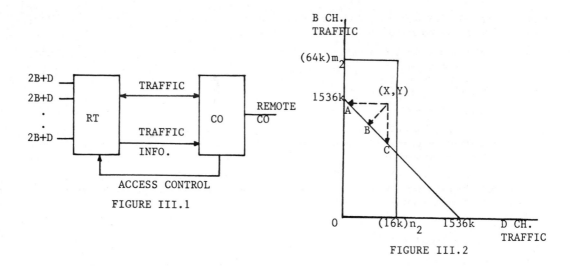

FIGURE III.1

FIGURE III.2

3.2 Congestion Control Strategy

When the necessary condition for non-congested traffic, as in (Eq III.1.2), is met, there is always a partition of DLC output capacity, $\{r_x(k), r_y(k)\}$ such that the sufficient condition for a non-congested traffic as in (Eq III.1.3) and (Eq III.1.4) are satisfied. When (Eq III.1.2) is not met, especially for large m_2 and n_2,

$$P[X(k) + Y(k) > 1536000] > 0 \qquad \text{(Eq III.2.1)}$$

This implies either

$$P[X(k) > r_x(k)] > 0 \qquad \text{(Eq III.2.2)}$$

or,

$$P[Y(k) > r_y(k)] > 0 \qquad \text{(Eq III.2.3)}$$

or, both. This is illustrated in Figure III.2. Since the realized point $\{X(k), Y(k)\}$ is located outside of the DLC potential capability region, it must be moved (by the control strategy) into the region to correspond to a realizable transmission. Of course, it will cause some congestion of B channel and

D channel traffic, depending on the congestion control strategy used. Of course, such a situation may yield some traffic congestion.

For example,

1) When the operating point R is set to the point A, there will be congestion of D channel traffic only because all of $Y(k)$ is carried.

2) When the operating point R is set to the point C, it will yield congestion for B channel only because all of $X(k)$ is carried.

3) When the operating point R is set to the point B, it will yield congestions for both the D channel traffic and the B channel traffic.

A specific congestion control strategy should be designed and implemented to provide the desired quality of service. Clearly, trade-offs are involved.

We propose that the control strategy adhere to the following policies:

I) For B channel traffic, the in-progress B channels can not be interrupted by the access congestion control.

II) D channel traffic will be queued in the buffer *only when* all transmission capacity is in use and a contention between B and D channel traffic occurs.

III) After satisfying the above, D channel traffic has a priority over B channel traffic if a contention still exists. New incoming B channel traffic will be blocked if no capacity can be allocated.

In fact, we use a straightforward congestion control strategy and assumptions about the control dynamics to the computer simulation for numerical results.

Most access concentration architectures now being considered allow for D channel packet queueing (and delay), but do not provide for B channel queueing. Therefore, (Eq III.2.2) can be relaxed by queueing the traffic in the buffer, while (Eq III.2.3) can not be relaxed. That is, the probability in (Eq III.2.2) can be significantly reduced as:

$$P[\ X(k) > r_x(k) + W\ ] < P[\ X(k) > r_x(k)\ ]$$

where W is a buffer length available. When queueing is performed, the traffic congestion must be further investigated in terms of delay and, possibly, blocking when the buffer size is not sufficiently large to hold all the delayed traffic.

Then, in summary, the objective control for congested traffic is that $r_x(k)$ and $r_y(k)$ should be determined in such a way that the delay and blocking for D channel traffic, and blocking for B channel traffic are minimized (or are within a tolerable range).

4. COMPUTATIONAL RESULTS

Given the numbers of B channels and D channels plugged in the RT and the transmission rate of the DLC is set at the DS1: i.e., 1536 kbps for user message transportation and 8 kbps for network control and maintenance, the traffic comparison parameters introduced in the Chapter II are computed for each of access alternatives that combine multiple end-users. In this initial analysis, we consider only a few examples, as being illustrative of the potential benefits of our approach. More extensive studies would be required for complete understanding.

4.1 Assumptions

For the TDM access, the number of end users is set at 10 and 2B+D is assumed for all users. Then, $m_0 = 20$ and $n_0 = 10$. For the concentrated access and the adaptive access concentration cases, the numbers of D channels and B channels are 40 and 80, respectively. In fact, this is equivalent to 40 end-users, each having 2B+D. Then, $m_1 = m_2 = 80$ and $n_1 = n_2 = 40$. In order to characterize the traffic demand, in a static sense, we assume that each incoming D channel traffic, X_i, $i = 1, 2, ..., n$, has an average offered load of 0.1, and each incoming B channel traffic, Y_i, $i = 1, 2, ..., m$, has an average offered load of 0.2. Furthermore, it is assumed that all the incoming channel traffics are mutually independent. Then, 10% of the plugged-in D channels and 20% of the plugged-in B channels are seeking access capacity at any time (or on the average).

Hence, the expected number of offered D channels and B channels would be $\lambda_D = (40)(0.1) = 4$ and $\lambda_B = (80)(0.2) = 16$.

For a dynamic traffic characterization, we can assume that the number of D channels and B channels offering traffic in a time interval is Poisson distributed. That is, in a time interval T,

$$P[X = (16000)l] = P[n = l]$$
$$= e^{-(\lambda_D T)} \frac{(\lambda_D T)^l}{l!}$$

where $T = 1$ and $0 \leq l \leq 40$ and, it is assumed that:

$$\sum_{l=0}^{40} P[n = l] \cong 1$$

Similarly,

$$P[Y = (64000)l] = P[m = l]$$
$$= e^{-(\lambda_B T)} \frac{(\lambda_B T)^l}{l!}$$

where $T = 1$ and $0 \leq l \leq 80$ and, it is assumed that:

$$\sum_{l=0}^{80} P[m = l] \cong 1$$

For the concentrated access case, DS0 (64 kbps) is assumed for the RT output capacity that is allocated for D channel traffic and, therefore, the remaining 1472 kbps will be dedicated to B channel traffic. However, for the adaptive concentration, no limitation is set for RT output allocation for the D and B channel traffic, although the initial allocations will be the same as for the concentrated access case.

For simplicity, D channel packet length is assumed to be always 128 octets and the traffic increase due to framing and address information is ignored for both the concentrated case and for the adaptively concentrated case. For each of numerical computation and a straightforward comparison among the access alternatives, an infinite buffer length is assumed, where applicable. Hence, the traffic congestion on the B channel will be compared in terms of the blocking probability and the traffic congestion on the D channel will be compared in terms of only the average delay reflected by the average queue length. For an adaptive access concentration, the congestion control strategy described in Section III.2 is applied.

The time unit, T, will be represented by 1 and the controller processing delay is also assumed to be a time unit, T. Furthermore, the propagation delay between the RT and the CO is assumed to be negligible. Finally, the traffic performance requirement is set as follows:

Blocking Probability on B Channel Traffic ≤ 0.5 %
Average Delay on D Channel Traffic ≤ 50 msec.

4.2 Numerical Results

In this section, the performance measures introduced in the Chapter II will be computed. In addition, a computer simulation is performed to obtain the average queue length for the D channel traffic and the blocking probability for B channel traffic.

4.2.1 Multiplexed RT

From (Eq II.2.3),

$$Facility\ Efficiency = \frac{(16000)(10)(0.1) + (64000)(20)(0.2)}{(1536000)}$$
$$= 0.1771$$

From (Eq II.2.4), $TrafficEfficiency = 1.0$. From (Eq II.2.5) and (Eq II.2.6), the Traffic Congestions are: $U_B = U_D = 0.0$.

4.2.2 Concentrated RT

From (Eq II.3.3),

$$Facility\ Efficiency\ =\ 1.0\ -\ \frac{(16000)\sum\limits_{k=0}^{4}(4-k)P[n=k]\ +\ (64000)\sum\limits_{k=0}^{23}(23-k)P[m=k]}{1536000}$$

$$=\ 0.6965$$

From (Eq II.3.4),

$$Traffic\ Efficiency\ =\ P[X\le 64000,\ Y\le 1472000]$$
$$=\ P[n\le 4,\ m\le 23]$$
$$=\ 0.6057$$

From (Eq II.3.5) and (Eq II.3.6), the Traffic Congestions are:

$$U_B\ =\ P[m>23]\ =\ 0.0367$$
$$U_D\ =\ P[n>4]\ =\ 0.3712$$

Note that these are the probabilities of traffic congestion *without queueing* for the B channel and D channel traffic, respectively.

With queueing, from the computer simulation, the average queue length for the D channel traffic is found as 8.733 packets with an average delay of 139.73 msec. and the blocking probability for B channel traffic is found as 0.0036. Note that the blocking probability can also be calculated as follows:

$$Blocking\ Probability\ =\ \sum\limits_{k=24}^{\infty}P[m=k]\cdot(\frac{k-23}{k})$$

$$=\ 0.0033$$

This analytical result agrees closely with the one found by the computer simulation. Since the average delay on D channel traffic violates the assumed performance objective, two and three DS0 are tried for the RT output capacity allocated for D channel traffic. For those cases, there would be 1408 kbps and 1344 kbps dedicated for B channel traffic, respectively. The numerical results for these trials are included in Table I.

4.2.3 Adaptive Concentration

To compute the performance measures defined in Chapter II, a perfectly adaptive controller was assumed. However, for the computer simulation, the adaptive controller described briefly in the Chapter III, was used. System time units are in packet transmission times.

From (Eq II.4.3),

$$Facility\ Efficiency\ =\ 1.0\ -\ \sum\limits_{i=0}^{40}\sum\limits_{j=0}^{80}\{1536000-(16000)(i)-(64000)(j)\}^{+}\cdot$$
$$P[X=(16000)(i),\ Y=(64000)(j)]\ /\ (1536000)$$

$$=\ 0.7045$$

From (Eq II.4.4),

$$Traffic\ Efficiency\ =\ P[X+Y\le 1536000]\ =\ 0.9549$$

From (Eq II.4.5), the Traffic Congestion is:

$$U_{B,D}\ =\ P[X+Y>1536000]\ =\ 0.0451$$

From the computer simulation with an identical input applied to the concentrated RT case, it is found that the average queue length for D channel traffic is 0.1885 packets with an average delay of 0.38 msec. and the blocking probability for B channel traffic is 0.0019. These statistics meet out objectives.

4.2.4 Discussion

First, we find that, as motivated and expected, the static concentration method improves Facility Efficiency significantly, but at the expense of Traffic Efficiency, relative to the fully multiplexed case. Notice that the D channel traffic is heavily congested as compared to the B channel traffic.

As shown in Table I, when $r_x = (8)(16k) = 128$ [kbps] and $r_y = (22)(64k) = 1408$ [kbps], there is a big improvement in the Traffic Efficiency and a negligible average queue length and average delay. However, this modification degraded the B channel performance to a point at which it violated the requirement assumed. This clearly suggests the potential benefit of frequent adjustments of the output capacity allocated to the D channel and the B channel traffics. In fact, for the adaptive concentrated case, the B channel blocking probability as well as the D channel average delay are found to be satisfactory because of this frequent adjustment.

The key point is that the adaptive concentration technique improves facility utilization over the static concentrated technique at its *best* with Traffic Efficiency nearly the same as the essentially dedicated TDM access procedure.

In addition, the average queue length and the average delay are nearly negligible. That is, the RT with adaptive access concentration, indeed, effectively utilizes "room" created by the B channel traffic fluctuations to transport the bursty D channel traffic. It results in a very small average queue length and, hence, would not necessitate a large buffer in the RT.

STATIC TRAFFIC PERFORMANCE				
ACCESS METHOD	OUTPUT ALLOCATION	FACILITY EFFICIENCY	TRAFFIC EFFICIENCY	CONGESTION PROBABILITY
TDM $m_0 = 20$ $n_0 = 10$	$r_y = 1280\ kbps$ $r_x = 160\ kbps$	0.1771	1.0	$U_B = 0.0$ $U_D = 0.0$
CONC. $m_1 = 80$ $n_1 = 40$	$r_y = 1472\ kbps$ $r_x = 64\ kbps$	0.6965	0.6058	$U_B = 0.0367$ $U_D = 0.3712$
	$r_y = 1408\ kbps$ $r_x = 128\ kbps$	0.7019	0.9216	$U_B = 0.0582$ $U_D = 0.0214$
	$r_y = 1344\ kbps$ $r_x = 192\ kbps$	0.6985	0.9105	$U_B = 0.0892$ $U_D = 0.0003$
ADAPTIVE CONC. $m_2 = 80$ $n_2 = 40$	VARIABLE	0.7045	0.9549	$U_{B,D} = 0.0451$

DYNAMIC TRAFFIC PERFORMANCE				
ACCESS METHOD	OUTPUT ALLOCATION	BLOCKING PROBABILITY (B CHANNEL)	AVERAGE QUEUE LENGTH (D CHANNEL)	AVERAGE DELAY [msec] (D CHANNEL)
TDM $m_0 = 20$ $n_0 = 10$	$r_y = 1280\ kbps$ $r_x = 160\ kbps$	0.0	0.0	0.0
CONC. $m_1 = 80$ $n_1 = 40$	$r_y = 1472\ kbps$ $r_x = 64\ kbps$	0.0036	8.733	139.73
	$r_y = 1408\ kbps$ $r_x = 128\ kbps$	0.0062	0.0524	0.42
	$r_y = 1344\ kbps$ $r_x = 192\ kbps$	0.0092	0.0	0.0
ADAPTIVE CONC. $m_2 = 80$ $n_2 = 40$	VARIABLE	0.0019	0.1885	0.38

Table I. A numerical comparison for ISDN "mixed" access architectures.

5. SUMMARY

A number of "mixed" access architectures for the RT/DLC system in an ISDN environment are investigated and compared by computing several traffic performance indices that depend on demand traffic characteristics. All of the access architectures could be designed such that *traffic performance* is satisfactory but, in some cases, only by limiting the number of input channels or subscribers.

However, because facility utilization is an important measure of *economic* efficiency, a technique that provides acceptable traffic performance at high levels of facility utilization may be optimal. We propose such a scheme employing adaptive concentration methods to improve on time division multiplexing and static concentration access architectures. The approach allows the largest number of input channels, among the alternatives studied in this paper, while maintaining acceptable traffic performance.

The proposed technique provides an improvement of facility utilization with little or no increase in congestion relative to the other access techniques. Such improvements would be much more dramatic if the demand were more volatile, the number of subscribers time-varying, and demands less uniform. The cost of providing the adaptive controller function was not considered thus far.

REFERENCES

[1] Engineering and Operations in the BELL system: Second Edition, AT&T Bell Laboratories, Murray Hill, N.J., 1984.

[2] IEEE Journal on Selected Areas in Communications, vol. SAC-4, no. 3, "Special Issue on ISDN: Recommendations and Field Trials-I," May 1986.

[3] Eleventh International Teletraffic Congress, Proceeding 1 & 2, Kyoto, Japan, Sep. 1985.

TRAFFIC ENGINEERING for ISDN Design and Planning
M. Bonatti and M. Decina (Editors)
Elsevier Science Publishers B.V. (North-Holland)
449

NONBLOCKING MULTIRATE SWITCHING NETWORKS

Gerd NIESTEGGE

SIEMENS AG, N ZL SV 23
P.O. Box 70 00 76
D-8000 Munich 70, Federal Republic of Germany

It is of great importance for the introduction of broadband ISDN that it be possible to switch connections with different bitrates through a common switching network (multirate switching). One way of achieving this is to use multichannel circuit switching. The paper studies a type of nonblocking multistage switching networks for multichannel connections. The problem of maintaining bit sequence integrity on multichannel connections is solved by always feeding the single-channel connections making up the multichannel connection via a common multiplex system (incoming highways and interconnection links).

Main Statements. A type of nonblocking multistage switching networks for connections with different bitrates, suitable for broadband ISDN exchanges, is studied.

1. Introduction

1.1 Broadband ISDN Channel Types

The upgrading of the ISDN to a broadband ISDN will mean that the narrowband services will be supplemented by services with bitrates up to 140 Mb/s (videophone, high-speed data transmission etc.). The CCITT has completed the standardization of bitrates up to 2 Mb/s [1]. The bitrates for broadband services above 2 Mb/s are still being discussed [2]. In the following, the notation given in tab. 1 is used.

USA		Europe	
B	64 kb/s	B	64 kb/s
H0	384 kb/s	H0	384 kb/s
H11	1.5 Mb/s	H12	1.9 Mb/s
H2	45 Mb/s	H2	35 Mb/s
H3	90 Mb/s	H3	70 Mb/s
H4	140 Mb/s	H4	140 Mb/s

Tab.1: Broadband ISDN Channel Types

1.2 Multirate Switching

It would be too expensive to use a separate switching network for each type of channel in a switching system. It is therefore of great importance for the introduction of broadband ISDN that it be possible to switch connections with different bitrates through the same switching network (multirate switching). One way of achieving this is to use multichannel circuit switching. The problem of maintaining bit sequence integrity on multichannel connections can be solved by always feeding the single-channel connections making up the multichannel connection via a common

multiplex system (**parallel** switching of multichannel connections). Another way of multirate switching which is not discussed
here is asynchronous time division (ATD).

1.3 Nonblocking Switching Networks

The following investigates nonblocking multistage switching networks for multichannel connections switched in parallel. Two
actual examples for switching B, H0 and H1 or H2, H3 and H4
channels, respectively, are presented.

Nonblocking multistage switching networks were introduced by A.
Clos [3]. At that time interest was taken only in space division.
Nonblocking switching networks with space and time division were
treated by A. Jajszczyk [4]. A nonblocking switching network in
an exchange can naturally only be implemented with a much larger
outlay than that necessary for a switching network for which
small losses are permitted; it does however provide a series of
advantages from the point of view of operation and planning. It
is, for example, possible to switch nailed-up connections together with dial-up connections via the switching network without any
restrictions; this is particularly important when nailed-up
connections are created by subscriber procedures as it is the
case with the ISDN.

2. Nonblocking Switching Networks for Multichannel Connections

2.1 Two-Stage Reversed Switching Arrangements

Fig. 1 shows a two-stage reversed (one-
sided) switching arrangement. It has ac
incoming highways. A switching matrix of
the A stage is connected with every
switching matrix of the B stage via an
interconnection link. The incoming highways and interconnection links are operated as duplex circuits so that only
one path has to be specified for a
single-channel connection requiring one
channel for each speech direction. We
assume that the connections between two
incomimg highways connected to the same
switching matrix of the A stage are
switched within this matrix and do not
occupy interconnection links.

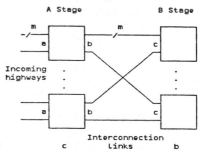

Fig. 1: Two-Stage Re-
versed Arrangement

Each direction of each incoming highway and interconnection link
is provided with a multiplex system having m channels. The
transport bit rate of the multiplex system is m times the bit
rate which can be transmitted in a channel. The number m is known
as the multiplex rate. The switching matrixes can provide
arbitrary combinations of space and time switching.

2.2 Multichannel Switching

Connections with different bit rates are achieved by switching
multichannel connections, which, depending on the bit rate,
occupy different numbers of channels (multichannel switching).
The possible bit rates are then whole multiples of the bit rate
which can be transmitted over one channel. A differentiation must
be made between:

Independent switching of multichannel connections: the single-channel connections making up a multichannel connection are always switched through the switching network independently of each other (see fig. 2).

Parallel switching of multichannel connections: The single-channel connections making up a multichannel connection are always fed together via a common multiplex system (incoming highways and interconnection links). In the multiplex system, they occupy arbitrary channels. This means that a multichannel connection consists of a maximum of m single-channel connections (the maximum bit rate of a multichannel connection is then the transport bit rate of a multiplex system) and that the single-channel connections making up the multichannel connection are all fed via the same switching matrix of the B stage (see fig. 3).

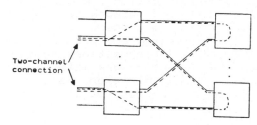
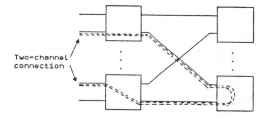

Fig.2: Independent Switching of   Fig.3: Parallel switching of a
     a Multichannel Connection   multichannel connection

The task of maintaining bit sequence integrity on multichannel connections can be achieved much more easily in the case of parallel switching of multichannel connections than in the case of independent switching. Parallel switching is therefore more practicable. On the other hand, internal blocking occurs more frequently in the case of parallel switching of multichannels than in the case of independent switching. The following investigates when switching networks are nonblocking in the case of parallel switching of multichannel connections.

2.3 Nonblocking Parallel Switching of Multichannel Connections

Multistage switching networks are nonblocking if the well-known condition as per Clos [3] or the more general form of this condition for digital switching networks as per Jajszczyk [4] is met. These conditions can be applied if only connections with a fixed bitrate are switched or if multichannel connections are switched independently. If multichannel connections with different numbers of channels are switched in parallel, the condition described in the following must be substituted for these.

We assume that an arbitrary traffic mixture of single-channel and multichannel connections with maximum channel number s (s $\leqslant$ m) is fed to the switching network in fig. 1. Multichannel connections are switched in parallel. Then, internal blocking in the switching network does not occur if the following condition is met:

$$(1) \qquad b \geq 2 \left[\frac{am - s}{m - s + 1} \right] + 1$$

(where [x] denotes the greatest integer less than or equal to a real number x; e.g. [7.34] = 7).

Proof: If the two lines to be interconnected are terminated on the same switching matrix of the A stage the connection can be switched through the matrix without occupying interconnection links. No blocking is caused here.

Let us now look at a request for an s-channel connection between s idle channels on two incoming highways which are terminated on different switching matrixes of the A stage. We assume the most unfavourable condition, i.e. all other channels on the incoming highways terminated on the two switching matrixes are already seized (see fig. 4). A total of (a-1)m+(m-s) = am-s channels are then occupied on the incoming highways of each of the two switching matrixes. The same number of channels are maximally occupied on the b interconnection links which are attached to each of the two switching matrixes (it may be less since connections between highways terminated on the same switching matrix of the A stage do not occupy any channels on the links).

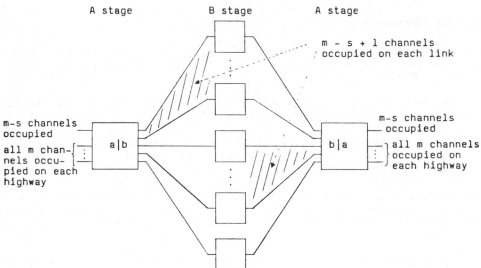

Fig. 4: Path Network

Since parallel switching is used, a switching matrix of the B stage must be specified for the s-channel connection and the s single channels making up the connection are fed via this. A minimum of s channels must still be free on the two links between the two switching matrixes of the A stage on which the two incoming highways are terminated and this switching matrix of the B stage. A link is no longer available for the s-channel connection if more than m-s (i.e. at least m-s+1) of the m channels are already occupied. The ma-s occupied channels on each of the two switching matrixes of the A stage can block a maximum of

$$\left[\frac{ma - s}{m - s + 1} \right]$$

interconnection links and the same number of switching matrixes of the B stage for an s-channel connection.

In the most unfavourable case, the switching matrixes of the B stage, which, because of a lack of idle channels on the interconnection links, cannot be reached from the first switching matrix of the A stage and those which cannot be reached from the second switching matrix of the A stage are disjunct. As a result, a maximum of

$$
2 \left[\frac{ma - s}{m - s + 1} \right]
$$

switching matrixes of the B stage, for the s-channel connection are no longer available. If (1) is met, there is at least one switching matrix of the B stage, via which a path can be set up for an s-channel connection.

Finally, it should be noted, that, if no internal blocking occurs in the switching network in the case of an s-channel connection, no blocking will occur with an r-channel connection with $1 \leqslant r \leqslant s$.

2.4 Some Comments on the Above Condition

In the case m=s=1 (only one channel per line, only single-channel connections), condition (1) conforms to the condition as per Clos: $b \geqslant 2a-1$.

The number b of the necessary switching matrixes in the B stage is naturally a function of the parameter a. In addition, it is, as in (1), dependent on the quotient s/m and not to any great extent on m and s themselves. (The multiplex rate m and the number s of the single-channel connections which can make up a multichannel connection mainly determine the complexity of the switching matrix). The quotient s/m corresponds to the ratio of the maximum bit rate of a connection (multichannel) to the transport bit rate of the multiplex system. The necessary number b of switching matrixes in the B stage increases as this ratio increases.

An unfavourable situation arises when the maximum bit rate of a connection corresponds to the transport bit rate of the multiplex system (s=m). This results in: $b \geqslant 2s(a-1)+1$. The traffic is expanded by a factor $b/a \approx 2s$ in the A stage of the switching network. The B stage is almost as large as the total of all the B stages of s separate switching networks (one for each type of connection) which comply with the condition as per Clos (expansion factor 2). If one considers that, generally, only k-channel connections are permitted for selected k between 1 and s (e.g. 2 to the power of an integer), separate switching networks for the individual types of connection are more favourable. We will come back to the case s=m in connection with "nonblocking in the wide sense" (section 4.1).

The situation is different when the multiplex rate m is large in comparison to the maximum number of channels permitted for a connection (m >> s). In such a case, the expansion factor is hardly greater than 2. The B stage is only a bit larger than the B stage of a nonblocking switching network for nonmixed traffic which complies with Clos' condition. A few actual examples are given in section 3.

It is also possible to envisage switching networks with a
different multiplex rate on the incoming highways to that on the
links. Condition (1) is also valid for this case when m in the
numerator of the fraction is equal to the multiplex rate of the
incoming highways and m in the denominator of the fraction is
equal to the multiplex rate of the links. Naturally, in the case
of parallel switching of multichannel connections, the maximum
number of single-channel connections making up a multichannel
connection is then determined by the lowest value of the two
multiplex rates.

Condition (1) is also valid for symmetrical three-stage straight
(two-sided) switching networks; the proof can easily be applied
to this case.

2.5 Three-Stage Reversed Switching Networks

Nonblocking, three-stage reversed (one-sided) switching networks
are obtained if each of the switching matrixes of the B stage in
a two-stage reversed network described above is replaced by a
nonblocking two-stage reversed switching arrangement (see
fig. 5).

Nonblocking reversed switching networks for a large number of
incoming highways can be realized with three stages. The three-
stage reversed switching network also offers the advantage of
greater modularity; in the case of small, partial-capacity
stages, the third stage and a large part of the second stage can
be omitted and these stages can then be supplemented when the
system is supplemented.

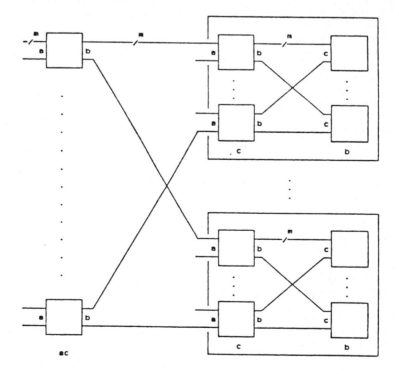

Fig. 5:   Three-Stage Reversed Arrangement

3. Switching Networks For Broadband ISDN Channel Types

3.1 Uniform Switching Matrixes

Duplex connections must be switched by the switching matrixes used for the reversed arrangements considered here. Switching matrixes of this kind can best be designed with a folded configuration of directional switching matrixes with N inputs and N outputs (multiplex systems with m channels), which can switch Nxm (single-channel) simplex connections. One input and one output together make one duplex circuit termination; this results in a switching module with N terminations, each providing one duplex circuit (see fig. 6).

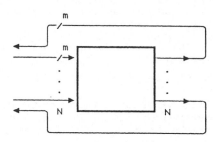

Fig. 6: Folded Congiguration of a Directional Switching Matrix

In the two-stage reversed switching network described above (fig. 1) a module with N=a+b terminations is required for the A stage and a module with N=c terminations is required for the B stage. In order to keep the outlay for the development and mass production as low as possible, it is advisable to use a uniform switching module as switching matrix in all stages of the switching network. This requires that a+b=c. This is a further restriction as far as the selection of suitable switching network structures is concerned.

The possibility of using a uniform switching module as switching matrix in each stage of a reversed arrangement is an advantage which straight arrangements do not have.

3.2 Example A

The following describes arrangements for nonblocking switching networks suitable for switching H2, H3 and H4 connections and operated on the basis of H2 channels (see tab. 1).

We assume that the transmit and receive directions of highways and links (duplex operation) are each provided with a multiplex system having a transport bit rate of 560 Mb/s (optical fibre). The bit rate which can be transmitted in a channel corresponds to that of the H2 channel; this is 35 Mb/s or 45 Mb/s, respectively. The multiplex rate m then amounts to 12 H2 channels in the American case and 16 in the European case. H4 connections are 4-channel connections (Europe, s=4) or 3-channel connections (USA, s=3); in both cases, H3 connections are 2-channel connections. Multichannel connections are switched in parallel.

These prerequisites and the demand for a standard switching module severely limit the number of possible structures for nonblocking switching networks able to switch H2, H3 and H4 connections. Selection of parameter a automatically specifies the other parameters of a two- or three-stage arrangement if parameter b (number of switching matrixes in the second stage) is to be selected to be as suitable as possible, i.e. as small as possible.

Fig. 7 shows an example of a two-stage arrangement which is nonblocking in both cases (European and American standard). The example is based on a time division multiplex switching module with 30 terminations for 560 Mb/s systems, which can be operated as time division multiplex systems with 12 or 16 H2 channels, respectively.

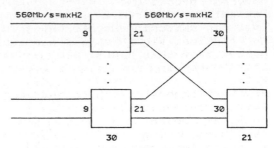

Fig. 7: 2-Stage Reversed Arrangement with 270 Incoming Highways of 560 Mb/s, i. e. 3240 (USA, m = 12) or 4320 (Europe, m = 16) H2 channels, respectively.

The nonblocking three-stage reversed arrangement which is based on the same module (fig. 5: a=9, b=21, c=30) results in a switching network with 2430 incoming highways of 560 Mb/s; i.e. 29160 H2 channels (USA) or 38880 H2 channels (Europe), respectively.

In connection with different standards in the USA and Europe, it should be noted that one switching network does not necessarily have to be nonblocking in both the American and European cases. The two-stage reversed arrangement (fig. 1) with parameters a=10, b=23 and any c is nonblocking for the American case (m=12, s=3) but not for the European case (m=16, s=4): the condition (1) is met in the first case but not in the second.

3.3 Example B

Fig. 8 gives an example of an arrangement for a nonblocking switching network suitable for switching B, H0, H11 and H12 channels (see tab. 1). It is operated on the basis of B channels. The incoming highways and interconnection links are time division multiplex systems which have a transport bitrate of 8 Mb/s and which are used for transmitting 128 B channels. 32 8-Mb/s-systems of this type can be connected to the switching module.

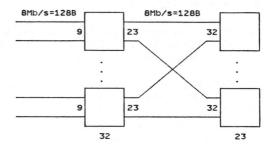

Fig. 8: 2-Stage Reversed Switching Arrangement for 288 Highways (8 Mb/s), i.e. 36864 B channels

In the case of parallel multichannel connection switching, the arrangement in fig. 8 is nonblocking for multichannel connections with up to 35 B channels (s=35). An arbitrary traffic mixture of connections with all the channel types discussed can therefore be switched up to 2 Mb/s in this switching network; an H0 connection occupies 6 B channels, an H11 connection 24 B channels and an H12 connection 30 B channels. The switching network has a termination capacity of more than 36 000 B channels. If only B channel connections, H0 connections and H11 connections are switched (no H12, s=24), a number of 21 switching matrixes would even suffice in the B stage (b=21).

4. Topics for Further Study

4.1 Arrangements Nonblocking in the Wide Sense

A switching network is nonblocking in the wide sense if a path searching algorithm exists which, when used, does not result in internal blocking of the switching network (see [5]). This term was defined for conventional switching networks which are only used for switching single-channel connections. It is, however, of no practical significance since, as far as I know, no switching networks of this kind exist which are not nonblocking but which are nonblocking in the wide sense.

If multichannel connections are switched in parallel by a switching network, it is easy to find examples of switching networks which are nonblocking in the wide sense but which are not nonblocking. Let us examine an example of a two-stage reversed arrangement with parameters m=4, a=4, b=14 and c=4 (see fig. 9):

This network switches single- and four-channel connections (no two- and three-channel connections) in parallel. In order for it to be nonblocking, the number of switching matrixes in the B-stage must, according to the condition (1), be at least 25; it is not therefore nonblocking.

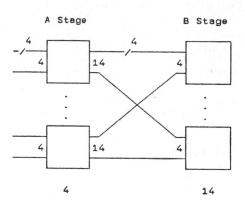

Fig. 9: A Switching Network Which is Not Nonblocking but Which Is Nonblocking in the Wide Sense for Single- and Four-Channel Connections

Let us now look at the following path search algorithm:

When a single-channel connection has to be switched, the switching matrixes in the B stage are hunted from top to bottom, always starting at the first matrix of the B stage. When a four-channel connection is switched, hunting is again from top to bottom, this time starting at the eighth matrix of the B stage.

In the case of nonmixed traffic (only single-channel connections or only four-channel connections), the switching network with b=7 switching matrixes in the B stage would be nonblocking. In the path search algorithm described above, 7 switching matrixes are available in the B stage for each of the two types of connection, each of which is only used by one type of connection. Internal blocking does not therefore occur in the switching network if the path search algorithm described above is used. The switching network is therefore nonblocking in the wide sense.

The question still has to be answered as to whether this path search algorithm is the optimal one or whether another with less than 14 switching matrixes in the B stage (with the same parameters a, c and m) can be used without blocking occurring. It is conjected that 13 switching matrixes will suffice in the B stage if, following every connection request, they are hunted from top to bottom and if, irrespective of the type of connection, hunting always starts at the first switching matrix.

It would seem that the expression "nonblocking in the wide sense" and the determination of an optimal path search algorithm for switching networks which would allow variable numbers of channels to be switched in parallel play a much more important role than they do in the case of conventional switching networks. Finding a condition enabling one to determine whether switching networks of this kind are nonblocking in the wide sense or not and finding optimal path search algorithms represent problems which still have to be solved and which still require further study.

4.2 Rearranging Multichannel Connections

Another interesting aspect is that of examining the relation between parallel switching of multichannel connections in a switching network and rearranging.

Rearranging refers to the rearranging of existing connections in a switching network in order to eliminate internal blocking when a new call arrives. A switching network is said to be "rearrangeable" if inner blocking can be eliminated by rearranging (see [5]).

It can be assumed that rearranging in switching networks for parallel switching of multichannels plays an important role and that switching networks of this kind which are rearrangeable are to construct with considerably less outlay (less switching matrixes and interconnection links) than are switching networks which are nonblocking or nonblocking in the wide sense.

References

[1] CCITT Red Book, Fascicle III.5, Rec. I.412, 1984

[2] CCITT Study Group XVIII - Report R 19 (C),
    Geneva, July 1986

[3] Clos, C.: A Study of Non-Blocking Switching Networks;
    Bell Syst. Tech. J., vol. 32, no. 2, 1953

[4] Jajszczyk, A.: On Non-Blocking Switching Networks Composed
    of Digital Symmetrical Matrices;
    IEEE Trans. on Com., vol. com-31, no. 1, 1983

[5] Benes, V.E.: Mathematical Theory of Connecting Networks and
    Telephone Traffic; Academic Press, New York London 1965

TRAFFIC ENGINEERING for ISDN Design and Planning
M. Bonatti and M. Decina (Editors)
Elsevier Science Publishers B.V. (North-Holland)
© IAC, 1988

A PERFORMANCE STUDY OF LAPD FRAME-RELAY PROTOCOLS FOR PACKETIZED DATA TRANSFER OVER ISDN NETWORKS

Kiran M. Rege
Kim-Joan Chen

AT&T Bell Laboratories
Holmdel, New Jersey 07733

ABSTRACT

It has been proposed that the LAPD data-link protocol be used for packetized data transfer on the bearer channels of ISDNs. Since LAPD allows multiplexing at layer 2, it will eliminate the need to process layer 3 headers during switching which is expected to make for a more efficient network operation. Among the various possible implementations of LAPD, the frame-relay and edge-terminated implementations are of particular interest. In this paper, we present a comparison of the throughput-delay performance of these implementations. We also demonstrate how a "stop-duration" congestion control scheme with properly chosen parameters can effectively protect LAPD frame-relay networks from overloads.

Main Statement: The frame-relay implementation of LAPD can potentially result in a significant improvement of the network performance and provides a frame-work in which excellent congestion control schemes can be designed.

1. INTRODUCTION

The current standards for ISDN propose the LAPD data-link protocol for the signaling channel only. It has been suggested that the LAPD protocol be used on the bearer channels as well for packetized data transfer [1]. Since LAPD allows multiplexing at layer 2, this would make it possible to move to layer 2 several functions currently performed at layer 3 in LAPB based protocols such as X.25. For example, in networks using LAPB as the layer 2 protocol, the information required for switching packets has to be gleaned from layer 3 headers. LAPD will make this information available at layer 2, thus enabling networks to perform switching without having to process layer 3 headers. It is believed that eliminating layer 3 processing for packet transport will make for a more efficient network operation.

A LAPD based protocol can be implemented in several ways. For example, one may terminate the layer 2 protocol (LAPD) at every node, or at a few selected nodes (e.g. edge nodes), or at no network nodes at all. A node where LAPD is terminated is required to perform all LAPD functions such as maintaining layer 2 timers and frame counts, generation of acknowledgements, window rotation and retransmission. On the other hand, a node where LAPD is not terminated performs a minimal set of functions - error checking and switching - which are absolutely essential in a packet-switching environment. This is often called "frame-relay" operation.

Among the various possible implementations of LAPD in data networks, of particular interest are the "frame-relay" and "edge-terminated" implementations. In a frame-relay implementation, LAPD is terminated at the end-systems only with all network nodes operating in a frame-relay mode. Since the frame-relay operation requires a minimal amount of processing, it increases the capacity of the protocol handlers in network nodes which may be particularly important in high speed networks where the processing capacity of the network nodes rather than trunk speeds might determine how much traffic the networks are able to handle. On the other hand, since the protocol is not terminated anywhere in the network, new procedures may have to be developed to monitor and control user traffic. In an edge-terminated implementation, LAPD is terminated at the end-systems as well as at the edge nodes, while all nodes inside the network operate in a frame-relay mode. This implementation makes it easier to monitor and control user traffic at entry; however, additional processing capacity and intelligence are required at the edge-nodes.

The question that naturally arises is how much and under what circumstances does the increased packet handling capacity in a frame-relay implementation result in a significant improvement in the overall network performance? Also, does terminating the protocol at the edges result in a more robust network operation? These questions are addressed in Section 3 of this paper by presenting a comparison of the performance of the frame-relay and edge-terminated implementations of LAPD over a wide range of traffic levels.

Another issue of interest is whether one can develop an effective congestion control scheme to protect LAPD frame-relay networks which do away with link-by-link flow control. There is a large body of literature dealing with flow control and congestion control. (See [2] for a bibliography.) Flow control usually means "speed matching" between a "sender" and a "receiver" [3] and is typically implemented by introducing a "window" between communicating entities which limits the number of packets/frames that the sender can transmit without receiving an acknowledgement from the receiver. Congestion control, on the other hand, refers to the actions taken by the network to protect its resources from the sometimes disastrous effects of overload. While flow control can indirectly help control congestion, by itself it is often inadequate. Consequently, additional control actions are required to prevent network congestion. Some of the congestion control schemes discussed in the literature are described below.

In some networks, the network may deliberately withhold/delay acknowledgements to ease congestion. However, this scheme requires that the protocol (layer 2 or layer 3) be terminated at the edges at least and the corresponding time-out interval be large. None of these conditions are met in a LAPD frame-relay network. Another method employs adaptive windows, which has been analyzed in the context of local area networks in [4]. In this method, the sender adjusts its window, using an adaptive mechanism, according to its perception of congestion. A limitation of this scheme is that it cannot be used if the end-systems employ un-numbered information (UI) frames for communication. A third method discussed in literature employs "choke packets" [5]. In this method, each network node monitors its critical resources for indications of congestion. If the monitoring mechanism indicates congestion on a path leading to some destination, whenever a packet arrives at that node to be routed to the congested path, a choke packet is sent to the source of that packet. On receipt of this choke packet, the source reduces traffic submitted to the network.

The congestion control scheme to be studied in this paper is similar to this scheme and to the one described in [6]. It works as follows: For each virtual circuit "class" there is an "onset threshold". Whenever a frame transmitted on a virtual circuit enters a buffer in a node and the buffer contents are above the corresponding onset threshold, a "stop-message" is sent to the end-system that generated that frame, asking it to stop all layer 3 traffic in the direction in which congestion was encountered. The stop-message carries in it a duration parameter, the value of which may be fixed or chosen randomly from a set of fixed duration values. The end-system stops all layer-3 traffic for the duration indicated in the stop-message. If an end-system in this state receives another stop-message with a stop-duration value larger than the remaining time in its present stop-duration, the latter is replaced with the new stop-duration value. At the end of the stop-duration, the end-system is free to resume layer 3 traffic as before. A performance study of this scheme in the context of LAPD frame-relay networks is presented in Section 4.

2. A SIMULATION MODEL OF LAPD BASED PACKET SWITCHING NETWORKS

2.1 Model Features

To study the issues described in the previous section, a simulation model of LAPD based packet switching networks was developed. This model focuses on a linear segment of the network. Since it was meant to be used as a tool for studying the performance of the data transfer phase of LAPD, it completely ignores the control aspects such as call set-up and tear-down.

As shown in fig. 1, the linear segment of the network comprises nodes 1, 2, ... , N which are connected by full duplex "links" (trunks). As shown in fig. 2, each node consists of a "node processor", a "receive buffer" and a "trunk buffer" for each out-going link. Terminals, work-stations, etc. (referred to as terminals in this paper) are connected to the end nodes (nodes 1 and N) via full duplex "access lines". A "host" is assumed to be connected to each of the end nodes via a full duplex "host link". It is assumed that each terminal communicates with the host at the far end of the network over a virtual circuit. It is possible for an access line to carry several virtual circuits connecting different terminals to the far-end host. In addition to the traffic on these virtual circuits, the model allows some background traffic to be included as simple, open streams of data frames.

The traffic on all virtual circuits is explicitly flow controlled at layers 2 and 3. In all virtual circuits, layer 3 rides end-to-end, while the layer 2 protocol (LAPD) may be terminated at an arbitrary set of nodes. If LAPD is not terminated at any of the network nodes, we have a frame-relay implementation of LAPD. Since the virtual circuits are multiplexed at layer 2, separate layer 2 windows, sequence numbers and timers are maintained for each virtual circuit. The model does not allow piggybacking of acknowledgements at layer 2 or layer 3. Consequently, each layer 2 or layer 3 acknowledgement is carried in a separate frame.

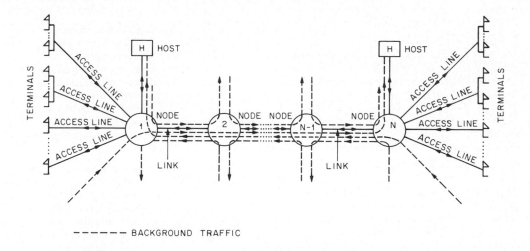

FIG. 1: A SCHEMATIC OF THE NETWORK MODEL

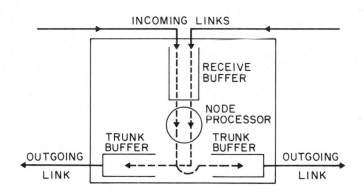

FIG. 2: MODEL OF A NETWORK NODE

The virtual circuits are characterized by their state transitions. At any time, a virtual circuit is in the idle state (called "think" state) or one of three active states - "stream mode", "block mode" or "file mode". On leaving the think state, a virtual circuit enters one of the three active states. In the stream mode, it generates a (random) number of (short) frames in a renewal stream. In the block and file modes, it generates a block of data or a file, which consist of a (random) number of data frames. In each of the active modes, after successfully transmitting all data frames (subject, of course, to window flow control) and receiving acknowledgements, the virtual circuit re-enters the think state where it remains for a random amount of time. By judiciously selecting the parameters of these states a wide variety of traffic patterns can be created.

The model incorporates several features of the LAPD protocol [7], which are believed to have significant performance implications. These include dropping out-of-sequence frames, layer 2 timers, rejects, poll frames and responses to polls (i.e. command/response frames with the P/F bit on). Although the loss of frames due to transmission errors is not included in the model, frames can be lost because of buffer overflow. Out-of-sequence frames are dropped at those nodes where LAPD is terminated or at the end-systems where LAPD is always terminated. Reject frames are sent on receiving the first out-of-sequence frame. At this time, a "reject condition" flag is turned on. While this flag is on, further out-of-sequence frames are simply ignored. This flag is cleared when the next "in-sequence" frame is received. A poll frame is sent when the layer 2 timer times out. The response to this frame is simply a frame carrying the sequence number of the last correctly received frame. All unacknowledged frames are retransmitted on receiving a reject frame or a response to a poll frame. The model also includes the "stop-duration" congestion control scheme described earlier.

2.2 Work-load Characterization

Since LAPD based networks will conceivably carry a wide variety of traffic patterns, the traffic mix used in this study was chosen to make it representative of this wide variety. It consisted of traffic patterns generated by three kinds of virtual circuits - "character interactive", "block interactive" and "file transfer" type.

On a character interactive virtual circuit, a terminal connected at one of the end nodes was assumed to generate, on an average, a stream of 14 short data frames (10 bytes each), which, on being delivered to the host at the far end, would evoke a response consisting of a single 136 byte data frame which would be returned to the terminal. This cycle was assumed to repeat once every 20 seconds. On a block interactive virtual circuit, the "terminal" at one end would typically send a message consisting of a 136 byte frame, and, on receiving this message, the host at the far end would respond with, on an average, four 136 byte frames. Such exchanges were assumed to occur once every 32 seconds for each virtual circuit of this type. On a file transfer type virtual circuit, it was assumed that a file would be transmitted, on an average, once every 30 seconds either from the host to the terminal or the other way round. The mean number of frames in a file was 125, with a 136 byte frame length.

These three kinds of traffic patterns were modeled using three virtual circuit classes. It was assumed that character interactive virtual circuits used 16 kbps access lines with a single virtual circuit per access line. For block interactive and file transfer type virtual circuits, the access line speed was 64 kbps, with 8 virtual circuits per access line. All network links and host links were 64 kbps. The layer 2 window was 3 and the layer 2 timer was 1 second. At each node operating in a frame-relay mode, the protocol processing time was assumed to be 0.5 ms per frame (independent of the frame-length). If LAPD was terminated at a node, the per frame protocol processing time was increased by 0.5 or 2.0 ms. All receive and trunk buffers were 4 kbytes each. A symmetric configuration was assumed, i.e. the same number of virtual circuits of each type were assumed to be established from each end of the network.

Throughout this study, the same basic traffic mix was used. In this mix, the numbers of virtual circuits of the three types were roughly in the proportion 2 : 1 : 1. To create different load levels, we simply varied the number of virtual circuits of each type, keeping their relative proportions fixed. The traffic intensity was measured in terms of the "nominal offered load", denoted by ρ. This was defined as the average load the network would have carried (in either direction) if all the links and processors in the network had infinite capacity and all propagation delays were zero, divided by the capacity of the bottleneck link in the network. One should note that because of window flow control, the actual load offered to the network is always less than ρ. The latter, however, is a measure of how much load the users would have imposed on the network in the absence of any capacity constraints.

3. A COMPARISON OF THE PERFORMANCE OF THE FRAME-RELAY AND EDGE-TERMINATED IMPLEMENTATIONS OF LAPD WITHOUT CONGESTION CONTROL

To compare the performance of the frame-relay and edge-terminated implementations of LAPD without congestion control, several sets of simulation runs were made. In particular, there were two sets of runs with the frame-relay implementation in which the network consisted of 2 and 4 nodes respectively. In addition, there were two sets of runs with the edge-terminated implementation. In both of these, the network consisted of 2 nodes; however, the additional per frame protocol processing time at the nodes where LAPD was terminated was 0.5 ms in the first set of runs and 2 ms in the second set. Using the basic traffic mix described in the previous section, the nominal offered load, ρ, was varied from 0.5 to 2.5 by suitably varying the number of virtual circuits of each type. A nominal offered load of 0.5 represents normal operating conditions while a nominal offered load of 2.5 is representative of fairly heavy congestion.

Some of the results of these runs are displayed in figs. 3 and 4. In fig. 3, the effective layer-3 throughput has been plotted against the nominal offered load for all four sets of runs. This performance measure is defined as the total number of bits in layer 3 packets (including layer 3 acknowledgements) delivered correctly and "in sequence" to the end-systems every second, divided by the trunk capacity expressed in bits per second. This is one of the most important performance measures from the network's point of view as it indicates how efficiently the network resources are being utilized to carry user generated data.

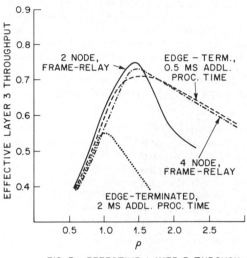

FIG. 3: EFFECTIVE LAYER 3 THROUGH-
PUT V/S LOAD

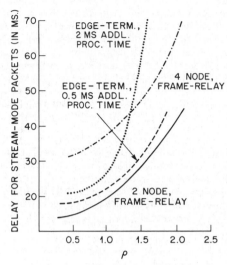

FIG. 4: STREAM-MODE PACKET
DELAY

All four curves in fig. 3 display similar trends - initially, the throughput rises with ρ; however, as ρ goes beyond a certain level, the throughput falls with an increase in ρ. This phenomenon has been noticed elsewhere in similar contexts.(See [3] or [8], for example.) This clearly shows that in the absence of congestion control schemes, both the frame-relay and the edge-terminated implementations can be vulnerable to overloads which lead to frames being lost requiring repeated retransmissions not only of the lost frames but also those which may be received out of sequence. This results in a loss of throughput.

There is very little qualitative difference between the curves in fig. 3, which correspond to the frame-relay implementation. The curve corresponding to the 2-node case has a slightly higher peak (75%) than the one which corresponds to the 4-node case (73%), while the latter falls a little less sharply under overloads than the former. This difference may be attributed to the fact that the additional network latency in the 4-node configuration slows down the entry of new frames into the network, which reduces the throughput under normal conditions but softens the impact of overloads during congestion. The curve which corresponds to the edge-terminated implementation with 0.5 ms additional processing time has a slightly lower peak than both of the frame-relay curves and falls more slowly than both of them under overloads. Here, too, the difference may be attributed to the additional delay introduced by terminating the protocol at the edges, which slows down the entry of new frames under normal conditions as well as during congestion. In this set of runs, although the time required to process a frame at the edge nodes was larger than in the runs where the frame-relay implementation was used, it was not so large as to make the protocol handlers, rather than the trunks (as in the frame-relay case), the bottleneck. Consequently, even with the termination of LAPD at the edge nodes, we do not see a significant drop in the throughput. The fourth curve in fig. 4 represents the case where terminating LAPD at the edges increases the protocol handling time to such an extent that it is the protocol handlers in the nodes which limit the system throughput. In this case, with 2 ms additional processing time at the edge nodes, the peak throughput is significantly lower than for the frame-relay implementation. Also, the nominal offered load at which this peak is achieved is considerably lower than for the frame-relay implementation. This curve demonstrates the potentially serious degradation of throughput when the additional complexity in protocol handlers increases the processing times to such an extent that the protocol handlers become the bottleneck.

Figure 4 shows the mean end-to-end delay for the short frames generated by character interactive virtual circuits as a function of the nominal offered load for the four sets of runs described earlier. Because of smaller processing times at network nodes, the frame-relay implementation results in lower end-to-end delays for the short frames. Also since the character interactive and block interactive virtual circuits have a higher priority than the file transfer type virtual circuits, even during heavy overloads we do not see a more severe degradation of these delays for the frame-relay implementation that we observed in the context of the total layer 3 throughput.

To summarize, we note that the frame-relay implementation of LAPD performs significantly better than the edge-terminated implementation when the additional processing time for terminating LAPD is large enough to make the protocol handlers rather than the trunks the throughput limiting resource. In this case, even if the offered load is less than the trunk capacity, the throughput can deteriorate because frames waiting for the protocol handlers are lost due to overflowing "receive buffers". This situation may arise in high-speed networks where protocol processing at network nodes could be considerably slower than the trunk speeds. Also, if most of the traffic consists of small frames, the protocol handlers are likely to be the bottleneck, especially if they are required to do complete LAPD processing.

4. PERFORMANCE OF THE FRAME-RELAY IMPLEMENTATION OF LAPD WITH STOP-DURATION CONGESTION CONTROL

In this section, we examine the effectiveness of the stop-duration congestion control scheme in protecting LAPD frame-relay networks from overloads. To test the effectiveness of this congestion control scheme and to see what values of the stop-duration may be appropriate at different levels of congestion, several simulation runs were performed. By suitably choosing the number of virtual circuits of each type, the nominal offered load was set at 3.0 which is representative of very heavy congestion. The network model consisted of four nodes operating in a frame-relay mode and the receive and trunk buffers at each node were 4 kbytes each. The onset threshold for all virtual circuit classes was set at 1.5 kbytes.

With this configuration several possible implementations of the stop-duration scheme were tried. In particular, there were two fixed-duration implementations with stop-durations of 2 and 5 seconds respectively; also, there were four random duration implementations with duration value sets (2,4,...,10), (0.5,1.0,1.5,...,5), (1,2,...,10) and (0.5,1.0,1.5,...,10) respectively. Some important performance measures for these simulation runs are shown in Table I.

TABLE I

A COMPARISON OF CONGESTION CONTROL SCHEMES - OFFERED LOAD 3.0

Performance Measure	No Control	Fixed Duration		Random Duration			
		Duratn. 2 Secs.	Duratn. 5 Secs.	Dur.Set (2,4,..,10)	Dur.Set (1,2,..10)	Dur.Set (.5,1,..,5)	Dur.Set (.5,1,..,10)
Effective L3 Throughput	0.558	0.681	0.571	0.654	0.702	0.694	0.701
Frames Lost Per Second	52.8	5.82	3.51	0.075	0.025	1.32	0.0
Frms Rejctd Per Second	10.0	2.72	0.99	0.11	0.007	0.35	0.0
# Retrnsmsns Per Second	63.20	7.59	3.85	0.053	0.025	1.32	0.0
# Time-outs Per Second	32.61	32.85	16.9	7.39	7.01	27.68	13.85
# Stop-msgs Per Second	0.0	138.6	72.7	27.0	25.0	115.7	50.0

One can clearly see that in the absence of any form of congestion control, the effective layer-3 throughput is 56% which is considerably lower than its peak level of about 73% which was achieved with a nominal offered load of 1.5. One can also see that the number of frames lost because of buffer overflow, the number of retransmissions and time-outs are all high, indicating a wastage of band-width. During overloads, the effective layer 3 throughput assumes an added significance - in the case of a temporary surge in user traffic causing an overload, it is a measure of how quickly the surge will be depleted returning the network to normalcy.

With a fixed stop-duration of 2 seconds, one can see that the effective layer-3 throughput is 68%. While this represents a substantial improvement, other performance measures for this run indicate that there is still some room for improvement. With a fixed stop-duration of 5 seconds, the effective layer-3 throughput drops to 57% while all other performance measures show a marked improvement over the simulation run with a stop-duration of 2 seconds. This appears to be a case of over-reacting to the perceived congestion, or not reacting quite intelligently. With a large, fixed stop-duration, such as 5 seconds for this level of congestion, a number of virtual circuits may be asked to stop all layer-3 traffic within a short time after the onset threshold is exceeded, and they remain shut off for a long time as determined by the stop-duration. In this case, because a number of virtual circuits are forced into an idle state, the network may actually run out of user traffic. On the other hand, at the end of the stop-duration, all of these virtual circuits become active almost simultaneously, pushing the network back into congestion. The network may thus oscillate between congestion and idleness, resulting in a loss of throughput.

Table I shows that all the four random stop-duration schemes studied here result in a marked improvement in all or most of the performance measures compared to the two fixed-duration schemes. Among these, the scheme with the duration value set (2,4,...,10) results in the lowest layer-3 throughput of about 65% while the schemes with duration value sets (1,2,...,10) and (0.5,1,1.5,...,10) have the highest layer-3 throughput of about 70%. Note that this latter throughput is close to the peak value of about 73%. One can also see that while all four schemes have fairly low frame loss, frame rejection and retransmission rates, these performance measures are virtually equal to zero for the two schemes with duration value sets (1,2,...,10) and (0.5,1,...,10). As far as the number of time-outs per second is concerned, the former scheme has about half as many time-outs per second as the latter. The same is true for the number of stop messages generated every second. These two performance measures are also important from the network's point of view since a virtual circuit timing out repeatedly may lead to the dropping of that connection which might be viewed as a serious degradation of service by the customer, and the number of stop messages generated every second is a measure of the additional load created by the congestion control scheme to cope with the overload situation. Considering all of these observations, the random stop-duration scheme with the duration value set (1,2,...,10) appears to be the best among all the congestion control schemes considered in this study when the nominal offered load is about 3.

To study the sensitivity of the "optimum" parameters of the stop-duration scheme to the level of congestion, another set of simulation runs was made with a nominal offered load of 4.5. Three fixed stop-duration implementations were tried with stop-durations of 2, 5 and 10 seconds respectively. Also, three random stop-duration schemes were tried with duration value sets (1,2,...,10), (0.5,1,1.5,...,10) and (1,2,...,20) respectively.

TABLE II

A COMPARISON OF CONGESTION CONTROL SCHEMES - OFFERED LOAD 4.5

Performance Measure	No Control	Fixed Duration			Random Duration		
		Duratn. 2 Secs.	Duratn. 5 Secs.	Duratn. 10 sec.	Dur.Set (1,2,..,10)	Dur.Set (.5,1,..,10)	Dur.Set (1,2,..,20)
Effective L3 Throughput	0.49	0.624	0.647	0.556	0.704	0.718	0.714
Frames Lost Per Second	69.3	35.4	14.8	5.63	1.01	0.46	0.0
Frames Rjctd Per Second	12.2	6.82	3.55	1.50	0.26	0.2	0.0
# Retrnsmsns Per Second	78.9	34.1	15.1	6.42	1.03	0.66	0.0
# Timeouts Per Second	73.9	62.0	30.9	16.6	15.4	16.0	7.11
# Stop-msgs Per Second	0.0	326.9	121.9	69.5	62.5	66.2	24.5

Table II shows all the performance measures that were investigated for this set of runs. One thing that immediately stands out from these observations is that at this level of congestion, without congestion control, all performance measures have degraded even more than when the nominal offered load was 3.0 - the effective layer-3 throughput has dropped to 49% from 56% and the frame-loss, rejection and retransmission rates and the number of time-outs have all increased considerably. Another interesting fact is that for the fixed-duration scheme with a stop-duration of 2 seconds, the effective layer-3 throughput has dropped to 62% from 68% while for the scheme with a stop-duration of 5 seconds, the layer-3 throughput has increased from 57% to 65%. This means that if one has to use a fixed duration scheme, the stop-duration will have to be tailored to the existing level of congestion. The stop-duration value which works well for a certain level of congestion, will be inadequate for a higher level of congestion resulting in high frame-loss and retransmission rates, while at lower rates of congestion, it may unnecessarily force the network into idleness for long periods of time. Note that at this level of congestion, the scheme with a fixed stop-duration of 10 seconds represents this latter case where the length of the stop-duration is a little too large, resulting in a loss of throughput because of forced idleness.

The three random stop-duration schemes included in Table II show uniformly better performance than the three fixed duration schemes. In all three of these schemes, the throughput is between 70 and 72% which is close to its peak value while the frame loss, rejection and retransmission rates are very low. At this level of congestion, the random scheme with the duration value set (1,2,...,20) appears to be the best although, except for the number of time-outs and stop-messages generated every second, the random scheme with the duration value set (1,2,...,10) has a comparable performance.

In summary, then, we observe that without congestion control the performance of LAPD-based (or any other protocol, for that matter) networks can deteriorate severely under heavy overloads. The policy of sending short poll messages rather than retransmitting all outstanding frames on timer expiry reduces wastage of band-width due to repeated retransmissions. However, as our analysis indicates, it is not enough to keep the effective layer-3 throughput from deteriorating severely under heavy overloads. One may also argue that if a sufficiently large buffer-space is provided, congestion control may not be required at all since, ultimately, the window flow control will ensure that the number of frames in transit will not increase indefinitely. While, to an extent, this is true, it overlooks the fact that with large buffers at network nodes, the delays in getting frames acknowledged can become large under heavy loads. This may lead to repeated time-outs, ultimately resulting in the connections being dropped. This would be perceived by the users as a serious degradation of service.

The stop-duration congestion control scheme with a fixed stop-duration improves network performance to a certain extent. However, the optimum value of the stop-duration for such a scheme appears to be quite sensitive to the level of congestion - if the duration is small for the existing level of congestion, the control action is not adequate, resulting in a wastage of band-width because of frame-loss and retransmissions; on the other hand, if the duration is too large, it may force the network into idleness for long periods of time leading to an underutilization of the network resources.

The random stop-duration schemes with a reasonably fine granularity in the stop-duration values and a moderately large number of duration values appear to be the best suited for controlling congestion in LAPD-based data networks. They seem to be more robust than their fixed duration counterparts - over a wide range of congestion levels they appear to be able to maintain a high level of throughput while holding the frame loss and retransmission rates to low values. Also, over this range they seem to perform better than the best fixed duration scheme for each level of congestion. By randomizing the stop-durations, these schemes ensure that different sets of virtual circuits remain idle for different periods of time and, consequently, become active in different periods of time. Thus, in effect, the total load in the network in each period is reduced to a level where it can be handled efficiently by the available network resources.

For the random stop-duration scheme to perform well over the range of possible congestion levels, the duration values need to be selected judiciously. If the granularity of the stop-duration values (the difference between consecutive duration values) is large, there is a danger of forcing the network into idleness for long periods of time. On the other hand, with a small granularity, virtual circuits forced to stop layer-3 traffic become active too soon, increasing the number of stop messages the network has to send to keep the load under control. How large or small the granularity should be depends on several factors - the network latency in conveying stop-messages to the end-systems, the layer-2 time-out interval, the buffer-space provided at network nodes etc. Given the granularity of the duration value set, the number of duration values in that set depends on the highest level of congestion the scheme is meant to combat - the higher this level, the larger should be the size of the duration value set since the load during overload surges will have to be divided among that many more periods. For the range of congestion levels considered in this study (along with the network parameters used here), granularity of about 1 second and

10-15 duration values appear to be the right combination.

5. CONCLUSION

This study demonstrates that under normal operating conditions the frame-relay implementation of the LAPD protocol outperforms the edge-terminated implementation. The additional protocol processing time required at the edge nodes results in larger end-to-end and round-trip delays in the edge-terminated implementation. This additional delay has a slight side benefit in that during overloads it delays entry of new packets into the network, thus somewhat softening the impact of the overload. However, as we have seen earlier, in the absence of congestion control, both the frame-relay and the edge-terminated implementations can experience a serious degradation of throughput under heavy overloads.

The real performance advantage of the frame-relay implementation over the edge-terminated implementation can be seen when the additional processing time at the nodes where LAPD is terminated is large enough to make the protocol handlers, rather than the transmission facilities, the bottlenecking resource. Such a situation is likely to arise in high-speed data networks or in those environments where the bulk of the traffic consists of small frames. In such cases, the edge-terminated implementation would limit the achievable throughput to well below the trunk capacity.

The stop-duration congestion scheme with properly chosen stop-duration values can effectively protect the network and maintain a high level of throughput over a wide range of congestion levels. If this scheme is implemented with a fixed stop-duration, the optimum value of this duration is sensitive to the existing level of congestion. Random stop-duration implementations of this scheme, in contrast, are more robust over a wide range of congestion levels. Such an implementation with a reasonably fine granularity and a moderately large number of stop-duration values distributes the load over disjoint intervals of time, which can then be delivered with minimal wastage of network resources. The granularity and the number of stop-duration values depend upon the buffer size, the network latency for the stop-messages and the range of congestion levels over which the control scheme is meant to protect the network. In our study, we found that, in general, congestion should be detected early (i.e. setting not-to-high "onset thresholds"); however, there should be adequate back-up buffer space beyond the onset threshold to prevent buffer overflows between the time congestion is detected and the time the effects of the congestion control actions are felt.

The random stop-duration scheme can also be implemented in a cyclic manner. Whenever a stop-message is to be sent, instead of choosing the stop-duration randomly from the set of duration values, one can "cycle" through this set. It is also possible to couple the random (or cyclic) stop-duration scheme with an adaptive mechanism which tracks the level of congestion. With a fixed granularity, the number of stop-duration values can be varied with the perceived level of congestion. One could, for example, start with a small number of duration values. If the buffer occupancy is found to persist above the onset threshold, one can gradually increase this number. On the other hand, this number can be gradually lowered if the buffer contents are found to be consistently low. The fixed duration scheme can also be coupled with such a mechanism.

There are several ways in which the stop-messages can be conveyed to the end-systems. For example, one may use either the signaling channel or the bearer channel itself for this purpose. Then there is the issue of ensuring user compliance with the intended control actions. These are all basically implementational issues which are beyond the scope of this paper. What this study demonstrates is that LAPD frame-relay networks provide a frame-work in which excellent congestion control schemes can be implemented.

ACKNOWLEDGEMENTS

The authors wish to thank Bharat Doshi and Han Nguyen for their help during the course of this work.

REFERENCES

[1]   "Frame-Relay Service: A Proposed New Packet Mode Bearer Service", CCITT SG XVIII, Contribution D717.

[2]   M.Gerla and L.Kleinrock, "Flow Control: A Comparative Survey", IEEE Trans. on Commun., vol. COM-28, no. 4, April 1980, pp. 553-574.

[3]   A.S.Tanenbaum, 'Computer Networks', Prentice-Hall, Englewood Cliffs, New Jersey, 1981.

[4]   W.Bux and D.Grillo, "Flow Control in Local-Area Networks of Interconnected Token Rings", IEEE Trans. on Commun., vol. COM-33, no. 10, October 1985, pp. 1058-1066.

[5]   J.C.Majithia, M.Irland, J.L.Grange, N.Cohen and C.O'Donnell, "Experiments in Congestion Control Techniques", in 'Flow Control in Computer Networks', Eds. J.L.Grange and M.Gien, pp. 211-234, North Holland, 1979.

[6]   A.R.Modarressi and R.A.Skoog,"Performance Considerations of Signaling Networks in an ISDN Environment", Proceedings of the 4th ITC Seminar on ISDN, Brussels, Belgium, May 1986.

[7]   CCITT Recommendation Q.921, April 1, 1986.

[8]   L.Kleinrock, 'Queueing Systems - Volume II: Computer Applications', John Wiley and Sons, New York, 1976.

TRAFFIC ENGINEERING for ISDN Design and Planning
M. Bonatti and M. Decina (Editors)
Elsevier Science Publishers B.V. (North-Holland)
© IAC, 1988

EFFECT OF A GAP PERIOD MECHANISM ON THE DASS1 PROTOCOL PERFORMANCE

S.E.Swedan, D.G.Smith, and J.L.Smith

Department of Electronic and Electrical Engineering
University of Strathclyde
Royal College Building
204 George Street
Glasgow G1 1XW

The performance of the DASS1 protocol is examined when a gap is
introduced between transmission and retransmission.   The effect of
gap size is analysed.   Results are presented to demonstrate the
increased efficiency that is produced when a gap of optimal size
is used.

1.   INTRODUCTION

Plans for the UK basic ISDN are currently being formulated.   Due to the
increasing need for a reliable and efficient signalling communication system for
user access to the ISDN (i.e. between the NTE and the LE), system performance
and the development of an efficient system protocol (Digital Access Signalling
System - DASS) is an interesting subject.
The link access procedure (LAP) used within the DASS1 protocol (the first
version of DASS protocol)is based on 'compelled' signalling in that a confirm-
atory response is required to each transmitted message, which is sent continuously until the response is recognised.   Such continuous retransmission
increases channel occupancy so that the link will be busier and that leads to
long delay in message transfer.
This paper examines an aspect of the retransmission procedure.
The signalling transfer time and channel load in the LAP-DASS1 protocol has
been analysed in [1] for continuous retransmission.   In addition, that paper
suggests a method of improving the performance of such a signalling link, the
ABORT technique option is proposed and the effect of this procedure has been
described.
This paper concentrates its discussion on another method that can be used to
improve the protocol performance.
The objective of the present investigation is to study the performance of the
DASS1-LAP when it is operated with a gap delay between retransmission frames.
We are interested in identifying the effect of the gap and the length of gap
which gives best performance.   In the next section, the flow control and error
recovery of the DASS1-LAP, and the development of the retransmission procedure
are described.
In section 3 , the system is modelled.   The model is analysed in section 4
and the performance is discussed in terms of maximum throughput, mean transfer
time, and total channel load.
Two points have been distinguished:
a. the effect of the gap period, and
b. the degradation due to one frame error.
Finally, in section 5, numerical examples are given and the results obtained
from analysis and simulation are discussed.

2.   FLOW CONTROL PROCEDURES

DASS1 follows the layered model for a data transfer system proposed by ISO [3].
Messages are formatted by the LAP into HDLC type frames.   Each message is
transferred by preparing a level 2 information-command frame containing address,
control, information and FCS fields.
Modulo 2 sequence numbers in the control field of the information frames (the
so-called send sequence number $N(P)$ and receive sequence number $N(F)$) and the
state variables at each end - $V(P)$ and $V(F)$ - are used to control the flow of
frames.
An NTE or LE can have only one unacknowledged frame outstanding at any time.

2.1. Error Recovery

Each originating I-frame is transmitted repeatedly.   A correctly received
frame is acknowledged by a response (ACK) frame.   Once the ACK frame is
received, the sending end will stop further retransmission of the current
frame.   During this process, the state variables at each end are updated ready
for the next I-frame.
If an I-frame is received containing a transmission error, this is detected
using the FCS and then the frame is discarded, but the next (or a subsequent)
retransmission should get through without error and be acknowledged.
The retransmission frames received out of sequence (due to the updating of a
state variable) are discarded.
If level 2 receives no acknowledgement after NL retransmissions, the link is
reset by transmitting an SABMR frame.   This frame is retransmitted until
either a reset response UA frame is received or the SABMR has been sent NL
times; in this case the line is taken out of service.

2.2. System Developments

The DASS1 documents describe a continuous retransmission strategy for error
control.   This strategy could be inefficient, since so much of the channel
capacity is wasted in retransmission.
This inefficiency might be reduced by either or both of two developments.
The first development of using an ABORT technique is analysed in [1].
The second development is by adding a pause before retransmission.
In this strategy, a frame is first transmitted and then the transmitter waits
for a certain time G.   Then either the next frame is transmitted or the same
frame is retransmitted again (if unacknowledged).
The chance of receiving the acknowledgement, before the gap period G expires
and retransmission starts, will be greater when the gap period is long.
On the other hand, if the originating frame is discarded due to its transmission error, the receiving end will wait for the next retransmission.   Hence,
a long gap period may cause a long delay in transferring the message.   We
have to balance the advantage against the disadvantage.

3.   LINK ACCESS PROCEDURE MODEL

At each end (NTE and LE), the call control messages arrive for transmission
randomly, with rates λ_a and λ_b respectively.   We assume that each message
is of variable length with truncated exponential distribution.   The messages
are transmitted according to FCFS, one message per frame.
As described in [1], the transmission channel can be represented by a single
server with two priority levels.   The ACK frame is given the first priority
for transmission, while the frame kept in the service room (SR) takes the
second priority.

3.1. Gap Function Algorithm

a) A copy of each command frame sent will be kept in the SR.
b) At the moment when the copy frame is stored, the SR is closed for a gap period.
c) During the closed period the held frame cannot be transmitted even if the transmitter is free.
d) After the gap period, the SR will be reopened and its frame will be ready to transmit according to the priority scheme.
e) When the acknowledgement for the current frame has been received, the SR is released and opened, and remains open until it is occupied by a new message.

4. ANALYSIS APPROACH

4.1. Theoretical Analysis

In this section the principle methods for calculating the maximum message throughput and the mean transfer time of a message, for one way traffic flow, are summarised. Some derivations of analytical expressions are given in Appendix A.
The analysis is based on the same assumptions as in [1].

4.1.1. Notation

The following symbols are used
L = signalling message length - the number of information bits in an I-frame.
$\bar{L}$ = nominal mean message length (mean value of exponential distribution of length).
L_h = overhead length

V = channel transmission rate
α = transmission time of maximum message length (max.length is 45 bytes).
c = normalising factor.
L_o = actual mean message length, $(l_o = \bar{L} - \alpha V.(c-1))$
$\bar{b}$ = nominal mean message transmission time, $\bar{b} = \bar{L}/V$
h = overhead bits transmission time
λ_a = input message arrival rate

T_a = ACK frame transmission time

D = propagation + processing delay

t_i = information frame transmission time

G = gap period between transmissions

P_f = probability that a frame is received in error. P_f depends on the independent bit error probability P_b, the message length, and the overhead length;

$$P_f = 1 - (1 - P_b)^{\bar{L}+L_h}$$

4.1.2. Virtual Transmission Time

The virtual transmission time represents the effective channel occupancy by one message including repeated transmission and idle times due to the gap mechanism.
The virtual transmission time t_v is defined in the following way: the virtual transmission time of an I-frame begins with the start of its first transmission. It terminates either at the end of its last repeated transmission or at the

moment of the ACK frame reception acknowledging this frame (depending on whether the ACK frame is received after or before a retransmission starts). It is partitioned into two possible durations (figure 2a and b):

t_1, represents the service time of an I-frame which is correctly received

t_2, represents the duration which will be added if the original frame contains an error.

The expectation of the virtual transmission time of an I-frame which has been disturbed exactly once before it is received correctly is [2]

$$E[t_v] = E[t_1] + P_f \cdot E[t_2] \tag{1}$$

4.1.3 Throughput

The information throughput H is defined as the transfer number of information bits in a unit of time on the channel. We calculate the channel throughput for a one-way traffic flow system under the assumption that the send buffer has messages to send at any time (saturated message buffer).

The mean time to serve successfully an I-frame with a mean message length L_o is given in equation 1. Therefore, the maximum information throughput H_o is given by

$$H_o = \frac{L_o}{E[t_v]} \tag{2}$$

The throughput can be normalised by the transmission rate V. Thus, we get the normalised throughput

$$(H_o)_{nor} = \frac{L_o}{E[t_v] \cdot V} \tag{3}$$

The evaluation of $E[t_v]$ is outlined in Appendix A.

4.1.4 Transfer Time

Now, we assume that the channel is only loaded to a fraction of its full capacity.

The transfer time of the transmitted messages represents the essential measure of performance. The transfer time T_f is defined here as the time from the arrival of a message at the send buffer of the sending end until its successful reception at the other end. That means, the transfer time encompasses the waiting time of a message and all the transmissions that are necessary for successful transfer plus any gaps.

The transfer time analysis is also based on the notion of the virtual transmission time, as defined in 4.1.2.

The mean transfer time of the message can be determined by using well-known results from the theory of the M/G/1 queue. The mean transfer time $E[T_f]$ of a message can be evaluated with the aid of the Polaczek-Khintchine formula [4]

$$E[T_f] = \frac{\lambda_a \cdot E[t_v^2]}{2(1 - \lambda_a \cdot E[t_v])} + E[t_1] + P_f \cdot E[t_2] + D \tag{4}$$

This formula requires us to determine the first two moments of the virtual transmission time t_v. This is described in Appendix A.

4.2 Simulation Model

In order to investigate performance under two-way traffic flow, the link access procedure model has been implemented by a discrete-event simulation. The gap mechanism was implemented, according to the algorithm described above, with this simulation study.

The parameters describing the traffic generated by a sending source can be varied to measure both the maximum message throughput and the system performance at loads less than the maximum.

The simulation program allows the free choice of a number of options, namely
- the gap period,
- mean value of the distribution of inter-arrival times of call control messages,
- mean value of the distribution of message lengths,
- transmission rate and error rate probabilities.
The model further assumes:
a. the link has already been initialised,
b. each end may be transmitting and receiving simultaneously (full-duplex
   transmission).
The quantities measured during the simulation are:
- maximum throughput of the signalling messages. To achieve this measurement
   the send buffer has been made a saturated queue (i.e. it has a message to
   send at any time.)
- mean transfer time
- total channel load.
The measure of throughput of the protocol is computed as

$$H_o = \frac{1}{T} \sum_{m=1}^{M} L_m$$

where T is the duration of the simulation,
      M is the number of the messages serviced during T, and

L_m is the length of mth message (bits)

5.   RESULTS

Numerical values of the system performance measures have been obtained by
analysis and simulation.
Two different situations are studied:
a. Only channel A to B is loaded whereas the reverse channel does not carry
   any information bits.   Results are obtained by both analysis and simulation.
b. Both channels are assumed to be loaded and the input traffic is symmetric
   (note that the figures show the average results obtained from both ends).
   These results are obtained by simulation only.
Throughout this section we assume that message arrivals obey a Poisson law
and the length distribution is a truncated exponential with mean 12 bytes.
We further assume that D = zero.
We summarize the behaviour of the link access retransmission procedure at
different gap periods as follows.
In two-way traffic flow, each channel may have an idle period after sending
its frame, due to the gap mechanism.   There are two cases to discuss.
- at the instant when end A (NTE) finishes transmitting a frame, end B (LE)
  is in course of transmitting a frame.
- at the instant when end A finishes transmitting a frame, end B is idle.
We have the following 4 points.
1.   (First case, figure 3a) a retransmission of A's frame will be avoided
     provided the time period r is less than G and B's frame is correctly
     received.   The benefit from this saving will increase with increasing
     G up to a maximum value (when G = transmission time of a maximum frame
     length).
2.   (Second case, figure 3b) a retransmission of A's frame will be avoided
     provided $G > T_a$.   In this case no further benefit will result as G is
     increased.
3.   It must be noted (figure 3c) that increasing G carries with it the dis-
     advantage of delaying a retransmission when one is required because of
     a frame in error.
4.   In one-way traffic flow, end B will always be idle when receiving an I-
     frame.   So retransmission will be avoided when $G > Y_a$ exactly as in 2
     above.

5.1 Maximum Throughput Results

For two-way traffic flow, figure 7 shows the maximum throughput of information bits per second H_o, relative to the transmission rate V, as a function of the gap period G.
We observe a strong dependence of the throughput on the gap period.   The curves show a small rise when increasing the gap period up to T_a.   This is due to the small probability of the behaviour mentioned in point 1.   Increasing the gap period $(G > T_a)$ yields an improvement of the maximum throughput which is due to the increasing probability of the points 1 and 2 occuring, but for a higher error rate the need for retransmitting frames increases and the maximum throughput drops as the gap increases (behaviour of point 3).
Figure 4 shows the normalised maximum throughput curves for one-way traffic flow.   As we described in point 4, whilst $G < T_a$, nothing can be saved.
On the contrary, the virtual transmission time increases and the maximum throughput will drop.   At $G = T_a$, all retransmissions are saved (except if the original frame has been discarded), and the best value of maximum through-put can be obtained.
Increasing the gap may cause a drop in throughput (in the case of error) which increases as the gap period increases.

5.2. Mean Transfer Time Results

In figure 8, the normalised mean transfer time is depicted as a function of the gap period for two-way traffic flow, with the input message rate held constant at 20 messages/sec.   In the case of P_b = zero and with increasing gap period, the mean transfer time decreases.   When $G = T_a$, the curve shows a sudden drop which is due to the behaviour as mentioned in point 2.   The same behaviour can be seen from the curves with error but with more delay.
The reason for the mean transfer time increasing at a long gap period is due to the behaviour mentioned in point 3.
Figure 5 shows the normalised mean transfer time as a function of the gap period for one-way traffic flow at the same input rate (20 messages/sec).
Contrary to figure 8, the mean transfer time increases as the gap increases in the region up to $G = T_a$, since the virtual transmission time increases.
The minimum transfer time can be obtained at $G = T_a$, with no effect from a further increase of the gap period, except in the case of error transmission, where the normalised mean transfer time increases as the gap period increases.

5.3. Total Channel Load Results

Figure 9 shows the total channel load as a function of the gap period for the same example mentioned in figure 8.   The total channel load decreases as the gap period increases.   This improvement depends on the saved load in re-transmission.   When $G > T_a$, more improvement can be obtained due to the be-haviour which is described in point 2.
The curves show no effect at further increase of gap (after $G = 8T_a$) because either all retransmissions have been saved and each message is transmitted only once (in the case of error free transmission) or, the number of trans-missions due to frames in error has reached its final value.   Figure 6 shows the total channel load as a function of the gap period for one-way traffic flow at an input rate of 20 messages/sec.   The figure shows two values of channel load for each curve:
a. when $G < T_a$, each message is transmitted twice (or three times in the case of error).
b. when $G > T_a$, one of the retransmissions can be saved.
This is quite clear from equation 14 below.

6. CONCLUSION

The main contribution of this paper is to propose the introduction of a gap between transmission and retransmission of the DASS1 link access protocol, and to examine the most important aspects of the resulting performance. From the diagrams, it can be seen that:

i. The gap period has an important effect on the system performance degradation.

ii. At a small gap period $(G < T_a)$, the performance can be improved in two-way traffic flow, while in one-way traffic flow this leads to performance degradation.

iii. An increase of gap does not always produce an improvement of the performance, as demonstrated by the results on transmission error.

When the gap function option is used on a DASS1 link controller, the optimal value of gap period should be set so that it is just sufficient for receiving an acknowledgement response frame before the transmitter starts to send a copy.

* In one-way traffic flow, the optimal value of gap period equals $T_a + 2D$.

* In two-way traffic flow, the suitable value of gap seems to be from the mean value of the frame transmission time to a little more, where both of the transmission cases (error free and high error rate) should be considered.

APPENDIX A

In this analysis it is assumed that the frame transmission time has a density function

$$\Phi(t) = P_r(t_1 = t) = \frac{c}{\bar{b}} EXP\left(- \frac{t - h}{\bar{b}}\right) \qquad H < t < \alpha + h$$

$$= zero \qquad \qquad \qquad otherwise \qquad (5)$$

$$where \ c = \frac{1}{1 - EXP\left(- \frac{a}{\bar{b}}\right)} \qquad (6)$$

The average frame transmission time $E[t_i] = \bar{b} + h - \alpha.(c-1)$.

The virtual transmission time of an error-free frame is t_1, and the virtual transmission time of a frame that is in error on the first attempt to transmit is $t_1 + t_2$.

To determine the duration t_1, two cases have to be distinguished:

a. when the gap period expires before the ACK frame is recognised (figure 2.a)

b. when the ACK frame is recognised before the gap period expires (figure 2.b)

The figures show that

$$t_1 = 2t_i + G \qquad \qquad G < T_a + 2D$$

$$= t_i + T_a + 2D \qquad \qquad G \geq T_a + 2D \qquad (7)$$

$$t_2 = t_i + G \qquad \qquad Always \qquad (8)$$

With probability $(1 - P_f)$, there is no error in the first transmission, and the virtual transmission time is t_1.

With probability P_f, there is an error in the first transmission and then the virtual transmission time will be $t_1 + t_2$.

So the density function of the virtual transmission time is

$$f_v(t) = (1 - P_f) \cdot f_1(t) + P_f \cdot f_2(t) \qquad (9)$$

where

$$
f_1(t) = \begin{cases}
\dfrac{c}{2\bar{b}} \cdot \text{EXP}\left(-\dfrac{t - (G + 2h)}{2\bar{b}}\right) & \begin{array}{l}(2h+G)<t<(2(h+\alpha)+G)\\ \text{and} \qquad G<(T_a+2D)\end{array} \\[4ex]
\dfrac{c}{\bar{b}} \cdot \text{EXP}\left(-\dfrac{t - (T_a + 2D + h)}{\bar{b}}\right) & \begin{array}{l}(h+T_a+2D)<t<(h+\alpha+T_a+2D)\\ \text{and} \qquad\qquad G\geq(T_a+2D)\end{array} \\[4ex]
\text{zero} & \text{otherwise}
\end{cases}
\tag{10}
$$

$$
f_2(t) = \begin{cases}
\dfrac{c}{3\bar{b}} \cdot \text{EXP}\left(-\dfrac{t - (2G + 3h)}{3\bar{b}}\right) & \begin{array}{l}(3h+2G)<t<(3h+\alpha)+2G)\\ \text{and} \qquad G<(T_a+2D)\end{array} \\[4ex]
\dfrac{c}{2\bar{b}} \cdot \text{EXP}\left(-\dfrac{t - (T_a + 2D + G + 2h)}{2\bar{b}}\right) & \begin{array}{l}t>(2h+T_a+2D+G)\\ t<(2(h+\alpha)+T_a+2D+G)\\ \text{and} \qquad G\geq(T_a+2D)\end{array} \\[4ex]
\text{zero} & \text{otherwise}
\end{cases}
\tag{11}
$$

The first two moments of the virtual transmission time are

$$
E[t_v] = \begin{cases}
(2 + P_f) \cdot E[t_i] + G \cdot (1 + P_f) & G<(T_a+2D) \\[2ex]
(1 + P_f) \cdot E[t_i] + T_a + 2D + P_f \cdot G & G\geq(T_a+2D)
\end{cases}
\tag{12}
$$

$$
E[t_v^2] = \begin{cases}
(4 + 5P_f) \cdot (X_1 - \alpha(c-1)X^2) + (1+2P_f) \cdot (4E[t_i] + G) \cdot G & G<T_a+2D \\[2ex]
(1 + 3P_f) \cdot (X_1 - \alpha(c-1)X^2 + 2t_m(1+P_f) \cdot E[t_i] \\[1ex]
\quad + P_f \cdot G(4E[t_i] + G + 2t_m) + t_m^2 & G>T_a+2D
\end{cases}
\tag{13}
$$

where $X_1 = 2\bar{b}^2 + h^2 + 2h\bar{b}$,

$X_2 = \alpha + 2(h + \bar{b})$,   and

$t_m = T_a + 2D$.

The total channel load T_c, defined as bits per second transmitted over the physical channel of level 1, relative to the transmission rate V, can be evaluated from figure (2a and b) as

$$
T_c = \begin{cases}
\lambda_a \cdot (2 + P_f) \cdot E[t_i] & G<(T_a+2D) \\[2ex]
\lambda_a \cdot (1 + P_f) \cdot E[t_i] & G\geq(T_a+2D)
\end{cases}
\tag{14}
$$

REFERENCES

[1] Swedan,S., Smith, D.G. and Smith, J.L. Introduction of an Abort Function
     into the DASS Protocol in ISDN. To be published.
[2] Bux, W. and Truong, H.L., High Level Data Link Control-Traffic Considera-
     tions. in Proc. 9th ITC Torremolinos, Spain, Oct. 1979.
[3] Hoppitt, C.E., Integrated Digital Access - A step by step Description of
     the Network Termination Equipment. British Telecommunication Engineering
     J., vol 2, Oct. 1983.
[4] Kleinrock, L., Queueing System vol. 1: Theory, New York Wilely 1975.

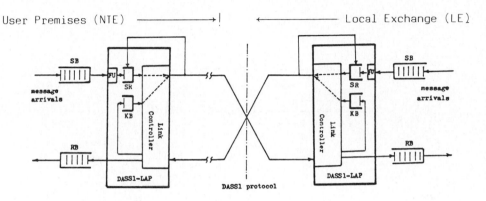

Figure 1 : DASS1 - Link Access Procedure Simulation Model

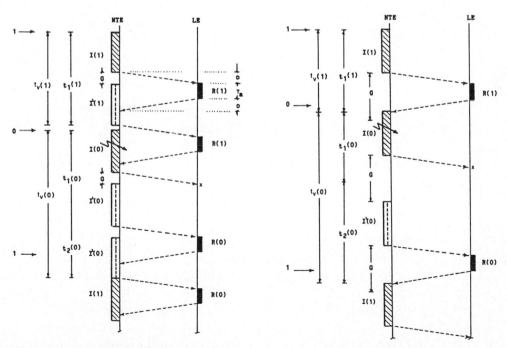

Figure 2a: Virtual Transmission Time t_v
    (DASS1-LAP with gap function)
    $G < (T_a + 2D)$

Figure 2b: Virtual Transmission Time t_v
    (DASS1-LAP with gap function)
    $G \geq (T_a + 2D)$

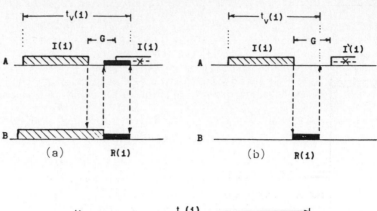

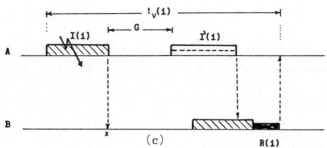

Figure 3

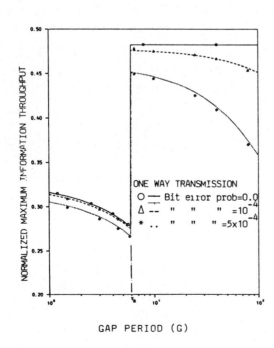

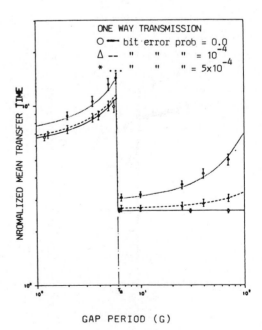

Figure 4
Normalized Maximum Information
Throughput vs. Gap Period
(λ_a = 20 mes./s)
(DASS-LAP PROTOCOLS)

Figure 5
Normalized Mean Transfer Time vs.
Gap Period
(λ_a = 20 mes./s)
(DASS-LAP PROTOCOLS)

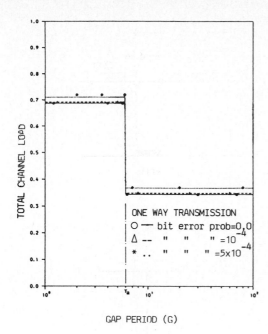

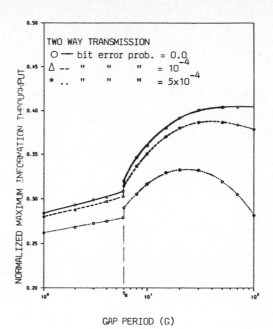

Figure 6
Total channel Load vs. Gap Period
(λ_a = 20 mes./s)
(DASS-LAP PROTOCOLS)

Figure 7
Normalized maximum information
throughput vs. Gap Period
(λ_a = 20 mes./s)
(DASS-LAP PROTOCOLS)

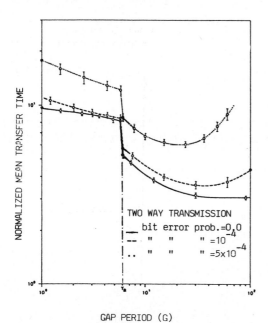

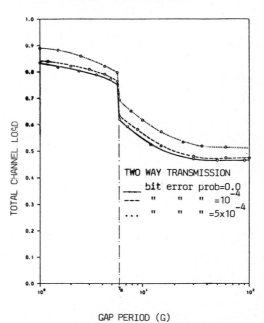

Figure 8
Normalized mean transfer time vs.
Gap Period
(λ_a = 20 mes./s)
(DASS-LAP PROTOCOLS)

Figure 9
Total channel load vs. Gap Period
(λ_a = 20 mes./s)
(DASS-LAP PROTOCOLS)

TRAFFIC ENGINEERING for ISDN Design and Planning
M. Bonatti and M. Decina (Editors)
Elsevier Science Publishers B.V. (North-Holland)
© IAC, 1988

ANALYTICAL APPROACH TO AVAILABILITY PERFORMANCE OF LOCAL GRADE ISDN SECTIONS

Harro L. Hartmann and Peter Protzel

Institut für Nachrichtensysteme, Technical University of Braunschweig, Braunschweig, FRG

Abstract

This paper presents a mathematical model to describe the availability performance of local grade sections of international hypothetical reference connections (HRX) with respect to an ISDN. Based on this model, availability performance parameters are defined in order to distinguish between quality of service (QOS) from the user's viewpoint and network performance (NP) from the provider's viewpoint. An analytical relationship between this QOS and NP parameters is derived and numerical results are given for an example of a local grade broadband ISDN with optical fibers and an digital switching system for 800 subscribers.

Main Statements

A mathematical model with the definition of appropriate availability performance parameters allows a comprehensive description of the outage process in local grade ISDN sections.

1. Introduction

The importance of availability questions is increased with the introduction of modern electronic equipment in communication systems, especially in ISDN. Therefore, availability performance is an essential question in current CCITT discussions. The main problems are the definition of qualified availability performance parameters and the development of methods for dealing with availability performance in a network /1/. The urgent demand of contributions on these questions is emphasized in /2/ as well as the importance of availability performance for network planning and system design of ISDN.

The overall performance concept due to the quality of service distinguishes between trafficability and availability performance /3/. While trafficability performance describes network congestion and traffic overload phenomena, availability performance is concerned with network equipment failures. Thus a QOS degradation results with respect to the subscribers /4/. However, the definition of appropriate performance parameters must distinguish between trafficability and availability performance in view of the different statistical features of the underlying processes. This differentiation corresponds to the most recent CCITT discussion about primary and secondary performance parameters /5/. Primary performance parameters are used to describe traffic performance and secondary performance parameters are based on thresholds of the primary performance parameters. Availability is a secondary performance parameter and describes QOS and NP for all time intervals when the service or connection is available or unavailable, respectively /5/.

Because of the difference between the traffic and the outage process the numerical values of the corresponding parameters are of quite different order, e.g. mean connection time of about some minutes but mean down time of about some hours. Therefore, a combined analytical consideration of both influences can lead to misunderstanding conclusions, e.g. that the impact of outages on the traffic performance seems to be neglectable, cf. /6/. To avoid this difficulties in the interpretation of the results, a separate consideration of the different phenomena must be performed. Especially in local network sections with no alternative routing capability for the subscriber lines, the loss of function for a single subscriber or a group of subscribers under failure condition does not affect the traffic performance of the remaining subscribers. Only if this mutual dependance exists in networks due to the capability of alternative routing, e.g. in medium and long distance networks, a combined consideration of both influences may be studied with caution. For example, medium and high grade network sections recover from trunk or node failures in a multiple of mean down time than in case of traffic overload with enhanced recovering in a multiple of mean connection time. This paper deals with the availability performance of local grade network sections. In case of equipment failures the isolated subscriber senses blocking for a down time interval in the order of hours but not in the order of minutes.

2. Availability Measures for Local Communication Networks

In the presented model of local communication networks it is assumed that failures of single network-components affect a definite number of subscribers and cause the loss of function for these subscribers during the down time of the failed components. Therefore, in accordance with other studies /7/, the number of subscribers affected under failure condition is used as a measure of the failure effect. Because of the stochastic nature of the failure and repair process the number of subscribers affected is a random variable which is called X. A complete description of the availability performance can be obtained by the computation of the probability distribution of this random variable. Thus, in a network with n subscribers, $P(X=k)$ denotes the probability of loss of function for exactly k out of n subscribers.

From this probability distribution a set of availability performance parameters can be derived. $P(X=0)$ yields the complete availability A_0, i.e. all subscribers can perform their function. Because of A_0 is usually near to 1, it is often more convenient to use the unavailability $U_0=1-A_0=P(X>0)$ as the probability that at least one subscriber has lost its function. The total unavailability $U_n=P(X=n)$ denotes the probability of loss of function for all subscribers. An interesting new parameter results from the conditional expected value $E(X|X>0)$ and is called the effective failure range (EFR). The EFR specifies the mean number of subscribers affected in case of network equipment failure and is a direct measure for the degree of centralization of the network's structure.

In order to describe the provider's load due to necessary maintenance actions another time oriented parameter is defined. This load is increasingly determined through failures of redundant components, especially in switching systems, which do not cause a system outage but require a maintenance action /8/. Therefore, the parameter $MTBF_P$ (mean time between failures from the provider's viewpoint) is defined by the inverse value of the sum of all failure rates including those of redundant components. The $MTBF_P$ can be interpreted as the mean time between maintenance actions.

The previous defined parameters describe the network performance (NP) from the provider's point of view. An important quality of service (QOS) parameter from the user's viewpoint is the probability of loss of function for any single subscriber. This probability is called service unavailability U_S. It can be shown that U_S results from the mean number of subscribers affected related to the total number, i.e. $U_S=E(X)/n$. This equation shows the feasibility to measure U_S by the determination of $E(X)$. For that purpose it must be recorded for which time how many subscribers have loss of function. Actually, such recordings are automatically performed in digital switching systems /9/. Another remarkable relationship between the NP and QOS parameters can be obtained from $EFR=E(X|X>0)=E(X)/P(X>0)=nU_S/U_0$.

3. Combined Availability Models for Local Transmission and Switching Systems

Figure 1 shows the underlying model of a local grade network section including both a subscriber line network and a switching system. Each subscriber is connected to the switching system by his own line. The single lines are partioned into several sections and are conducted in common cableways. The fault of a line section which is mainly due to forcible damage by external influences /10/ causes the loss of function for all those subscribers whose lines are conducted in this line section. Failures of switching system components also cause the loss of function for a definite number of subscribers depending on the systems structure. The model allows the analysis and the comparison of different switching control architectures from which three major structures are shown in figure 1.

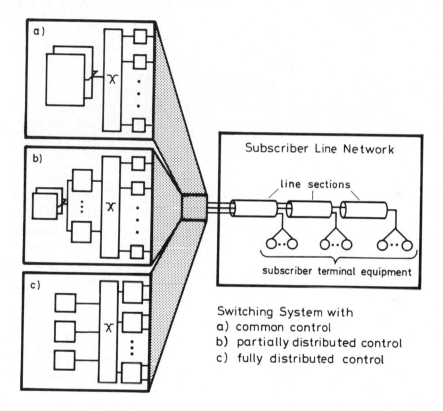

Switching System with
a) common control
b) partially distributed control
c) fully distributed control

FIGURE 1

Model of a local grade network section with different structures of switching control systems.

The computation of P(X=k) is performed under the assumption of stationary conditions and the system components are described through time invariant failure and repair rates or failure probabilities, respectively. Statistical dependencies due to a limited number of repairmen can be considered for the number of subscriber terminal equipment. Otherwise the components are assumed to be statistically independent relating to the failure and repair process. For the analysis, all combinations of component failures and their corresponding effect on the number of subscribers affected must be taken into account. The analysis is accomplished with a combined method using both markoff models and a decomposition approach with conditional probability distributions. The great number of possible combinations of component failures leads to very high computing times in the numerical evaluation of P(X=k). The model proceeds from /11/ and /12/ and a full description can be found in /13/.

4. Example of a Local Grade Broadband ISDN with Different Service Levels

As an example of the model's application a local grade broadband ISDN section for 800 subscribers will be considered. A switching system with fully distributed control is assumed which contains a total of 19 processors. Three of them are working in upper hierarchical levels with hot standby redundancy for safety reasons. The subscriber line network contains five line sections with a length of 0.4 km. Figure 2 shows the more detailed structure of the subscriber line module and the subscriber terminal equipment. The electronic multiplex-demultiplex operations and the electro-optical conversions are separately performed for the broadband (BB) and the basic access (BA) carrier signals. This independance is important because of the greater susceptibility to failure of the more complex BB components. The assumed numerical values for the failure and repair rates are based on field experiences as far as possible.

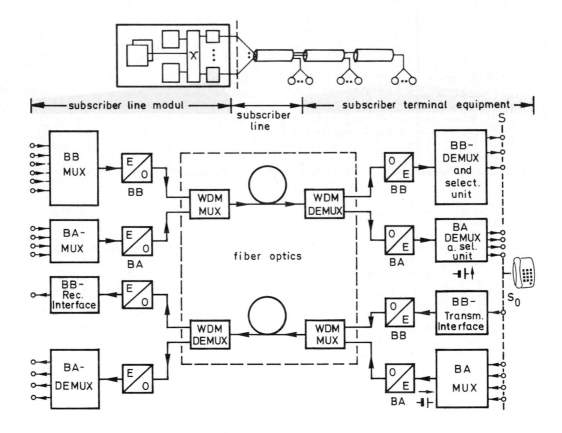

FIGURE 2

Subscriber line modul and subscriber terminal equipment for a local grade broadband ISDN section.

For the definition of availability performance parameters, especially of ISDN, it is necessary to distinguish between different levels of service. In this example it is meaningful to differentiate between the three levels, BA-services available, BB-services available, and all services available. A further differentiation is not useful because of the common equipment for the BA- or BB-services respectively which affects the entire class in case of failure. The computation of $P(X=k)$ must be performed for each service level separately. Table 1 shows numerical results for the defined availability performance parameters concerning the BA-services. Note the dominating influence of the subscriber line network to the overall values. The probability of total outage U_n is almost exclusively determined by failures of the line sections. The service unavailability U_S is mainly determined by failures of the subscriber terminal equipment.

TABLE 1

Exemplary results for the availability performance parameters concerning the basic access (BA).

Result for / Parameter	Switching System	Subscriber Line Network	Local Network (overall)
NP $U_o = P(X > 0)$	5,9 d/a	24,6 d/a	30,0 d/a
$U_n = P(X = n)$	0,03 h/10a	0,77 h/10a	0,8 h/10a
$EFR = E(X \mid X > 0)$	2,0	1,6	1,7
$MTBF_P$	5,1 d	2,5 d	1,7 d
QOS $U_s = E(X)/n$	0,4 h/a	1,2 h/a	1,5 h/a

5. Conclusions

The presented approach and the analytically founded definitions of corresponding parameters will be helpful for further discussions and future recommendations to availability performance in the ISDN. The model can be used to substantiate the definition of availability requirements as well as to comment and to compare different system structures. As one result, it has been shown that the major influence of the subscriber line network to the overall availability performance should be taken into account for further considerations.

References

/1/ CCITT Study Group XVIII: Rapporteur's Report. Special Rapporteur for Question 17/XVIII - Availability Performance. Temp. Doc. No. 28-E(XVIII/6), July 1986, pp. 1-2.

/2/ CCITT Study Group XVIII: Considerations on Definitions and Parameters on Network Outage Duration. Sub-Working Party on Question 17/XVIII - Availability Performance. Temp. Doc. No. 31-E(XVIII/6), July 1986, pp. 1-4.

/3/ CCITT Recommendation G.106: Concepts, Terms and Definitions Related to Availability and Reliability Studies. COM CMBD-R 6, March 1984, pp. 10-107.

/4/ CCITT: General Network Planning. Geneva, 1983.

/5/ CCITT Study Group XVIII: Part B of the Report of the Geneva Meeting of Working Party XVIII/6 (Performance Aspects). COM XVIII-R 24(B), August 1986, pp. 1-89.

/6/ Fischer, K.; Tuppy, W.; Bär, M.: Nachrichtenverkehrstheorie unter Berücksichtigung störanfälliger Bedienungskanäle. ntz-Archiv, Bd. 3, 1981, H. 10, pp. 277-283.

/7/ CCITT Study Group XVIII: Availability Performance Plan. Contribution No. RW, Swedish Administration, June 1983, pp. 1-27.

/8/   Maurer, W.: Betriebserfahrungen der Deutschen Bundespost mit dem Analogver-
      mittlungssystem EWSA. telcom report, Bd. 5, 1982, H. 6, pp. 343-348.

/9/   Schlag, R.; Seeger, H.: Automatische Messung der Betriebsgüte im Digitalver-
      mittlungssystem EWSD. telcom report, Bd. 8, 1985, H. 6, pp. 367-371.

/10/ CCITT Study Group XV: The Influence of the Cable and the Line System on
      the Reliability and Availability of Analogue Line Sections. COM XV-32 E, April
      1985, pp. 1-3.

/11/ Badach, A.; Protzel, P.: Service Availability Evaluation of Hierarchical Systems.
      ntz-Archiv, Bd. 7, 1985, H. 5, pp. 109-118.

/12/ Hartmann, H.L.; Protzel, P.; Ebbecke, H.A.: Leistungsmerkmale diensteintegrie-
      render Digitalnetze - Teil 1: Fehlerwahrscheinlichkeiten und Verbindungs-Nicht-
      verfügbarkeiten. ntz-Archiv, Bd. 7, 1985, H. 5, pp. 101-108.

/13/ Protzel, P.: Zuverlässigkeit von Nahbereichs-Kommunikationsnetzen. Dissertation,
      TU Braunschweig, 1987, in print.

TRAFFIC ENGINEERING for ISDN Design and Planning
M. Bonatti and M. Decina (Editors)
Elsevier Science Publishers B.V. (North-Holland)
© IAC, 1988

TRAFFIC STUDY ON HIGH SPEED/MULTIPLEXED ISDN USER-NETWORK INTERFACE

Kou MIYAKE

NTT Electrical Communications Laboratories
9-11 Midori-Cho 3-Chome, Musashino-Shi
Tokyo 180 Japan

ABSTRACT High speed/multiplexed ISDN user-network interface is one
version of the ISDN user-network interface recommended by the
CCITT. It supports high speed digital services. The purpose of
this paper is to propose a queueing model for this interface and to
study the model from the view point of traffic characteristics.

1. Introduction

The main feature of an ISDN user-network interface is its ability to support
a wide range of services in the same network by offering users end-to-end
digital connections. The high speed/multiplexed ISDN user-network interface
is one version of the ISDN user-network interface recommended by the
International Telegraph and Telephone Consultative Committee (CCITT). The
transmission capacity of this interface is greater than 1.5Mb/s and high
speed access (i.e. 384Kb/s, 1.5Mb/s) and multiplexed access (nx64Kb/s) are
transparently supported. It supports high speed facsimile, file
transmission, PBX and other high speed digital services.

The development of a traffic design method for this interface is of
considerable importance. However, few results have been reported so far.
The purpose of this paper is to propose a queueing model for this interface
and to study the model from the view point of traffic characteristics.
The queueing model is first described and the call arrival process and
queueing model are defined. Then the Markovian state equations and the
product form solutions for the number of calls in the system are derived.
Furthermore, the call congestion probability is obtained and it is shown that
the stationary distribution of the number of busy servers in the queueing
system depends only on the mean of the service time. Finally, some numerical
examples are shown and traffic characteristics are also discussed.

2. Queueing model description

2.1 Outline of the model

The model studied in this paper has the following properties.
(1) Several terminals are connected to an access line, and each terminal
requires a heterogeneous transmission speed. An access line is shared by
several terminals.
(2) A call request from each terminal occurs according to Poissonian process,
if and only if there remains a transmission capacity greater than the
required call speed on the access line.
(3) A call request from each access line is connected to a transit line
through a concentrator switch, if and only if there remains sufficient
transmission capacity, greater than the required call speed on the transit
line. If the call encounters congestion, it is lost and cleared. The
transit line must be accessible from every access line which is connected to
the concentrator.

2.2 Definitions and notations

Throughout this paper, the required call speed, access line speed, and transit line speed are defined by multiples of some basic speed. In the formulation, the following notations are used.

K: number of terminal speed classes which are connected to access line.
$v_{\ell j}$: terminal speed of speed class ℓ, and access line j.
$m_{\ell j}$: number of class ℓ terminals connected to access line j.
S_j: capacity of access line j.
$\lambda_{\ell j}$: mean arrival rate of calls from access line j with speed class ℓ terminal.

$\mu_{\ell j}$: mean service rate of calls from access line j with speed class ℓ terminal.
M: number of access lines connected to the concentrator.
N: capacity of transit line.

In section 3.1 and 3.2, the service time distribution for each call is assumed to be an exponential distribution. This assumption will be relaxed later in order to form a general distribution.

3. Analysis

3.1 Stationary distribution of the number of calls in the system

Assuming that the transit line capacity is infinite, then the stationary distribution of the number of calls in the system depends only on the state of each access line. Therefore, we consider an access line j which is defined with the following notations:

(i) $Q_{\ell j}$: the number of calls with speed class ℓ in access line j.

(ii) $\underline{i}_j = (i_{1j}, ---, i_{Kj})$: state representation of the number of calls in access line j, where $i_{\ell j}$ is the number of calls which occurs from access line j and speed class ℓ.

(iii) $A_j = \left\{ \underline{i}_j : \sum_{u=1}^{K} i_{uj} \cdot v_{uj} \leq S_j \right\}$: state space of $\underline{i}_j$.

(iv) $\Pi_j(\underline{i}_j) = \Pr\{ Q_{\ell j} = i_{\ell j}, \ell = i, ---, K \}$: stationary probability of calls in access line j.

(v) R_ℓ^+: operator to act upon state $\underline{i}_j$, defined by $R_\ell^+ \underline{i}_j =$
$$(i_{1j}, ---, i_{\ell j}+1, ---, i_{Kj})$$

(vi) $q(\underline{i}_j, \underline{i}_j')$: transition probability for state $\underline{i}_j$ to $\underline{i}_j'$.

The transition probability $q(\underline{i}_j, \underline{i}_j')$ is given as follows.

(1) $q(\underline{i}_j, \underline{i}_j') = 0$ if $|\underline{i}_j - \underline{i}_j'| \geq 2$ or $(A_j \not\ni \underline{i}_j$ or $A_j \not\ni \underline{i}_j')$

(2) $q(\underline{i}_j, R_\ell^+ \underline{i}_j) = (m_{\ell j} - i_{\ell j}) \cdot \lambda_{\ell j}$ if $A_j \ni \underline{i}_j$, $R_\ell^+ \underline{i}_j$

(3) $q(R_\ell^+ \underline{i}_j, \underline{i}_j) = (i_{\ell j}+1) \cdot \mu_{1j}$ if $A_j \ni \underline{i}_j$, $R_\ell^+ \underline{i}_j$

The following theorem can be obtained.

Theorem-1

Let,

$$\Pi_j(\underline{i}_j) = C \cdot \prod_{u=1}^{K} \binom{m_{uj}}{i_{uj}} \cdot \left(\frac{\lambda_{uj}}{\mu_{uj}}\right)^{i_{uj}} \qquad \text{--------(3.1)}$$

where C is the normalizing constant on state space A_j.

Then $\Pi_j(\underline{i}_j)$ satisfies the following detailed balance condition.

$$\Pi_j(\underline{i}_j) \cdot q(\underline{i}_j, \underline{i}_j') = \Pi_j(\underline{i}_j') \cdot q(\underline{i}_j', \underline{i}_j) \qquad \text{--------(3.2)}$$

for all $\underline{i}_j$, $\underline{i}_j' \in A_j$.

It follows from Kelly's results[1], that the above theorem indicates that the stationary distribution of $\{Q_{\ell j}, (\ell=1,---,K)\}$ is given by (3.1). Furthermore, $\{Q_{\ell j}, (\ell=1,---K)\}$ is a reversible process.

Suppose now that the transit line capacity is finite. Then, the stationary distribution of the number of calls in the system, which is the stationary distribution of $\{Q_{ij}, (i=1,---,K;j=1,---,M)\}$, is also a reversible process truncated on the state space of $\{\underline{i}_j : j=1,---,M\}$.

Therefore, the stationary distribution of the number of calls in the system can be obtained by the following corollary.

Corollary-1

Let $\Pi(\underline{i}_1,---,\underline{i}_M)$ be the stationary distribution of the number of calls in the system be expressed as

$$\Pi(\underline{i}_1,---,\underline{i}_M) = \Pr\{Q_{\ell j} = i_{\ell j}, \quad \ell=1,---,K, \quad j=1,---,M\}.$$

Then

$$\Pi(\underline{i}_1,---,\underline{i}_M) = C \cdot \prod_{u=1}^{M} \Pi_u(\underline{i}_u) \qquad \text{--------(3.3)}$$

where $\Pi_u(\underline{i}_u) = \prod_{v=1}^{K} \binom{m_{uv}}{i_{uv}} \cdot \left(\frac{\lambda_{uv}}{\mu_{uv}}\right)^{i_{uv}}$ and C is the normalized constant

on the state space $\{\underline{i}_j ; j=1,---,M\}$.

3.2 Call congestion probability

Let $\widetilde{\Pi}_{\ell j}(\underline{i}_1,---,\underline{i}_M)$ be the stationary distribution of the number of calls in the system when a call attempts, which is initiated from access line j and whose speed class is ℓ. The following theorem can then be derived using the result of corollary-1.

Theorem-2

$\widetilde{\Pi}_{\ell j}(\underline{i}_1,---,\underline{i}_M)$ is the same distribution as $\Pi(\underline{i}_1,---,\underline{i}_M)$ with one less terminal whose speed class is ℓ and connected to access line j.

According to this result, the call congestion probability can be obtained from the distribution of calls in the system when a call attempts, which is initiated from access line j and whose speed class is ℓ.

3.3 Insensitive property

In this section, the service time distribution assumption is relaxed to the general distribution. Using the Burman's restricted flow equation method[2], the following insensitivity property can be obtained for the stationary distribution of calls in the system.

Theorem-3

The stationary distribution of the number of calls in the system in this

queueing model depends only on the mean of the service time. The distribution
is given by (3.3).

4. Numerical examples

Call congestion probabilities for the queueing model are shown in tables 1,
and 2. In these examples, there exist two terminal types whose speed is
different and the total traffic potential is fixed. Call congestion
probabilities are shown for each type when the number of
access lines is changed. Furthermore, the results of the infinite source
model[3] are also shown in comparison with these examples. From these
examples, the following properties can be derived.
(1) When the number of access lines is small, the call congestion
probability for each type of call is small.
(2) As the number of access lines increases, the call congestion
probability begins to approximate that of an infinite source model.

References
[1] F.P.Kelly :"Reversibility and Stochastic Networks", John Wiley and Sons
(1979).
[2] D.Y.Burman :"Insensitivity in Queueing System", Adv. Appl. Prob., 13,
pp.846-859 (1981).
[3] L.A.Gimpelson :"Analysis of Mixtures of Wide- and Narrow-Band Traffic",
IEEE. Trans. Communication Technology, Vol.13, No.3, pp.258-266 (1965).

Table-1 Congestion probability

number of access lines		10	20	30	$+\infty$
congestion probability	B_1	1.49×10^{-3}	2.71×10^{-3}	3.22×10^{-3}	4.24×10^{-3}
	B_2	6.32×10^{-3}	1.01×10^{-2}	1.16×10^{-2}	1.45×10^{-2}

transit line capacity: 8   access line capacity: 2
type-1 terminal speed: 1   type-2 terminal speed: 2
number of type-1 terminals for each access line: 2
number of type-2 terminals for each access line: 1
traffic potential for type-1 calls: 1
traffic potential for type-2 calls: 1
congestion probability for type-1 calls: B_1
congestion probability for type-2 calls: B_2

Table-2 Congestion probability

number of access lines		10	20	30	$+\infty$
congesion probability	B_1	4.24×10^{-4}	8.23×10^{-4}	1.01×10^{-3}	1.42×10^{-3}
	B_2	6.67×10^{-3}	1.03×10^{-2}	1.17×10^{-2}	1.46×10^{-2}

transit line capacity: 16   access line capacity: 4
type-1 terminal speed: 1   type-2 terminal speed: 4
number of type-1 terminals for each access line: 4
number of type-2 terminals for each access line: 1
traffic potential for type-1 calls: 2
traffic potential for type-2 calls: 2
congestion probability for type-1 calls: B_1
congestion probability for type-2 calls: B_2

TRAFFIC ENGINEERING for ISDN Design and Planning
M. Bonatti and M. Decina (Editors)
Elsevier Science Publishers B.V. (North-Holland)
© IAC, 1988

DISCUSSION

1 Overload and Flow Control Strategies. (P.E. Wirth)

1.1 Bursty Traffic Performance.

L. Berry (University of Adelaide) asked about performances in case
of bursty traffic: with bursty arrivals it is also possible to have
lower delays than those shown by the main curve; is the bursty curve
presented in the paper (fig. 1) qualitative? if not, how was it
obtained?

P.E. Wirth confirmed that the bursty curve is qualitative: "A delay
curve was drawn above the main curve to indicate that even if a
particular level of "burstiness" in the arrival stream is predicted,
a larger burstiness can be experienced with a certain probability
that depends on the accuracy of our forecasting. A lower burstiness
is also possible; however, since this produces lower delays, it
should not be of concern in determining the level of provisioning.".

1.2 Degraded Performances.

Both R. Pandya (BNR) and G. Gosztony (BHG) referred to the authors
proposal of either

> 1) providing uniformly degraded performance to all services

or

> 2) providing better performance to some services and highly
>   degraded performance to the remaining services, on some
>   priority basis,

under proccessor overload.

R. Pandya asked how the second proposal could be implemented, given
that the switching control will not know apriori the type of service
the subscriber has requested, till it accepts and analyses (using
real-time resources) the call setup message.

G. Gosztony asked if a cost dependent priority scheme could be
applied implementing the second proposal, instead of a simple
priority scheme such as users grouping, traffic types
differentiation etc. "Operating companies are interested in
economical optimization! Some considerations about the Income
Loss.vs. Rejected Calls figure would very likely be required before
call rejection"

P. Wirth answered to R. Pandya question, observing that the second
proposal can be implemented in a number of ways depending on the
hardware and software architecture of the system as well as the user
protocols. For example, signaling information and data packets are
carried on distinct logical links on the D-channel. Only a small
amount of processing would be required to distinguish frames

arriving on these links and give priority to one. An additional mean of implementing this is through cooperation of the various processors in the system, as discussed in the paper.

A cost optimizing scheme – surely highly desirable from an operating company point of view – seems to P. Wirth too difficult to implement unless the "optimal" traffic to retain in an overload (from a cost viewpoint) could be mapped into call types that can be readily distinguished by processing elements. This may also have protocol implications.

1.3 Frequency of overload control instances.

S. Katz (AT&T Bell Laboratories) asked comments on the frequency with which overload control of switching systems is tipically esperienced: "I assume that we wish to estimate capacity with sufficiently liberal resources, so that few instances of switching overload are encountered. This is particularly true for the new data services which we are trying to nurture".

"Overload controls are infrequently invoked in current switching systems due to our understanding of the traffic and to the ability to engineer for the expected load" answered P. Wirth. "In the new ISDN environment it is imperative that we liberally engineer the system so that customers experience good service. However, it is also important to implement overload controls, such as call denial and data throttling to protect switch resources in case the liberally engineering was insufficient to get the system more tolerant to unexpected events."

2 Multirate Switching Networks. (G. Niestegge)

2.1 "Wide-sense" non-blocking.

C. Halgreen (Jutland Telephone Company) asked if for "wide-sense" non-blocking we can virtually replace the maximum channel number S by the number of different bandwidth classes. The importance of this number in constructing multiservice networks seems very high.

G. Niestegge recognised that this number plays an important role referring to "wide-sense" non-blocking switching networks. But we cannot simply replace the needed parameters by this number, and it is no longer sufficient to take into account only the maximum channel number S. We have to take into account the combination of all the channel numbers allowed for multichannel connections.

2.2 Possible switching network simplification.

A. Buchheister (SEL) observed that G. Niestegge maintains TSSI by taking only a limited number of paths into consideration. "How much simpler the switching network would be if TSSI had not to be maintained?".

G. Niestegge answered that if TSSI is not maintained, the single-channel connections making up a multichannel connection can be switched independently of each other. In this case, the switching network is non-blocking for multichannel connections, if it is nonblocking for single-channel connections only, i.e. if the Clos'condition holds ($b \geq 2a-1$). The expansion factor in the first stage then amounts to 2. If TSSI must be maintained, it lies between 2 and 2S (S = maximum number of channels allowed for a connection) depending on the ratio of the maximum bit rate allowed for a connection and the transport bit rate of the multiplexes. If this ratio is small, the switching network does not become much simpler. But the situation is different if the ratio approximates 1.

3 LAPD Frame–Relaying Protocols. (K.M. Rege)

3.1 Variable .vs. fixed frame size.

Referring to the ongoing discussion in CCITT SG XVIII on frame–relay procedures as a future integrated transport mechanism for packet switched and circuit switched applications, and especially to the need of an early standardization referring to the variable .vs. fixed frame size issue, R. Pandya (BNR) asked about the effect of this parameter on the results presented in the paper.

"One of the main results presented in the paper" – underlined K.M. Rege – "is a demonstration that LAPD Frame-Relay networks can be adequately protected with a properly designed (randomized) "stop-duration" congestion control scheme. Moreover, it was observed that once the parameters of this scheme were properly chosen, it performed robustly over a wide range of congestion levels. These results were obtained from simulation runs using a traffic mix consisting of frames whose size varied from 8 bytes to 136 bytes – a variable frame-size environment. While it is possible that the effectiveness of the congestion control scheme will depend, to some extent, on the frame-size and the traffic mix, the observed robustness of its performance seems to suggest that it can handle a fairly large variety of traffic patterns. With a fixed frame-size, the traffic will be more "homogeneous" than when a variable frame-size is allowed. In our opinion, this should help improve the effectiveness of the congestion control scheme. Of course, with a fixed frame-size, the network will have to carry more traffic (because of increased overheads) for the same level of user activity. However, in view of observed "flat" response characteristic of the stop-duration congestion control scheme, it should be able to cope well with this additional load".

4 Gap Period Mechanism in DASS1 Protocol. (J.L. Smith)

4.1 Impact of the processing/queueing time at the Local Exchange.

P. Wirth (AT&T Bell Laboratories) asked on the impact of processing time or queueing time at the Local Exchange on the results.

"The results are based on the delays caused by gaining access to the transmission channel, under the DASS protocol" – answered J.L.

Smith — "The models did not consider delays at the Local Exchange due to processing or queueing for a processor. Limited queue size at the processor in the Local Exchange must mean that some correctly received signalling messages are discarded. These would have to be recovered by some higher level protocol. The effect would presumably be to increase the load on the signalling channel".

TRAFFIC ENGINEERING for ISDN Design and Planning
M. Bonatti and M. Decina (Editors)
Elsevier Science Publishers B.V. (North-Holland)
© IAC, 1988

CONTROL POLICIES AND NETWORK COST

(Chairman Conclusions to the Afternoon Session on Systems)

Jacques Labetoulle

CNET, France

I will point out three main aspects out of this session, on which significant and new results were obtained and presented by the authors.

1) Switching system modelling:

    For that aspect, I mention here the paper presented in the morning's session, on the modelling of the ATD technique, which represents a major contribution. The paper by Niestegge represents also a very original contribution on an important subject: the non blocking multirate switching networks. In particular, this paper treats the problem of TSSI whose importance was pointed out the first day by J. Roberts.

2) Protocol and access scheme analysis:

    Here also we had various presentation (by Kim, Skoog, Smith and Rege) showing efficient methods to get numerical results proving how it is possible to optimize the utilization of system.

3) Control strategies:

    As pointed out by Pat Wirth, general architecture or basic control architectures are of fundamental importance. But in this field, if we had a very interesting overview on the methodology to follow, we have not seen through this conference practical examples of what to do.

    If I come back to Skoog's analysis of CCS 7, where the queue build-up after a detection of an error on a link has been analysed, it can be considered that the effect of this accumulation of packets will be smoothed and shared over a certain number of links if the routing authorized it. So here also, the architecture of the system and the routing policy will greatly affect the control strategy.

    Since future ISDN networks will have to respect predefined quality of service in various conditions on mixing of traffics, or overloads, it seems clear that the cost of networks will be greatly influenced by the efficiency of control policies. And my conclusion today is that this area is far to be completed and that there is a lot of job to be done, and this job is certainly of an extreme difficulty.

TRAFFIC ENGINEERING for ISDN Design and Planning
M. Bonatti and M. Decina (Editors)
Elsevier Science Publishers B.V. (North-Holland)
© IAC, 1988

CLOSING SESSION

Concluding Reports and Discussion

Chairman: Prof. Dr.-Ing. P. Kuehn, University of Stuttgart, FRG

Panelists: Mr. G. Robin, Alcatel, Belgium
             Mr. D. Songhurst, British Telecom, UK
             Mr. K. Kawashima, NTT, Japan
             Dr. R. Pandya, BNR, Canada
             Dr. H. Heffes, AT&T Bell Laboratories, USA
             Dr. J. Labetoulle, CNET, France
             Dr. M. Bonatti, Italtel Research Laboratories, Italy

Concluding Reports have been delivered by the Session Chairmen on ISDN Services, Networks and Systems during the Closing Session. Major issues and achievements have been addressed and, in particular, open problems have been indicated which should be subjected to further study or basic research.

One of the key results of the Seminar has been the unique statement that Traffic Engineering plays a central role in

- supporting system development
- planning networks and services and
- network management and service provisioning.

A whole set of new questions have been discovered which could not adequately be coped with by traditional Traffic Engineering methods and practices due to the broad spectrum of service parameters, network features, and traffic character- istics.

It has also been discovered that there is a strong impact of technology on the development of services and networks, and that Traffic Engineering must benefit from cross-fertilization between adjacent fields like computer system perfor- mance, dynamic systems research, operations research, and reliability theory. Those aspects have been excellently addressed by invited speakers who tried hard to report on the state of the art of their related fields.

ISDN SERVICES

The report on ISDN Services was given by Mr. Robin and Mr. Songhurst. The presented papers addressed the development of telecommunication services, their characteristics and network requirements. Specific topics have been discussed, such as mathematical description of the traffics of new services, forecasting of demands, system reaction in response to bulk resource demands, and the definition of 'reference models' for new ISDN subscribers as a basis for net- work planning.

Future issues are:

- finding a stable development scenario of new services, their
  requirements, and their dependence on new technologies

- modelling the interaction of services and network

- development of practical methods to predict and parameterize
  new services.

There exists no doubt about such general requirements whereas different conclusions can be drawn for specific issues, such as handling of multi-slot
connections with time slot sequence integrity (endsystem or network responsibility?) or reservation strategies for multi-slot connections.

ISDN NETWORKS

The reports on the Sessions on ISDN Networks were given by Mr. Kawashima and
Dr. Pandya. The complexity of ISDN networks results not only from topology but
also from features such as dynamic routing schemes, performance requirements,
bandwidth allocation strategies, connection types (point-to-point and point-
to-multipoint) or dynamic structures as in mobile networks. The comparison with
neural networks of biological systems is fascinating, although significant
differences exist between nature and technical analogy. It has been stated that
Traffic Engineering may contribute to the development of ISDN networks by

- GOS parameter definitions for various CS and PS based services

- modelling of the signalling protocols and mechanisms

- assessment of the potential capabilities of new transfer modes,
  such as frame relaying or fast packet/fast circuit switching

- studies on the implications of routing and call processing
  in SPC based networks.

Other important problems, such as interworking between ISDN and non-ISDN networks, had not been addressed at all.

SYSTEMS

System aspects of ISDN has been the third major topic which had been summarized
by Dr. Heffes and Dr. Labetoulle. These sessions provided a number of studies
on detailed problems, such as subscriber access and interoffice signalling
channels, performance of packet-oriented transmission, such as frame relaying
or asynchronous transfer modes, impact of service mixtures on protocol performance, dynamic schemes for traffic concentrators or overload control as well
as nonblocking multi-slot switching networks.

Similarities between telecommunication switching networks and highly modularized multiprocessing computer systems are visible; in fact, self-routing
interconnection networks, developed at first for multiprocessor systems, are
becoming extremely useful in connection with the new ATM networks for future
broad band integration. All detailed models revealed difficulties which can
hardly be attacked by classical methods. It seems really necessary to reduce
the model complexity to find basic mechanisms and their related "generic"
models which can be thouroughly analyzed to gain inside into the interaction
of parameters and their influence on the global performance. First general
results are visible.

Dr. Bonatti put forward a very valuable comment on technology influences and
trade-off studies for service design and planning.

DISCUSSION

The summary of the seminar gave rise to a lively discussion. Mr. R.R. Phillips
(GTE) recommended that similar basic issues have already been discovered in
connection with packet switched networks, and that certain solutions might be
well applicable. (The full comment is printed at the end of this section).

Dr. S. Katz (AT&T) made an enthusiastic statement on the success gained by Traffic Engineering in the past of Bell Laboratories Scientists and Engineers. He also strongly advocated for a careful evaluation of the real problems and on new issues arising with complex services, in particular within a competitive environment. Dr. J.M. Holtzman (AT&T) pointed to a set of new problems created by the complexity of todays system design.

Dr. G. Gosztony (BHG, Hungaria) gave the advise to concentrate on the solution of basic problems, and to make use of the mutual benefit from cooperation with computer performance analysis. Mr. C. Rasmussen (Copenhagen Telecom) addressed the complex issue resulting from the inclusion of varying charging rates as control and design parameters.

There were many more short comments contributing to this discussion which cannot be given here in detail. The general evaluation of the seminar, however, was quite positive. The seminar contributed largely to

- the understanding of the major new issues
- the elucidation of the state of the art in analysis, forecasting, and network planning, and
- the understanding of open and future issues.

This has not only been achieved by the high quality of papers but also by the unique atmosphere of the environment and the way the seminar was organized.

TRAFFIC ENGINEERING for ISDN Design and Planning
M. Bonatti and M. Decina (Editors)
Elsevier Science Publishers B.V. (North-Holland)
© IAC, 1988

CLOSING SESSIONS COMMENTS BY ROBERT R. PHILLIPS (GTE)

ISDN is not the integration of voice and data, but the decomposition of the
information into its key parts for timely transmission. There is really not
voice and data, but different types of data because many of the new types
of information have many of the same characteristics as does real time
voice. Voice now can be stored and transmitted as data; therefore, it does
not appear that ISDN should address the categories of voice and data. The
advent of the powerful workstation also is changing the nature of data
communications. Data transfers are now becoming high speed bursts of
information instead of continous streams of low speed information
processed in a central host. The hosts now are acting as file servers
providing files of information that the workstation is to process. These
high speed bursts of information will probably be the most difficult for
the networks to carry since they are of short duration and little indication
of when they are to be transmitted.

It appears that the different forms of information consist of two basic
types data. One is a low speed (small packet) type for control purposes
and the other is a higher speed (large packet) type for the transfer of the
information. The control data begins before and ends after the higher
speed data and involves both the control data for the network, as well as,
the control data between the user's terminal equipment. We have
developed a test bed which routes both the high speed file transfers and
voice between various workstations. This test bed has shown that the
control data needs to have immediate response and flexible routing.,
whereas the higher speed data has a longer response (or connect) time, but
requires the wider bandwidths. Also the time this bandwidth is required
is usually predicable. The test bed, as well as, the modeling of computer
networks has indicated that two networks are desirable, if not required.
One is a low speed short packet type that is packet switched and the other
a high speed variable bandwidth type that has large or variable length
packets which could be circuit or packet switched. Packet networks in
order to operate with the desired response times usually have a 50%
utilization. This means with wide bandwidths that a lot of possible data
capacity is lost. However, if the control network is used to manage the
data transfer on the high data rate network then its efficiency can be
much higher than 50%. The control network still would be limited to the
50%, but the total loss in bandwidth would be much less.

The papers presented this week for the most part addressed the modeling of a particular network format or protocol which is not going to be the real case. If there is not real standardization for ISDN, the networks will be a combination of protocols that can have adverse effects on the user. Present telecommunications networks are spared from this problem because they provide the user with a link level protocol that does not introduce any changes in the format of the user's data. If networks for ISDN employ packet protocols to transmit data then the user could (and probably will) experience severe throughput problems due to the various changes in protocols his data will experience going through the networks. These problems are already experineced by users of X.25 and other types of packet networks. The developers of these equipments have had to design various types of PADs to interface the different user protocols to their particular network protocol. Telecommunication providers could very easily get involved in similar problems if packet protocols are used. It does not appear that any network will have the same protocol throughout its service area if packet type transmissions schemes are used because the subscriber and trunk circuits wil require different formats.

The issues of error correction and network control cannot be ignored in the design of ISDN networks. The trend appears to place error correction on the user, but he has to be guaranteed a bit error rate to know how good his system will perform. Some of the discussion this week suggested that the loss of data (particularly small packets) was not critical. However, if the data lost is the user's error correction information it will degrade his end-to-end performance. Network control cannot be replaced by the use of packet protocols because this function has to occur regardless of the type of protocol used. All of the large packet network providers have extensive network control systems to keep their networks operating and service the user's trouble requests.

For future meetings I would like to recommend that the packet network and computer companies be invited to present their findings. They have done extensive modeling of various packet networks which should be of use to the ISDN process. I also would recommend that the network modeling examine the end-to-end case which includes more than one protocol in determining the overall performance. And last, I would like to recommend that the evaluation of ISDN approaches include tradeoffs not just between packet type systems, but between packet and switched networks.

PAPER COMMITTEE MEMBERS,
SPEAKERS and DISCUSSANTS

Roger G. Ackerley
British Telecom,
R15.2   MLB5/53
Martlesham Heath
Ipswich IP5 7RE
United Kingdom

L.F.   Agnati
Istituto Fisiologia Umana
Universita' di Modena
Via Campi 287
41100 Modena

Gerald R. Ash
AT&T Bell Laboratories ,
Crawfords Corner Road
Holmdel, New Jersey 07733
U.S.A.

Les   Berry
Teletraffic Research Centre
The University of Adelaide
GPO Box 498
Adelaide, SA 5001
Australia

Vladimir   Bolotin
Bell Communication Research
2X-104,331 Newman Springs Rd,
Red Bank, N.J.07701-7020
U.S.A.

Mario Bonatti
Italtel
Research Laboratories CL4B
20019 Settimo Milanese (MI)
Italy

Albrecht Buchheister
Standard Elektrik Lorenz AG
Lorenzstrasse 10
D-7000 Stuttgart 40, FRG

Fulvio   Casali
FACE Finanziaria
Via Monte Rosa, 15
20149 Milano
Italy

Beatriz   Craignou
CNET - PAA / ATR
38-40 Rue du General Leclerc
92131 - Issy-Les-Moulineaux
France

Maurizio Decina
Italtel
Via A. di Tocqueville, 13
20154 Milano
Italy

Paolo Ing. De Ferra
STET
Via Aniene 31
00198 Roma
Italy

dr. Berth   Eklundh
Ericsson Radio Systems
S-223 70 LUND
Sweden

Prof. Mario   Gerla
Computers Science Dept.
University of California
Boelter Hall 3732
Los Angeles, CA 90024
USA

Lester A.   Gimpelson
Alcatel
Avenue Louise 480
1050 Bruxelles
Belgium

Oscar   Gonzalez Soto
Alcatel
Josefa Valcarcel, 27
28027 Madrid
Spain

G.   Gosztony
BHG Telecom Works
Development Institute
P.O. Box 2
1509 Budapest
Hungary

Davide   Grillo
Fondazioni Bordoni
Teletraffic Engineering Group
Room 210
Via B. Castiglione 59 (EUR)
00142 Roma

M.   Gruszecki
Bell Telephone Manufacturing
Francis Wellesplein, 1
B-2018 Antwerpen
Belgie

Christian   Halgreen
Jutland Telephone Company
Sletvej 30
DK-8310 Artus-Tranbjerg J
Denmark

Prof. Harro L. Hartmann
Institut fuer
Nachrichtensysteme
Hans Sommer Str. 66/11 OG.
Postf. 33 29
D-300 Braunschweig
Germany

Harry   Heffes
AT&T Bell Laboratories
HO 3L-304
Crawfords Corner Road
Holmdel, New Jersey 07733
U.S.A.

Jack M.   Holtzman
AT&T Bell Laboratories
Room 2M629
Crawfords Corner Road
Holmdel, New Jersey 07733
U.S.A.

Prof. Arne   Jensen
IMSOR -
The Technical University
of Denmark
Building 349
2800 Lyngby
Denmark

Arik N.   Kashper
AT&T Bell Laboratories
WB 3B-126
Crawfords Corner Road
Holmdel, New Jersey 07733
U.S.A.

Steve   Katz
AT&T Bell Laboratories
SPC Center
Crawfords Corner Road
Holmdel, New Jersey 07733
U.S.A.

Konosuke   Kawashima
Senior Staff Engineer
Teletraffic Section
Switching Technology
Development Division
Nippon Telegraph and Telephone Corp.
3-9-11 Midoi-Cho 3 Chome
Musashino-Shi, Tokyo 180
Japan

Noshik   Kim
Bell Communication Research
331 Newman Springs Rd.
NVC-1F249
Red Bank - New Jersey 07701
U.S.A

Ruth Kleinewillinghoefer-Kopp
Research Institute of the DBP
Postfach 5000
D-6100 Darmstadt
Germany

Paul   Kuehn
Inst. f. Nachrichtenvermittlung und
Datenverarbeitung
University of Stuttgart
Seidenstrasse, 26
7000 Stuttgart 1
Germany

Jacques   Labetoulle
CNET - PAA - ATR
38-40 Rue du General Leclerc
92131 - ISSY-LES-MOULINEAUX
France

Pierre   Le Gall
CNET - DICET
38-40 Rue du General Leclerc
92131 - ISSY-LES-MOULINEAUX
France

Karl   Lindberger
Swedish Telecomminications Network Dept.
S-123 86 Farsta
Sweden

Jean-Raymond Louvion
Centre National d'Etudes
des Telecom.
LAA/SLC/EVP
BP40 22301 Lannion Cedex
France

Prof. C. Marchetti
International Institute for
Applied Systems Analysis
Schlossplaz 1
2361 Laxenburg
Austria

Lorne Mason
INRS - Telecommunications
3 Place du Commerce, Verdun
Quebec
Canada

Jun   Matsuda
Switching Technology Develo
Nippon Telegraph and Teleph
9-11 Midoi-Cho 3 Chome
Musashino-Shi, Tokyo 180
Japan

E.J. McCarthy
Bell Canada
Room 1000, 220 Laurier Ave.
Ottawa - Ontario K2A 2R4
Canada

Prof. John F. Meyer
Dept of Electrical Eng.
The University of Michigan
1079, East Engineering
Ann Arbor, MI 48109
USA

Gerd   Niestegge
Siemens N ZL. SV 23
Hofmannstr. 51
8000 Muenchen 70
Postfach 700076
Germania

Krister   Nivert
Televerket
Room C437
Faernebogatan 81-87
S-12386 FARSTA
Sweden

Raj   Pandya
Bell Northern Research
P.O. box 3511 Station C
Ottawa - Ontario K1Y 4H7
Canada

Roberts Phillips
GTE System Corp.
1700 Research Boulevard
Rockville, ME 20850
USA

Karsten Rasmussen
The Copenhagen Telephone Co.
Noerregade 21
1199 Copenhagen K.
Denmark

Kiran M.   Rege
AT&T Bell Laboratories
Crawfords Corner Road
Holmdel, New Jersey 07733
U.S.A.

Philip   Richards
Bell Northen Research
P.O. box 3511 Station C
Ottawa - Ontario K1Y 4H7
Canada

James   Roberts
CNET - DICET
38-40 Rue du General Leclerc
92131 - ISSY-LES-MOULINEAUX
France

Gerard   Robin
Alcatel
Avenue Louise 480
1050 Bruxelles
Belgium

Dr. Rudolf Schehrer
Univeristy of Dortmund
Lehrstuhl fuer Elektronische
und Vermittlungstechnik
Otto-Haln-Strasse, P1-01-111
D 4600 Dortmund 50
BRD / FRG

Jila   Seraj
Ericsson Telecom
S-12625 Stockholm
Sweden

Ronald A. Skoog
AT&T Bell Laboratories
Crawfords Corner Road
Holmdel, New Jersey 07733
U.S.A.

D.G. Smith
Department of Electronic Engineering
University of Strathclyde
George Street
Glasgow
U.K.

David   Songhurst
R15.2   MLB5/53
British Telecom Research,
Martlesham Heath
Ipswich IP5 7RE
United Kingdom

Craig   Stanfill
Thinking Machines Corp.
245 First Street
Cambridge MA 02142
U.S.A.

Bengt   Stavenow
Ericsson Radio Systems
S-223 70 Lund
Sweden

Jonathan S. Turner
Washington University
Computer Science Dept., Box 1045
St. Louis, MO 63130
USA

Yu   Watanabe
Kokusai Denshin Denwa Co. LTD.
Research and Dev. Lab.
2-1-23 Nakameguro 2 -
Chome, Meguro-KU,
Tokyo 153
Japan

Dietmar Weber
SIEMENS AG K PN EAP
Hofmannstrasse 51,
P.O. Box 70 00 77
D-8000 Muenchen 70
Germania

Jens Weber
Telenorma TN Gmbh
Postfach 102160
6000 Frankfurt/Main 1
West Germany

Patricia E. Wirth
AT&T Bell Laboratories
Crawfords Corner Road
Holmdel, New Jersey 07733
U.S.A.